ESSAYS IN THE
HISTORY OF
POLITICAL THOUGHT

ESSAYS IN THE
HISTORY OF
POLITICAL THOUGHT

Edited by
ISAAC KRAMNICK
Yale University

PRENTICE-HALL, INC., *Englewood Cliffs, New Jersey*

PRENTICE-HALL INTERNATIONAL, INC., *London*
PRENTICE-HALL OF AUSTRALIA, PTY. LTD., *Sydney*
PRENTICE-HALL OF CANADA, LTD., *Toronto*
PRENTICE-HALL OF INDIA PRIVATE LTD., *New Delhi*
PRENTICE-HALL OF JAPAN, INC., *Tokyo*

13–283598–3

Library of Congress Catalog Card Number: 69–12974

Current printing (last digit):
10 9 8 7 6 5 4 3 2 1

Printed in the United States of America

PREFACE

The study of the history of political thought has survived the revolution in the social sciences which has swept the universities in our age. It has, to be sure, been pushed aside from its traditional place at the center of the political science curriculum by the quest for scientific explanation and a methodological concern with quantitative analysis. But all indications point to a revival of concern with the questions raised by the great writers on politics and with such concepts as representation, authority, citizenship, loyalty, and obligation, a revival which has itself been enriched by the work of the empirical school. An incipient disillusionment with the barrenness of "value-free" inquiry and the heightened awareness of our own troublesome times have led the political science fraternity back to the respectability of normative inquiry. "What ought to be" is now as often discussed as "what is," "what will be," and "how it came" or "will come to be"; and once attention has returned to the normative realm where noncumulative principles of knowledge apply, the study of the speculations of great thinkers in the past becomes again a respectable enterprise.

The pursuit of values in the political world requires the choice between and among competing and often irreconcilable norms. This procedure is, of course, not unique to the contemporary world. Great writers on politics have always done this, and it is only natural that their efforts be studied, criticized, and learned from. What the great political philosophers have done is to look at more than the facts of political systems. Their central concern has been with the "ought"—the description and defense of the most desirable political order. Sheldon Wolin has, in the first selection of this book, best described the activity which characterizes the writings of the political philosophers. He suggests that they approach the political world with a rare quality of imaginative vision. Their genius is an ability to envision a right and good pattern of political order and then to project this vision onto the pages of their writings. In Wolin's words, "At the center of the enterprise of political theory was an imaginative element, an ordering vision of what the political system ought to be and what it might become."[1]

The political philosopher is perpetually stating preferences: who should govern; what, if any, are the limits on governors; when men should obey; what is a just order; what are the boundaries of freedom; what is the proper relationship of the individual and the state, of the state and economic life. On these and many other issues political philosophers take positions indicating what occurs to them as the most desirable, the most just, the most pleasing. But they do more than simply state preferences. Plato does more than proclaim the value of rule by an educated elite, Locke more than the desirability of a limited government whose sole concern is protecting individual and property rights. The normative position is bound to an argument much more subtle than the single and bald statement of a particular preference. Complex logical webs are woven; intricate philosophical, legal, or historical arguments are constructed which give the political philosopher's basic position a timeless and universal quality and remove it from whatever particular events in the real world have provoked the writer to the normative response which is his central motivation. Thus Plato's preference is surrounded by complex metaphysical speculations on the nature of reality, and Locke's with hypothetical models of prepolitical existence and abstract speculations on the imperatives of a universally perceived law of nature. The theorist's combination of preference and intricate argument by which he hopes to recommend his preference present us with writings which transcend

---

[1] Sheldon S. Wolin, *Politics and Vision: Continuity and Innovation in Western Political Thought* (Boston: Little, Brown and Company, Inc., 1960), p. 35.

the historical setting and give Plato and Locke, for example, meaning and relevance, not only for the Athenian city-state or the England of the Exclusion Crisis, but for all time.

It is customary to trace the great tradition in political philosophy as extending from Plato to Hegel and Marx in the nineteenth century, the span covered in the readings in this volume. This century has seen an apparent decline of great political theory in terms of great normative statements. It may be that intellectual reflexes are such that to be considered part of a great tradition the theorist must, by definition, be a figure in the past. There seem to be, however, more objective forces at work which explain the evident demise of the tradition represented by the theorists in this book.

There is first the obvious influence and prestige of science and its impact on the study of government. The scientific quest for knowledge for its own sake has turned men away from uttering ethical judgments lest they be seen as somehow unscientific. A second factor contributing to the disinclination of men to offer normative speculations on politics is surely the post-Enlightenment, post–French Revolution disenchantment with politics so heavily reinforced by the spectre of twentieth-century totalitarianism. This has left in the minds of many the belief that normative political activity is not only futile but downright dangerous. This reaction, combined with that of the skeptical descendants of Burke, has led many to ridicule any effort to be purposive in politics, any effort to offer imaginative visions for the political world. The tremendous appeal of Marxism is another factor contributing to the decline of political theory. Though it is itself the paradigmatic normative vision seeking to reorder the political world, it sets a veil of suspicion upon any other less than apocalyptic vision. Another possible factor would be the predominance of America in the modern world, and the related lack of genuine political philosophy here. In a country where, as Louis Hartz argues, all tend to agree on the norms of politics, there is little genuine effort at normative speculation; men in agreement seldom write against one another.[2] The assumption that management, experts, or bureaucrats can solve all political problems also has contributed to the decline of political theory. To the extent that it appears there are rational political solutions which experts or public administrators can perceive, the role of normative theorists to propose alternative visions is undermined. There is, I think, one final factor contributing to the decline of normative political theory which is related to

---

2 Louis Hartz, *The Liberal Tradition in America* (New York: Harcourt, Brace and Co., 1955).

the change in the nature of the men who are political philosophers. No longer are such men, by and large, men of the real world operating in practical and real crises. Today the theorist is primarily an academic—in the university— whose bias is away from action, choice, and commitment, and whose predominant concern is that of his colleagues and his profession, objectivity and impartiality. Such traits are inimical to political philosophy as I have described it and as practiced by the figures in the great tradition.

All of these tendencies notwithstanding, one can detect today a resurgence of normative thinking on politics. Few single thinkers of the stature of those found in the great tradition have emerged; still there is no doubt that the activity itself is experiencing a resurgence of exciting and impressive dimensions. Far from the death of this tradition, we are witnessing its renaissance in the outpourings of writings from many different schools. Isaiah Berlin has recently pointed to an impressive list of such normative speculations: neo-Marxism, neo-Thomism, nationalism, historicism, existentialism, anti-essentialist liberalism and socialism, the transferral of notions of natural right and natural law into empirical terms.[3] It is in this context, then, of a renewed interest in political philosophy, that this anthology on the classical figures in the tradition is offered.

The need for such an anthology seems quite evident to me. In preparing reading lists for courses in the history of political thought the first imperative is that the theorist be allowed to speak for himself; healthy chunks of primary material are in order. It is then useful to present secondary comments upon the theorists in which trained minds analyze ideas and draw attention to the refinements of meaning and intention. In survey courses this presents particular difficulties. Should one assign a single book which seeks to do this, to cover the entire span of western political thought? To do this would be to investigate only one man's reactions to large numbers of theorists. It would seem better to offer the students different opinions from various scholars. But this has usually meant assigning bits and pieces from different books and journals. This book brings together in one volume some of the best writings on the great political thinkers and thus offers a single accompanying text to the reading of the various theorists themselves.

The decision on which theorists to cover has been less than arbitrary. To a great extent a consensus exists on who belongs in the inner circle of

---

[3] Isaiah Berlin, "Does Political Theory Still Exist?" in *Philosophy, Politics and Society* (2nd series), ed. P. Laslett and W. G. Runciman (New York: Barnes & Noble, Inc., 1962).

great political theorists. Most scholars agree on including Plato, Aristotle, Augustine, Aquinas, Machiavelli, Hobbes, Locke, Rousseau, Burke, Mill, Hegel, and Marx. Limiting the volume to these figures still involves, of course, the omission of others, for whose importance a strong case could easily be made. Thus we have been forced to omit Cicero, Luther, Calvin, Bodin, Spinoza, Hume, Harrington, Bentham, and Kant.

Deciding which essays to use, on the other hand, has been much more difficult. Here no conventional wisdom exists, no ready ordering of valuable and useful commentary. What I have done, then, is to comb the literature in an effort to find commentary that would serve the purposes of most survey courses in the field. The result is a collection of scholarship, for the most part contemporary, from America, England, France, Italy, and Germany. The criterion I have applied is that the selections be the best available commentary on a level fit for both beginning students and specialists. I have chosen the two essays on each man, not because they are contentious and present competing interpretations, but because the selections present stimulating and learned treatment of the figure under discussion. I have therefore favored no one school of thought nor sought to emphasize any particular themes or concerns. The result is a set of essays of varying approaches. Some stress a close formal study of a thinker's ideas, the logical consistency and intrinsic meaning of his arguments. Some stress the historical and social context within which the writer operates and its relevance for his ideas. Some point to the writer's significance and influence, others to the sources of the thinker's ideas. All the pieces are intended to provoke the student who has already read the texts to look at the theorists afresh in the new perspectives offered by another, perhaps more learned, reader. The student may then find something new, or he may not; he may agree or disagree with the author of the selection. But if by reading the selection he has been brought more closely into the normative vision projected by the theorists, then the intent of this volume will have been realized.

ISAAC KRAMNICK

CONTENTS

ESSAYS IN THE
HISTORY OF
POLITICAL THOUGHT

1

PLATO

Plato (428–347 B.C.) was born into the comfortable life of an Athenian aristocratic family; he claimed descent, through his mother's family, from Solon, the great lawgiver of Athens. During the first twenty-four years of his life the Athenian polis was beset by the upheaval and political confusion of the Peloponnesian Wars. The disorder and chaos of the Athens of his youth would have an enduring influence on his attitudes toward politics, as would the trial and execution of his beloved teacher Socrates.

Sheldon Wolin, a professor of government at the University of California at Berkeley, contends in his book, *Politics and Vision,* that the *Republic* is an antipolitical manifesto, an effort by Plato to forever banish politics as commonly understood and to replace it with the certainty and finality of philosophy. Wolin also contends that in the *Republic* one can best see the projective quality which is the essence of great political theory, for Plato's imaginative vision on the proper ordering of society is a powerful one to which men have continually returned in the millenia since Plato's era. David Grene, a professor of social thought at the University of Chicago, draws attention in the selection reproduced below to the historical context in which Plato wrote and to the influence of these events on his writings. He then follows the arguments of the *Republic,* critically analyzing its vision of philosophic rule in light of Plato's own flirtation with such rulers and his second thoughts in the *Laws.*

SHELDON S. WOLIN

Plato: Political Philosophy Versus Politics*

PHILOSOPHY AND SOCIETY

This takes us to the heart of Plato's conception of political philosophy. The ideas of Plato provide the first full mirroring of the dramatic encounter between the ordering vision of political philosophy and the phenomena of politics. Never has the art of ruling been clothed in a higher dignity: "What art is more difficult to learn? But what art is more important to us?"[1] Never have the claims of political philosophy been advanced in more sweeping fashion: it "will not only preserve the lives of the subjects, but reform their characters too, so far as human nature permits of this."[2] And never has it been more strongly insisted that the rightful place of political philosophy ought to be at the throne of political power: "...the human race will not see better days until either the stock of those who

rightly and genuinely follow philosophy acquire political authority, or else the class who have political control be led by some dispensation of providence to become real philosophers."[3]

If, however, political philosophy were to fulfill this architectonic role, two prior assumptions about the nature of politics had to be accepted. The whole range of political phenomena must be considered fully comprehensible to the human mind and malleable to human art. There must be no doubts, such as those expressed by Santayana, of the wisdom of trying "to harness this wild world in a brain-spun terminology."[4] If there existed a true pattern for the whole life of the community, and if political philosophy possessed the true science that could transform a diseased polity into a thing of beauty and health, then it must be assumed that the concepts and categories of philosophy could

---

* From *Politics and Vision: Continuity and Innovation in Western Political Thought* by Sheldon S. Wolin. Copyright, ©, 1960, Little, Brown and Company, Inc. Reprinted by permission of the publishers, and by permission of George Allen and Unwin Ltd. (London).
1 *Statesman*, 292 d.
2 *Ibid.*, 297 b.

3 *Epistle VII*, in L. A. Post, *Thirteen Epistles of Plato* (Oxford: Clarendon Press, 1925), 326 a–b.
4 *Three Philosophical Poets* (Cambridge: Harvard University Press, 1944), p. 139. See also the remarks of Sorel along these same lines in *Réflexions sur la violence*, pp. 208–212. Compare Plato, *Sophist*, 235 C.

comprehend and penetrate to all of the varied aspects of political and social phenomena. Similarly, if it were claimed that through the master science of political philosophy the political order could be shaped by an eternal truth, then the materials of that order must be highly plastic to the impress of the right design.

Thus from the very beginnings of political philosophy, a duality was established between the form-giving role of political thought and the form-receiving function of political "matter." Political knowledge, like all true knowledge, was essentially a science of order, one that traced the proper relationship between men, indicated the sources of evil in the community, and prescribed the overarching pattern for the whole. It aimed not at describing political phenomena, but at transfiguring them in the light of a vision of the Good. The two words, *eidon* and *idea,* which Plato used to represent the eternal objects of knowledge, both contained the root-meaning of "vision." The effect of this was to impart to political philosophy a projective quality. The political philosopher, by an act of thought, strove to project a more perfect order into future time. "In dealing with a plan for the future...he who exhibits the model on which an undertaking should be fashioned should abate nothing of perfect excellence and absolute truth..."[5] Thus at the center of the enterprise of political theory was an imaginative element, an ordering vision of what the political system ought to be and what it might become. In later centuries, other political thinkers, such as Hobbes and Comte, recurred to this notion of thought as the ordering agency of political life, but no one has ever surpassed Plato in insisting upon the moral urgency and centrality of political vision:

There can be no question whether a guardian who is to keep watch over anything needs to be keen-sighted or blind. And is not blindness precisely the condition of men who are entirely cut off from knowledge of any reality, and have in their soul no clear pattern of perfect truth, which they might study in every detail and constantly refer to, as a painter looks at his model, before they proceed to embody notions of justice, honour, and goodness in earthly institutions or...to preserve such institutions as already exist?[6]

The element of political imagination, as developed in Plato's thought, was never intended as an exercise in utopia-building. The spirit of playfulness that marked many of the dialogues, those moments where Plato appeared astonished at his own boldness, and, at the opposite extreme, those passages brooding with disillusion—none of these moods displaced his basic conviction that men could effect a junction between truth and practice. Towards the end of his life, he did despair of seeing the ideal polity take hold in an actual society, yet he still insisted that there could be no marked improvement in existing polities unless men had an ideal pattern at which to aim. Political knowledge of the best remained absolutely essential if men were to share even that slight participation in reality allowed by the gods.[7] The shortcomings of the existential order of things did not destroy the claim of political philosophy to being a severely practical enterprise of the most serious kind. Political science was "the knowledge

---

[5] *The Laws of Plato,* trans. A. E. Taylor (London: Dent, 1934), V, 746; *Republic,* VI, 503.

[6] *The Republic of Plato,* trans. Francis Macdonald Cornford (London: Oxford University Press, 1945), VI, 484 (all translations from the *Republic* will be from this edition); *Laws,* XII, 962.

[7] *Laws,* I, 644 E–645.

by which we are to make other men good."[8] Its ultimate ministry was the human soul. Statecraft was, in Samuel Butler's word, "soul-craft"; and the true ruler, an architect of souls.

The task of fashioning souls was not to be accomplished, however, by the ruler working directly on the human psyche. The essential problem was to establish the right influences and the most salutary environment wherein the soul could be attracted towards the Good. Plato, unlike some later Christian thinkers, never believed that the soul could be perfected in defiance of the surrounding political and social arrangements. In a society where naked ambition, acquisitiveness, and cleverness were encouraged, the best of characters could not remain uncorrupted.[9] Regeneration, like its opposite, was a social process, and the saving political knowledge had to be as wide-ranging as the life of the community itself. From this it also followed that the sphere of the political art was coextensive with all of the influences, public and private, that affected human character.[10]

The creation of a rightly ordered society promised the solution of still another problem, one that was intimately related to the other goals of moral regeneration and political stability. Some of the most moving passages in the dialogues occur where Plato reflected upon the deep antagonism existing between philosophy and society. It was not only that the practices of society were in fundamental contradiction to the teachings of philosophy; the real crime of society was to make a life devoted to philosophy impossible, or, at best, hazardous. Given the shape of existing societies, to pursue a life of philosophy was to invite martyrdom. Where the philosopher was not scorned, he was humiliated, as Plato had been by the tyrant Dionysius; where he was not humiliated, he was corrupted, as Alcibiades and Critias had been; where he could not be corrupted, he was condemned to death, as Socrates had been. We moderns need only substitute the "intellectual" for the philosopher, and we have a timeless document portraying the lot of the intellectual in society: rejected, enticed, never fully accepted, a lonely figure whom Plato compared to a traveller taking shelter under a wall from the swirling storm, "content if he can keep his hands clean from iniquity while this life lasts ...."[11] To make a world safe for philosophy was as fully important a motivation in Plato's political theory as the reform of society and the moral improvement of its members. In fact, all three purposes were intertwined. For if the features of Plato's society appear harsh, and if the moral and intellectual stature of many of its members seem stunted, this was not the revenge of an intellectual nursing the angry hurts inflicted by society. All of these were the outcome of a deep conviction that a city of reason ruled by philosophy would be the salvation, not only of philosophers and philosophy, but of all its members. The fate of philosophy and the fate of mankind were as closely united as the twins of Hippocrates who flourished and suffered as one. A city hospitable to philosophy, *ipso facto*, would be a city following the principle of virtue and developing the best in its members.

---

8 *Euthydemus,* 292 B–C (Jowett translation); *Laws,* VI, 771. The serious nature of political philosophy has been well brought out by Leo Strauss, *Natural Right and History* (Chicago: University of Chicago Press, 1953), pp. 120ff.

9 *Statesman,* 297 b; *Laws,* I, 650.

10 *Republic,* VI, 491–496; *Laws,* VI, 780 A; VII, 788 A, 790 A; X, 902–904; XI, 923.

11 *Republic,* VI, 496 D.

The common assumption underlying Plato's strictures against existing societies, as well as his schemes for political regeneration, was that any political system, good or bad, was the direct product of the beliefs held by its members. This conviction concerning the sovereign role of beliefs was supported, in Plato's eyes, by the activities of the Sophists in the democratic politics of Athens. In undertaking to instruct men in the techniques of political success and in promising to outfit men for coping with the demands of "real" life, the Sophists, in effect, were asserting that they possessed a form of true knowledge. The assertion, Plato insisted, was a serious one, for it advocated that men reorder their behavior according to certain beliefs. It followed, whether the Sophists recognized it or not, that they had implicitly assumed a responsibility for the stability of the political order and a responsibility for the human soul. The superficiality of their teachings, however, had led only to confusion—confusion in the city and confusion in the soul.[12] More precisely, there had been disorder in the city and in the lives of the citizens because in both cases the Sophists taught not knowledge, but mere "opinion" (doxa). Disastrous as this experience had been, it testified, nevertheless, to the supreme importance of beliefs. If the power of mere opinion could create so much harm, then, Plato reasoned, true belief might work just as powerfully in the opposite direction. Here was further support for the proposition that political philosophy was a pursuit of the utmost urgency and practicality.

Plato's belief in the practical character of political philosophy received its classic expression in the dictum concerning the necessity for rulers being philosophers or philosophers, rulers. Yet in the dialogue *Politicus,* there was still a more striking assertion, that the political philosopher was deserving of the title "statesman" even though he might never possess the reality of political power.[13] From one angle this could be taken to mean that the basic distinction lay between those who had the true political knowledge and those who, like the Sophist and the "politician," had only a pretense of knowledge. In this sense, the true philosopher and the true statesman were alike. Considered from another angle, however, Plato was saying something much more significant about the nature of political philosophy. To grasp the true idea of political theory was to attain an intellectual position wherein the chaos of political life had been remoulded by the informing vision of the Good.[14] By virtue of the transforming power of political theory, the philosopher had already accomplished in thought what the ruler in practice had yet to do: he had cured the ills of the community and ordered it to a pattern of perfection. If, then, the drama of political transformation had been enacted previously at the level of mind, and if the philosopher possessed the knowledge whereby this drama might be enacted in actual political life, the Platonic alliance between philosophy and political power appears in a different light. The philosopher acquiring power or the ruler acquiring philosophy did not symbolize a harnessing of opposites but a blending of two kinds of power, a joining of complements. The perfect form of political power was to be achieved by a combina

---

[12] *Euthydemus* 305 B–306 D.

[13] *Statesman,* 295 a–b; 293 a.

[14] This aspect of Plato's thought was grasped by Nietzsche. See the remark cited in H. J. Blackham, *Six Existentialist Thinkers* (London: Routledge, 1952), p. 24. For Plato's view that philosophy was a totally ordering science, see *Republic* 531 D, 534 E; *Sophist* 227 B.

tion of the two, the power of thought prescribing the right pattern, the power of the ruler effecting it. In contrast, the commands of the tyrant or the persuasive arts of the political rhetorician were denied to be true forms of power. By definition, a power ought to bring some good to its possessor, but this occurred only when he had a true knowledge of the good and the just towards which to direct his power.[15]

Now in Plato's general philosophy, true knowledge exhibited certain general characteristics, and these exerted a profound influence over the categories which he attached to political thought. These characteristics were summed up in his conception of the nature of the true model: "Whenever the maker of anything looks to that which is unchanging and uses a model of that description in fashioning the form and quality of his work, all that he thus accomplishes must be good. If he looks to something that has come to be and uses a generated model, it will not be good."[16] Genuine knowledge, then, was derived from the stable realm of immaterial Forms.[17] The world of sense and matter, in contrast, was a world in movement, always in flux, and therefore unable to rise above the plane of

"opinion" to that of knowledge; it was a world filled with maddeningly elusive half-truths and distorted perceptions. Each of these realms was to be approached in a different way, for each had its own set of categories. In the one case, the categories were shaped to express certainty, repose, permanence, and an objectivity unaffected by the vagaries of human taste; the sensible world, on the other hand, was to be understood through categories adapted to its nature, categories of uncertainty, instability, change, and variety. The categories descriptive of the Forms we might call "categories of value," while those relating to the world of sense perception, "categories of disvalue."

When carried over into political theory, the categories of disvalue were at once descriptive and evaluative of the existential world of politics, while the categories of value were indicative of what that world might become under the guidance of philosophy. Stability, timelessness, harmony, beauty, measure, and symmetry—all of these categories derived from the nature of the Forms were to be the angles of vision, the enclosing moulds for capturing political phenomena and reducing them to the proper shape. Thus the immutability of the Forms—"ever to be the same, steadfast and abiding, is the product of the divinest things only"[18] —was translated into the political category of stability; its final issue was the principle that "any change whatever, except from evil, is the most dangerous of all things."[19] Again, since knowledge of the Forms represented an insight into eternal beauty, the political order was to be transformed in the light of aesthetic categories: "...the true lawgiver aims only at that on which some eternal

15 *Gorgias*, 466–470.
16 *Plato's Cosmology; the Timaeus of Plato*, trans. F. M. Cornford (New York: The Library of Liberal Arts, No. 101, 1957), 28 a–b. Reprinted by permission of the publishers.
17 See in general the discussion in F. M. Cornford, *Plato's Theory of Knowledge* (New York: Humanities Press, 1951) ; Sir David Ross, *Plato's Theory of Ideas,* 2nd ed. (Oxford: Clarendon Press, 1951), which stresses the changes in Plato's thinking on this subject. For a critical analysis, K. R. Popper, *The Open Society and Its Enemies,* 2 vols. (London, Routledge, 1945), Vol. I, especially Chs. 3–4; and for a response to Popper see Ronald B. Levinson, *In Defense of Plato* (Cambridge: Harvard University Press, 1953), pp. 18, 454, 522, 595–596, 627–629.

18 *Statesman,* 269 d ; *Theaetetus,* 181 B–183 C ; *Philebus,* 61 E.
19 *Laws,* VII, 797; also VI, 772 ; VIII, 846.

beauty is always attending. . ."[20] And as a final example, the perfect unity and harmony exhibited by the Forms had their political counterparts in Plato's obsessive preoccupation with the unity and cohesion of the city:

Does not the worst evil for a state arise from anything that tends to rend it asunder and destroy its unity, while nothing does it more good than whatever tends to bind it together and make it one?. . .And are not citizens bound together by sharing in the same pleasures and pains, all feeling glad or grieved on the same occasions of gain or loss; whereas the bond is broken when such feelings are no longer universal, but any event of public or personal concern fills some with joy and others with distress?[21]

POLITICS AND ARCHITECTONICS

Although Plato has commonly been regarded as the archetype of the political thinker who has his feet planted firmly in the clouds, the recognition of "politics" was indicative of Plato's strongly empirical vein. It was here that he spoke directly to the Greek political experience. Conflict and change, revolution and faction, the dizzy cycle of governmental forms—these were not the invention of philosophical fancy but the stuff of Athenian political history. Moreover, the dimension of "politics" had been further broadened by the establishment of democratic institutions and practices during the fifth century. As new groups were granted the privileges of citizenship, which included the right to deliberate in the public assemblies and law courts, the circle of political participation was widened and thereby the element of "politics" became more pervasive. Accordingly, the "politician" made his appearance, the skilled manipulator who fashioned power from the grievances, resentments, and ambitions festering the community. With him came the Sophists, the logical accompaniment to democratic participation, promising to instruct men in the art of political persuasion.[22]

The intensity of factional strife, the conflict between social classes, and the loss of confidence in traditional values had worked to create a situation where the political order appeared forever to tremble on the brink of self-destruction.

After a contest for office, the victorious side engrosses the conduct of public affairs so completely. . .that no share whatever of office is left to the vanquished, or even to their descendants; each party watches the other in jealous apprehension of insurrection. . .Such societies. . .are no constitutional states. . .men who are for a party, we say, are factionaries, not citizens, and their so-called rights are empty words.[23]

In this competition for power, woven out of rival ambitions and jarring interests, lay the disturbing factor of "politics," the source of instability and change, and the inevitable product of a condition where political forms and relationships were allowed to flourish with a minimum of preconceived direction and a maximum of spontaneity. The prevalence of politics had dissolved political life into a "whirlpool," an "incessant movement of shifting currents."[24]

For Plato, the flux of political life was symptomatic of a diseased polity; the spontaneity, variety, and turbulence of Athenian democracy, a contradiction of every canon of order. Order was the product of the subordination of the lower to the higher, the rule of wisdom over naked ambition, and of knowledge

---

[20] *Laws*, IV, 706 (Jowett translation).
[21] *Republic*, V, 461.

[22] On the Sophists, see W. Jaeger, *Paideia*, Vol. 1, 286–331; Mario Untersteiner, *The Sophists*, trans. Kathleen Freeman (Oxford: Blackwell, 1954).
[23] *Laws*, IV, 715 (Taylor translation).
[24] *Epistle*, VII, 325 e.

over appetite. Yet in existing polities, a ruling group would base its credentials to rule on anything but wisdom—on birth, wealth, or democratic right. At every turn, the world of politics violated the dictates of the world of Forms. Where the world of Forms marked the triumph of unchanging Being over the flux of Becoming, the immutable nature of the Good over the ever-changing world of appearances, actual political practice was plagued by constant innovations as first one class, then another, tinkered with the constitution, altering here, modifying there, but never establishing the basic arrangements on a secure basis. Again, where the realm of Forms testified to a truth of majestic simplicity, existing independently of human tastes and desires, political life followed a frenzied path from one "opinion" to another, sampling first this, then that way of life, and finding rest only in a scepticism about all political values. Where the Idea of the Good taught the necessity of a harmonious mixture unstreaked by faction,[25] a necessity that reappeared in the imperative that the best polity was one that insured the happiness of the whole and not the disproportionate advantage of the part, existing regimes were torn by the bitter struggles between groups and classes, each straining to impose its special advantage.[26] Where the true pattern was a design of beauty, a whole where each part had been shaped to symmetry and softened by temperance—characteristics that pointed to the conclusion that "happiness can only come to a state when its lineaments are traced by an artist working after the

divine pattern"[27]—actual political institutions were disfigured by an ever-changing ugliness and distortion as successive ruling groups tipped the scales in their own favor. Where the world of the Forms knew only regular, ordered motion, the political condition was one of random movements, jerking this way and that, as the wild energy of demagogues and revolutionaries seized the *polis*, or as a tolerant democracy allowed its citizens a limitless freedom to follow their own preferences.

As a kind of standing antithesis to the world of Forms, the world of politics testified to what life was like when it was unredeemed by that vision that "sheds light on all things."[28] Without an illuminating vision of the Good, the members of a community were condemned to live in a cave of illusions, vainly following distorted images of reality and ceaselessly driven by irrational desires. A visionless life further gave rise to struggles that wracked the community, for "all goes wrong when, starved for lack of anything good in their own lives, men turn to public affairs hoping to snatch from thence the happiness they hunger for. They set about fighting for power, and their internecine conflict ruins them and their country."[29] Far from being a "real" world, political societies dwelt in a shadowy realm, a dream world "where men live fighting one another about shadows and quarreling for power, as if that were a great prize. . ."[30]

At this point we must pause to consider some of the implications of Plato's argument. In particular we must ask: what meanings has he fastened upon "politics" and the "political"? Stated in summary form, Plato understood *political* philosophy to mean knowledge pertaining to the good life at the public

---

[25] *Philebus,* 63 e–64 a.

[26] *Republic,* IV, 421; V, 465; *Laws,* IV, 715; X, 902–904; XI, 923. These passages should be compared with Plato's discussion of the nature of the forms in *Philebus,* 65 A; *Gorgias,* 474; *Timaeus,* 31 C.

[27] *Republic,* VI, 500.   [28] *Ibid.,* VII, 540.
[29] *Ibid.,* VII, 521.   [30] *Ibid.,* VII, 520.

level and *political* ruling to be the right management of the public affairs of the community. One may quarrel with Plato's definition of the good life and with his conception of rulership, but it is difficult to deny that Plato displayed a sure sense that the political, whether it be philosophy or ruling, has to do with what is public in the life of a society. This cannot be said, however, of his conception of "politics." Plato understood "politics" largely in the sense that I have used it earlier. He was aware of the struggle for competitive advantage, of the problem of distributing the good things of life among the various groups in society, and of the instabilities engendered by changing social and economic relationships among the members. He chose to treat these phenomena as the symptoms of an unhealthy society, as the problem against which political philosophy and the political art had to contend. Political philosophy and ruling alike had as their objectives the creation of the good society; "politics" was evil, and hence the task of philosophy and of ruling was to rid the community of politics. Thus the Platonic conception of political philosophy and ruling was founded on a paradox: the science as well as the art of creating order were sworn to an eternal hostility towards politics, towards those phenomena, in other words, that made such an art and science meaningful and necessary. The paradox had serious consequences for both thought and action. A science that is at odds with its own subject-matter, one that tries to get rid of the distinctive context in which the problems of that science take shape, is an instrument ill-adapted for theoretical understanding. Similarly, action designed to extirpate what are the inescapable givens of social existence will be driven to using the harsh methods that Plato himself grudgingly admitted were neces-

sary. These criticisms suggest that the central weakness in Plato's philosophy lay in the failure to establish a satisfactory relationship between the idea of the *political* and the idea of *politics*. The problem is not how the one can eliminate the other, but rather how can we gain the necessary knowledge of politics to enable us to act wisely in a context of conflict, ambiguity, and change?

In this connection, Plato's fascination with the art of medicine leads to a quite misleading analogy: the body politic does not experience "disease," but conflict; it is beset not by harmful bacteria but individuals with hopes, ambitions, and fears that are often at odds with the plans of other individuals; its end is not "health," but the endless search for a foundation that will support the mass of contradictions present in society. Unless the distinctively political context is preserved, political theory tends to vanish into larger questions, such as the nature of the Good, the ultimate destiny of man, or the problem of right conduct, thereby losing contact with the essentially political questions that are its proper concern: the nature of political ethics, that is, right conduct in a political situation, or the question of the nature of the goods that are possible in a political community and attainable by political action. Similarly, the neglect of the political context is likely to produce a dangerous kind of political art, especially when it is motivated by an animus against "politics." The art of ruling becomes the art of imposition. A truly political art, on the other hand, would be one framed to deal with conflict and antagonism; to take these as the raw materials for the creative task of constructing areas of agreement, or, if this fails, to make it possible for competing forces to compromise in order to avoid harsher remedies. The business of the

political art is with the politics of conciliation; its range of creativity is
defined and determined by the necessity
of sustaining the on-going activities of
the community. Its restless search for
conciliation is, at bottom, inspired by
a belief that the art of imposition ought
to be confined to those situations where
no other alternative exists.

Implicit in the politics of conciliation
is a notion of order markedly different
from that held by Plato. If conciliation
is a continuing task for those who
govern—and the nature of "politics"
would seem to dictate that it is—then
order is not a set pattern, but something akin to a precarious equilibrium,
a condition that demands a willingness
to accept partial solutions. For Plato,
however, order was in the nature of a
mould shaped after a divine model; a
concept to be used for stamping society
in a definite image. But what kind of
an order could issue from a political
science dedicated in large measure to
the eradication of conflict; that is, to
the elimination of politics? If order
could only flourish in the absence of
conflict and antagonism, then it followed that the order thus created had
surrendered its distinctively political
element; order it might be, but not
a "political" order. For the essence of
a "political" order is the existence of a
settled institutional arrangement designed to deal in a variety of ways with
the vitalities issuing from an associated
life: to offset them where necessary, to
ease them where possible, and, crea-
tively, to redirect and transmute them
when the opportunity allows. This is
not to say that a society cannot achieve
order by imposition, but only that such
a society is not "political." It also
follows from this conception of a "political" society that the art of politics
ought to proceed on the assumption that
order is something to be achieved *within*
a given society; that is, between the

various forces and groups of a community. The ideal of order must be
fashioned in the closest connection with
existing tendencies, and it must be
tempered by the sober knowledge that
no political idea, including the idea of
order itself, is ever fully realized, just
as few political problems are ever irrevocably solved.

Plato, however, was convinced that
the political realm was inherently prone
to disorder and that the contraries of
disorder—stability, harmony, unity, and
beauty—would never develop out of the
normal course of political events. They
did not exist immanently within the
materials of politics, but had to be
brought in from the "outside." "The
virtue of each thing, whether body or
soul, instrument or creature, when given
to them in the best way, comes not to
them by chance but as the result of
the order and truth and art which are
imparted to them...And is not the
virtue of each thing dependent on order
or arrangement?"[31] Order, in all of its
facets of harmony, unity, measure, and
beauty was the positive creation of art;
and art, in turn, was the province of
knowledge. Political order was produced
by an informing vision which came
from the "outside," from the knowledge of the eternal pattern, to shape
the community to a pre-existent Good.

The outside vision was of crucial importance to Plato's distinction between
the true statesman and the philosopher,
on the one hand, and the politician and
the Sophist on the other. In the dialogue
Gorgias, the great political leaders of
Athens, such as Themistocles, Cimon,
and Pericles, were severely criticized on
the grounds that they had failed in the
supreme test of statesmanship, the improvement of the citizenry. The reason
for their failure, as well as the explanation of their power, was attributed by

---

[31] *Gorgias,* 506 (Jowett translation).

Plato to a false view of the political art. They had been content to manipulate and play upon the desires and opinions of the citizens. They had never risked the loss of power and esteem by attempting to transmute popular wants and opinions into something loftier; nor had they been willing to impose a correct but unpopular policy. The result was not only a degraded citizenry, but the degradation of the leaders as well:

But if you suppose that any man will show you the art of becoming great in the city, and yet not conforming yourself to the ways of the city, whether for better or worse, then I can only say that you are mistaken, Callicles; for he who would deserve to be the true natural friend of the Athenian Demus...must be by nature like them, and not an imitator only.[32]

The true statesman, on the other hand, looked not to "politics" for his inspiration, but to the true dictates of his art; he sought not for the clever combination of existing political tendencies but for their transformations:

[The older crop of politicians] were certainly more serviceable than those who are living now, and better able to gratify the wishes of the State; but as to transforming those desires and not allowing them to have their way, and using the powers which they had, whether of persuasion or of force, in the improvement of their fellow-citizens, which is the prime object of the truly good citizen...they were [not] a whit superior to our present statesmen...[33]

The crucial difference between the "democratic" leader and the Platonic ruler centers around the constituency that each "represents," or, if this word

[32] *Ibid.*, 513; *Republic*, IV, 426.
[33] *Gorgias*, 517. In this connection, there is an implicit similarity between Plato's conception of the poet and his strictures against politicians. Like the latter, the poet does not possess true knowledge; hence, he can only reproduce what pleases the multitude. *Republic*, X, 602 A.

suffers from later associations, the constituency to which each is responsive. The popular leader owed his power to an ability to sniff the moods and aspirations of the populace, to juggle a wide variety of variables, and to strive for the *ad hoc* solution. His constituency, in short, was the community: its wants, demands, and humors insofar as these had political manifestations. His "virtues" were agility, shrewdness, and a calculating eye for the changing disposition of political forces within the community. Even in the hostile pages of Plato, he emerges as the true "political" man, the leader whose problems are defined by the ever-changing patterns of "politics" and whose knowledge is pragmatic and empirical, because he aims not at pursuing an absolute principle but at discovering a policy whose duration depends on the alignment of political forces at any moment. His was the politics of reconciliation, sometimes of the crudest sort. As a politician, his existence became possible only under certain conditions, such as when men were exhausted by bitter conflicts over principles; or when they had ceased to believe in immutable truths; or, finally, when they are, as Balfour put it, "so at one they can safely afford to bicker."

In contrast, the Platonic ruler had a different constituency, for he was not first and foremost a "political man" but a philosopher endowed with political power. As a philosopher, his loyalty was to the realm of truth, "a world of unchanging and harmonious order." As a ruler, he had an obligation to bring the community into a closer approximation with that realm, "to mould other characters besides his own and to shape the patterns of public and private life into conformity with his vision of the ideal."[34] Yet, in the Pla-

[34] *Republic*, VI, 500.

tonic formulation, there could be no conflict of interest or duty between the two roles. The ruler, in following the true art of statesmanship, was conforming to the knowledge made possible by philosophy and discharging the obligation of the philosopher to pursue the truth. And in following the dictates of his art, rather than the wishes of the community, the philosopher qua ruler satisfied the demands of rulership, because the ends of his art coincided exactly with the true interests of the community. His constituency was not the community, that is, it was not a political constituency that claimed his loyalty, but rather the Idea of the good community. "An art is sound and flawless so long as it is entirely true to its own nature as an art in the strictest sense..."[35]

This aspect of constituency becomes clearer when it is related to the motivations of the Platonic ruler. In the Platonic scheme, the community occupied a middle position between the impulse motivating the ruler and the pattern of the Good at which his art was aimed. The true ruler was inspired by an urge which, in the single role of philosopher, he could not satisfy; not merely to know the real, but to bring it into existence, to shape political actualities to conform with the divine pattern. The community supplies the aesthetic medium for the satisfaction of this impulse towards beauty. The motivation of the ruler, then, was not that of the politician—to retain power and to enjoy the prestige and rewards of office—but that of the aesthetician seeking to impress on his materials the image of perfect beauty. The aesthetic element in the political art connoted form, determinate shape, rational harmony, and all that was antithetical to the untidiness, dissymmetries, and

moral ugliness of "politics." Its triumph was the victory of the Apollonian principle of harmonious order over the Dionysiac tendencies of political life.[36]

These considerations were further pointed up by the analogies drawn by Plato between the ruler and the physician, weaver, and artist.[37] The practice of each of these arts involved three elements: the active agency of the skilled practitioner; the Idea at which he aimed, such as health or beauty; and the passive material receptive to the impress of the Idea. The materials in each case possessed no "claim" of their own, because the only way that the sick body, the unshaped marble, and the unwoven strands could attain their respective ends was through the skilled art of the practitioner. The criteria for judging the product of each art were dominantly aesthetic: harmony between the parts; symmetry of proportion; a moderate blend of diversities. All of these aspects, in turn, were carried over by Plato into his conception of rulership. Like the artist, the statesman too was inspired by a pattern of beauty, which issued in the impulse

---

[35] *Republic*, I, 342.

[36] See Nietzsche's famous discussion of the Apollonian and Dionysian spirits in *The Birth of Tragedy;* Guthrie, *The Greeks and Their Gods,* pp. 183ff.; Jane Harrison, *Prolegomena to the Study of Greek Religion,* 3rd ed. (New York: Meridian, 1955), p. 439.

[37] For Plato's conception of analogy, see the *Statesman,* 277 a–279 a. The weaver analogy dominates the *Statesman;* the artistic examples are especially prominent in the *Republic;* the medical recurs in both dialogues and in the *Laws.* On medicine, see Jaeger, *Paideia,* Vol. III, pp. 3–45, 215–216, and on the arts generally, see Rupert C. Lodge, *Plato's Theory of Art* (London: Routledge, 1953). The limitations inherent in Plato's use of analogy are discussed by Renford Bambrough, "Plato's Political Analogies," *Philosophy, Politics, and Society,* ed. Peter Laslett (Oxford: Blackwell, 1956), pp. 98–115. See also on this topic the brilliant study by Richard Robinson, *Plato's Earlier Dialectic,* 2nd ed. (Oxford: Clarendon Press, 1953), pp. 202ff.

to create an ordered harmony by assigning the "parts" of the community to their rightful functions. Harmony of the whole, unity of design, and the shunning of extremes—all of these became imperatives governing the actions of the statesmen as well as prescriptions for the institutions of society. The end of the royal art was the greatest of all human achievements, a community bound together in

a true fellowship by mutual concord and by ties of friendship. It is the first and best of all fabrics. It enfolds all who dwell in the city, bond or free, in its firm contexture. Its kingly weaver maintains his control and oversight over it, and it lacks nothing that makes for human happiness so far as happiness is obtainable in a human community.[38]

Like any skilled practitioner, the ruler was justified by the end of his art in removing the obstacles that blocked the way to the realization of the true Form. Just as the physician might be compelled to amputate a member to preserve the body or the weaver to discard defective materials, so the ruler could purge the body politic of its deformed "members" by whatever means suitable.[39]

This concern with the condition of the "materials" of art led Plato to strain to the utmost the analogy between the ruler and the other skilled professions. No art could be fully realized and no aesthetic impulse truly satisfied if the materials were resistant to the "design of pure intelligence."[40] When translated into political terms, this meant that the "royal weaver" ought to take special pains in selecting the human nature from which the bonds of community were to be woven. He could not combine the bad with the good—for this would issue in a product both useless and ugly—but the various forms of virtue, such as courage and moderation, were the proper materials. The other human characters were to be discarded; that is, put to death, expelled, or so severely disgraced as to be deprived of any influence.[41]

This quest for the suitable materials was essentially a search for a political *tabula rasa,* and in the *Republic* Plato made it a necessary condition for political success that all of the members of the community who were over ten years old ought to be banished; the remainder would be shaped and moulded to the desired form by the institutions of society, especially by the educational system.[42] Then and then only would the political artist be able to paint with a free hand on a fresh canvas:

He will take society and human character as his canvas, and begin by scraping it clean. That is no easy matter;...unlike other reformers, he will not consent to take in hand either an individual or a state or to draft laws, until he is given a clean surface to work on or has cleansed it himself.[43]

The search for a fresh beginning also preoccupied Plato in his latest work, the *Laws,* which many commentators still persist in regarding as a more "practical" political scheme. In this dialogue, he confronts the imaginary legislator with a choice: will the art of the legislator function more effectively in an established society where it could capitalize on the existing sense of community created by a common language, laws, worship, and a spirit of friendship developed over a long period of living together, or would the chances

---

38 *Statesman,* 311 c.
39 *Republic,* III, 399; IV, 410 A; VIII, 564, 568; *Statesman,* 293 d, 309 a; *Laws,* V, 735.
40 *Statesman,* 310 a.

41 *Ibid.,* 309 a.
42 *Republic,* VII, 540.
43 *Ibid.,* VI, 500.

for success be greater if the legislator were to sacrifice these advantages of a going concern and seek instead the fresh situation where the disadvantages of a going concern would also be absent? Any society which lacked the informing hand of the philosopher-ruler would be etched instead by entrenched interests, standing antagonisms, and engrained superstitions.[44] It would, in short, present an unaesthetic medium, as well as a less plastic material. It is not surprising that before the dialogue had progressed very far one of the participants bursts in to announce—with something of the style of second-rate melodrama—that he had recently been commissioned to draw up a constitution for a new colony. Here, *mirabile dictu,* was the great opportunity of a "clean" political situation, one devoid of the blemishing disproportions of wealth, debt, and the resulting social antagonisms.[45] All that was lacking was the master hand to shape the receptive materials to order. But instead of the philosopher educated for political power, which had been the motif of the *Republic,* Plato advocated a philosopher-legislator who would act vicariously through the agency of a young and pliable tyrant; that is, a kind of idealized Dionysius. It was, however, the same formula of absolute power yoked to absolute knowledge.[46]

Once the proper situation had been defined, the political art could then set about constructing institutional arrangements. The detailed prescriptions concerning political institutions, economic

arrangements, the family, education, religion and cultural life, which were so prominent in the political dialogues, were governed by two broad objectives. The first was to establish points of political fixity or unalterable fundamentals capable of withstanding the pressures of political change. Included among these points of rigidity were the size of the *polis* itself, its population, the structure of vocations, the institutions of property, marriage, and education, and moral and religious doctrines. When taken together, these various topics constitute a kind of catalogue of the areas of community life with the greatest potentialities for causing political disorder.[47] They were, in short, the main sources of political disagreements and conflicts. By attending to their close regulation, it would be possible to regularize human behavior and to eliminate, as far as possible, its unpredictable elements. In this way, the stability and unity reflective of the ideal pattern of community would be reproduced at the human plane.

The obverse side of these political fundamentals was more positive. They were the means for enabling the community to approximate the pattern of the Good, to become a medium for the expression of an eternal truth. This conception logically excluded the notion that the political fundamentals of a community constituted an index of agreements among the members. For in this latter view, the community in its political organization was the expression of a social consensus which, by its nature, would fall short of speculative truths.

One of the major techniques for establishing points of fixity was mathematics. If social stability and coherence were important goals, what could be

<hr/>

44 *Laws,* IV, 708. See controls over immigration in *Ibid.,* V, 736.

45 *Laws,* III, 684; V, 736.

46 *Ibid.,* IV, 709–712. Plato's relationship to Dionysius is discussed in Ludwig Marcuse, *Plato and Dionysius; A Double Biography,* trans. Joel Ames (New York: Knopf, 1947); and Jaeger, *Paideia,* III, p. 240.

<hr/>

47 *Republic,* V, 463–464.

a more suitable basis for political action than that knowledge that dealt with fixed objects of unrivalled symmetry and consistency?[48]

The legislator must take it as a general principle that there is a universal usefulness in the subdivisions and complications of numbers...All must be kept in view by the legislator in his injunction to all citizens, never, so far as they can help it, to rest short of this numerical standardization. For alike in domestic and public life and in all the arts and crafts there is no other single branch of education which has the same potent efficacy as the theory of numbers...[49]

This belief, that the political art could transfer the properties of numbers to society and thereby create a more harmonious and regular life, was particularly influential in the political scheme described in the *Laws*. For example, the citizen-body was to be fixed at 5040 because this figure represented not only the optimum size, but also the most useful basis for political calculations. As the figure with "the greatest number of successive divisions," it could be used to divide the citizens for purposes of war, peace, taxation, and administration. By the use of numbers, then, the life of the community would come to reflect the mathematical properties of stability and precision.

· · ·

POLITICAL OBLIGATION

Because of the dominating position which he assigned to knowledge, obligation was not a peculiarly political

problem for Plato. The knowledge of the Good, which it was the function of the ruler to apply to the community so as to bridge the gap between political existence and true reality, was not really a form of political knowledge at all. It was not a knowledge concerning political matters, such as conflict between groups, the operation of political institutions, the art of leadership, or the problem of when to act and when not to act;[50] rather it was an extra-political knowledge which the ruler came to know, not by observing or acting in politics, but by an education that covered every important subject except the political one. At the same time, Plato maintained that the political association formed a proper vehicle for the realization of the ultimate good. Why was this true? Plato's answer was that the Good was a true good for everyone; that is, it represented the true interest of each. Moreover, since no one would ever knowingly refuse to follow his own true interests, it followed that an art, like the political, which was based on a knowledge of man's true interest, could never injure anyone as long as it was being faithfully observed.[51] Once political authority was armed with this kind of knowledge, it became irrelevant to ask why a subject was obligated to obey its commands. To pose the question in this context would be comparable to asking men to choose between salvation and damnation; it would be neither a question with a real choice, nor a question that was properly political.

---

48 *Philebus,* 51; *Republic,* VII, 527. There are discussions of the relationship between mathematics and politics in Robert S. Brumbaugh, *Plato's Mathematical Imagination* (Bloomington: Indiana University Press, 1954), pp. 47ff.; Maurice Vanhoutte, *La Philosophie politique de Platon dans les "Lois"* (Louvain, 1953) p. 44.

49 *Laws,* V, 747.

50 It ought to be noted, however, that the outlines of a theory of political action, closer to that put forward here, were latent in Plato's discussion of the "second-type of measurement" in *Statesman,* 284 e. Unfortunately, the discussion remained imperfect because of Plato's tendency to consider the problem of action solely through the categories of "excess," "deficiency," and the "mean."

51 *Statesman,* 293 a–c; 296 a–e.

The problem of political obligation emerges when conflicting considerations are recurrent, when it is seen that the acceptance of authority involves the individual in a real choice between competing goods, as well as competing evils. Interestingly enough, this had been brought out by Plato himself in the dialogue *Crito*. The condemned Socrates is faced with the choice of escaping the unjust judgment of the city or of taking the hemlock. Suppose he were to take the first alternative, what would be the reply of the city that had wronged him and was now to deprive him of life itself?

Tell us, Socrates, what are you about? are you not going by an act of yours to overturn us—the laws, and the whole state, as far as in you lies? Do you imagine that a state can subsist and not be overthrown, in which the decisions of law have no power, but are set aside and trampled by individuals?...Since you were brought into the world and nurtured and educated by us, can you deny that you are our child and slave, as your fathers were before you?...And because we think it right to destroy you, do you think you have any right to destroy us in return?...Will you then flee from well-ordered cities and virtuous men? and is existence worth having on those terms?[52]

In making the possibility of injustice the price of civilized living, a genuine problem of political obligation was posed, but in the later dialogues, such as the *Republic* and the *Laws*, it was replaced by a problem of another order: what was the obligation of the philosopher to society? Plato's answer, that the philosopher had an obligation, one that he could be compelled to fulfill only in a society that had encouraged the development of the philosopher, was not an answer to a political question. Political obligation concerns man in his capacity as citizen; whether he is an artisan, a doctor, or a philosopher is not strictly relevant. As a doctor, for example, he may have a duty to his patients or to "society," but in any case, it is not a political duty. The issue of political obligation, then, is not one concerning the philosopher as a citizen, but the citizen who may incidentally be a philosopher.

Plato was led to formulate the question of obligation in terms of the philosopher because of his own belief, mentioned earlier, that the interests of the philosopher and the true interests of society were synonymous. Once the premise was adopted that the true interests of all classes and individuals would be satisfied when society and philosophy were no longer in conflict, then the task became one of insuring that society was ruled by philosophy; that is, ruled not by men but by the principles of true knowledge. But since it was impossible to escape government by men, the primary aim of all social arrangements, and especially of the educational institutions, was to create an elite which would rule not as ordinary men but as selfless instruments.[53] This dream of a vision armed with power, of a small group whose special excellence and knowledge coincided with the good of the whole society, is one that has assumed a variety of forms in the history of political thought. It had been latent in the familiar Greek idea of the Great Legislator, an idea that had fused together myth, legend, and memory to create the archetype of the political hero, the symbol of what uninhibited greatness might accomplish. From the great deeds attributed to a Draco, Solon, Lycurgus, and Cleisthenes, there was drawn the towering figure of the law-giver, suddenly intruding to save the disintegrating life of the *polis* and to re-establish it on a fresh foundation.

---

[52] *Crito*, 50–53 (Jowett translation).

[53] *Republic*, I, 342, 345–346; IX, 591.

The notion that the image of the good society might be so deeply etched into political realities by the hand of a great statesman as to withstand almost indefinitely the eroding forces of conflict and disruption was one that Plato also seemingly shared. In reality, however, he added a new element which was to have a profound impact on later thought. This was the conception of the ruler as the agent of a divine and timeless idea, "in constant companionship with the divine order of the world," and not merely a man of surpassing wisdom or virtue. His task was to mediate between divinity and society, to transform men and their relationships, and to make human society in the image of the divine exemplar. This notion of the ruler as the political embodiment of a *logos* was revived in Hellenistic thought where the king was viewed as the transmitter of a life-giving force, infusing a new élan into men and revitalizing their communities. The ruler, declared Ecphantus, "in so far as he has a sacred and divine mentality he is truly a king; for by obeying this mentality he will cause all good things, but nothing that is evil."[54] Early Christian writers, such as Eusebius, Arian, and Cyril of Jerusalem, carried forward the ancient idea that the good ruler ruled his realms as God ruled the universe, and that the ruler who subordinated himself to the truth announced by Christ could act as a holy instrument in purifying society.[55] In terms of later political thought, it is important to separate and distinguish

some of these tangled skeins, because not all of the later writers visualized the Great Legislator or the Divine Ruler in the same way. Some later writers, such as Machiavelli and Harrington, recurred to the old notion of the great law-giver, but they viewed the legislator not as the agent of a divine idea but as a man of intelligence blessed with a golden opportunity.

As no man shall show me a Commonwealth born straight, that ever became crooked; so no man shall show me a Commonwealth born crooked that ever became straight... a Commonwealth is seldom or never well turned or constituted, except it have been the work of one man.[56]

Others, like James I of England and many of the Royalist writers who supported his cause, disclaimed the argument from the intellectual virtue of the ruler, as well as the conception of the ruler as the intermediary of the *logos*. They were content to claim that kings had been sent by God to supply the political universe with the same kind of direction and control that God displayed in His cosmic realm. Like God, the King was an unmoved mover.

Many of these strands were gathered together in Rousseau's attempt to combine the notion of the Great Legislator with a new vision of the community as the active medium for the expression of the *logos*. To the Legislator was assigned the task of preparing the way for the *logos* by instilling in the citizenry an awareness that each is "part of a greater whole from which in a manner he receives his life and being."[57] But the *logos* itself is only expressed through the will of the members when, and only when, that will fulfills the criterion of generality; when, that is, the individuals transcend their private

---

54 Cited in Erwin R. Goodenough, "The Political Philosophy of Hellenistic Kingship," *Yale Classical Studies*, Vol. I, pp. 55–102 (1928) at p. 86.

55 Eusebius, *De Laudibus Constantini*, I, 6; III, 4–5; V, 1; and the references in George H. Williams, "Christology and Church-State Relations in the Fourth Century," *Church History*, Vol. 20 (1951), pp. 3–33.

56 *The Commonwealth of Oceana*, ed. Henry Morley (London, 1887), pp. 71, 173.
57 *Social Contract*, II, vii.

selves to will the general good of the society. The political order was, in short, potentially self-redemptive. These ideas were given a different form when Marx transferred the actualization of the *logos* from society to a class. The triumph of the proletariat was to mark the realization of a truth that had been immanent in history. When it became necessary to find a more catalytic agent of the *logos*, Lenin advanced the theory of the selfless revolutionary elite. The cycle was now complete, for in the Leninist theory of the Party that guides and prods a lethargic proletariat, we find faint echoes of the divine ruler of Hellenistic thought who labors to infuse into men a *logos* of which they are only dimly conscious.[58]

THE QUESTION OF POWER

In order to understand Plato's relationship to these ideas, we must bear in mind the two considerations which governed his choice of the philosopher as the selfless instrument of a divine truth. One was the conviction that no political order could long endure unless its rulers sought to govern in the interests of the whole community. The other related to Plato's deep and abiding suspicion of absolute power, a consideration that has been frequently passed over by Plato's critics.[59] Plato's argument for entrusting the philosopher with absolute power did not originate in

a naïve attitude towards the temptations of power, much less in the secret craving for *étatisme*. It came, instead, from two entirely blameless aims, the good of the whole and the avoidance of tyranny. In the figure of the philosopher-statesman these two objectives were to be reconciled. As a philosopher the ruler possessed a knowledge of the true ends of the community. He was the servant of a truth untouched by his own subjective preferences or desires; of a truth he had discovered but not invented.[60] At the same time, the character of the ruler was to be tempered by influences that would supplement the discipline of philosophy, by strict control over education, family life, living arrangements, and property. These were intended as part of a conditioning in self-denial and austerity which would produce selfless rulers, impervious to those temptations of power and pleasure that goaded the tyrant beyond endurance.

...Whom else can you compel to undertake the guardianship of the commonwealth, if not those who, besides understanding best the principles of government, enjoy a nobler life than the politicians and look for rewards of a different kind?[61]

The real difficulty, Plato suggested, would lie in persuading the philosophers to abandon their contemplation of eternal objects for a turn of duty in the "cave" of politics. Yet the reluctance of the philosopher would be proof of his selflessness, and his ultimate commitment to philosophy the guarantee of his disinterestedness. "You can have a well-governed society only if

---

58 Compare Goodenough's discussion (*op. cit.,* pp. 90–91) of the Hellenistic notions of the relationship between the ruler and his subjects with Lenin's famous remarks about "trade union consciousness" in "What is to be Done?" *Selected Works,* 12 vols. (London: Lawrence and Wishart), Vol. 2, pp. 62–66, 98–107, 151–158.

59 For some of Plato's attitudes towards power, see the following: *Gorgias,* 470, 510, 526; *Laws,* III, 691, 693, 696; IV, 713–714; IX, 875.

60 On this point, see the discussion of Michael B. Foster, *The Political Philosophies of Plato and Hegel* (Oxford: Clarendon Press, 1935), pp. 18ff. For some critical remarks on Foster's approach, see H. W. B. Joseph, *Essays in Ancient and Modern Philosophy* (Oxford: Clarendon Press, 1935), pp. 114ff.

61 *Republic,* VII, 521.

you can discover for your future rulers a better way of life than being in office. . ."[62] That the very loftiness of the philosophic life might leave the future ruler ill-equipped for the rough-and-tumble of political life was a thought which Plato never seriously entertained.

The beneficence of Plato's ruler was not the product of a passionless nature. The philosopher by definition had a "passion for wisdom" which could not be stilled until he had come to know the essential nature of each thing.[63] His was the only vocation where "acquisitiveness" could be allowed, because the knowledge of the Good for which he strove was a type of knowledge that contained inherent limits; that is, a knowledge of the Good, by definition, did not entail knowledge for evil. Unlike those who panted after wealth and power, the lover of wisdom was not in competition with his fellow-citizens, nor did he gain his ends at the expense of his neighbor's. His was the only appetite that benefited the community as a whole. Whereas in most polities the political contests arose out of a competition for the limited goods of power, office, wealth, and prestige, the Platonic rulers would direct their acquisitive instincts toward the inexhaustible and immaterial goods of knowledge. The realm of philosophy knew no "politics"; ambition had been sublimated into the quest for wisdom.

The passionate nature ascribed to the philosopher throws an interesting light on Plato's conception of the community. The philosopher's quest for knowledge was fired by *eros,* and this deep longing of the purified soul not only drove the philosopher to seek unity with knowledge but also created a deep bond with those dedicated to a similar end. Yet while the seekers of knowledge were thus unified by a common impulse, the unity of the society at large was a vicarious benefit of the philosopher's search. Thus *eros* might bind philosophers together, but not them to the community, or the members of the community to each other. It required the Christian notion of *agape* before there could be an idea of love as a force fusing together a community.[64]

It was also Plato's belief that a selfless ruling group, dedicated not to politics but to philosophy, would solve the problem of absolute power. In existing societies, where the rulers were selected by irrational methods, absolute power was bound not only to corrupt the rulers, but to degrade the citizenry as well. The citizen of the Platonic community, however, would be benefited by the exercise of absolute power, because, in the last analysis, he would be compelled and controlled not by a personal power but by the impersonal agents of a timeless truth. The subject was to be under "the same principle as his superior, who is himself governed by the divine element within him."[65] The truth superior over ruler and ruled alike was by definition in the true interests of both. Since no man seeks to will other than his true interests, it followed that no man's will was being compelled when it was made to conform to these interests. The political principle that flows from these con-

[62] *Ibid.* For the apolitical character of the philosopher, see *Theaetetus,* 173 A–E.

[63] The problem of knowledge and *eros* is discussed by F. M. Cornford, *The Unwritten Philosophy,* ed. W. K. C. Guthrie (Cambridge: Cambridge University Press, 1950), pp. 68–80; Jaeger, *Paideia.,* II, pp. 186ff.; Levinson, *op. cit.,* pp. 81ff.

[64] See Anders Nygren, *Agape and Eros,* trans. Philip S. Watson (Philadelphia: Westminster Press, 1953), especially pp. 166ff.; and from a Thomist position, M. C. D'Arcy, *The Mind and Heart of Love* (New York: Meridian, 1956), pp. 62–96.

[65] *Republic,* IX, 590.

siderations is that when political power is joined to knowledge it loses its compulsive element. In this way, political power becomes etherealized into principle.

This argument also held some important implications for the community. By transforming power into principle, Plato could define the citizen as one who shared in the benefits flowing from that principle. This stands in contrast to the Aristotelian notion of the citizen as one who shared in the power of the *polis*. In Plato's scheme, there was no power to share; what was sharable was the Form of the Good written into the structure of the community. The results of this line of argument were two-fold: the idea of citizenship was severed from the idea of meaningful participation in the making of political decisions; and the idea of the political community, that is, a community that seeks to resolve its internal conflicts through political methods, is replaced by the idea of the virtuous community devoid of conflict and, therefore, devoid of "politics." Plato did not deny that each member of the community, no matter how humble his contribution, had a right to share the benefits of the community; what he did deny was that this contribution could be erected into a claim to share in political decision-making.

This marked one of the crucial points at which Aristotle diverged from his master. In rejecting Plato's sharp demarcation between an active ruling group and a politically passive community, Aristotle came closer to the practice of Athenian democracy where the basic distinction had been between those who were citizens and those who were not. This is not to make of Aristotle a partisan of democracy, but rather to insist on the significance of his returning to the notion that the political community was synonymous with the whole of the citizenry. A citizen, in Aristotle's definition, was one who participated in legislative and judicial deliberations.[66] The claim to participate flowed from the contribution made by the citizen to the true end of the political association. What saved this definition from the narrowness of Plato's was the tolerant admission by Aristotle that there were several kinds of goods proper to a political community. Neither knowledge nor virtue, much less wealth or birth, were defensible foundations for an exclusive claim to political power.[67] Goodness might have a higher claim than any other virtue, yet the nature of the political association was that of a self-sufficient whole, and this end of self-sufficiency was possible only through diverse contributions. The claim to participate, therefore, arose from a person's contribution to the civilized life of the community. From the citizen's point of view, however, it represented something more. Citizenship connoted the right of an individual to live in the only form of association that allowed him to develop his capacities to the fullest. In this sense, participation was

---

[66] *Politics*, III, ii, 15, 1276 a; III. iii, 7, 1276 b.

[67] *Politics*, III, xi, 1281 b 6–9; III, xiii, 1283 a 1–4; III, xiii, 1283 b 9–12. This is not to deny that Aristotle thought some claims were superior to others and that a man of pre-eminent virtue ought to be given full power. But it is also significant that the last conclusion comes only after a long argument which raises doubts as to whether such a person was likely to appear frequently enough to raise a real problem. The question of the value of some claims over others is perhaps not to be resolved satisfactorily on a theory of contribution, as Aristotle held, yet it is difficult to see the superiority of modern democratic theories which begin from the premise of equal claims. The problem inherent in the democratic approach is that the distributive role thrust on the political order militates against the equal treatment of competing claims.

a claim flowing from the nature of man. In Aristotle's words, man was born for citizenship.[68]

Plato's criticism of political participation grew directly out of his distinction between political knowledge and political "opinion." In the Platonic scale, "opinion" occupied an intermediate position between knowledge and incorrect belief. It was a compound of half-truths and correct beliefs imperfectly understood. It also represented the sort of crude notions carried around in the head of the average person. To allow the average person to participate in political decisions was to pave the way for government by "opinion." In other words, "opinion" did not constitute a relevant form of political knowledge; this could come only from a true science of politics.

POLITICAL KNOWLEDGE AND POLITICAL PARTICIPATION

Plato's distrust of political participation, then, rested on a definite notion of what constituted a relevant source of political knowledge. If a case is to be made for popular participation, it would have to be shown that Plato's conception of political knowledge was unduly narrow and that a more adequate conception, one that would be more in keeping with the nature of political decisions, is directly connected to a more inclusive scheme of participation. The first thing to be noted is that Plato vastly exaggerated the degree of precision that political knowledge might attain. The belief that political science was a body of absolute knowledge was closely connected with the static character that Plato attributed to the objects of knowledge; there could be no valid

---

68 *Ethics,* I, vii, 1097 b 11–12.

knowledge where the objects of thought were changing and lacking in proportion. Conversely, because the true objects of thought were fixed, unchanging, and symmetrical, it was possible for thought to achieve an absolute precision and accuracy. But Plato's argument about the absolute character of political knowledge was not the consequence of a close examination of politics or of political situations, but was drawn from other fields, from mathematics or the skilled arts, like medicine or weaving or piloting. This is not to say, as some writers have, that Plato was singularly blind to political experience; this would be to ignore not only Plato's personal acquaintance with the political personalities and problems of his own day, but also the way in which this experience is reproduced at many points in the dialogues. The contention, instead, is that his notion of an absolutely valid political philosophy was not, in the first instance, shaped by the nature of political phenomena. It was inspired by the impressive precision attained in science, mathematics and medicine. But if one were to assert that the possible precision in a particular discipline is conditioned by the nature of its subject-matter, then a certain humility is in order. At no time in the history of political thought has this point been made so tellingly as by Plato's greatest pupil:

Our discussion will be adequate if it has as much clearness as the subject-matter admits of, for precision is not to be sought for alike in all discussions, any more than in all the products of the crafts. Now fine and just actions, which political science investigates, admit of much variety and fluctuation of opinion...We must be content, then, in speaking of such subjects and with such premises to indicate the truth roughly and in outline, and in speaking about things which are only for the most part true and with premises of the same kind to reach conclusions that are no better ...It is the mark of an educated man to look for precision in each class of things just so far as the nature of the subject admits; it is evidently equally foolish to accept probable reasoning from a mathe-

matician and to demand from a rhetorician scientific proofs.[69]

---

[69] *Ibid.,* I, iii, 1094 b 12–29; I, vii, 1098 a 20–34 (trans. W. D. Ross) in *The Basic Works of Aristotle,* ed. Richard McKeon (New York: Oxford University Press, 1941).

DAVID GRENE

Man In His Pride[*]

1

That Plato can actually isolate for separate treatment matters of political theory in certain of the early and middle dialogues is our justification for a similar separation. Yet we must notice that the casual ingressive quality of the narrative in these dialogues, the fashion in which, for instance, the nature of the perfect state comes to be part of a discussion which starts with why Cephalus is happy in old age and other men are not,[1] is not an accidental thing or merely a literary device in the simplest sense of that term. It is to be

---

Ch X The Teamster and
    the Team
[1] *Republic,* 328E ff.

understood as the sign of something deeper: that political life does not exist, as a subject for discussion, apart from metaphysics, or the theory of knowledge, or ethics, or, indeed, as we see from the *Timaeus,* cosmology or physiology. Plato in these earlier dialogues has perhaps found the only means to isolate what is for his philosophy isolable in political theory, while the framework of the dialogue with its immediate human context, and the digressions of its human participants, keeps alive in our minds the sense of endless continuity between this and all other subjects. The dialogue thus becomes in itself an artefact expressing the intellectual limits within which politics can be discussed, not an essay teaching Plato's political doctrines.

To put it another way, Plato's political doctrine is implicit in the entire canvas, prelude, debate, and conclusion; persons, manner of debate, and shifts in argument; and not in the isolation of a particular argument or a particular position. I do not know if Professor Cornford is correct in assuming that "the *Republic*...is intended, not primarily for students of philosophy, but for the educated public, who would certainly not read the *Parmenides* and would find the *Theaetetus* and the *Sophist* intolerably difficult,"[2] but there is this much truth in the statement: that it is the grasp of the whole human situation in dramatic (and hence popular) terms in the *Republic* which enlightens Plato's readers on his political beliefs and that later in his life, in the *Sophist* and the *Statesman,* understanding is more a matter of following the logic of the argument and its principle of discussion in order to see what Plato himself is saying about politics.

But, when we set about the business of trying to piece together a Platonic theory of politics and understand it, we are inevitably introducing an element of distortion in that we cannot, in the course of an argument on Plato's political beliefs, make simultaneously an adequate allowance for the constant confluence of the other elements in his philosophy which, if we are sensitive to his meaning, keep complicating and deepening seemingly simple statements of political fact. To take an example: anyone who knows all the dialogues— and this is, indeed, the only way to understand the political dialogues—can see a connection between the doctrines of the immortality and divinity of the soul, the reality of the forms divorced from the world of becoming, the artificial or unrealizable character of the state which is to be the "pattern laid up in heaven" in the *Republic,* and the rigid "harmonies" which are to appear later in the *Laws.* Yet it is impossible,

in dealing with statements in the *Republic* which combine all these aspects of the Platonic philosophy, to discuss them all satisfactorily at one and the same time. Necessarily then to make explicit the position of Plato on basic political questions is to distort certain other aspects of his philosophy or at best to foreshorten or attenuate them. What must and can be avoided, however, is the distortion of emphasis. Considering the nature of the subject matter, the raising and explication of these problems in Plato involves a failure to set them with due detail in their philosophic context; yet we must try to avoid a falsity of emphasis such that, for instance, we are led to identify Plato superficially with certain modern political doctrines because specific parts of his total picture recall them.[3] There are very few individual items of belief in a political philosophy which in themselves justify the drawing of similitudes and comparisons with that of another; it is only the totality of the intellectual picture which can be so likened or compared. We must not distort the emphasis in that total picture.

2

The dominant feature of Plato's political theory at all stages of its life is the root-and-branch character of the change it advocates in existing Greek institutions. Almost from the moment when he began to observe political life and certainly since he began to write of it, he did not want any piecemeal renovation of an existing structure or even any series of four or five central

---

[2] F. M. Cornford, *Plato's Theory of Knowledge* (London: Routledge & Kegan Paul, 1935), p. 2.

[3] Cf., e.g., R. H. S. Crossman, *Plato Today* (London: G. Allen & Unwin, 1937), or in part even the much more illuminating book of Karl Popper, *The Open Society and Its Enemies,* Vol. I: *The Spell of Plato* (London: G. Routledge & Sons, Ltd., 1945). Popper, as a matter of fact, considers that he is chiefly carrying further the work begun by Crossman (*ibid.,* p. 28).

reforms but a transformation of the state in the light of an entirely new concept. This concept was a new philosophical formulation of the objectives of man's existence and the state as the expression of such objectives.

To form a state entirely on a theoretical and philosophical foundation or to remake the constitution of an existing state in a similar way was more frequent in the political experience of Greece than that of later Western civilization. Aristotle in his *Politics* says that in deciding on the nature of the best state he must take account not only of such well-governed states as exist but also of such theoretical structures as men have created from time to time in their search for the best form of political community.[4] Earlier than Plato's days apparently both Sparta and Crete had adopted "planned" constitutions which to a greater or lesser extent continued to exhibit the main features of their authors' original plans.[5] And within Plato's own lifetime, not only do we find Plato himself trying to create the Sicilian state anew,[6] but it seems that the Academy was treated as a sort of political workshop to which at times the Greek city-states applied for lawgivers or constitution-framers.[7]

This tendency is something that we can readily understand, but we have not seen many instances of it in later European history. The work of the American Constitution-makers and the founders of the French Republic is perhaps closest. Yet in both these cases there does appear to be a lesser, or at least a derived, emphasis on philosophical speculation about the nature of the state and a closer relation to a given historical situation. The eyes of both the Frenchmen and the Americans concerned are on the defects and merits of existing governments; their theories spring from such observation and never completely abandon it. The American concept of liberty brought forth on this continent a new nation; their belief in liberty implied an opposition to, a rejection of, the systems of the Old World and shows this in its formulation.

The fifth-century Greek, on the other hand, was strikingly unhistorical in his attitude politically. Apparently he tended to view political experiment as a series of explorations of logical possibility within the framework of a fixed human nature. If he had gone wrong with one possibility, he would try a new and entirely different one without an awareness of traditional links binding him to the past. He would, in fact, start all over again. This is not true of all Greece, or at all times. The progress of the Athenian democracy from the beginning of the sixth to the end of the fifth century does follow an observable pattern in which certain steps are taken gradually, and the transformations within the democracy are made as slowly and with as little violence as we are accustomed to in America and Britain. But in many states, notably rich commercial states, like Corcyra and the cities of the Ionian seaboard, and in Athens herself by the end of the fifth century, there are frequent examples of abrupt changes from one kind of government to another, with new constitutions and new theories of political life continually appearing. It may be that the fact of the internal strife between the rich and poor sharpened the theoretical faculty

---

[4] Aristotle, *Politics*, 1260 b 30.

[5] Cf. the reference to the origin of the Cretan and Spartan legal systems in the opening of the *Laws*, 624A ff.; also Book iii. 682E ff.

[6] Cf. chap. xii.

[7] Cf. chap. ix, n. 11 above. On this characteristic of Plato's political views cf. also Wilamowitz-Moellendorf, *Platon* (2e Auflage; Berlin, 1920), I, 394: "Es ist keine Reform des Bestehenden, sondern ein Neubau, der kein anderes Fundament haben soll als die Natur des Menschen."

in the body politic. A change from democratic to oligarchic or oligarchic to democratic government could not be made gradually. It must come with violence, and the violence brought with it a demand for a new theory of government, not just an emended version of what was wrong before, but a new view of the meaning of the state as the instrument of man's desires.

It is against such a background that we must see Plato as a political theorist. He, too, felt the struggle between rich and poor as the chief disease of the states of his day.[8] But whereas the sharp changes in political fortune drove others to formulate constitutions which would more effectively serve the interests of their class or the external advantage of their country, the observation of the same factors made him see the state as an expression of what was wrong with man himself. Plato's theoretical states, then, are nothing less than the projection of a new consummation for what is truly human in the best meaning of human, as he understood it. It therefore involves a radical readjustment of teaching and education; it involves a reconsideration of the meaning of justice until it takes in the whole significance of human nature. This is why the discussion of the state, in the *Republic,* is only introduced as an annex of the argument about justice in the individual, as an example where the dimensions of the quality would be larger and more discernible than in the single man.[9]

3

Let us see how Plato tells the story of his own approach to politics in the *Seventh Letter.* He was, of course, an old man when he wrote the following words, but I believe he probably is not misinterpreting this younger self who comes before him as he writes:

When I was a young man [he says], I felt as many young men do: I thought that the very moment I attained my majority I should engage in public affairs, and there came my way an opportune turn of political events that I will tell you of. The democratic constitution, then loudly decried by many people, was abolished, and the leaders of the revolution set themselves up as a government of fifty-one men— eleven in charge of Athens proper, ten in charge of the Peiraeus, each of these commissions to handle matters of administration in the market at Athens and the surrounding villages; and over all, with supreme authority, there was set up a government of thirty. Some of these men, you must understand, were relatives of my own and well known to me, and, what is more, they actually invited me at once to join them, as though politics and I were a fit match. I was very young then, and it is not surprising that I felt as I did: I thought that the city was then living a kind of life which was unjust and that they would bend it to a just one and so administer it; so I eagerly watched to see what they would do. And, you must know, as I looked, I saw those men in a short time make the former democratic government seem like a golden age. I will say nothing of their other crimes but of one only: my old friend Socrates, whom I would not hesitate to call the justest man of that day, they sent along with others to arrest a certain citizen then abroad and bring him home to his death; they did this simply in order to involve Socrates, willingly or otherwise, in their actions. He refused, however, and risked the final punishment rather than share their crimes. All of this I saw, I tell you, and much else that was not slight, and my blood boiled at it. So I refused to have anything to do with what was going on.

Some time afterward the government of the Thirty fell and with it their whole constitution. The urge to public service and political ambition drew me slower now, but it drew me still. There were at this time,

8 *Republic,* 421D–423B.
9 *Ibid.,* 368D–369B.

too, many offensive things happening, as was inevitable at such a moment of confusion, and it would not have been surprising in the revolution if some crueler revenge had been wreaked on many by their opponents. Yet the returned democrats actually showed considerable leniency. But by some chance it was again my friend Socrates who got into trouble; some of those who were in high places threw him into jail on the vilest of charges and one least fitting Socrates. For they indicted him of impiety, condemned him, and executed him—this man who had refused to share in the arrest of one of their own friends when he was a fugitive and when *they* were the political party in trouble and in exile, because this arrest was unjust. I looked at this, you see, and at the men who were in politics, at the laws and the customs; and the more I looked and the older I grew, the more difficult it seemed to me to administer political affairs rightly. For you cannot do so without friends and comrades you can trust and such existing it was not easy to find, for our city no longer lived in the fashion and ways of our fathers, and it was impossible to get new friends with any degree of facility, as the corruption of both law and traditional behavior went on apace and increased extraordinarily; finally, eager though I had been at first to go into politics, as I looked at these things and saw everything taking any course at all with no direction or management, I ended by feeling dizzy. I did not abandon my interest in watching political life to discover how it might be bettered in other respects and especially in the whole matter of constitutional government, and I was perpetually waiting my opportunity. But at last I saw that as far as all states now existing are concerned, they are all badly governed. For the condition of their laws is bad almost past cure, except for some miraculous accident. So I was compelled to say, in praising true philosophy, that it was from it alone that one was able to discern all true justice, public and private. And so I said that the nations of men will never cease from trouble until either the true and genuine breed of philosophers shall come to political office or until that of the rulers in the

states shall by some divine ordinance take to the true pursuit of philosophy.[10]

Here we have in Plato's own words the way he saw his interest in politics, viewed from the very end of his life. It is the attempt of the Thirty to enmesh his friend and the execution of that friend by the restored democracy which colored all Plato's further speculations on political life. In seeing the attempt to entrap Socrates as an accomplice in crime, in seeing him condemned and executed, Plato not only saw an innocent man condemned unjustly, but the pain he experienced in his friend's suffering was no ordinary wound.

Socrates was, I say again, for Plato a kind of portent, a revelation of a truth that could only be brought to life, in all its ambiguity, in Socrates. As the combination of his outer ugliness and his inner beauty is full of hidden meaning, so are his life and the end of that life. I can imagine that at this time when Plato was still a very young man the paradox of Socrates' ugly beauty had only been felt as a kind of repulsive magnetism, a puzzle which was to yield its full meaning later. But the facts of the end of Socrates' life, the paradox of the man's quality and its reward, politically and socially, were clear. Because the conduct of Socrates was constantly dictated by an inner knowledge and an inner rightness which was not part of the external political world, there was an irreconcilable conflict between him and Athens, the most flexible and sensitive and consequently changeable of existing states. Thus he falls foul first of an oligarchic and then of a democratic government. The conclusion which impressed itself on Plato's mind and which later experience hardened into dogmatic conviction is that all existing states were ordered with no conscious relation to the pattern of jus-

10 *Seventh Letter,* 324B–326B.

tice. If it seems that this was a hasty and unwarranted judgment, that Plato had no reasonable ground for generalizing from the conduct of two successive governments in Athens toward a single person to the nature of all governments everywhere, the answer lies in the person of Socrates and Plato's relation to him. A great deal of understanding can be compressed into a single experience if the event is rich and the observer sensitive enough. That an administration composed of extreme oligarchs who cared nothing for public opinion and another composed of democrats who lived by giving the people exactly what they wanted should both have tried to remove from his unique position of difference this strange man was what Plato saw and noted. When in later years the young man's conviction of Socrates' innocence and justice was deepened into the understanding of what such justice was, the last years of Socrates' life and his treatment by the two successive governments became more significant that ever.

Yet it would be quite false to interchange the role of Socrates in the earlier dialogues and the context of his political observations with the political position or views of Plato himself. If we do that, we miss entirely the peculiar value which the figure of Socrates has for Plato in his political setting. The dialogues as they represent the old philosopher's life and conversations again and again stress the difference of this life from the social organization which surrounded it. Socrates is the most just and wisest of men in a society which felt his justice and wisdom as a thing alien and at last eliminated it. Socrates as he is dramatized by Plato is the individual in the light of whose virtues the true state should be founded. Paradoxically, such a new state would automatically remove the need for or the occurrence of Socrates, as he actually lived in this world. For it is his sense of difference from others which is not the least potent influence in making him what he was. But Socrates as Plato wrote of him proved in lifelike dimensions *why* the existing states could not admit of the just man or be transformed readily by ordinary political means into just states. Plato is always the man who from outside Socrates' society saw in that society the evidence of the necessity of an order of political life completely different, and the political discussions of Socrates and his friends and enemies are, in their harmony and opposition, the arguments for the necessity of that change.

There are two aspects of Socrates, in the early dialogues, which perhaps reveal Plato's keenest interest in the historical figure. In the first place, Socrates was entirely indifferent, intellectually and morally, to the complexities of the world of becoming and completely true to his vision and understanding of the world of being. In other words, unlike Plato himself, he did not try to change the times in which he lived in the light of his inner vision. When his vision and the existing political necessity conflicted—as in the case of Leon of Salamis[11]—he unhesitatingly followed his vision. Thus the destruction of the destructible part of Socrates in this political world is for Plato an all-significant illustration of the ultimate incompatibility of such "justice, wisdom, and goodness" with the ordinary social life of a Greek state. Socrates, as far as they would let him, did not meddle in politics and tried to "save his own soul." But in the Greek society of his time the conflict between his standards and theirs must necessarily become explicit.

---

11 *Apology,* 32C–E.

Yet despite his vision Socrates, without trying to change his political and social world, implicitly admitted its rights over him, however painful this exercise might be.[12] This is what makes the *Crito* one of the most important early dialogues of Plato. Socrates, faced with the injustice of his judges in this world, will compromise on nothing in his intellectual discussion with them; but he will not escape from the consequences of their verdict because he is a citizen and they represent the laws of his state, and this is the natural relation of man in this world. However corrupted or defaced, this is the basic pattern of justice. This acceptance by Socrates of moral obligations which he regards as truly conceived, amid an intellectual structure which he rejects, is to be the keynote of Plato's thought for a long time.

.   .   .

4

The *Republic* stands by itself among Plato's works in that it is the dramatic presentation of his own dilemma. That is, in the combination and composition of the parts he is laying bare the dilemma itself.[13]

An old man at the extreme limit of life speculates on what it is that makes men happy at the last. In the ensuing discussion it appears that happiness depends more on the character of the particular man than on various general conditions of life. Justice seems the most complete statement of the requisite human virtue which makes the soul of the possessor happier both in this world and in the next.

It is suggested that one will see more clearly the dimensions and outline of justice in a state than in an individual man.[14] And the model of justice in the state, and consequently the just state, is outlined. The interlocutors ask the essential question: *Can* it come into being in this world?[15] The answer is that it can—if a philosopher can become a king or a king a philosopher.[16] There follows a discussion of the progress toward knowledge which it takes to make the philosopher who will be king.[17] Lastly, Plato demonstrates that even the just state, if it should come to pass, will in course of time and at the juncture of the fulfilment of a certain number and a certain kind of man in the state decline.[18] An imaginary and highly schematic process is then described in which the original just state is transformed into the four variations of state Plato's world knew— timocracy, oligarchy, democracy, and tyranny—as the personal character of the inhabitants and the constitutional construction of the state interact. Here the identity of the big and the little, the state and the individual, in virtue and vice are very painstakingly articulated. The book ends with an epilogue amplifying the earlier treatment of the subject of art and government in the ideal

---

12 *Crito,* 50B–53A.

13 The *Republic* can be dated only very roughly. John Burnet, for example, puts it "either before the foundation of the Academy or very shortly after" (*Greek Philosophy,* Part I: *From Thales to Plato* [London, 1914], pp. 223–24)—i.e., in the 380's. Wilamowitz-Moellendorf (*Platon* [Berlin, 1920], I, 393) places it "about 374." For the popular German hypothesis that the first book formed an earlier, unpublished dialogue, the *Thrasymachus* (cf. Ritter, *Untersuchungen über Platon* [Stuttgart, 1888], pp. 34–47; Wilamowitz-Moellendorf, *op. cit.,* II, 81–85), there is not sufficient stylistic evidence, and there is every philosophic and artistic evidence against it.

14 *Republic,* 368D ff.
15 *Ibid.,* 471C ff.
16 *Ibid.,* 473D.
17 *Ibid.,* 474C–483E, 504A–511E.
18 *Ibid.,* Books viii and ix (543A–588A).

state and with the myth which is the likeness of the journey of man's soul after death.[19]

Anyone who reads the *Republic* intelligently will see how clearly its outline reveals Plato's predicament in politics. The book has three phases, in its strictly political parts. In the first the model state is described with the clarity and certainty that belong to Plato's vision of what should be. The second is separated from the first by the decisive question: Can it be made to work?[20] And Plato's answer is: It can. He vehemently asserts the truth and significance of the model even if it should never be born among men, but that there must be a *possibility* of such realization is essential to *him* if not to the truth of what he asserts.[21] Because if there is no possibility of it, his one function, that of an artist in the lives of men and women, is negatived. As to how the change can come to pass he has no detailed answer. That is, he is certain that the philosopher-king is to be the agent of change, and he shows how the philosopher-king can be trained, but he does not know (and later in Sicily did not know) how the conjunction of the trained philosopher-

king and his future people can be accomplished. This, the moment when the dreams become actual life, he cannot see.[22] The third movement is the recognition that even the model state, brought as near realization among men as it can be, making allowance for the difference between word and act, will perish, like all things man-made, and enter into the cycle of imperfection inherent in its humanity. The whole political story of Plato is here: the picture of the model state, of the trained ruler, the faltering hesitation as to how to bring not one but two dreams together, the desperation at the thought that failure can be construed as precluding the possibility of success, the certainty increasing all the time as he grows older that there is an element in all man-made things that makes for death and change and that the dreams of static perfection are only dreams.

5

If we were to ask Plato, "What is the state?" in a certain sense the answer would not differ widely from that of Aristotle. The formulation of the latter,

---

[19] *Ibid.,* 614B ff.

[20] The sharp break in the dialogue marked by the "three waves of paradox" is seldom given sufficient attention; apparently the third wave is thought simply, as Wilamowitz explains (*op. cit.,* I, 446–47), "to set metaphysics at the center of the dialogue" (cf. also Ritter, *Die Kerngedanken der Platonischen Philosophie* [München, 1931], pp. 48 ff.). The introduction of "metaphysics," however, does not serve so much to complete a dialectical structure of being or reality as to turn our attention from the formal articulation of the model state to the need for its realization (cf., e.g., 502C, 540D); it is for the purpose of realizing the model that the philosopher-king, with his knowledge of the really real, is necessary.

[21] *Republic,* 499C.

[22] It is precisely the desperate concern with the problem of realization, without the sure means of accomplishing it, that characterizes Plato's argument. Hildebrandt's analysis of the *Republic,* as the last appeal to his city by a Plato quite seriously wanting and even half-expecting to be made philosopher-king of Athens, involves an amazing misunderstanding both of the spirit of the *Republic* and of the possibilities of Athenian politics (cf. Kurt Hildebrandt, *Platon: Der Kampf des Geistes um die Macht* [Berlin, 1933], p. 271). It was one thing to try to turn a Sicilian tyrant into a philosopher-king—though that was itself a sufficiently dubious undertaking—but it was inconceivable (as Plato himself has said: *Republic* 407A–B) that the philosopher-king should be superimposed on any of the totally antimonarchical (as well as antiphilosophical) constitutions of Greece proper.

that the state is a combination of men that come together for the sake of living and continue for living well, is very nearly the best statement we could make in summing up the *Republic* to answer this question.[23] But a closer examination of the *Republic* will also show the important respects in which the expansion of the common statement would alter its meaning for Plato. It cannot be too much emphasized that in this dialogue the state is discussed only because it is felt that being larger than the individual, while still exhibiting precisely the same proportional dimensions, it may be easier to see justice in operation in the state than in the individual soul. Therefore, we are asked to join a kind of mechanical game in which the interlocutors create in the imagination a state, first in bare essentials and then with greater complexities, and set it to working. When it works and we set aside the virtues which can be most simply and unequivocally determined and named, the residual virtue, it is assumed, will be justice. It is very important to notice that this toy model created by the investigators of justice has in a sense a dual personality, for it is at once *a* state and the just state. These two aspects are combined in the dialogue, for good reasons as we shall see. But analytically we need to see them distinct to be clear as to what Plato is doing: When first Socrates and his friends set about "creating" the state, it would seem to have no "model" character. It appears to be only a question of how people come to live in communities and how the rules of the community increase in complexity as the community itself grows. But this is precisely the community in which we are going to

find justice—as it is *not* possible to find it in the current Greek states. Therefore, when completed, the state created by Socrates will be the just state and as such will represent the theoretical projection, politically, toward which the philosopher-king, in the second half of the dialogue, will look when he tries to realize the true state in this world.

Of course, the assumptions here are so large that it is quite absurd to treat the argument of the *Republic* in logical terms. For instance, we must assume, to start with, that there is a limited number of virtues, four in this case, both in the organization of man's soul and in that of the state. When we have separated out three, the fourth is justice.[24] Moreover, in order to discover the nature of this fourth virtue, we are asked to agree, on the basis of a rather unsubstantial argument, to the definition of three parts of the soul (and the state), the rational, the passionate, and the appetitive.[25] But all this is exactly as it should be. It must be said again: The dialogues are not treatises designed to teach the reader by the rigor of logic; they are not exhaustive as Aristotle tried to make his treatments of particular subject matters. They are rather designed to make the reader understand imaginatively one point of view and neglect others. He cannot

---

23 *Politics,* 1252 b 5, 1252 a 25. Cf. 1279 a 30.

24 *Republic,* 432B.
25 Even if, because of the resemblance to the *Phaedrus* myth, the tripartite division of the soul is generally taken as a constant of Platonic "psychology" (cf., e.g., Burnet, *op. cit.,* Part I, p. 177, where it appears as Socratic; or Wilamowitz-Moellendorf, *op. cit.,* I, 396), the whole apparatus here (four virtues and three parts of the soul) is introduced much too arbitrarily to be taken as "proved." It is rather, as most Platonic arguments are, intended to turn the interlocutors' attention in the proper direction; in this case, to the nature of justice as a harmony.

learn Plato's doctrine from pieces of
the dialogue; he cannot learn the
methods of Plato's philosophic peda-
gogy. But he may be persuaded that
one way of seeing politics is truer than
another.[26]

Here, then, we see our mechanical
model of a state being put together and
into action. There is the hypothetical
gathering of farmer, artisans, etc., and
the formation of a community. In other
words, economic needs dictate the formation of the state. Several men will
survive, in unison, where one man will
starve. So far we can call the origin
of the state, according to Plato, and
the thing created "natural."

There has been some discussion of
whether one has any right to say of
Plato that this is his theory of the
"historical" origin of states. Some have
thought that we must not assume this,
that it is only a theoretical sketch, a
working model designed to introduce
to us the political elements which the
argument requires.[27] This is largely
true, and yet we would do well not to
forget Plato's description of historical
cycles at a primitive level in the *Statesman*.[28] There we are told that as a
result of flood and various forms of
natural destruction the beginnings of
civilization have been made many times
over. The particular details of the initial
organization in the *Republic* are admittedly chosen to illustrate the later argu-

ment. Plato certainly did not conceive
of a civilization starting up with a full
complement of necessary artisans. In
fact, his discussion of the process in the
Statesman, tracing the series of steps
through the nomadic way of life to
agriculture and beyond that, is a much
more sophisticated analysis than this.
But the notion of a state beginning with
bare economic needs and out of them
generating a social and moral order is,
I believe, not purely a device of philosophic exposition but roughly approxi-
mates what he conceives of as a historical process.

When the organization of human
beings in the community agrees to the
principle of specialization and the
peaceful combination of specialists, the
seeds of justice are planted. Justice is,
for Plato, the combinative virtue which
exists not simply in the possession of
one class in the community but in the
union of all. It is, as he says, a kind
of harmony; and the essential life of
the state is in justice—is, in other
words, in the need to be a harmony.[29]
And since this, the higher organization
of the state, is by agreement of men
in accordance with certain principles to
live peacefully with an end in view, we
can also call the state "artificial." Yet
neither "natural" nor "artificial" is a

26 Cf. Leo Strauss, "On a New Interpretation of Plato's Political Philosophy," *Social
Research,* XIII (1946), 326–47: "Plato composed his writings in such a way as to prevent
for all time their use as authoritative texts.
His dialogues supply us not so much with an
answer to the riddle of being as with a most
articulate imitation of that riddle" (p. 351).
27 This view is implicit, e.g., in the discussion of Paul Shorey, "Introduction" to *Republic* (Loeb ed.; Cambridge: Harvard University Press, 1937), pp. xiv and xv.
28 *Statesman,* 269C–274E.

29 It is hardly necessary to point out the
importance of the conceptions of order and
harmony for Plato. This has been done and
overdone in the discussions of the connections
of Plato and Pythagoreanism from Aristotle
and the Neo-Platonists on (cf., e.g., Burnet,
op. cit., Part I, p. 91, and F. M. Cornford,
Plato's Theory of Knowledge [London, 1935],
pp. 9–10). All that is needed is to point, for
example, to the tenor of the argument against
Callicles in the *Gorgias* (cf. 506D) or the
whole treatment of the well-ordered soul in
the *Republic* itself: 399E–401A, the effect of
rhythms on the soul; 430E, the definition of
temperance; 443C–444E, the definition of
justice—to mention only a few of the many
relevant texts.

term which is useful applied to the Platonic scheme of the state. It is exactly Plato's purpose to convey in this dialogue that there is no true break between the first stage of man's economic association and his later more developed community. The need for the simplest economic co-operation already suggests the image of the harmony. All that is done later is to label the elements in the harmony, describe their most effective combination, and, of course, by the complication of the structure, render the whole working model more significant in ordinary human terms.[30]

This interpretation is further justified, perhaps, by observing the pains to which Plato goes to insist that the primitive city, that is, the city of simple economic needs and simple economic co-operation, is the healthy city—in spite of the title "city of pigs" which the interlocutor gives it.[31] The more developed, luxurious, "fevered" city is that in which our discovery of justice will have more importance for the discussion, for it will be more like an ordinary city, but the primitive city already exhibits the harmonic structure and as such is a *true* city and is "healthy." Thus we can see a considerable difference between the fashion in which Plato describes the state and Aristotle's statement. The latter conceived of a state bred of economic needs which in a second totally distinct stage of growth, a more "civilized" stage, discovers, the principle of justice and "living well." For Plato the essential quality of the

state is discovered when men combine in an economic unit, when a harmony, however crude, is born.

6

According to Plato, all objects in the world, and conceivably certain qualities or relationships between objects, are the image or reflection of ideas or perfect forms of the same objects, qualities, or relationships, eternally existent and immutable outside the world of sense.[32] There are various ambiguities in the scanty evidence of the theory that even the whole body of the dialogues affords us, such, for instance, as whether there are forms of both natural and artificial objects. In the *Parmenides* it looks as though only "natural" objects had correspondent forms; in the *Republic,* however, there is mentioned a form of such an artificial object as the bed made by a carpenter.[33] We will disregard these disputable matters and concentrate on the undoubted fact that Plato believed in the form of a state. Thus the true state in this world is that which would approximate most closely to the form of the state, eternal, immutable, and apprehensible by pure reason.

The great problem concerning the forms and the world of sense is, of course, and always has been to determine in what way the sensible objects "participate in" or "share in" or even "recall" their eternal and abstract forms.[34] This difficulty is peculiarly sharp in the world of politics, where the relation of the abstract harmony, governed by its principle of order, to the continuous confusion of the separate

---

30 It is the conception of the state as existing in and through a harmony that accounts for Plato's emphasis on the rigid division of labor, for in a harmony the component parts must be pure and distinct. Cf. *Republic* 433A–434C, also 414B ff. (the "noble lie") and 421A.

31 *Republic,* 372D.

32 See chap. ix, n. 55, and the analysis by Cornford cited there.

33 *Parmenides,* 128E–F; *Republic* 597A; cf. *Seventh Letter,* 342D.

34 The best text for this problem is Plato's own: *Parmenides,* 130E ff.

aims and separate interests of the aggregate of individuals in a political community is at its hardest to determine adequately.[35] Allowing for certain changes in emphasis, the pattern of Plato's political philosophy from the comparatively early days of the *Republic* to the period of the *Statesman* and *Sophist* and last of all the *Laws* is very consistent. The consistency in inherent in the belief that there is a true and vital relationship between the soul of the individual man, the state, and the perfect form, which is the pattern of both. In the *Republic* Plato conceives both of the individual soul and of the state as a combination of elements involving a natural hierarchy and a natural subordination and authority. This picture is exactly the same in the *Laws*. In both dialogues, just as the intellect exercises despotic authority over the passions and the appetites for the good of the unit, so in the state a class of guardians which represents the intellect controls the other classes of the community in the interests of the whole city.

The variable element in his political theory, as, for instance, determined by the *Republic,* is inherent in Plato's relation to its realization. For Plato the tantalizing and torturing thing is the gap between the inner stimulus and the creation to which it forces man. The prophet, the poet, and the lover are all men inspired; that is, the passion that possesses them makes them the vehicle of what in man is greater and more perfect than he. But these passions, like the capacity for recollection, are only the sign of what is hidden in the midst of human imperfection. When the poet would re-create in words or the statesman would try to trans-

figure in men and women and buildings and territory the image of beauty and human truth which has haunted him, he is moving from what is natural and independent of mortality to what is artificial, man-made, and doomed to imperfection and death.

It is for the moment of such creation that, in Plato's eyes, the rational understanding is all-important. That the poet or the statesman shall be able to give an account of himself is the only clear proof, in terms of his human fallibility, that he has not allowed his inspiration to exhaust itself and been self-impelled by vanity into the regions where he imitates "that which is not." So the statesman who would bring to life the model of the early books of the *Republic* must be a philosopher, one who by dint of training in abstract disciplines had acquired a critical, rational self-control. When, at the time that he wrote the *Republic,* Plato was still earnestly bent on trying, at least, to bring his state into existence, the training of the philosopher-king is all-important. The preliminary sketch of the model state in the *Republic can* be a mere sketch—for it is of the nature of the philosophic wisdom of the philosopher-ruler that he should be able to meet particular contingencies in the light of general principles. His will be the task of bringing the state into being and of formulating the manner in which it should conduct its affairs.

But there is another political domain in which Plato is interested— that which lies beyond the formation of the true state by the philosopher. Plato does not believe in the continuous emergence of rulers with the kind of original and creative gift which the first philosopher, who founds the state, possesses. There must then be provision for the future, with two political elements involved— laws which embody permanently what-

---

[35] *Phaedrus,* 250B (cf. chap. ix, n. 51 above).

ever can be laid down as principles in the political wisdom of the philosophic founder, and one or more governors who continue to administer these laws in a spirit of devotion and constancy. Thus there is an inevitable coincidence between the model state of the early books of the *Republic* and the so-called "practical" state of the *Laws*. They are together, in theory, and only separated by the political tragedy of Plato's life—his total inability to bring his state into being. The "practical" treatise of the *Laws* can be deeply concerned about all the minutiae of administration —because it belonged to the never-never land that lay the other side of the failure in Sicily. It is more "practical" than the model state of the *Republic* only in that the early essay is really subordinate, in Plato's interests at the time, to the hope of realization which depends on the philosophic ruler and his education. When the drive to realization is spent, he can give thought and care to the details of what will never come to pass.

But from beginning to end the important thing in the earthly imitation of the perfect form is the harmony which is the objective if mechanical image of the true harmony of the perfect form. This harmony is very largely independent of the actual understanding of the truth by the lower members of the political unit and, strange as it may seem, partly independent of such understanding even by the rulers themselves. In the *Republic*, when discussing the mechanical toy model which develops from the city of pigs, Socrates urges the famous "noble lie" as the foundation of the community. This is the legend which we have already quoted which asserts that men are born gold, silver, or bronze and that their worth to the community and place in it must be determined in accordance with these "natural" characteristics.[36] Now it must be clearly understood that Socrates and his friends are acting like engineers with their model. They are pulling the strings, seeing the puppets work, and, on the basis of this, discovering what are their true and natural movements, always construing "true" and "natural" as pertaining to the interests of the community as a whole and viewing this whole as a kind of biological entity the destruction or survival of which constitutes the difference between good and bad, true and false, natural and unnatural. As an engineer of this kind Socrates says: Let us convince of the truth of this (noble lie) first and best the rulers if possible, but if not the rulers at least the rest of the people.[37] What matters apparently to the puppet reproduction of the "true" state is that certain motions should be gone through, almost ritualistically, and it is at least not of supreme importance that the people executing the motions do so out of an understanding belief in the truth of their doctrine. In other words, the harmony, in the mechanical toy, is the all important element of resemblance between it and the eternal form, not the subjective understanding of the participants in the political unit. Socrates is at this point able to say "convince of the falsehood" first and best the rulers, because it is only the model that is being considered. When later the philosopher-king enters as the instrument of realization, the nature of the latter, we are told, will admit of no falsehood in any form. But the belief in falsehood on the part of the rulers does not interfere, from Plato's point of view, with the validity of the toy model as a suggestive representation of the eternal form of the state.

---

36 *Republic,* 414B ff.
37 *Ibid.,* 414C.

There are further hints in the *Republic* and elsewhere which reinforce this impression. For instance, in excising certain passages in the poets from the scheme of education in the toy model, Socrates says: We will not have the poets say such things, first, because they are not true, and, *even if they were*, it would not suit the interests of our state to have our young men taught them.[38] It is possible, of course, to explain this conditional statement by claiming that Plato cannot anticipate the question, "What is truth?" until he has written the parts of the dialogue on the knowledge line, but he is not writing a treatise in the fashion of Aristotle in which the steps follow one another logically. What is brought out by this passage is Plato's conviction of the value of certain beliefs and certain actions and ways of life resulting from them irrespective of whether the individual believers really understand what they believe or even of whether the things they believe are objectively so or not. The harmony and the ritual are the important elements in the earthly approximation of the eternal form.

The discussion of the philosopher-king, occupying the later parts of the *Republic,* is introduced as the final wave of paradox.[39] After the sketch of the, mechanical-toy state, his interlocutors ask Socrates for an expansion of certain details of that state and finally: Is the whole state possible? The answer to this is to investigate the smallest possible change in existing states which will permit the model of the ideal state to come to life. This change is the introduction of the philosopher-king, and the statement that the true state will exist only when and where the ruler becomes a philosopher,

or a philosopher becomes a ruler, is Socrates' third and great "wave of paradox." It is therefore essential to notice that the philosoher-king—and that means the ruler who can admit of no compromise with falsehood, at least in his own understanding—belongs to the part of the work which deals with the realization of the eternal form in this political world.

Weak spots in the theory of the autocratic philosopher-ruler are already clearly apparent in the *Republic*. One is the difficulty of getting him into the position of supreme authority, and the other is keeping him there. The first is shown by the brilliant study of how easily a man of philosophic gifts can be corrupted in seeking power, the historical example in Plato's mind being, probably, Alcibiades.[40] The second appears in an appeal of Socrates to his auditors where one can hear the almost desperate anxiety of Plato himself: Do you not think, he says, that the many, when they understand that the philosopher-ruler wants nothing for himself and is not bent on robbing or plundering them but rules only for their good, will submit and gladly accept his leadership?[41]

These weaknesses in his plans affecting the inception and continuity of the philosophic ruler are to be painfully demonstrated in his experiment in Sicily. It is in accordance with the general picture of Plato that, faced with the necessity of using violence to impose something approximating his pattern, he is quite incapable of doing so. "No authority achieved with even the smallest number of deaths and banishments is any good,"[42] he says at the very end of his life; but in the

---

38 *Ibid.,* 378A.
39 *Ibid.,* 472A.

40 *Ibid.,* 490E–495B.
41 *Ibid.,* 499E; 500C.
42 *Seventh Letter,* 351C.

Laws, in the projected state, once it is established, the heretic or rebel is to be cut off like a diseased limb.[43] The failure of his efforts to make of Dionysius the example of the existent ruler turned philosopher, and the failure of the government of Dion, Plato's friend and student, as the philosopher turned ruler, also left a very deep mark on Plato. What is powerfully suggested by the *Laws* is that, as Plato abandoned the possibility of realization for his state by the philosopher-king, the "first and best way,"[44] as he says himself, he turned back to the mechanical-toy state the *Republic* and with minor modifications tried to convert this into another and more "lifelike" model (though one still belonging strictly to the unrealized), by a system of unchangeable laws freezing the life of the state into immobility.

This impression is strengthened if we notice that in the *Laws* again, as in the *Republic,* the devisers of the political structure are outside the framework itself. In the *Republic* Socrates and his friends were the engineers of the toy model. They say, "Let *us* convince, first and best, the guardians," etc. In the *Laws* a Spartan, a Cretan, and an Athenian are confronted with the task of constructing a system of laws for a new state. Thus, in both cases, political questions are not being raised from the inside of the drama, as it were—as, for instance, is the case in the *Gorgias* or the *Protagoras*—but from the outside. The harmonic structure of the state, the rigidity of the class system, the immutability of the several parts are essential, mechanically and otherwise, to the state which would bear resemblance to the eternal form. The infallibility of the builder of the state

must be assumed, and this holds equally well for both the philosopher-king, who may bring the toy model to life, or Socrates and his friends who set up the model itself. When we come to the *Laws,* we find that here, too, the three interlocutors are themselves thought of as *knowing* the truth, and this is now being permanently legislated into existence in a code of laws with preambles explaining in each case the general principles involved.[45]

But in the imitation of the eternal model it is the structure of the state and its unchangeability which are essential; it is not essential that from moment to moment or generation to generation even the ruler, much less the bulk of the population, should understand the truth which underlies this organization. It will do very well if they follow a pattern which in the first place was well laid out. It is perhaps because of this that in the *Republic* the ultimate downfall even of the perfect state is envisaged. At the completion of the appropriate number a deterioration will take place in the governing class, and the progress downward to timocracy, oligarchy, democracy, and tyranny has begun. It is not necessary to take this part of the *Republic* as a completely worked-out cyclical theory of history. There is no reason to assume that Plato thought that it was certain that each change in the social organization inevitably followed. Obviously, in his own time, certain states like Sparta had partially accepted all the changes and remained with a mixed constitution. Others, such as Thessaly, had frozen in one of the earlier stages. But it is probably important to notice that the perfect state, or the state which approaches the greatest perfection on earth, will neces-

---

43 *Laws,* 907D–909D.
44 Cf. *ibid.,* 710A–B; *Statesman,* 297E.
45 *Ibid.,* 719E ff.

sarily one day change and change as a result of the emergence of a different and hence wrong kind of man in the governing class. And this I suggest is because the crucial value of the state is not in the understanding of its governing class or of the rest of the population but in the virtually ritualistic organization and functioning of the state as a whole.[46]

---

[46] On the other side, in contrast to this highly formalized conception of the best state and the philosophic necessity for its decay even were it once realized, it is interesting to notice the very particular and Athenian character of Plato's account of the shifts from one form of degenerate state to the next. The change in the constitution is brought about by the change in psychological conditioning in the individual, and that, in turn, is brought about by the continuous sense of other people living around him in a fashion different from his own: that is just the mark of a democracy, which, as Socrates says, exhibits within herself a pattern of every sort of state—and he is certainly thinking of Athens as the supreme example of a democracy. As Pericles said in the Funeral Speech: "We bear our neighbor no grudge for going his own way even if it is not ours, and we refrain from inflicting on him not only legal penalties but private animosity which may or may not be painful but is always vexatious." The oligarch who perceives the power of money to be more powerful than the old value of honor is not a figure taken from Thessaly or Corinth; instead he is a certain kind of young Athenian, a son of the older order. He is tempted, obviously, by seeing all around him young men and older men who have more influence than his own father, in virtue of the money they possess. The democratic son of this oligarch emerges amid the general atmosphere of license within his society and the sense of the cramping restrictions of his money-hungry father. Lastly, the tyrant son of the democratic father appears as the *reductio ad absurdum* of the liberty and want of discipline of his democratic father.

2

ARISTOTLE

Raphael's painting, "The School of Athens," depicts Plato with hand stretched up pointing to the sky, and Aristotle with hand outstretched, palm down, indicating his concern with this world. Such has been the traditional interpretation of Aristotle. He is the scientist, the realistic observer of things as they are, and not the visionary dreamer of things as they ought to be. A biologist himself, and son of a physician, Aristotle (384–322 B.C.) spent twenty years as student to Plato. After Plato's death Aristotle became teacher of the young Alexander the Great. Aristotle founded his own school in Athens some thirteen years before his death; here he produced most of his writings and lectures, the source of those texts which ultimately survived.

In his two most important political works, the *Politics* and the *Nicomachean Ethics*, Aristotle is much more than the disinterested observer. In both works he offers normative ideals which have had an enduring influence on western civilization. Hans Kelsen, the distinguished legal theorist, investigates the *Ethics* of Aristotle in his essay in order to describe Aristotle's notion of justice. Moving from Aristotle's views on the golden mean to the famous

discussion in Book V of distributive and retributive justice, Kelsen concludes
with Aristotle's ideas about political justice and equality before law. The
second selection offered here, by William T. Bluhm, a professor at the University of Rochester, deals with Aristotle's vision of the best political order
as well as with his views on actual governments and the dynamics of their
transformations, be these natural or revolutionary.

HANS KELSEN

Aristotle's Doctrine of Justice

1

Aristotle tries to develop his moral philosophy, in his *Ethics,* on a thoroughly rationalistic basis, in spite of the fact that his philosophical system includes a true metaphysics which, in the last analysis, is not without strong moral implications. It is true that his metaphysics presents itself as an ontology, that is as a science of being, a cognition of reality, a knowledge of the nature, the properties, and relations of being as such; it is concerned with that which *is*—and not in the first place with that which *ought* to be or to be done. He characterizes his metaphysics as a science which deals with the primary causes and principles.[1] He says, "the things which are most knowable are first principles and causes; for it is through these and from these that other things come to be known." But he adds that the science of first principles and causes is supreme because it knows "for

what end each action is to be done, that is, the Good in each particular case, and in general the highest Good in the whole of nature." Knowledge of the principles and causes of that which *is* coincides with knowledge of that what *ought to be or to be done,* that is the knowledge of the good, "for the Good, that is, the end, is one of the causes."[2] Thus, in Aristotle's metaphysics—as in any true metaphysics—the dualism of the *is* and the *ought,* of reality and value, is abandoned. For Aristotle's—as any true metaphysics—aims in its last instance at the concept of God, who is at the same time the *first cause* and the ultimate end, namely, the *absolute good.*

The starting point of the speculation leading to the Aristotelian idea of God is the concept of motion, or, more exactly, the antagonism of the movable and the immovable. The movable is the realm of nature and hence the object of natural science; the immovable, so far as it exists apart, is the object of another science, the metaphysics, the "first philosophy," which Aristotle characterizes in another connection expressly as "theology,"[3] that is, as the knowledge of God. This science is "the most honorable," the highest one, and as

* Reprinted from Hans Kelsen, *What is Justice* (Berkeley: University of California Press, 1957), pp. 110–36, by permission of the publisher.

[1] Aristotle, *The Metaphysics,* 981b. Translations used: Hugh Tredennick, Loeb Classical Library (London: 1936), and *The Works of Aristotle,* ed. by W. D. Ross, 2nd edition (Oxford: 1928), VII.

[2] *Ibid.,* 982b.   [3] *Ibid.,* 1026a.

such superior to the other sciences; for its object is higher than that of the others. "The most honorable" (highest) science must deal with the "most honorable" (highest) class of subjects. Hence the antagonism of movable and immovable implies an order of values. The metaphysics or theology stands above the other sciences because the object of the former has a higher value than the objects of the latter. As the task of the first philosophy or theology Aristotle states here: "to consider being *qua* being—both what it is and the attributes which belong to it—*qua* being."[4] Thus the abstraction "being" is hypostatized as a separate entity and at the same time established as supreme, and that means as value. This ontology has the tendency to turn into an ethical theology.

If there is motion or change, there must exist something that is moved or changed and something that causes the motion or change. "Everything that changes is something, and is changed by something and into something."[5] There is something which always moves the things that are in motion; and the first mover must itself be unmoved."[6] "There is, then, something which is always moved with an unceasing motion, which is motion in a circle. This is plain not in theory only but in fact. Therefore the first heaven must be eternal. There is therefore also something which moves it. And since that which is moved and moves is intermediate, there is a mover which moves without being moved, being eternal, substance, and actuality."[7] The first mover is the final cause of the motion and is itself unmovable. But it is at the same time the absolute good. "For the final cause is (a) some being for whose good an action is done, and (b) something at which the action aims. . . . The final cause, then, produces

motion as being loved [and the object of rational love is the good], but all other things move by being moved. . . . The first mover, then, of necessity exists; and so far as it exists by necessity, its mode of being is good, and in this sense a first principle. For the necessary has all these senses—that which is necessary perforce because it is contrary to natural impulse; that without which the good is impossible; and that which cannot be otherwise but is absolutely necessary";[8] which implies that the unmoved mover is the absolute good.

The Aristotelian metaphysics shows a clear tendency of personifying its first principle, presented as the unmoved mover and the absolute good. Life and happiness and activity are attributed to it, and its activity is characterized as thinking. "It is a life [the life of the unmoved mover, the first principle] such as the best which we [human beings] enjoy, and enjoy but for a short time. For it is ever in this state (which we cannot be) since its actuality is also pleasure." It is highly significant that Aristotle, in describing the happy life of the unmoved mover expressly speaks of it as of God. "If, then, God is always in that good state in which we sometimes are, this compels our wonder; and if in a better, this compels it yet more. And God *is* in a better state. And life also belongs to God; for the actuality of thought is life, and God is that actuality; and God's self-dependent actuality is life most good and eternal. We say therefore that God is a living being, eternal, most good, so that life and duration continuous and eternal belong to God; for this *is* God."[9]

Since God's actuality is thinking, the question arises: what is the contents of his thinking? Since God is the absolute good, this question is equivalent to the question: what is the contents of the

---

4 *Ibid.*, 1003a.   5 *Ibid.*, 1069b.
6 *Ibid.*, 1012b.   7 *Ibid.*, 1072a.   8 *Ibid.*, 1072b.   9 *Ibid.*, 1072b.

absolute good? It is evident, says Aristotle, that God "thinks that which is most divine and precious."[10] Since the "most divine and precious" is only God himself, God can think only himself, or, what amounts to the same, his own thinking. "Therefore," says Aristotle, "it must be of itself that the divine thought thinks (since it is the most excellent of things) and its thinking is a thinking on thinking."[11] The divine thinking will be one with the object of its thought."[12] That means that the question concerning the object of the divine thought, which in the Aristotelian metaphysics represents the absolute good, is not answered, but eliminated. The answer amounts to an empty tautology. The contents of the thinking is thinking, the good is the good.

At the end of book xii of his *Metaphysics*, which is the most informative part of this work, Aristotle raises the question "in which of two ways the nature of the universe contains the good and the highest good, whether as something separate and by itself, or as the order of the parts"; that means: whether the good is a value transcendent to empirical reality; or immanent in empirical reality. And his answer is: "Probably in both ways."[13] To illustrate this statement he compares the universe with an army, and states: "Its good is found both in its order and in its leader, and more in the latter."[14]

There can be no doubt that the leader of the army, in whom the highest good is found even more than in the army itself, is the unmoved mover. And Aristotle concludes: "The world must not be governed badly: 'The rule of many is not good; let one be the ruler.' "[15] The unmoved mover of the universe, the God of Aristotelian meta-physics is the personal ruler of the world. This ontology implies a mono-theistic theology and as such a meta-physical ethics.

But this metaphysics has no essential influence on that part of Aristotle's system which is particularly devoted to the problem of morality and especially to that of justice, his treatise on moral science, his *Ethics*. We have three versions of his *Ethics*: the so-called *Nicomachean Ethics*, the *Eudemian Ethics*, and the *Great Ethics*. Nicomachus was Aristotle's son who fell in battle while still young; Eudemus was a pupil of Aristotle. The *Nicomachean Ethics*[16] is considered to be the authoritative statement of Aristotle's moral philosophy.

It is true that Aristotle starts his *Ethics* with the statement that "the good is that at which all things aim,"[17] which is almost identical with the main thesis of his *Metaphysics*, that "the end for which each action is done is the good, the good in each particular case, and in general the highest good in the whole of nature";[18] that he character-izes the good to which his *Ethics* refers us an "ultimate end," as "the supreme good," and that he defines the task of this science as: to "comprehend in out-line what exactly this supreme good is."[19] This is the object of his *Meta-physics*. But he separates his *Ethics* from his *Metaphysics* by emphasizing that it is "the good for man,"[20] and not the transcendent good of the unmoved mover, which his *Ethics* intends to determine. In opposition to Plato he rejects—for the purpose of his *Ethics*—the idea of an absolute good existing separately in another world. He states

---

10 *Ibid.*, 1074b.   11 *Ibid.*, 1074b.
12 *Ibid.*, 1075a.   13 *Ibid.*, 1075a.
14 *Ibid.*, 1075a.   15 *Ibid.*, 1075b.

16 Aristotle, *The Nicomachean Ethics,* trans. H. Rackham, Loeb Classical Library (London: 1926), and *The Works of Aristotle*, ed. by W. D. Ross (Oxford: 1925), IX.
17 *Nicomachean Ethics,* 1094a.
18 *Metaphysics,* 982b.
19 *Ethics,* 1094a.   20 *Ibid.*. 1094b.

that "good is not a general term corresponding to a single idea."[21] He admits that different things are called good not merely by chance; that they possibly are called good "in virtue of being derived from one good, or because they all contribute to one good." But he dismisses this question as belonging to another science[22]—the first philosophy, his *Metaphysics*. Of Plato's idea of the good he says: "If the goodness predicated of various things in common actually is a unity or something existing separately and absolute"—which definition applies also to the concept of God established in his *Metaphysics* —"it clearly will not be practicable or attainable by man." And he adds: "But the Good which we are now seeking is a good within human reach."[23] And in another connection he says: "We instinctively feel that the Good must be something proper to a man and not easily taken from him."[24]

Since the good which his *Ethics* has to define is a final end, something "for the sake of which everything else is done,"[25] it must be happiness. For "happiness above all else appears to be absolutely final in this sense, since we always choose it for its own sake and never as a means for something else."[26] "To say, however, that the Supreme Good is happiness will probably appear a truism; we still require a more explicit account of what constitutes happiness."[27] The result of this inquiry is that happiness is identified with virtue.

This identification is a characteristic feature of a certain type of moral philosophy. Its starting point is man's desire for happiness as a definite state of mind, the unattainable state of complete satisfaction of all wishes. In order to induce those at whom the moral norms are directed to conform their behavior to these norms (and that means, to be virtuous) this moral philosophy maintains that through such behavior they will—in accordance with the principle of retribution—obtain the desired happiness. This happiness appears as the reward for virtue. If you are virtuous, that is to say, if you behave as you ought to behave, you will be happy. This is the teaching of this moral philosophy. However, since in reality the virtuous man is very often unhappy, and the wicked man happy, and since this philosophy is not able to change the reality of happiness, it is forced to change its concept. For this purpose, the happiness at which men actually aim, is distinguished, as a mere apparent, deceptive, and false happiness, from a real, genuine, and true happiness at which men ought to aim. Since this philosophy is not able and not willing to procure man the former, it promises him the latter; and it can do so without any risk, because it promises only that what it requires. For the true happiness is nothing else but virtue itself. Thus virtue—by its fictitious identification with happiness— becomes its own reward. The fundamental principle: If you are virtuous, that is to say, if you behave as you ought to behave, you will be happy, is still maintained. But since "to be happy" means now to be virtuous, to behave as one ought to behave, the principle amounts to the tautology: If you are virtuous, you are virtuous. However, it is a peculiarity of this ideology that the fiction on which it is based, may turn into reality. If somebody believes in the affirmation of this moral philosophy that virtue, and only virtue, makes man happy, then the consciousness of having behaved morally, of having fulfilled his moral duty, may produce in him the same feeling of satisfaction which is constituted by that happiness which the moral philosophy—because it cannot

---

21 *Ibid.*, 1096b. 22 *Ibid.*, 1096b.
23 *Ibid.*, 1096b–1097a. 24 *Ibid.*, 1095b.
25 *Ibid.*, 1097a. 26 *Ibid.*, 1097b.
27 *Ibid.*, 1097b.

procure it to man as reward for his virtue—tries to replace by virtue itself.

When Aristotle takes happiness as the starting point of his ethics, because it is the supreme good, the good which is always chosen for its own sake, he first accepts this concept in its usual sense, as a real state of mind, as that condition of satisfaction which is actually desired by man. He is far from identifying it with virtue. He expressly rejects the doctrine that virtue is the end of life, "since it appears possible to possess virtue while you are asleep, or without putting it into practice throughout the whole of your life; and also for the virtuous man to suffer the greatest misery and misfortune— though no one would pronounce a man living a life of misery to be happy, unless for the sake of maintaining a paradox."[28] And when he characterizes happiness as something desired for its own sake, he opposes happiness to virtue: "Happiness," he says, "we choose always for itself and never for the sake of something else; but honor, pleasure, reason, and every virtue we choose, indeed, for themselves (for if nothing resulted from them we should still choose each of them) but we choose them also for the sake of happiness, judging that by means of them we shall be happy."[29] Happiness is here evidently conceived of as consequence or reward of virtue, and not at all as identical with it.

The transformation of happiness into virtue takes place while asking what happiness really is. Aristotle tries to answer this question "by ascertaining what is man's function."[30] By this he understands the specific function of man in general, in contradistinction to the function a man has in his capacity as a carpenter, a shoemaker, or the like. This specific function of man is, accord-

ing to Aristotle, "the practical life of the rational part of man," the function of his rational faculty, the activity of his reason; and happiness is activity in conformity with reason. It is "an activity of soul which follows or implies a rational principle"; and "the function of a good man is to perform this activity well and rightly." Since a "good man" is a virtuous man, and to perform an activity "well and rightly" is to perform it in accordance with virtue, the just-quoted statement amounts to the redundancy: a virtuous man is the one who acts in accordance with virtue. On this, rather problematical, basis he arrives at the following definition of happiness as the supreme human good. It is "activity of the soul in accordance with virtue—if there is more than one virtue, in accordance with the best and most complete."[31] The good is happiness and happiness is virtue. "Our definition accords with the description of the happy man as one who 'lives well' or 'does well'; for it has virtually identified happiness with a form of good life or doing well." Aristotle expressly admits that his definition is in agreement "with those who pronounce happiness to be virtue, or some particular virtue."[32] He even declares, in fact, that "no supremely happy man can ever become miserable. For he will never do hateful or base actions, since we hold that a truly good and wise man will bear all kinds of fortune in a seemly way, and will always act in the noblest manner that the circumstances allow."[33] But he does not go so far as to ignore completely the importance of external goods for happiness. A revised definition of happiness reads as follows: That man is happy "who realizes complete virtue in action, and is adequately furnished with external goods, not for any casual period but throughout a com-

28 *Ibid.*, 1095b, 1096a.   29 *Ibid.*, 1097b.
30 *Ibid.*, 1097b.

31 *Ibid.*, 1098a.   32 *Ibid.*, 1098b.
33 *Ibid.*, 1101a.

plete lifetime."[34] But later Aristotle returns to the first definition of happiness as "a certain activity of the soul in conformity with perfect virtue" as a starting point of his investigation into the nature of virtue. And again he insists that "the virtue that we have to consider is clearly human virtue, since the good or happiness which we set out to seek is human good and human happiness."[35]

2

Thus the good, the moral value, is humanized; it is presented as virtue of man. Consequently the *Ethics* of Aristotle aims at a system of human virtues, among which justice is the "chief of the virtues," the "perfect virtue."[36] How to determine the moral value, or, in Aristotle's language, the moral virtues? At the beginnings of his *Ethics,* Aristotle emphasizes that "the

same exactness must not be expected in all departments of philosophy alike, any more than in all the products of arts and crafts." In the field of ethics "we must be content if, in dealing with subjects and starting from premises thus uncertain [as the concepts of the good and of justice], we succeed in presenting a rough outline of the truth..." "It is the mark of an educated mind to expect that amount of exactness in each kind which the nature of the particular subject admits. It is equally unreasonable to accept merely probable conclusions from a mathematician, and to demand strict demonstration from an orator."[37] Nevertheless, Aristotle applies

---

34 *Ibid.*, 1101a.

35 *Ibid.*, 1102a. Later, Aristotle characterizes virtue as "disposition" (1106a). In answering the question as to "what species of disposition" virtue is, he says: "Excellence or virtue in a man will be the disposition which renders him a good man and also which will cause him to perform his function well." This definition, too, is tautological. Since "virtue in a man" is identical with goodness as a man's quality, the definition amounts to the statement that the goodness of a man is the disposition which renders him a good man and causes his work to be a good work. Of the same type is the statement: "Inasmuch as moral virtue is a disposition of the mind in regard to choice, and choice is deliberate desire, it follows that, if the choice is to be good, both the principle must be true and the desire right, and that desire must pursue the same things as principle affirms.... The attainment of truth" in so far as "practical intelligence" is concerned, "is the attainment of truth corresponding to right desire," (1139a). That means: the choice (i.e. deliberate desire) is good if it is right—which means: if it is good. Another statement of the same kind: "To like and to dislike the right things is thought to be a most important element in the formation of a virtuous character" (1172a).

36 *Ibid.*, 1129b.

37 *Ibid.*, 1094b. Although Aristotle presents his ethics as a department of politics (1094b) and characterizes politics as "the most authoritative science" whose purpose is "the knowledge of the supreme good," as a science which "lays down laws as to what people shall do and what things they shall refrain from doing" (1094b), he states in the second book of his *Ethics:* "our present study, unlike the other branches of philosophy, has a practical aim (for we are not investigating the nature of virtue for the sake of knowing what it is, but in order that we may become good, without which result our investigation would be of no use)" (1103b), thus confusing ethics, as the science of morals, with its object, that is, morals as a normative order. It seems that he denies the possibility of describing this object in terms of general rules. For he says that "the whole theory of conduct is bound to be an outline only and not an exact system, in accordance with the rule we laid down at the beginning [referring to the statement quoted in the text] that philosophical theories must only be required to correspond to their subject matter; and matters of conduct and expediency have nothing fixed or invariable about them, any more than have matters of health. And if this is true of the general theory of ethics, still less is exact precision possible in dealing with particular cases of conduct; for these come under no science or professional tradition, but the agents themselves have to consider what is suited to the circumstances of each occasion, just as is the case with the art of medicine or of navigation" (1104a). If, as Aristotle asserts, "scientific knowledge is a mode of conception dealing with universals

a mathematical-geometrical analogy to solve the central problem of his ethics, to answer the question as to what is virtue. It is his famous Doctrine of the Mean (*mesótes*). Virtue is a mean state between two extremes, which are vices, one of excess and one of deficiency. "Virtue is a mean state in the sense that it aims at hitting the mean . . . excess and deficiency are a mark of vice, and observance of the mean a mark of virtue."[38]

This formula is—as Aristotle himself admits—instigated by a commonplace, "the common remark about a

_____

and things that are of necessity" (1140b), and if ethics cannot describe its object in terms of general rules because "action"—the object of a theory of morals—"deals with particular things" (1141b), ethics is not only no sicence but altogether impossible. For what else could a "theory" of morals present but general rules indicating that under certain conditions a certain human behavior ought to take place? And how can an acting individual know how to act morally in a concrete case if he does not know a general rule prescribing a definite conduct under definite conditions, identical with those under which he is acting? What the acting individual has to decide for himself is only the question as to whether the conditions determined by the general norm exist in his case—he has to decide the *questio facti*, not the *questio juris* (the latter is the question how to act if his action is to be considered as morally good, i.e., in conformity with a general rule of morals). The value judgment that a concrete action is morally good or morally bad consists in nothing else but in the judgment that it is or is not in conformity with a general norm presupposed by the judging subject as valid. As a matter of fact, Aristotle presents in his *Ethics* many general rules of morals, thus when he states that "to seek death in order to escape from poverty, or the pangs of love, or from pain or sorrow, is not the act of a courageous man, but rather of a coward" (1116a); or: "Falsehood is in itself base and reprehensible, and truth noble and praiseworthy" (1127a). The fact that some general rules are valid only with certain exceptions means that there is a conflict between two general rules and that, therefore, the one is restricted by the other, as Aristotle shows in *Ethics*, IX, 1.

38 *Ibid.*, 1106b.

perfect work of art: that you could not take from it nor add to it"; which—according to Aristotle—means "that excess and deficiency destroy perfection, whereas adherence to the mean preserves it."[39] Aristotle chooses this commonplace as starting point of his inquiry because in it the quality of value is presented as quantity; and the application of a mathematical-geometrical method in ethics is possible only if the moral value is transformed from a quality into a quantity. If the criterion of that what is good in a work is: that one cannot take away from it nor add to it, then the good is characterized in the same way as the point by which a line is divided into two equal parts. The moralist can find the virtue which he is looking for just as the geometrist can find the point equidistant from the two ends of a line. The tendency to quantify the moral value in order to render a mathematical-geometrical or quasi mathematical-geometrical method possible is very clear in the statement: "Now of everything that is continuous and divisible, it is possible to take the larger part or the smaller part, or an equal part, and these parts may be larger, smaller, and equal either with respect to the thing itself or relatively to us; the equal part being a mean between excess and deficiency. By the mean of the thing I denote a point equally distant from either extreme; which is one and the same for everybody; by the mean relative to us, that amount which is neither too much nor too little, and this is not one and the same for everybody."[40] In another connection Aristotle says of the two vices between which, as between two extremes, the virtue as the mean lies: "The greatest degree of opposition exists between the two extremes. For the extremes are farther apart from each other than from the mean, just as great is farther from small and small from great than either from

_____

39 *Ibid.*, 1106a.   40 *Ibid.*, 1105b.

equal."[41] That Aristotle intends to present his method of determining the moral good or virtue as a quasi mathematical-geometrical operation is shown by his saying that although it is possible to find what is good or a virtue, it is not easy: "It is a hard task to be good, for it is hard to find the middle point in anything: for instance, not everybody can find the center of a circle, but only someone who knows geometry."[42] To determine the good is, in principle, the same problem as to determine the middle point of a straight line or the center of a circle.

The quantification of the moral value, the three-partite scheme of "too much," "mean," "too little," the essential presupposition of a mathematical-geometrical method of determining the good, is a fallacy. In the realm of moral values there are no measurable quantities as in the realm of reality as object of natural science. Ethics deals with qualities only—with the qualities of good and evil, right and wrong, just or unjust, virtuous or vicious; that is to say, with conformity and nonconformity to a norm presupposed as valid. The statement that a definite human behavior is good or evil, right or wrong, just or unjust, virtuous or vicious, presupposes the assumption that something ought to be done. The statement that something ought to be or to be done, is a norm. It is a way to express the idea that something is an end, not a means to an end. It is a value judgment. The statement that a human behavior is good or evil, right or wrong, just or unjust, virtuous or vicious, means that this behavior is in conformity with a presupposed norm, or is not in conformity with it, that is, in contradiction to the presupposed norm. If a man's behavior is in conformity with a norm presupposed to be valid, we say: he obeys the norm; if his behavior is not

in conformity with the norm, because it contradicts the norm, we say: he violates the norm.

The statement that a virtue is the mean between a vice of deficiency and a vice of excess, as between something that is too little and something that is too much, implies the idea that the relationship between virtue and vice is a relationship of degrees. But, since virtue consists in conformity, and vice in nonconformity of a behavior to a moral norm, the relationship between virtue and vice cannot be that of different degrees. For with respect to this conformity or nonconformity no degrees are possible. A behavior can neither "too much" nor "too little" conform, it can only conform or not conform to a (moral or legal) norm; it can only contradict or not contradict a norm. If we presuppose the norm: men shall not lie, or—expressed positively—men shall tell the truth, a definite statement made by a man is true or is not true, is a lie or is not a lie. If it is true, the man's behavior is in conformity with the norm; if it is a lie, the man's behavior is in contradiction to the norm. But the behavior cannot be in different degrees in conformity with or in contradiction to the norm. It cannot be more or less and, hence, not too much or too little in conformity or contradiction to the norm. Aristotle's differentiation of three degrees or "amounts"—excess, mean, deficiency—does, in truth, not refer to the moral value, the quality of being good or evil, a virtue or a vice, but to a psychic reality. He says: Moral virtue "is concerned with feelings and actions, in which one can have excess or deficiency or a due mean. For example one can be frightened or bold, feel desire or anger or pity, and experience pleasure and pain in general, either too much or too little, and in both cases wrongly; whereas to feel these feelings at the right time, on the right occasion, toward the right people, for the right

---

[41] *Ibid.,* 1108b.   [42] *Ibid.,* 1109a.

purpose, in the right manner, is to feel the best amount of them which is the mean amount—and the best amount is, of course, the mark of virtue."[43] Applied to the virtues of temperance and courage, the *mesótes* doctrine is presented as follows: "The observance of the mean of fear and confidence is courage. The man that exceeds in fearlessness is not designated by any special name (and this is the case with many of the virtues and vices); he that exceeds in confidence is Rash; he that exceeds in fear and is deficient in confidence is Cowardly. In respect of pleasures and pains—not all of them, and to a less degree in respect of pains—the observance of the mean is Temperance, the excess Profligacy. Men deficient in the enjoyment of pleasures scarcely occur, and hence this character also has not been assigned a name, but we may call it Insensible."[44] Cowardice is a "vice of deficiency," because it is characterized by too little confidence. Rashness is a "vice of excess," because it is characterized by too much confidence. Profligacy is a vice of excess, because it is characterized as too much indulgence in pleasure. Insensibleness is a vice of deficiency, because it is characterized by too little enjoyment of pleasure. The feeling which accompanies or causes a certain behavior may be capable of different degrees of intensity but not the conformity or nonconformity of this behavior with the moral norm which constitutes the virtue or the vice, the quality of being right or wrong. Neither of these degrees or amounts is, in itself, "too much" or "too little," or represents excess or deficiency. To be "too much" or "too little," are value judgments which are possible only if one presupposes that a certain degree or "amount" is the "right" one. And a certain degree or amount of feeling is "right" because the behavior accompanied or caused by

this feeling is right, that is, in conformity with the moral norm. What is right or wrong is the behavior in its relation to the moral norm; and this relation is not capable of degrees. This is why Aristotle cannot consistently maintain his statement that the virtue is a mean, and, as such, opposed to the extremes, but has to admit that virtue is an extreme itself. He is compelled to modify his doctrine of the mean by saying that virtue is "the observance of the mean" only "in respect of its essence and the definition that states its original being," but "in point of excellence and rightness it is an extreme."[45] The point of excellence and rightness is in truth the only point which counts, for virtue is by its very

43 *Ibid.,* 1106b.   44 *Ibid.,* 1107b.

45 *Ibid.,* 1107a. In another connection we read: "The middle states of character are in excess as compared with the defective states and defective as compared with the excessive states, whether in the case of feelings or of actions. For instance, a brave man appears rash in contrast with a coward and cowardly in contrast with a rash man; similarly a temperate man appears profligate in contrast with a man insensible to pleasure and pain, but insensible in contrast with a profligate" (1108b). Hence virtue may be not only a mean but also an excess as well as a deficiency. But there are virtues and vices to which, according to Aristotle's express statement, the *mesótes* doctrine does not apply at all. "Not every action or feeling however admits of the observance of a due mean. Indeed the very names of some essentially denote evil, for instance malice, shamelessness, envy, and, of actions, adultery, theft, murder. All these and similar actions and feelings are blamed as being bad in thmselves; it is not the excess or deficiency of them that we blame. It is impossible therefore ever to go right in regard to them—one must always be wrong" (1107a). Among the virtues to which the *mesótes* doctrine is not applicable, temperance and justice are mentioned: "Just as there can be no excess or deficiency in temperance and justice, because the mean is in a sense an extreme, so there can be no observance of the mean nor excess nor deficiency in the corresponding vicious acts." Nevertheless, later the *mesótes* doctrine is applied to temperance as well as to justice.

nature "excellence and rightness." The ideas of "too much" and "too little," designating a quantitative distance from the good, are merely figures of speech, a special metaphor in presenting the relation of a human behavior to a moral (or legal) norm. Aristotle compares the fact that a certain behavior corresponds to a presupposed norm with the middle point of a line, and the fact that a behavior does not correspond to a pre-supposed norm with the two ends of the line. When the phenomenon is described without using a metaphor, the tripartite scheme of the *mesótes* formula must immediately be replaced by a bipartite scheme: the antagonism of good and evil, right and wrong, conformity and nonconformity. "Too much" and "too little" are not—as the doctrine of the mean presents them—two different quantities of the same moral substra-tum, but two different expressions designating one and the same quality, namely nonconformity—the fact that a certain behavior contradicts a norm. Virtue means: to comply with a moral norm, vice: to violate a moral norm.

To distinguish between two different vices as two different "extremes" is pos-sible only if there are two different norms regulating human behavior. It seems that this is the situation at least in some cases to which the *mesótes* formula is applied. A typical example is the virtue of courage as a mean be-tween the vice of cowardice as "too little" and the vice of rashness as "too much" (confidence). By characterizing the vice of cowardice as compared with the virtue of courage as "too little" we express figuratively the idea that the behavior in question contradicts the norm whose fulfillment constitutes the virtue that the coward violates, the norm prescribing courage. By character-izing the vice of rashness compared with the virtue of courage as "too much" we express the idea that the behavior con-tradicts a norm other than the one whose fulfillment constitutes the virtue concerned. Only rashness, the "too much," not cowardice, the "too little," is a violation of the norm prescribing courage. A rash man is courageous, whereas a coward is not. The former is courageous but he has too much con-fidence. In this sense he is "too" cour-ageous; and that means that he, by being courageous, violates another norm, the one prescribing prudence, the duty to take into consideration the pos-sibility of success, the principle that the value we risk to destroy should be in a certain proportion to the value we try to realize by our action. "Too" just is, according to a widespread opinion, he who applies a certain rule of inter-national morality in a certain case even to the disadvantage of his own country, who in applying this rule violates the norm expressed in the well-known say-ing: "right or wrong, my country." In one of the two "too's" of the *mesótes* formula nonconformity to one norm, in the other nonconformity to another norm is expressed. In the spatial meta-phor that virtue is the mean between two vices as two extremes, one con-formity is brought in relation to two nonconformities, without expressing the fact that there are two different norms which the two patterns of behavior, characterized as "vices," are violating. The *mesótes* doctrine creates the ap-pearance as if it were one and the same norm which one violates by, so to speak, remaining below, or by going beyond the line determined by it. The *mesótes* formula veils the problem it pretends to solve. Since the norms of a given moral system are very often in conflict with one another, it is necessary, in order to act morally, to restrict the sphere of validity of the different norms in the proper way. That "virtue" is the "mean" between two vices means that morally correct is only the behavior by which the one of the conflicting norms is obeyed without the other being violated. The true problem is to show how this is possible, how, for example, a man's behavior can conform to the norm of courage and at the same time to that of prudence. To this question the *mesótes* doctrine gives no answer; nor to any question aiming at a determination of the moral value.

It claims to be such an answer by pretending to furnish a method by which the moralist can find the good by finding the mid point between two vices, just as geometry furnishes a method to find the middle point between two extreme points of a line. If the *mesótes* formula is a determination of the good at all, it is it only if the virtue is a mean in the same sense as a line is bisected at a point equidistant from its two ends. But this Aristotle cannot maintain. For the two vices between which the virtue lies are not extremes in the same sense as the two ends of a line bisected at a point equidistant from them. This is shown by an example Aristotle himself presents. He says: "Suppose that ten pounds of food is too much for anybody and two pounds too little, it does not follow that a trainer will prescribe six pounds [which is the exact mean], for perhaps even this will be too much or too little for the particular athlete who is to receive it."[46] If the "extremes"—ten and two—can be characterized only as "too much" and as "too little," any quantity greater than ten—that is, the one characterized as "too much"—is also too much, and any quantity smaller than two—that is, the one characterized as "too little"—is also too little, and the correct quantity may be any of the infinitely many magnitudes between ten and two. This is the reason why Aristotle distinguishes between the

mean in an objective sense and the mean in a subjective sense of the term, between the "mean with respect to the thing" which is the real mean, and "one and the same for everybody," and the "mean with respect to us," which "is not one and the same for everybody." That expresses that the "mean with respect to us" is not determined and not determinable as the point equidistant from the two ends of the bisected line. Virtue is a mean between two vices in the sense of the "mean with respect to us." Since the two "extremes" between which virtue lies as a "mean with respect to us" are not so determined as the two extreme points of a line must be determined in order that we can determine the point equidistant from them—since the two vices are characterized only as "too much" and "too little"—all we can say of the virtue we are looking for is that it lies somewhere between them. There is no reason to assume that the virtue lies exactly in the middle and not nearer to the one or the other vice. Aristotle admits: "In some cases the defect, in others the excess, is more opposed to the mean; for example, Cowardice, which is a vice of deficiency, is more opposed to Courage than is Rashness, which is a vice of excess; but Profligacy, or excess of feeling, is more opposed to Temperance than is Insensibility, or lack of feeling."[47] Later he says: "Thus much then is clear, that it is the middle disposition in each department of conduct that is to be praised, but that one should lean sometimes to the side of excess and sometimes to that of deficiency, since this is the easiest way of hitting the mean and the right course."[48] If one leans to the side of excess or to the side of deficiency, one does not hit the mean, but one may hit the right course. Hence, virtue is

---

[46] *Ibid.*, 1106a, b.

[47] *Ibid.*, 1109a.   [48] *Ibid.*, 1109b.

not the "mean" but the "right course." One of the definitions of virtue runs as follows: "Virtue, then, is a settled disposition of the mind as regards the choice of actions and feelings, consisting essentially in the observance of the mean relative to us, this being determined by a rational principle, that is, as a man of practical wisdom would determine it."[49] According to the original formula of the *mesótes* doctrine, the mean is determined by the two extremes. But the "mean relative to us" is not determined in this way and hence no "mean" at all. It is determined by "practical wisdom," and "practical wisdom issues commands, since its end is what ought to be done or not to be done"[50]—it coincides in Aristotle's ethics with the moral order. Hence virtue is that disposition of men that is in conformity with the moral order. This is the true meaning of the statement that virtue is the observance of the mean relative to us.

The statement that a virtue lies somewhere between two vices is a figure of speech. Its meaning, without the use of a metaphor, is: if we compare a virtue with two vices, the virtue is neither the one nor the other vice. The *mesótes* formula amounts to the tautology that: if something is correct it is not too much and not too little—or, in other words, that a virtue is not a vice, that good is not evil, right is not wrong.

But even if the two moral extremes were as completely determined as the two extreme points of a line bisected at a point equidistant from the two ends, and even if the moral mean were not a "mean with respect to us, but a mean with respect to the thing," and consequently as determined and determinable as the point equidistant from the two ends of the bisected line, the *mesótes* formula were no determination of the moral good. The alleged determination of the good consists in the statement that the virtue is a mean between two opposite vices. The existence of these vices Aristotle takes for granted. He does not prove that the two extremes, as for instance rashness and cowardice, are evils or vices; his ethics presupposes it as self-evident; just as a geometrist presupposes a circle or the two extreme points of a line as given in order to determine the center or the point by which the line is divided into two equal parts. The circle or the two extreme points being given, that is, predetermined, the determination of the center or the bisecting point is automatically implied. The center is determined by the given circle, the middle point of a line by the two given extreme points.

If an ethical doctrine presupposes all possible vices, it presupposes, together with those vices, all possible virtues. If we know what is evil, we thereby know what is good, and then nothing new remains to be determined. Even if the virtue determined according to the *mesótes* formula as a mean between two "given" vices, were "a mean with respect to the thing" and hence "one and the same for everybody," the formula could proclaim only a redundancy. For its meaning were, in this case too, nothing else but that the good is opposite to the evil; and the evil is not determined but presupposed by the formula.

Although the ethics of the *mesótes* doctrine pretends to establish in an authoritative way the moral value,[51] it leaves the solution of its very problem to another authority: the determination of what is evil or a vice, and, consequently, also the determination of what is good or a virtue. It is the authority

---

49 *Ibid.*, 1107a.   50 *Ibid.*, 1143a.   51 Cf. n. 37 and quotation n. 50.

of the positive morality and the positive law—it is the established social order. By presupposing in its *mesótes* formula the established social order, the ethics of Aristotle justifies the positive morality and the positive law which, as a matter of fact, determine what is "too much" and what "too little," what are the extremes of evil or wrong, and thereby what is the mean, that is, good and right. In this justification of the established social order lies the true function of the tautology which a critical analysis of the *mesótes* formula reveals.[52]

3

The book v of Aristotle's *Ethics,* devoted to the problem of justice, begins with the question: "In regard to justice and injustice (*dikaiosýne* and *adikía*) we have to inquire what sort of actions precisely they are concerned with, in what sense justice is the observance of a mean, and what are the extremes between which that which is just is a mean. Our inquiry may follow the same procedure as our preceding investigations."[53] It is the procedure of the *mesótes* doctrine. Aristotle first distinguishes justice in a general and justice in a particular sense. There are, he maintains, two concepts of justice: lawfulness and equality. "The term 'unjust' is held to apply both to the man who breaks the law and the man who takes more than his due, the unfair man. Hence it is clear that the law-abiding man and the fair man will both be just. 'The just' therefore means that which is lawful and that which is equal or fair, and 'the unjust' means that which is illegal and that which is unequal or unfair."[54] As to the relationship between lawfulness and equality, Aristotle says that the two concepts are not identical, lawfulness being the broader, equality the narrower concept: Not everything unlawful is unequal, though everything unfair is unlawful. Equality is related to lawfulness "as part to whole."[55] Consequently justice in the sense of lawfulness is "not a part of virtue but the whole of virtue";[56] it is perfect virtue "with a qualification, namely that it is displayed toward others."[57] That means that justice in the sense of lawfulness is a social virtue. By lawfulness Aristotle undoubtedly understands conformity to positive law. He says: "We saw that the lawbreaker is unjust and the law-

---

[52] The fact that Aristotle's ethics in determining the moral value, that is, virtue, presupposes the established social order, results also from his assertion that moral virtue is not the product of instruction, but of habit. "We become just by doing just acts, temperate by doing temperate acts, brave by doing brave acts. This truth is attested by the experience of states: lawgivers make the citizens good by training them in habits of right action" (1103b). If we, without previously being instructed by an ethical theory, can act morally and can become virtuous by acting morally, the moral action can only be that action which is usually considered to be such. The habit which makes a man virtuous can only be that habit by which the moral order actually prevailing in his society is maintained, the positive moral order under which he is actually living. The reference to the positive law is highly characteristic. Not only because here its concordance with morals is presupposed as self-evident, but because the law produces the desired disposition of man to act in conformity with the law not through instruction but by attaching to the contrary behavior specific sanctions. The "habit of right action" becomes possible only after the positive law prescribing this action has been established. Similarly, the habit of moral action is possible only if a positive moral order is established; and just as the right action is the one prescribed by positive law, the moral or virtuous action at which Aristotle's ethics is aiming is the one prescribed by the positive moral order presupposed to be valid at a certain time and in a certain place.

[53] *Ibid.,* 1129a.   [54] *Ibid.,* 1129a.
[55] *Ibid.,* 1130b.   [56] *Ibid.,* 1130a.
[57] *Ibid.,* 1129b.

abiding man just. It is therefore clear that all lawful things are just in one sense of the word, for what is lawful is decided by legislature, and the several decisions of legislature we call rules of justice." The *nómimon* is identical with the *díkaion,* law identical with justice (in one sense of this term). But is *nómos,* the law, really to be understood as the positive law—any positive law? This question must certainly be answered in the affirmative. For Aristotle continues: "Now all the various pronouncements of the law aim either at the common interest of all, or at the interest of a ruling class determined either by excellence or in some other similar way; so that in one of its senses the term just is applied to anything that produces and preserves the happiness, or the component parts of the happiness, of the political community."[58] But the "happiness" may be the happiness "of all" or only of "a ruling class." It is this justice in the general sense of lawfulness which Aristotle characterizes as the "perfect virtue" and the "chief of virtues, and more sublime than the evening or the morning star."[59] Which amounts to an unconditional glorification of positive law. But Aristotle is not a positivist. He does not confine his inquiry to an analysis of positive law, he does not renounce the use of the two concepts of justice and law, the *díkaion* and the *nómimon;* he maintains the dualism, but only to identify positive law with justice, to justify the *nómimon* as *díkaion.*

Of the particular justice, which consists in equality, there are also two kinds: distributive and corrective justice. Distributive justice "is exercised in the distribution of honor, wealth, and the other divisible assets of the community which may be allotted among its members in equal or unequal shares"

by the legislator. Corrective justice is "that which supplies a corrective principle in private transactions...those which are voluntary and those which are involuntary."[60] The corrective justice is exercised by the judge in settling disputes and inflicting punishments upon delinquents. The principle of distributive justice is proportional equality. That "justice involves at least four terms, namely two persons for whom it is just and two shares which are just. And there will be the same equality between the shares as between the persons, since the ratio between the shares will be equal to the ratio between the persons: for if the persons are not equal, they will not have equal shares."[61] Thus the principle of distributive justice is expressed in a mathematical formula: If a right a is alloted to an individual A, and a right b to the individual B, the requirement of distributive justice is fulfilled if the ratio of value a to value b is equal to the ratio of value A to value B. If the individuals A and B are equal, the rights to be allotted to them must be equal too. However, there are in nature no two individuals who are really equal, since there is always a differences as to age, sex, race, health, wealth, and so forth. There is no equality in nature. Nor is there equality in society. Equality as a social category, the statement that two individuals are socially equal, does not mean that there are no differences between these individuals, but that certain differences which really exist, as for instance differences concerning age, sex, race, wealth, are considered to be irrelevant. The decisive question as to social equality is: Which differences are irrelevant? To this question Aristotle's mathematical formula of distributive justice has no answer. Nor to the other essential question as to

---

58 *Ibid.,* 1129b.   59 *Ibid.,* 1129b.   60 *Ibid.,* 1131a.   61 *Ibid.,* 1131a.

which rights the legislator ought to allot to the individuals in order to be just. Is it just to confer upon the citizens the right of private property, or is it just to establish communism? Is it just to confer upon the citizens political rights, that is, to establish democracy, or is it just to confer upon the citizens no political rights at all, to establish autocracy? Aristotle's formula of distributive justice says only, that *if* rights are allotted, and *if* two individuals are equal, equal rights shall be allotted to them. According to this formula a capitalistic as well as a communistic legal order is just, and a legal order which confers political rights only to men who have a certain income, or who belong to a certain race, or are of noble birth is as just as a legal order which confers the same rights to all human beings who are of a certain age without regard to other differences. Any privilege whatever is covered by this formula. When a legal order reserves all possible rights to one single individual (the ruler) and assigns only duties to all others (the ruled), such a legal order too is just, since the difference between the ruler and the ruled is considered to be decisive, so that the ruled cannot be considered as equal to the ruler.

To illustrate his formula of distributive justice Aristotle refers to the "principle of assignment by desert." He says: "All are agreed that justice in distributions must be based on desert of some sort, although they do not all mean the same sort of desert; democrats make the criterion free birth; those of oligarchical sympathies, wealth or, in other cases, birth; upholders of aristocracy make it virtue." But his moral philosophy is not capable and considers itself not competent to answer the question which of these criteria is the just one. This, however, is the very question of justice.

The answer to this question Aristotle's *Ethics* leaves to the authority of positive law. Only if it is supposed that the positive law decides the question which rights shall be conferred upon citizens, and which differences between them are relevant, Aristotle's mathematical formula of distributive justice is applicable. As a postulate it means nothing else but that positive law shall be applied according to its own meaning. The equality of this justice is the equality before the law, which means merely legality, lawfulness. Aristotle's definition of distributive justice is but a mathematical formulation of the well-known principle *suum cuique*, to each his own, or to each his due. But this tautology has the important function of legitimizing the positive law which, as a matter of fact, fulfills the task, which legal philosophy is not capable of fulfilling—to determine what is everybody's due.

"Corrective" justice is exercised by the judge in deciding cases of "voluntary or involuntary transactions." "To go to a judge is to go to justice, for the ideal judge is, so to speak, justice personified."[62] Aristotle's distinction between "voluntary" and "involuntary" transactions probably coincides by and large with our distinction between civil and criminal law. He says: "Examples of voluntary transactions are selling, buying, lending at interest, pledging, lending without interest, depositing, letting for hire; these transactions being termed voluntary because they are voluntarily entered upon. Of involuntary transactions some are furtive, for instance, theft, adultery, poisoning, procuring, enticement of slaves, assassination, false witness. Others are violent, for instance, assault, imprisonment, murder, robbery with violence, maiming, abusive language, contumelious treat-

---

62 *Ibid.*, 1132a.

ment."[63] All these acts are crimes which are punishable under positive law. Corrective justice, too, is equality; but it is equality not according to geometrical but according to arithmetical proportion;[64] it is not equality of two ratios, it is equality of two things, especially of two losses or two gains. A typical example is barter, which may stand for any voluntary transaction. Corrective justice requires that the service and counterservice constituting the barter should be equal. The loss of one party by doing a service to the other party ("doing a service" comprising also making a gift to the other party) shall be equal to the loss of the latter by doing a return service ("doing a return service" comprising also giving a return gift); and vice versa: the gain of one party in receiving service from the other should be equal to the gain of the latter by receiving a return service from the former. The same equality shall prevail in the relation between crime and punishment. To do a service to another without receiving from him an adequate return service amounts to the same injustice as to commit a crime without receiving the adequate punishment. The problem of this kind of justice is: what is the adequate, correct, just return service, the adequate, correct, just punishment? Aristotle tries to answer this question, too, by a mathematical-geometrical formula. He compares the situation when a man has done to another a service without receiving a return service, or when a man has committed a crime injuring another, with a line divided into unequal parts. "The unjust being here the unequal, the judge endeavors to equalize [the inequality] ...the judge endeavors to make them [the two parts of the line] equal by the penalty or loss he imposes, taking away the gain."[65]

Now the judge restores equality: if we represent the matter by a line divided into two unequal parts, he takes away from the greater segment that portion by which it exceeds one-half of the whole line, and adds it to the lesser segment. When the whole has been divided into two halves, people then say that they 'have their own,' having got what is equal. . . . The equal is a mean by way of arithmetical proportion between the greater and the less. For when of two equals a part is taken from one and added to the other, the latter will exceed the former by twice that part, since if it had been taken from the one but not added to the other, the latter would exceed the former by once the part in question only. Therefore the latter will exceed the mean by once the part, and the mean will exceed the former, from which the part was taken, by once that part.[66]

The two equal parts of a bisected line and the two halves of a whole are evidently only a metaphor for the relationship of equality which should be established between service and return service, crime and punishment. The metaphor is no solution of the problem of just return service and just punishment. It is only another way of presenting the problem. Aristotle, however, thinks that by stating that the judge has to find the mean in the same way a geometrist divides a given line into two equal parts, has solved the problem of corrective justice. He says with reference to the just quoted passage: "This process then will enable us to ascertain what we ought to take away from the party that has too much and what to add to the one that has too little."[67] That means: the process enables us to determine the just return service and the just punishment; "we must add to the one that has too little the amount whereby the mean between them exceeds him, and take from the greatest of the three the amount by which the mean is exceeded by him." All this

63 *Ibid.*, 1131a.   64 *Ibid.*, 1131b.
65 *Ibid.*, 1132a.

66 *Ibid.*, 1132a.   67 *Ibid.*, 1132b.

says nothing else but that service and return service, that crime and punishment should be equal. This equality is certainly not a mathematical quantitative equality. An exchange between two persons takes place if both need different things. Aristotle says: "An association for interchange of services is not formed between the physicians, but between a physician and a farmer, and generally between persons who are different [i. e., who are able to do different services] and who may be unequal [with respect to their services] though in that case they have to be equalized."[68] That means: service and return service have to be equalized, since they are in themselves not and cannot be, equal in the sense the two halves of a line are, nor can crime and punishment be equal in this sense.

This is why Aristotle is compelled finally to give up his mathematical formula according to which "equality" is established by corrective justice. In discussing the Pythagorean doctrine that justice is reciprocity (*antipeponthós*) he says that reciprocity is sometimes at variance with corrective justice. But he admits: "In the interchange of services justice, in the form of reciprocity, is the bond that maintains the association; reciprocity, that is, on the basis of proportion, not on the basis of equality. The very existence of the state depends on proportionate reciprocity, because men demand that they shall be able to requite evil with evil (if they cannot, they feel they are in the position of slaves) and to repay good with good (failing which, no exchange takes place, and it is exchange that binds them together)."[69] The principle of retribution —or more generally formulated, reciprocity—is the rule to return evil for evil, good for good, like for like. The punishment shall be equal to the crime,

the reward equal to the merit. The decisive question, what is evil and what is good, is not answered by this formula; nor the question, what is "like" or equal. Positive law is, by its very nature, a coercive order. It provides coercive acts—forcible deprivation of life, freedom or property—as sanctions to be executed against the individual who commits a delict, that is, behaves in a way considered by the legislator to be harmful to society. The different legal orders differ very much in their determination of the delicts as well as the sanctions; but all correspond to the principle of retribution, which is at the basis of the social technique we call law. That retribution is considered as a principle of justice may be explained by the fact that it originates in one of the most primitive instincts of man, his desire for revenge. Aristotle's objection against the rule "like for like" as principle of justice, is that the relation between merit and reward, crime and punishment is not equality but proportionality. Return service shall not be equal to the service, the punishment not equal to the crime—this is impossible— but "proportional," which means that the one should be in an adequate proportion to the other. But this again is merely a presentation, not the solution, of the problem. The decisive question as to what is corrective justice remains unanswered. The pretended answer is a mere sham answer. It is again the tautology of the formula, "To each his own."[70]

Although the discussion of the problem of justice starts with the question in what sense justice is the observance of a mean, the *mesótes* doctrine plays but a subordinate role in Aristotle's legal philosophy. The application of the *mesótes* formula to the problem of justice is superficial and not very consistent. The sense of the statement that

---

68 *Ibid.*, 1133a.
69 *Ibid.*, 1132b–1133a.

70 Cf. quotation n. 66.

justice is a mean is not always the same. The main statement is: "Just conduct is a mean between doing and suffering injustice, for the former is to have too much and the latter to have too little."[71] It is evident that one of the two extremes (doing injustice and suffering injustice), namely, suffering injustice, is no vice. The *mesótes* formula has here a meaning different from that which it has in the discussion of the other virtues. This is admitted by Aristotle himself. He says: "Justice is a mode of observing the mean, though not in the same way as the other virtues are."[72] The difference is of no interest here, since the *mesótes* formula in its application to the problem of justice has the same character of a tautology as in its application to the other moral values. This character is here even more obvious. Doing injustice and suffering injustice are not two different degrees of one and the same substratum; they are not even two different facts between which a third fact can be situated. One man's doing injustice implies another man's suffering injustice. The one cannot be separated from the other. To say that justice is a mean between doing and suffering injustice, is a figurative expression of the judgment that justice is not injustice, neither the injustice which is done, nor the injustice which is suffered, which, however, are both one and the same injustice.

It might seem as if Aristotle himself was not completely satisfied with the result of his doctrine of justice. For in book viii of his *Ethics,* where he discusses the virtue of friendship, a certain tendency appears to complete the more or less empty idea of justice by the more substantial idea of peace. Here we read the astonishing passage: "Friendship appears to be the bond of the state; and lawgivers seem to set

more store by it than they do by justice; for to promote concord, which seems akin to friendship, is their chief aim; while faction [discord], which is enmity, is what they are most anxious to banish. And if men are friends there is no need of justice between them; whereas merely to be just is not enough; a feeling of friendship also is necessary."[73] "Concord" means peace; and to establish peace rather than justice seems to be—according to this statement—the essence of the state. Aristotle does not disapprove that legislators aim chiefly at peace, not at justice; and where peace prevails there is no need of justice. Justice is not enough! Is that the same justice of which Aristotle so enthusiastically speaks at the beginning of his inquiry into the nature of this virtue, proclaiming it "the chief of virtue," and "more sublime than the evening or the morning star"? Since to establish peace is certainly a function of the law, the stress Aristotle lays on the idea of peace corresponds to his identification of justice with law. "Justice," says Aristotle in his *Politics,* "is a function of the state. For the law is the order of the political community; and the law determines what is just."[74] If it is the law which determines what is just, justice is lawfulness; and if justice is equality, it is only equality before the law.[75]

[73] *Ibid.,* 1155a.
[74] *Politics,* 1253a.
[75] This essay is not dealing with the question as to whether and to what extent Aristotle's philosophy contains a natural-law doctrine. For Aristotle does not identify natural law with justice. In the *Nicomachean Ethics* (1134a) a distinction is made between "natural justice" (*physikón dikaion*) and "legal justice" (*nomikón dikaion*) as between two kinds of "political justice." Political justice "is found among men who share their life with a view of self-sufficiency," that is to say, within the state. "For justice exists only between men whose mutual relations are governed by law" (1134a). By a rule of natural justice Aristotle

[71] *Ibid.,* 1133b.   [72] *Ibid.,* 1133b.

This definition of justice as equality before the law implies the substitution of the logical value of truth for the moral value of justice.

Since a rationalistic moral philosophy is not capable of determining the content of a just order, of answering the questions what is good and what is evil, which differences between individuals are relevant and which irrelevant, who is equal and what is equal, it must presuppose these determinations. This means: leave it to the state (that is, to the positive legislator) who establishes a legal order, a system of general norms to be applied by the judge. When the legislator has established an order, when, for example, he has stipulated that every male citizen more than 24 years old may participate in the election of the magistrates, or that every individual more than 14 years old who commits theft shall be punished, and so on, then moral philosophy is in a situation to ascertain that it is just to allow not only A but also B to exercise a right of voting, provided that both are equal, that is, male citizens, 24

years of age; and that it is just for the judge to punish not only C but also D, provided that both individuals are equal, namely, both are more than 14 years old and both have committed theft. This is the principle of justice in the sense of lawfulness or in the sense of equality; this is equality before the law. And this kind of equality is established by any general norm. Equality before the law is maintained when the general norm is applied according to its own meaning. This is why this kind of equality is identical with lawfulness. If the judgment is valid that every individual more than 14 years old who has committed theft shall be punished, and if C and D are both individuals more than 14 years old who have committed theft, then the judgment is true that not only C but also D shall be punished. It is true as a conclusion from the general to the particular, which is implied in the application by a judge of a general norm to a particular case. If a judge, pretending to apply a general rule of law, states that C shall be punished and D shall not be punished, he presupposes in the first case the general judgment: Every individual more than 14 years old who has committed theft shall be punished; and in the second case, the general judgment: Not every individual more than 14 years old who committed theft shall be punished. These two general judgments constitute a logical contradiction. The judgment that it is not just to decide that C shall be punished but D shall not be punished, only means: it is contradictory. The principle of justice in the sense of equality before the law or lawfulness is nothing but the logical law of contradiction with reference to the application of a general norm of positive law to particular cases. This is the only concept of justice which Aristotle's moral philosophy—as any other rational philosophy—is able to define.

---

understands a norm "that has the same validity everywhere and does not depend on our accepting or not"; by a rule of legal justice a norm "that in the first instance may be settled in one way or the other indifferently, though having once been settled it is not indifferent" (1134b). But such a norm, too, represents "justice." Aristotle does not say that a norm of positive law, if it is not in conformity with natural justice, is not to be considered as valid; nor does he indicate the requirements a norm must fulfill in order to be in conformity with natural justice. Although he asserts the existence of natural justice, this concept does not play an essential part in his *Ethics*, of which only a few lines are devoted to this problem. Besides, the assertion of a "natural justice" is hardly compatible with the statement made in connection with the doctrine that moral virtue is the product of habit: "it is clear that none of the moral virtues is engendered in us by nature, for no natural property can be altered by habit" (1103a).

It is obvious that this concept of justice, as a law of thought, is totally different from the original ideal of action we understand by justice. This ideal does not aim at a logically, but a morally satisfactory normative system. A totally noncontradictory order as a system of general rules may be totally unjust in the original sense of the ideal. The substitution of the logical value of noncontradiction for the moral value of justice, inherent in the definition of justice as equality before the law, is the result of the attempt to rationalize the idea of justice as the idea of an objective value. Although this substitution is no solution, but an elimination of the problem of justice, it seems that the attempt will never be abandoned— perhaps, because of its important political implication. This type of rationalistic philosophy, pretending to answer the question what is just, and hence claiming authority to prescribe to the established power how to legislate, ultimately legitimizes the established power by defining justice as equality before the law and thus declaring the positive law to be just.

Since the concept of justice produced by a rationalistic moral philosophy has no definite content, it must not necessarily be used in a conservative tendency, to legitimize the given social order, to justify the validity of positive law. It may be used—although the intellectual history of mankind shows that this is only exceptionally the case —in a reformatory, or even revolutionary, tendency, to deny the validity of a given social order by declaring it unjust. A very interesting example is the legal philosophy of Aurelius Augustinus, who was a bishop of the Christian Church in an African province of the Roman Empire at a time when this empire was not yet a firmly established province of Christianity. Augustine identifies law and justice, just as

Aristotle identifies the *nómimon* and the *dikaion;* but he does so, not as Aristotle did, in order to strengthen the authority of the former by that of the latter. He propounds the thesis that a social order is law only if it is just, in order to destroy the authority of Roman law. "Where there is no true justice"[76] he says, "there can be no law. For what is done by law is justly done, and what is unjustly done cannot be done by law. For the unjust inventions of men are neither to be considered nor spoken of as laws; for even they themselves say that law is that which flows from the fountain of justice, and deny the definition which is commonly given by those who misconceive the matter, that right is that which is useful to the stronger party. Thus, where there is not true justice there can be no assemblage of men associated by a common acknowledgment of law," that is, a state. "If there is no law where there is no justice then most certainly it follows that there is no state where there is no justice." "Justice taken away, then, what are states but great robberies?"[77]

But what is justice? To this question Augustine answers with the same formula which Aristotle used to an exactly opposite purpose. "Justice is that virtue which gives everyone his due." But what is everyone's due? The Greek philosopher left the answer to the authority of the positive moral and legal order accepted by the majority of his society, the Christian bishop to the positive religious order of the minority to which he belonged. According to Augustine, justice is Christianity, injustice paganism. "Where, then, is the justice of man, when he deserts the true God and yields himself to impure demons? Is this to give every one his

---

[76] *The City of God (Civitas Dei)*, Bk. XIX, chap. 21.
[77] *Ibid.*, Bk. IV, chap. 4.

due? Or is he who keeps back a piece of ground from the purchaser, and gives it to a man who has no right to it, unjust, while he who keeps back himself from the God who made him, and serves wicked spirits, is just?...Hence, when a man does not serve God, what justice can we ascribe to him?...And if there is no justice in such an individual, certainly there can be none in a community composed of such persons." Consequently—and the Sain does not hesitate a moment to face this consequence—there never was a Roman State. Which amounts to saying: there never was a Roman law.

This is a very interesting result of a doctrine of justice based on the empty tautology of the formula "To every one his due." It is interesting not so much because this formula enables the one who is willing to use it to deny to an empire (by which, during many hundred years, a great and the most civilized part of mankind, was organized) the character of a state, and to a law (which was so to speak the mother of all modern law) the character of law; it is so interesting because it shows the unlimited possibility of using this formula to any purpose whatever.

WILLIAM T. BLUHM

Immanent Good: Aristotle's Quest for the Best Regime*

The focus of Aristotle's political thought, just as Plato's, is on the *polis*. Indeed, the title of his great treatise, *Politike,* ought to be translated "the

* Reprinted from William T. Bluhm, *Theories of the Political System* © 1965, by permission of Prentice-Hall, Inc., Englewood Cliffs, New Jersey, and, in modified form, from "The Place of the 'Polity' in Aristotle's Theory of the Ideal State," *The Journal of Politics,* XXIV, No. 4 (November 1962), 743–53, by permission of the editors and the author.

theory of the common life of the *polis,*" rather than by our word "politics."[1] And the first object of his analysis is to pin down the function or purpose of the *polis.* (In comparison with other forms of human association, what is it that the *polis* does, or produces, which is uniquely characteristic of it?) Aristotle does not separate out for inquiry

[1] Ernest Barker, ed., Introduction to *The Politics of Aristotle,* New York: Oxford University Press, Inc., 1958, p. lxvi.

the purpose of the political system of the *polis,* as modern students of politics do. His work is at one and the same time a sociology and a political science.

How did Aristotle proceed? He was aware that the *polis* had not always existed, but that it had a historical beginning and was preceded by more rudimentary village and family associations which continued to exist to his own day as "sub-organs" of the polis. This was common knowledge among learned Greeks of his time, as we have seen from our study of Thucydides and Plato. Placing these three entities side by side, and in order of historical development as three forms of the broader category "human association," Aristotle proceeded to ask whether a teleological development could be discerned in the phenomena. Could movement toward an end, or fulfillment, be discerned? He concluded that it could, that society seemed ordained to make possible for men the good and complete life, a life in which their highest capacities, and hence happiness, could be realized. This also was a common notion of the time, and Aristotle's own review of the facts confirmed it for him. Each level of society had something to contribute to human happiness, and the comprehensive society of the *polis,* which contained all the partial associations, was the form of social order in which complete fulfillment could be achieved. (This is the meaning of the famous Aristotelian dictum that "Man is a political animal.") The family and village existed for the sake of life, the *polis* for the good life. The *polis* is thus the culmination, the *telos,* of human society.

When we come to the final and perfect association, formed from a number of villages, we have already reached the *polis*— an association which may be said to have reached the height of full self-sufficiency; or rather...we may say that while it *grows*

for the sake of mere life,... it *exists*... for the sake of a good life....

Because it is the completion of associations existing by nature, every polis exists by nature, having itself the same quality as the earlier associations from which it grew. It is the end or consummation to which those associations move, and the "nature" of things consists in their end or consummation.... Again...the end, or final cause, is the best. Now self-sufficiency ...is the end, and so the best.[2]

Now, at this point a modern student might throw up his hands and exclaim that Aristotle's analysis was hopelessly subjective and "culture-bound," and of no use for us today. Modern city-states like Andorra, Luxembourg, Liechtenstein are merely rather comical vestigial remains of an earlier historical order, and to think of them as the culmination of social development is ridiculous. But this would be dealing over-hastily and superficially with Aristotle's thought. For the notion of *"polis"* was to him not primarily a conception of territorial size, though size was an important factor, but rather a set of social and political principles which are capable of embodiment in geographical units of various size. The extent of the territorial unit in which they can be embodied is largely a function of technology. And given the technology of Aristotle's day, the *polis* seemed a better realization of these principles than any other political unit.

Yves Simon, a modern student of politics who stands in the Aristotelian tradition, writes that in our own time "dependence upon things, persons, and social structures lying outside one's own state or federal nation have become such a common and important occurrence that it may be wondered whether any society smaller than the world has the character of a civil society [i.e., a

---

[2] *Politics,* 1252b 27–1253a 1.

society of temporal fulfillment], except in a strongly qualified sense. Such a situation raises the problem of the world-state but does not demonstrate its possibility."[3]

The first of the principles of the perfect society is self-sufficiency, or autarky. Aristotle seeks to understand the form of social organization which contains within itself all things requisite for the complete happiness of its members. But what is the nature of that happiness, and how does Aristotle determine it?

Aristotle on the "Good Life"

Aristotle expounded his idea of the good life in detail in two treatises on ethics. And the last paragraph of the second of these works, the *Nicomachean Ethics*, points to a sequel on social organization, the *Politics*. What goes into the making of a good and sufficient life, a happy life? It is more than security from injury, and material well-being. The end of the *polis* does not consist merely in providing an "alliance for mutual defence against all injury, or to ease exchange and promote economic intercourse." If this were the case, a *polis* could not be distinguished from other forms of alliance or from trade associations. "The Etruscans and the Carthaginians would be in the position of belonging to a single *polis;* and the same would be true of all peoples who have commercial treaties with one another."[4] The proper end of the *polis* is rather to make men good. And human goodness, just as the goodness of any creature, must be sought for in function. To know what the good human life is like, we must ask what the characteristically human activity is. What is it

that a man does which distinguishes him from the rest of creation? The answer is the exercise of reason. Along with the lower animals, man has the faculties of nutrition, sensation, local movement, and perception. But in addition he has reason. "The function of man is an activity of soul which follows or implies a rational principle."[5] And so the good of man lies in the excellent (virtuous) performance of this activity.

But now we come to a new departure. For Aristotle has something new to say about what "reason" means. He distinguishes two kinds of reason, while Plato had spoken only of one. On the one hand, there is the reason which "contemplates the kinds of things whose originative causes are invariable." And on the other, there is the reason which regards "variable things." The objects of the contemplative reason comprise what we would today call the objects of scientific, mathematical, and metaphysical inquiry. The object of the practical reason is the good for man. The end of the contemplative reason is understanding only, theory. But that of the practical reason is moral action. The practical reason works out broad criteria of moral choice and also guides the particular choices of the moral agent. Practical wisdom is "a true and reasoned state of capacity to act with regard to the things that are good or bad for man."[6] Thus the rational activity of man will have two kinds of excellence, intellectual excellence and moral excellence.

Of the two activities, contemplation is the highest, because it is the activity of pure reason. It is a self-sufficient activity, because reason is a divine thing, because its objects are the best knowable objects, and because its pleasures are the purest and most enduring.

[3] Yves Simon, *Philosophy of Democratic Government,* Chicago: University of Chicago Press, 1951, pp. 67–68.
[4] *Politics,* 1280a 35–40.
[5] *Nicomachean Ethics,* 1098a 7–8.
[6] *Ibid.,* 1140b 5–6.

And its purpose can be achieved in perfect isolation, apart from all human society. By contrast, moral virtue, which is a "state of character concerned with choice, lying in a mean...determined by a rational principle," involves our whole composite nature, the passions as well as reason. It is the excellence of that which is specifically human in us. And it requires society for its development. "The just man needs people towards whom and with whom he shall act justly, and the temperate man, the brave man, and each of the others is in the same case."[7] It also requires abundant material goods. Liberality, for example, needs wealth for its exercise.

To a degree, Aristotle identifies the life of thought and the life of action as the lives of two different kinds of men, the philosopher and the man of affairs (*politikos*). But the separation is not complete, for the philosopher is not given leave to retire into the isolation of the wilderness. If he is to develop his humanity, even the philosopher must depend on society. "In so far as he is a man and lives with a number of people, he chooses to do virtuous acts; he will therefore need such aids to living a human life."[8] Society, then, and specifically the *polis,* exists to make possible one aspect of the life of reason—the life of practical reason and moral virtue —which is a life according to the principle of the mean.

Some actions are to be deemed bad in themselves and to be avoided altogether, such as envy, adultery, theft, murder. But in most things one should guide the appetites, or passions, which activate us, by the principle of the mean, which is as good a rule as there is available in the world of "variable things" and contingencies, which is the

world of moral choice. For example, with reference to feelings of fear and confidence, the excellent man is neither cowardly nor rash, but courageous. In matters of honor he will take proper pride in his accomplishments, and be neither unduly humble nor vainglorious. In the use of wealth he will be liberal, not miserly or prodigal. In bodily pleasures he will be neither ascetic nor self-indulgent, but temperate. With regard to pleasantness in social intercourse, the virtuous man is neither obsequious nor surly, but friendly.

How are the moral virtues, which make this good life possible, acquired? Not by teaching, Aristotle tells us. Intellectual virtue may be so acquired, but moral virtue is a result of habit. And good habits are acquired through the practice of good actions. As in the arts, we learn by doing. "We become just by doing just acts, temperate by doing temperate acts, brave by doing brave acts."[9]

But how are men brought to the performance of the noble actions from which good habits, a permanent disposition to act well, will arise? This is the question which leads us from the *Ethics* to the *Politics*. For it is the job of the laws and of the statesman to implant these habits in men. The statesman should receive his own education in these things from a study of the politico-ethical experience embodied in the laws and customs of mankind.

We have clarified the first principle of Aristotle's perfect social order, autarky. The perfect society contains within itself all the means for producing men who lead lives of noble action guided by the principle of the mean. And if the *polis* is sufficient for the good life, it will make its members good. What does the experience of mankind

---

[7] *Ibid.,* 1106b 35–1107a 1, 1177a 29–34.
[8] *Ibid.,* 1178b 5–7.

[9] *Ibid.,* 1103b 1–2.

tell us about how the perfect society is to be ordered? What are its structural principles?

A beginning of a revelation of the principles peculiar to "political" government is made in Book I of the *Politics* by a genetic analysis, which Aristotle calls his "normal method."[10] To understand the *polis,* we must understand the social forms out of which it emerged, the family and village. As these are only rudimentary and partial associations, they will be functionally and structurally different from the *polis.* And by seeing what these characteristics are, we shall, in a negative way, begin to understand what the *polis* is as we watch it grow out of them.[11]

It is a mistake to believe that the statesman...is the same as the monarch of a kingdom, or the manager of a household, or the master of a number of slaves. Those who hold this view consider that each of these persons differs from the others not with a difference of kind, but...according to the number, or the paucity, of the persons with whom he deals.... This view abolishes any real difference between a large household and a small *polis;* and it also reduces the difference between the "statesman" and the monarch to the one fact that the latter has an uncontrolled and sole authority, while the former exercises his authority in conformity with the rules imposed by the art of statesmanship and as one who rules and is ruled in turn. But this is a view which cannot be accepted as correct.[12]

Aristotle describes the family or household group as an association whose primary object is to support life. Thus property as well as procreation comes within the sphere of the household, since property (i.e., things, instruments) is necessary for life.

In this section Aristotle includes a long discussion of the slave as an "animate article of property," which has been much deplored in the commentaries and treated as a skeleton in the closet of an otherwise virtuous house. For Aristotle presents a justification of the institution of slavery as natural, in the teleological sense of the word "natural." All men who "differ from others as much as the body differs from the soul, or an animal from a man...are by nature slaves."[13] And it is best for them to be ruled by another, for being without reason, they are incapable of governing themselves. This is not the same as a justification of the *legal* institution of slavery, however, or an argument that everyone who is by law a slave is properly one by nature also. In fact Aristotle specifically says that nature's intention often miscarries, so that natural slaves have the status of free men, while men who should be free are bound in slavery.[14] In a sense even the very egalitarian philosophy of modern liberalism admits the conception of "slaves by nature" when it sanctions prisons for criminals and institutions for the confinement of the insane.

At any rate, Aristotle's main point in bringing up the whole question of slavery, an important established institution of his time, was not to praise or justify it, but by identifying the authority of the master as an aspect of household management, to distinguish it from the kind of authority properly exercised by a statesman over the citizens of a *polis.*

The argument makes it clear that the authority of the master and that of the states-

---

10 *Politics,* 1252a 20.

11 Book I appears to be incomplete, as it closes after a discussion of the elements of household management. There is no consideration at all of the village, here or elsewhere in the *Politics.*

12 *Ibid.,* 1252a 17–18.

13 *Ibid.,* 1254b 15–18.

14 *Ibid.,* 1255a 3–1255b 15.

man are different from one another, and that it is not the case that all kinds of authority are, as some thinkers hold, identical. The authority of the statesman is exercised over men who are naturally free; that of the master over men who are slaves.[15]

It is all essentially a rebuttal of Plato's argument for a three-class *polis*. The *polis* as the association of human fulfillment must be an association of "freemen and equals," whose equality resides primarily in their common reason.

In discussing the other two interpersonal relations which are found in the household group, that between husband and wife, and that between father and child, Aristotle stresses the same point. The natural equipment of the persons in each of these relationships is different. Reason is developed only in the mature male. In the woman it takes a form "which remains inconclusive." (Aristotle merely asserts but does not defend this proposition.) And in the child it is immature. Hence hierarchy rather than equality is the applicable principle here. The husband and father is the naturally superior and should therefore rule, over his wife as "a statesman over fellow citizens," but with permanent tenure, over his children as "a monarch over subjects."[16] Moral goodness will be found in slave, wife, and child, to the extent that the person in question fulfills the duties of his status, which are primarily to obey the commands of the master or father. In none of these cases, however, do we find the perfection of human goodness. That is found only in the good master and father, whose reason is fully developed, and these are the citizens of the *polis*. Since the *polis* exists to make the good life possible, it must ideally offer a life of mature reason enjoyed equally by all its members. "The members of a political association aim by their very nature at being equal and differing in nothing."[17]

We have left Plato's elitist utopia far behind. The good life is not a life lived by most men in subjection to the dictates of a few philosophic Guardians who have achieved intellectual and spiritual communion with the "Good." It is a life lived by most men in subjection to the dictates of their own practical reason, which sees what is good for man in a rather imprecise way, guided only by the principle of the mean. But, with the help of a well-formed disposition to act aright, good habit, it is a life which moves prudently from problem to problem through the maze of moral choice. It is a life, for most men, of self-government rather than other-government.

Having completed this brief genetic analysis of the *polis*, Aristotle proceeds to elaborate his study with other methods. His object now is to discover that system, or constitution (*politeia*), which is ideal. And by ideal he means that one which best realizes the *telos* of the *polis*, the good life shared in common. The emphasis is now entirely on form and matter, the formal cause and the material cause. (The final cause has been sufficiently established.) Already we have some indications as to what it will be like. For in the genetic analysis, equality and rationality were posited as fundamental structural principles.

Book II pursues a formal cause analysis by reviewing what other writers have said about the best constitution, and by describing the characteristic institutions of actual states commonly reputed to be well organized. (Such a survey of the existing body of knowledge and opinion was a usual procedure of Aristotle in every field of inquiry.)

15 *Ibid.*, 1255b 16–20.
16 *Ibid.*, 1259b 9–12.

17 *Ibid.*, 1259b 6–7.

His purpose is to point up the utter inadequacy in every respect of existing theory of the good regime. First he mercilessly criticizes Plato's *Republic,* as we have already seen, then the *Laws* as well; next he points out the defects of the utopias of half a dozen other writers, and finally he criticizes the constitutions of Sparta, Crete, and Carthage. The discussion is loose and rambling.

A large part of Book III is also devoted to an evaluation of current opinion. But the discussion this time is focused on the material cause, and the opinions surveyed are not those of academic theorists, or even of statesmen, but rather of social interests. Since the ideal must be found growing in the empirical world, rather than in the heaven above the heavens, it must be constituted out of matter which really exists, not out of imaginary stuff. Therefore one must see what materials are available, and what claims are made on behalf of each type.

Aristotle asks what claims to political power are commonly made, and which of them are valid. What is the best "matter" for the ruling class of the good *polis?* He introduces the theme by remarking that the citizens of a *polis,* whom he defines as those who "share in the offices and honors of the state" (from juryman to general), are the parts of a *polis.* And as the raw material out of which the parts are made varies, so will the whole. The character of the citizens determines the character of the constitution of the city in the broadest sense. "The civic body [the *politeuma,* or body of persons established in power by the polity] is everywhere the sovereign of the state; in fact the civic body is the polity (or constitution) itself."[18] The way of life of the citizens—their values, habits, virtues, vices—will be

the way of life of the city. If it is a good and proper way of life, the *telos* of the city will be realized. If not, the city will be a poor thing. One must pay special attention to the composition of the "sovereign" authority.[19]

Claims are made on behalf of the "one," the "few," and the "many." The claim of the "one" (which establishes monarchy) is usually a claim of pre-eminent goodness, or virtue, though it may be the claim of the tyrant, which rests on force. The claim of the "few" may be that of the wealthy commercial minority, urging that wealth should rule (oligarchy). Or it may be that of the hereditary landed aristocracy, the patrician families, claiming greater goodness and capacity than others as the basis of their claim. The claim of the "many" is the claim of numbers, that the freeborn majority should rule (democracy or polity).

Something can be said for and against each of these actual claims to power. For the wealthy, it can be said that since the *polis* has need of financial resources for its very existence, their large share of these resources seems to constitute a valid claim to power. There is merit also in the claim of the "better sort," the aristocracy. Their social position always gives them prestige, and it is observable that noble families do in fact produce offspring of great merit and noble character, which is always the best claim to power. And since virtue is a sovereign claim, if one man in a *polis* is found to be pre-eminent over all others in goodness and statesmanship, who can deny him the right to rule over all, and be above all law, which is made for equals? The tyrant, presumably, can urge with some cogency that might is right and by superior force get his

---

18 *Ibid.,* 1278b 11–12.

claim called legitimate. Aristotle actually does not detail his claim, though he lists the tyrant among the claimants. So far as "the people" or the "many" are concerned, it can be urged that though no one of them taken alone might be worth much, collectively they possess wisdom and an excellence of judgment which is of a superior sort.

But there are also important objections to each of these claims. The "many" are usually the poor, who have often in practice abused sovereign power by employing it to despoil the rich minority of their wealth, an act of manifest injustice and the ruination of a state. But a wealthy minority in the seat of power may as well use its authority to plunder the "many." Also, it is plain that the democratic conception of justice, that equality in the one point of free birth means equality in all things, and that of the oligarchs, that inequality in point of wealth means absolute inequality, are both mistaken notions. And neither conception takes cognizance of the true end of the *polis,* which is goodness, not mutual defense or the protection of property. So far as the rule of "the better sort" is concerned, though in a sense it is beneficial, by definition it bars all the rest of the community from public office and honors. And, by implication, this is an evil. Aristotle does not spell out the nature of the evil here. But we have already seen in Book I that the political relation, by its nature, and by contrast with those of the household, implies an equality among the members of the *polis.* And so to arrogate all authority to those few who are best is a slight to all the rest who by virtue of their rationality as mature freemen have a claim to power.

To accept the sovereignty of the one best man has the same disadvantage, since it disbars even more people from a share in the making of community decisions. And though Aristotle at the end of this section continues to argue that when such a god among men appears, all others are truly obligated to accept his rule, he plainly does not apprehend this as an ideal circumstance. In fact he is hardly ready to call such an association a *polis.* The man of singular goodness, he says, cannot "be treated as part of a [*polis*]." And in one place he gives qualified approval to the policy of ostracism, which was designed to prevent such a person from developing in a *polis;*[20] though usually, he notes, this policy has been applied in a spirit of faction, rather than in the disinterested spirit of Aristotle's analysis.

Where does this leave matters? What then *are* valid claims to power? Aristotle seems reluctant to answer the question flatly. All the *usual* claims have both merits and defects. All are valid, all are invalid. Much depends on the circumstances. Certainly in the case of any particular *polis* the decision would have to depend on its circumstances. But is there an *ideal* claim, corresponding to an *ideal* set of circumstances?

Aristotle seems particularly well disposed toward the "many," though not on the basis of the *usual* claim made on their behalf—numbers and free birth —but on the ground of a claim which *he* puts forward for them. Four times he speaks of the special claim which can be made for the "many's" right to sovereignty.[21] All of these defenses of the "many" embody the notion that,

---

20 *Politics,* 1284b 15–34.

21 The first time is in Chapter XI, which follows upon the discussion in Chapter X of the particular defects of all the usual claims. The second is toward the beginning of Chapter XIII, following a listing of the virtues of the various claims. The third is later in Chapter XIII, following a further evaluation of the conflicting claims which concludes that no one principle urged by itself—wealth, birth, goodness, number—is adequate. And the fourth is in Chapter XV, which evaluates in detail the claim on behalf of absolute monarchy.

at least under *some* circumstances, the many can urge *all* the claims on their behalf, which the "one" and the "few" can never do. "The many may urge their claims against the few: taken together and compared with the few they are stronger, richer, and better."[22] Aristotle notes that these virtues will not be found in "all popular bodies and all large masses of men." But when they are found, then the many should rule. For example, "in a group whose members are equals and peers it is neither expedient nor just that one man should be sovereign over all others."[23]

Thus, when taken together, *all* the kinds of claims in the empirical order, not the claim of virtue alone, are valid for the ideal order. And an existing social group has been found which, under certain circumstances, can be considered the ideal ruling class, or *politeuma*.

A METHOD FOR STUDYING ACTUAL REGIMES

Book III has revealed that Aristotle is not content to think only in terms of ideal circumstances and ideal regimes. Observation made it evident that ideal circumstances were seldom, if ever, realized in human affairs, by contrast with physical nature, and that few, if any, actual states could be found which measured up to an ideal standard.[24] Aristotle and his students had the evidence of studies of more than 150 different *poleis* that this was so. Yet there were many governments which, despite a certain amount of internal strife, were plainly going concerns, had some measure of worth, and were as good as circumstances permitted.

Aristotle's empiricism brought with it a strong appreciation of necessity in social relations. The social world, in all its variety, seemed much more fixed, much less plastic, than it had to Plato. The area in which human freedom might consciously mold conditions to its desire was very small. And "good" therefore had to contain a large element of the relative. "Good" must be measured in terms of that which rigid and various circumstance decrees as possible. Plainly, a comprehensive political science would have to take account of the normal persistence of actual regimes markedly different from the ideal regime, and some kind of relative standard of judgment would have to be found in addition to the standard of the *telos*. In one place, for example, he remarks that some men "come together and form and maintain political associations, merely for the sake of life; for perhaps there is some element of good even in the simple act of living, so long as the evils of existence do not preponderate too heavily."[25]

One standard which produces a very general but still useful principle of classification is that of the general interest. Governments which aim at the common interest are to be deemed right and just forms (even though the conception of interest they possess is not the same as the absolute good?), while those which seek only the private good of the rulers are wrong and perverted forms. This yields the six-fold classification of monarchy, aristocracy, polity (governments of the one, the few, and the many in the general interest), and tyranny, oligarchy, democracy (governments of the one, the few, and the many in the interest of the rulers). This is not original with Aristotle but is much like the commonly employed system of classification of the time.

It is also inadequate. Another stan-

---

22 *Ibid.*, 1283a 40–1283b 1.
23 *Ibid.*, 1288b 1–3.
24 See George Boas, "Some Assumptions of Aristotle," *Transactions of the American Philosophical Society,* New Series, Vol. XLIX, Part 6, 1959, pp. 44, 48, 49, 54, 56.

25 *Ibid.*, 1278b 25–27.

dard of comparison is required. At the beginning of Book III, Aristotle tells us that we must distinguish the "good man" from the "good citizen." Only in the case of the ideal state will they be the same. In all other cases, the "good citizen" will be one who plays his proper role in the *polis* of which he is a member, thus contributing to its maintenance. And so stability, the continued endurance of a regime, is introduced by Aristotle as a third standard of evaluation.

A bridge toward Naturalism

The need for this more elaborate analysis, going beyond a consideration of the ideal, is spelled out by Aristotle at the beginning of Book IV.

First, [politics] has to consider which is the best constitution, and what qualities a constitution must have to come closer to the ideal when there are no external factors...to hinder its doing so. Secondly, politics has to consider which sort of constitution suits which sort of civic body. The attainment of the best constitution is likely to be impossible for the general run of states; and the good law-giver and the true statesman must therefore have their eyes open not only to what is the absolute best, but also to what is best in relation to actual conditions. Thirdly, politics has to consider the sort of constitution which depends upon an assumption. In other words, the student of politics must also be able to study a given constitution, just as it stands and simply with a view to explaining how it may have arisen and how it may be made to enjoy the longest possible life.... Fourthly,...politics has also to provide a knowledge of the type of constitution which is best suited to states in general.[26]

In Book IV, Aristotle continues to employ formal and material cause analysis but in a more complex way than in the earlier books. He is still seeking to delineate the structure of the

ideal state which has been only partly completed. But he has indicated that the ideal structure is possible only in rare cases, under special circumstances, and that other structures may be considered good relative to the various nonideal circumstances which abound in the empirical world.

At this point, what began as a theory of the best regime has joined to it a theory of the empirical order. Aristotle catalogs all of the kinds of political systems which were in operation in his day. And as he shows what constitutions are suited to the various kinds of social circumstances, what "forms" go with what kinds of "matter," the language of freedom (the language of "good" and "ought") passes into the language of necessity. This is well illustrated in 1296b, for example, which begins the discussion of this question. Aristotle asks: "What and what sort of constitution is suited to (*symphero*) what sort of persons?"[27] The Greek word *symphero* implies the notion of utility and advantage, which is the language of "good." But a few lines later, as the answers begin to emerge from the inquiry, we have such statements as:

Where the number of poor is more than enough to counterbalance the higher quality of the other side, *there will naturally be* (*pephuken*) a democracy.... If they are mechanics and day-labourers, *we shall have* the extreme form.... Where the number of the members of the middle class outweighs that of both the other classes...a polity *can be* permanently established.[28]

These are purely descriptive, not evaluative, terms. Aristotle's theory of actual states, instead of being a theory of relative goods, turns out to be a theory of empirical correlations—what would today be called "scientific description."

The four-cause scheme of analysis

---

26 *Ibid.*, 1288b 21–35.

27 *Ibid.*, 1296b 13–14.
28 *Ibid.*, 1296b 25–40. (Emphasis supplied.)

remains a useful instrument for the new enterprise. In place of perfection, the *telos* or final cause of the actual type becomes survival. ("There is some element of good even in the simple act of living.") And formal cause analysis, in place of a unique structure, must describe all the different types of system which are observed to survive in the empirical world. We are in a Darwinian order now. The material cause reveals what social groupings produce what kinds of structures and the efficient cause tells us what behavior is characteristic of the various regimes, and the processes by which they change from one into another.

Aristotle's theory of the actual order seems very close both in its method and in its conclusions to that of the typical naturalist. The focal norm in each case is the survival of any given kind of system. It is a norm which is merely posited. And it corresponds to no noumenal purpose or entelechy. As far as it rests on a conception of the good, the particular good involved plays as large a role in the naturalistic as in the noumenalist theory of value. Aristotle assumes that most people desire preservation rather than destruction, a principle on which the arch-materialist Hobbes later erected his entire political theory. And it is this value, preservation, as related to *mere* order rather than the order of moral perfection, around which Aristotle constructs his theory of Books IV to VI of the *Politics*. It is a theory of the various ways in which a preservation-order is produced in the empirical world. Later, in Book VI, Aristotle combines with this theory of actual polities a theory of rational (or efficient) order which could also have been erected on purely naturalistic foundations. He considers the problem of constructing each of the actual systems in such a way as to make them more stable than they usually are found to be in their historical embodiments. We might state the theme in these terms: "Given the limitations which can be stabilized, how, in any given situation, can the appropriate constitution be constructed so as to guarantee the maximum of stability?" A naturalist would frame the problem no differently.

A dual analysis

While Aristotle first announces the necessity for a dual analysis (of the empirical as well as of the ideal order) only at the beginning of Book IV, he actually begins to perform it in the last chapters (XIV–XVIII) of Book III. There he describes in considerable detail five different kinds of monarchy found to exist and indicates the conditions under which each should be considered "appropriate." He examines and finds wanting the claim of those who say that monarchy is the absolutely best form of government. But he tells us that there are special circumstances under which it can be considered good, or appropriate:

The society appropriate to kingship is one of the sort which naturally tends to produce some particular stock, or family, preeminent in its capacity for political leadership. . . . Where it happens that a whole family, or even a single person, is of merit so outstanding as to surpass that of all the rest, it is only just that this family should be vested with kingship and absolute sovereignty, or that this single person should become king.[29]

Then he describes five other existing varieties of monarchy and indicates the conditions under which each actually arises—to indicate the conditions under which each is "suitable." The difference between the good order and the empirical order simply evaporates in the course of description.

[29] *Ibid.*, 1288a 8–19.

Book IV deals in this fashion with all the other forms of constitution. Most space is given to oligarchy and democracy, the forms most common in the Greek world of the time. The name "oligarchy" applies to any system in which the "rich and better born" (does he mean to include the hereditary aristocracy?), who are also a minority, control the government. And "democracy" is a constitution in which the free-born and poor, being also a majority, rule. In this section we again have evidence of Aristotle's empirical bent and of his feeling for the multiformity of political phenomena; for we discover that we have not two, but actually nine, different kinds of constitution—five varieties of democracy and four of oligarchy. As to form, they are distinguished in each case by the kinds of qualification for office they employ and by the relative status of basic laws and decrees of the deliberative assembly. As to matter, they are distinguished by the social composition of the *poleis* in which they arise. For example, if the population is predominantly made up of small farmers, there will usually be a low property qualification. Meetings of the assembly will be kept to a minimum, since the people have little leisure to devote to politics because of the pressure of earning a living. But they are able to live by their moderate means. And as a consequence of these things, the fundamental law is supreme over and limits the scope of popular decrees. This is the first or "peasant form" of democracy. If the bulk of the population are mechanics and day labourers, there will be no property qualification. And a system of state payment for attendance at the assembly will provide leisure for the common man to engage in political activity. In this society the well-to-do will absent themselves from political meetings because of business affairs. As a consequence, decrees of

the assembly will be paramount to law. This is the last form of democracy, which Aristotle calls the "extreme form."

The discussion of democracies and oligarchies is followed by a description of the system called "polity," which Aristotle defines as a "mean" between democracy and oligarchy, and as a mixture of the two.[30] Polities combine the institutions proper both to democracies and oligarchies. For example, a polity will adopt a rule fining the rich if they do not take part in the work of the law courts (an oligarchical rule), and combine it with a provision to pay the poor so that they may also sit in the courts (a democratic rule). Or it may combine the device of the lot (considered democratic) with that of election (an oligarchic institution) in the choice of executive officers.

In terms of its social base, the polity is also, in a sense, a mixture of democracy and oligarchy. For polity appears in societies which have a middle class that is larger and stronger than either the class of the very wealthy or of the very poor. Thus it combines the principles of numbers and free birth, which are characteristic of democratic government, with that of wealth, which is proper to oligarchy. That is, the dominant class is strong both in numbers and in material substance.

Aristotle returns to the question of the ideal order in this portion of Book IV and showers great praise on the middle-class polity as the "constitution —short of the ideal—[which] is the most generally acceptable and the most

---

30 This is different from the definition in the classification of constitutions of Book III, where "polity" is the general-interest form of rule by the "many." The democracies of Book IV, in which law is described as paramount over popular decree, seem to represent the polity of Book III, while that term now identifies another kind of regime.

to be preferred."[31] And from the description of the polity we come to see more clearly than we have to this point what the ideal order itself is like. Unlike Plato's state of the *Laws,* it is not an artificial construct, self-consciously created out of elements salvaged from the historical wreckage of an originally ideal order. It is rather the unselfconscious product of natural development toward the *telos* of the *polis.* The polity actually contains all the structural principles of the ideal order, though in an imperfectly developed form. To use a physical metaphor, it is like a late stage of development in an evolutionary series, like Cro Magnon man in comparison with modern man. The metaphor is not perfect, since an evolutionary series presumably has no fixed *terminus ad quem.* And our figure makes modern man just such a terminus, or rather *telos.* Yet, with this modification, the metaphor is a good way to illustrate Aristotle's thought. The polity is a close approximation to the formal cause of the ideal *polis,* and probably the closest that a historical state will come to its realization.

What are its great virtues? First, the members of its ruling class lead the best kind of social life. The introduction to this section is misleading. For Aristotle says that he intends to employ a standard of excellence not "above the reach of ordinary men, or a standard of education requiring exceptional endowments or equipment, or the standard of a constitution which attains an ideal height." He will be concerned with "the sort of life which most men are able to share and the sort of constitution which it is possible for most states to enjoy."[32] This seems to reject the *telos* or the ideal as a measure. But then he goes on to employ the standard of the mean, as he had worked it out in the *Ethics.*

If we adopt as true the statements made in the *Ethics*—(1) that a truly happy life is a life of goodness lived in freedom from impediments, and (2) that goodness consists in a mean—it follows that the best way of life is one which consists in a mean, and a mean of the kind attainable by every individual. Further, the same criteria which determine whether the citizen body have a good or bad way of life must also apply to the constitution; for a constitution is the way of life of a citizen body.[33]

And so he does after all advance an ideal standard of measurement. The way of life of the philosopher may be the highest way. But it is really a divine rather than a human life, as we have seen. And the philosophic activity itself is a lonely activity. We are here concerned with the ideal *society,* and so the way of life of the polity, if it is a life according to the mean, must be the way of life of the ideal *polis* as well as of the ruling class of the best actual *polis.*

Legislators, whose function is to inculcate virtue in others, must be preeminently virtuous men if they are to legislate well. And Aristotle tells us that the best legislators have come from the middle class. The material circumstances of the middle class are conducive to the virtuous life. They are subject to none of the psychological pressures which make for vice in the very rich and the very poor. "Those who belong to either extreme...find it hard to follow the lead of reason." Virtue is a middle-class affair.[34]

The men of the middle class understand both how to rule and how to obey—a virtue, as we saw in Book III, both of the good man and of the citizen of the ideal state. And this too is a

---

31 *Ibid.,* 1289b 15–18.
32 *Ibid.,* 1295a 25–31.

33 *Ibid.,* 1295a 36–40.
34 *Ibid.,* 1295b 6–9.

result of their middling condition. For "those who enjoy too many advantages ...are both unwilling to obey and ignorant how to obey." They are fit only to be slave masters. At the other end of the social scale are the "mean and poor-spirited," who only know how to obey, and that as slaves.[35] This knowledge of the combined art of ruling and of obeying, and willingness both to rule and be ruled make for friendship and community in the middle classes, while the envious poor and the contemptuous rich have capacity for friendship neither with one another nor with the other classes.

Polity is also the most stable of constitutions and the freest of all from factions. This is particularly true of large polities where the middle class is more numerous than in small ones. Its chief strength lies not in the fact that it has the support of a majority, however, but that "no single section in all the state...would favour a change to a different constitution."[36] Its institutions and ideals have a general-interest appeal. It is therefore best in the order of perfection. The polity is the keystone of the arch of Aristotle's bridge from the noumenal to the naturalist world.

Lastly, the men of the dominant middle class are peers and equals, as are the citizens of the ideal state. For a "state aims at being as far as it can be, a society composed of equals and peers."[37]

It seems, then, that the only difference between the polity and the ideal state is a purely quantitative one. The ruling class of the polity, its way of life, its political institutions, are like those of the ideal state. The many, when thus organized, combine all three of the valid claims to power—numbers, wealth, and virtue. They are a true

aristocracy. But while this class is only a majority in the polity, in the ideal state it would be coextensive with the entire society. Aristotle does not expressly say this, but it is quite compatible with what he does say about the principles of the ideal state in Books VII and VIII.

Thus by the end of Book IV we have seen fully revealed the structural principles of the ideal order, of the best order which has actually been constructed, and of *all* the main kinds of systems which have been historically constructed.[38] We have analyzed the final, the formal, and the material causes of the *polis* in both its ideal and empirical forms. (The analysis of empirical forms is organized, we have seen, around the same norm used by the naturalists, "survival.") Efficient causes remain to be discussed. To this subject Aristotle turns in Book V.

THE EFFICIENT CAUSE: POLITICAL CHANGE

To study the "efficient cause" is to study the "how" of a thing, i.e., the mechanical order of all the little interrelated steps or events which end in a given result. It is therefore to study activity and change—"process" in today's terminology. The reader will recall that this was the sole concern of Thucydides' political science, a science

---

35 *Ibid.,* 1295b 14–19.
36 *Ibid.,* 1294b 38–39.
37 *Ibid.,* 1295b 25–26.

38 I think it better to speak of the polity as the "best system which has actually been constructed" rather than, as Barker does, of the "most practicable state," or as Aristotle himself does, of the "best constitution for the majority of states and men." For while in a sense this is a goal at which a majority of states may aim, its achievement will be rare. Aristotle specifically says that the policy is a rare occurrence: "A middle or mixed type of constitution has never been established—or, at the most, has only been established on a few occasions and in a few states." *Ibid.,* 1296a 36–37.

of the dynamics of empire. In Aristotle's work it is only part of an elaborate theoretical structure, and it is only incompletely treated. Aristotle was particularly interested in that aspect of the political process which involves the creation, destruction, and stabilization of organizations, i.e., the phenomenon of constitutional change. But he says virtually nothing about the processes of the stable system.

The causes of revolution

Book V opens with a discussion of the most general causes of change, both evolutionary and revolutionary, with emphasis on the latter. Aristotle tells us that the primary causes, or motor forces, are psychological, and are twofold—certain ideologies or "attitudes of mind," and certain drives or desires. As to the first, he suggests that revolutions are never made merely for material interest but always in the name of some ideal of justice. And a regime whose legitimating ideology carries conviction only with a particular social class is radically unstable and open to attack from many quarters. What we may term "radical oligarchy" and "radical democracy," the two most prevalent systems of Aristotle's time, were therefore peculiarly susceptible to sedition (*stasis*) because of the class ideologies of their ruling groups.

Democracy arose in the strength of an opinion that those who were equal in any one respect were absolutely equal, and in all respects. (Men are prone to think that the fact of their all being equally free-born means that they are absolutely equal.) Oligarchy similarly arose from an opinion that those who were unequal in some one respect were altogether unequal. (Those who are superior in point of wealth readily regard themselves as absolutely superior.) Acting on such opinions, the democrats proceed to claim an equal share in everything, on the ground of their equality; the oligarchs proceed to press for more, on the ground that they are unequal—that is to say, more than equal. . . .
But a constitutional system based absolutely, and at all points, on either the oligarchical or the democratic conception of equality is a poor sort of thing. The facts are evidence enough: constitutions of this sort never endure.[39]

Democracy is the more stable of the two, being plagued only by differences between the rich and the poor, while oligarchy suffers from factions within the wealthy classes as well. But more stable still is the regime whose legitimating principles have a universal appeal by recognizing numerical equality in some cases but "equality proportionate to desert" in others. The polity has just such a universal ideology and is the most stable of governments, as we have already noted.

Ideology does not operate alone to cause revolution. Associated with every such "attitude of mind" which disposes people to seek change are certain universal drives—the drive for material gain, the drive for prestige or status, the fear of loss and disgrace. (The reader will recall that Thucydides identified these as "the three greatest things" in his explanation of political motivation.) And both ideological protest and the quest for material advantage through revolution are activated by still another type of cause—certain kinds of catalytic events which Aristotle calls "occasions and origins of disturbances." One is the distribution of income and prestige in a way which strikes an important social group as unjust. Another is "a disproportionate increase in some part of the state"—the sudden growth of a social class in numbers, wealth, or other power, or an unusual increment of power in a certain political office. Election intrigues may

---

39 *Ibid.*, 1301a 28–35, 1302a 3–5.

set in motion the psychological causes of revolution, as may what Aristotle calls "dissimilarity of elements" in the makeup of a *polis*—ethnic or national heterogeneity in a population.

Revolutions sometimes are occasioned by the negligence of the ruling class. Men disloyal to the constitution may find their way into high positions which they then employ to subvert the entire order.

The objects of revolution

The object of sedition (*stasis*) according to Aristotle is not always a wholesale revolution of the regime. It may be to get control of the government into the hands of the party of change, while leaving the machinery of government intact. Or it may be to change only some parts of the constitution, so as to heighten or diminish the general character of the system, e.g., to make a democracy more or less democratic.

Particular causes of revolution

Aristotle follows his description of the general causes of revolution with a consideration of particular causes. These are catalytic events or circumstances peculiarly associated with each kind of regime. In democracies it is frequently the confiscatory policies of demogogues which precipitate sedition by the rich. When demagogues were also military men, the regime was often converted into a tyranny, though in Aristotle's time the coincidence of a popular following and military command was less frequent. He attributed this to the use of rhetoric as an art (the art of propaganda in the fourth century B.C.) which placed power over the mob in the hands of people with a glib and persuasive tongue. But such people, lacking military force, were unable to establish tyrannical power. Oligarchies are susceptible to a variety of threats arising both outside of and within the ruling class. Monarchies are overturned when the king loses moral authority—the respect of his subjects—or when the royal family is divided, or when the king attempts to enlarge his prerogative and move entirely beyond the restrictions of law. The discussion of the downfall of monarchies brings to mind aspects of three great modern upheavals, the English, French, and Russian revolutions.

Aristotle's discussion of revolution includes a critique of the Platonic theory of constitutional change set forth in Books VIII and IX of the *Republic*. His chief argument is that the cycle of change described by Plato, aristocracy–timocracy – oligarchy – democracy – tyranny, is empirically incorrect. Observation showed that democracies are more often and more readily converted into oligarchies than into tyranny. And tyrannies, instead of changing into philosophic monarchies, as Plato's theory implies, and thus inaugurating a new cycle, change rather into other forms of tyranny or into democracy or some other form. This criticism is in a way quite beside the point, because Plato did not intend to depict a process of empirical change but rather an ideal cycle—the logical process of corruption of the best system generated in imagination, the logic of moral decay. That Aristotle did not appear to understand this is further evidence of the empirical bent of his mind, and of his persuasion that discussions of politics in terms of purely abstract models, quite devoid of empirical reference, are not very rewarding affairs.

Conditions of stability

Parallel to the problem of the cause of change is of course the question of the cause of stability. And this is Aristotle's next theme. Once more he reviews the various kinds of regime one by one and describes the policies which maintain them. The discussion is cast in the form of a structure-process analysis (formal and efficient causation), which carries us through the last half of Book V and all of Book VI. Book IV described regimes as they are actually found to exist. In Books V and VI we are given a picture of the "rational" form (i.e., the most stable structure) of each kind of government, and of the measures necessary to create and maintain it.

What Herbert Spiro, a modern student of comparative government, calls "constitutional engineering" will go a certain way toward stabilizing a regime. In every state, for example, where the ruling class is relatively large, certain democratic institutions are desirable, even though the constitution is not democratic. There should be provisions for restricting the tenure of office to short periods, so that as many of the "peers" as possible have the right to enjoy office—status and glory must thus be well distributed in the ruling orders. And it is less easy for factions to get control of the governmental apparatus. This blocks one method whereby tyrannies are created in oligarchies and democratic states. In oligarchies and polities which use a property qualification, the property assessments underlying the qualification should be changed as the poorer class increases in wealth or as inflation occurs, else the regime will be automatically converted into a democracy. Increases in the property of one particular segment of the population pose problems which can be partially offset by constitutional engineering. Groups outside the prosperous circle may be compensated for their misfortune with the perquisites of public office. Measures to prevent the embezzlement of public funds are of the greatest importance.

All of the stabilizing devices recommended by Aristotle are designed to build social support for the political system, not to substitute for it. And Aristotle also recognizes their limited value in this area. Pure class rule, he points out, can never be stabilized by constitutional engineering. At least *some* access to control over policy must be provided for all major groups. Measures should be taken to build up the middle classes as a buffer in the antagonisms of rich and poor. Leaders must learn to speak for the interests of classes other than their own. The most important stabilizer of regimes is adequate education of the citizens in the spirit of the constitution. There must be institutions for the political socialization of the population.

Aristotle on tyranny

Aristotle's desire to be exhaustive in his analysis of political systems led him to examine the conditions of stability of even the tyrannical regime. Are there some circumstances under which tyranny can be considered a good order? It was certainly a *common* phenomenon in Aristotle's time, and certain kinds of circumstance seemed to generate it as a natural product. (We have already noticed how the notions of mechanical necessity and relative good tended to coalesce in Aristotle's mind.) Though its appearance under certain conditions might not be avoided, perhaps the worst aspects of tyrannical government could be mitigated. It is significant that the recipes which Aristotle puts forward for increasing the stability of tyrannies are all based on the principle that the successful tyrant should in his actions *appear* like the just king.

The analysis of tyranny begins with a description of the usual practices of tyrants in the maintenance of their power, "the method of government still followed by the majority of tyrants."

The traditional policy aims at the prevention of opposition through social disorganization. Outstanding personalities in the country who might assume rival leadership positions are "lopped off." Social communication which might bind individuals together and produce community spirit is disrupted by the prohibition of all private societies for cultural purposes—the citizens are made strangers to one another and measures are taken to sow enmity and distrust between individuals and social groups. Efforts are even made to divide families, and set wife against husband. Public gatherings under government auspices are held frequently to facilitate surveillance of the population and to foster psychological dependence of the people on the ruler. A secret-police network is maintained to detect covert attempts at political communication and organization. Financial resources which might go into the development of an opposition organization are drained into the public treasury by heavy taxes and expended by the tyrant on showy public buildings. And the tyrant diverts the public mind from domestic ills and increases the general sense of dependence on his leadership by constant war-mongering.

After recounting the measures usually taken by tyrants to stabilize their regimes, Aristotle offers his own prescription, which, he argues, promises greater stability than the traditional methods. The tyrant should counterfeit the just king, "subject to the one safeguard that the reformed tyrant still retains power, and is still in a position to govern his subjects with or without their consent." He should deal responsibly with the public funds. He should seem grave without being harsh, and should seek to inspire awe rather than fear. He should display military prowess to engender respect. He should restrain his desires, and avoid giving offence to his subjects by molesting their women and children. In all his pleasures he should be moderate—or at least appear to his subjects to be so. He should appear godly. He should honor good men among his subjects, though avoiding the concentration of authority in any single pair of hands. The tyrant should attempt to satisfy both the rich and the poor, but if he is forced to choose one, he should be sure to base his power on the strongest social groups. In all things, so far as possible, he should appear a "trustee for the public interest, not a man intent on his own." Such a regime will be as good as the circumstances permit. It will be both morally better and more stable than the common tyranny.

THE IDEAL *POLIS*

The last two books of the *Politics* take up once more and carry through to completion the theme of the ideal state. In Book I we were told that the *polis* in its ideal form is based on the principle of equality. It is a government by the many rather than by the few. In Book III we learned that the many may rightly lay claim to power when they are collectively richer and better, as well as more numerous, than the few; that the coincidence of these qualities in the many produces the ideal ruling class. And we were told that in the ideal *polis* the good man and the good citizen are identical. In Book IV we were shown this ideal order partly developed in the polity, a system governed by the many in the form of a large middle class which possesses the qualities of the ideal ruling class. These good citizens of the polity are also good men. They lead the sort of moral life described in the *Ethics* as the best life for man in society.

Throughout the *Politics*, intertwined with his analysis of actual states (both in their empirical and "rational" forms),

Aristotle has been developing for us a picture of the ideal order. And he has identified elements of that order in the historical polity. We have been told a good deal about the final, material, and formal causes of the good *polis,* though nothing has been said of the efficient causes which establish the good order. Thus in the last two books the subject of the good *polis* needs only to be rounded out. The discussion proceeds on all four levels, but with emphasis on efficient causes.

Aristotle reaffirms the final cause of the best *polis* to be the realization of the good human life. "We may . . . expect that—unless something unexpected happens—the best way of life will go together with the best constitution possible in the circumstances of the case." Some scholars have been puzzled by the last words in this sentence. Ernest Barker, for example, writes:

It is not quite clear . . . why Aristotle adds the words of qualification. The ideal constitution . . . presupposes ideal conditions or circumstances. . . . And it is not adjusted to given conditions or circumstances, such as an imperfect heterogeneous society.[40]

But if we keep Aristotle's metaphysic clearly in mind, this difficulty, I think, disappears. The metaphysic holds that the ideal order *is* adjusted to "given conditions." The Form must dwell in an empirical context if it is to be at all. It is a meaningless dream apart from the limiting conditions of that context. One may imagine in constructing an image of the best *polis* the best circumstances, but they must be real human circumstances, not those of a Platonic utopia. The "circumstances of the case" are the circumstances of the human case as we observe them to exist. It must be clear that the laws of efficient causation in the empirical world are capable of producing our imaginary system.

The good social life is the life of noble action guided by rational principle, which was described in detail in the *Ethics,*[41] and which we have already seen operating in the life of the ruling class of the polity. But now the notion "noble action" is given a new connotation. In the *Ethics,* the god-like life of thought was contrasted with the best human life, that of the virtuous man of action, in order to demonstrate that only the second way of life depended on society for its realization. But this seemed to imply that the philosopher, by virtue of his contemplative activity, had to be alien to the city, had to be an isolated, lonely, and passive being. Aristotle was not willing to conclude this. The contemplative reason, the divine faculty, might not need society for its development. But perhaps society could be served by philosophy. And surely the philosopher, to be fulfilled as a *man,* needed society. To resolve his dilemma, Aristotle in Book VII of the *Politics* tells us that philosophy is best understood as itself a kind of action, and thus may be assimilated to the life of action which is the life of the city.

But the life of action need not be, as is sometimes thought, a life which involves relations to others. Nor should our thoughts be held to be active only when they are directed to objects which have to be achieved by action. Thoughts with no object beyond themselves, and speculations and trains of reflection followed purely for their own sake, are far more deserving of the name of action. "Well-doing" is the end we seek: action of some sort or other is therefore our end and aim; but, even in the sphere of outward acts, action can also be predicated . . . of those who, by their

---

40 Barker, *The Politics of Aristotle,* p. 279, footnote 2.

41 See *Politics,* 1332a 8–10, in which Aristotle makes specific reference to the standard set down in the *Ethics.*

thoughts, are the prime authors of such acts.[42]

This does not mean, of course, that Aristotle has changed his conception of the final cause of the *polis* in the last pages of the *Politics*. He has not concluded that society exists for the sake of philosophy, nor that in the best *polis* every man will be a philosopher. He has simply tried to establish a place for the philosopher—*a* place among many, and not the *foremost* place—in the social life of man.

Out of what kind of material will the best *polis* be constructed? Under this heading Aristotle deals with the size and character of the population and of the territory of the good society. The population should consist of the "greatest surveyable number required for achieving a life of self-sufficiency," a population large enough to support itself in all things but small enough so that its members can be well acquainted with one another and know each other's character. The people should have a natural endowment of spirit and intelligence, the foundation of courage and wisdom. And the territory should be large enough to make possible a life of leisure for the citizenry—the physical foundation of wisdom—and a life combining liberality with temperance, two of the other virtues of the good man.

Very little is said about formal causes —the social and political organization of the best *polis*. Perhaps Aristotle assumed that the description of the polity had supplied enough on this head. The economy is to be a "mixed one"; some property is to be state-owned, some privately. The citizens are all to be property owners, for the virtue of the man of action requires external goods for its development—"We have to remember that a certain amount of

equipment is necessary for the good life, and while this amount need not be so great for those whose endowment is good, more is required for those whose endowment is poor."[43] Apparently they will all lead the leisure life of the gentleman farmer. For farm labor and all commercial and manufacturing functions are performed by slaves or serfs. "The truly good and happy man...has advantages at hand."[44] The state property is to be used to support the worship of the gods and such community-building institutions as common meals. This will allow the poor man, who can afford to make no financial contribution to their support, to take part in the activities of the city's common life.

The form of government is a democracy—all citizens share equally in the government. And all have the leisure necessary for participation in civic affairs, the noble actions through which human excellence is developed and made manifest. Aristotle divides these political functions into three parts and assigns each to a different age group. To the young citizen is given the responsibility of defending the state, the military function and the politics of force. To the older, and wiser, belongs the politics of words—the deliberative function. The oldest men staff the priesthood which fosters the cult of the gods of the community.

The resemblance of these citizens of the ideal state to the middle-class rulers of the polity (the entelechy in the process of development) is marked. Both groups are martial people and men of substance. Both groups are "peers and equals." Both groups know how to obey as well as rule. And they rule and are ruled in turn. The life enjoyed by the dominant class of the

42 *Ibid.*, 1325b 17–23.

43 *Ibid.*, 1329a 19–20; 1331b 40; 1332a 2.
44 *Ibid.*, 1332a 20–25.

developing ideal is shared by all the citizenry of the *polis* in its fullest development.

Aristotle deals with all these questions concerning final, formal, and material causes in the first half of Book VII. The rest of the *Politics* is devoted to the problem of efficient causes. How is the endowment of our *polis* with excellent matter, both natural and human, and with excellent form, to be turned to account? How is this static potential to be converted into an actuality of virtuous activity, into "a perfected activity functioning without interference from outside?"[45] What is the efficient cause of the good *polis?* The answer is, of course, a process— education. Only the right kind of education can guarantee that the good matter and good form will not be wasted but rightly used.

Aristotle's scheme of ideal education begins with the act of procreation. The first concern is to ensure a good physique for each generation, which requires regulation of marriage relations. The regulations are few, however, and relate chiefly to the ages and physical fitness of the marriage partners. There is no attempt à la Plato to distinguish types of moral character and to breed "gold" only with "gold," though it is assumed that all the parents are persons of spirit and intelligence. Monogamous family organization is the rule, and adultery is to be severely punished.

The next section deals with the nurture of the young until the age of seven, and reads like a combination of the handbooks for modern parents by Doctors Spock and Gesell. In Aristotle's *polis*, of course, this would be a handbook for the public authorities charged with the oversight of all matters of child-rearing, as well as for parents, since the early training is carried on in the home. Only good models of behavior should be placed in the child's way. And all contact with things indecent, vulgar, or low must be avoided. In this way, right habits are implanted in the young. Play is supervised in institutions vaguely resembling the modern nursery school and kindergarten.

Formal education begins at seven, and lasts to age twenty-one. The basic subjects are reading, writing, physical training, and "music" (poetry, song, and instrumental music as a single discipline). The first two are useful for most of the ordinary concerns of life, but have little value for character building, the most important matter. And Aristotle excludes from his curriculum for "gentlemen citizens" all purely useful mechanical arts—what we today call "vocational training." "Music" is the important thing, for it is "music" which liberates the mind and soul and builds the good way of life. It serves to amuse us, to inculcate virtuous habit, and also contributes to the "cultivation of our minds and to the growth of moral wisdom"—the development of the practical reason.[46]

The discussion of education ends at this point. Nothing is said about the higher education, and most students of Aristotle believe that the section is incomplete. But we must remember that the *telos* of the *polis* is realized in producing men of practical reason. And "musical" education, to Aristotle, was the basic ingredient of moral training. The higher studies of the speculative intellect do not have the influence on character and on the quality of a citizen's life which Plato attributed to

45 John Herman Randall, *Aristotle,* New York: Columbia University Press, 1960, p. 52.

46 *Politics,* 1339a 11, 1340b 20.

them. The *polis* does not exist to produce philosophers, nor is it ruled by them, as we have seen.

The *Politics* closes with this sketch of education as the chief efficient cause of the good *polis*. Of all the processes which affect the character of political systems, the learning process, to Aristotle, was the most significant single cause, for a political system is more than "an arrangement of offices." It embodies a set of values, indeed, an entire way of life. And as its education varies, so will the manners and morals of the *polis*. The emphasis was typically Greek, and one which, despite other marked differences in their work, Aristotle shared with his teacher Plato.[47]

[47] See Werner Jaeger, *Paideia: The Ideals of Greek Culture,* 3 vols., Gilbert Highet, trans., Oxford: Basil Blackwell, 1939.

3

CHRISTIAN
POLITICAL THOUGHT

The hegemony of Christian thought in western Europe produced two centrally important writers on politics, both saints of the Roman Catholic Church. St. Augustine (355–430) lived in North Africa in that part of the Roman Empire which now comprises Tunisia. During his lifetime two turning points in western civilization occurred. Rome fell to the barbarian invaders, and Christianity became the official religion of the Empire. Whereas Augustine's life, after its sinful prelude, was spent as bishop in the midst of the active life of the church, Aquinas (1225–1274) led a comparatively uneventful life as Dominican monk and scholar. Born near Naples, he spent most of his life either in Paris or Italy leading the intellectual defense of the recently revived Aristotelian learning in its assault on the ascendance of Augustinian ideas over the church.

These Augustinian ideas on politics and the state are ably described in the selection by Herbert Deane, professor of politics at Columbia University. The state, according to Augustine, is a repressive tool designed by God to curb the misery of unregulated life among sinful men. Obedience is owed to the princely sword, for it is God's agent in the passing world of Babylon. The distinguished Italian professor and political theorist, A. P. D'Entrèves, describes in his essay how Aquinas repudiates the central place Augustine has given to sin in the origin of the state and how, in turn, he revives Aristotelian notions of the naturalness of sociability and political institutions themselves. D'Entrèves' essay not only discusses Aquinas and his theory of law, which is so characteristic of Catholic political thought, but he also speculates on how Aquinas' revival of classical political thought laid the foundation for more modern views of the state.

HERBERT A. DEANE

The Political and Social Ideas
of St. Augustine*

Despite its emphasis upon the individual soul and the unique relation between each soul and God, Christianity has also insisted, from the beginning, that man is naturally and inherently a social being. The *ecclesia* itself is regarded as a fellowship or society of believers, and the world outside the church is viewed as a community of sinners. The essence of Augustine's conception of two cities or two societies the heavenly city and the earthly city—is found in the Christian tradition at least as far back as St. Paul.

Augustine follows this traditional Christian doctrine that society and social life are natural to mankind, and hence are to be sharply distinguished from the state and the political and legal order. As we shall see, the latter are not natural, but are remedial institutions ordained by God after the Fall in order to deal with the changed condition of sinful man. Even before the Fall, however, God intended man to

be a social creature. As soon as He had created Adam, He saw that it was not good for man to be alone; He therefore formed Eve as a wife and companion for him. This bond between husband and wife, later extended to include their children, is the primary "natural bond of human society." In addition, men are endowed with a great natural good, the power of friendship; by nature they are sociable beings who are inclined to love their fellow men.

. . .

Since Augustine insists that human fellowship and social life are natural to man, it is not surprising that he follows St. Paul and the Church Fathers in recognizing the existence of a law of nature, a basic moral law that is written in the hearts of all men, and that is distinct from human laws or divinely revealed laws. The basic precept of this natural law, which should guide men in all their dealings with others, is the Golden Rule in its negative form, that is, "Do not unto others what you would not have others do unto you." Augustine states the precept in a number of ways, for example, "What thou wouldest not have done to

* Reprinted from Herbert A. Deane, *The Political and Social Ideas of St. Augustine* (New York: Columbia University Press, 1963), pp. 78, 85–87, 92–96, 136–47, 151–53, by permission of the publisher. The footnotes found in the original have been omitted here.

thyself, do not to another," "What thou art unwilling to suffer, be unwilling to do," or "That which to thyself thou wouldest not have done, do not thou to another." In this principle are embodied the basic moral rules that govern man's conduct toward others, such as the prohibitions against murder, violence, theft, fraud, and lying. It is by this law of nature that men judge whether any particular action is righteous or unrighteous, just or unjust, and this law is implanted in the conscience of every rational man, no matter how wicked his own conduct may be. He recognizes the law of nature and expects other men to observe it even if he flagrantly violates it himself.

Theft is punished by thy law, O Lord, and by the law written in men's hearts, which not even ingrained wickedness can erase. For what thief will tolerate another thief stealing from him? Even a rich thief will not tolerate a poor thief who is driven to theft by want.

Since natural law or the law of conscience is innate in man, it has existed since the creation of Adam. Therefore, it precedes the Fall and the introduction of sin into the world, and it antedates and is distinguished from the written law given directly by God to the Jews through Moses as well as the law of Christ in the Gospels. The Ten Commandments and the Gospel precepts do not contradict or annul the law of nature; rather, they make it more explicit and overt and give it the greater force of God's direct commandment to men. Although it is innate and not "learned," the law of nature is not perceived or recognized by the young child, but when a child has grown up he discovers, by the use of his reason, this law in his rational soul, that is, in his conscience. The basic precept of the natural law—"That which therefore to thyself thou wilt not have to be done, do not thou to another"—follows

necessarily for any rational man from his unwillingness to suffer hurt or injury and from his recognition of the inevitable fact that he must live and work with other men.

Come, if thou art not willing to suffer these things, art thou by any means the only man? dost thou not live in the fellowship of mankind? He that together with thee hath been made, is thy fellow; and all men have been made after the image of God, unless with earthly covetings they efface that which He hath formed.... For thou judgest that there is evil in that, which to suffer thou art not willing; and this thing thou art constrained to know by an inward law; that in thy very heart is written.

The natural law, since it is discoverable by all men by the use of reason, without special revelation, is a universal law, and by it the Gentiles, to whom the law of Moses was not given, are judged and found to be transgressors.

Augustine also speaks of this law of nature as "the eternal law of God [*lege Dei aeterna*]," written in "the hearts of the godly," and says that from this eternal law was copied the law given to the Jews through Moses. The law of nature is God's eternal law because the source of these rules that rational men discover in their consciences is God's Truth.

Where indeed are these rules [*regulae*] written, wherein even the unrighteous recognizes what is righteous, wherein he discerns that he ought to have what he himself has not? Where, then, are they written unless in the book of that Light which is called Truth? whence every righteous law [*omnis lex justa*] is copied and transferred (not by migrating to it, but by being as it were impressed upon it) to the heart of the man that worketh righteousness; as the impression from a ring passes into the wax, yet does not leave the ring.

. . .

Augustine's insistence upon the fact that men are by nature social creatures bound together by ties of equality and fraternity, and his frequent references to the natural law of moral conduct which man can discover by the use of reason may seem difficult to reconcile with his description of human life in this world as "this hell upon earth" and with his graphic portrayal of the strife and conflict that result from the clash of men's avaricious and ambitious strivings. We must always remember that when he says that "the laws of man's nature move him to hold fellowship and maintain peace with all men so far as in him lies," he is talking about the natural state of man before the Fall and the introduction into the world of sin and its consequences. Once the nature of man has been corrupted by sin each man seeks to gain possessions and wealth at the expense of others and each seeks to gain mastery over others. When we observe their actions and attitudes, we may well be forgiven for forgetting that these creatures are brothers descended from the same parents and that they were intended to live together in concord and harmony. Augustine's comment on the hatred and conflict that rage among men is bitterly sorrowful: "For there is nothing so social by nature, so unsocial by its corruption, as this race." Into such enormities of sin—cruelty, murder, war—has man fallen that

even the beasts devoid of rational will... would live more securely and peaceably with their own kind than men, who had been propagated from one individual for the very purpose of commending concord. For not even lions or dragons have ever waged with their kind such wars as men have waged with one another.

Only among the small number of men who have been redeemed by God's grace do we find the true unity and concord that are natural to man. They are made one by Him in Himself, and become members of the one Body of which Christ is the Head. Among them are found true love of and service to others, since each of them loves God and makes Him the center of his life and each loves other men as sons of God. Left to themselves, fallen men are, in contrast, incapable of unity and concord, "separated as they are one from another by divers pleasures and desires and uncleannesses of sin. . . ."

Moreover, sin and unrighteousness have almost effaced from men's hearts the natural law that God has implanted, although some faint traces of that law still remain. Ignorance and misguided will, the two primary defects of fallen man, make it difficult for him to know what he ought to do and impossible for him to do what he may know that he should do. Even in his corrupt state man retains some ability to ascertain what is right and wrong, just and unjust, and he can see the force of the fundamental precept of the natural law —"What thou wouldest not have done to thyself, do not to another"—especially when he is observing and judging the actions of other men. But he has an extraordinary capacity to ignore this voice of conscience and to fail to apply the moral law when he is contemplating an action of his own or considering it after the event. He usually manages to distinguish his own case from the general rule and to rationalize as necessary or even praiseworthy actions which he would instantly condemn if another man were to perform them. When he is about to act, he listens to the clamorous demands of cupidity, pride, lust, and hatred and ignores the small voice of conscience and God's eternal law. He treats other men as instruments for the satisfaction of his own desires and often employs treachery, deceit, and coercion in his dealings with them. In a word, he reverses the central precept of the natural law by treating other men in exactly the manner in which he does *not* want to be treated by them.

Once sin entered the world through Adam's disobedience and radically corrupted all his descendants, it became absolutely impossible for any man to lead a good life or to attain salvation by attempting to carry out the precepts of the law of nature. As St. Paul said, even the law of God given to the Jews through Moses cannot bring fallen men to true virtue or to salvation; indeed, it simply adds to the burden of man's sin by adding to the original evil action the crime of transgressing God's law. The natural law is even less capable of serving as the vehicle of salvation. If either the natural law or the law of Moses could lead men to eternal life, then, in St. Paul's phrase, "Christ died in vain." "If, however, Christ did not die in vain, then human nature cannot by any means be justified and redeemed from God's most righteous wrath—in a word, from punishment—except by faith and the sacrament of the blood of Christ." Without faith, faith in Christ, it is impossible to please God and to be saved. Therefore, no unbeliever can ever attain true virtue by means of a perfect obedience to the precepts of natural law. As long as we remain unregenerate we do not do what we know we ought to do or what, in a sense, we may want to do, since there is another law—the law of sin and lust—that overcomes the law of God within us. Only faith in Christ, given by God's grace, can bring us to repentance and to a new life, in which we die to sin and begin to carry out the commandments of God. In his polemic against Julian and his semi-Pelagian doctrines, Augustine says: "You introduce a race of men who can please God by the law of nature without the faith of Christ. This is the chief reason why the Christian Church detests you."

Since the fraternity and concord natural to human society have been shattered by the egoism of sinful men, and the natural law regulating human relations has been all but effaced from the human heart, how is society—which is essential to man's existence—to be maintained? God's grace which brings regeneration and ransom from the captivity to sin cannot serve as the basis for social organization since, as we have seen, it liberates only a small minority of the mass of sinners. Since most men —whether they are heathen or nominal Christians—are unredeemed and will be so until the end of the world, new means must be provided to introduce a measure of order, stability, and peace in the midst of the strife and conflict that mark earthly life. Even to disobedient, prideful man God has been most merciful; He has established new institutions, adapted to the new conditions of sinful existence, in order to keep a check on human greed and violence and to prevent society from collapsing into complete anarchy and chaos. These institutions, such as private property and the entire legal and political order, are divinely ordained as both punishments *and* remedies for the sinful condition of man. Although they provide an element of order, stability, and peace in social life that would be completely absent without them, the earthly peace and order that they make possible are no longer natural and spontaneous, but must be maintained by coercion and repression.

In view of the condition of sinful man, the peace, concord, and justice that are maintained by these economic, legal, and political institutions are supremely important. Yet they are only imperfect images or reflections of the natural, uncoerced peace, order, and justice that existed in Paradise or of the true and abiding concord, peace, order, and justice that will reign for all eternity in the heavenly city, the society built upon the love of all its members for God and for one another in God. As we have already seen, Augustine says that even the godless are able to make some moral judgments, judgments about what is right and wrong and about how men ought to behave, despite the fact that their own lives and minds are unrighteous. He also says that the ideas or norms of justice and righteousness which enable them to make such judgments are "images" or "impressions" of God's Truth and Righteousness. If the image of God and the law of God were completely obliterated from man's soul by sin, if no "faint outlines" of the original remained, men would have no conception of justice, righteousness, or peace to use as the foundation of the human standards of equity, fair-dealing, and order that are the pillars of civilized society.

. . .

...The justice that emerges in the well-ordered state is a most imperfect replica or image of true justice, no matter how good the intentions of the rulers may be. Most overt crimes are punished; but some are never detected and others are never solved; sometimes the wrong man is punished, and the guilty go scot free. The rulers and the citizens are only men, fallible, prejudiced, and ignorant of much that they need to know. Even when they do the best they can, their best is far from true justice; and, often, what they do is far from their best. Rulers are, as St. Paul said, God's ministers, avengers against those that do evil. But a province or a state can only be ruled by instilling fear in those who are ruled, and the fear of punishment can never produce true righteousness or justice. By their fear of the laws and of the punishments attached to them, men can be kept from performing certain injurious actions, but they cannot be made

good or righteous by these means. Civil laws do not "bring men to make a good use of their wealth," but "those who make a bad use of it become thereby less injurious." Augustine states the kernel of the problem in one sentence: "But, ruling a province is different from ruling a Church; the former must be governed by instilling fear, the latter is to be made lovable by the use of mildness."

Of course, these dilemmas would not exist and this very imperfect, rough "justice" of the state would be converted into true justice if not only the rulers but all the subjects were truly pious and just men, who obeyed the commandments of Christ, and, as a consequence, preferred common interests to their egoistic, private interests. If this were possible, we could have the "Christian state," the truly just society, based on God's law, that some commentators seem to think that Augustine regarded as feasible or necessary. It is perfectly clear, however, that the conditions *sine qua non* for the existence of such a state can never be realized on this earth. Moreover, if they were to be realized, the result would not be a Christian or truly just state but rather the complete absence of the state as we know it. Since the entire apparatus of law, punishment, coercion, and repression that constitutes the heart of the state would be totally unnecessary, the state would indeed "wither away" and be replaced by the anarchist's paradise —a spontaneous, noncoercive order of love, which would embody true justice, true peace, and true harmony, with no need for armies, courts, policemen, judges, jailers, and hangmen.

In other words, a truly just society would be the City of God brought down from heaven to earth, and that for Augustine is an absolute impossibility. Even when he is defending Christianity against pagan charges that it is incompatible with patriotism and the well-being of the state, he is careful to retain the contrary-to-fact conditional form in speaking of the possibility of a state made up of true Christians.

Wherefore, let those who say that the doctrine of Christ is incompatible with the State's well-being, give us an army composed of soldiers such as the doctrine of Christ requires them to be; let them give us such subjects, such husbands and wives, such parents and children, such masters and servants, such kings, such judges—in fine, even such taxpayers and tax-gatherers, as *the Christian religion has taught that men should be,* and then let them dare to say that it is adverse to the State's well-being; yea, rather, let them no longer hesitate to confess that *this doctrine, if it were obeyed, would be the salvation of the commonwealth.*

Augustine is perfectly explicit about the purpose of the earthly state and of the coercion and punishment it employs. The heavy hand of the state and its dreadful instruments of repression are necessary because they are the only methods by which sinful men can be restrained; the fear of punishment is the only safeguard of general peace and security. Only by such means can the wicked be kept from destroying one another as their competing egoisms clash, and discouraged from open assaults upon the minority of good and pious men.

Surely, it is not without purpose that we have the institution of the power of kings, the death penalty of the judge, the barbed hooks of the executioner, the weapons of the soldier, the right of punishment of the overlord [*dominantis*], even the severity of the good father. All those things have their methods, their causes, their reasons, their practical benefits. *While these are feared, the wicked are kept within bounds and the good live more peacefully among the wicked.* However, men are not to be called good because they refrain from wrongdoing through their fear of such things—*no one is good through dread of punishment but through love of righteousness*—even so, it is not without advantage that human recklessness should be confined by fear of the law so that innocence may be safe among evil-doers, and the evil-doers themselves may be cured by calling on God when their freedom of action is held in check by fear of punishment.

By the laws that it enforces the state protects from the encroachments of other men the things that each citizen properly regards as "his"—his body and bodily goods, his liberty (that is, his right as a free man to have no master), his household, his citizenship, and his possessions. The function of the temporal law is to insure that "men may possess the things which may be called 'ours' for a season and which they eagerly covet, on condition that peace and human society be preserved so far as they can be preserved in earthly things." The law determines what the citizen may lawfully possess, and then by its sanctions it secures to each citizen the enjoyment of his proper "possessions." Thereby, it moderates the intensity of the inevitable conflict among earthly men for goods and for glory, and prevents the clash of egoistic interests from totally disrupting the peace and harmony of society. The law operates through the instrument of fear. It has no effect on the men who are subject to it except through the medium of those very goods and possessions that it exists to protect and regulate. In other words, the sanction by means of which the state attempts to insure conformity to the conduct prescribed by the laws consists in the ability to deprive the offender of one or more of these possessions—his property, his liberty, his citizenship, or, in the last resort, his life. Since the men of the earthly city regard these possessions as the highest good, they are afraid of being deprived of any or all of them. Therefore, each man somewhat restrains his unlimited desire to acquire more possessions and more power at the expense of other members of the society, because he feels that the chance of greater gain and satisfaction is outweighed by the deprivations that he will suffer if he is punished for violating the law that protects the property of all.

It is sufficient to see that the authority of this law in punishing does not go beyond depriving him who is punished of these things or of some of them. It employs fear as an instrument of coercion, and bends to its own ends the minds of the unhappy people to rule whom it is adapted. So long as they fear to lose these earthly goods they observe in using them a certain moderation suited to maintain in being a city such as can be composed of such men [quendam modum aptum vinculo civitatis, qualis ex huiuscemodi hominibus constitui potest]. The sin of loving these things is not punished; what is punished is the wrong done to others when their rights are infringed.

Augustine sees that the legal system with its sanctions and punishments does not change, and does not attempt to change, the basic desires and attitudes of the men whose conduct it seeks to regulate. In fact, the system works precisely because these lovers of earthly goods are *not* transformed into lovers of real or eternal goods; unless they continued to place their affections in the things of this world, the law and its punishments would inspire no fear in them and so would have no effect on their behavior. The law can effectively punish only those men who love the possessions that can be taken from them against their will. "You see also that there would be no punishment inflicted on men either by injury done them or by legal sentence if they did not love the things that can be taken from them against their will."

These reflections about the state's purpose—the maintenance of external peace and order—and about the means that it employs to achieve this end—punishment and the deprivation of possessions, liberty, and life—exhibit one of the most characteristic features of Augustine's thoughts about man and his life on earth—his keen awareness of the paradoxes and ironies that mark every aspect of the human condition, and especially of political life. There is a constant danger that men will destroy one another as they seek to accumulate more and more possessions and power by robbing, cheating, or injuring their fellows. They are kept from this mutual injury and annihilation only by being threatened with the loss of the goods that they love and seek to acquire. The very sin of loving earthly goods thus supplies, to some extent, its own corrective and remedy, with the result that human society, which is essential to man's survival, is not completely dissolved and at least a minimum of security and peace is maintained.

Throughout the entire course of the world, order is imposed, through God's Providence, even upon the willful actions of evil men who seek to disrupt or destroy the natural order. Acts of political governance and the penalties imposed by the legal system represent striking examples of this process whereby order is recreated and restored out of disorder.

Some man, for instance, has chosen to be a house-breaker: the law of the judge knows that he has acted contrary to the law: the law of the judge knows where to place him; and orders him most properly. He indeed has lived evilly; but not evilly has the law ordered him. From a house-breaker he will be sentenced to the mines; from the labour of such how great works are constructed? That condemned man's punishment is the city's ornament.

The same point is made even more strikingly when Augustine refers to the "cruel and ferocious" hangman who is, nevertheless, an indispensable element in the order of a well-regulated state.

What more hideous than a hangman? What more cruel and ferocious than his character? Yet he holds a necessary post in the very midst of laws, and he is incorporated into the order of a well-regulated state [*bene moderatae ciuitatis*]; himself criminal in character, he is nevertheless, by others' arrangement, the penalty of evildoers.

The state's legal and punitive system does not *require* good and just men as its legislators, judges, jailers, or executioners; this is fortunate since only a small minority of its officers can be expected to be truly good. If true Christians happen to occupy these offices, they will punish evildoers not with vengeance but with the love and good will "which a father has towards his little son, whom by reason of his youth he cannot yet hate." Since the correction of evildoers is a duty, especially for those who are magistrates or hold other public posts, the imposition of legal penalties upon those who have violated the law does not contravene the Gospel precepts which forbid us to recompense evil for evil and which command us to turn the other cheek. Provided that the Christian keeps patience and benevolence in his heart as he punishes and disciplines the criminal for his own good and for that of society, he commits no sin "in correcting with a certain benevolent severity, even against their own wishes, men whose welfare rather than their wishes it is our duty to consult; and the Christian Scriptures have most unambiguously commended this virtue in a magistrate." Just as fathers and heads of households have a duty to correct by admonition or punishment their children and their servants so that, if possible, they may

be improved and domestic harmony may be maintained, or, at least, they may be restrained from further crimes and others may be deterred from evil actions, so those who have political or judicial authority must punish those citizens who violate the law. But judges and law-enforcement officers must, if they are Christians, remember that they themselves are sinners who need God's mercy; they must therefore show mercy to those whom they have the authority to punish or even to kill. Also, rulers and judges should remind themselves that power and exalted office, no less than great wealth, bring with them special dangers to the eternal wellbeing as well as the earthly happiness of their possessors.

The state and its instruments of coercion and punishment are, in Augustine's view, divinely ordained institutions designed as remedies as well as punishments for the sinful condition of fallen man. God uses the evil desires of fallen man as means for the establishment of earthly peace and order and for the just punishment of his vices. The state is thus a gift of God to man, despite the inadequacies and imperfections that necessarily mark the peace and justice that it can maintain among the unredeemed. The authority of the ruler over his subjects is therefore derived from God. The king or prince is established by God, no matter how wicked or unjust he may be, and Augustine allows no scope for any limitations of his power by his subjects or for any disobedience or resistance to his commands.

One of his favorite texts is the famous thirteenth chapter of St. Paul's Epistle to the Romans:

Let every person be subject to the governing authorities. For there is no authority except from God, and those that exist have been instituted by God. Therefore he who resists the authorities resists what God has appointed, and those who resist will incur judgment. For rulers are not a terror to good conduct, but to bad.... But if you do wrong, be afraid, for he does not bear the sword in vain; he is the servant of God to execute his wrath on the wrongdoer. Therefore one must be subject, not only to avoid God's wrath but also for the sake of conscience.

Any one who resists "duly constituted authority" resists "the ordinance of God." In order to make clear the divine origin of political power Augustine also refers to Christ's statement to Pilate: "You would have no power over me unless it had been given you from above." Christians therefore have a solemn duty to obey the laws and the commands of the rulers and to submit to all taxes and imposts. They owe to rulers, no matter how wicked or tyrannical they may be, not only obedience and reverence but respect and love, and they are obliged to see to it that their families, servants, and friends refrain from lawbreaking and crime. When Christians render obedience to rulers they are really obeying God rather than men, since it is God who establishes rulers and who orders that they be obeyed.

One of the primary reasons why Augustine insists so strongly on the divine origin of political authority and on the subjects' duty of absolute obedience to it is that, like Hobbes, he is so keenly aware of the need for a strong power to restrain the boundless appetites and ceaseless conflicts of men. He would agree with Hobbes's warning that any suggestion that resistance or disobedience to established rulers may be permissible or desirable in certain circumstances would serve as an invitation to anarchy. Factious, self-seeking individuals and groups would use such doctrines in order to rationalize their own desires to evade the laws, to escape punishment for their evil deeds, and

to acquire domination for themselves. Once egoism and ambition are unleashed in this way, the intricate fabric of social peace and order is in danger of being rent apart, and the dreadful specter of unending civil strife roams the land.

So all men, including Christ's saints, "are enjoined to be subject to the powers that are of man and of earth." The seventy-year period of the captivity of the Jews in Babylon signifies and prefigures this subjection of mankind to the kings of this world. Only at the end of time will this need for human authority and for absolute obedience to it come to an end. Only then will the Church "be delivered from the confusion of this world" and pass over from this world with its sufferings and its coercive, remedial order to the heavenly kingdom of perfect bliss and an order based upon perfect freedom and perfect love. In the meantime, all men must give absolute obedience to God's ministers, the kings and rulers of this earth, no matter how impious or wicked they may be. It is God who sends men tyrannical and cruel rulers in furtherance of His own designs. He uses the evil actions of wicked rulers, for which they alone are responsible and which hurt only themselves, to punish the transgressions of the sinful and to try the patience and fidelity of the good. The fact that a king may "rage with tyrannical cruelty" provides no excuse for condemnation of "the order of royal power" or for disobedience to his commands, just as the fact that a usurper may rule with benevolence and justice does not mean that his rebellion against the constituted authority is to be praised.

If wicked, sinful men occupy positions of power and authority as judges or kings, they are to be obeyed and their cruelty is to be accepted as divinely ordained discipline and punishment, while "the honour due to their power must needs be shown them." If anyone attempts to rebel against the established ruler, he is not to be aided but rather opposed and, if possible, punished, even if he seems to be a better and wiser man than the present king. However, it is God who, by His control over human actions, even over the actions of wicked men, determines the destinies of states and of rulers. It is a logical consequence of this belief in Providence that if a rebellion is successful and the former ruler is killed or routed, the usurper becomes the rightful ruler. He is then to be obeyed and honored as his predecessor was, although his act of usurpation and rebellion is not thereby rendered right or meritorious. Nevertheless, even his sinful action would not have been successful had God not chosen to use him and his wickedness as a way of punishing the previous ruler or of chastening the people, and as a demonstration that He can, when He will, humble the mighty and the proud who fail to recognize that their power is from Him and that they are His ministers.

The kings and princes of the earth, those who occupy "exalted stations" in this world, are sometimes good powers and fear God and sometimes evil powers and fear not God; but in either case they are to be obeyed and honored as long as they retain their authority. In this life the pilgrims from the City of God often have to endure as superiors men who are their inferiors;

we endure those whom we would not, we suffer for our betters those whom we know to be worse.... And it is a good thing to consider ourselves to be sinners, and thus endure men set over our heads: in order that we also to God may confess that deservedly we suffer.... God seemeth to be wroth, when He doeth these things: fear not, for a Father He is, He is never

so wroth as to destroy. When ill thou livest, if He spareth, He is more angry. In a word, these tribulations are the rods of Him correcting, lest there be a sentence from Him punishing.

Indeed, Augustine insists that the Christian ought to show to evil rulers a respect even greater than the deference exhibited to them by sinful, earthly men.

While Augustine does not use the phrase *legibus solutus* to describe the power of the king or ruler of a state, he recognizes that kings possess sovereignty (*imperium*), which he refers to as "the highest point of his [man's] desire," and he seems to regard a king as free to enact any laws that he believes to be necessary for the preservation of the peace and good order of the society over which he is ruling. He explicitly states that in making law the king is not limited by the precedents of his own prior enactments or those of his predecessors.

For it is lawful for a king, in the state over which he reigns, to command that which neither he himself nor anyone before him had commanded. And if it cannot be held inimical to the public interest to obey him, —and, in truth, it would be inimical if he were not obeyed, since *obedience to princes is a general compact of human society* [*generale quippe pactum est societatis humanae oboedire regibus suis*]—how much more, then, ought we unhesitantly to obey God, the Governor of all his creatures!

Since obedience to rulers is clearly in the public interest, all the laws promulgated by the ruler must be obeyed by all citizens, with the sole execption of laws or commands that run contrary to God's ordinances. Although Augustine believes that such laws are impious and wicked and insists that the Christian must not obey them, he never argues that the Christian has a right not to be punished when he refuses to obey a law or an order of this kind. The ruler has the right to punish anyone who refuses to obey his commands, whether the refusal is motivated by criminality, self-interest, or obedience to God, but only the man who refuses to obey because the order is contrary to God's ordinance is justified in his disobedience. Even this man, however, cannot claim a right not to be punished for his failure to comply with the law.

Christians owe the same obedience and honor to non-Christian kings that they must render to Christian rulers. Augustine notes that St. Paul taught us to make "supplications, prayers, intercessions, . . . for all men, for kings and for all who are in high positions, that we may lead a quiet and peaceable life, godly and respectful in every way." If even the rulers who persecuted the faithful were to be obeyed, honored, and prayed for, how much more are obedience and devotion due to those Christian kings who aid and cherish the Church and provide "the secure quiet of peace," so that "the Churches might be built up, and peoples planted in the garden of God, and that all nations might bring forth fruit in faith, and hope, and love, which is in Christ."

. . .

When one considers human frailty, one may rightly "despise the falling pinnacles of an earthly kingdom"; all the pomp, majesty, and power of temporal rule are trivial and ephemeral when compared to God's eternal kingdom. And for the sake of that kingdom, the only kingdom "which does not totter like all temporal dignities, but stands firm on eternal foundations," "the opposition of all earthly kingdoms should be patiently borne." Augustine notes that although the imperial office has lasted for a long time, each of its occupants has held it only briefly, and during his brief tenure each emperor has been subject to heavy cares and burdens; the office has been "filled by a constant succession of dying men." The powerful and mighty ones of this world, no less than their subjects, are merely creatures of a brief moment, "dying men."

The fact that this earth is a land of "dying men," all mortal and all subject to sin, suffering, and misfortune, is at the root of Augustine's political and social quietism. There is little room in his thought for the idea that power may be used to improve the lot of man on earth or to lessen his misery, and certainly no room at all for the view that one form of government should be abolished or a particular ruler replaced so that a better social and political order may be instituted. A relatively peaceful society and good rule are gifts of God to men; social disturbances, cruel and tyrannous rulers, and civil and foreign wars are punishments that He visits upon men when He sees that they require such chastisements. Since everything that takes place, whether "good" or "bad," is part of God's plan for the world and is, therefore, ultimately good, there is little or no impulse toward social or political reconstruction or amelioration. This life is only the anteroom to eternal life, a place of suffering and punishment for sin and a testing-ground for the virtues of the faithful. The institutions of social, economic, and political life have no real positive value. Their essential contribution is that they hold down the dark passions of sinful men and provide a measure of peace and stability. The breakdown of social and political order through disobedience or rebellion is therefore the worst of all possible earthly evils.

As long as the rulers do not force

their subjects into impiety or disobedience to God, they should be obeyed
quietly and without complaint.

For, as far as this life of mortals is concerned, which is spent and ended in a few
days, *what does it matter under whose
government a dying man lives,* if they who
govern do not force him to impiety and
iniquity [*quid interest sub cuius imperio
uiuat homo moriturus, si illi qui imperant
ad impia et iniqua non cogant*]?

We should not worry too much about
the fact that we may be in bondage
to evil rulers, or to evil masters if we
are slaves, for both king and subject,
master and slave, are on this earth for
only a brief period, and the only really
important concern is man's eternal
salvation. Servitude to the devil and
his angels is to be feared far more than
temporal—and temporary—servitude to
men; the former is servitude of the mind
and soul and will last unto all eternity,
while the latter is merely servitude of
the body in this life. Moreover, no
matter how we may be treated by
human rulers and masters, we have
"inner freedom," freedom of our
thoughts and minds and souls.

Anyone can easily see that under a human
lord we are allowed to have our thoughts
free. We fear the lordship of demons because it is exercised over the mind in which
is found our only means of beholding and
grasping the truth. Wherefore, though we
be enchained and subjected to all the
powers given to men to rule the state, provided we "render unto Caesar the things
that are Caesar's and to God the things
that are God's," there is no need to fear
lest anyone should exact such service after
we are dead. The servitude of the soul is
one thing, the servitude of the body quite
another.

Finally, it should be noted that when
Augustine is discussing the relations
between rulers and subjects he often
expresses a strongly paternalistic view
of the position of the ruler. The ruler
is not simply a man who occupies an
office that is necessary and useful; he
is, almost literally, "the father of his
people," and it is for him to decide
what they should do and how they
should do it. He does not ask the
people what they want, any more than
a father tries to ascertain the desires of
his young children before he tells them
what they must do. Augustine reveals—
perhaps unconsciously—his paternalistic conception of political authority
by his frequent use of the analogy
between the ruler and the father who
regulates and punishes the behavior of
his children. The king may be a good
and wise father, or a cruel and tyrannous father, but in either case his subjects must not only obey but honor
and respect him. Augustine does not
conceive of the citizens as mature,
rational persons who have a right to be
consulted about their wishes. Most of
them are willful, passionate children,
who must remain permanently under
the firm tutelage of a stern master. In
one of his letters he argues that

we confer a benefit upon others, not in
every case in which we do what is request-
ed, but when we do that which is not hurtful to our petitioners. *For in most cases we
serve others best by not giving, and would
injure them by giving, what they desire
[nam pleraque non dando prosumus et
noceremus, si dedissemus]*. Hence the proverb, "Do not put a sword in a child's
hand...." We are convicted of unfaith-
fulness towards those whom we profess to
love, if our only care is lest, by refusing
to do what they ask of us, their love towards us be diminished—and what becomes
of that virtue which even your own [i.e.,
pagan] literature commends, in the ruler
of his country who studies not so much
the wishes as the welfare of his people [*et
ubi est, quod et uestrae litterae illum
laudant patriae rectorem, qui populi utili-
tati magis consulat quam uoluntati*]?

A. P. D'ENTRÈVES

Thomas Aquinas[*]

Thomas of Aquino (1225–74) is not only the greatest representative of Scholastic philosophy and the most constructive and systematic thinker of the Middle Ages. He is also and foremost the typical exponent of what a recent historian has called the catholic mind. To him we owe an elaborate programme of that thorough christianization of human life which inspired the medieval ideal, and was soon to be celebrated in the immortal poem of Dante. In the formidable apparatus of his work all the aspects and issues of that programme are discussed, all the means of historical, scientific, and philosophical knowledge of the time are used to secure its realization. It is sometimes lamented that St. Thomas should not have left us a clear and definite account of his own political theory; but it is fairly easy to reconstruct the main outlines of that theory from the several indications which are contained in his work, provided that we never forget the general frame into which they fit, and from which they draw their significance. Such indications are to be found

in almost all of St. Thomas's works, from the Commentary on the *Sentences* of Peter Lombard to the great *Summae,* from the Commentaries on the *Ethics* and *Politics* of Aristotle to the little treatise *De Regimine Principum.* The latter writings would at first sight appear the most appropriate source for the knowledge of Thomistic political theory; but the use which we can make of them is hampered by the doubts which have been raised as to the authenticity of some of their parts, and by the very limitation of the problems which are dealt with in them. However, the particular aspects of the doctrine matter much less than the fundamental problem around which the whole of Aquinas's political thought can be said to centre, and this in turn can only be understood in relation to the main body of Thomistic philosophy. This fundamental problem is that of the nature and value of political experience.

I have endeavoured in the preceding lecture to illustrate the different issues which this problem raised to the medieval mind. As in all other fields of philosophical speculation, the rediscovery of Aristotelian philosophy in the thirteenth century had a profound and sudden effect in the field of political theory. The classical conception of the

* Reprinted from A. P. D'Entrèves, *The Medieval Contribution to Political Thought* (New York: Humanities Press Inc., 1959, and London: Oxford University Press), by permission of the publishers. The footnotes found in the original have been omitted here.

state, which was contained in the writings of Aristotle, was in its very essence
opposed to the body of ideas and
doctrines which had constituted the
traditional starting-point of Christian
political thought. Dr. Carlyle, in his
*History of Mediaeval Political Theory
in the West,* has given us some striking
examples of the tenacity with which
these older ideas held ground down to
the very eve of the recovery of Aristotelian political theory. He has provided evidence of their presence in the
works of Albert the Great, the teacher
of St. Thomas Aquinas, by whom the
grafting of Aristotelianism on to the
body of Christian thought was begun;
a task which his famous pupil was to
complete. The proper meaning and the
historical significance of the political
theory of Thomas Aquinas thus appear
strictly correlative to his great enterprise of reconciling Aristotelianism and
Christianity, and to the philosophical,
or rather metaphysical premises which
seemed to make that conciliation possible. This metaphysical premiss must be
mentioned briefly, for it has a direct
bearing upon the essence and meaning
of Thomistic political thought. It is
the idea of a fundamental harmony
between human and religious values,
between reason and faith. In giving a
clear formulation to this idea, Thomistic
philosophy appeared to express the deep
and intimate aspiration of medieval
Christianity, so different in its attitude
towards the world and nature from the
diffidence and hostility of the early
Christian, and the rigid alternatives
which had been stressed by St. Augustine. Human values and truths are not
necessarily obliterated by the revelation of higher ones; however modest
and low, they deserve to be considered
as possible tools for the great task of
building up Christian civilization. In
St. Thomas's assertion, *gratia non tollit
naturam, sed perficit,* there is the

recognition of the existence and dignity
of a purely 'natural' sphere of rational
and ethical values. This essentially
'human' standard of justice is not vitiated by sin nor absorbed in the glare
of absolute and divine justice; it is
rather the first and necessary step in
the long ascent towards the fulfilment
of the Christian ideal. This sphere of
natural and human values finds its complete expression in the idea of natural
law, which thus appears as the proper
ground upon which social and political
relations can be secured and comprehended.

A complete analysis of the Thomist
idea of natural law is out of the question. The best description of its purpose
and meaning is perhaps that which has
been made many times, of a bridge
thrown, as it were, across the gulf which
divides man from his divine Creator.
In natural law is expressed the dignity
and power of man, and thus of his
reason, which allows him, alone of
created beings, to participate intellectually and actively in the rational order
of the universe. This explains the stress
which is laid in Thomistic philosophy
upon the ideas of reason and order
(*ordinatio*), which in turn are developed
into a complete and elaborate philosophy of law. Law itself is conceived as
the expression not so much of the will
as of the reason of the legislator: it is,
in St. Thomas's well-known expression,
aliquid rationis, an *ordinatio rationis.*
This definition itself has momentous
theological, as well as legal implications. It has remained ever since as the
highest expression of an 'intellectual-
istic' as against a 'voluntaristic' theory
of law. It is the key to a proper understanding of that 'rationalistic' bent
which is one of the distinctive features
of Thomistic philosophy. Its decisive
influence is to be felt in every aspect
of St. Thomas's political theory. But
above all, it explains his attitude to-

wards the problem of political obligation, and his acceptance of a theory,
like that of Aristotle, which involved
a rational explanation of the state and
attributed a positive value to social
and political institutions, as being
grounded in the very nature of man.
As Dr. Caryle has pointed out, St.
Thomas did not in all respects directly
and categorically contradict the older
explanation of those institutions as the
result of, and divine remedy for, sin.
The idea of sin and of its consequences
remained for him, and could not but
remain, a fundamental dogma of the
Christian faith. But, as St. Thomas
expressly puts it, sin itself has not
invalidated *ipsa principia naturae*. Its
consequences, therefore, only concern
the possibility of man's fulfilling the
dictates of the *naturalis ratio*, not his
capacity of attaining to their knowledge: in other words they do not shat-
ter in the least the existence of a sphere
of purely natural ethical values, and it
is in this sphere that the state and
political relations find their *raison
d'être*. It has been rightly remarked
that the different manner of conceiving
the necessity and foundation of the
state, before and after St. Thomas,
derives from a different conception of
human nature: instead of considering
the state as an institution which may
well be necessary and divinely appointed, but only in view of the actual
conditions of a corrupted mankind,
Thomas Aquinas followed Aristotle in
deriving the idea of the state from the
very nature of man. But here again the
idea of natural law, and the conception
of a harmonious correspondence between the natural and the revealed
order which it expressed, provided a
solid ground for further developments.
For the Aristotelian conception, with
its insistence upon the 'natural' character of the state and its exaltation of
the state itself as the fulfilment and

end of human nature, contained at bottom a challenge to the Christian idea
of the existence of higher and ultimate
values, and of the inadequacy of merely
human means for their attainment. The
natural order, which comprises and
sufficiently justifies political experience,
is for St. Thomas only a condition and
a means for the existence of a higher
order, as natural law is but a part of
the eternal law of God. If *gratia non
tollit naturam*, certainly also *natura
non tollit gratiam*, and nature requires
to be perfected by grace. Thus the
action and value of the state, as part of
the natural order, must be considered
in the general frame of the divine direction of the world, and is entirely subservient to that direction. The recognition of the value of political experience
is thus subjected to a very important
qualification. But it is this clear-cut
delimitation which made it possible for
St. Thomas to attempt his conciliation
of the classical and of the Christian
ideal of the state, and, within these
well-drawn limits, the influence of
Aristotelian ideas caused a deep and
thorough-going reconstruction of medieval political thought.

Political institutions are, then, according to St. Thomas, an aspect or
part of 'natural' morality. As such they
can be considered and justified on a
purely human plane, independently of
religious values, which do not alter the
natural order of which the state is
a necessary expression. This implies
that even a non-Christian or pagan
state is endowed with a positive value,
as against St. Augustine's conception of
the pagan state as the embodiment of
the *civitas terrena* and the work of sin.
This idea is expressed in a well-known
passage of the *Summa Theologica*.

It must be granted that government and
authority are derived from human law,
while the distinction between believers and
unbelievers is introduced by divine law.

Now the divine law, which is founded on grace, does not abolish human law, which derives from natural reason. Hence the distinction between believers and unbelievers, considered in itself, does not abolish the government and authority of unbelievers over believers. Such a right of government or authority can, however, be justly abolished by the decision of the Church: for unbelievers, on account of their unbelief, deserve to lose their power over believers, who are become the sons of God. But this the Church sometimes decrees and sometimes not.

It is here very clearly stated that political authority has a value of its own, independent of religious belief; and it has such value as the expression of a natural and rational order. The intervention of the spiritual power, of the Church, may sometimes deprive the non-Christian ruler of his authority; but such intervention is justified on the ground of that general mission of control of the Church upon the temporal sphere which will be examined shortly. It in no way qualifies the statement that political authority is in itself fully justified as an expression of human and natural law. Let us notice once again how the question is referred back to the fundamental principle that grace does not abolish nature: the justification of the state and of political institutions must thus be sought in the very nature of man.

This is precisely the leading idea which St. Thomas derives from Aristotle. Few expressions are repeated so often, every time St. Thomas approaches the problem of politics, as that, *homo naturaliter est animal politicum et sociale (ut Philosophus dicit, ut probatur in I° Politicae,* &c.). I must leave it to better philologists than myself to ascertain whether and up to what point the Thomist expression *animal sociale et politicum* may be said to correspond to the Aristotelian πολιτικὸν ζῷον. But if, as I believe, the Aristotelian notion

of the political nature of man, as developed in the first book of *Politics,* somehow includes the notion of a social consciousness, and of the necessity for the state having its deepest roots in social experience—over and against the opposite and Machiavellian conception of the state as a work of art, the creation of a powerful but single will—the Thomist expression can be said to render fairly adequately the more important aspect of the Aristotelian conception of politics. The importance which St. Thomas attributes to that conception is explained by him over and over again. In one place he describes man as subject to a *triplex ordo,* divine law, reason, and political authority: this last is necessary in view of the social and political nature of man, for if indeed man had been by nature a solitary animal, the order of reason and that of revealed law would have been sufficient. Hence the necessity, if man is to attain his proper end and realize the highest form of life and virtue, of his sharing in political life, and of his practising the *virtutes politicae.* It is extremely interesting in this respect to observe St. Thomas's attitude in his Commentary on the *Politics* of Aristotle towards the Aristotelian doctrine of the 'monstrous' condition of man deprived or abstracted from political life. St. Thomas was forced to make an express reservation in favour of asceticism, in favour of the idea of a higher degree of perfection to be attained by retiring from the world rather than by participating in it. But he did not fail to emphasize the exceptional character of a life of this kind, and the necessity, for the attainment of such an ideal, of more than human capacities:

If any man should be such that he is not a political being by nature, he is either wicked—as when this happens through the corruption of human nature—or he is better than man—in that he has a nature more perfect than that of other men in general, so that he is able to be sufficient to himself without the society of men, as were John the Baptist and St. Anthony the hermit.

The idea of the social and political nature of man leads to an emphatic assertion of the full and harmonious integration of individual life in the life of the community:

Since therefore each man is a part of the city, it is impossible that any man should be good unless he is well-proportioned to the common good.

But what is the ultimate meaning of such 'integration'? Does it not imply in some way a belittlement, if not actually a denial of the value of human personality? Does it not lead to a complete absorption of individual life in that of the state? Here lay one of the greatest dangers of the return of the pagan conception of the state, which, as was shown by further development of the Aristotelian influence, menaced the fundamental Christian idea of the supreme value of human personality. If the whole is prior to its parts, if the end of the individual is inferior to that of the community, how can the value of human personality be secured? Does not the state become a sort of Leviathan which devours and annuls the individual? That such views are radically incompatible with the Christian teaching is clear not only to the modern student; it was realized very soon by medieval writers, and it was on this very ground that the charge of heresy was brought against so good a Thomist as Dante. It is therefore of the greatest importance that we should correctly understand and interpret St. Thomas's teaching on this momentous issue. But this is far from being an easy task. According to St. Thomas, the common good is undoubtedly more important than that of the individual: *majus et divinius est bonum multitudinis quam bonum unius*. But what is the real

difference between the one and the other? In a passage of the *Summa Theologica,* quoting Aristotle, St. Thomas seems to conceive of a difference in quality:

The common good of the city and the individual good of each person not only differ as being, the one more, the other less, but they are different in kind. The essence of the common good is different from that of the individual good, as that of the whole differs from that of the part. And hence the Philosopher in the first book of the Politics says that it is wrong to assert that the city and the household and other similar associations differ only in quantity and not in kind.

The doctrine that the end of the whole is of a different quality from that of the part is a dangerous one, as the Dominican critic of Dante, Guido Vernani, writing in the early fourteenth century, was at pains to demonstrate on the evidence of St. Augustine, St. Thomas, and Aristotle themselves. Yet on the other hand, in the *De Regimine Principum,* resuming the elaborate theory of ends which is expounded in the third book of the *Summa contra Gentiles*, St. Thomas openly acknowledges that the end of the single individual and that of the whole cannot and must not be judged on different standards ('idem autem oportet esse judicium de fine totius multitudinis et unius'), and that in fact the end of the one and the other are substantially the same ('oportet eundem finem esse multitudinis humanae qui est hominis unius'). This must mean that the difference between the end of the individual and that of the whole can only be a difference in quantity, and not in quality; that, in other words, the 'integration' of the individual in the whole must be conceived of as an enlargement and an enrichment of human personality, not as a degradation of the individual to the mere function of a part with no value of its own.

Thus the Christian idea of the value of individual personality appears to be safeguarded, and is further reasserted in the conception, which has been analysed above, that however paramount and important the state may appear for the fulfilment of human nature, political life is in its turn but a condition and means for the attainment of a higher type of perfection. This again implies that the individual can never be completely absorbed by the state, that something in him is reserved for a higher end: 'man is not formed for political fellowship in his entirety, and in all that he has...but all that a man is, and can do, and has, must be directed to God'. Clearly, the revival of the classical and pagan ideal of the state called for very important and substantial qualifications.

And yet, notwithstanding such qualifications, the teaching of Aristotle bore in the political thought of Aquinas some remarkable fruit. This is well seen in St. Thomas's treatment of the origin of the state and political institutions. According to Aristotle, the problem of the origin of the state is entirely independent of that of its rational justification. The doctrine of the political nature of man primarily implies the idea that, whatever the earliest conditions of mankind, the political condition is its 'natural' one. It is therefore quite pointless to argue about the causes of some supposed change in man, and to seek in them an explanation and justification of the state and political institutions. There is no place in such a doctrine for a contrast between 'nature' and 'convention'. The influence of this doctrine upon St. Thomas is clearly apparent in his treatment of the idea of a state of nature or *status innocentiae*, which is the object of careful discussion in the first part of the *Summa Theologica*. The whole tradition of Stoic and Christian political philoso-

phy was consonant and dogmatic on this point. The teaching of the Fathers could leave no doubts on the subject of the original condition in which mankind had been placed by God. St. Augustine, in a well-known passage which St. Thomas does not fail to remember, had stated that God made the rational man to be the master of other animals, not of his fellow men, thus showing by visible signs what is the proper order of nature and what are the consequences of sin. The traditional doctrine of the law of nature, transmitted in the works of the Roman lawyers and in Justinian's *Corpus Iuris,* had even more emphatically asserted the original freedom and equality of all men, and contrasted the institutions which can be referred to the *ius naturale* with those, such as property, slavery, and existing political organization, which are grounded upon the *ius gentium*. Here again St. Thomas does not directly and categorically contradict these conceptions. His answer to the difficulty raised by the contrast of two opposite modes of thought clearly shows his efforts of adaptation and the balance of his mind. It may be scorned as a typical instance of scholastic *distinguo,* but the distinction is important and far-reaching in its results. The fundamental equality of human nature, a capital tenet of the Christian faith, cannot be doubted. But the actual inequalities which are inherent in social and political conditions must be carefully assessed. St. Thomas here distinguished between *subiectio servilis* and *subiectio civilis.* The first is undoubtedly contrary to nature, and can therefore only be explained as a consequence of sin. But the latter, the relationship of authority and obedience between men which is necessary for the attainment of the good of all, in a word, political relationship, is by no means a consequence of sin, for it is founded upon the very nature of man. Such a relationship would therefore no doubt exist even if the *status innocentiae* had been preserved. The reason for this is again that, according to Aristotle, man is a social, and hence a political animal. The combination of the two opposite doctrines is clearly apparent, but it is important that the idea of sin, without being rejected, should be confined to narrow limits, merely to explain some necessary hardships of social and political experience, such as the penal character of laws, or the existence of tyrants. But the idea of sin has no part in the rational justification of the state, and the way is thus clear for the reception of a large part of Aristotelian teaching.

The same balance between opposite doctrines, and the same understanding of the value of Aristotle's ideas, appears in the remaining sections of St. Thomas's political theory. In these he is concerned more directly with practical issues, such as the sources of authority, the duty and limits of obedience, the forms and aspects of government. St. Thomas's views with regard to these several problems have been the object of much, and not always discriminating discussion. The causes of this particular interest lie in the fact that since the acceptance of Aquinas's teaching as representing somehow the official expression and foundation of the teaching of the Catholic Church, it has become of the highest importance to ascertain its proper meaning, and to explain how St. Thomas's authority has been claimed to support widely different attitudes, varying from the maintenance of almost democratic tenets at the time of the Counter-reformation to the almost unconditional acceptance of absolutism in later days. Our Italian liberals of the period of the *Risorgimento,* such as Bertrando Spaventa, did not fail to point out this apparently inexplicable contradiction. Here again St. Thomas's position can only be understood by distinguishing the different lines of approach which he endeavoured to reconcile.

With regard to the problem of the foundation and sources of authority, it is fairly easy to distinguish the various doctrines which have left their traces on St. Thomas's thought. The idea that the foundation of political power, or to use expressions more consonant with the medieval vocabulary, the source of the authority of the law, lies in the community, is, as Dr. Carlyle has never tired of warning us, one of the chief principles of medieval political thought. It is one to which, as he again has conclusively shown, both the older view of the supremacy of customary law and the revival of Roman conceptions equally contributed. For however different in their premises and practical implications, they could both be interpreted, and were in fact interpreted, as expressing the idea that the people is the only ultimate source of law and of political authority. But although this idea can undoubtedly be traced in several passages of St. Thomas's works, we are by no means authorized to read into his teaching, as some interpreters have done, an assertion of the idea of popular sovereignty. Although clearly admitting that the proper foundation of law and authority is the will, or at least the consent of the community, St. Thomas nowhere committed himself to anything which may be said to approach even remotely the idea of an 'original' or 'natural' right of the people. Hence the acknowledgement of the human source of authority can be reconciled with the fundamental Christian idea of its divine and sacred character; if 'dominium et praelatio introducta sunt ex iure humano', it is also true that 'non est potestas nisi a Deo'. This distinction and reconciliation assumes in one place the aspect of a typically scholastic distinction between 'form' and 'substance', between the *causa formalis* and the *causa materialis* of authority. The ultimate divine source of all authority (*causa formalis*) does not exclude, but on the contrary requires a determination of its actual human and historical origin (*causa materialis*). But there is a third motive, along with these two traditional ones, whose influence is clearly to be felt in St. Thomas's theory of the foundation of power: it is the Aristotelian idea that, since political relationship is grounded in nature, the real foundation of the *ordo inter homines* must be sought in the different capacities of men, in their 'natural' inequality. Hence the best *ordinatio* of the *humanum regimen* is that which corresponds most closely to that inequality, and respects that *praeeminentia intellectus* which is the real justification of power. This lends to St. Thomas's teaching a much more aristocratic than democratic flavour.

When from the problem of the source of authority we turn to that of obedience, it is obvious that the influence of Aritotelian ideas will not be so clearly visible, for this problem assumed in Christian political theory an importance unknown to the classical world. This is the direct result of the Christian ideas of divided allegiance and of the religious value of obedience. And yet it is of great interest to notice that, according to St. Thomas, the duty of obedience is not only a precept of divine law, directly traceable to the biblical texts which have already been quoted, but also a precept of natural law. This precept allows of a rational justification, which is grounded precisely upon the Aristotelian argument of the natural foundation of the political relationship. With regard to the limits of obedience, the detailed analysis of the several issues raised in St. Thomas's careful

discussion cannot be attempted here. It is enough to remember the main principle which St. Thomas develops, that, as the duty of obedience to authority is grounded both upon divine and upon natural order, its limits are necessarily fixed by the correspondence of human authority with divine and natural law, that is, with justice. This leading idea is developed in the discussion of the value of human law in the section *De Legibus* of the *Summa Theologica,* and formulated with all possible clearness in the section *De Obedientia*:

It must be said that a man is so far obliged to obey secular princes, as the order of justice requires; hence if their authority is not just but usurped, or if they command that which is unjust, a subject is not obliged to obey, except, according to the circumstances, to avoid scandal or peril.

The practical applications of this principle, the determination of the modes and consequences of an eventual refusal of obedience, necessarily lead to a complex casuistry. The most discussed instance is that relating to the possibility of active resistance, which to some interpreters has appeared to imply nothing less than an authorization of tyrannicide: a theory which, as is well known, found some famous applications in the hands of Catholic writers of later days. In my opinion, although St. Thomas's apparent justification of tyrannicide is accompanied by important qualifications which practically amount to a flat disavowal of it, there can be no doubt of his acknowledgement not only of the right, but of the duty of resistance to an unjust power. His teaching on the subject can thus be said to bear witness to that transformation of the Christian doctrine of obedience into a doctrine exactly opposed to the theory of passive obedience held by older and later Christian political thinkers. I have already pointed out that this transformation is one of the most characteristic features of medieval political theory.

We find ourselves again in touch with Aristotelian ideas when, from the discussion of authority and obedience, we turn to the determination of the forms and aspects of political organization and to the definition of the nature and essence of the *communitas perfecta,* or what we should call the attributes of the state. The decisive influence of the Aristotelian definition of the state upon the development of medieval political thought has been vividly depicted by Gierke. It is evident, he notes, that as soon as men take this definition in earnest, only some among the various subordinated and superordinated communities can be regarded as being states. Thus the revival of the classical conception of the state helped to destroy the medieval ideal of a universal community or *imperium mundi*; and it prepared the way for the modern idea of the particular and sovereign state. St. Thomas's teaching affords a striking confirmation of this trend of ideas which has been described by Gierke. The state, as the *communitas perfecta,* is, according to St. Thomas, of an intrinsically different nature from all other communities. This difference can be inferred from the state's capacity for making laws endowed with a *potestas coactiva,* and its possession of a 'sufficientia ad omnia necessaria vitae', the two Aristotelian attributes of autonomy and autarchy. These requisites are fulfilled by two main types of organization, the *civitas* and the *regnum,* which thus deserve the name of *communitates perfectae*; clearly, the Aristotelian notion of the πόλις undergoes a noteworthy extension. But in its essence, it is the Aristotelian notion of the particular state which bears full sway. There is no open mention, in the whole of St. Thomas's work, of the idea of a universal empire. Many explanations have been given of this curious fact, and they may all contain some part of the truth. But, strange though it is that St. Thomas should have been silent on an issue usually considered as the very backbone of medieval political thought, the causes of this silence are not so important as its implications. Does it imply a complete abandonment of the ideal of a superior unity of mankind, transcending the particularism of single political units and expressing an aspiration for absolute values? This, and this alone, would be a sign that the continuity of medieval thought had undergone a sudden and far-reaching interruption. But this is certainly not the case with St. Thomas. The idea of the fundamental unity of human life, for one thing, undoubtedly inspires the whole of St. Thomas's philosophy of law, with its assertion of the unity and universal value of the supreme principles of justice, from which the several systems of positive law derive their substance and value. The same idea is preserved in the conception of the *corpus mysticum ecclesiae* and of the *unus populus christianus,* which embraces and unites the widest variety of countries and nations. But above all it is preserved in the idea of the supreme divine government of the world, which is the highest expression of that *principium unitatis,* of that *ordinatio ad unum* which, as Gierke again pointed out, assumed in medieval eyes the value of a constituent principle of the universe. Thus behind or above the manifold human types of life and political experience there is a fundamental oneness: as St. Thomas expressly puts it, 'esti sint multi regentes, eius (scil. Dei) regimini omnes subduntur'.

When from the definition of the state and its attributes we turn to consider its organization and structure, we are confronted with a further confirmation of the tenacity with which medieval conceptions still hold their ground in St. Thomas's political theory. The influence of Aristotelian ideas is here practically neutralized, as appears from the very method with which St. Thomas sets about to determine the best form of government. This, as is expressly set forth in the second chapter of the *De Regimine Principum,* must be determined in accordance with the highest and most abstract metaphysical premisses, of which the lesson of experience can only provide a confirmation. Thus the arguments in favour of monarchy as the best form of government are mainly of a deductive character: first and foremost among them is the argument derived from the *principium unitatis,* upon which Dante was soon to base his abstract deductions in the first book of the *Monarchia.* Yet, when it comes to defining the organization of monarchy, and to facing some fundamental issues such as the relation of the ruler to the law, or the nature of tyranny, the influence of, and the reference to, actual historical experience are deep and continuous. I am afraid that I shall have to omit a complete analysis of this interesting section of St. Thomas's political theory, and content myself with a brief summary of what in my opinion are its more important aspects. With regard to the problem of tyranny, the teaching of St. Thomas in the *Commentary on the Sentences* appears to contain the germ of a distinction which bore its fruits in later thinkers. This is the distinction between tyranny *ex parte exercitii* and tyranny *ex defectu tituli,* of which the important developments in fourteenth- and fifteenth-century Italian political theory, from Bartolus to Coluccio Salutati, are well known. With regard to the relation of the prince to the law, St. Thomas's discussion of the Roman

principles 'quod principi placuit legis habet vigorem' and 'princeps legibus solutus', is of capital importance for the history of the influence of Roman legal ideas upon medieval political thought. I have pointed out in my preceding lecture that the reconstruction and appreciation of that influence by the modern historian appears to me to be vitiated by an undue simplification of its complexity, and by the attribution to it of the largest share of responsibility for the spread of those 'absolutist' ideas which led to the final disruption of medieval political theory. An attentive study of St. Thomas's position should be a safeguard against such tendentious interpretations. For St. Thomas shows a thorough understanding of the Roman doctrine of the superiority of the prince (or of whoever has the function of making law, which may also belong to the whole multitude) to the law from the point of view of mere legal experience; that is to say, with regard to positive law. It is from the authority of the prince, or, generally speaking, from the *potestas publica,* that law derives its *vis coactiva,* its positive legal value. Hence, with regard to this *vis coactiva,* the *potestas publica* is really *legibus soluta.* This acknowledgement of a principle which, without qualification, is substantially nothing else than the principle of sovereignty, ought to induce reflection in the many who still repeat the old slogan that 'there was no conception of sovereignty in the Middle Ages'. Yet in St. Thomas the principle is at once qualified by the important proviso that, *quantum ad vim directivam,* the prince is no doubt subject to the law, albeit nobody except God can compel him to submit to it. Further, the *voluntas principis* has *vigorem legis* only inasmuch as it is *ratione regulata.* Both the *vis directiva* and the *regula rationis* are indeed nothing else than the expression of that natural and rational order of justice which limits the sovereignty of the particular state.

Moreover, along with this fundamental limitation to the 'absoluteness' of sovereignty, St. Thomas conceives of other possible limitations within the state itself, and is even at pains to show their necessity. This is clear in his theory of the practical organization of political power. The real meaning of St. Thomas's teaching on that point, or rather its bearing upon the actual historical possibilities and problems of his time, have recently been an object of careful inquiry, especially with regard to the curious theory which he expounds about the excellency of a 'mixed constitution'. On this point, the main features of the *regimen mixtum,* which is referred to in the *Summa Theologica,* should be considered in connexion with the discussion as to the most convenient establishment of the *regimen unius* which is found in the first book of the *De Regimine.* It is fairly easy to see that the best structure of a political régime is, according to St. Thomas, some form of limited monarchy. This limitation implies the dependence of the prince on the rule of law as the expression of the will of the community. Political power, though in essence, and according to the Roman teaching, *legibus solutus,* must be constitutionally limited. The mutual interaction of opposite doctrines and of the main issues of medieval political experience are thus clearly apparent in St. Thomas's teaching, and it is significant that it was precisely to his authority that, two centuries later, one of the first theorists of the English constitutional system, Sir John Fortescue, repeatedly referred, when he defended limited monarchy, not only as the traditional system inherited of old, but as the best of all possible forms of government.

Finally, there remains to be examined St. Thomas's attitude towards the problem of the relation between the temporal and the spiritual powers. Unfortunately his thought on this subject is nowhere systematically expounded. As Cardinal Bellamin was later to complain on this point, 'de Sancto Thoma quid senserit non est tam certum'. The clearest account of St. Thomas's position is contained in the fourteenth chapter of the first book of the *De Regimine Principum.* It is the doctrine of the necessity of a dual direction in human affairs, of the insufficiency of the *humanum regimen* and of its integration with the *divinum regimen.* This duality is reflected in the *regnum* and *sacerdotium.* There is no need to point out the traditional character of this doctrine, although, as Grabmann has remarked, its connexion with the Aristotelian doctrine of ends is undoubtedly a novelty in the development of medieval theory. It is with a view to the full attainment of human ends, which culminate in the *fruitio divina,* that the necessity of the two powers is shown; and although this duality converges into unity in Christ, who is both *rex* and *sacerdos,* in this world the two powers are committed separately, the one to earthly kings, the other to priests, and principally to the Roman pontiff, 'ut a terrenis essent spiritualia distincta'. The different value of these ends necessarily implies a subordination of the one power to the other, of the *regnum* to the *sacerdotium,* and hence it follows that to the *summus sacerdos,* the successor of Peter, the vicar of Christ, the Roman potiff, 'omnes reges populi Christiani oportet esse subditos'.

However clear and definite in its outlines, this doctrine is far from being free of all ambiguity. Let us remark for one thing that St. Thomas does not conceive of a relation between two different societies, between state and church in any modern sense, but of a distinction of functions (*gubernationes, regimina, ministeria, potestates*). But it is the relationship itself which leaves the field open to uncertainty. To some interpreters, the assertion which is made in the *De Regimine* of the necessary 'subjection' of the temporal rulers to the authority of the Pope, has seemed to imply an unconditional acceptance of that so-called 'theocratic' doctrine which found its celebrated assertion less than half a century later at the hands of Boniface VIII and of his supporters. But such an interpretation is, according to the best Thomist authorities, quite inaccurate. It is enough to consider attentively the argument of the *De Regimine Principum*, to convince oneself that the subordination or *subiectio* of the civil to the spiritual power of which St. Thomas speaks, is such only with regard to the end.

The Thomist doctrine of the two powers and of their relationship can thus be taken to express the normal medieval doctrine, and to summarize that particular interpretation which medieval Christianity contrived to give of the fundamental Christian idea, to which I have referred in the introduction. It is a doctrine which must not be confused with later interpretations, which in turn represent other and different developments of the Christian ideal. It can be called a theocratic doctrine, but only in the sense that it admits of the necessary and supreme unity of all power in God. It is a very

different doctrine from that which is usually called 'theocratic' and which asserts the actual sovereignty, the *plenitudo potestatis* of the Pope over the world. A reference to this latter idea which, as Professor Scholz has conclusively shown, marks in many ways the end of medieval conceptions proper, can be found in the third book of the *De Regimine Principum*, which is commonly attributed to Ptolemy of Lucca. According to the most authoritative interpreters, the teaching of Aquinas only implies the assertion of an indirect power of spiritual over civil authority, a power of guidance and control, which is a consequence of the superiority in value of the ends to which spiritual rule is directed. But, on the other hand, the fully developed theory of the *potestas indirecta,* the typical doctrine of the post-tridentine Church, is a later development of the Christian ideal, a development of which no doubt the germs are already contained in St. Thomas's teaching, but which represents an adaptation of the Catholic doctrine to a social and political condition greatly different from that of the Middle Ages. It implies the definite abandonment of the medieval idea of unity, which had provided the ground for the Gelasian principle and for the notion of the *respublica christiana,* and the recognition of a new problem unknown to the Middle Ages, the modern problem of the relation between church and state.

4

MACHIAVELLI

Niccolò Machiavelli (1469–1532) grew up in the Florence of Lorenzo de' Medici, the golden age of the Florentine Renaissance. When the Republic was reestablished he served it as secretary and diplomat. Schooled in the art of statecraft, Machiavelli learned well the lessons of political reality. The failure of the Republic, however, found Machiavelli out of favor and led him, some have contended, to the authorship of *The Prince* as an effort to recommended himself to the restored Medici rulers of Florence. His *Prince* has left an indelible impression on the western mind, and with it the unfavorable connotations involved in the term "Machiavellian." Shakespeare's Iago is representative of supposedly Machiavellian man. But Machiavelli's political writings are concerned with much more than the amorality his name evokes.

The selections on Machiavelli are from works by two important German scholars of this century. Both Friedrich Meinecke and Ernst Cassirer are concerned with Machiavelli's important role in breaking away from the medieval tradition of political writing. Meinecke's concern is also with

Machiavelli's parentage of the vastly influential concept of *raison d'état*. Perhaps the most fascinating part of Meinecke's essay is his analysis of Machiavelli's theory of *virtù* and the all important role it plays in his political thought. Cassirer in his selection describes the historical and intellectual setting of Machiavelli's writings and also comments on their novel methodological aspects. His major concern, however, is the impact of Machiavelli's ideas on the evolution of attitudes to, and the conception of, the state, subjects about which Cassirer has great misgivings.

FRIEDRICH MEINECKE

Machiavelli*

Whatever the circumstances the business of ruling is, as we have remarked, always carried out in accordance with the principles of *raison d'état*. *Raison d'état* may be deflected or hindered by real or imaginary obstacles, but it is part and parcel of ruling. It is not realized, however, as a principle and an idea until a particular stage of development has been reached; namely when the State has become strong enough to break down those obstacles, and to lay down its own unqualified right to existence in the face of all other vital forces. An account of this process from the standpoint of universal history would have to embrace and compare all cultures; it would have to begin by examining the idea of *raison d'état* in the ancient world, and analysing its relationship with the spirit of that epoch. For both the free city-states and the monarchies of antiquity are teeming with the problems of *raison d'état* and with attempts to formulate it. In the dialogue between the Athenians and the citizens of Melos, given by

* Reprinted from Friedrich Meinecke, *Machiavellism*, trans. Douglas Scott (New Haven: Yale University Press, 1957, and London: Routledge & Kegan Paul Ltd.), pp. 25–45, by permission of the publishers. The footnotes found in the original have been omitted here.

Thucydides in Book 5 (ch. 85 ff.), the harsh and frightening aspects of *raison d'état* and power politics are stated very succinctly. In his *Phoenician Virgins,* Euripides makes Eteocles say: 'For if one must do evil, then it is good to do it for the sake of authority; but otherwise one ought to act rightly.' In Book 5 of his *Politics,* Aristotle gives a picture of the rationally conceived way in which a tyrant can rule. In Book 3 of *De officiis,* Cicero discussed fully from the Stoic point of view the conflict between morality and what is useful to the State, and stated regretfully: *Utilitatis specie in republica saepissime peccatur* (ch. 11). The great historical works of Tacitus are steeped in the idea of *raison d'état*; as evidence of this we may quote one statement, from the lips of Cassius in Book 14 of the Annals: *Habet aliquid ex iniquo omne magnum exemplum, quod contra singulos utilitate publica rependitur.* Subsequently, after he had been republished by Justus Lipsius in 1574, Tacitus became the great teacher of *raison d'état* (though not to any great extent for Machiavelli, who drew chiefly on Livy, Aristotle and Xenephon); then for a whole century there blossomed a literature of Tacitists who exploited him politically. Justus Lipsius himself put together his grammar of politics

(*Politicorum sive civilis doctrinae libri sex, qui ad principatum maxime spectant,* 1589) entirely out of maxims from antiquity, principally from Tacitus; he thus made available a mine of information (which is still valuable today) about the opinions of the ancient world on the subject of *raison d'état*. And even if the ancients had not coined for it any particular expression which was in general use, yet we frequently meet with *ratio reipublicae* in Cicero, and *ratio et utilitas reipublicae* in Florus.

Polytheism and a secular view of human values were what nourished *raison d'état* in antiquity. At the period when the city-state was flourishing, the thing most worth living for was the State itself. The ethics of individual and of national conduct thus coincided, and so there was no conflict between politics and ethics. There was also no universal religion, to try and restrict by its commands the free exercise of State powers. The national religion which existed tended rather to favour this free exercise, by glorifying heroism. As the city-state began to dissolve, the heroic ideal passed over into the new form which power assumed in the State where men struggled fiercely, each for himself; this was the State of the ruthless man of power, classically portrayed by Plato in Callicles of the *Gorgias*. Altogether the ancient conception of *raison d'état* remained at this time firmly fixed in personalities, and served to vindicate the mode of action which was forced on contemporary rulers by pressure of the situation. It never seemed to rise (or at least not at all consistently) towards the conception of a supra-individual and independent state personality, which would stand over against the actual rulers of the time.

An epilogue and a final crushing judgment on the ancient view of *raison d'état* was given by Christianity, when Augustine said: *Remota justitia quid sunt regna nisi magna latrocinia.* The new universal religion set up at the same time a universal moral command, which even the State must obey, and turned the eyes of individual men on otherworldly values; thus all secular values, including heroism as the herald of power politics and *raison d'état*, were caused to give ground. Then in the Middle Ages Germanic jurisprudence combined with Christian ethics in keeping down the State. The State certainly existed in the Middle Ages, but it did not rank supreme. Law was set above it; it was a means for enforcing the law. 'Politics and *raison d'état* were not recognized at all in the Middle Ages.' Naturally, of course, the general practice was different from this theoretical view. Therefore, 'since there was no place in the legal and constitutional theory of mediaeval times for the demands of policy, these forced their own elemental way out'.

But in the later Middle Ages these irregular outlets began to be regularized. The struggle between Church and Papacy fostered the conscious power politics of great rulers like the Emperor Frederick II and Philip IV of France. The Emperor Charles IV in Germany and King Louis XI in France were examples of a thoroughly unscrupulous and rational art of government, based on their own authority. Even the Church itself, by its inner transformations, by the progressive permeation of the Papacy with worldly political interests, by the often very utilitarian approach of the Church Councils, and by the rational perfecting of Papal finance, paved the way for a new spirit in the art of government. The strongest motive for this, however, still lay in the incipient growth of national States, and in the struggles of the more important dynasties, whose possessions had been amassed by feudal methods, to safeguard these possessions by non-feudal means, by adhesive methods of government. The universal ideas of this mediaeval *corpus christianum* moved continuously towards a new centre of Will concentrated in the State.

Late mediaeval thought began further to distinguish the ideal law of Nature from statute law, and thereby to diminish the influence which Germanic jurisprudence had hitherto exerted on the State. 'Henceforth the power of the State is set above statute law, and comes under natural law. Thus it is no longer the case that every insignificant individual right is placed outside the grasp of the State; it is only the great fundamental principles of Natural Law that remain beyond its reach.'

Here and there at this time one notices a few basic admissions of the new conception of necessity of State. In the fourteenth century Philipp von Leiden, a priest in the service of the Count of Holland, wrote *de cura reipublicae et sorte principantis;* he advanced the proposition that a territorial ruler ought to revoke a privilege which he had granted to a single town or to a single person, if it was injuring the *publica utilitas.* In an even more general manner Jean Gerson declared in 1404 that if any laws conflicted with the aim of maintaining the peace (which was the supreme purpose of the State in the Middle Ages), then the laws ought to be interpreted more in accordance with that aim, or they would have to be completely abolished, since *necessitas legem non habet.* Even more audacious was a certain doctor of theology in the service of the Duke of Burgundy, named Jean Petit. In a long and exceedingly sophistical dissertation, which he delivered in Paris in March 1408, he defended his master for having caused the murder of Duke Louis of Orleans; and he went on to say that promises and alliances between noblemen did not need to be kept, if keeping them would entail injury to the ruler and to the commonwealth. He even said that to keep such promises would be completely against the laws of God and Nature.

A systematic search among the sources and authors of the late Middle Ages would probably discover still further opinions of this kind, and thus throw light on the gradual and continuing loosening up of the mediaeval feudal barriers. But a theory on a grand scale has not yet grown up out of it.

Nevertheless the modern Western world has inherited one legacy of extraordinary importance from the Christian and Germanic Middle Ages. It has inherited a sharper and more painful sense of the conflict between *raison d'état* on the one hand, and ethics and law on the other; and also the feeling which is constantly being aroused, that ruthless *raison d'état* is really sinful, a sin against God and divine standards, a sin against the sanctity and inviolability of the law of the good old times. The ancient world was already familiar with these sins of *raison d'état*, and did not omit to criticize them, but without taking them very much to heart. The very secularity of human values in the ancient world made it possible to view *raison d'état* with a certain calmness and to consider it the outcome of natural forces which were not to be subdued. Sinfulness in antiquity was still a perfectly naïve sinfulness, not yet disquieted and frightened by the gulf between heaven and hell which was to be opened up by Christianity. This dualistic picture of the world, which was held by dogmatic Christianity, has had a deep influence even on the period of a Christianity that is growing undogmatic; and it has given the problem of *raison d'état* this deeply felt overtone of tragedy, which it never carried in antiquity.

It was therefore a historical necessity that the man, with whom the history of the idea of *raison d'état* in the modern Western world begins and from whom Machiavellism takes its name, had to be a heathen; he had to be a man to whom the fear of hell was unknown, and who on the contrary could set about his life-work of analysing the essence of *raison d'état* with all the naïvety of the ancient world.

Niccolò Machiavelli was the first to do this. We are concerned here with the thing itself, not with the name for it, which he still did not possess. Machiavelli had not yet compressed his thoughts on *raison d'état* into a single slogan. Fond as he was of forceful and meaningful catch-words (coining many himself), he did not always feel the need to express in words the supreme ideas which filled him; if, that is, the thing itself seemed to him self-evident, if it filled him completely. For example, critics have noticed that he fails to express any opinion about the real final purpose of the State, and they have mistakenly deduced from this that he did not reflect on the subject. But, as we shall soon see, his whole life was bound up with a definite supreme purpose of the State. And in the same way his whole political way of thought is nothing else but a continual process of thinking about *raison d'état*.

Machiavelli's system of thought was brought into being by an absolutely special and sublime, and at the same time extraordinary, conjunction of events: the coinciding of a political collapse with a spiritual and intellectual renaissance. In the fifteenth century Italy enjoyed national independence, and was, in the pregnant words of Machiavelli (*Principe*, ch. 20), *in un certo modo bilanciata* by the system of five States which kept each other within bounds: Naples, the Papal States, Florence, Milan and Venice. There was growing up in Italy, fostered by all the realistic elements in Renaissance culture and directly promoted by the arrangement (which was just coming into fashion) of having permanent embassies, a form of statecraft which was carried on according to fixed and definite rules. This statecraft culminated in the principle of *divide et impera,* it taught that everything ought to be considered with a view to its usefulness, it surmounted all religious and moral limitations in a naïvely playful manner, but itself functioned by means of relatively simple and mechanical operations and thought-processes. Only the catastrophes which overtook Italy after 1494, with the invasion by the French and the Spanish, the decline of Neapolitan and Milanese independence, the precipitate change in the form of government in Florence, and most of all the collective impact of foreign countries on the entire Apennine peninsula—only these catastrophes succeeded in maturing the spirit of politics to that point of passionate strength, depth and acuteness, which is revealed in Machiavelli. As a secretary and diplomat of the Florentine Republic until the year 1512, he learnt everything that Italian statecraft had achieved up to that time, and he was also beginning already to shape his own original thoughts on the subject. What caused them to pour out suddenly after 1512 was the crushing fate which overtook both him and the republic in that year. As a member of the party which had been overthrown and was being temporarily persecuted, Machiavelli, in order to re-establish himself, was forced to seek the favour of the new rulers, the Medicis, who were once more in power. Thus a conflict arose between his own personal and egotistical interests, and the ideals of republican freedom and the city-state which he had held up to now. It is indeed the greatness of Machiavelli that he strove now to settle this conflict, and bring it to a final issue. Against the obscure and not particularly attractive background of his own naïve and unscrupulous egoism, there came into being the new and masterly reflections on the relation between republic and monarchy, and about a new national mission of monarchy; it was in a context of all this that the whole essence of *raison d'état*, compounded of mingled ingredients both pure and impure, both lofty and hateful, achieved a ruthless expression. He had reached his fortieth year —the age at which productive scientific minds often give of their best—when after 1513 he wrote the little book about the prince and the *Discorsi sopra la prima deca di Tito Livio*.

A spiritual and intellectual renaissance must also, as we said, have been a formative influence. Machiavelli did not by any means absorb the whole of the Renaissance movement. He did not share its religious needs, or its urge towards speculative philosophy; and, although unconsciously steeped and bathed in its aesthetic spirit, he still did not value its artistic attempts particularly highly. His passionate interest was the State, the analysis and computation of its different forms, functions and conditions for existence; and thus it was that the specifically rational, empirical and calculating element in Italian Renaissance culture reached its peak in him. But a mere cool consideration of questions of political power would not have signified any complete spiritual and intellectual renewal. The faith and energy necessary to sustain it, and out of which the ideal of a rebirth could grow, were, so far as Machiavelli shared in them, of ancient origin. The spirit of antiquity was certainly not signalized in him (as it was in so many humanists of the Renaissance) by a merely learned and literary regeneration, with the bloodless

rhetorical inspiration of a schoolmaster. Often his enthusiasm for the heroes and thinkers of antiquity shows a somewhat classicist lack of independence and judgment. But in the main the element of antiquity in him rose anew out of the tradition and hereditary feeling, which in Italy had never been entirely lost. In spite of his outward respect for the Church and for Christianity (frequently mingled with irony and criticism), and in spite of the undeniable influence which the Christian view had on him, Machiavelli was at heart a heathen, who levelled at Christianity the familiar and serious reproach (Disc., II, 2) of having made men humble, unmanly and feeble. With a romantic longing he gazed towards the strength, grandeur and beauty of life in antiquity, and towards the ideals of its *mondana gloria*. He wanted to bring back once again that united strength of sense and intellect in the natural genuine man, where *grandezza dell'animo* and *fortezza del corpo* combined together to create heroism. He broke then, with the dualistic and onesidedly spiritualizing ethic of Christianity, which depreciated the natural impulses of the senses. Although indeed he retained some of its structural ideas about the difference between good and evil, he strove principally for a new naturalistic ethic which would follow the dictates of nature impartially and resolutely. For whoever follows these dictates (as he said once) can find no fault in carrying on lighthearted amorous affairs in the midst of serious business—even Nature is full of change and contradiction.

This kind of naturalism can easily lead to a harmless and unreflecting multiplicity in the question of human values. But (in spite of the offering which he gladly brought to the altar of Venus) Machiavelli concentrated all his real and supreme values in what he called *virtù*. This concept is exceedingly rich in meaning, and although it was taken over from the tradition of antiquity and humanism, it had been felt and elaborated in a quiet individual manner; ethical qualities were certainly embraced in it, but it was fundamentally intended to portray something dynamic, which Nature had implanted in Man— heroism and the strength for great political and warlike achievements, and first and foremost, perhaps, strength for the founding and preservation of flourishing States, particularly republics. For in the republics, of which Rome in its great republican period seemed to him an ideal example, he saw the conditions most favourable for the generation of *virtù*. It therefore embraced the civic virtues and those of the ruling class; it embraced a readiness to devote oneself to the common good, as well as the wisdom, energy and ambition of the great founders and rulers of States. But the *virtù* which the founder and ruler of a State had to possess counted for Machiavelli as *virtù* of a higher order. For in his opinion this kind of *virtù* was able, by means of appropriate 'regulations', to distil out of the thoroughly bad and wretched material of average specimens of humanity the other kind of *virtù* in the sense of civic virtue; to a certain extent the latter was *virtù* of a secondary quality, and could only be durable if it was rooted in a people whose spirit was naturally fresh and unspoilt. This separation of *virtù* into two types, one original and the other derived, is of exceptional significance for a complete understanding of the political aims of Machiavelli. For it shows that he was a long way from believing uncritically in the natural and imperishable virtue of a republican citizen, and that he viewed even the republic more from above, from the standpoint of the rulers, than from underneath, from the standpoint of broad-based democracy. He appreciated

the proverb, which was popular in his time, that *in piazza* your opinions were not the same as they were *in palazzo* (Disc., II, 47). His republican ideal therefore contained a strain of monarchism, in so far as he believed that even republics could not come into existence without the help of great individual ruling personalities and organizers. He had learnt from Polybius the theory that the fortunes of every State are repeated in a cycle, and that the golden age of a republic is bound to be followed by its decline and fall. And so he saw that, in order to restore the necessary quantum of *virtù* which a republic had lost by sinking to such a low point, and thus raise up the State once again, there was only one means to be adopted; namely, that the creative *virtù* of one individual, of one *mano regia*, one *podestà quasi regia* (Disc., I, 18 and 55), should take the State in hand and revive it. Indeed he went so far as to believe that for republics which were completely corrupt and no longer capable of regeneration, monarchy was the only possible form of government. Thus his concept of *virtù* formed a close link between republican and monarchical tendencies, and, after the collapse of the Florentine Republic, enabled him without inconsistency to set his hopes on the rule of the Medicis, and to write for them the Book of the Prince. In the same way it made it possible for him immediately afterwards to take up again in the *Discorsi* the strain of republicanism, and to weigh republic and monarchy against one another.

Moreover his own special ethic of *virtù*—a product of the joyous worldly spirit of the Renaissance—begins now to throw light on the relation in which he stands to the ordinary Christian, and so-called genuine, morality; this relationship has been the cause of much dispute and a continual subject of reproof to Machiavelli. We have already remarked that he retained the basic Christian views on the difference between good and evil. When he advocated evil actions, he never denied them the epithet evil or attempted any hypocritical concealment. Nor did he dare to embody direct traits of morally wicked behaviour in his ideal of *virtù*. In Chapter 8 of the *Principe,* which deals with Agathocles, he says that to murder one's co-citizens, to betray one's friends, to be lacking in loyalty, piety and religion, cannot deserve the name of *virtù,* these things can achieve mastery; but no glory. And yet in Agathocles, who behaved in this way, he recognized at the same time a real *virtù* and *grandezza dell'animo,* i.e. great virtues of a ruler. The ethical sphere of his *virtù* therefore lay in juxtaposition to the usual moral sphere like a kind of world of its own; but for him it was the higher world, because it was the vital source of the State, of the *vivere politico,* the supreme task of human creativity. And because it was for him the higher world, so it could be permitted to trespass and encroach on the moral world in order to achieve its aims. These encroachments and infringements, these 'sins' in the Christian sense, never ceased to be judged by him as immoral, and did not indeed constitute *virtù* itself—but they could in the last resort (as we shall soon see more clearly) arise out of *virtù*.

Let us first look more closely at his theory of *virtù,* and at the striking mixture of pessimism and idealism, of mechanistic and vitalistic elements, which go to compose it. In the *Discorsi* (I, 4), he says that of their own accord men will never do anything good, unless they are driven to it by some 'necessity'. Hunger and poverty, he goes on, make men industrious, and laws make them good. The penalties imposed on any infringement of the laws lead on towards a recognition of justice. For him, therefore, moral goodness and justice were produced and could be produced by the constraining power of the State. How high his opinion was of the State, and how little he thought of individual human beings! But this rigid positivist causal nexus was relaxed through the medium of *virtù,* and by a belief in the creative powers of great men, who, through their own *virtù* and the wise regulations which they made, were able to raise up the average level of humanity to a new, secondary form of *virtù*. Then too it was another mechanistic and fatalistic belief of his that, since the world always remained the same and all things were repeated in a cycle, *virtù* did not exist in the world in unlimited supply, but was passed round in the world continually, and now this, now that people was privileged to possess it. This was echoed by Hegel three hundred years later when, in his theory about the 'dominant peoples of world history' (who are entrusted by the World Spirit from time to time with the task of directing its affairs in the world), he made the fatalistic element part of a sublime philosophy of progress and ascent. Machiavelli however contented himself with stating resignedly that only in ancient times did it happen that a single nation was blessed with a preponderance of this *virtù,* in modern times it was divided up amongst a number of nations. This brings out very clearly the similarity and the difference between the centuries. Surrounded by the collapse of the political world in which they lived, both thinkers cast longing eyes on the representatives of strength and efficiency in world history —Hegel with an optimistic belief in progress, the result of the century of the Enlightenment, Machiavelli with the old belief in the everlasting similarity of historical life, a belief which had always been fostered by the Christian disdain for this world and which the vital energy of the Renaissance had not been able to break down. But this vital energy was still strong enough not to lose courage even amid the collapse and in the face of the contempt of humanity, and strong enough to watch out for fresh *virtù*. For the development and creation of *virtù* was for Machiavelli the ideal, and completely self-evident, purpose of the State. To raise his own nation by means of *virtù* from the low point to which it had sunk, and to regenerate the State, if this was still possible (he continually wavered between doubting this and believing it), became his life interest. But this new political idealism was now indeed burdened with the serious problematical element which was inherent in the character of *raison d'état*. This brings us nearer to our real task.

It was certainly impossible, once the moral and religious bond had been severed which held together the mediaeval Christian ideal of life, to set up immediately a new worldly system of ideals which would have the same inner unity and compactness. For, to minds freshly released from the restraints of the Middle Ages, so many provinces of life were now opened up simultaneously that it was not possible at once to find a distinctive point of view, from which the secularized world could be grasped and comprehended once again as a harmonious unity. One made discoveries, first in one place, then in another; one devoted oneself enthusiastically and often quite wholeheartedly to the discovery of the moment and became so completely taken up with it, that one had no opportunity to examine the contradictions and discrepancies between the experiences one had newly acquired and the human values which had held up till now. Machiavelli possessed this one-sided passion for discovery to an extraordinary degree. He

threw himself on his particular aim of the moment in such a way that occasionally all he himself had previously thought and said was entirely forgotten. In a quite undaunted, now and then almost fanatical manner, he deduced the most extreme, and sometimes the most terrible consequences from the truths which he had found, without ever testing their reaction on other beliefs he held. In the course of his experimental discoveries he was also fond of changing his standpoint, and identifying himself for the moment with widely different interests in the political struggle, so that for each interested party, whether it be a prince or an enemy of princes, he could devise some powerful remedy, some *medicina forte* (and wherever possible a *regola generale*). His occasional recipes, then, should often be taken as having a certain degree of relativity. And these tendencies of his should be kept firmly in view.

The most serious discrepancy in his system of thought—a discrepancy which he never succeeded in eliminating and which he never even tried to eliminate— lay between the newly discovered ethical sphere of *virtù*, and of the State animated by *virtù*, on the one hand, and the old sphere of religion and morality on the other. This *virtù* of Machiavelli was originally a natural and dynamic idea, which (not altogether unhappily) contained a certain quality of barbarity (*ferocia*); he now considered that it ought not to remain a mere unregulated natural force (which would have been in accordance with the spirit of the Renaissance) but that it ought to be raised into a *virtù ordinata*, into a rationally and purposively directed code of values for rulers and citizens. The *virtù ordinata* naturally set a high value on religion and morality, on account of the influence they exerted towards maintaining the State. In particular, Machiavelli spoke out very forcibly on the subject of the indispensability of religion (Disc., I, 11 and 12); at any rate, he was strongly in favour of a religion which would make men courageous and proud. He once named 'religion, laws, military affairs' together in one breath, as the three fundamental pillars of the State. But, in the process, religion and morality fell from the status of intrinsic values, and became nothing more than means towards the goal of a State animated by *virtù*. It was this that led him on to make the double-edged recommendation, which resounded so fearsomely down the centuries to come, inciting statesmen to an irreligious and at the same time dishonest scepticism: the advice that even a religion tinged with error and deception ought to be supported, and the wiser one was, the more one would do it (Disc., I, 12). Whoever thought like this was, from a religious point of view, completely adrift. What final certainty and sure foundation was there left in life, if even an unbelieved and false religion could count as valuable, and when moral goodness was seen as being a product of fear and custom? In this godless world of Nature man was left alone with only himself and the powers Nature had given him, to carry on the fight against all the fateful forces wielded by this same Nature. And this was exactly what Machiavelli conceived his own situation to be.

It is striking and forceful to observe how he strove to rise superior to it. On the one side *fortuna,* on the other *virtù*—this was how he interpreted it. Many people today (he says in ch. 25 of the *Principe*), in the face of the various blows of Fate and unsuspected revolutions we have experienced, are now of the opinion that all wisdom is entirely unavailing against the action of Fate, and that we must just let it do what it likes with us. He admits that even he himself has occasionally felt like this, when in a gloomy mood. But he considered it would be lacking in *virtù* to surrender to the feeling. One must rouse oneself and build canals and dams against the torrent of Fate, and then one will be able to keep it within bounds. Only half our actions are governed by Fortune; the other half, or almost half, is left to us. 'Where men have not much *virtù,* then *fortuna* shows its strength clearly enough. And because it is full of change, so there are numerous changes in republics and states. And these will always go on changing, until sooner or later there will come a man who so loves antiquity, that he will regulate *fortuna*; then it will not be able to show every twenty-four hours how much it is capable of accomplishing' (Disc., II, 30). *Fortuna* has got to be beaten and bruised like a woman one wants to possess, and boldness and barbarity will always be more successful there than coldness. But this boldness has got to be united with great cunning and calculation, for each situation of fate demands a method specially suited for dealing with it. He began to meditate very deeply on just this particular problem, for it showed up very clearly both the powers and the limitations of *virtù*, and of humanity altogether. The individual agent cannot escape the nature he is born with. He acts in such and such a way because this nature requires it. Hence it arises that, according to the disposition of Fate, this same method which his character dictates will turn out well one day, and badly the next (Disc., III, 9). An insight of this kind could lead back to fatalism. But the effect on him of all these doubts and impulses was like the bending of a taut-strung bow. He let fly his arrows with all the more force.

Enemies learn to use each other's weapons. *Virtù* has the task of forcing back *fortuna*. *Fortuna* is malicious, so *virtù* must also be malicious, when there is no other way open. This expresses quite plainly the real spiritual origin of Machiavellism: the infamous doctrine that, in national behaviour, even unclean methods are justified, when it is a question of winning or of keeping the power which is necessary for the State. It is the picture of Man, stripped of all transcendent good qualities, left alone on the battlefield to face the daemonic forces of Nature, who now feels himself possessed too of a daemonic natural strength and returns blow for blow. In Machiavelli's opinion, *virtù* had a perfectly genuine right to take up any weapon, for the purpose of mastering Fortune. One can easily see that this doctrine, which appeared so dualistic on the outside, had really sprung from the background of a naïve Monism, which made all the powers of life into forces of Nature. It now became a presupposition for the discovery which Machiavelli had made about the essence of *raison d'état*.

But in order to make this discovery, yet another theory was needed—one which he thought out and applied just as clearly and consistently as he did the theory of the struggle between *virtù* and *fortuna*. This was the theory of *necessità*. *Virtù*, *fortuna* and *necessità* are three words which keep on sounding again and again throughout his writings with a kind of brazen ring. These words, and perhaps also the refrain of the *armi proprie* (which sums up the demands he made on the State in the way of military matters and power politics), show his ability to condense the wealth of his experience and thought, and how the rich edifice of his mind rested on a few, quite simple, but solid pillars. For him *virtù* and *necessità* were related in a way very similar to that in which, in modern philosophy, the sphere of values is related to the sphere of causal

connection; i.e. where the causal connection provides the means and possibility of realizing the values. If *virtù* was the vital power of men, a power which created and maintained States, and gave them sense and meaning, then *necessità* was the causal pressure, the means of bringing the sluggish masses into the form required by *virtù*. We have already heard how he traced back the origin of morality to 'necessity'. We have discussed fully (so he says in the *Discorsi*, III, 12) how useful *necessità* is for human actions, and to what glory it can lead on. And (as several moral philosophers have written) the hands and speech of Man—which are the two principal tools for his ennoblement— would never have functioned completely, and human achievements would never have reached their present high level, if they had not been pushed to it by *necessità*. The old military commanders recognized the *virtù di tal necessità* and used it to instil into their soldiers the dogged spirit of combat, when they planned to put them in a situation where they would *have* to fight. Come with me, a Volscian leader shouts to the soldiers round him, in Livy (4, 28), *virtute pares, quae ultimum ac maximum telum est, necessitate superiores estis*. These were words to warm Machiavelli's heart. The more *necessità* there is, he insists in the *Discorsi*, I, 1, the more *virtù* there will be also, and *necessità* can bring us to many things, which reason is not strong enough to drive us to (Disc., I, 1). And alongside the conception of *virtù ordinata* he placed the equally characteristic conception of *necessità ordinata dalle leggi* (Disc., I, 1) as engendering first-class human material for the State. Thus it is always a question of following the natural forces of life, but also at the same time of regulating them by means of reason. If one were to adopt for a moment the unlovely nomenclature of '-isms', one could call his system a triad of naturalism, voluntarism and rationalism. But without his belief (rooted in universal history) in the positive *blessing* of *necessità,* without the real warmth which he gave it, he would never have come to proclaim with such determination and conviction that which one can call the *curse* of *necessità,* of necessity of State.

One more trait of his personality must have contributed: namely, the quite unconventional and at the same time radical nature of his thought, which never shrank back before any abyss. Certainly his contemporaries too had long learnt never to shrink back before any moral abyss, and to wade quite cheerfully through any filth. For if it had not been for the general stultifying of moral feeling in life, and without the examples offered by the Papacy from the time of Sixtus IV and Alexander VI, with his frightful son Cesar Borgia, Machiavelli would never have had the milieu required for his new ideas about the use of immoral methods in politics. They were indeed not new as regards content; but they were new in the sense that he dared to express them, and to combine them into a system which embraced a universal outlook. For up till now theory had only limped after practice. The selfsame humanists who, like Pontanus at the court of Naples, saw clearly all the dark side of the new statecraft, were indeed prepared to permit cunning and deception when it was for the good of the community; but after that they fell back once more on the formal pattern of the figure of the Prince, filled in with classic phrases. If I am to offer something really useful, says Machiavelli, it seems to me more suitable to follow the real truth of things, rather than the imaginary picture one has of them. Many people have imagined for themselves republics and principalities, the

like of which one has never seen or even thought possible; for the difference between what one actually does and what one ought to do is so great that whoever, in considering how people ought to live, omits to consider how they behave, is riding for a fall. That is to say, the man who makes it a rule in all circumstances to perform nothing but good actions, is bound to go under amongst so many who are evil. Therefore it is 'necessary' for a prince, if he is to maintain his position, to learn also how not to be good, and then to utilize or not utilize this knowledge, as *necessità* prescribes.

It is worthy of notice that Machiavelli did not introduce near the beginning of his essay on the Prince this new principle of method—a principle which was to break fresh ground for so many centuries, and which was so purely empirical and so completely free from presuppositions. He does not bring it in till much further on, in Chapter 15. For he himself underwent development, during the course of his work on the book. Chapter 15 belongs (as we have tried to prove elsewhere), not to the original conception of the *Principe,* but rather to an extension of it which probably came soon afterwards. Henceforth he always exercised the new principle, which was closely akin to the aesthetic honesty and directness of Florentine art. Then, when he was in the full spate of work, he suddenly became conscious that he was treading new paths. It was the climax of his life, and at the same time also a turning point for the history of European thought. And in this matter history of thought touched very closely upon the history of nations; they were both struck by the *same* electric shock. Even if the statesmen themselves learnt nothing new from it, the very fact that it was *being taught* was still new. For it was not until after it had been grasped as a principle that the historical tendencies achieved their full power of impact, and reached the stage when they could be called ideas.

But the initial application of the new scientific method, and its effect on historical life, were frightful and shattering. A prince must also learn how not to be good—this was the requirement of *necessità,* by which all human life was governed and constrained. But it was quite another matter to decide whether, on the one hand, the moral law should be broken only in the practice of politics, or whether, on the other hand, it was permissible to justify (as from now on became possible, and in fact more and more tended to happen) such an infringement by the plea of an unavoidable 'necessity'. In the first instance the moral law itself had, in its sanctity as a supra-empirical necessity, remained entirely unimpaired. But now this supra-empirical necessity was broken down by an empirical necessity; the force of evil was fighting for a place alongside that of good, and was making out that it was, if not an actual power of good, then at least an indispensable means for obtaining a certain kind of goodness. The forces of sin, which had been basically subdued by the Christian ethic, now won what was fundamentally a partial victory; the devil forced his way into the kingdom of God. There now began that dualism under which modern culture has to suffer: that opposition between supra-empirical and empirical, between absolute and relative standards of value. It was now possible for the modern State, following its own inmost vital impulse, to free itself from all the spiritual fetters that had constrained it; it was possible for it, as an independent power acknowledging no authority outside this world, to effect the admirable accomplishments of rational organization, which would have been unthinkable in the Middle Ages, but were now due to increase from century to century. But it already contained the poison of an inner contradiction, from the very moment it began its ascent. On the one hand religion, morality and law were all absolutely indispensable to it as a foundation for its existence; on the other hand, it started off with the definite intention of injuring these whenever the needs of national self-preservation would require it. But surely (it will be asked) Machiavelli must have felt this contradiction, and the serious consequences it was bound to have?

He was not able to feel it, for the reason that his cast-iron theory of *necessità* concealed it from him, or because (as he believed, at least) the theory of *necessità* resolved the contradiction. The same force which impelled princes to refrain from being good under certain circumstances, also impelled men to behave morally; for it is only from necessity that men perform good actions (*Principe,* ch. 23). Necessity was therefore the spear which at the same time both wounded and healed. It was the causal mechanism which, provided that *virtù* existed in the State, saw to it that the necessary morality and religion were present, and that any failings in that respect were made good. Thus the theory of the struggle between *virtù* and *fortuna,* and the theory of *necessità,* worked together very closely to justify the prince in the use of underhand measures, and to prevent this from being harmful in his opinion.

For all the time Machiavelli held firmly to the absolute validity of religion, morality and law. Even in the most evil and notorious chapter of the *Principe,* Chapter 18, which justifies breach of contract, and declares that a prince (and especially a new prince), for the purpose of maintaining the

State, 'is often obliged (*necessitato*) to act without loyalty, without mercy, without humanity, and without religion' —even in this chapter he still emphasizes that a prince, when he *can,* should not leave the path of morality, but only that he should, in case of necessity (when *necessitato*), also know how to tread the path of evil. Bad indeed was the infamous advice which he gives here: that it is not necessary for the prince to possess all the good moral qualities of loyalty, sincerity, etc., but that he must always appear to have them, because the former case, in which they would always be exercised, would be harmful, but the latter case where he appeared to have them would be useful. With this he helped to make any hypocritical scoundrel secure on a throne. It would throughout have been perfectly in keeping with his purposes and with the main line of his thought, to demand from the prince himself a certain inner moral restraint, even if it were united with the power to take upon himself, in a case of necessity of State, the entire conflict between State-interest and individual morality, and thus make a tragic sacrifice. But perhaps this kind of solution to the problem (one which Frederick the Great was to give later on) was still entirely alien to the intellectual climate of the period and to Machiavelli's own way of thought. The ability to think in terms of inner conflicts, violations and tragic problems, presupposes a more modern and sophisticated mentality, which perhaps only began with Shakespeare. It was in the spirit of the time to delight in tracing precise and rectilinear paths; and in opposition to the straight path of Christian morality Machiavelli laid down another path, just as straight in its own way, a path which was directed exclusively towards the goal of what was useful for the State. He then proceeded, with a pleasure which was characteristic

of him, to draw from it the most extreme consequences.

But was it then, one cannot help challenging him once more—was it then really the well-being of the State, which he had in mind when he wrote the *Principe?* Or was it merely a breviary for the Medicis, whose favour he needed and to whom he dedicated the book, in order to found for himself a new principality by recommending the methods of the frightful Cesar Borgia? We have tried to prove elsewhere that this interpretation is much too narrow. The personal and contemporary political motives which induced him to write the book are undeniable; but from far back there also entered in his entire philosophy of the State, and also his longing to see Italy freed from the Barbarians. Cesar Borgia, with his rational exercise of cruelty and bad faith, must certainly have offered a model for the practical methods of power politics in the situation as it then existed. But the ideal and supreme pattern for the new princes in Italy must have been the great national liberators and founders of States, such as Moses and Cyrus, Theseus and Romulus. The whole book from beginning to end, even including the last chapter (which is sometimes erroneously taken to be an appendix and not an integral part of the book), grew up out of one uniform and fundamental conception, and is built up on the great theme of the struggle between *virtù* and *fortuna.*

It is certainly true that, as regards its technical chapters, the *Principe* can easily arouse the feeling that Machiavelli is only watching out for the personal advantage of the prince. In this respect Machiavelli yielded to his passion for one-sided emphasis and excessive subtlety in dealing with the *thema probandum* of the moment. But if his work is taken together with the *Discorsi* and the other writings and treated as a whole, then this impression entirely disappears. One sees clearly what is the real central idea in Machiavelli's life: namely, the regeneration of a fallen people by means of the *virtù* of a tyrant, and by means of the levering power of all the measures dictated by *necessità*.

This is what is peculiar of Machiavelli, and at the same time constitutes the historical power of his work—the fact that he, the first person to discover the real nature of *raison d'état,* did actually succeed in taking the measure of all the heights and depths to which it led on. He knew its depths, which lead down to the bestial element in Man—'thus it is necessary for a prince, that he should have a proper understanding of how to make use of the brute as well as the man' (*Principe,* ch. 18). He could in the process, as we already saw, when drawn on by his deep-rooted passion for analysis, sink much more deeply into the filth of bestiality than was strictly necessary in order to make a proper use of that bestiality. He knew also that a case of necessity of State (where perhaps a republic which is threatened by dangerous neighbours might be obliged to adopt a policy of conquest) did not represent merely a simple factual necessity, but contained in addition certain elements of power-drive and power-appetite—'molestation by others will give rise to the desire and necessity for conquering' (*la voglia e la necessità dello acquistare,* Disc., II, 19). But he despised a mere insensible greed for power, the *brutta cupidità di regnare* (Disc., III, 8), and he always returned once more to the utilitarian middle way of *raison d'état.* Keep your head clear, he advised, so that you only wish for what is attainable; do not become presumptuous after victory, but, if you have a stronger opponent, take care to make peace at an opportune moment

(Disc., II, 27). Nor should you exasperate an enemy with threats or insult him in words; threats make him more cautious, while insults will increase his hatred (Disc., II, 26). To draw hatred on oneself without getting any benefit from it, is indiscreet and unwise (Disc., III, 23). Under no circumstances should a system of government be built up on a permanent hatred amongst the people. It would be better even to provoke an attack from the nobles, because there are only a few of them, and they can therefore be more easily subdued; but even here he advocated a rationally balanced procedure, 'to refrain from reducing the nobles to despair and to satisfy the people' (Princ., ch. 19).

Political utilitarianism was also at the same time a policy of relativity. Nowadays, he taught, it is necessary to pay attention to the subject peoples, because the peoples are of more significance than the armies. The Roman emperors, on the other hand, had to accommodate themselves to the soldiers rather than the people, because the soldiers could do more at that time than the people could (Princ., ch. 19). Fortified castles may be useful or not, according to the state of the times; but not to be hated by one's people is better than any fortified castle (Princ., ch. 20). But each thing always has concealed in it some special evil that is peculiar to it (Disc., III, 11); therefore whenever one is acting in accordance with *raison d'état,* one must always be conscious of the spheres of uncertainty, of change, and of two-fold consequences, in which it works. 'No State ought to think that it can adopt a course which is absolutely secure, but it ought to reflect rather that all are doubtful; because it is in the order of things, that one can never avoid an evil without running into another one. Wisdom therefore consists in distinguishing between different qualities of evil, and in accepting the lesser evil as good' (Princ., ch. 21).

As we have already seen, he adopted a relativist view, when considering the various forms which the State could take. The contrast between the monarchist bias in the *Principe* and the republican tinge of the *Discorsi* is only apparent. The quantity of *virtù*, which existed in a people, was the factor that decided whether a monarchy or a republic was the more suitable. So it was only consistent that, for his disjointed times, he demanded a monarchical despot and took this to be a necessity of State. The fact that the thing he was asking for might cut both ways was perfectly clear to him; he knew quite well that the tool of monarchical power, which with supreme art he was putting into the hands of the prince, could be misused in the interests of a purely personal greed for power. One can understand why he does not proceed to treat this problem in the *Principe*. But in the *Discorsi* he gives it quite openly as his really sincere opinion, that only in a republic can it be ensured that public good will take precedence of private advantage, and thus make it possible for the State to achieve greatness (Dics., II, 2). With the passionate exaggeration into which he sometimes fell, he was capable of laying down, with reference to a city-state ruled by a prince, the following proposition: that what the prince did for his own advantage, would in most cases injure the State, and that what he did for the benefit of the State, would injure him. Yet immediately afterwards he went on to modify his own crude conception, and contrasted the barbaric type of oriental ruler with the pattern of the Western prince; in that, if the latter be of a normal human stamp, then he will have a uniform paternal love for the cities which come under his care, and he will leave their old constitutional arrangements undisturbed. It is also in the essence of Machiavellian *raison d'état,* as one can see, that with regard to the inner life of the State it should still wish to behave in a relatively conservative and considerate manner. But ruthless acts of interference, when they were necessary to protect power against direct threats, were not thereby excluded. Certainly there also appeared on the horizon of his political imagination the wish-fantasy of a great regenerator of fallen States, 'who, either through his own *virtù*, or by means of the *virtù* of a regulation' (i.e. of a general reform), would breathe new life into these States. The practical needs and possibilities of his time, however (and he generally based his calculations on these), did not go beyond the suppression of actual resistance inside the State, i.e. did not go beyond a rational and at the same time thorough opposition, by direct and indirect means, to all conspiracies. The aims of the later type of absolutism, with its levelling tendencies, were still completely foreign both to himself and to his time. Machiavellism had certainly opened up the road which led to them, but they themselves had not yet come in sight. It is for this reason that we see no signs in Machiavelli of *raison d'état* taking precedence over statute law, which in the seventeenth century (as we shall see presently) was to constitute the principal importance of *raison d'état*. On the contrary a fundamental respect for the existing laws was part of the very essence of his rational autocracy. 'It is well that princes should know that, in the very hour when they begin to break the laws, and disturb old arrangements and customs under which men have long lived, in that hour they begin to lose the State' (Disc., III, 5). All this shows that he moved on the ethical heights of a *raison d'état* which within the limits of his time could only have limited aims indeed, but which was capable of a vital consciousness of the good of the community, the *bene comune* of the whole people. And ultimately he was even capable of rising to the highest ethical feeling which is possible for action prompted by *raison d'état;* this sacrifice consists in taking on oneself personal disgrace and shame, if only it offers a means of saving the Fatherland. Occasionally he would express it in the very same breath with his prosaic utilitarianism: 'It will always be difficult to win the masses over to such conclusions as these, which appear to indicate cowardice and defeat, but do in reality signify salvation and gain' (Disc., I, 53). But the heights and depths of his *raison d'état* are united in the most powerful manner by that phrase, which is to be found at the end of his *Discorsi* (III, 41), and which must surely have sounded in the ears of a certain great German statesman during the First World War: that one may save the Fatherland even *con ignominia*. 'When it is a question of saving the Fatherland, one should not stop for a moment to consider whether something is lawful or unlawful, gentle or cruel, laudable or shameful; but, putting aside every other consideration, one ought to follow out to the end whatever resolve will save the life of the State and preserve its freedom.'

It has been the fate of Machiavelli, as of so many great thinkers, that only one part of his system of thought has been able to influence historical life. It is true that he exerted a powerful and lasting influence through his new method of building politics upon a foundation of experience and history— although even this did not immediately replace the previous scholastic and humanistic methods, but only, through the course of nearly two centuries, intermingled with the older methods, and was able gradually to supersede them. But his ideal of *virtù* soon faded; because the heathen mood of the Renaissance, from which it had sprung, was not able to survive in the period which followed the *sacco di Roma*. And with that too the ethical aim of his statecraft, the idea of regeneration, paled into insignificance. Attention was indeed paid to his republican ideals, but they were misinterpreted in many ways, as for instance in the opinion which was soon expressed that, by giving a sincere picture of the *Principe* he had wanted to unmask tyranny and give a warning against the danger he was pointing out. But generally speaking he was seen first and foremost as having prepared the poison of autocracy; as such, he was publicly condemned and secretly made use of. As we have seen, Machiavelli is to blame for this himself, on account of his method of isolating in a one-sided manner whatever problem he happens to be dealing with at the moment. The chief thing was, however, that the idea of political regeneration was altogether beyond the capabilities and the wishes of the peoples and the rulers of that time, and hence it fell to the ground. The struggle which was to rage around religious values took up entirely all the higher spiritual power of men; and Machiavelli's ancient heathen idealism of the State was no longer understood by the men of the Counter-Reformation period—not even by the Free-thinkers, who took over the secular spirit of the Renaissance.

ERNST CASSIRER

The Triumph of Machiavellism and Its Consequences[*]

MACHIAVELLI AND THE RENAISSANCE

Notwithstanding the widely different opinions about Machiavelli's work and his personality there is at least one point in which we find a complete unanimity. All authors emphasize that Machiavelli is "a child of his age," that he is a typical witness to the Renaissance. This statement is, however, of no avail as long as we have no clear and unambiguous conception of the Renaissance itself. And in this regard the situation seems to be hopelessly confused. In the last decades the interest in Renaissance studies has steadily increased. We are now provided with an astoundingly rich material, with new facts collected by political historians and by historians of literature, art, philosophy, science, and religion. But as to the main question, the question of the "meaning" of the Renaissance, we still seem to be in the dark. No modern writer could repeat the famous formulae by which Jakob Burckhardt tried to describe the civilization of the Renaissance. On the other hand all those descriptions that have been given by the critics of Burckhardt's work are equally objectionable. There are many scholars, and scholars of high authority in their special fields, who decided to cut the Gordian knot. They warn us against the use of the very term "Renaissance." "What is the use in questioning the Renaissance," wrote Lynn Thorndike in a recent discussion of the subject. "No one has ever proved its existence, no one has really tried to."[1]

But we should not discuss merely names and terms. That the Renaissance is not a mere *flatus vocis,* that the term corresponds to a historical reality, is undeniable. If we were in need of proving this reality it would be enough to summon two classical witnesses and to point to two works: Galileo's *Dialogues Concerning Two New Sciences* and Machiavelli's *Prince*. To connect these two works may, at first sight, appear to be very arbitrary. They deal with en-

[1] *Journal of the History of Ideas,* IV, No. 1 (January, 1943), with contributions by Hans Baron, Ernst Cassirer, Francis R. Johnson, Paul Oskar Kristeller, Dean P. Lockwood, and Lynn Thorndike.

tirely diverse subjects; they belong to different centuries, they were written by men who were widely divergent in their thoughts, in their scientific interests, in their talents, and in their personalities. Nevertheless the two books have something in common. In both of them we find a certain trend of thought which marks them as two great and crucial events in the history of modern civilization. Recent research has taught us that both Machiavelli and Galileo had their precursors. Their works have not jumped, ready made and in full armor, out of the heads of their authors. They needed a long and careful preparation. But all this does not detract from their originality. What Galileo gave in his *Dialogues* and what Machiavelli gave in his *Prince* were really "new sciences." "My purpose," said Galileo, "is to set forth a very new science dealing with a very ancient subject. There is, in nature, perhaps nothing older than motion concerning which the books written by philosophers are neither few nor small; nevertheless I have discovered by experiment some properties of it which are worth knowing and which have not hitherto been either observed or demonstrated."[2] Machiavelli would have been perfectly entitled to speak of his book in the same way. Just as Galileo's Dynamics became the foundation of our modern science of nature, so Machiavelli paved a new way to political science.

In order to understand the novelty of both these works we must begin with an analysis of medieval thought. That in a mere chronological sense we cannot separate the Renaissance from the Middle Ages is obvious. By innumerable visible and invisible threads

the Quattrocento is connected with scholastic thought and medieval culture. In the history of European civilization there never was a break of continuity. To seek for a point in this history in which the Middle Ages "end" and the modern world "begins" is a sheer absurdity.[3] But that does not do away with the necessity of looking for an *intellectual* line of demarcation between the two ages.

The medieval thinkers were divided into various schools. Between these schools, the dialecticians and the mystics, the realists and the nominalists, there were interminable discussions. Nevertheless there was a common center of thought that remained firm and unchangeable for many centuries. To grasp the unity of medieval thought there is perhaps no better and easier way than to study the two books Περὶ τῆς οὐρανίας ἱεραρχίας and Περὶ τῆς ἐκκλησιαστικῆς ἱεραρχίας (*On the Celestial Hierarchy* and *On the Ecclesiastical Hierarchy*). The author of these books is unknown. In the Middle Ages they were generally attributed to Dionysius Areopagita, the disciple of St. Paul, who was converted and baptized by him. But this is only a legend. The books were probably written by a Neo-Platonic writer, a disciple of Proclus. They presuppose the theory of emanation that had been developed by Plotinus, the founder of the Neo-Platonic school. In order to understand a thing we must, according to this theory, always go back to its first principle and we must show in what way it has evolved from this principle. The first principle, the cause and origin of all things is the One, the Absolute. This absolute One develops

---

[2] Galileo, *Dialogues Concerning Two New Sciences,* Third Day. English trans. by H. Crew and Alfonso de Salvio (New York: The Macmillan Co., 1914; now Evanston and Chicago: Northwestern University, 1939), p. 153.

[3] In the following paragraphs I have repeated some remarks contained in a paper, "The Place of Vesalius in the Culture of the Renaissance," *The Yale Journal of Biology and Medicine,* XVI, No. 2 (December, 1943), 109ff.

into the multiplicity of things. But that is not a process of evolution, in our modern sense, it is rather a process of degradation. The whole world is held together by a golden chain—that *aurea catena* of which Homer spoke in a famous passage of his *Iliad*. All things whatsoever, spiritual and material things, the archangels, the angels, the seraphim and cherubim and all the other celestial legions, man, organic nature, matter, all of them are bound in this golden chain about the feet of God. There are two different hierarchies; the hierarchy of existence and that of value. But they are not opposed to each other; they correspond to each other in perfect harmony. The degree of value depends on the degree of being. What is lower in the scale of existence is also lower in the ethical scale. The more a thing is remote from the first principle, from the source of all things, so much the less is its grade of perfection.

The pseudo-Dionysian books about the celestial and ecclesiastic hierarchies were widely and eagerly studied throughout the Middle Ages. They became one of the principal sources of scholastic philosophy. The system developed in these books not only influenced the thoughts of men but was also connected with their deepest feelings, and it was expressed, in different ways, in the whole ethical, religious, scientific, and social order. In Aristotelian cosmology God is described as the "unmoved mover" of the universe. He is the ultimate source of motion—being at rest himself. He transmits his moving force first to the things that are next to him: to the highest celestial spheres. From here this force descends, by different degrees, to our own world, to the earth, the sublunar world, the world below the moon. But here we no longer find the same perfection. The higher world, the world of the celestial

bodies, is made of an imperishable and incorruptible substance—the ether or the *quinta essentia,* and the movements of these bodies are eternal. In our world everything is perishable and liable to decay; and every movement comes, after a short time, to its standstill. There is a sharp discrimination between the lower and the higher worlds; they do not consist of the same substance and they do not follow the same laws of motion. The same principle holds for the structure of the political and social world. In religious life we find the ecclesiastical hierarchy that reaches from the Pope as the summit, to the cardinals, the archbishops, the bishops down to the lower degrees of the clergy. In the state the highest power is concentrated in the Emperor, who delegates this power to his inferiors, the princes, the dukes, and all the other vassals. This feudal system is an exact image and counterpart of the general hierarchical system; it is an expression and a symbol of that universal cosmic order that has been established by God and which, therefore, is eternal and immutable.

This system prevailed throughout the Middle Ages and proved its force in all spheres of human life. But in the first centuries of the Renaissance, in the Quattrocento and Cinquecento, it changed its form. The change did not come all of a sudden. We do not find a complete breakdown, an abrogation or an open denial of the fundamental principles of medieval thought. Nevertheless, one breach after another is made in the hierarchical system that seemed to be so firmly established and that had governed the thoughts and feelings of men for many centuries. The system was not destroyed; but it began to fade away and lose its unquestioned authority.

The Aristotelian cosmological system was replaced by the astronomical system of Copernicus. In the latter we no longer find a distinction between the "higher" and the "lower" world. All movements whatever, the movements of the earth and those of the celestial bodies, obey the same universal rules. According to Giordano Bruno, who was the first thinker to give a metaphysical interpretation of the Copernican system, the world is an infinite whole, pervaded and animated by the same infinite divine spirit. There are no privileged points in the universe, no "above" or "below." In the political sphere, too, the feudal order dissolved and began to crumble. In Italy new political bodies of a quite different type appeared. We find the Renaissance tyrannies, created by individual men, the great *condottieri* of the Renaissance, or by great families, the Visconti or Sforzas in Milan, the Medici in Florence, the Gonzagas in Mantua.

THE MODERN SECULAR STATE

That scene was the general political and intellectual background of Machiavelli's *Prince*, and if we approach his book from this angle, we have no difficulty in determining its meaning and its right place in the development of European culture. When Machiavelli conceived the plan of his book the center of gravity of the political world had already been shifted. New forces had come to the fore and they had to be accounted for—forces that were entirely unknown to the medieval system. When studying Machiavelli's *Prince* we are surprised how much his whole thought is concentrated upon this new phenomenon. If he speaks of the usual forms of government, of the city-republics or of the hereditary monarchies, he speaks very briefly. It is as if all these old and time-honored forms of government could hardly arouse Machiavelli's curi-

osity—as if they were unworthy of his scientific interest. But when Machiavelli begins to describe the new men and when he analyzes the "new principalities," he speaks in an entirely different tone. He is not only interested but captivated and fascinated. We feel this strong and strange fascination in every word about Cesare Borgia. Machiavelli's narration of the method taken by Cesare Borgia to rid himself of his enemies, is, both in style and thought, one of his most characteristic writings.[4] And long after the fall of Cesare Borgia he still felt the same way. The "Duca Valentino" always remains his classical example. He frankly confesses that, if he had to found a new state, he would always follow the famous model of Cesare Borgia.[5]

All this cannot be explained by a personal sympathy for Cesare Borgia. Machiavelli had no reason to love him; on the contrary he had the strongest reasons to fear him. He always objected to the temporal power of the Pope, in which he saw one of the greatest dangers for Italy's political life. And nobody had done more to extend the temporal dominion of the Church than Cesare Borgia. On the other hand Machiavelli knew very well that the triumph of Cesare Borgia's politics would have meant the ruin of the Florentine Republic. How was it that, in spite of all this, he spoke of this enemy of his native city not only with admiration but with a kind of awe—with a reverence that perhaps no other historian ever felt for Cesare Borgia? This is only understandable if we bear in mind that the real source of Machiavelli's admiration was not the man himself

---

[4] *Descrizione del modo tenuto dal duca Valentino nell' ammazzare Vitellozzo Vitelli,* etc. English trans. by Farneworth, "The Works of Nicholas Machiavel," II, 481–490.

[5] *Lettere familiari,* CLIX, ed. Ed. Alvisi (Florence, 1883), p. 394.

but *the structure of the new state* that had been created by him. Machiavelli was the first thinker who completely realized what this new political structure really meant. He had seen its origin and he foresaw its effects. He anticipated in his thought the whole course of the future political life of Europe. It was this realization that induced him to study the form of the new principalities with the greatest care and thoroughness. He was perfectly aware that, when compared to former political theories, this study was to be regarded as a certain anomaly—and he apologized for the unusual course of his thought. "It ought not to appear strange to anyone," he says in the sixth chapter of *The Prince,*

if in what I am going to say concerning Principalities and Princes and States, altogether new, I shall quote great and eminent examples...I say then, that the possession of a Principality newly acquired by one who was not a Prince before, is more or less difficult to be maintained, in proportion to the abilities of the person that acquires it. Now as it argues a great share of valour and conduct, or good fortune at least, to raise one's self from a private condition to the rank of a Prince; either that valour and conduct, or that good fortune, in all probability, will enable the same person to surmount many other ensuing difficulties.[6]

Of those states that are based upon mere tradition and the principle of legitimacy Machiavelli speaks with a certain disdain or with an open irony. The ecclesiastic principalities, he declares, are very fortunate; for as they are fortified by religious constitutions of ancient and venerable authority they maintain themselves easily. "But as they are under the immediate superintendence and direction of an Almighty Being who both raised and supports

them, and whose operations are far above the comprehension of our weak understanding, it would be rash and presumptuous in any mortal man that should pretend to account for these things: and therefore I may very well be excused from entering into any solution of that kind."[7] To attract Machiavelli's interest something different from these quiet and peaceful forms of commonwealth was needed—a body politic that had been created by force and was to be maintained by force.

Yet this political aspect is not the only one. In order to understand the whole purport of Machiavelli's theory we must see it in a much broader perspective. To the political we must add the philosophical point of view. This side of the problem has been unduly neglected. Politicians, sociologists, and historians have vied with each other in analyzing, commenting, and criticizing Machiavelli's *Prince*. Yet in our textbooks of the history of modern philosophy we find no chapter on Machiavelli. That is in a sense understandable and justifiable. Machiavelli was no philosopher in the classical or medieval sense of this term. He had no speculative system, not even a system of politics. Nevertheless his book had a very strong indirect influence upon the general development of modern philosophical thought. For he was the first who, decidedly and unquestionably, broke away from the whole scholastic tradition. He destroyed the cornerstone of this tradition—the hierarchic system.

Time and again the medieval philosophers had quoted the saying of St. Paul that all power is of God.[8] The divine origin of the state was generally acknowledged. In the beginning of the modern era this principle was still in full vigor; it appears, for instance, in

---

[6] *The Prince,* chap. vi, op. cit., II, 223f.

[7] *Idem,* chap. xi, *op. cit.,* II, 281.
[8] See St. Paul, Romans, 13.1.

its full maturity in the theory of Suárez.[9] Even the strongest champions of the independence and sovereignty of the temporal power did not dare to deny the theocratic principle. As to Machiavelli he does not even attack this principle; he simply ignores it. He speaks from his political experience; and his experience had taught him that power, real and factual political power, is anything but divine. He had seen the men who were the founders of the "new principalities" and he had keenly studied their methods. To think that the power of these new principalities was of God was not only absurd, it was even blasphemous. As a political realist Machiavelli had, once for all, to give up the whole basis of the medieval political system. The pretended divine origin of the rights of kings seemed to him to be entirely fantastic. It is a product of imagination, not of political thought. "It now remains to show," says Machiavelli in the fifteenth chapter of *The Prince*,

in what manner a prince should behave to his subjects and friends: but as many have written upon this head already, it may seem arrogant in me, perhaps, to offer any thing further, especially as I shall differ widely in my opinion from that of others. However, since I write only for the instruction of such, as I would have thoroughly acquainted with the nature of things, I thought it better to represent them as they really are in fact, than to amuse the imagination with visionary models of Republics and Principalities (as several have done) which never did nor can exist.[10]

Machiavelli does not follow the usual ways of a scholastic disputation. He never argues about political doctrines or maxims. To him the facts of political life are the only valid arguments. It is

enough to point to "the nature of things" to destroy the hierarchic and theocratic system.

Here too we find a close connection between the new *cosmology* and the new *politics* of the Renaissance. In both cases the difference between the "lower" and the "higher" world vanishes. The same principles and natural laws hold for the "world below" and the "world above." Things are on the same level both in the physical and in the political order. Machiavelli studied and analyzed political movements in the same spirit as Galileo, a century later, did the movement of falling bodies. He became the founder of a new type of science of a political static and a political dynamics.

On the other hand it would be incorrect to say that the only aim of Machiavelli was to describe certain political facts as clearly and exactly as possible. In this case he would have acted as a historian not as a theoretician of politics. A theory demands much more; it needs a constructive principle to unify and synthesize the facts. The secular state had existed long before the times of Machiavelli. One of the earliest examples of a complete secularization of political life is the state founded by Frederick II in the south of Italy; and this state had been created three hundred years before Machiavelli wrote his book. It was an absolute monarchy in the modern sense; it had emancipated itself from any influence of the Church. The officials of this state were not clerics but laymen. Christians, Jews, Saracens had an equal share in the administration; nobody was excluded for merely religious reasons. At the court of Frederick II a discrimination between sects, between nations or races was unknown. The paramount interest was that of the secular, the "earthly" state.

That was an entirely new fact, a fact

[9] See von Gierke, *Natural Law*, quoted above (Chapter IX, p. 107, n. 4). English trans., pp. 71ff.

[10] *The Prince, op. cit.*, II, 320.

that had no equivalent in medieval civilization. But this fact had not yet found a theoretical expression and justification. Frederick II was always regarded as an arch heretic. He was twice excommunicated by the Church. Dante, who felt a great personal admiration for him and saw in him the very model of a great monarch, nevertheless condemned him in his *Inferno* to the flaming sepulchers of the heretics.[11] The Lawbook of Frederick II has been styled "The Birth Certificate of Modern Bureaucracy." Yet although modern in his political actions Frederick was by no means modern in his thoughts. When he speaks about himself and about the origin of his empire he speaks not as a skeptic or heretic but as a mystic. He always claims an immediate personal relation to God. It is this personal relation that makes him entirely independent of all ecclesiastic influences and demands. As his biographer describes his thoughts and feelings,

divine Providence had singled him out, him only, and elevated him directly to the throne, and the marvel of her grace had enveloped the last of the Hohenstaufens in a mist of magic glory far beyond that of any other prince, far from the ken of the profane. The purposeful active Foresight of God did not enshroud the Emperor but revealed herself in him as the highest Reason: "Leader in Reason's path" he has been called.[12]

RELIGION AND POLITICS

To Machiavelli all such mystical conceptions had become entirely unintelligible. In his theory all the previous theocratic ideas and ideals are eradicated root and branch. Yet he never

meant on the other hand to separate politics from religion. He was an opponent of the Church but he was no enemy of religion. He was, on the contrary, convinced that religion is one of the necessary elements of man's social life. But in his system this element cannot claim any absolute, independent, and dogmatic truth. Its worth and validity depend entirely on its influence on political life.

By this standard, however, Christianity occupies the lowest place. For it is in strict opposition to all real political *virtù*. It has rendered men weak and effeminate. "Our religion," says Machiavelli, "instead of heroes canonizes those only that are meek and lowly" whereas the "Pagans deified none but men full of worldly glory, such as great commanders and illustrious governors of commonwealths."[13] According to Machiavelli this pagan use of religion was the only rational use. In Rome religion could become, instead of a source of weakness, the chief source of the greatness of the state. The Romans always availed themselves of religion in reforming their state, in prosecuting their wars, and in composing tumults.[14] Whether they did this in good faith or by calculation is of no importance. It was a proof of great political wisdom in Numa Pompilius that he derived his laws from a supernatural source and that he convinced the people of Rome that these laws had been inspired by his conversations with the nymph Egeria.[15] Even in Machiavelli's system, therefore, religion is indispensable. But it is no longer an end in itself; it has become a mere tool in the hands of the political rulers. It is not the foundation of man's social life but a powerful weapon in all political struggles. This weapon

---

11 *Dante, Inferno*, X, 119ff.

12 See Ernst Kantorowicz, *Frederick the Second*. English version by E. O. Lorimer (London: Constable & Co., 1931), p. 253. For all details see chap. v, pp. 215–368.

13 *Discourses*, Bk. II, chap. II.

14 *Idem*, Bk. I, chap. XIII.

15 *Idem*, Bk. I, chap. XI.

must prove its strength in action. A merely passive religion, a religion that flees the world instead of organizing it, has proved to be the ruin of many kingdoms and states. Religion is only good if it produces good order; and good order is generally attended with good fortune and success in any undertaking.[16] Here the final step has been taken. Religion no longer bears any relation to a transcendent order of things and it has lost all its spiritual values. The process of secularization has come to its close; for the secular state exists not only de facto but also de jure; it has found its definite theoretical legitimization.

THE ISOLATION OF THE STATE AND ITS DANGERS

The whole argument of Machiavelli is clear and coherent. His logic is impeccable. If we accept his premises we cannot avoid his conclusions. With Machiavelli we stand at the gateway of the modern world. The desired end is attained; the state has won its full autonomy. Yet this result has had to be bought dearly. The state is entirely independent; but at the same time it is completely isolated. The sharp knife of Machiavelli's thought has cut off all the threads by which in former generations the state was fastened to the organic whole of human existence. The political world has lost its connection not only with religion or metaphysics but also with all the other forms of man's ethical and cultural life. It stands alone—in an empty space.

That this complete isolation was pregnant with the most dangerous consequences should not be denied. There is no point in overlooking or minimizing these consequences. We must see them face to face. I do not mean to say that

16 *Ibid.*

Machiavelli was fully aware of all the implications of his political theory. In the history of ideas it is by no means unusual that a thinker develops a theory, the full purport and significance of which is still hidden to himself. In this regard we must, indeed, make a sharp distinction between Machiavelli and Machiavellism. There are many things in the latter that could not be foreseen by Machiavelli. He spoke and judged from his own personal experience, the experience of a secretary of the State of Florence. He had studied with the keenest interest the rise and fall of the "new principalities." But what were the small Italian tyrannies of the Cinquecento when compared to the absolute monarchies of the seventeenth century and with our modern forms of dictatorship? Machiavelli highly admired the methods used by Cesare Borgia to liquidate his adversaries. Yet in comparison with the later much more developed technique of political crimes these methods appear to be only child's play. Machiavellism showed its true face and its real danger when its principles were later applied to a larger scene and to entirely new political conditions. In this sense we may say that the consequences of Machiavelli's theory were not brought to light until our own age. Now we can, as it were, study Machiavellism in a magnifying glass.

There was still another circumstance that prevented Machiavellism from coming to its full maturity. In the centuries that followed, in the seventeenth and eighteenth centuries, his doctrine played an important role in practical political life; but, theoretically speaking, there were still great intellectual and ethical forces which counterbalanced its influence. The political thinkers of this period, with the single exception of Hobbes, were all partisans of the "Natural Right theory of the state." Crotious, Pufendorf, Rousseau,

Locke looked upon the state as a means, not as an end in itself. The concept of a "totalitarian" state was unknown to these thinkers. There was always a certain sphere of individual life and individual freedom which remained inaccessible to the state. The state and the sovereign in general were *legibus solutus*. But this meant only that they were free from legal coercion; it did not mean that they were exempt from moral obligations. After the beginning of the nineteenth century, however, all this was suddenly called in question. Romanticism launched a violent attack against the theory of natural rights. The romantic writers and philosophers spoke as resolute "spiritualists." But it was precisely this metaphysical spiritualism that paved the way for the most uncouth and uncompromising materialism in political life. In this regard it is a highly interesting and remarkable fact that the "idealistic" thinkers of the nineteenth century, Fichte and Hegel, became the advocates of Machiavelli and the defenders of Machiavellism. After the collapse of the theory of natural rights the last barrier to its triumph was removed. There was no longer any great intellectual or moral power to check and counterbalance Machiavellism, its victory was complete and seemed to be beyond challenge.

THE MORAL PROBLEM IN MACHIAVELLI

That Machiavelli's *Prince* contains the most immoral things and that Machiavelli has no scruples about recommending to the ruler all sorts of deception, of perfidy, and cruelty is incontestable. There are, however, not a few modern writers who deliberately shut their eyes to this obvious fact. Instead of explaining it they make the greatest efforts to deny it. They tell us that the measures recommended by Machiavelli,

however objectionable in themselves, are only meant for the "common good." The ruler has to respect this common good. But where do we find this mental reservation? *The Prince* speaks in quite a different, in an entirely uncompromising way. The book describes, with complete indifference, the ways and means by which political power is to be acquired and to be maintained. About the *right use* of this power it does not say a word. It does not restrict this use to any consideration for the commonwealth. It was only centuries later that the Italian patriots began to read into Machiavelli's book all their own political and national idealism. In any word of Machiavelli, declared Alfieri, we find the same spirit, a spirit of justice, of passionate love for freedom, of magnanimity and truth. He who understands Machiavelli's work in the right way must become an ardent enthusiast for liberty and an enlightened lover of all political virtues.[17]

This is, however, only a rhetorical answer to our question, not a theoretical one. To regard Machiavelli's *Prince* as a sort of ethical treatise or a manual of political virtues is impossible. We need not enter here into a discussion of the vexed problem whether the last chapter of *The Prince*, the famous exhortation to deliver Italy out of the bonds of barbarians, is an integral part of the book or a later addition. Many modern students of Machiavelli have spoken of *The Prince* as if the whole book were nothing but a preparation for this closing chapter, as if this chapter were not only the climax but also the quintessence of Machiavelli's political thought. I think this view to be erroneous, and, as far as I see, the

---

[17] "Chiunque ben legge e nell' autore s'immedesima non può riuscire se non un focoso entusiasta di libertà, e un illuminatissimo amatore d' ogni politica virtù." Alfieri, *Del Principe e delle lettere,* cap. VIII.

onus probandi rests in this case with the advocates of the thesis. For there are obvious differences between the book taken as a whole and the last chapter, differences of thought and differences of style. In the book itself Machiavelli speaks with an entirely detached mind. Everyone may hear him and make what use he will of his advice which is available not only to the Italians but also to the most dangerous enemies of Italy. In the third chapter Machiavelli discusses at great length all the errors committed by Louis XII in his invasion of Italy. Without these errors, he declares, Louis XII would have had no difficulty in attaining his end, which was to subjugate the whole of Italy. In his analysis of political actions Machiavelli never gives vent to any personal feeling of sympathy or antipathy. To put it in the words of Spinoza he speaks of these things as if they were lines, planes, or solids. He did not attack the principles of morality; but he could find no use for these principles when engrossed in problems of political life. Machiavelli looked at political combats as if they were a game of chess. He had studied the rules of the game very thoroughly. But he had not the slightest intention of changing or criticizing these rules. His political experience had taught him that the political game never had been played without fraud, deception, treachery, and felony. He neither blamed nor recommended these things. His only concern was to find the best move—the move that wins the game. When a chess champion engages in a bold combination, or when he tries to deceive his partner by all sorts of ruses and stratagems, we are delighted and admire his skill. That was exactly Machiavelli's attitude when he looked upon the shifting scenes of the great political drama that was played before his eyes. He was not only deeply interested; he was fascinated. He could not help giving his opinion. Sometimes he shook his head at a bad move; sometimes he burst out with admiration and applause. It never occurred to him to ask by whom the game was played. The players may be aristocrats or republicans, barbarians or Italians, legitimate princes or usurpers. Obviously that makes no difference for the man who is interested in the game itself—and in nothing but the game. In his theory Machiavelli is apt to forget that the political game is not played with chessmen, but with real men, with human beings of flesh and blood; and that the weal and woe of these beings is at stake.

It is true that in the last chapter his cool and detached attitude gives way to an entirely new note. Machiavelli suddenly shakes off the burden of his logical method. His style is no longer analytical but rhetorical. Not without reason has that last chapter been compared to Isocrates' exhortation to Philip.[18] Personally we may prefer the emotional note of the last chapter to the cold and indifferent note of the rest of the book. Yet it would be wrong to assume that in the book Machiavelli has concealed his thoughts; that what is said there was only a sham. Machiavelli's book was sincere and honest; but it was dictated by his conception of the meaning and task of a *theory* of politics. Such a theory must describe and analyze; it cannot blame or praise.

No one has ever doubted the patriotism of Machiavelli. But we should not confuse the philosopher with the patriot. *The Prince* was the work of a political thinker—and of a very radical thinker. Many modern scholars are liable to forget or, at least, to underrate this radicalism of Machiavelli's theory. In their efforts to purge his name from all

---

[18] See L. A. Burd's notes in his edition of *Il Principe*, p. 366.

blame they have obscured his work. The have portrayed a harmless and innocuous but at the same time a rather trivial Machiavelli. The real Machiavelli was much more dangerous—dangerous in his thoughts, not in his character. To mitigate his theory means to falsify it. The picture of a mild or lukewarm Machiavelli is not a true historical portrait. It is a "fable convenue" just as much opposed to the historical truth as the conception of the "diabolic" Machiavelli. The man himself was loath to compromise. In his judgments about political actions he warned over and over again against irresolution and hesitation. It was the greatness and the glory of Rome that in Roman political life all half measures were avoided.[19] Only weak states are always dubious in their resolves, and tardy resolves are always hateful.[20] It is true that men, in general, seldom know how to be wholly good or wholly bad. Yet it is precisely this point in which the real politician, the great statesman, differs from the average man. He will not shrink from such crimes as are stamped with an inherent greatness. He may perform many good actions, but when circumstances require a different course he will be "splendidly wicked."[21] Here we hear the voice of the real Machiavelli, not of the conventional one. And even if it were true. that all the advice of Machiavelli was destined only for the "common good," who is the judge of this common good? Obviously no one but the prince himself. And he will always be likely to identify it with his private interest: he will act according to the maxim: *l'état, c'est moi.* Moreover, if the common good could justify all those things that

are recommended in Machiavelli's book, if it could be used as an excuse for fraud and deception, felony and cruelty, it would hardly be distinguishable from the common evil.

It remains, however, one of the great puzzles in the history of human civilization how a man like Machiavelli, a great and noble mind, could become the advocate of "splendid wickedness." And this puzzle becomes the more bewildering if we compare *The Prince* with Machiavelli's other writings. There are many things in these other writings that seem to be in flagrant contradiction with the views exposed in *The Prince.* In his *Discourses* Machiavelli speaks as a resolute republican. In the struggles between the Roman aristocracy and the plebeians his sympathy is clearly on the side of the people. He defends the people against the reproach of inconstancy and fickleness;[22] he declares that the guardianship of public freedom is safer in the hands of the commons than in those of the patricians.[23] He speaks in a very disparaging tone of the *gentiluomini,* of those men who live in opulence and idleness on the revenues of their estates. Such persons, he declares, are very mischievous in every republic or country. But even more mischievous are those who are lords of strongholds and castles besides their estates, and who have vassals and retainers who render them obedience. Of these two classes of men the Kingdom of Naples, the Romagna and Lombardy were full; and hence it happened that in these provinces no commonwealth or free form of government ever existed; because men of this sort are the sworn foes to all free institutions.[24] Taking everything into consideration, declares Machiavelli, the

---

19 *Discourses,* Bk. II, chap. XXIII.
20 *Idem,* Bk. II, chap. XV; Bk. I, chap. XXXVIII.
21 *Idem,* Bk. I, chap. XXVII.

22 *Idem,* Bk. I, chap. LVIII.
23 *Idem,* Bk. 1, chaps. IV, V.
24 *Idem,* Bk. I, chap. LV.

people are wiser and more constant than a prince.[25]

In *The Prince* we hear very little of these convictions. Here the fascination of Cesare Borgia is so strong that it seems completely to eclipse all republican ideals. The methods of Cesare Borgia become the hidden center of Machiavelli's political reflections. His thought is irresistibly attracted to this center. "Upon a thorough review of the Duke's conduct and actions," says Machiavelli,

I see nothing worthy of reprehension in them; on the contrary, I have proposed them and here propose them again as a pattern for the imitation of all such as arrive at dominion by the arms or fortune of others. For as he had a great spirit and vast designs, he could not well have acted otherwise in his circumstances: and if he miscarried in them, it was entirely owing to the sudden death of his father, and the desperate condition in which he happened to lie himself at that critical juncture.[26]

If Machiavelli reprehends anything in Cesare it is not his character; it is not his ruthlessness, his cruelty, his treachery and rapacity. For all this he has no word of blame. What he blames in him is the only grave error in his political career: the fact that he allowed Julius II, his sworn enemy, to be elected Pope after the death of Alexander VI.

There is a story according to which Talleyrand, after the execution of the Duke of Enghien by Napoleon Bonaparte, exclaimed: "C'est plus qu'un crime, c'est une faute!" If this anecdote be true then we must say that Talleyrand spoke as a true disciple of Machiavelli's *Prince*. All judgments of Machiavelli are political and moral judgments. What he thinks to be objectionable and

unpardonable in a politician are not his crimes but his mistakes.

That a republican could make the Duca Valentino his hero and model seems to be very strange: for what would have become of the Italian Republics and all their free institutions under a ruler like Cesare Borgia? There are however two reasons that account for this seeming discrepancy in Machiavelli's thought: a general and a particular one. Machiavelli was convinced that all his political thoughts were entirely realistic. Yet when studying his republicanism we find very little of this political realism. His republicanism is much more "academic" than practical; more contemplative than active. Machiavelli had served, sincerely and faithfully, the cause of the city-state of Florence. As a secretary of the state he had combated the Medici. But when the power of the Medici was restored he hoped to retain his post; he made the greatest efforts to make his peace with the new rulers. That is easily understandable. Machiavelli did not swear by the words of any political program. His was not a stern unyielding and uncompromising republicanism. He could readily accept an aristocratic government; for he had never recommended an ochlocracy, a dominion of the populace. It is not without reason, he declares, that the voice of the people has been likened to the voice of God.[27] But on the other hand he is convinced that to give new institutions to a commonwealth, or to reconstruct old institutions on an entirely new basis, must be the work of one man.[28] The multitude is helpless without a head.[29]

Yet if Machiavelli admired the Roman plebs, he had not the same

[25] *Idem*, Bk. I, chap. LVIII.
[26] *The Prince*, chap. VII (VI in Farneworth trans. is a misprint), cf. chap. XIII. Farneworth trans., p. 247, cf. p. 304.

[27] *Discourses*, Bk. I, chap. LVIII.
[28] *Idem*, Bk. I, chap. IX.
[29] *Idem*, Bk. I, chap. XLIV.

belief in the power of the citizens of a modern state to rule themselves. Unlike many other thinkers of the Renaissance he did not cherish the hope of restoring the life of the ancients. The Roman Republic was founded upon the Roman virtù—and this virtù is lost, once for all. The attempts to resuscitate ancient political life appeared to Machiavelli as idle dreams. His was a sharp, clear, and cool mind; not the mind of a fanatic and enthusiast like Cola di Rienzi. In Italian life of the fifteenth century Machiavelli saw nothing to encourage his republican ideals. As a patriot he felt the strongest sympathies for his fellow citizens, but as a philosopher he judged them very severely; his feeling bordered on contempt. Only in the North he was still able to find some traces of love of freedom and the ancient virtù. The nations of the North, he says, have to a certain degree been saved because they did not learn the manners of the French, the Italians, or the Spaniards—this corruption of the world.[30] This judgment about his own times was irrevocable. Machiavelli did not even admit that it could be questioned by anyone. "I know not," he says,

whether I may not deserve to be reckoned in the number of those who deceive themselves, if, in these discourses of mine, I render excessive praise to the ancient times of the Romans while I censure our own. And, indeed, were not the excellence which then prevailed and the corruption which prevails now clearer than the sun, I should proceed more guardedly in what I have to say. . . . But since the thing is so plain that everyone sees it, I shall be bold to speak freely all I think, both of old times and of new, in order that the minds of the young who happen to read these my writings may

be led to shun modern examples, and be prepared to follow those set by antiquity whenever chance affords the opportunity.[31]

Machiavelli was by no means especially fond of the *principati nuovi*, of the modern tyrannies. He could not fail to see all their defects and evils. Yet under the circumstances and conditions of modern life these evils seemed to him to be unavoidable. There is no doubt that Machiavelli personally would have abhorred most of the measures he recommended to the rulers of the new states. He tells us in so many words that these measures are most cruel expedients, repugnant not merely to every Christian, but to every civilized rule of conduct and such as every man should shun, choosing rather to lead a private life than to be a king on terms so hurtful to mankind. But, as he adds very characteristically, whoever will not keep to the fair path of virtue, must, to maintain himself, enter the path of evil.[32] *Aut Caesar aut nihil*—either to lead a private, harmless and innocuous life, or to enter the political arena, struggle for power, and maintain it by the most ruthless and radical means. There is no choice between these two alternatives.

When speaking of Machiavelli's "immoralism" we must, however, not understand this term in our modern sense. Machiavelli did not judge human actions from a standpoint "beyond good and evil." He had no contempt for morality; but he had very little esteem for men. If he was a skeptic, his skepticism was a human rather than a philosophical skepticism. The best proof of this ineradicable skepticism, of this deep mistrust of human nature, is to be found in his comedy *Mandragola*. This masterpiece of comic literature

---

30 *Idem,* Bk. I, chap. LV. "Perchè non hanno possuto pigliare i costumi, nè franciosi, nè spagnuoli, nè italiani; le quali nazioni tutte insieme sono la corruttela del mondo."

31 *Idem,* Bk. II, Preface. Thomson trans., p. 191.
32 *Idem,* Bk. I, chap. XXVI.

reveals perhaps more of Machiavelli's judgment about his contemporaries than all his political and historical writings. For his own generation and his own country he saw no hope. And in his *Prince* he tried to inculcate the same conviction of the deep moral perversion of men upon the minds of the rulers of states. This was an integral part of his political wisdom. The first condition for ruling men is to understand man. And we shall never understand him as long as we are suffering from the illusion of his "original goodness." Such a conception may be very humane and benevolent; but in political life it proves to be an absurdity. Those that have written upon civil government lay it down as first principle, says Machiavelli, and all historians demonstrate the same, that whoever would found a state, and make proper laws for the government of it, must presuppose that all men are bad by nature, and that they will not fail to show that natural depravity of heart, whenever they have a fair opportunity.[33]

This depravity cannot be cured by laws; it must be cured by force. Laws are, indeed, indispensable for every commonwealth—but a ruler should use other and more convincing arguments. The best foundations of all states, whether new, old, or mixed, says Machiavelli, are good laws and good arms. But since good laws are ineffective without arms, and since, on the other hand, good arms will always give due weight to such laws, I shall here no longer argue about laws but speak about arms.[34] Even the "saints," the religious prophets have always acted according to this principle as soon as they became rulers of states. Without this they were lost from the very beginning. Savonarola failed to attain his end, because he had

neither power to keep those steady in their persuasion who acknowledged his mission nor to make others believe who denied it. Hence it comes that all the prophets who were supported by an armed force succeeded in their undertakings, whereas those that had not such a force to rely on were defeated and destroyed.[35]

Of course Machiavelli prefers by far the good, the wise, and noble rulers to the bad and cruel ones; he prefers a Marcus Aurelius to a Nero. Yet if you write a book that is destined solely for these good and just rulers, the book itself may be excellent but it will not find many readers. Princes of this kind are the exception, not the rule. Everyone admits how praiseworthy it is in a prince to keep faith, and to live with integrity. Nevertheless, as matters stand, a prince has also to learn the opposite art: the art of craft and treachery.

A prince ought to know how to resemble a beast as well as a man, upon occasion: and this is obscurely hinted to us by ancient writers who relate that Achilles and several other princes in former times were sent to be educated by Chiron the Centaur; that as their preceptor was half-man and half-beast, they might be taught to imitate both natures since one cannot long support itself without the other. Now, because it is so necessary for a prince to learn how to act the part of a beast sometimes, he should make the lion and the fox his patterns: for the lion has not cunning enough of himself to keep out of snares and toils; nor the fox sufficient strength to cope with a wolf: so that he must be a fox to enable him to find out the snares, and a lion in order to terrify the wolves.[36]

This famous simile is highly characteristic and illuminating. Machiavelli did not mean to say that a teacher of princes should be a brute. Yet he has

---

[33] *Idem*, Bk. I, chap. III.
[34] *The Prince*, chap. XII.

[35] *Idem*, chap. VI.
[36] *Idem*, chap. XVIII, *op. cit.*, II, 340.

to do with brutal things and must not recoil from seeing them eye to eye and from calling them by their right names. Humanity alone will never do in politics. Even at its best politics still remains an intermediary between humanity and bestiality. The teacher of politics must therefore understand both things: he must be half man, half beast.

No political writer before Machiavelli had ever spoken in this way. Here we find the clear, the unmistakable and ineffaceable difference between his theory and that of all his precursors— the classical as well as the medieval authors. Pascal says that there are certain words which, suddenly and unexpectedly, make clear the sense of a whole book. Once we meet with these words we no longer can have any doubt about the character of the book: all ambiguity is removed. Machiavelli's saying that a teacher of princes must be *un mezzo bestia e mezzo uomo* is of such a kind: it reveals, as in a sudden flash, the nature and purpose of his political theory. No one had ever doubted that political *life*, as matters stand, is full of crimes, treacheries, and felonies. But no thinker before Machiavelli had undertaken to teach the *art* of these crimes. These things were done, but they were not taught. That Machiavelli promised to become a teacher in the art of craft, perfidy, and cruelty was a thing unheard of. And he was very thorough in his teaching. He did not hesitate or compromise. He tells the ruler that since cruelties are necessary they should be done quickly and mercilessly. In this case, and in this case alone, they will have the desired effect: they will prove to be *crudeltà bene usate*. It is no use postponing or mitigating a cruel measure; it must be done at one blow and regardless of all human feelings. A usurper who has won the throne must not allow any other man or woman to stand in his way; he must extirpate the whole family of the legitimate ruler.[37] All these things may be called shameful; but in political life we cannot draw a sharp line between "virtue" and "vice." The two things often change places: if everything is considered we shall find that some things that seem to be very virtuous, if they are turned into actions, will be ruinous to the prince, whereas others that are regarded as vicious are beneficial.[38] In politics all things change their place: fair is foul, and foul is fair.

It is true that there are some modern students of Machiavelli who see his work in quite a different light. They tell us that this work was by no means a radical innovation. It was, after all, a rather commonplace thing; it belonged to a familiar literary type. *The Prince*, these writers assure us, is only one of the innumerable books that, under various titles, had been written for the instruction of kings. Medieval and Renaissance literatures were full of these treatises. Between the years 800 and 1700 there were accessible some thousand books telling the king how to conduct himself so that he may be "clear in his great office." Everyone knew and read these works: *De officio regis, De institutione principum, De regimine principum*. Machiavelli simply added a new link to this long list. His book is by no means *sui generis;* it was rather a typical book. There is no real novelty in *The Prince*—neither a novelty of thought nor a novelty of style.[39]

Against this judgment we can, how-

---

37 *Discourses*, Bk. III, chaps. IV, XXX; cf. *The Prince*, chap. III: "a possederli sicuramente basta avere spenta la linea del principe che li dominava."
38 *The Prince*, chap. XV.
39 See Allan H. Gilbert, *Machiavelli's "Prince" and Its Forerunners. "The Prince" as a Typical Book "de Regimine Principum"* (Duke University Press, 1938).

ever, appeal to two witnesses: to the witness of Machiavelli himself and to that of his readers. Machiavelli was deeply convinced of the originality of his political views. "Prompted by that desire which nature has implanted in me fearlessly to undertake whatsoever I think offers a common benefit to all," he wrote in the Preface to his *Discourses*, "I enter on a path which, being untrodden by any though it involve me in trouble, may yet win me thanks from those who judge my efforts in a friendly spirit."[40] This hope was not disappointed: Machiavelli's readers judged likewise. His work was read not only by scholars or by students of politics. It had a much wider circulation. There is hardly one of the great modern politicians who did not know Machiavelli's book and who was not fascinated by it. Among its readers and admirers we find the names of Catarina de' Medici, Charles V, Richelieu, Queen Christina of Sweden, Napoleon Bonaparte. To these readers the book was much more than a book; it was a guide and lodestar in their political actions. Such a deep and permanent influence of *The Prince* would hardly be understandable if the book were only a specimen of a well-known literary type. Napoleon Bonaparte declared that of all political works those of Machiavelli were the only ones worth reading. Can we think of a Richelieu, a Catarina de' Medici, a Napoleon Bonaparte as enthusiastic students of works such as Thomas Aquinas' *De regimine principum*, Erasmus' *Institutio principis Christiani* or Fénélon's *Télémaque?*

In order to show the striking contrast between *The Prince* and all the other works *De regimine principum* we need, however, not rely on personal judgments. There are other and better reasons to prove that there is a real

gulf between Machiavelli's views and those of all previous political writers. Of course *The Prince* had its forerunners; what book has not? We may find in it many parallels to other writers. In Burt's edition most of these parallels have been carefully collected and annotated. But literary parallels do not necessarily prove parallels of thought. *The Prince* belongs to a "climate of opinion" quite different from that of previous writers on the subject. The difference may be described in two words. The traditional treatises *De rege et regimine, De institutione regis, De regno et regis institutione* were *pedagogical* treatises. They were destined for the education of princes. Machiavelli had neither the ambition nor the hope of being equal to this task. His book was concerned with quite different problems. It only tells the prince how to acquire his power and how, under difficult circumstances, to maintain it. Machiavelli was not naïve enough to assume that the rulers of the *principati nuovi,* that men like Cesare Borgia, were apt subjects for "education." In earlier and later books that called themselves *The King's Mirror* the monarch was supposed to see, as in a mirror, his fundamental duties and obligations. But where do we find such a thing in Machiavelli's *Prince?* The very term "duty" seems to be missing in his book.

THE TECHNIQUE OF POLITICS

Yet if *The Prince* is anything but a moral or pedagogical treatise, it does not follow that, for this reason, it is an immoral book. Both judgments are equally wrong. *The Prince* is neither a moral nor an immoral book: it is simply a technical book. In a technical book we do not seek for rules of ethical conduct, of good and evil. It is enough if we are told what is useful or useless.

---

40 Thomson trans., p. 3.

Every word in *The Prince* must be read and interpreted in this way. The book contains no moral prescripts for the ruler nor does it invite him to commit crimes and villainies. It is especially concerned with and destined for the "new principalities." It tries to give them all the advice necessary for protecting themselves from all danger. These dangers are obviously much greater than those which threaten the ordinary states—the ecclesiastic principalities or the hereditary monarchies. In order to avoid them the ruler must take recourse to extraordinary means. But it is too late to seek for remedies after the evil has already attacked the body politic. Machiavelli likes to compare the art of the politician with that of a skilled physician. Medical art contains three parts: diagnosis, prognosis, and therapy. Of these a sound diagnosis is the most important task. The principal thing is to recognize the illness at the right moment in order to be able to make provision against its consequences. If this attempt fails the case becomes hopeless. "The physicians," says Machiavelli,

say of hectic fevers, that it is no hard task to get the better of them in their beginning, but difficult to discover them: yet in course of time, when they have not been properly treated and distinguished, they are easily discovered, but difficult to be subdued. So it happens in political bodies; for when the evils and disturbances that may probably arise in any government are foreseen, which yet can only be done by a sagacious and provident man, it is easy to ward them off; but if they are suffered to sprout up and grow to such a height that their malignity is obvious to every one, there is seldom any remedy to be found of sufficient efficacy to repress them.[41]

All the advice of Machiavelli is to be interpreted in this spirit. He foresees

the possible dangers that threaten the different forms of government and provides for them. He tells the ruler what he has to do in order to establish and to maintain his power, to avoid inner discords, to foresee and prevent conspiracies. All these counsels are "hypothetical imperatives," or to put it in the words of Kant, "imperatives of skill." "Here," says Kant, "there is no question whether the end is rational and good, but only what one must do in order to attain it. The precepts for the physician to make his patient thoroughly healthy, and for a poisoner to ensure certain death, are of equal value in this respect, that each serves to effect its purpose perfectly."[42] These words describe exactly the attitude and method of Machiavelli. He never blames or praises political actions; he simply gives a descriptive analysis of them— in the same way in which a physician describes the symptoms of a certain illness. In such an analysis we are only concerned with the truth of the description, not with the things spoken of. Even of the worst things a correct and excellent description can be given. Machiavelli studied political actions in the same way as a chemist studies chemical reactions. Assuredly a chemist who prepares in his laboratory a strong poison is not responsible for its effects. In the hands of a skilled physician the poison may save the life of a man—in the hands of a murderer it may kill. In both cases we cannot praise or blame the chemist. He has done enough if he has taught us all the processes that are required for preparing the poison and if he has given us its chemical formula. Machiavelli's *Prince* contains many

---

[41] *The Prince,* chap. III, *op. cit.,* II, 200f.

[42] See Kant, *Fundamental Principles of the Metaphysics of Morals.* English trans. by T. K. Abbott in *Kant's Critique of Practical Reason and Other Works on the Theory of Ethics* (6th ed., New York and London: Longmans, Green & Co., 1927), p. 32.

dangerous and poisonous things, but he looks at them with the coolness and indifference of a scientist. He gives his political prescriptions. By whom these prescriptions will be used and whether they will be used for a good or evil purpose is no concern of his.

What Machiavelli wished to introduce was not only a new science but a new *art* of politics. He was the first modern author who spoke of the "art of the state." It is true that the idea of such an art was very old. But Machiavelli gave to this old idea an entirely new interpretation. From the times of Plato all great political thinkers had emphasized that politics cannot be regarded as mere routine work. There must be definite rules to guide our political actions; there must be an art (*technē*) of politics. In his dialogue *Gorgias* Plato opposed his own theory of the state to the views of the sophists —of Protagoras, Prodikos, Gorgias. These men, he declared, have given us many rules for our political conduct. But all these rules have no philosophical purport and value because they fail to see the principal point. They are abstracted from special cases and concerned with particular purposes. They lack the essential character of a technē —the character of universality. Here we grasp the essential and ineradicable difference between Plato's technē and Machiavelli's *arte dello Stato*. Plato's technē is not "art" in Machiavelli's sense; it is knowledge (*epistēmē*) based on universal principles. These principles are not only theoretical but practical, not only logical but ethical. Without an insight into these principles no one can be a true statesman. A man may think himself to be an expert in all problems of political life, because he has, by

long experience, formed right opinions about political things. But this does not make him a real ruler; and it does not enable him to give a firm judgment, because he has no "understanding of the cause."[43]

Plato and his followers had tried to give a theory of the *Legal* State; Machiavelli was the first to introduce a theory that suppressed or minimized this specific feature. His art of politics was destined and equally fit for the illegal and for the legal state. The sun of his political wisdom shines upon both legitimate princes and usurpers or tyrants, on just and unjust rulers. He gave his counsel in affairs of state to all of them, liberally and profusely. We need not blame him for this attitude. If we wish to compress *The Prince* into a short formula we could perhaps do no better than to point to the words of a great historian of the nineteenth century. In the introduction to his *History of English Literature* Hippolyte Taine declares that the historian should speak of human actions in the same way as a chemist speaks of different chemical compounds. Vice and virtue are products like vitriol or sugar and we should deal with them in the same cool and detached scientific spirit. That was exactly the method of Machiavelli. To be sure he had his personal feelings, his political ideals, his national aspirations. But he did not allow these things to affect his political judgment. His judgment was that of a scientist and a technician of political life. If we read *The Prince* otherwise, if we regard it as the work of a political propagandist, we lose the gist of the whole matter.

---

[43] See Plato, *Republic,* 533 B; cf. above, Chapter VI, p. 70.

5

HOBBES

Despite his eloquent description of man's obsessive fear of sudden death, Thomas Hobbes had the distinction of living ninety-one years (1588–1679). The bulk of his writings on politics, including his major work, the *Leviathan,* was produced late in life, in the years 1640–1656. This was the period of the violence and disorder of the English civil war, a fact which may help to explain his equally obsessive concern for order. It was Hobbes' fate to be author of a political doctrine which was pleasing to neither of the major contending forces in the revolutionary upheaval. He rejected, on the one hand, traditional religious and hierarchical arguments for the origin of government. Like the Puritan revolutionaries he also argued from nature and emphasized the role of consent and the flow of power coming from below to the political leadership. This could hardly appeal to the royalist defenders of the Stuart cause. On the other hand, his final doctrine emphasized centralized authority and unconditional submission to authority from above, views much closer to the royalists than the revolutionaries.

In his article on Hobbes, Sterling Lamprecht very carefully plots a Hobbes whose views are quite different from those usually assumed to be his. For this latter conventional picture Lamprecht pens the name Hobbism. While delineating a somewhat less repellent Hobbes than the traditional figure, Lamprecht still is led to question some of the views of his subject. In his piece Professor Strauss of the University of Chicago offers a penetrating study of Hobbes' novelty. He outlines, and criticizes, what he describes as Hobbes' decisive break with the classical notion of natural law and his creation of a new and morally inferior notion of natural rights. With Hobbes, Strauss contends, we are at the birth of individualist political thought, at the center of which is the protection of rights instead of the performance of duties.

STERLING P. LAMPRECHT

Hobbes and Hobbism[*]

Fearful of a committee appointed by the House of Commons to investigate the current tendencies towards atheism and profaneness, Hobbes in 1666 burned some of his private papers. The Great Plague and the Great Fire of London had just occurred. While many Englishmen were prone to blame the fire on those whom they considered the "treacherous Catholics," they tended to regard the plague as obviously an act of God. The House of Commons shared this widespread attitude and, desirous of ridding the country of the causes of the divine displeasure, named several persons whose wickedness might be the occasion of the display of God's wrath against the English people. The House included Hobbes in the list and specifically mentioned his *Leviathan*. Moreover, some bishops of the Church of England, at about the same time, suggested that it might be well to burn Hobbes as a heretic.[1] Nothing came of the parliamentary investigation; indeed, the investigation seems not to have been begun. And no fires were lighted except that in which Hobbes saw fit, as has been said, to burn some of his private papers.

It is interesting to conjecture, however, what the name of Hobbes would mean in the history of ideas if his works had happened all to perish in 1666 and we, then, had to judge him through the literature which his works provoked. The word *provoked* may here be used advisedly. For an amazing number of hostile writings against Hobbes were printed during his life-time and immediately after his death. Richard Blackbourne, in his *Vitae Hobbianae Auctarium* (1681), lists thirty-five authors who attacked Hobbes prior to that date, and then added: "In Hobbii defensionem unicum solummodo reperio scriptum, idque anonymum"![2] Of the thirty-five hostile writers, twenty-nine were concerned with Hobbes's political ideas, especially with the *Leviathan;* and the single favorable tract was, if not written by a foreigner, at least published in Amsterdam in defense of the *De cive*. After Blackbourne's report in 1681, the number of hostile references to Hobbes increased. The editor of *The Moral and Political Works of Thomas Hobbes of Malmesbury, Never Before Collected Together* (1750) has two long

* Reprinted from *The American Political Science Review*, No. 34 (1940), pp. 31–53, by permission of *The Review* and the author. The footnotes found in the original have been abridged for this edition.

1 Aubrey, *Brief Lives* (Oxford, 1898), I, p. 339.

2 P. 112.

foot-notes to a preliminary biographical sketch in which, depending largely upon Blackbourne's list, he goes on to add eight more hostile writers and only one further (again a foreign) favorable writer.[3] These lists are not exhaustive. Eight other hostile treatments of Hobbes can be given from the period of Hobbes's own lifetime and the ensuing decade.[4] Added together, the lists give us fifty-one hostile and two favorable treatments.[5]

Were we to formulate Hobbes's political theories from this contemporary literature about him (as, for example,

we have to formulate our ideas of the Christian gnostics of the second century largely from the writings of the church fathers who attacked them), we should get a system of political philosophy which may be properly referred to as Hobbism—something quite different in most fundamental points from the theories Hobbes set forth in his writings, yet issuing from those writings as those writings were read by and impressed themselves on the minds of Hobbes's contemporaries. This system of Hobbism would in summary be as follows. (1) God made man such a beast and rascal that he inclines universally to malice and fraud. Man's typical acts, when he is unrestrained, are violent and ruthless, savagely disregarding the persons and property of his fellows. His greatest longing is to preserve himself by gaining power over others. And he deems the exercise of power honorable, no matter for what ends it be exercised. (2) There is no real distinction between moral right and moral wrong. Moral distinctions are artificial suppositions foisted upon the generality of men by some superior power; they are arbitrary conventions which rulers impose upon their subjects and have no validity beyond the frontiers within which those rulers exercise control. The state is thus the original of what men have come to deem virtue; and apart from the state there would be no moral distinctions or principles at all. (3) A *de facto* ruler is always justified in all his ways. Since the distinction between good and bad arises from the dictate of princes, the commands of princes are *ipso facto* the criterion of right and wrong for those whom they are strong enough to command. A ruler, being himself the source of morality, cannot be immoral. (4) Appeal to law as a protection of popular rights is essentially invalid. For not

---

[3] Pp. xxv and xxvi.

[4] These eight writings, arranged according to dates of publication, are:

Philip Scot, *A Treatise of the Schism of England. Wherein Particularly Mr. Hales and Mr. Hobbs are Modestly Accosted.* 1650.

Luke Fawne, *A Beacon Set on Fire.* 1652.

Thomas Pierce, *Autokatakrisis, or, Self-Condemnation, Exemplified...with Occasional Reflexions on...Master Hobbs.* 1658.

Roger Coke, *Justice Vindicated from the False Forms Put upon it, by Thomas White Gent., Mr. Thomas Hobbs, and Hugo Grotius.* 1660.

William Lucy, *Observations, Censures and Confutations of Notorious Errours in Mr. Hobbes his Leviathan, and Other his Books.* 1663.

Sir Matthew Hale, *Reflections by the Lrd. Chiefe Justice Hale on Mr. Hobbes his Dialogue of the Lawe.* 1675.

William Sherlock, *Their Present Majesties Government Proved to be Thoroughly Settled, and That We May Submit to it, Without Asserting the Principles of Mr. Hobbs.* 1691.

Ja. Lowde, *A Discourse Concerning the Nature of Man...With an Examination of Some of Mr. Hobbs's Opinions Relating Thereunto.* 1694.

[5] One should not forget, however, that Hobbes had many friends and warm admirers in England during his lifetime. The editor of the 1750 edition of Hobbes's writings mentioned ten persons who held high opinions of Hobbes. And Hobbes's patrons, the Earls of Devonshire, inscribed on the marble slab over his grave the words: "Vir probus et fama eruditionis domi forique bene cognitus."

simply are there no popular rights, but the passing whims of rulers are of more force than what is alleged to be law.

These four points might well be taken as constituting the system of political Hobbism. Along with them would go the further position that both religion and personal character are to be despised by the discerning. Religion is a sham and a trick, whereby shrewd rulers buttress their wills by playing cleverly upon the fears of superstitious men. Character, too, is an idle notion. Men's inner motives are indifferent. What a man really seeks, what he hopes or wishes, what he secretly thinks, these are of no consequence provided that his outward acts conform to his ruler's will. No man can sin as long as he obeys his prince. On all matters on which he is not expressly forbidden to commit a deed, he is both legally and morally free to act as he chooses. As men are born savage beasts, so they remain savage beasts to the end, however much their bestiality is concealed beneath that thin veneer of legal conformity which can only ironically be called civilization.

Hobbism, thus defined, can find substantiation in the works of Hobbes, when those works are read hastily or separate sentences out of them are quoted out of context. That Hobbes was in his own day generally deemed a Hobbist is quite intelligible in the light of the psychology of the turbulent days of the Commonwealth and Restoration. That Hobbes continued to be deemed a Hobbist by many historians in subsequent centuries has been due both to the force of tradition and to the wide acceptance of a rival political philosophy which was sponsored with great power by Locke and was congenial to the currents of political change since the Glorious Revolution of 1688. Hobbes challenged, not merely with deep penetration but with caustic wit, many cherished political beliefs and party professions of his time; and his ideas run diametrically counter to much that is basic in the "natural rights" movement that gave constitutionalism its characteristic form in several of the great nations in the eighteenth and nineteenth centuries. He influenced the utilitarians and other nineteenth-century writers on specific points; but he has generally remained suspect, even to our own day, and is still pictured with many lingering traces of the Hobbism with which he was from the outset confused.

Among the factors which have tended to make Hobbes seem a Hobbist, three are perhaps most prominent. In the first place, Hobbes had a remarkable gift for trenchant utterance and a glee in exploiting this gift to the irritation of his opponents. During the years of his voluntary exile from his own country, he deliberately indulged his wit in antagonizing the clerical and royalist forces that had gathered in Paris about the person of the prince who later became Charles II. But he was not partial to any group in administering telling blows. Simultaneously with his expressions of anti-clericalism, he uttered defiances of the parties who were struggling for power in the Commonwealth at home—Presbyterians, Independents, agitators like the Levellers, republicans like Harrington. Consider, for example, the famous jibe that the papacy is "the ghost of the deceased Roman Empire, sitting crowned upon the grave thereof."[6] Or the ironic condemnation of the

---

6 *Leviathan*, pp. 697–98. (References are given to the pages of that volume of the Molesworth edition of *The English Works* in which the particular writing occurs. This Molesworth edition remains the one most generally accessible for Hobbes's writings as a whole.)

Presbyterians as, jointly with the Roman clergy, "authors of this darknesse in religion."[7] Or the attack upon the universities because they did no more than impose upon their students "the frivolous distinctions, barbarous terms, and obscure language of the Schoolmen," in order to "make men mistake the *ignis fatuus* of vain philosophy, for the light of the Gospel."[8] Or the assault upon, not merely the preachers, but also the gentry of England, whose opinions, Hobbes said, were derived "from the venime of heathen politicians, and from the incantation of deceiving spirits."[9] Or the cutting sarcasm in the brilliant half-truth that "the naturall seed of religion" lies "in these four things, opinion of ghosts, ignorance of second causes, devotion towards what men fear, and taking of things casuall for prognostiques."[10] Could any author more directly and unsparingly assail every one of the respectable groups of his time? Could any author who so assailed these groups hope to escape in his turn the vitriolic misrepresentations to which his own words, wrested from their context, were capable of being put? It is no wonder that contemporary opinion about Hobbes was controlled more by indignation than by analysis and that subsequent opinion should follow along the lines of the hostile tradition that treated Hobbes as a Hobbist. Hobbism may not have been Hobbes's position; but the fury that led to its formulation was excited by the relentless irony of his barbed shafts and would not soon die out.

In the second place, Hobbes was

known to his contemporaries, and even more generally to all subsequent generations, primarily by the *Leviathan*. The *Leviathan* is his greatest contribution to *belles lettres:* in suitability of style to content and in vigor of trenchant and dramatic utterance, it ranks among the finest classics of any literature. But intellectually and philosophically it is not as fine as the *De cive*. Eloquent as it is when taken paragraph by paragraph, quotable as it is when taken sentence by sentence, it lacks reasoned integrity and scholarly poise. It was written in the heat of controversy. It does not stay to achieve that balance of statement that is requisite to calm and fair consideration. Begun in a spirit of moderation, it passes in its middle chapters to passionate rhetoric, and closes in a burst of fury against the entrenched foes of Hobbes's program for securing a modicum of human happiness. The *De cive* indicates by its divisions the essential lines of its author's system of thought; the *Leviathan* indicates rather the intensity of his hates. Constructive teaching is in the *Leviathan* submerged beneath the insistent fire of destructive attacks. It is still, even in these days when Hobbes is little more than the historian's subject of discourse, an insolent and provocative book. It chooses to state its thesis in its most controversial context, namely, in emphasis upon its claim that all churches are entirely subordinate to the power of civil authorities. It even indicates by its famous frontispiece opposite the title-page that it would humble the churches by making them merely an arm of secular jurisdiction. It thus drives many readers into protest before it informs them of its due intent, and this is true today to only a somewhat less extreme degree than in Hobbes's lifetime. There is no change in essential doctrine from

---

[7] *Idem.*, p. 691. Cf. also *Behemoth*, p. 167, where the clergy of the land are put first in a list of "seducers of various sorts."

[8] *Leviathan*, pp. 540–41.

[9] *Idem.*, p. 713.

[10] *Idem.*, p. 98.

the *De cive* to the *Leviathan*. But the *De cive* ought to be more read: it ought especially to be read as introductory to the later work. The *De cive*, if less eloquent in its rhetoric, is very much more methodical and clear in its philosophical import.[11]

In the third place, Hobbes, as is typical of many another among the systematic philosophers, conceived an inclusive schematism which would enable him to place his political principles within the framework of a total theory of the universe. According to this schematism, the only ultimate facts are matter and motion; all else is but some special case of the basic realities of matter and motion. The schematism would, Hobbes thought, have three main parts, theory of body, theory of living body, theory of social body. So he wrote books with the titles *De corpore*, *De homine*, and *De cive*. The three books appeared in reverse order to their place in the allegedly controlling schematism, *De cive* in 1642, *De homine* in 1650, and *De corpore* only in 1655. Of course this matter of chronology is not conclusive; for Hobbes announced his general schematism in the "Preface to the Reader" of the *De cive*, and is known to have conceived it even earlier. Internal evidence, however, makes it highly probable that Hobbes did not deduce his political principles from his materialistic schematism, but derived them from observance of the actual actions of men and states and from his reading of others' (e.g., Thucydides's) similar observations.[12] The grandiose schematism served, Hobbes hoped, to give his political principles the added convincingness that would ensue if they fell easily into their place in a comprehensive body of scientific knowledge; for were they not the political analogue to the new science that Galileo and Robert Boyle and others were making popular among the enlightened minds of the century? If such were Hobbes's hopes, such were not his actual reception and fate. His fate has been that his views on mathematics and physics have been regarded as unimportant. And his reception has been that his political principles, taken as corollaries of his materialistic scheme, have drawn from their place in that schematism only increased opprobrium. Hobbes's political ideas gain, when taken as deductive consequences of his physics, only an added brutality which his passionate statement of his principles had already suggested. And thus the tendency to treat Hobbes as a Hobbist, which arose in his own day from the controversial fury of his utterances, has persisted to our own day from the alleged dependence of them upon a schematism that was an afterthought, or at most a reinforcing addendum.

The distinction which has been asserted between Hobbism and Hobbes's

---

[11] I find my estimate of the importance of the *De cive* expressed in Professor A. E. Taylor's recent article on Hobbes in the journal *Philosophy* for October, 1938 (Vol. 13, pp. 406–24). I cannot agree with most of what Professor Taylor says in analysis of Hobbes, as the conclusion of my paper will reveal to those who have read his article.

[12] The argument of Leo Strauss in his *The Political Philosophy of Hobbes*, pp. 8–29, seems to me conclusive on this point. Yet the point remains one, and probably must remain one, on which even the most competent critics will differ. For example, Professor George H. Sabine, in his *A History of Political Theory*, takes the opposite view to that of Strauss and that here maintained. Professor Sabine believes that the evidence Hobbes adduced for his political theory "was in no sense empirical" (p. 458), but was rather "the first whole-hearted attempt to treat political philosophy as part of a mechanistic body of scientific knowledge" (p. 460).

genuinely intended meaning can best be exemplified by considering Hobbes's views in connection with each of the four points of Hobbism already summed up above. But before taking up these four points in turn, some preliminary remarks are needed about Hobbes's primary concern and practical objective. The central theme of Hobbes is that the raw material of human nature is such that it can be transformed into a degree of civilized decency through only one practical means, namely, through the provision of a genuinely sovereign authority within society. This theme is dramatically and symbolically portrayed in the superb frontispiece of the first (privately printed) edition of the *De cive*.[13] In the upper part of the frontispiece is given a more or less conventional representation of the Last Judgment, with Christ in the center, the redeemed on his right, and the damned on his left. Probably no one will suppose that Hobbes wished to have his readers understand that his use of the traditional Christian iconography was indicative of his literal acceptance of the Christian mythology about the Last Judgment. Rather it doubtless means that whatever final and authoritative judgment can be passed upon human affairs will be in the light of the contrast between the two figures who stand respectively underneath the redeemed and the damned. Beneath the redeemed is the figure of *Imperium:* she is stately woman, strong and fair; in her right hand are the scales of justice and in her left a drawn sword to enforce her decisions; on her head is a royal crown; behind her opens out an idyllic countryside where men reap in security the crops they had sown, and a noble

city rests securely on a distant hill. Beneath the damned is the figure of *Libertas:* she is an old hag, sour in face, dejected in posture, mean in apparel; her weapons are primitive; behind her is visible a sordid vista, where assault and rape occur, and only a crude stockade offers a precarious refuge to the victims of open crimes. Hobbes seems to have wished to indicate that the antithesis of *imperium* and *libertas* is what the separation of redeemed and damned symbolizes. His intent is quite clearly to point out that we must choose irrevocably between *imperium* and her blessings on the one hand and on the other *libertas* and her attendant dangers. And if we translate Hobbes's Latin terms into current English, we cannot properly say that he is contrasting Empire and Liberty; for these words carry implications today that depart from his intent. We should rather say that he is contrasting Sovereignty and Anarchy. He is contrasting the possibilities of human life when firm rule establishes security for human enterprises with the doom that threatens all men alike when confusion and war are unrestrained.

The question that Hobbes raised in this frontispiece is an old one; the theme that he offers in its solution is a radical and uncompromising one. The question was how to guide the raw material of human nature into the ways of civilized life. This question confronts all serious and thoughtful moralists who do not entertain the notion that the human race began in a Garden of Eden and is subsequently guided by revelation and inspiration. Neither single men nor social groups originally possess such endowments as nobility, excellence, beauty, virtue. Men and societies come from barbarous backgrounds: they come with animal lusts, violent prejudices, wild passions, impulses which, uncontrolled, make for strife and discord. Whatever men come to exhibit in

---

[13] I have found only one copy of this edition (Paris, 1642) in the libraries I have been able to consult. Unfortunately, the frontispiece was so altered in the 1647 editions of *De cive* that its significance is utterly lost.

the way of worthy characters and ordered institutions and fine arts— whatever, in other words, they achieve in the way of civilization—is precarious in status and fragile in existence. This question of how to promote civilized ways in a precarious social world is a fundamental concern of many thinkers in all ages. But the solutions offered have varied considerably. Some thinkers have put their trust in educational schemes; others, in reliance upon natural reason; many, in supplications for divine grace; some, in appeal to law, whether *lex naturae* or Common Law;[14] a credulous few, in the automatic balance of a welter of independent forces into an eventual happy synthesis. Hobbes brushed such solutions aside. Education is prone to corruption; reason is weak; divine grace is a bone of contention and a cause of controversy; law is often flouted when it is good and enforced when it is bad; custom is subject to periodic breakdowns; and the idea that the anarchy of individual lusts will iron themselves out into universal harmony is a silly dream. The only technique of order is discipline, discipline imposed from above, discipline that comes from power that cannot be challenged by either passion or ignorance. Sovereignty is thus the *sine qua non,* not merely of peace, but also of all

excellence, both for individual men and for social groups.

In comparing Hobbes's position with Hobbism, one ought always to remember that all details in Hobbes's writings are subservient to a pressing home of this his central theme.[15] Hobbes knew quite well that he fell at times into overstatement, but he evidently valued overstatement as useful to shock his readers out of their complacency. For example he prefaced his first published work on political philosophy with the following very revealing words:[16]

Wherefore if ye shall meet with some things which have more of sharpness, and less of certainty than they ought to have, since they are not so much spoken for the maintenance of parties as the establishment of peace, and by one whose just grief for the present calamities of his country may very charitably be allowed some liberty; it is his only request to ye, Readers, ye will deign to receive them with an equal mind.

Of course Hobbes's contemporaries did not observe this warning and were shocked into violent opposition instead of into patient attention. But Hobbes's intent is none the less clear.

On the first point of Hobbism as outlined above, Hobbes was far from being a Hobbist. The picture which he gave of "man in the state of nature" is, to be sure, far from flattering. Every

---

14 Critics have sometimes maintained against Hobbes that he failed to appreciate how generally men, even savage men, normally act within the framework of accepted custom or "ancient law." Certainly Hobbes omits from his discussions any considerable attention to this important point. Yet the criticism seems unjustifiable. For Hobbes's problem was not to weigh the degree of social efficacy which reason, custom, education, and prudent self-interest might respectively have in the history of political developments. His problem was to carry social analysis to its last and final stages, and to inquire what technique of control was possible when reason was frustrated, custom broken down, education corrupt, and self-interest imprudent.

15 Perhaps one exception might be made to the general statement in the text above. The growing hatred of Hobbes for the Roman Catholic Church in particular and all clerical forces in general led him, especially in the second half of the *Leviathan,* to long diatribes that are not strictly germane to his central theme. But even here there is no inconsistency between the central theme and the diatribes.

16 *De cive,* "Preface to the Reader," pp. xxiii–xxiv. (Quotations from the *De cive* are given from Hobbes's own translation of the work into English under the title *Philosophical Rudiments Concerning Government and Society.*)

man in the state of nature is enemy to every other man; he exists in a constant state of war, friendless, neither giving nor receiving sympathy, beset by dire fears, driven by a lust for power after power that ceaseth only in death.[17] But what is seldom noticed by Hobbes's readers is that the picture of "man in the state of nature" is not meant by Hobbes as a complete picture of human nature.[18] The idea of man in a state of nature is, like the idea of a state of nature, not historical but analytical. Hobbes did not regard the state of nature as an early historical period from which men later departed; he rather regarded it as a permanent factor within society, with which therefore all sound social theory must be constantly occupied—that is, as an ever-present menace against which men must be on their guard in both theory and practice. So the idea of man in a state of nature is an emphasis on an aspect of all human nature, an aspect that may be at times competently controlled but can never possibly be eradicated. Man in the state of nature is what man would be in the absence of all the normal associations of social life. It is really a

---

[17] Cf. *Leviathan,* Chap. 13, or *De cive,* Chap. 1. The most famous and most quoted passage in Hobbes is probably that in Chap. 13 of the *Leviathan,* p. 113, which concludes with the magnificent phrase that the life of man in the state of nature is "solitary, poor, nasty, brutish, and short." Unfortunately, critics have usually quoted this eloquent passage before pausing to analyze the purport of the chapter, and have thus perverted the meaning of the passage by taking it out of its legitimate context.

[18] The annihilating attack on Hobbes's "egoism" and selfish view of man was carried through with great thoroughness by the eighteenth-century British moralists, notably Bishop Butler. This entire line of criticism, constructively effective as it may be, was far from just to Hobbes's intent and is probably a major reason for the persistence of the notion that Hobbes gave a wholly egoistic picture of man.

picture of man as he is perhaps never, certainly seldom, found, though as he is in part forever tending to become. The idea is analogous to the scientific description of a body as continuing in a state of rest or of uniform motion in a straight line unless influenced by outside forces.[19] Actually there is no such body, because all bodies are continually influenced by outside forces. Yet the concept of a body as it would be if left to itself is useful in enabling us to make more exact calculations of the various outside forces that influence any particular body we may wish to study. So the concept of man in the state of nature is useful in enabling us to estimate the importance of the social ties that qualify the conduct of any and every man we may wish to study. Hobbes was not so poor a psychologist as to overlook man's genuinely social interest. But the concept of man in a state of nature is important because it makes evident the gravity of the problem of securing a stable, and even moderately decent, society. Men do have lusts that do not easily submit to discipline; they are in continual need of being remade and controlled. The irruption of bestiality into human affairs is not to be glibly explained away as an unfortunate effect of bad social conditions: it is too often the very source of those bad conditions. We actually find men who are neither pure samples of man in the state of nature nor clear embodiments of perfect virtue. We have men of varying degrees of crudity and refinement; and our problem is to understand the causes of the crudity in order that we may then increase the amount of the refinement. A clear idea of man in the state of nature is a prerequisite to any formulation of an effec-

---

[19] This analogy I owe to the brilliant characterization of Hobbes by Professor F. J. E. Woodbridge in his *Hobbes: Selections* (New York, 1930), pp. xx–xxi.

tive technique of social control; for the difficulties of social life are not functions of man's better aspects but rather functions of his basest lusts. The world is turbulent because men lie and cheat and murder. Thus the idea of man in a state of nature, while not a psychologically adequate analysis of human nature (which it was not Hobbes's purpose to give), is just that analysis of man that is most relevant to the political problem with which Hobbes is grappling.

Hobbes explicitly states that men are not naturally evil.[20] But they are naturally passionate; and in the absence of means of security they are naturally the prey of haunting fears. Men's passions and fears may make them evil if conditions force them to aim primarily at defense against treachery and secret plotting. Men's passions will be qualified, however, and their fears may in large part be dissipated, if conditions surround them with ordered custom and lawful procedures. One cannot persuade water to run up hill, but one may pump it some distance upwards. So one cannot persuade men to be passionless; but one may so organize a state that men will gratify their passions within the definable bounds of civilized ways. In brief, excellence comes, not from romantic trust in human nature, but from realistic knowledge of what the forces are which require control. Hobbes really did for political theory at this point what scientific investigation of moving bodies was doing in the seventeenth century for mechanics. He did not discover any such existing person as a man in the state of nature, just as no one discovered a body that moved without influence from without. But he revealed what the nature is of that which we

have to control, as others revealed the nature of that which outside forces affect. Hobbes therefore differs entirely from Hobbism, since he is not giving a picture of human nature in its entirety, but is fashioning a concept that is explicitly relative to the central theme of securing a society in which incentives to violence are few and encouragements to virtue may abound.

The second point of Hobbism as outlined concerns the basis of morality. According to Hobbism, morality is the creature of the arbitrary fiat of princes and lacks all validity apart from sovereign control. It is easy to find the phrases in Hobbes, repeated from book to book and recurrently within each book, which led men to classify Hobbes as a Hobbist. For example, there are such passages as the following:

Nature hath given all to all. From whence we understand likewise, that in the state of nature profit is the measure of right.[21]

Irresistable might, in the state of nature, is right.[22]

Before the institution of sovereign power, *meum* and *tuum,* implied no propriety, but a community, where every man had right to every thing.[23]

Seeing then that a just action...is that which is not against the law; it is manifest that before there was a law, there could be no injustice; and therefore laws are in their nature antecedent to justice and injustice.[24]

Where there is no common-wealth, there is nothing unjust. So that the nature of justice, consisteth in keeping of valid covenants: but the validity of covenants begins not but with the constitution of a civill power sufficient to compel men to keep them.[25]

---

20 Cf. for example the passage in *De cive,* p. xvi: "But this, that men are evil by nature, follows not from this principle."

21 *De cive,* p. 11.
22 *De corpore politico,* p. 86.
23 *Ibid.,* p. 207.
24 *A dialogue of the common laws,* p. 29.
25 *Leviathan,* p. 131.

These and other such phrases in Hobbes's writings are challenging. But they do not properly mean Hobbism. Two things need to be said in order to establish a correct interpretation of Hobbes's meaning. First, Hobbes is speaking in legal, not in moral, terms. Justice and right are being defined in terms of enforcement of a conformity to law. It is then an analytical proposition and admits of no dispute that where there is no law there can be no question of justice and right at all. Justice then begins only where law exists. And in the absence of law, might makes right, not in the sense that might proves wisdom or virtue to be resident in him who exercises the might, but in the sense that might, when irresistible, is the beginning of a régime in which the distinction between ruler and subjects is emerging, in which, hence, the existence of law is beginning to manifest itself and conformity to law is incipiently involved.

Secondly, and almost by corollary from the preceding remark, it is also clear that Hobbes is insisting that any significant morality is social in character and presupposes the occurrence of regularized procedures.[26] Morality is not significantly present when men are considered in their separateness as atomic individuals; it is significantly present when men are considered in their interrelations in an integral situation in which questions of social adjustment arise. If one wants to press the point

and insist that some minor problems of morality might arise in connection with the conduct of a single man in isolation from his fellows, Hobbes would grant the point. Indeed, he did expressly grant the point in a revealing fashion. Some critic evidently pressed this very point against Hobbes when the first privately printed edition of the *De cive* appeared in Paris in 1642. For in the Elzevir editions of 1647 footnotes appeared in answer to this criticism. Hobbes did not consider the point important enough to make any alterations in the text proper, but he did quite explicitly answer the criticism. Even apart from social institutions, a man may well find some conduct wiser and other conduct more foolish, so that "the laws of nature," i.e., the principles of reason or morality, apply to him considered alone. In his own words:[27]

There are certain natural laws, whose exercise ceaseth not even in time of war itself. For I can not understand what drunkenness or cruelty, that is, revenge which respects not the future good, can advance towards peace, or the preservation of any man. Briefly, in the state of nature, what is just and unjust, is not to be esteemed by the actions but by the counsel and conscience of the actor.

There is here no reluctance to admit a minor kind of morality apart from social institutions; but Hobbes evidently considered such morality as of slight moment because hardly pertinent to any existing situation in which men actually live. All significant moral problems arise in the complex adjustments of men in civil society. So dominantly social is morality that one can practically equate the social and the moral; and Hobbes felt no compunction at such inconsequential over-statements as he, deeply stirred by his important

---

[26] Critics often accuse Hobbes of failing to distinguish between government and society, or between state and society. The same type of reply may well be made in behalf of Hobbes at this point that we made in connection with the point dealt with in footnote 14. The distinction between state and society is not relevant to Hobbes's problem. Hobbes was not writing a textbook that had to give proportionate amounts of space to all the twentieth-century problems of a systematic treatment of political science.

[27] Pp. 45–46.

theme, had made in the main text of his book.

The two comments just made in exposition of Hobbes's position are intimately involved in each other. It is precisely because justice and right have an important meaning as legal terms that morality can be viewed as a genuinely social affair. If men lived without a known law and a civil power to enforce it, they would have no guide except their individual judgments; consequently, opinions would clash, strife would ensue, and chaos would result. To recognize this is not to endorse ruthless, anti-social, and passionate acts: it is rather to indicate the indispensable rôle of law in the pursuit of the good life. If we supposed that individual men in their individuality are so many separate seats of moral prerogatives and moral obligations, then the nature of morality would be fixed antecedently to the enactment of laws, and the duty of law-makers would be merely to frame laws consistent with this fixed and antecedent standard. Such a philosophy would be an utterly superficial view of the intimate involvement of morals and law in each other. Not simply is it true that "where there is no judge, there is no end of controversy; and therefore the right of hostility remaineth,"[28] so that without law chaos would ensue and the possibility of genuinely moral achievement be annulled by universal strife. But also and more fundamentally it is true that the establishment of law creates a new situation in which sound reason or sound moral principle (two terms for the same idea) requires decisions such as would be ridiculous if there were no law or if there were a different law. Law does not by fiat create moral distinctions, and Hobbes never said that it did. But law does create significant moral situations, and Hobbes saw this more clearly than any prior political philosopher of modern times.

That Hobbes never regarded law as by fiat creating moral distinctions is so often overlooked that the point requires amplification. Hobbes repeatedly said that "the laws of nature," i.e., the principles of reason, "are the sum of moral philosophy."[29] But for good and sufficient reason the law of nature demands the establishment of civil society (which of course includes law) and the operation of men within the structure thus established. As Hobbes said:[30]

Theft, murder, adultery, and all injuries, are forbid by the law of nature; but what is to be called *theft*, what *murder*, what *adultery*, what *injury* in a citizen, this is not to be determined by the natural, but by civil law.

For the principles of reason are all of them abstract, and the acts of men are all of them concrete; and the passage from abstract principle to concrete act is possible only when considered in the social situation in which the concrete acts occur. Hobbes was far from the position of the Hobbist, who assumed that moral distinctions are artificial suppositions foisted upon men by arbitrary power. He was dramatically stressing the point that morality (aside from a few trivial exceptions) arises in social life as manifest in the existence of social instrumentalities or institutions to regularize human relations, of laws to define and modify these relations, and of authorities to enforce their observance. So far from being a denier of genuine moral distinctions, he was alert to specify exactly what the conditions of morality are, in what context moral problems occur, and by what means some kind of practical solution of moral difficulties may be reached.

This fact anticipates and involves the third point on which Hobbes again

---

28 *De corpore politico*, p. 106.

29 *De cive*, p. 49.   30 *Ibid.*, p. 85.

must be distinguished from what has been called Hobbism. According to Hobbism, the lawmaker, since he creates moral distinctions, is *ipso facto* always morally justified in all of his acts, and a bad lawmaker is thus a contradiction in terms. Again, as in the case of the former point, it is easy to find the phrases in Hobbes's works which led hasty readers or prejudiced critics to interpret him as asserting this kind of Hobbism. Consider, for example, the following:

Legitimate kings therefore make the things they command just, by commanding them, and those which they forbid unjust, by forbidding them.[31]

It belongs to the same chief power to make some common rules for all men, and to declare them publicly, by which every man may know what may be called his, what another's, what just, what unjust, what honest, what dishonest, what good, what evil.[32]

There are no authentical doctrines concerning right and wrong, good and evil, besides the constituted laws in each realm and government.[33]

Whatsoever he [i.e. the sovereign] doth, it can be no injury to any of his subjects; nor ought he to be by any of them accused of injustice.[34]

These, again, are strong words; for Hobbes wished to drive home his point with vigor and to leave no loopholes for those who deem their private opinions superior to law. In one phrase, namely, in making the sovereign competent to determine good and evil, Hobbes might properly be said to have gone beyond his intent. For good and evil are ethical terms, even in Hobbes's usage; and his inclusion of them in the second and third sentences just quoted indicates how easy it was for Hobbes to slip into

overstatement. With this exception granted, however, the passages quoted are thoroughly sound in the sense in which Hobbes used the terms. Hobbes was clearly employing the words in their strictly legal sense. His meaning is that the source of law can hardly be contrary to law (except in certain technical details, explanation of which he did not take time or burden himself to give). Civil society carries with it the obligation that it be respected as such. Even bad law is law, and even good citizens cannot properly flout bad law as if it were not really law at all. Since law establishes, in part at least, the situations which define our moral problems, it cannot, in any competent and incisive moral conduct, be treated as either inconsequential or irrelevant. He who ignores the legal purport of his acts *ipso facto* destroys the moral legitimacy of those acts.

Hobbes proceeded in all his writings to repudiate the Hobbist contention that "the king can do no wrong." He had much to say "concerning the duties of them who bear rule," to quote one of his chapter titles.[35] Though a sovereign cannot, by definition, act unjustly, he "may diverse ways transgress against the other laws of nature, as by cruelty, iniquity, contumely, and other like vices."[36] A sovereign, as much as any other man, is subject to the law of nature or the dictates of reason; indeed he has greater responsibilities to these laws than other men because he is by function the person who "hath taken into his hands any portion of mankind to improve."[37] "The duty of a sovereign," said Hobbes, "consisteth in the good government of the people."[38] Good government involves provisions to increase the number of the people, to

---

[31] *De cive*, p. 151.   [32] *Ibid.*, p. 77.
[33] *Ibid.*, p. xiii.   [34] *Leviathan*, p. 163.

[35] *De cive*, Chap. 13.   [36] *Ibid.*, p. 101.
[37] *De corpore politico*, p. 215.
[38] *Ibid.*, p. 213.

preserve peace at home, to provide defense against attack from without, and generally to safeguard "the commodity of living." And by commodity of living Hobbes meant such regulations as will give encouragement to trade, abundant opportunity for labor, ample supplies of food and other necessities, and such liberty of movement and of private affairs as is compatible with maintenance of public order.[39] Not simply may a sovereign violate his responsibilities to his people through indulgence in vice or through neglect, but even a conscientious sovereign may commit such vital mistakes of judgment that his rule involves serious moral disasters. All this Hobbes reiterated so frequently that at no point is he more obviously to be distinguished from Hobbism. One may agree or disagree with Hobbes on such points as whether increase of population is a good; but one can hardly identify him with Hobbism without ignoring long chapters of his political writings.

On the fourth point of Hobbism as outlined above, Hobbes may be said to have come fairly close to being a Hobbist. Yet even here a distinction must be carefully made. Hobbes did deny popular rights to the generality of men when they live in civil society. He granted to citizens only such rights as are conferred by law or as are not in any way dealt with by law. No rights inhere in citizens by virtue of their civil status which it would then be unjust to change or annul. Sovereign power must be, not only great, but also absolute. No check can be imposed on sovereign power; for then that person or group that imposes the check would be the sovereign, and the official on whom the check was imposed would be but a subordinate and dependent instrument.

"The sovereign power...implieth an universal impunity."[40]

Now it is only fair to grant to Hobbes all the validity that his words may have; and there are two things, in connection with this point, which ought to be said in his behalf and support. The first of these is that social problems often admit of no settlement by conference, by compromise, by mutual reconciliation of conflicting claims. In such cases, we have to choose between open strife and imposed settlement. Wise rulers, even prudent citizens, will seek to prevent the occasions of such embittered opposition. But rulers are not always wise nor citizens prudent; and even where wisdom and prudence are found in some men, intransigent discord may be found among others of their fellows. Often, perhaps usually, imposed settlement is in these cases preferable to continuance of strife. Well might Hobbes say: "The condition of man in this life shall never be without inconvenience."[41] One of the conditions of civil life is the habit of conforming to governmental decisions as binding, whether they are or seem to be wisely made or not. To deny that civil authority is entitled to determine policy even when it cannot give adequate demonstration of the soundness of that policy is to "make it impossible for any nation in the world to preserve themselves from civil war."[42]

The second thing to be said in Hobbes's support on the present point is that sovereign will inevitably lies behind law. Appeal from sovereign will to some law is virtually appeal from a present sovereign to a past sovereign; it is therefore virtually appeal to a fixed sovereignty and implies that past decisions of a former sovereign are prefer-

[39] Cf. *De corpore politico*, pp. 213–19; *De cive*, pp. 167–73.

[40] *Ibid.*, p. 205. Cf. *De cive*, pp. 78ff.
[41] *Leviathan*, p. 195.
[42] *Liberty, Necessity, and Chance*, p. 260.

able to decisions of a present sovereign who may take cognizance of changed conditions. Law is important, and no one saw this more clearly than Hobbes. But also no force in society is more human in its origin than law, more experimental in its course, more tentative in its objectives, more dependent in its meaning upon the authorities who use it. Veneration for law, whether common law, written or unwritten constitutions, or statutes of any kind, is a virtue which, pressed to an extreme, easily becomes a vice.[43] Hobbes is at this point in sharp contrast with Locke, and is, it may well be maintained, the wiser political philosopher. The most significant thing about Locke's *Treatise of Civil Government* is really not what it says but what it avoids saying. Locke's most notable trait is that he could compose an entire treatise on government without so much as mentioning the word or introducing the idea of sovereignty. He hoped that laws might govern instead of men; and "liberals" have generally followed his lead. Locke evidently thought that an original contract could so determine for all time the best conditions for all future society that further exercise of sovereign power could be eliminated from government in both theory and practice. He dared to hope that government might thus become merely the continued application of principles firmly established for every possible contingency. Hobbes had too much realism, too penetrating an insight, to entertain any such position. Even if he erred in overstatement, even

if he made too little distinction between a sovereign's passing caprice and his studied decision, he is at least sound in refusing to take law as a final court of appeal. The complexity of social needs demands some authority other than law and custom to impose settlement and enforce it with power. Legalism ties a society to precedent, to the level of past achievement. Hobbes's appeal to sovereignty, with all the faults of its tendency to harsh overstatement, is in theory a release from outworn precedent. It is in theory a turning to the ultimate source of law in the interest of securing beter and more pertinent law.

There yet remains something ruthless in Hobbes's words that sovereign power implies universal impunity, something ruthless enough to make it natural for hasty readers to misinterpret his words as a mere expression of Hobbism. Hobbes put the sovereign above not merely law but also criticism. Counsellors a sovereign may choose; but no one may offer unsolicited advice. Hobbes wrote that the subjects of a sovereign are not called upon to renounce their "natural reason,"[44] or to give "a submission of the intellectual faculty to the opinion of any other man."[45] But he insisted upon such full obedience of every subject to his sovereign in all respects that for practical purposes he refuses to admit the right of independence of thought.[46] We may well enjoy Hobbes's ironic comment that "in mat-

---

[43] Confusion over this contention of Hobbes is doubtless due today to the fact that people often identify a sovereign with a monarch, even with an absolute monarch. That Hobbes favored absolute monarchy leads them to identify his theory of sovereignty with his defense of monarchy. Hobbes, of course, recognized that the sovereign may be one man, several men, or all men. What he had to say about sovereignty is quite independent of his preference for monarchy.

[44] *Leviathan,* p. 359.   [45] *Ibid.,* p. 360.

[46] Hobbes could, in discussing the problem of the relation of individual conscience and civil rule, go so far as to say: "There can therefore be no contradiction between the laws of God, and the laws of a Christian commonwealth" (*ibid.,* p. 601). But even then he had to grant that there may be a contradiction between what a person took to be the laws of God and the laws of a commonwealth that was not Christian. And in such a case he went so far as to say that no man is even then entitled to resist his prince, but has no remedy except to "go to Christ by martyrdom" (*De cive,* p. 316).

ter of government, when nothing else is turned up, clubs are trumps."[47] We may even grant the truth behind the irony. But we can hardly brook the pretense of Hobbes that a sovereign is responsible to God alone, and hence beyond the legitimate right of human criticism. Hobbes seems too ready to let the sovereign use clubs as trumps on any and every occasion. The appeal to force may need to be implicit in any civil organization; but surely the exercise of force ought to be only a last resort when reason fails.

And exactly here is to be found that major fault that mars Hobbes's entire political philosophy. Hobbes's appeal to force was insistent because his distrust of human reason was excessive. Hobbes analyzed "the law of nature" with great skill and effect; but he did not believe that men are intelligent enough to follow the paths of reasonableness.[48] Hu-

man reason may be fallible, as Hobbes pointed out; but so is any constituted authority or any *de facto* sovereignty. Because reason does not control men sufficiently, Hobbes denied it any proper play in human affairs. Hobbes had no sense for the social value of what we may call "His Majesty's Opposition." He had no sense for either the privilege or the duty of a sovereign to provide for criticism, to permit the free exchange and discussion of ideas to assist in clarifying policy and defining purposes. Since such criticism must at times be suspended, Hobbes would deny it altogether. Hobbes, himself given to forceful reasoning, yet regarded reasoning as weak and ineffective. He treated reasoning as sedition against authority, criticism as treason, discussion of policy as a mark of the dissolution of commonwealth. Hence he supported the strange thesis that strong government is one in which reasoning and criticism and discussion are not visible. When he wrote that "toleration of a professed hatred of tyranny, is a toleration of hatred to commonwealth in general,"[49] he so defined tyranny as to safeguard his statement. But he none the less gives even a sympathetic reader the impression that he would prefer an arbitrary fiat from any sovereign at all to a reasoned debate on matters of public policy. Only on such a supposition can one explain how he came to say that "the commands of them that have the right to command, are not by their subjects to be censured, nor disputed,"[50] or that "the law is all the right reason we have, and...the infallible rule of moral goodness."[51] Hobbes, it might justifiably be said, took the same pessimistic view of human reason that was prevalent among the early Protestant reformers. But whereas the Protestant reformers looked to God's grace to re-

---

[47] *Dialogue of the Common Laws*, p. 122.

[48] On this point I find myself unable to accept the analysis which Professor Sabine gives of Hobbes's philosophy. Professor Sabine states with great precision that "the laws of nature really meant for Hobbes a set of rules according to which an ideally reasonable being would pursue his own advantage, if he were perfectly conscious of all the circumstances in which he was acting and was quite unswayed by momentary impulse and prejudice." But then he immediately adds that Hobbes "assumes that in the large men really do act in this way." Cf. *A History of Political Theory*, p. 461. The striking thing about Hobbes, it seems to me, is rather that, after elaborating what the laws of nature require, he assumes that men would not ordinarily act according to those laws and have to be coerced contrary to their inclinations. The motive power in men, Hobbes supposed, was, not the laws of nature or of reason, but "a general inclination of all mankind, a perpetual and restless desire of power after power, that ceaseth only in death" (*Leviathan*, pp. 85–86). Professor Sabine seems to withdraw from the position I criticize when, on pp. 464–67 of his book, he speaks of reason and desire as two opposed principles of human nature, and adds (p. 468) that, according to Hobbes, reason "is too weak to offset the avarice of men in the mass."

---

[49] *Leviathan*, p. 706.   [50] *Ibid.*, p. 194.

[51] *Liberty, Necessity, and Chance*, p. 194.

endow human reason with more power, Hobbes looked to sovereign power to make human reason unnecessary.

An estimate of Hobbes's significance for political theory is possible by comparing his position with that of Plato. Plato held that "the best thing is, not that the laws prevail, but that a man prevail who has wisdom and royal quality."[52] Here is the mean between Locke's appeal to law in fear of tyranny and Hobbes's appeal to tyranny in fear of anarchy. The historian may excuse Hobbes's fear of anarchy when he recalls the confusion of affairs in the seventeenth century and Hobbes's consequent desire to get something settled with finality. But the critic must weigh the merits of what the historian explains. And the critic may well see in Hobbes's distrust of reason a threat that Hobbes's political theory may easily slip into that very Hobbism from which Hobbes is carefully distinguished. For if reason be effete and insignificant, then the "natural man" tends to become the entire man, moral distinctions tend to become arbitrary fiats, and any sovereign may be justified in all his ways. Had the opponents of Hobbes focused their attack upon Hobbes's distrust of reason, they would have been able to make out a trenchant case. But of course

they, too, distrusted reason, preferring to appeal to some principle of legitimacy or some ecclesiastical authoritarianism or some hereditary institution. Hobbes was so eager to solve the problem of political life that he chose one possible means of settlement of issues, one possibly correct means for the settlement of some issues. But he erred in generalizing about this means which competent reason might ratify relatively to some specific situations, and so regarded it as superseding for all occasions that critical reason which alone could justify it to a degree and for certain selected situations. We may need at times to enforce old law, to insist on some *de facto* settlement of moot issues, to precipitate revolution at the risk of disorder. But we cannot make ourselves victims of established law or submissive subjects of absolute power of facile inciters to violence. The one thing that Hobbes needed to complete his theory and to make it a defensible interpretation of civil and social life was an understanding of the rôle that reason may play in human affairs. With that addition, his political philosophy would become a definitive theory; but without that it still remains a monumental contribution that deserves to be differentiated from Hobbism, even while it is recognized as that from which hasty readers would be repelled as from Hobbism.

---

[52] *The Statesman,* 294n.

LEO STRAUSS

On the Spirit of Hobbes'
Political Philosophy[*]

1

Thomas Hobbes regarded himself as the founder of political philosophy or political science. He knew of course that the great honor which he claimed for himself was awarded, by almost universal consent, to Socrates. Nor was he allowed to forget the notorious fact that the tradition which Socrates had originated was still powerful in his own age. But he was certain that traditional political philosophy "was rather a dream than science."

Present-day scholars are not impressed by Hobbes' claim. They note that he was deeply indebted to the tradition which he scorned. Some of them come close to suggesting that he was one of the last schoolmen. Lest we overlook the wood for the trees, we shall reduce for a while the significant results of present-day polymathy into the compass of one sentence. Hobbes was indebted to tradition for a single but momentous idea: he accepted on trust

* Reprinted from *La Revue Internationale de Philosophie*, IV, No. 14 (1950), 405–31, by permission of *La Revue* and the author. The footnotes found in the original have been abridged for this edition.

the view that political philosophy or political science is possible or necessary.

To understand Hobbes' astonishing claim means to pay proportionate attention to his emphatic rejection of the tradition on the one hand, and to his almost silent agreement with it on the other. For this purpose one must first identify the tradition. More precisely one must first see that tradition as Hobbes saw it and forget for a moment how it presents itself to the present-day historian. Hobbes mentions the following representatives of the tradition by name: Socrates, Plato, Aristotle, Cicero, Seneca, Tacitus, and Plutarch. He then tacitly identifies the tradition of political philosophy with a particular tradition. He identifies it with that tradition whose basic premises may be stated as follows: the noble and the just is fundamentally distinguished from the pleasant, and is by nature preferable to it; or, there is a natural right that is wholly independent of any human compact or convention; or, there is a best political order which is best because it is according to nature. He identifies traditional political philosophy with the quest for the best regime or for the simply just social order, and therefore with a pur-

163

suit that is political not merely because it deals with political matters but above all because it is animated by a political spirit. He identifies traditional political philosophy with that particular tradition that was public spirited or—to employ a term which is loose indeed but at present still easily intelligible—that was idealistic.

When speaking of earlier political philosophers, Hobbes does not mention that tradition whose most famous representatives might be thought to be "the sophists," Epicurus, and Carneades. The anti-idealistic tradition simply did not exist for him—as a tradition of political philosophy. For it was ignorant of the very idea of political philosophy as Hobbes understood it. It was indeed concerned with the nature of political things and especially of justice. It was also concerned with the question of the right life of the individual and therefore with the question of whether or how the individual could use civil society for his private, non-political purposes: for his ease or for his glory. But it was not political. It was not public-spirited. It did not preserve the orientation of statesmen while enlarging their views. It was not dedicated to the concern with the right order of society as with something that is choiceworthy for its own sake.

By tacitly identifying traditional political philosophy with the idealistic tradition, Hobbes expresses then his tacit agreement with the idealistic view of the function or the scope of political philosophy. Like Cicero before him he sides with Cato against Carneades. He presents his novel doctrine as the first truly scientific or philosophic treatment of natural law: he agrees with the Socratic tradition in holding the view that political philosophy is concerned with natural right. He intends to show "what is law, as Plato, Aristotle, Cicero, and divers others have done": he does not refer to Protagoras, Epicurus, or Carneades. He fears that his *Leviathan* might remind his readers of Plato's *Republic*: no one could dream of comparing the *Leviathan* to Lucretius' *De Rerum Natura*.

Hobbes rejects the idealistic tradition on the basis of a fundamental agreement with it. He means to do adequately what the Socratic tradition did in a wholly inadequate manner. He means to succeed where the Socratic tradition had failed. He traces the failure of the idealistic tradition to one fundamental mistake: traditional political philosophy assumed that man is by nature a political or social animal. By rejecting this assumption, Hobbes joins indeed the Epicurean tradition. He accepts its view that man is by nature or originally an a-political and even an a-social animal, as well as its premise that the good is fundamentally identical with the pleasant. But he uses that a-political view for a political purpose. He gives that a-political view a political meaning. He tries to instill the spirit of political idealism into the hedonistic tradition. He thus became the creator of political hedonism, a doctrine which has revolutionized human life everywhere on a scale never yet approached by any other teaching.

The epoch-making change which we are forced to trace to Hobbes was well understood by Edmund Burke. "Boldness formerly was not the character of atheists as such. They were even of a character nearly the reverse; they were formerly like the old Epicureans, rather an unenterprising race. But of late they are grown active, designing, turbulent, and seditious." Political atheism is a distinctly modern phenomenon. No premodern atheist doubted that social life requires belief in, and worship of, God or gods. If we do not permit ourselves to be deceived by ephemeral phenomena, we realize that political atheism and political hedonism belong together. They arose together in the same moment and in the same mind.

For in trying to understand Hobbes' political philosophy we must not lose sight of his natural philosophy. His natural philosophy is of the type classically represented by Democritean-Epicurean physics. Yet he regarded, not Epicurus or Democritus, but Plato as "the best of the ancient philosophers." What he learned from Plato's natural philosophy was not that the universe cannot be understood if it is not ruled by divine intelligence. Whatever may have been Hobbes' private thoughts, his natural philosophy is as atheistic as Epicurean physics. What he learned from Plato's natural philosophy was that mathematics is "the mother of all natural science." By being both mathematical and materialistic-mechanistic, Hobbes' natural philosophy is a combination of Platonic physics with Epicurean physics. From his point of view, pre-modern philosophy or science as a whole was "rather a dream than science" precisely because it did not think of that combination. His philosophy as a whole may be said to be the classic example of the typically modern combination of political idealism with a materialistic and atheistic view of the whole.

Positions that are originally incompatible with each other can be combined in two ways. The first way is the eclectic compromise which remains on the same plane as the original positions. The other way is the synthesis which becomes possible through the transition of thought from the plane of the original positions to an entirely different plane. The combination effected by Hobbes is a synthesis. He may or may not have been aware that he was in fact combining two opposed traditions. He was fully aware that his thought presupposed a radical break with all traditional thought, or the abandonment of the plane on which "Platonism" and "Epicureanism" had carried on their secular struggle.

Hobbes as well as his most illustrious contemporaries were overwhelmed or elated by a sense of the complete failure of traditional philosophy. A glance at present and past controversies sufficed to convince them that philosophy, or the quest for wisdom, had not succeeded in transforming itself into wisdom. This overdue transformation was now to be effected. To succeed where tradition had failed, one has to start with reflections on the conditions which have to be fulfilled if wisdom is to become actual: one has to start with reflections on the right method. The purpose of these reflections was to guarantee the actualization of wisdom.

The failure of traditional philosophy showed itself most clearly in the fact that dogmatic philosophy had always been accompanied, as by its shadow, by skeptical philosophy. Dogmatism had never yet succeeded in overcoming skepticism once and for all. To guarantee the actualization of wisdom means to eradicate skepticism by doing justice to the truth embodied in skepticism. For this purpose, one must first give free rein to the most extreme skepticism: what survives the onslaught of the most extreme skepticism is the absolutely safe basis of wisdom. The actualization of wisdom is identical with the erection of an absolutely dependable dogmatic edifice on the foundation of extreme skepticism.

The experiment with extreme skepticism was then guided by the anticipation of a new type of dogmatism. Of all known scientific pursuits, mathematics alone had been successful. The new dogmatic philosophy must therefore be constructed on the pattern of mathematics. The mere fact that the only certain knowledge which was available is not concerned with ends, but "consists in comparing figures and motions only" created a prejudice against any teleological view, or a prejudice in favor of a mechanistic view. It is perhaps more accurate to say that it strengthened a prejudice already in existence. For it is probable that what was foremost in Hobbes' mind was the vision, not of a new type of philosophy or science, but of a universe that is nothing but bodies and their aimless motions. The failure of the predominant philosophic tradition could be traced directly to the difficulty with which every teleological physics is beset, and the suspicion arose quite naturally that, due to social pressures of various kinds the mechanistic view had never been given a fair chance to show its virtues. But precisely if Hobbes was primarily interested in a mechanistic view, he was inevitably led, as matters stood, to the notion of a dogmatic philosophy based on extreme skepticism. For he had learned from Plato or Aristotle that if the universe has the character ascribed to it by Democritean-Epicurean physics, it excludes the possibility of any physics, of any science; or, in other words, that consistent materialism necessarily culminates in skepticism. "Scientific materialism" could not become possible if one did not first succeed in guaranteeing the possibility of science against the skepticism engendered by materialism. Only the anticipatory revolt against a materialistically understood universe could make possible a science of such a universe. One had to discover or to invent an island that would be exempt from the flux of mechanical causation. Hobbes had to consider the possibility of a natural island. An incorporeal mind was out of the question. On the other hand, what he had learned from Plato and Aristotle made him realize somehow that the corporeal mind composed of

very smooth and round particles with which Epicurus remained satisfied, was an inadequate solution. He was forced to wonder whether the universe did not leave room for an artificial island, for an island to be created by science.

The solution was suggested by the facts that mathematics, the model of the new philosophy, was itself exposed to skeptical attack and proved capable of resisting it by undergoing a specific transformation or interpretation. To "avoid the cavils of the skeptics" at "that so much renowned evidence of geometry...I thought it necessary in my definitions to express those motions by which lines, superficies, solids, and figures, were drawn and described." Generally stated, we have absolutely certain or scientific knowledge only of those subjects, of which we are the causes, or whose construction is in our power or depends on our arbitrary will. The construction would not be fully in our power if there were a single step of the construction that is not fully exposed to our supervision. The construction must be conscious construction: it is impossible to know a scientific truth without knowing at the same time that we have made it. The construction would not be fully in our power if it made use of any matter, i.e. of anything that is not itself our construct. The world of our constructs is wholly un-enigmatic because we are its sole cause and hence we have perfect knowledge of its cause. The cause of the world of our constructs does not have a further cause, a cause that is not, or not fully, within our power: the world of our constructs has an absolute beginning or is a creation in the strict sense. The world of our constructs is therefore the desired island that is exempt from the flux of blind and aimless causation. The discovery or invention of that island seemed to guarantee the possibility of a materialistic and mechanistic philosophy or science, without forcing one to assume a soul or mind that is irreducible to moved matter. That discovery or invention permitted eventually an attitude of neutrality or indifference towards the secular conflict between materialism and spiritualism. Hobbes had the earnest desire to be a "metaphysical" materialist. But he was forced to rest satisfied with a "methodical" materialism.

We understand only what we make. Since we do not make the natural beings, they are strictly speaking unintelligible. According to Hobbes, this fact is perfectly compatible with the possibility of natural science. But it leads to the consequence that natural science is and will always remain fundamentally hypothetical. Yet this is all we need in order to make ourselves masters and owners of nature. Still, however much man may succeed in his conquest of nature, he will never be able to understand nature. The universe will always remain wholly enigmatic. It is this fact that ultimately accounts for the persistence of skepticism and justifies skepticism to a certain extent. Skepticism is the inevitable outcome of the unintelligible character of the universe or of the unfounded belief in its intelligibility. In other words, since natural things are as such mysterious, the knowledge or certainty engendered by nature necessarily lacks evidence. Knowledge based on the natural working of the human mind is necessarily exposed to doubt. For this reason Hobbes parts company with pre-modern nominalism in particular. Pre-modern nominalism had faith in the natural working of the human mind. It showed this faith especially by teaching that *natura occulte operatur in universalibus,* or that the "anticipations" by virtue of which we take our bearings in ordinary life and in science, are products of nature. For Hobbes, the natural origin of the universals or of the anticipations was a compelling reason for abandoning them in favor of artificial "intellectual tools." There is no natural harmony between the human mind and the universe.

Man can guarantee the actualization of wisdom since wisdom is identical with free construction. But wisdom can not be free construction if the universe is intelligible. Man can guarantee the actualization of wisdom, not in spite of, but because of the fact that the universe is unintelligible. Man can be sovereign only because there is no cosmic support for his humanity. He can be sovereign only because he is absolutely a stranger in the universe. He can be sovereign only because he is forced to be sovereign. Since the universe is unintelligible, and since control of nature does not require understanding of nature, there are no knowable limits to his conquest of nature. He has nothing to lose but his chains and, for all he knows, he may have everything to gain. Still, what is certain is that man's natural state is misery; the vision of the City of Man to be erected on the ruins of the City of God is an unsupported hope.

It is hard for us to understand how Hobbes could be so hopeful where there was so much cause for despair. Somehow the experience as well as the legitimate anticipation of unheard of progress within the sphere which is subject to human control, must have made him insensitive to "the eternal silence of those infinite spaces" or to the crackings of the *moenia mundi.* In fairness to him one must add that the long series of disappointments which subsequent generations experienced have not yet succeeded in extinguishing the hope which he, together with his most illustrious contemporaries, has kindled. Still less have they succeeded in breaking down the walls which he erected as if in order to limit his vision. The conscious constructs have indeed been replaced by the unplanned workings of "History." But "History" limits our vision in exactly the same way in which the conscious constructs limited the vision of Hobbes: "History" too fulfills the function of enhancing the status of man and of his "world" by making him oblivious of the whole or of eternity. In its final stage, the typically modern limitation expresses itself in the suggestion that the highest principle which as such has no relation to any possible cause or causes of the whole, is the mysterious ground of "History" and, being wedded to man and to man alone, is so far from being eternal that it is coeval with human history.

To return to Hobbes, his notion of philosophy or science has its root in the conviction that a teleological cosmology is impossible and in the feeling that a mechanistic cosmology fails to satisfy the requirement of intelligibility. His solution is that the end or the ends without which no phenomenon can be understood, need not be inherent in the phenomena: the end inherent in the concern with knowledge suffices. Knowledge as the end supplies the indispensable teleological principle. Not the new mechanistic cosmology, but what later on came to be called epistemology becomes the substitute for teleological cosmology. But knowledge cannot remain the end if the whole is simply unintelligible: *Scientia propter potentiam.* All intelligibility or all meaning has its ultimate root in human needs. The end, or the most compelling end posited by human desire is the highest principle, the organizing principle. But if the human good becomes the highest principle, political science, or social science, becomes the most important kind of knowledge, as Aristotle had predicted. In the words of Hobbes, *Dignissima certe scientiarum haec ipsa est, quae ad Principes pertinet, hominesque in regendo genere humano occu-*

patos. One cannot leave it then at saying that Hobbes agrees with the idealistic tradition in regard to the function and scope of political philosophy. His expectation from political philosophy is incomparably greater than the expectation of the classics: no Scipionic dream illumined by the true vision of the whole reminds his readers of the ultimate futility of all that men can do. Of political philosophy thus understood, Hobbes is indeed the founder.

2

It was Machiavelli, that greater Columbus, who had discovered the continent on which Hobbes could erect his structure. When trying to understand the thought of Machiavelli, one does well to remember the saying that Marlowe was inspired to ascribe to him: "I... hold there is no sin but ignorance." This is almost a definition of the philosopher. Besides, no one of consequence ever doubted that Machiavelli's study of political matters was public spirited. Being a public spirited philosopher, he continued the tradition of political idealism. But he combined the idealistic view of the intrinsic nobility of statesmanship with an anti-idealistic view, if not of the whole, at any rate of the origins of mankind, or of civil society.

Machiavelli's admiration for the political practice of classical antiquity and especially of republican Rome is only the reverse side of his rejection of classical political philosophy. He rejected classical political philosophy, and therewith the whole tradition of political philosophy in the full sense of the term, as useless: Classical political philosophy had taken its bearings by how man ought to live; the correct way of answering the question of the right order of society consists in taking one's bearings by how men actually live. As one would expect, Machiavelli understood the intention of classical political philosophy. It had been the quest for the political order which agrees with the requirements of virtue, or human excellence, or the perfection of human nature. It had demanded that the best political order, in order to be a reasonable goal, must be possible, but it had not regarded its actualization as necessary or even as probable: its actualization was thought to depend on chance. The best or simply just political order is the object of a wish or prayer; it is of its essence to exist in speech as distinguished from deed. Since classical political philosophy had taken its bearings by the perfection of human nature, it necessarily and consciously culminated in the elaboration of a utopia. Machiavelli's "realistic" revolt against tradition led to the substitution of patriotism or merely political virtue for human excellence or, more particularly, for moral virtue and the contemplative life. It entailed a deliberate lowering of the ultimate goal. The goal was lowered in order to increase the probability of its attainment. Just as Hobbes later on abandoned the original meaning of wisdom in order to guarantee the actualization of wisdom, Machiavelli abandoned the original meaning of the good society or of the good life in order to guarantee the actualization of the good society or of the good life. What would happen to those natural inclinations of man or of the human soul whose demands simply transcend the lowered goal was of no concern to Machiavelli. He disregarded those inclinations. He limited his horizon in order to get results. And as for the power of chance, Fortuna appeared to him in the shape of a woman who can be forced by the right kind of men: chance can be conquered.

Machiavelli justified his demand for a "realistic" political philosophy by reflections on the foundations of civil society, and this means ultimately by reflections on the whole within which man lives. There is no superhuman, no natural support for justice. All human things fluctuate too much to permit their subjection to stable principles of justice. Necessity rather than moral purpose determines what is in each case the sensible course of action. Therefore, civil society cannot even aspire to being simply just. All legitimacy has its root in illegitimacy; all social or moral orders have been established with the help of morally questionable means; civil society has its root not in justice but in injustice. The founder of the most renowned of all commonwealths was a fratricide. Justice in any sense is possible only after a social order has been established; justice in any sense is possible only within a man-made order. Yet the founding of civil society, the supreme case in politics, is imitated, within civil society, in all extreme cases. Machiavelli takes his bearings not so much by how men live, as by the extreme case. He believes that the extreme case is more revealing of the roots of civil society and therefore of its true character than is the normal case. The root or the efficient cause takes the place of the end or of the purpose.

It was the difficulty implied in the substitution of merely political virtue for moral virtue, or the difficulty implied in Machiavelli's admiration for the lupine policies of republican Rome, that induced Hobbes to attempt the restoration of the moral principles of politics, i.e. of natural law, on the plane of Machiavelli's "realism." In making this attempt he was mindful of the fact that man can not guarantee the actualization of the right social order if he does not have certain or exact or scientific knowledge of both the right social order and the conditions of its actualization. He attempted therefore in the first place a rigorous deduction of the natural or moral law. To "avoid the cavils of the skeptics," natural law had to be made independent of any natural "anticipations" and therefore of the *consensus gentium*. The predominant tradition had defined natural law with a view to the end or the perfection of man as a rational and social animal. What Hobbes attempted to do on the basis of Machiavelli's fundamental objection to the utopian teaching of the tradition, although in opposition to Machiavelli's own solution, was to maintain the idea of natural law but to divorce it from the idea of man's perfection: only if natural law can be deduced from how men actually live, from the most powerful force that actually determines all men, or most men most of the time, can it be effectual or of practical value. The complete basis of natural law must be sought, not in the end of man, but in his beginnings, in the *prima naturae* or rather in the *primum naturae*. What is most powerful in most men most of the time is not reason but passion. Natural law will not be effectual if its principles are distrusted by passion or are not agreeable to passion. Natural law must be deduced from the most powerful of all passions.

But the most powerful of all passions will be a natural fact, and we are not to assume that there is a natural support for justice or for what is human in man. Or is there a passion, or an object of passion, which is in a sense antinatural, which marks the point of indifference between the natural and the non-natural, which is, as it were, the *status evanescenti* of nature and therefore a possible origin for the conquest of nature, or for freedom? The most powerful of all passions is the fear of death, and more particularly, the fear of violent death at the hands of others: not nature, but "that terrible enemy of nature, death," yet death insofar as man can do something about it, i.e. death

insofar as it can be avoided or avenged, supplies the ultimate guidance. Death takes the place of the *telos*. Or, to preserve the ambiguity of Hobbes' thought, let us say that the fear of violent death expresses most forcefully the most powerful and the most fundamental of all natural desires, the initial desire, the desire for self-preservation.

If then, natural law must be deduced from the desire for self-preservation, if, in other words, the desire for self-preservation is the sole root of all justice and morality, the fundamental moral fact is not a duty but a right: all duties are derivative from the fundamental and inalienable right of self-preservation. There are then no absolute or unconditional duties: duties are binding only to the extent to which their performance does not endanger our self-preservation. Only the right of self-preservation is unconditional or absolute. By nature, there exists only a perfect right and no perfect duty. Since the fundamental and absolute moral fact is a right and not a duty, the function as well as the limits of civil society must be defined in terms of man's natural right and not in terms of his natural duty. The state has the function not of producing or promoting a virtuous life, but of safeguarding the natural right of each. And the power of the state finds its absolute limit in that natural right and in no other moral fact. If we may call liberalism that political doctrine which regards as the fundamental political fact the rights, as distinguished from the duties, of man, and which identifies the function of the state with the protection or the safeguarding of those rights, we must say that the founder of liberalism was Hobbes.

By transplanting natural law on the plane of Machiavelli, Hobbes certainly originated an entirely new type of political doctrine. The pre-modern natural law doctrines taught the duties of man; if they paid any attention at all to rights, they conceived of them as essentially derivative from his duties. As has frequently been observed, in the course of the seventeenth and eighteenth centuries a much greater emphasis was put on rights than ever had been done before. One may speak of a shift of emphasis from natural duties to natural rights. But quantitative changes of this character become intelligible only when they are seen against the background of a qualitative and fundamental change, not to say that such quantitative changes always become possible only by virtue of a qualitative and fundamental change. The fundamental change from an orientation by natural duties to an orientation by natural rights finds its clearest and most telling expression in the teaching of Hobbes, who squarely made an unconditional natural right the basis of all natural duties, the duties being therefore only conditional. He is the classic and the founder of the specifically modern natural law doctrine. The profound change under consideration can be traced directly to Hobbes' concern with a human guarantee for the actualization of the right social order or to his "realistic" intention. The actualization of a social order that is defined in terms of man's duties is necessarily uncertain and even improbable; such an order may well appear to be utopian. Quite different is the case of a social order that is defined in terms of the rights of man. For the rights in question express, and are meant to express, something that everyone actually desires anyway; they hallow everyone's self-interest as everyone sees it, or can easily be brought to see it. Men can more safely be depended upon to fight for their rights than to fulfill their duties. In the words of Burke, "The catechism of the rights of man is easily learned; the con-

clusions are in the passions." With regard to Hobbes' classic formulation, we add that the premises already are in the passions. What is required to make modern natural right effective is enlightenment or propaganda rather than moral appeal. From this we may understand the frequently observed fact that during the modern period, natural law became much more of a revolutionary force than it had been in the past. This fact is a direct consequence of the fundamental change in the character of the natural law doctrine itself.

The tradition which Hobbes opposed had assumed that man cannot reach the perfection of his nature but in and through civil society, and therefore that civil society is prior to the individual. It was this assumption which led to the view that the primary moral fact is duty and not rights. One could not assert the primacy of natural rights without asserting that the individual is in every respect prior to civil society or, more precisely, that there is a state of nature. According to Rousseau "the philosophers who have examined the foundations of civil society have all of them felt the necessity to go back to the state of nature." It is true that the quest for the right social order is inseparable from reflection on the origins of civil society or on the pre-political life of man. But the identification of the pre-political life of man with "the state of nature" is a particular view, a view by no means held by "all" political philosophers. The state of nature became an essential topic of political philosophy only with Hobbes who still almost apologized for employing that term. It is only since Hobbes that the philosophic doctrine of natural law has been essentially a doctrine of the state of nature. Prior to him the term "state of nature" was at home in Christian theology rather than in political philosophy. The state of nature was distinguished especially from the state of grace, and it was subdivided into the state of pure nature and the state of fallen nature. Hobbes dropped the subdivision, and replaced the state of grace by the state of civil society. He thus denied if not the fact, at any rate the importance of the Fall, and accordingly asserted that what is needed for remedying the deficiencies, or the "inconveniences" of the state of nature is, not divine grace, but the right kind of human government. This anti-theological implication of "the state of nature" can only with difficulty be separated from its intra-philosophic meaning, which is, to make intelligible the primacy of rights as distinguished from duties: the state of nature is originally characterized by the fact that in it there are perfect rights but no perfect duties.

The attempt to deduce the natural law or the moral law from the natural right of self-preservation or from the inescapable power of the fear of violent death led to very far-reaching modifications of the content of the moral law. The modification amounted in the first place to a considerable simplification. Sixteenth and seventeenth century thought in general tended toward a simplification of moral doctrine. To say the least, that tendency easily lent itself to absorption in the broader concern with the guarantee for the actualization of the right social order. One tried to replace the "unsystematic" multiplicity of irreducible virtues by a single virtue, or by a single basic virtue from which all other virtues could be deduced. There existed two well-paved ways in which this reduction could be achieved. In the moral teaching of Aristotle, "whose opinions are at this day, and in these parts of greater authority than any other human writings" (Hobbes), there occur two virtues which comprise all other virtues or, as we may say, two "general" virtues: magnanimity, which comprises all other virtues insofar as they contribute to the excellence of the individual, and justice, which comprises all other virtues insofar as they contribute to man's serving others. Accordingly, one could simplify moral philosophy by reducing morality either to magnanimity or else to justice. The first was done by Descartes, the second by Hobbes. Hobbes' choice had the particular advantage that it permitted of a further simplification of moral doctrine: the unqualified identification of the doctrine of virtues with the doctrine of the moral or natural law. The moral law, in its turn, was to be greatly simplified by being deduced from the natural right of self-preservation. Self-preservation requires peace. The moral law became therefore the sum of rules which have to be obeyed if there is to be peace. Just as Machiavelli reduced virtue to the political virtue of patriotism, Hobbes reduced virtue to the social virtue of peaceableness. Those forms of human excellence which have no direct or unambiguous relation to peaceableness—courage, temperance, magnanimity, liberality, to say nothing of wisdom—cease to be virtues in the strict sense. Justice (in conjunction with equity and charity) does remain a virtue, but its meaning undergoes a radical change. If the only unconditional moral fact is the natural right of each to his self-preservation, and therefore all obligations to others arise from contract, justice becomes identical with the habit of fulfilling one's contracts. Justice no longer consists in complying with standards that are independent of human will. All material principles of justice—the rules of commutative and distributive justice or the Second Table of the Decalogue—cease to have intrinsic validity. All material obligations arise from the agreement of the contractors, and therefore in practice from the will of the sovereign, which is the general will. For the contract that makes possible all other contracts is the social contract or the contract of subjection to the sovereign.

If virtue is identified with peaceableness, vice will become identical with that habit or that passion which is *per se* incompatible with peace because it essentially and, as it were, of set purpose issues in offending others; vice becomes identical for all practical purposes with pride or vanity or *amour-propre*. In other words, if virtue is reduced to social virtue or to benevolence or kindness or "the liberal virtues," "the severe virtues" of self-restraint will lose their standing. Here again, we must have recourse to Burke's analysis of the spirit of the French Revolution; for Burke's polemical overstatements were and are indispensable for tearing away the disguises, both intentional and unintentional, in which "the new morality" introduced itself. "...the Parisian philosophers...explode or render odious or contemptible, that class of virtues which restrain the appetite... In the place of all this, they substitute a virtue which they call humanity or benevolence." This substitution is the core of what we have called political hedonism.

To establish the meaning of political hedonism in somewhat more precise terms, we must contrast Hobbes' teaching with the non-political hedonism of Epicurus. The points in which Hobbes could agree with Epicurus, were these: the good is fundamentally identical with the pleasant; virtue is therefore not choiceworthy for its own sake but only with a view to the attainment of pleasure or the avoidance of pain; the desire for honor and glory is utterly vain, i.e. sensual pleasures are as such preferable to honor or glory. Hobbes had to oppose Epicurus in two crucial points in order to make possible political hedonism. In the first place he had to reject Epicurus' implicit denial of a state of

nature in the strict sense, i.e. of a pre-political condition of life in which man enjoys natural rights; for Hobbes agreed with the idealistic tradition in thinking that the claim of civil society stands or falls with the existence of natural justice. Besides, he could not accept the implication of Epicurus' distinction between natural desires which are necessary and natural desires which are not necessary; for that distinction implied that happiness requires an "ascetic" style of life. Epicurus' high demands on self-restraint were bound to be utopian as far as most men are concerned; they had therefore to be discarded by a "realistic" political teaching. The "realistic" approach to politics forced Hobbes to lift all restrictions on the striving for unnecessary sensual pleasures or, more precisely, for the *commoda hujus vitae*, with the exception of those restrictions that are required for the sake of peace. Since, as Epicurus said, "Nature has made (only) the necessary things easy to supply," the emancipation of the desire for comfort required that science be put into the service of the satisfaction of that desire. It required above all that the function of civil society be radically redefined: "the good life" for the sake of which men enter civil society, is no longer the life of human excellence but "commodious living" as the reward of hard work. And the sacred duty of the rulers is no longer "to make the citizens good and doers of noble things," but to "study, as much as by laws can be effected, to furnish the citizens abundantly with all good things...which are conducive to delectation."

It is not necessary for our purpose to follow Hobbes' thought on its way from the natural right of everyone, or from the state of nature, to the establishment of civil society. This part of his doctrine is not meant to be more than the strict consequence from his premises. It culminates in the doctrine of sovereignty, of which he is generally recognized to be the classic exponent. The doctrine of sovereignty is a legal doctrine. Its gist is not that it is expedient to assign plenitude of power to the ruling authority, but that that plenitude belongs to the ruling authority as of right. The rights of sovereignty are assigned to the supreme power on the basis, not of positive law or of general custom, but of natural law. The doctrine of sovereignty formulates natural public law. Natural public law—*jus publicum universale seu naturale*—is a new discipline that emerged in the seventeenth century. It emerged in consequence of that radical change of orientation which we are trying to understand. Natural public law represents one of the two characteristically modern forms of political philosophy, the other form being "politics" in the sense of Machiavellian "reason of state." Both are fundamentally distinguished from classical political philosophy. In spite of their opposition to each other, they are motivated by fundamentally the same spirit. Their origin is the concern with a right or sound order of society whose actualization is probable, if not certain, or does not depend on chance. Accordingly, they deliberately lower the goal of politics; they are no longer concerned with having a clear view of the highest political possibility with regard to which all actual political orders can be judged in a responsible manner. The "reason of state" school replaced "the best regime" by "efficient government." The "natural public law" school replaced "the best regime" by "legitimate government."

Classical political philosophy had recognized the difference between the best regime and legitimate regimes: the best regime is possible only under very favorable conditions and it is therefore legitimate only under those conditions; under more or less unfavorable conditions, only more or less imperfect regimes are possible and therefore legitimate. In contradistinction to the best regime, legitimate regimes are possible and morally necessary at all times and in all places. Classical political philosophy admitted then a variety of types of legitimate regimes: what type of regime is legitimate in given circumstances depends on the circumstances. Natural public law, on the other hand, is concerned with that right social order whose actualization is possible under all circumstances. It therefore tries to delineate that social order that can claim to be legitimate or just in all cases, regardless of the circumstances. Natural public law, we may say, replaces the idea of the best regime, which does not supply, and is not meant to supply, an answer to the question of what is the just order here and now, by the idea of the just social order which answers the basic practical question once and for all, i.e. regardless of place and time. Natural public law intends to give such a universally valid solution to the political problem as is meant to be universally applicable in practice. In other words, whereas, according to the classics, political theory proper is essentially in need of being supplemented by the practical wisdom of the statesman on the spot, the new type of political theory solves, as such, the crucial practical problem: the problem of what order is just here and now. In the decisive respect, then, there is no longer any need for statesmanship as distinguished from political theory. We may call this type of thinking doctrinairism, and we shall say that doctrinairism made its first appearance within political philosophy—for lawyers are altogether in a class by themselves—in the seventeenth century. At that time the sensible flexibility of classical political philosophy gave way to fanatical rigidity.

The political philosopher became more and more undistinguishable from the partisan. The historical thought of the nineteenth century tried to recover for statesmanship that latitude which natural public law had so severely restricted. But since that historical thought was absolutely under the spell of modern "realism," it succeeded in destroying natural public law only by destroying in the process all moral principles of politics.

As regards Hobbes' teaching on sovereignty in particular, its doctrinaire character is shown most clearly by the denials which it implies. It implies the denial of the possibility of distinguishing between good and bad regimes (kingship and tyranny, aristocracy and oligarchy, democracy and ochlochracy) as well as of the possibility of mixed regimes and of "rule of law." Since these denials are at variance with observed facts, the doctrine of sovereignty amounts in practice to a denial not of the existence, but of the legitimacy of the possibilities mentioned: Hobbes' doctrine of sovereignty ascribes to the sovereign prince or to the sovereign people an unqualified right to disregard all legal and constitutional limitations according to their pleasure, and it imposes even on sensible men a natural-law prohibition against censuring the sovereign and his actions. But it would be wrong to overlook the fact that the basic deficiency of the doctrine of sovereignty is shared, if to different degrees, by all other forms of natural public law doctrines as well. We merely have to remind ourselves of the practical meaning of the doctrine that the only legitimate regime is democracy.

The classics had conceived of regimes (*politeiai*), not so much in terms of institutions, as in terms of the aims actually pursued by the community or its authoritative part. Accordingly, they regarded the best regime as that regime whose aim is virtue, and they held that the right kind of institutions are indeed indispensable for establishing and securing the rule of the virtuous, but only of secondary importance in comparison with "education," i.e. the formation of character. From the point of view of natural public law on the other hand, what is needed in order to establish the right social order is not so much the formation of character as the devising of the right kind of institutions. As Kant put it in rejecting the view that the establishment of the right social order requires a nation of angels: "hard as it may sound, the problem of establishing the state [i.e. the just social order] is soluble even for a nation of devils, provided they have sense," i.e. provided they are guided by enlightened selfishness; the fundamental political problem is simply one of "a good organization of the state, of which man is indeed capable." In the words of Hobbes, "...when (commonwealths) come to be dissolved, not by external violence, but intestine disorder, the fault is not in men, as they are the matter, but as they are the makers and orderers of them." Man as the maker of civil society can solve once and for all the problem inherent in man as the matter of civil society. Man can guarantee the actualization of the right social order because he is able to conquer human nature by understanding and manipulating the mechanism of the passions.

There is a term that expresses in the most condensed form the result of the change which Hobbes has effected. That term is Power. It is in Hobbes' political doctrine that power becomes for the first time *eo nomine* a central theme. Considering the fact that, according to Hobbes, science as such exists for the sake of power, one may call Hobbes' whole philosophy the first philosophy of power. "Power" is an ambiguous term. It stands for *potentia* on the one hand,

and for *potestas* (or *jus* or *dominium*) on the other. It means both "physical" power and "legal" power. The ambiguity is essential: only if *potentia* and *potestas* essentially belong together, can there be a guarantee for the actualization of the right social order. The State is as such both the greatest human force and the highest human authority. Legal power is irresistible force. The necessary coincidence of the greatest human force and the highest human authority corresponds strictly to the necessary coincidence of the most powerful passion (fear of violent death) and the most sacred right (the right of self-preservation). *Potentia* and *potestas* have this in common, that they are both intelligible only in contradistinction, and in relation, to the *actus*: the *potentia* of a man is what a man *can* do, and the *potestas* or, more generally expressed, the right of a man, is what a man *may* do. The predominance of the concern with "power" is therefore only the reverse of a relative indifference to the *actus,* and this means to the purposes for which man's "physical" as well as his "legal" power is or ought to be used. This indifference can be traced directly to Hobbes' concern with an exact or scientific political teaching. The sound use of "physical" power as well as the sound exercise of rights depends on *prudentia,* and whatever falls within the province of *prudentia,* is not susceptible of exactness. There are two kinds of exactness: mathematical and legal. From the point of view of mathematical exactness, the study of the *actus* and therewith of the ends is replaced by the study of *potentia.* "Physical" power as distinguished from the purposes for which it is used is morally neutral and therefore more amenable to mathematical strictness than is its use: power can be measured. This explains why Nietzsche who went much beyond Hobbes and declared the will to be the essence of reality, conceived of power in terms of "quanta of power." From the point of view of legal exactness, the study of the ends is replaced by the study of *potestas.* The rights of the sovereign as distinguished from the exercise of these rights permit of an exact definition without any regard to any unforeseeable circumstances, and this kind of exactness is again inseparable from moral neutrality: right declares what is permitted as distinguished from what is honorable. Power as distinguished from the end for which power is used or ought to be used, becomes the central theme of political reflections by virtue of that limitation of horizon which is needed if there is to be a guarantee for the actualization of the right social order.

Hobbes' political doctrine is meant to be universally applicable and hence to be applicable also and especially in extreme cases. This indeed may be said to be the boast of the classic doctrine of sovereignty: that it gives its due to the extreme case, to what holds good in emergency situations, whereas those who question that doctrine are accused of not looking beyond the pale of normality. Accordingly, Hobbes built his whole moral and political doctrine on observations regarding the extreme case; for the experience on which his doctrine of the state of nature is based is the experience of civil war. It is in the extreme situation, when the social fabric has completely broken down, that there comes to sight the solid foundation on which every social order must ultimately rest: the fear of violent death, which is the strongest force in human life. Yet Hobbes was forced to concede that the fear of violent death is only "commonly" or in most cases the most powerful force. The principle which was supposed to make possible a political doctrine of universal applicability is then not universally valid, and therefore is useless in what from Hobbes' point of view is the most important case: the extreme case. For how can one exclude the possibility that precisely in the extreme situation the exception will prevail?

To speak in more specific terms, there are two politically important phenomena which would seem to show with particular clarity the limited validity of Hobbes' contention regarding the overwhelming power of the fear of violent death. In the first place, if the only unconditional moral fact is the individual's right of self-preservation, civil society can hardly demand from the individual that he resign that right both by going to war and by submitting to capital punishment. As regards capital punishment, Hobbes was consistent enough to grant that by being justly and legally condemned to death, a man does not lose the right to defend his life by resisting "those that assault him": a justly condemned murderer retains, nay, he acquires the right to kill his guards and everyone else who stands in his way to escape, in order to save dear life. But by granting this, Hobbes in fact admitted that there exists an insoluble conflict between the rights of the government and the natural right of the individual to self-preservation. This conflict was solved in the spirit, if against the letter, of Hobbes, by Beccaria, who inferred from the absolute primacy of the right of self-preservation the necessity of abolishing capital punishment. As regards war, Hobbes, who proudly declared that he was "the first of all that fled" at the outbreak of the Civil War, was consistent enough to grant that "there is allowance to be made for natural timorousness." And as if he desired to make it perfectly clear to what lengths he was prepared to go in opposing the lupine spirit of Rome, he continues as follows: "When armies fight, there is on one side, or both, a running away: yet when they do it not out of treachery, but fear, they are not esteemed to do it unjustly, but dishonorably." But by granting this, he destroyed the moral basis of what is now called national defense. The only solution to this difficulty which preserves the spirit of Hobbes' political philosophy is the outlawry of war or the establishment of a world-state.

There was only one fundamental objection to Hobbes' basic assumption which he felt very keenly and which he made every effort to overcome. In many cases the fear of violent death proved to be a weaker force than the fear of hell-fire or the fear of God. The difficulty is well illustrated by two widely separated passages of the *Leviathan*. In the first passage Hobbes says that the fear of the power of men (i.e. the fear of violent death) is "commonly" greater than the fear of the power of "spirits invisible" i.e. than religion. In the second passage he says that "the fear of darkness and ghosts is greater than other fears." Hobbes saw his way to solve this contradiction: the fear of invisible powers is stronger than the fear of violent death as long as people believe in invisible powers, i.e. as long as they are under the spell of delusions about the true character of reality; the fear of violent death comes fully into its own as soon as people have become enlightened. This implies that the whole scheme suggested by Hobbes requires for its operation the weakening, or rather, the elimination, of the fear of invisible powers. It requires such a radical change of orientation as can be brought about only by the disenchantment of the world, by the diffusion of scientific knowledge, or by popular enlightenment. Hobbes' is the first doctrine that necessarily and unmistakably points to a thoroughly "enlightened," i.e. a-religious or atheistic society as the solution of the social or political problem. This most important implication of Hobbes' doctrine was made explicit not many years after his death by Pierre Bayle, who attempted to prove that an atheistic society is possible.[1]

It is then only through the prospect of popular enlightenment that Hobbes' doctrine acquired such consistency as it possesses. The virtues which he ascribed to enlightenment, are indeed extraordinary. The power of ambition and avarice, he says, rests on the false opinions of the vulgar regarding right and wrong; therefore, once the principles of justice are known with mathematical certainty, ambition and avarice

will become powerless and the human race will enjoy lasting peace. For obviously, mathematical knowledge of the principles of justice (i.e. the new doctrine of natural right and the new natural public law that is built on it) can not destroy the wrong opinions of the vulgar, if the vulgar are not appraised of the results of that mathematical knowledge. Plato had said that evils will not cease from the cities if the philosophers do not become kings, or if philosophy and political power do not coincide. He had expected such salvation for mortal nature as can reasonably be expected, from a coincidence over which philosophy has no control, but for which one can only wish or pray. Hobbes, on the other hand, was certain that philosophy itself can bring about the coincidence of philosophy and political power by becoming popularized philosophy and thus public opinion. Chance will be conquered by systematic philosophy issuing in systematic enlightenment: *Paulatim eruditur vulgus.* By devising the right kind of institutions and by enlightening the citizen body, philosophy guarantees the solution of the social problem, whose solution cannot be guaranteed by man if it is thought to depend on moral discipline.

Opposing the "utopianism" of the classics, Hobbes was concerned with a social order whose actualization is probable and even certain. The guarantee of its actualization might seem to be supplied by the fact that the sound social order is based on the most powerful passion and therewith on the most powerful force in man. But if the fear of violent death is truly the strongest force in man, one should expect that the desired social order is always, or almost always, in existence, because it will be produced by natural necessity, by the natural order. Hobbes overcomes this difficulty by assuming that men in their stupidity interfere with the natural

[1] A good reason for connecting Bayle's famous thesis with Hobbes' doctrine rather than with that of Faustus Socinus, e.g., is supplied by the following statement of Bayle (*Dictionnaire,* Art. *Hobbes,* rem. D): "Hobbes se fit beaucoup d'ennemis par cet ouvrage (sc. *De Cive*): mais il fit avouer aux plus clairvoyants, qu'on n'avait jamais si bien pénétré les fondements de la politique."—I cannot prove here with the necessary detail that Hobbes was an atheist, even according to his own view of atheism. I must limit myself to asking the reader to compare *De Cive* XV, 14, with *English Works,* edited by Molesworth, IV, 349. Many present-day scholars who write on subjects of this kind do not seem to have a sufficient notion of the degree of circumspection, or of accommodation to the accepted views, that was required, in former ages, of "deviationists" who desired to survive or to die in peace. Those scholars tacitly assume that the pages in Hobbes' writings devoted to religious subjects, can be understood if they are read in the way in which one ought to read the corresponding utterances, say, of Lord Bertrand Russell. In other words, I am familiar with the fact that there are innumerable passages in Hobbes' writings which were used by Hobbes and which can be used by everyone else, for proving that Hobbes was a theist and even a good Anglican. The prevalent procedure would merely lead to historical errors, if to grave historical errors, but for the fact that its results are employed for buttressing the dogma that the mind of the individual is incapable of liberating itself from the opinions which rule his society.

order. The right social order does not normally come about by natural necessity on account of man's ignorance of that order. The "invisible hand" remains ineffectual if it is not supported by the *Leviathan* or, if you wish, by the *Wealth of Nations*.

There is a remarkable parallelism and an even more remarkable discrepancy between Hobbes' theoretical philosophy and his practical philosophy. In both parts of his philosophy, he teaches that reason is impotent and that it is omnipotent, or that reason is omnipotent because it is impotent. Reason is impotent because reason or humanity have no cosmic support: the universe is unintelligible, and nature "dissociates" men. But the very fact that the universe is unintelligible permits reason to rest satisfied with its free constructs and to anticipate an unlimited progress in its conquest of nature. Reason is impotent against passion, but it can become omnipotent if it cooperates with the strongest passion, or if it puts itself into the service of the strongest passion. Hobbes' rationalism rests then ultimately on the conviction that, thanks to nature's kindness, the strongest passion is the only passion which can be "the origin of large and lasting societies," or that the strongest passion is the most rational passion. In the case of the human things, the foundation is not a free construct but the most powerful natural force in man. In the case of the human things, we understand not merely what we make, but also, what makes our making and our makings. Whereas the philosophy or science of nature remains fundamentally hypothetical, political philosophy rests on a non-hypothetical knowledge of the nature of man. As long as Hobbes' approach prevails, "the philosophy concerned with the human things" will remain the last refuge of nature. For at some point nature succeeds in getting a hearing. The modern contention that man can "change the world" or "push back nature," is not unreasonable. One can even safely go much beyond it and say that man can expel nature with a hayfork. One ceases to be reasonable only if one forgets what the philosophic poet adds, *tamen usque redibit*.

6

LOCKE

John Locke (1632–1704), the great philosopher who authored the *Essay on Human Understanding* and the *Second Treatise on Government*, was, surprisingly enough, trained at Oxford in medicine. It is said that his entrance into political life resulted from his successful treatment of an abscess belonging to the Chancellor of the Exchequer, Lord Ashley, soon to be the first Earl of Shaftesbury. Locke became an important member of Shaftesbury's circle and it was for its efforts to exclude the future James II from the crown that he wrote the *Second Treatise*. To escape the repression which followed the failure of the exclusion effort, Locke was forced to flee to Holland, returning only after the fall of James in the Glorious Revolution of 1688.

The two selections offered here are quite different in emphasis. Professor Macpherson, from the University of Toronto, is concerned with the ideological thrust of Locke's writings. He outlines the class and social assumptions behind the ideas as well as the vision they convey of a bourgeois political order resting on certain assumptions concerning the relationship of property and individualism. Willmoore Kendall, in contrast to Macpherson, engages in a more formal analysis of Locke's arguments in the *Second Treatise*. Kendall's central theme is an examination of Locke's contribution to the theory of consent and the principles of majority rule and popular sovereignty.

C. B. MACPHERSON

The Social Bearing of
Locke's Political Theory*

SOME UNSETTLED PROBLEMS OF
LOCKE'S POLITICAL THEORY

The reference in the title of this paper is to be taken in a double sense. It marks a concern both with the social assumptions that carry the weight of Locke's political theory and with the type of society to which that theory pointed the direction. Not enough attention has been given to either of these problems, especially the first—the social assumptions. It is not entirely surprising that these assumptions have been neglected. The renewed discussion of Locke's political ideas in recent years is part of a revival of interest in natural law and in the meaning and possibilities of liberal democracy. But the current revival of interest in liberal-democratic principles contains its own dangers. It is, directly or indirectly, part of the Western defenses against communism. The consequent preoccupation with the broad validity of liberal democracy has inhibited any substantial notice of the class content of even seventeenth cen-

tury liberal theory. Attention has thus been diverted from the social assumptions of Locke's theory, insofar as they are assumptions about the class character of society, in a way which is unlikely to be conducive to a valid understanding either of his theory or of liberal-democratic principles.

The neglecting of social bases alone might not call for a reinterpretation of Locke, were it not that current interpretations leave at the heart of his political theory serious unexplained inconsistencies. Neglect of Locke's social assumptions and failure to explain contradictions in his political theory are not unrelated. This paper attempts in part to show that a closer analysis of these assumptions may render Locke's political theory more intelligible.

The prevailing view, it might fairly be said, is that Locke was primarily the theorist of the liberal state, of constitutional or limited government as opposed to arbitrary or absolute government, of government conditional on the consent of the governed, or of majority rule qualified by individual rights. It is usually implied that the problem Locke had set himself was either to build a universally valid general theory

* From *The Western Political Quarterly*, VII (1954), 1–22, reprinted by permission of the University of Utah, Copyright owners.

of political obligation or to provide a general validation of a particular constitutional position. In either of these versions, little attention is given to the social, as distinct from the constitutional, content of Locke's theory.

Such abstraction from social content has not always prevailed. A more realistic quality was given to the constitutional interpretation by those who saw Locke's state as, in effect, a joint-stock company whose shareholders were the men of property. This was the view taken by Leslie Stephen in his *English Thought in the Eighteenth Century* (1876), by C. E. Vaughan in his *Studies in the History of Political Philosophy* (1925), by Laski in his *Locke to Bentham* (1920) and his *Rise of European Liberalism* (1936), and by Professor Tawney in his *Religion and the Rise of Capitalism* (1926). There is one great difficulty in this view. Who were the members of Locke's civil society? If they were only the men of property, how could the social contract be an adequate basis of political obligation for all men? Yet undoubtedly the purpose of the social contract was to find a basis for all-inclusive political obligation. Here is an outstanding difficulty. That eminent historians of thought did not see it as such is probably because their interpretation was mainly in the constitutional tradition:[1] it emphasized the limits Locke put on government in the interests of property, rather than the very great power Locke gave to the political community (his "civil society") as against individuals.

Another view, with opposite emphasis, has made some headway in the last ten years, following the publication of Professor Kendall's study.[2] There a strong case is made that Locke's theory confers something very close to complete sovereignty on civil society, that is, in effect, on the majority of the people (though not, of course, on the government, which has only fiduciary power). Against this sovereignty of the majority, the individual has no rights. Impressive evidence can be shown for this reading of Locke. It leads to the striking conclusion that Locke was not an individualist at all, but a "collectivist" in that he subordinated the purposes of the individual to the purposes of society. He is made a forerunner of Rousseau and the General Will.[3] The case is a strong one. However, in concluding that Locke was a "majority-rule democrat," this interpretation overlooks all the evidence that Locke was not a democrat at all. It reads into Locke a concern with the democratic principle of majority rule, which was to be the focus of much American political thinking in the late eighteenth and early nineteenth centuries, as it is now. And it leaves a major problem: Does not majority rule endanger that individual property right which Locke plainly sought to protect? Moreover, it proposes a resolution of Locke's many inconsistencies by imputing to him an assumption ("that the chances are at least 50 plus out of 100 that the average man is rational and just"),[4] which Locke certainly did not hold unambiguously and which he specifically contradicted more than once.[5]

[1] Professor Tawney's, of course, was not, and he did draw attention to the decisive seventeenth century assumption that the laboring class was a race apart (R. H. Tawney, *Religion and the Rise of Capitalism* [Harmondsworth and New York: Penguin Books Ltd., 1940], pp. 175, 241, to which reference is made below, p. 186). However, the implications for the political theory of the period, not being central to his argument, were not explored.

[2] Willmoore Kendall, *John Locke and the Doctrine of Majority-Rule* (Urbana, Illinois: University of Illinois, 1941).

[3] *Ibid.,* pp. 103–6.

[4] *Ibid.,* pp. 134–35.

[5] *Second Treatise of Civil Government,* sections 21, 123; and see below, p. 194.

More recently, attempts have been made, notably by J. W. Gough,[6] to bring Locke back into the liberal-individualist tradition. However, these efforts are not conclusive. In trying to rescue Locke from the abstract logical treatment he has had at some hands and to restore his theory to its historical context, the emphasis is again put on his constitutionalism. But the context of political history overshadows that of social and economic history. At most, what is proposed is a compromise between Locke's individualism and his "collectivism," and major inconsistencies are left unexplained.

Indeed, almost all interpretations fail to account for radical contradictions in Locke's postulates. Why should Locke have said, and what could he have meant by saying, both that men on the whole are rational and that most of them are not; both that the state of nature is rational, peaceable and social, and that it is not essentially different from Hobbes's state of war?[7] To make consistency the first rule of interpretation is as unrealistic as to take comfort in the allegation that great minds are not consistent. Yet the contradictions that lie on the surface of the *Second Treatise of Civil Government* deserve more explanation than they have had. The fact that they cannot be resolved by logical analysis, or explained by constitutional historical analysis, suggests that they are the outcome of a deeper social contradiction. Therefore we may look to Locke's view of his own society for insight into the meaning of his political theory.

We shall find that his conception of that society, especially of its class differentiation, entered into his abstract postulates about the nature of society and man in a way that has not generally been noticed. This view goes far to account for the contradictions in Locke's political theory, and for the outstanding problems of its interpretation.

LOCKE'S SOCIAL PRECONCEPTIONS

Locke did not make all his social assumptions explicit. There is no reason why he should have done so. The assumptions which he and his contemporary readers absorbed from the thinking of their own time, and from their understanding of their own society, he could take for granted.

Here I want to direct attention to two preconceptions which Locke, in common with many others of his class and time, entertained about his own society. As assumptions about the nature of seventeenth century society they are explicit in various writings of Locke; as assumptions about society in general they are implicit in the *Treatise* and had a decisive influence in his political theory.[8]

These are (1) that while the laboring class is a necessary part of the nation, its members are not in fact full members of the body politic and have no claim to be so; and (2) that the members of the laboring class do not and cannot live a fully rational life. "Laboring class" is used here to include both the "laboring poor" and the "idle poor," that is, all who were dependent on employment or charity or the workhouse because they had no property of

    [6] J. W. Gough, *John Locke's Political Philosophy: Eight Studies* (Oxford, 1950).

    [7] *Rational* is used here in Locke's sense of governing oneself by the law of nature or law of reason (e.g., *Second Treatise*, § 6: Reason *is* the law of nature; § 8: To transgress the law of nature is to live by another rule than that of reason and common equity). For Locke's contradictory views of man's rationality, see below, pp. 193–95.

    [8] These two are not necessarily Locke's most fundamental social assumptions. First place should be given to his belief that every man is the sole proprietor of his own person and capacities. But as this is explicit in the *Treatise,* it does not demand the same attention here.

their own by which, or on which, they might work.

That these people were not, in fact or by right, full members of political society was the prevailing view in England in the second half of the seventeenth century. They were regarded not as citizens but as a body of actual and potential labor available for the purposes of the nation. Professor Tawney has summarized their position in the observation that the prevailing attitude of English writers after 1660 "towards the new industrial proletariat [was] noticeably harsher than that general in the first half of the seventeenth century, and...has no modern parallel except in the behaviour of the less reputable of white colonists towards coloured labour."[9] The working class was, in effect, in but not of civil society.

This attitude may be seen as a secularization, not only of the Puritan doctrine of the poor, but also of that Calvinist view in which the church, while claiming to include the whole population, held that full membership could be had only by the elect. The nonelect (who were mainly, though not entirely, coincidental with the non-propertied) were at once members and not members of the church: not full members sharing in the government of the church, but sufficiently members to be subject, rightfully, to its discipline.[10] This Calvinist position tended to exclude beggars, vagrants, and all unemployed poor from full citizenship, an implication of their exclusion from full membership in the church.

The secular view that came to prevail during the Restoration went much further. Not only the unemployed but also the employed poor were treated, not

as citizens but as objects of state policy. Economic writers of the day admitted, even insisted, that the laboring poor were the ultimate source of any nation's wealth, but only if they were compelled to continuous labor. That the arrangements for extracting this labor were not regarded as entirely satisfactory in 1688 is evident from Gregory King's famous statistical estimate of the population and income of England in 1688 (which, as Unwin has said, affords "better evidence of the common assumptions of the directing classes than of any objective social facts").[11] He divided the whole body of the people into those increasing and those decreasing the wealth of the kingdom, and put not only "cottagers and paupers" and "vagrants," but also the "labouring people and outservants" among the occupational classes, each of which decreased the wealth of the kingdom.[12]

The estimated size of the propertyless wage-earning and unemployed classes in 1688 need not be emphasized, though it is striking enough: King and D'Avenant put more than half the population in this category. What is more important is the assumption that the laboring class is to be managed by the state in order to make it productive of national gain. The laboring class's interests were not subordinated to the national interest; the class was not considered to have an interest. The ruling-class view of the national interest was the only one.

This attitude towards the working

---

[9] Tawney, *op. cit.*, pp. 240–41.

[10] For expression of this view in English Calvinism, see Christopher Hill, "Puritans and the Poor," *Past & Present*, II (November, 1952), 41.

[11] George Unwin, *Studies in Economic History* (ed. by R. H. Tawney, London, 1927), p. 345.

[12] King's estimate is conveniently reproduced in Dorothy George, *England in Transition* (Penguin edition, 1953), pp. 150–51. It is partially reproduced in G. N. Clark, *The Wealth of England from 1496 to 1760* (London, 1946), but without the division into those increasing and those decreasing. The full table is in D'Avenant's *Works* (1771), II, 184.

class, generally explicit in the economic writings of the period from 1660, is nicely exemplified in William Petyt's statement:

People are...the chiefest, most fundamental and precious commodity, out of which may be derived all sorts of manufactures, navigation, riches, conquests and solid dominion. This capital material being of itself raw and indigested is committed into the hands of supreme authority in whose prudence and disposition it is to improve, manage and fashion it to more or less advantage.[13]

The view that human beings of the laboring class were a commodity out of which riches and dominion might be derived, a raw material to be worked up and disposed of by the political authority, was fully shared by Locke. The evidence leaves no doubt that he regarded the working class as subject to, but without full membership in, the political society of seventeenth-century England. He assumed this not only as a matter of fact but as a matter of right. The moral assumption was that the laboring class does not and cannot live a rational life.

Evidence of these assumptions is scattered throughout Locke's writings. His proposals for the treatment of the able-bodied unemployed are fairly well known, although when they are mentioned by modern writers it is usually to deprecate their severity and excuse it by reference to the standards of the time. What is more to the point is the view which these proposals afford of Locke's assumptions. Masters of workhouses ("houses of correction") were to be encouraged to make them into sweated-labor manufacturing establish-

ments; justices of the peace were to make them into forced-labor institutions. Children of the unemployed "above the age of three" were unnecessarily a burden on the nation; they should be set to work, and could be made to earn more than their keep. All this was justified on the explicit ground that unemployment was due not to economic causes but to moral depravity. The multiplying of the unemployed, Locke wrote in 1697 in his capacity as a member of the Commission on Trade, was caused by "nothing else but the relaxation of discipline and corruption of manners."[14] There was no question in his mind of treating the unemployed as full or free members of the political community; there was equally no doubt that they were fully subject to the state. The state was entitled to deal with them in this way because they would not live up to the moral standard required of rational men.

Locke's attitude towards the employed wage-earning class has been noticed less often, though it is plain enough in various passages of his economic writings, particularly in *Some Considerations of the Consequences of the Lowering of Interest and Raising the Value of Money* (1691). There, incidentally to his technical arguments, Locke takes for granted that the wage-laborer constitutes a normal and sizable class in the nation,[15] that he has no property but is entirely dependent on his wages, and that, of necessity, his wages are normally at a bare subsistence level.[16]

---

13 William Petyt, *Britannia Languens* (1680), p. 23. This and similar passages from various writers of the period are quoted in E. S. Furniss, *The Position of the Laborer in a System of Nationalism* (New York: Houghton, 1920), pp. 16ff.

14 Quoted in H. R. Fox Bourne, *The Life of John Locke* (London, 1876), II, 378. Locke seems to have regarded the idle poor as depraved by choice, in contrast to the laboring poor, whom he considered incapable of a fully rational life because of their position. (See below, p. 196).

15 *Considerations,* in *Works* (1759 edition), II, 13–16.

16 *Ibid.,* p. 29.

Such a person "just lives from hand to mouth." One passage in particular deserves quotation:

...The labourer's share [of the national income], being seldom more than a bare subsistence, never allows that body of men, time, or opportunity to raise their thoughts above that, or struggle with the richer for theirs (as one common interest), unless when some common and great distress, uniting them in one universal ferment, makes them forget respect, and emboldens them to carve to their wants with armed force: and then sometimes they break in upon the rich, and sweep all like a deluge. But this rarely happens but in the male-administration of neglected, or mismanaged government.[17]

It is hard to say which part of these remarks is the most revealing. There is the assumption that the laborers are normally kept too low to be able to think or act politically. There is the assertion that maladministration consists not of leaving them there, but of allowing such unusual distress to occur as will unite them in armed revolt. And there is the conviction that such revolt is improper, an offense against the respect they owe to their betters.

Now the question: Who has the right of revolution? is a decisive question with Locke. The revolutionary right is to him the only effective test of citizenship, as he makes no provision for any other method of overthrowing an unwanted government. Although he insists, in the *Treatise*, on the majority's right to revolution, it does not seem to cross his mind here that the laboring class might have the right to make a revolution. Indeed there is no reason why such a thought should have occurred to him, for to him the laboring class was an object of state policy and of administration, rather than fully a part of the citizen body. Such a class was incapable

of rational political action, but the right to revolution depended essentially on rational decision.

The assumption that members of the laboring class are in too low a position to be capable of a rational life—that is, capable of regulating their lives by those moral principles Locke supposed were given by reason—is evident again in *The Reasonableness of Christianity*. The whole argument of that work is a plea that Christianity be restored to a few simple articles of belief "that the laboring and illiterate man may comprehend." Christianity should thus again be made

a religion suited to vulgar capacities; and the state of mankind in this world, destined to labour and travel.... The greatest part of mankind have not leisure for learning and logick, and superfine distinctions of the schools. Where the hand is used to the plough and the spade, the head is seldom elevated to sublime notions, or exercised in mysterious reasoning. 'Tis well if men of that rank (to say nothing of the other sex) can comprehend plain propositions, and a short reasoning about things familiar to their minds, and nearly allied to their daily experience. Go beyond this, and you amaze the greatest part of mankind....[18]

This is not, as might be thought, a plea for a simple rationalist ethical religion to replace the disputations of the theologians. On the contrary, Locke's point is that without supernatural sanctions the laboring class is incapable of following a rationalist ethic. He only wants the sanctions made clearer. The simple articles he recommends are not moral rules, but articles of faith. Belief in them is all that is necessary, for such belief converts the moral rules of the gospel into binding commands. Locke's problem is to frame the articles so that they will appeal directly to the

---

[17] *Ibid.*, p. 36.

[18] *The Reasonableness of Christianity*, last two pages; *Works* (1759), II, 585–86.

experience of the common people, who can thus believe.[19] The greatest part of mankind, he concludes, cannot be left to the guidance of the laws of nature or of reason; they are not capable of drawing rules of conduct from them. For "the day-labourers and tradesmen, the spinsters and dairy-maids...hearing plain commands, is the sure and only course to bring them to obedience and practice. The greatest part cannot know and therefore they must believe."[20]

Of course, Locke was recommending this simplified Christianity for all classes, as may be seen in his ingenuously mercantile observations on the surpassing utility of the Christian doctrine of rewards and punishments.

The [ancient] philosophers, indeed, shewed the beauty of virtue;...but leaving her unendowed, very few were willing to espouse her.... But now there being put into the scales on her side, 'an exceeding and immortal weight of glory'; interest is come about to her, and virtue now is visibly the most enriching purchase, and by much the best bargain.... The view of heaven and hell will cast a slight upon the short pleasures and pains of this present state, and give attractions and encouragements to virtue, which reason and interest, and the care of ourselves, cannot but allow and prefer. Upon this foundation, and

upon this only, morality stands firm, and may defy all competition.[21]

No doubt Locke's readers would appreciate this recommendation of Christianity more than would the laborers, who were not in a position to think in terms of making "the most enriching purchase." However, Locke regards as only a secondary advantage the ability of his fundamental Christian doctrine to satisfy men of higher capacities. His repeated emphasis on the necessity of the laboring classes being brought to obedience by a belief in divine rewards and punishments leaves no doubt about his main concern. The implication is plain: the laboring class, beyond all others, is incapable of living a rational life.

Clearly, then, when Locke looked at his own society he saw two classes with different rationality and different rights. It would have been strange had he not done so. Locke was no Leveller. His was not the democratic puritanism that had appeared during the Commonwealth, but the puritanism which had encountered no difficulty in accommodating itself to the exigencies of class rule in 1660. Locke had welcomed the Restoration not only because it had put an end to the turbulence of the Commonwealth,[22] but also because it had restored something that was positively good,

the protection of those laws which the prudence and providence of our ancestors established and the happy return of his Majesty hath restored: a body of laws so well composed, that whilst this nation would be content only to be under them they were always sure to be above their neighbours, which forced from this world this constant acknowledgment, that we

---

[19] The essential articles of belief are that there is a future life and that salvation can only be had by believing that Christ was raised from the dead to be the divine savior of mankind. Locke argues that this is a plain notion which, along with miracles, can readily be grasped by the illiterate in terms of their common experience: "The healing of the sick, the restoring sight to the blind by a word, the raising, and being raised from the dead, are matters of fact, which they can without difficulty conceive, and that he who does such things, must do them by the assistance of a divine power. These things lie level to the ordinariest apprehension: he that can distinguish between sick and well, lame and sound, dead and alive, is capable of this doctrine." (*Ibid.*, II, 580.)

[20] *Ibid.*, II, 580.

[21] *Ibid.*, II, 582.

[22] See the passages quoted from Locke's MS treatise of 1660 on the Civil Magistrate, in Gough, *op. cit.*, p. 178.

were not only the happiest state but the purest church of the latter age.[23]

From this unreserved approbation of the pre-Commonwealth constitution—not, of course, the constitution (of Church and State) as understood by James I and Charles I, but as understood by the Parliamentarians—he went on to state as a matter of principle that "the supreme magistrate of every nation what way soever created, must necessarily have an absolute and arbitrary power over all the indifferent actions of his people."[24] Locke showed himself to be truly conservative in 1660. From then on, his view of society was that of the men of substance.

---

[23] Preface to the treatise on the Civil Magistrate, 1660; Bodleian Library, MS Locke C 28, fol. 2 verso.

[24] *Ibid.*, fol. 3 recto. The difference between this and the position Locke took three decades later in the *Second Treatise* is not in the amount of power granted to the civil authority but in the locus of that power. The "absolute and arbitrary power" of 1660 is only over 'indifferent actions." Indifferent actions he defined as those not comprehended in the law of nature or divine revelation; in other words, those matters as to which man is naturally free. (See Locke's premises, quoted in Gough, *op. cit.,* p. 179.) These are precisely the matters which in the *Second Treatise* Locke has the individual hand over to the supreme civil authority, there the civil society itself.

But in 1660 Locke was willing to consider a monarch—or was it only the king-in-parliament?—as the supreme authority; the "magistrate" is defined as "the supreme legislative power of any society, not considering the form of government or number of persons wherein it is placed" (MS treatise on Civil Magistrate, Bodleian Library, MS Locke, c. 7, fol. 1, sidenote), whereas in 1689 Locke reserved supreme authority to the civil society itself. He was consistent throughout in wanting a civil authority which could secure the basic institutions of a class society. In 1660 this required the recall of the Stuarts and the doctrine of the magistrate's absolute and arbitrary power in things indifferent; in 1689 it required the dismissal of the Stuarts and the doctrine of the *Second Treatise*.

THE SOCIAL PRECONCEPTIONS GENERALIZED

It would be surprising if Locke's preconceptions about his own society did not somehow affect his premises about society and man as such. His unhistorical habit of mind presented no obstacle to his transferring assumptions about seventeenth-century society into a supposed state of nature. As he took his assumptions about his own society so much for granted that he felt no need to argue them, they could easily be carried into his premises without any consciousness of a problem of consistency. I shall argue that both of the assumptions about his own society—that of a class differential in rationality, and that of a class differential in rights—were generalized in Locke's thinking into implicit assumptions about human nature as such and about individual *natural* rights, and that these assumptions modified his explicit postulates about human nature and natural rights.

In Locke's initial statement of his postulates in the *Treatise* (and in his analysis of human nature in the *Essay Concerning Human Understanding,* which has to be considered also for a full statement of his general theory of human nature), there is nothing to suggest an assumption of class differentiation. However, before he used these postulates to deduce the necessary character of civil society, he put forward other arguments, especially in his treatment of property rights, which imply that he had already generalized his differential assumptions about his own society into abstract implicit assumptions of differential human nature and natural rights.

(1) Differential Rights. We have seen that Locke found in seventeenth-century society a class differentiation so deep

that the members of the laboring class had very different effective rights from the classes above them. They lived, and must live, "from hand to mouth," could never "raise their thoughts above that," and were unfit to participate in political life. Their condition was a result of their having no property on which they could expend their labor; their having no property was one aspect of the prevailing inequality which was grounded in "the necessity of affairs, and the constitution of human society."[25]

What Locke saw in his own society he considered typical of all civil society. But how did this become an assumption of differential *natural* rights, and where does it, as such an assumption, enter into the argument of the *Treatise?* It is certainly not present in the opening statements about natural rights; there the emphasis is all on the natural equality of rights (§§ 4, 5).[26]

The transformation of equal into differential natural rights comes to light in Locke's theory of property. In the chapter on property in the *Treatise,* he went out of his way to transform the natural right of every individual to such property as he needed for subsistence and to which he applied his labor, into a natural right of *unlimited* appropriation, by which the more industrious could rightfully acquire all the land, leaving others with no way to live except by selling the disposal of their labor.[27]

This transformation is not an aberration in Locke's individualism but an essential part of it. The core of his individualism is the assertion that every

man is naturally the sole proprietor of his own person and capacities (§§ 4, 6, 44, 123)—the absolute proprietor in the sense that he owes nothing to society for them—and especially the absolute proprietor of his capacity to labor (§ 27). Every man is therefore free to alienate his own capacity to labor. This individualist postulate is the one by which Locke transforms the mass of equal individuals (rightfully) into two classes with very different rights, those with property and those without. Once the land is all taken up, the fundamental right not to be subject to the jurisdiction of another is so unequal between owners and nonowners that it is different in kind, not in degree: those without property are dependent for their livelihood on those with property and are unable to alter their own circumstances. The initial equality of natural rights, which consisted in no man's having jurisdiction over another (§ 4) cannot last after the differentiation of property. In other words, the man without property in things loses that proprietorship of his own person which was the basis of his equal natural rights. Locke insists that disparity in property is *natural,* that is, that it takes place "out of the bounds of society, and without compact" (§ 50). Civil society is established to protect unequal possessions, which have already in the natural state caused unequal rights. In this way Locke has generalized the assumption of a class differential in rights in his own society into an implicit assumption of differential *natural* rights. This implicit assumption, as will be seen, did not replace the initial theory of equality: both were in Locke's mind at the same time.

(2) Differential Rationality. We have seen that Locke assumed in his own society a class differential in rationality which left the laboring class incapable

---

25 *Considerations, Works* (1759), II, 19.

26 This and subsequent references in the text are to the section numbers of the *Second Treatise of Civil Government.* Quotations are from the 1764 edition of the *Treatises.*

27 "Locke on Capitalist Appropriation," *Western Political Quarterly,* IV, 550–66.

of a fully rational life. The questions are: How did this become an assumption of differential rationality in general? And where did this enter the argument of the *Treatise?* It is clearly not present in the opening statements of postulates. There, rationality and depravity are dealt with abstractly and although rational men are distinguished from depraved men,[28] there is no suggestion that the distinction is correlated with social class. But as the argument proceeds and the postulates have to be made more specific, it becomes apparent that Locke has something else in mind. When he has to relate depravity and rationality to man's political needs, these qualities turn out to have meaning only in the setting of a particular kind of property institutions and to be closely related to ownership.

Whatever man's inherent depravity may be, Locke thinks it does not require any but the most rudimentary political society until there is extensive property. Where there was "the equality of a simple poor way of living, confining [men's] desires within the narrow bounds of each man's small property," there would be few controversies and few trespasses, and consequently no need of many laws or magistrates; there would be more fear of outsiders than of each other, and the main purpose of setting up government would be for security "against foreign force" (§ 107). A fully civil society of the kind which is the main concern of the *Treatise,* a society for the internal security of individual property, is required for the protection not of small equal properties but only of extensive unequal ones, not of a modest store of consumables or perhaps a few acres of land but of a substantial accumulation of resources. It is the propensity to accumulate property beyond the requirements of sub-

sistence that necessarily leads rational men to establish civil society.

Here we reach the crux of the matter. The propensity to accumulate, although it leads to quarrels, is itself not depraved but rational. Not only is the desire for accumulation rational, according to Locke, but accumulation is the essence of rational conduct. More precisely, the true nature of rational behavior is to expend labor improving the gifts of nature for subsequent enjoyment of greater real income or of greater power or prestige. This procedure, in Locke's view, requires private possession; and the measure of rational industriousness is the accumulation of possessions.

All this can be seen in the famous chapter on property in the *Treatise,* the burden of which is that the truly rational man is the industrious man. Rational behavior in temporal affairs is investing one's energies in the accumulation of real property and capital. "God gave the world to men in common; but...he gave it them...for... the greatest conveniencies of life they were capable to draw from it...." Therefore, He "gave it to the use of the industrious and rational," who would "improve" it (§ 34). Improvement without ownership is impossible: "The condition of human life, which requires labour and materials to work on, necessarily introduces private possessions" (§ 35). Not everyone in the state of nature could acquire property, for wherever money is introduced—and it is introduced in the state of nature (§50) the land is all appropriated (§ 45). That the appropriation leaves some men without any possibility of getting land does not disturb Locke because the day-laborer in a society where the land is all appropriated is better off than the greatest man in a primitive economy (§ 41).

Thus "the industrious and rational" are not all laborers, but only those who

---

28 See below, p. 194.

acquire property and improve it by their labor.[29] A further effect of the introduction of money is that the rational goal of a man's industry becomes accumulation beyond any requirements of consumption. "Different degrees of industry" give men different amounts of property, and the invention of money gives the more industrious man the opportunity "to enlarge his possessions beyond the use of his family, and a plentiful supply to its consumption" (§ 48). In short, rational conduct, in the state of nature, consists in unlimited accumulation, the possibility of which is open only to some. It follows that there was, in Locke's view, a class differential in rationality in the state of nature, inasmuch as those who were left without property after the land was all appropriated could not be accounted fully rational. They had no opportunity to be so. Like day laborers in civil society they were not in a position to expend their labor improving the gifts of nature; their whole energies were needed to keep alive. They could not "raise their thoughts above that," for they just lived "from hand to mouth."

THE AMBIGUOUS STATE OF NATURE

From the foregoing analysis it may be concluded that Locke read back into the state of nature, in a generalized form, the assumptions he made about differential rights and rationality in existing societies. Although the generalized assumptions modified in his own mind the initial postulates of the *Treatise*, they did not displace them. Locke entertained both at the same time, at differ-

ent levels of consciousness. Hence, the postulates on which he was operating were confused and ambiguous. All men were on the whole rational; yet there were two distinct classes of rationality. All men were equal in natural rights; yet there were two distinct orders of possession of natural rights. The source of the extraordinary contradiction in Locke's presentation of human nature is found here.

We customarily think that Locke held men to be essentially rational and social. Rational, in that they could live together by the law of nature, which is reason, or which at least (though not imprinted on the mind) is knowable by reason without the help of revelation. Social, in that they could live by the law of nature without the imposition of rules by a sovereign. This conception, indeed, is usually said to be the great difference between Locke's and Hobbes's views of human nature. If there is a significant difference it is here that one expects to find it, rather than in the theory of motivation. For Locke, like Hobbes, held that men are moved primarily by appetite and aversion; the appetites are so strong that "if they were left to their full swing, they would carry men to the overturning of all morality. Moral laws are set as a curb and restraint to these exhorbitant desires."[30] It is usually maintained that the difference between this and Hobbes's view is that Locke thought men capable of setting these rules on themselves, by perceiving their

---

29 The same conclusion is reached, from a different starting point, by Leo Strauss, in a penetrating recent article on natural law: "On Locke's Doctrine of Natural Rights," *Philosophical Review*, XLI (October, 1952), 495–96.

30 *Essay Concerning Human Understanding*, I, 3, § 3. Cf. Locke's Hobbesian reflection in 1678 that "the principal spring from which the actions of men take their rise, the rule they conduct them by, and the end to which they direct them, seems to be credit and reputation, and that which at any rate they avoid is in the greatest part shame and disgrace," and the consequences he draws for government. (Quoted from Locke's MS journal in Fox Bourne, *op. cit.*, I, 403–4.)

utility, without installing a sovereign.

The general theory presented at the opening of the *Treatise* affirms that men are naturally able to govern themselves by the law of nature, or reason. The state of nature, we are told, has a law of nature to govern it, which is reason (§ 6). The state of nature is contrasted flatly to the state of war: the two are "as far distant, as a state of peace, goodwill, mutual assistance and preservation, and a state of enmity, malice, violence and mutual destruction, are from one another. Men living together according to reason, without a common superior on earth, with authority to judge between them, is properly the state of nature" (§ 19). It is no derogation of this view of the state of nature to allow, as Locke does, that there are some men in it who will not follow the law of nature. Nature's law teaches only those who will consult it (§ 6); some men transgress it and, by so doing, declare themselves "to live by another rule than that of reason and common equity" and in this way become "dangerous to mankind" (§ 8); a man who violates the law of nature "becomes degenerate, and declares himself to quit the principles of human nature, and to be a noxious creature" (§ 10). The whole picture of the state of nature in chapter ii of the *Treatise* is one of a people abiding by natural law, with some natural criminals among them: Locke even uses the word criminal to describe the man in the state of nature who violates its law (§ 8).

But this representation is only one of two quite opposite pictures Locke has of the state of nature. As early as chapter iii of the *Treatise*, only a page after the distinction between the state of nature and the state of war, we read that where there is no authority to decide between contenders "every the least difference is apt to end" in the "state of war," and that "one great

reason of men's putting themselves into society, and quitting the state of nature" is "to avoid this state of war" (§21).[31] The difference between the state of nature and the Hobbesian state of war has virtually disappeared. Some chapters later, we read further that the state of nature is "very unsafe, very unsecure"; that in it the enjoyment of individual rights is "very uncertain, and constantly exposed to the invasion of others," and that it is "full of fears and continual dangers." All this danger occurs because "the greater part [are] no strict observers of equity and justice" (§ 123). What makes the state of nature unlivable, according to this account, is not the viciousness of the few but the disposition of "the greater part" to depart from the law of reason.

The contradiction between Locke's two sets of statements about natural man is obvious. It is a central contradiction in the explicit postulates on which his political theory is built. It will not do to say he simply echoes the traditional Christian conception of man as a contradictory mixture of appetite and reason. Locke no doubt accepted that view; and within it there is room for a considerable variety of

---

[31] This passage is not in the Everyman edition of the two Treatises (ed. by W. S. Carpenter) nor in the Appleton-Century edition of the *Second Treatise* and *Letter Concerning Toleration* (ed. by C. L. Sherman, New York, 1937). Each of these follows, at this point, a printing of the first edition of the *Treatises* which did not contain any § 21, and each has covered up the deficiency by arbitrarily dividing another section into two. (Sherman divides § 20; Carpenter divides § 36, so that all the sections in the Everyman edition from 21 to 35 are wrongly numbered.) The particulars of the two printings of Locke's first edition, and of their handling by modern editors, are given in Peter Laslett's "The 1690 Edition of Locke's *Two Treatises of Government:* Two States," *Transactions of the Cambridge Bibliographical Society,* IV (1952), 341–47.

belief as to the relative weights (or potentialities) of the two ingredients of human nature. Different exponents of Christian doctrine could take different views. What has to be explained is how Locke took not one position in this matter but two opposite positions.

One might say that he had to take both in order to make his case against Hobbes; he had to make men rational enough not to require a Hobbesian sovereign, yet contentious enough to necessitate their handing over their natural rights and powers to a civil society. However, to say this would be to accuse Locke, unjustly and unnecessarily, either of intellectual dishonesty or of extraordinary superficiality; besides, it would imply an underestimate of the extent to which Locke did subordinate the individual to the state.[32]

It seems more reasonable to conclude that Locke was able to take both positions about human nature because he had in mind simultaneously two conceptions of society, which, although logically conflicting, were derived from the same ultimate source. One was the seventeenth-century atomistic conception of society as a mass of equal, undifferentiated beings. The other was the notion of a society composed of two classes differentiated by their level of rationality—those who were "industrious and rational" and had property, and those who were not, who labored, indeed, but only to live, not to accumulate.

Locke was unconscious of the contradiction between these two conceptions of society because both of them (and not merely, as we have already seen, the second one) were elements transferred to his postulates from his comprehension of his own society. Ultimately it was Locke's comprehension of his own society that was ambiguous

and contradictory. It could not have been otherwise, for it was the comprehension of an emerging bourgeois society, reflecting the ambivalence of a society which demanded formal equality but required substantive inequality of rights.

As a bourgeois philosopher, a proponent of seventeenth-century individualism, Locke had to regard men as equal, undifferentiated units, and to consider them rational. The bourgeois order justified itself by assuming, first, that all men were intellectually capable of shifting for themselves, and secondly, that rational behavior in this sense was morally rational, in accordance with the law of nature. Thus a necessary part of the bourgeois vision pictured man in general in the image of rational bourgeois man. Locke shared this view, which gave him the account of the state of nature as rational and peaceable.

At the same time, as a bourgeois philosopher Locke necessarily conceived abstract society as consisting of two classes with different rationality. The two classes in Locke's England lived lives totally different in freedom and rights. The basic difference between them in fact was the difference in their ability to live by the bourgeois moral code. But to the directing class this appeared to be a differential capacity in men to live by moral rules as such. This conception of society gave Locke the picture of the state of nature as unsafe and insecure. For to say, as he did, that most men are incapable of guiding their lives by the law of reason, without sanctions, is to say that a civil society with legal sanctions (and a church with spiritual sanctions) is needed to keep them in order. Without these sanctions, i.e., in a state of nature, there could be no peace.

Both views of the state of nature flowed from the bourgeois concept of

---

32 See below, p. 199.

society, and both were necessary to it. Their common source obscured their contradictory quality. There was no question of Locke's basing his theory on an Aristotelian concept of two classes —masters and slaves—whose relative positions were justified by a supposed inherent difference in rationality. With Locke the difference in rationality was not inherent in men; it was socially acquired by virtue of different economic positions. But since it was acquired in the state of nature, it was inherent in society. Once acquired, that is to say, it was permanent, for it was the concomitant of an order of property relations which Locke assumed to be the permanent basis of civilized society. His notion of differential rationality justified as natural, not slavery,[33] but the subordination of one part of the people by their continual contractual alienation of their capacity to labor. In the bourgeois view men were free to alienate their freedom, and Locke, at least, thought that the difference in rationality was a result rather than a cause of that alienation. But the difference in rationality, once established, provided a justification for differential rights.

THE AMBIGUOUS CIVIL SOCIETY

We may now inquire how Locke's ambiguous position on natural rights and rationality enters and affects his theory of the formation of civil society. Men enter into civil society, Locke asserts, to protect themselves from the inconveniences, insecurity and violence of the state of nature. Or, as he declares

repeatedly, the great reason for men's uniting into society and putting themselves under government is to preserve their property, by which, he says, he means their "lives, liberties and estates" (§ 123, cf. § 173). When property is so defined, everyone has a reason to enter civil society, and everyone is capable of entering it, having some rights which he can transfer. However, Locke did not keep to this definition. He used the term in two different senses at points where its meaning was decisive in his argument. The property for the protection of which men oblige themselves to civil society is sometimes (e.g., §§123, 131, 137) stated to be "life, liberty and estate," but sometimes (e.g., §§ 138–140) it is clearly only goods or land.[34] Consequently, men without estate or goods, that is, without property in the ordinary sense, are rightfully both in civil society and not in civil society.

When the property for the protection of which men enter civil society is taken to be life, liberty and estate, all men (except slaves) are eligible for membership; when it is taken to be goods or estate alone, then only men who possess them are eligible. Locke interprets it both ways, without any consciousness of inconsistency. What has happened is understandable in the light of our analysis. Locke's recognition of differential class rights in his own society, having been carried into his postulates as an implicit assumption of differential natural rights and rationality, without displacing the formal

---

[33] Locke did, of course, justify slavery also, but not on grounds of inherently differential rationality. Enslavement was justified only when a man had "by his fault forfeited his own life, by some act that deserves death" (§ 23). Locke appears to have thought of it as a fit penalty for his natural criminals.

[34] A striking instance of the latter use is in § 138, where, after arguing that men in society must have property (since the purpose of their entering society was to preserve property), he concludes that "they have such a right to the goods which by the law of the community are theirs, that nobody hath a right to take their substance or any part of it from them without their own consent; without this they have no property at all."

assumption of general rationality and equal rights, has emerged at the level of the social contract in a crucial ambiguity about who are parties to the contract.

The question as to whom Locke considered to be members of civil society seems to admit only one answer. Everyone, whether or not he has property in the ordinary sense, is included, as having an interest in preserving his life and liberty. At the same time only those with "estate" can be full members, for two reasons: only they have a full interest in the preservation of property, and only they are fully capable of that rational life—that voluntary obligation to the law of reason—which is the necessary basis for full participation in civil society. The laboring class, being without estate, are subject to, but not full members of, civil society. If it be objected that this is not one answer but two inconsistent answers, the reply must be that both answers follow from Locke's assumptions, and that neither one alone, but only the two together, accurately represent his thinking.

This ambiguity about membership in civil society by virtue of the supposed original contract allows Locke to consider all men as members for purposes of being ruled and only the men of estate as members for purposes of ruling. The right to rule (more accurately, the right to control any government) is given only to the men of estate; it is they who are given the decisive voice about taxation, without which no government can subsist (§ 140). On the other hand, the obligation to be bound by law and subject to the lawful government is fixed on all men whether or not they have property in the sense of estate, indeed, whether or not they have made an express compact. When Locke broadens his doctrine of express consent into a doctrine of

tacit consent, he leaves no doubt about who are obligated. Tacit consent is assumed to have been given by "every man, that hath any possessions, or enjoyment, of any part of the dominions of any government...whether this his possession be of land, to him and his heirs forever, or a lodging only for a week; or whether it be barely travelling freely on the highway; and in effect, it reaches as far as the very being of any one within the territories of that government" (§ 119). Locke is careful to say (§ 122) that this does not make a man a full member of civil society, but only subjects him rightfully to its government: the men of no estate are not admitted to full membership by the back door of tacit consent.[35] Of course, Locke had to retreat to tacit consent because it was impossible to show express consent in the case of present citizens of an established state. However, his doctrine of tacit consent has the added convenience that it clearly imposes obligation, reaching to their "very being," on those with no estate whatever.

It appears from the foregoing anlysis that the result of Locke's work was to provide a moral basis for a class state from postulates of equal individual natural rights. Given the seventeenth-century individualist natural-rights assumptions, a class state could only be legitimized by a doctrine of consent which would bring one class within, but not make it fully a part of, the state. Locke's theory achieved this end. Its accomplishment required the implicit assumptions which he held. These assumptions involved him in the ambiguities and contradictions that pervade

---

35 We may notice incidentally that in his discussion of tacit consent, as well as in that of the supposed express entry into civil society by the contract, Locke lumps together life, liberty and estate under one term, and here the term is not even "property" but "possession" (§ 119, quoted above).

his argument. It is difficult to see how he could have persisted in such contradictions had he not been taking the class state as one desideratum and equal natural rights as another.

Locke did not twist deliberately a theory of equal natural rights into a justification for a class state. On the contrary, his honestly held natural-rights assumptions made it possible, indeed almost guaranteed, that his theory would justify a class state without any sleight of hand. The decisive factor was that the equal natural rights Locke envisaged, including as they did the right to unlimited accumulation of property, led logically to differential class rights and so to justification of a class state. Locke's confusions are the result of honest deduction from a postulate of equal natural rights which contained its own contradiction. The evidence suggests that he did not realize the contradiction in the postulate of equal natural right to unlimited property, but that he simply read into the realm of right (or the state of nature) a social relation which he accepted as normal in civilized society. The source of the contradictions in his theory is his attempt to state in universal (non-class) terms, rights and obligations which necessarily had a class content.

UNSETTLED PROBLEMS RECONSIDERED

When Locke's theory is understood in the sense here ascribed to it, some outstanding difficulties of its interpretation may be resolved.

(1) The problem inherent in the joint-stock interpretation of Locke's state is now no problem, for we have seen how Locke considers that the state consists both of property-owners only and of the whole population. He has no difficulty, therefore, in thinking of the state as a joint-stock company of owners whose majority decision binds not only themselves but also their employees. The laboring class, whose only asset is their capacity to labor, cannot take part in the operations of the company at the same level as the owners. Nevertheless, the laboring class is so necessary to the operations of the company as to be an organic part of it. The purpose of the company is not only to keep the property it has, but also to preserve the right and conditions which enable it to enlarge its property; one of these conditions is a labor force effectively submitted to the company's jurisdiction. Perhaps the closest analogue to Locke's state is the joint-stock company of merchants trading with or planting in distant lands, whose charter gives them, or allows them to take, such jurisdiction over the natives or the transplanted labor force as the nature of the trade requires.

(2) The implicit contradiction in that interpretation of Locke's theory which emphasizes the supremacy of the majority is also explained. The inconsistency, it will be remembered, was between the assertion of majority rule and the insistence on the sanctity of individual property. What would happen if the propertyless were a majority? This was no fanciful problem. It had been raised in the debates between the Levellers and the Independents in the parliamentary army during the civil wars.[36] It was a real difficulty in Locke's day, for it was thought that the propertyless were a majority.[37] We can now see that there is no conflict between the assertion of majority rule and of property right inasmuch as Locke was assuming that only those with property were full members of civil society and thus of the majority.

[36] A. S. P. Woodhouse, ed., *Puritanism and Liberty* (London: Dent, 1938), esp. pp. 53–63.
[37] Cf. King's estimate, cited above, n. 12.

(3) Various inconsistencies left unexplained in Locke by the liberal-individualist interpretation can also be resolved. Mr. Gough asks, for instance, whether Locke can really have believed, as he did (§ 140), "that the consent of a majority of representatives was the same as a man's own consent, from which it is., in fact, twice removed?"[38] Locke can easily have thought so if he was thinking primarily of the defense of property owners as a whole. His equation of a man's own consent with the consent of the majority makes sense only if he was thinking in this way. Locke was very well aware that there were differences of interest between the landed men, the merchants, and the monied men, differences which he saw sharply demonstrated in struggles over the incidence of taxation.[39] In these circumstances, the fact that he could identify individual and majority consent to taxation indicates that he was thinking of the defense of property as such. Locke could assume, as a man of property himself, that the common interest of propertied men was more important than their divergent interests as owners of land, or of money, or of mercantile stock.

(4) The debate about whether Locke was an individualist or a "collectivist," whether he put the purposes of the individual or the purposes of society first, now appears in a new light. When the fundamental quality of Locke's individualism is kept in mind, the controversy becomes meaningless. His individualism does not consist entirely in maintaining that individuals are by nature free and equal and can only be rightfully subjected to the jurisdiction of others by their own consent. The main significance of Locke's individualism is that it makes the individual the natural proprietor of his own person and capacities, owing nothing to society for them.

Such an individualism is necessarily collectivism (in the sense of asserting the supremacy of civil society over every individual). For it asserts an individuality that can be realized fully only in accumulating property, and, therefore, realized only by some at the expense of the individuality of the others. To permit such a society to function, political authority must be supreme over individuals; if it is not, there can be no assurance that the property institutions essential to this kind of individualism will have adequate protection. Individuals who have the means to realize their personalities (that is, the propertied) do not need to reserve any rights against civil society, since civil society is constructed by and for them, and operated by and for them. All they need to do is insist that civil society, or the majority of themselves, is supreme over any government, for a particular government might otherwise get out of hand. Locke did not hesitate to allow individuals to hand over to civil society all their natural rights and powers, including specifically all their possessions and land (§§ 120, 128, 136), or, what comes to the same thing, to grant all the rights and powers necessary to the ends for which society was formed (§§ 99, 129, 131), the majority being the judge (§ 97). The wholesale transfer of individual rights was necessary to get sufficient collective force for the protection of property. Locke could afford to propose this transfer because the civil society was to be in the control of the men of property. Under these circumstances individualism must, and could safely, be left to the collective supremacy of the state.

The notion that individualism and "collectivism" are the opposite ends of

---

38 *Op. cit.*, p. 69.

39 *Considerations*, in *Works* (1759), II, 36, 29.

a scale along which states and theories of the state can be arranged, regardless of the stage of social development in which they appear, is superficial and misleading. Locke's individualism, that of an emerging capitalist society, does not exclude, but on the contrary demands, supremacy of the state over the individual. It is not a question of the more individualism, the less collectivism; rather, the more thoroughgoing the individualism, the more complete the collectivism. Hobbes's theory is the supreme illustration of this relation, but his denial of traditional natural law and his failure to provide guarantees for property against the sovereign (whether a majority of the people or an absolute monarch) did not recommend his views to those who thought property the central social fact. Locke was more acceptable because of his ambiguity about natural law and because he provided some sort of guarantee for property rights. When the specific quality of seventeenth-century bourgeois individualism is seen in this light, it is no longer necessary to search for a compromise between Locke's individualist and collectivist statements; they imply each other.

(5) Locke's constitutionalism now becomes more intelligible; it need not be minimized or emphasized. It can be seen for what it is, a defense of the rights of expanding property rather than of the rights of the individual against the state.

We may notice, in this respect, that Locke did not think it desirable (whereas the Levellers in the Agreement of the People had thought it essential) to reserve some rights to the individual against any parliament or government. Locke's state does not directly protect any individual rights. The individual's only safeguard against arbitrary government lies in the right of the majority to say when a government has broken its trust to act always in the public good, never arbitrarily. Locke could assume that this supremacy of the majority constituted a sufficient safeguard for individual rights because he thought that all who had the right to be consulted were agreed on one concept of the public good: maximizing the nation's wealth, and thereby (as he saw it) its welfare. This agreement could be postulated only because he thought that the laboring class had no right to be consulted. Locke's constitutionalism is essentially a defense of the supremacy of property—not that of the yeoman only, but more especially that of the men of substance to whom the security of unlimited accumulation was of first importance.

Locke's insistence that the authority of the government ("the legislative") is limited and fiduciary, dependent on the consent of the majority of taxable persons, or on that majority's interpretation of the government's faithfulness to its trust, is not the primary part of his whole theory. He had to develop limitations on government because he had first constructed the other part, i.e., the total subordination of the individual to civil society. Both parts were necessary for any theory which sought to protect and promote the property institutions, and thereby the kind of society, which to secure a civil war, a restoration, and a further revolution had been necessary. If in 1689 the confinement of arbitrary government had a more obvious immediacy, subordination of the individual to the state had at least as lasting a significance. The Whig revolution not only established the supremacy of parliament over the monarchy but also consolidated the position of the men of property—specifically of those men who were using their property in the new way, as capital employed to yield profit—over the laboring class. Locke's theory served the Whig state in both respects.

We have seen how Locke, by carrying into his postulates the implicit assumptions of class differential rationality and rights (derived from his comprehension of his own society), reached an ambiguous theory of differential membership in civil society, a theory which justified a class state from postulates of equal individual natural rights. Ambiguity about membership concealed from Locke himself the contradiction in his indivualism, which produced full individuality for some by consuming the individuality of others. Locke could not have been conscious that the indi-

viduality he championed was at the same time a denial of individuality. Such consciousness was not to be found in men who were just beginning to grasp the great possibilities for individual freedom which lay in the advancement of capitalist society. The contradiction was there, but these men could not recognize it, let alone resolve it. Locke was at the fountainhead of English liberalism. The greatness of seventeenth-century liberalism was its assertion that the free rational individual was the criterion of the good society; its tragedy was that this very assertion necessarily denied individualism to half the nation.

WILLMOORE KENDALL

John Locke and the
Doctrine of Majority-Rule[*]

POPULAR SOVEREIGNTY

Since Locke certainly claimed (in reply to his question regarding the "way of designing and knowing the persons that have" political power) for the majority of the members of his political society

* Reprinted from Willmoore Kendall, *John Locke and the Doctrine of Majority-Rule* (Urbana, Ill.: University of Illinois Press, 1959), pp. 90–123, by permission of the publisher.

all the power which the society itself could rightfully exercise,[1] the validity of our thesis that he was an extreme majority-rule democrat is most likely to be questioned by those who regard his theory as one in which there is no room for the concept of sovereignty as we today understand it. Locke's majority, they may object, was to have its way only within certain carefully

[1] See below p. 220.

defined limits (*i.e.,* within the limits set by the natural rights which he attributes to the members of his society). If the majority (or the people) were to ignore these limits, it would find itself exercising powers which Locke denies to the society itself. Locke, in a word, could not possibly have countenanced the notion of an unlimited sovereignty, either in the whole people or in a majority of the people.

We have, as the reader will recall, taken the liberty of treating Locke's state of nature as an expository device, the purpose of which is to show what men's rights and duties would be in the absence of formal political organization. Proceeding on this assumption, we have attempted to analyze Locke's account of those rights and duties into irreducible first principles of ethics— always, however, emphasizing the fact that they are intended to apply to a situation in which, by definition, there is no political organization, and, wherever possible, calling attention to their mutual incompatibility.

We shall, in the same way, treat Locke's "compact" as an expository device, whose purpose is to lay bare the essential character of the rights and duties which belong to men as members of (legitimate) commonwealths.[2] That is, we shall proceed *as if Locke had said to the reader:*

---

[2] Cf. J. Allen Smith, *The Growth and Decadence of Constitutional Government* (New York: Henry Holt & Co., 1930) pp. 167–68: "[Locke] did not contend that the social contract was the origin of all governments, but merely of all legitimate governments.... A fair interpretation of his political philosophy justifies the assumption that any part which the social contract may have had in the remote past in the creation of political institutions was, in his opinion, of minor importance in comparison with the significance of the social contract doctrine as a theory of political organization."

A commonwealth, in my view, is simply a group of people occupying a given territory and, normally, obeying a common government. All of us are familiar with such groups of persons, and all of us are accustomed to distinguish in our minds between those situations in which the members of a commonwealth are under an obligation to obey their present government and those situations in which we are unable to perceive any such obligation. Or, if you like, physical power to promulgate and enforce laws sometimes, in this commonwealth or that one, gets into the hands of persons who have no right to exercise it, and use it to enforce rules which ought not to be obeyed. Unfortunately, however, our ideas on this question are extremely indefinite, thus greatly in need of clarification; and the need is all the greater because two recent writers, Filmer and Hobbes, have said things about it which, at least in my own opinion, are iniquitous. I believe myself to have discovered certain principles which will serve, for those of us who disagree with Filmer and Hobbes, as reliable criteria by which to distinguish governments which ought to be obeyed from those which ought not.

Briefly, the way in which I have arrived at these principles is as follows. I start out by assuming that organization for purposes of government is a necessity for human beings—a notion which we may express either by saying (as I sometimes do in a metaphorical sense) that men were not willing when they were in the state of nature (= in an unorganized condition) to remain in it, or by saying (what comes to the same thing) that they would not willingly return to the state of nature even if they were free to do so.

At the same time, I assume that they are not so eager for the benefits of life in an organized political society as to be willing to pay an unlimited price for them. They desire certain conveniences which can be had only through organization, *i.e.,* certain rights, and are willing to accept certain burdens (which we shall call duties) in order to assure themselves those conveniences; but if the onerousness of the burdens were obviously disproportionate to the desirability of the conveniences, they would not be willing to accept the former —nor would it be fair, in that event, to expect them to do so.

I assume, thirdly, that it is possible to infer, from what we know about people, what *inconveniences* would weigh most heavily upon them in the absence of political organization; and that it is proper for us to posit the removal of those inconveniences as the *minimum* which they ought (if the exchange is to be a fair one) to receive from their political society in return for the acceptance of any burdens whatever. Those inconveniences are, pretty obviously, the absence of any commonly accepted law defining men's rights and duties, the lack of an impartial judge to decide disputes regarding maters of right, and finally, the helplessness of the weak man with right on his side against the unjust man who happens to be strong.[3] We may, therefore, point to the following facilities which a political society must be able to offer to its members in return for the duties which it imposes upon them: promulgated, standing laws defining the rights and duties of all the members; arrangements for impartial decisions on matters of right; and unfailing protection of the members in the enjoyment of their rights.[4] A society which fails to provide these facilities is not really a political society at all, but a continuation of the state of nature. In other words, we shall regard men as organized only when they are organized in such a way as to be free of the inconveniences of the state of nature.

In the fourth place, having gone so far already as to speak in terms of a fair exchange between the society and its members, I assume that the most convenient method we can employ in describing the duties which the members must accept in order for the society to be able to provide the facilities set forth above is that of pretending that a contract has been negotiated between the members of the society, setting forth the burdens they are willing to shoulder in return for such facilities. In other words, I shall speak as if such a society could come into existence only by

virtue of a promise given by each of its members to accept certain duties and faithfully discharge them—which is only another way of saying that such a society can continue to exist only if it can count on its members to act *as if* they were under contract for the performance of certain duties.

I propose in this book, then, to expound my views as to the nature of the promise which individuals must be understood to have given if their society is really to deliver them from the inconveniences of life outside society—*i.e.*, the understandings which must exist between the individuals in a society in order for the latter to be capable of achieving the purposes for which it exists.

The chief of these understandings which Locke demands of the citizens of his commonwealth are (1) an understanding with regard to the *purpose* for which the society's power is to be used; (2) an understanding as to the kind of obedience which each member of the society may expect the other members to tender to the society's law; and (3) an understanding as to the way in which the society's laws are to be made.

The most immediately interesting of these understandings, for our present purposes, is the first. If the reader will turn back to Locke's definition of political power[5] he will observe that it contains the words "and all this only for the public good." It is, as it stands, an apparent limitation upon the power of the society (*i.e.*, the power of the society cannot be employed *except* for the promotion of the public good)— and, at the same time, a grant of power to the society (*i.e.*, to take action for the public good). Whether or not it *is*, in the treatment it receives at Locke's hands, a limitation upon the society's power, is a question to which we shall return at a later point, our present con-

---

[3] ix. 124–26. [4] ix. 131.

[5] Willmoore Kendall, *John Locke and the Doctrine of Majority-Rule* (Urbana, Ill.: University of Illinois Press, 1959), p. 66.

cern being to direct attention to Locke's failure to give an adequate account of what he understood the phrase to mean. There is no *a priori* objection to the notion (already mentioned briefly in our discussion of Locke's law of nature) that men may become so related to one another in a collectivity as to justify us in speaking in terms of a good which is that of the collectivity rather than that of its members regarded as individuals. Nor is there any objection *a priori* to the notion that men become so related to one another in a collectivity as to be willing to sacrifice their narrow interests as individuals to the broader interests of the collectivity. Much of the history of humankind would be incomprehensible but for the possibility of appealing to such an hypothesis, and the prospects for the future moral development of mankind would seem dismal indeed but for the possibility of indulging the hope that it is true. Nevertheless, to concede the utility of the concept is not to concede that it should be loosely used, and we cannot face too early, in our study of Locke, the fact that he was completely unaware of its presuppositions.[6] He should have seen (but did not) that if there is to be a good "public" to a group of individuals, they must have over a considerable area, interests which are really common, and that, conversely, where such common interests do not exist, there is no point in speaking of a public good. Rousseau was well aware of these presuppositions, and uses the concept of the *"bien public"* with notable preci-

sion.[7] Locke lacks Rousseau's insight into the fact that, were the men in a commonwealth without recognized common interests, the maintenance of authority would be impossible, while if their interests did not conflict authority would be unnecessary, that, therefore, a sort of equilibrium between centrifugal and centripetal tendencies is a logical presupposition of political society.[8] When, therefore, what he wants to show is that government is necessary, he speaks as if men's interests were so divergent as to deprive the notion of a good common to them of all meaning; and when what he wants to show is that obedience pays good returns, he simply takes for granted the existence of enough common interests to constitute a public good—and without realizing that this makes his conclusions inapplicable to situations where that assumption is not fulfilled. If, that is to say, Locke had been really aware of the area of common interests whose existence is assumed in his concept of a public good, he would have contented himself with arguing (as Rousseau does) that *in a certain kind of society* promoting one's own interest is the same thing as promoting the public good,[9] and thus would have made room in his political system both for the duty

---

[6] Cf. Lamprecht, *Moral and Political Philosophy of John Locke*, p. 135 n.: "Locke did not distinguish between the common good and the good of each separate person, but assumed always that the former included the latter. ... Locke does not give any indication of having realized that there is any problem in this identification of private and public interests."

[7] Cf. Rousseau, *Contrat social,* i. 5: "Que des hommes épars soient successivement asservis à un seul...je n'y vois point un peuple...; c'est, si l'on veut, une agrégation, mais non pas une association; *il n'y a là ni bien public, ni corps politique"* (italics mine). This is, clearly, to say that there are situations in which there is no good which is public.

[8] Cf. *ibid.,* ii. 1: 'Si l'opposition des intérêts particuliers a rendu nécessaire l'établissement des sociétés, c'est l'accord de ces mêmes intérêts qui l'a rendu possible. C'est ce qu'il y a de commun dans ces différents intérêts qui forme le lien social; et s'il n'y avait pas quelque point dans lequel tous les intérêts s'accordent, nulle société ne saurait exister."

[9] *Ibid.,* ii. 4.

to look well to one's own interests and that duty to promote the *public* interest which he demands of the members of his society. Or, to put the same point in another way, he would have seen that men must be related to one another in a certain way before we can conceive of their being willing to make this (first) of the three promises of which Locke is thinking[10]—and that, having posited the existence of such relations we must not, subsequently, exaggerate the extent to which their interests conflict.

With regard to the second and third of these understandings, the critic's most important task is to distinguish sharply between them; for, although they appear at first blush to come to much the same thing, they do not in fact do so. On the one hand Locke is saying (on our interpretation of the compact) that the idea of a society free from the inconvenience of the state of nature involves as a matter of course the recognition by the members of the society that the latter can act for the public good only by imposing certain uniformities of conduct upon its members, and that the members must stand ready to accept these impositions when they are in the public interest. There is, Locke is saying, an absolute and irrevocable obligation upon the members of a political society to discharge any duties which arise out of the community's needs, and to content themselves with such rights as attach to the performance of those duties. Implicit in this insistence is the notion that where men live together in a genuine community (*i.e.,* one with a good which is genuinely public) there arises a complex

of rights which ought to be respected and duties which ought to be performed, and that the law of the community ought to be a law which enjoins those duties and respects those rights—which is, be it noted, some such restatement of the second thesis above as we have already warned the reader to expect. On the other hand, Locke is saying that a society free of the inconveniences of the state of nature is possible only where men can count upon each other to obey all positive legal enactments made in a certain way; and our point, for the moment, is that the promise necessary for an understanding of this kind is a promise of an essentially different character from the promise to promote the public good and the promise to obey that law which is in fact necessary for the promotion of that good. For, the moment we begin to speak of legal enactments made in a certain way, we move from the world of concepts into the world of actualities, where methods for enacting positive rules must, if they are to be applied, be applied by human beings who are not only fallible intellectually, thus capable of conceiving incorrectly the uniformities of conduct demanded by the public interest, but also capable, upon occasion, of employing for their own selfish purposes whatever power is entrusted to them to determine the content of legal enactments.

It is only against the background of the essential difference between the *first two* of these three understandings and the third (to which we shall devote most of the remainder of this chapter) that we can appreciate the significance of the question Locke raises, at the very beginning of his book, as to who the *persons* are who have the right of making laws, *i.e.,* who the persons are who have the right to political power. For such a question, on the lips of a

---

10 Cf. viii. 107: *"Those who liked one another so well* as to join into society cannot but be supposed to have *some acquaintance and friendship* together, and some trust in one another"* (italics mine).

man who believes that the *real* duty of each man in a political society is to promote the public good and to obey laws calculated to promote the public good is, quite simply, a *question mal posée*. The remainder of the present chapter is, in the main, an elaboration of this criticism of Locke. We do not propose to find fault with his assumption that the relations between the members of a political society free from the disadvantages of the state of nature can properly be described in contractual terms, or to raise inconvenient questions as to whether or not such a contract was ever negotiated by the members of any political society. We do not propose, either, to question his assumption that political society is necessary, in the sense explained above, or his assumption that by imposing upon its members duties disproportionate to benefits conferred, a society might well cease to be (or fail to become) a society free of the inconveniences of an unorganized existence, or his assumption that the *minima* of a society free of those inconveniences are a uniform law (thus one which imposes equal duties on its members), an impartial judge, and adequate machinery for the enforcement of its decrees. Nor shall we press further our objections, already recorded, to Locke's loose thinking about the public good, or his cavalier assumption that in promoting the good of one's own political platoon one also promotes the good of humankind. Rather we shall fix attention upon the relation between the *third* understanding, the notion that the members of a political society have promised one another absolute obedience to all positive enactments made in a certain way, and criticize it exclusively on Locke's own principles. It will be shown (1) that, although he did not use these words, Locke does read into this third understanding, not only the concept of unlimited sovereignty, but also the concept of an unlimited sovereignty which

is *personal*; (2) that the promise necessary for such an understanding is prohibited by Locke's own theory of consent, thus would not (on his showing) be binding upon the members of his political society; and (3) that a society built upon such an understanding would not be free from the inconveniences which he attributes to the state of nature.

Most of the current misunderstandings about Locke's views on sovereignty can be attributed to (a) failure to distinguish between the powers of Locke's government (at any given moment) and the powers which (on his principles) the society can entrust to the government whenever it sees fit to do so, (b) failure to pay adequate attention to Locke's concrete proposals regarding political organization, (c) failure to face the implications of what Locke has to say about the right of revoltion, and (d) failure to appreciate the character of the obligation which Locke assigns to the individual *vis-à-vis* his society and its law. We propose to take up these points *seriatim*.

(a) The most significant thing about Locke's *Treatise of Civil Government*," writes Professor Lamprecht, "is really not what it says but what it avoids saying. Locke's most notable trait is that he could compose an entire treatise on government without so much as mentioning the word or introducing the idea of sovereignty."[11] And Professor Laski,

---

[11] Lamprecht, "Hobbes and Hobbism," p. 49. Cf. *Id., Moral and Political Philosophy of John Locke,* p. 148: "He did, to be sure, reject any government which does not rest in the consent of the governed; but he nowhere expounded a doctrine of popular sovereignty." Cf. Smith, *op. cit.,* p. 14: "The conception of the state which prevailed in the [American] Revolutionary period was very largely that which we find in the political writings of John Locke. His defense of the social compact was not a defense of unlimited power.... Sovereignty in the sense of unlimited power could have no place in the philosophy of the free state."

whose opinion regarding a question of this kind cannot lightly be set aside, can be cited to the same effect. "It is," he says, "not accident which makes him [Locke] construct a non-sovereign state."[12] "His state is nothing so much as a contract between a group of business men who form a limited liability company whose memorandum of association forbids to the directors all those practices of which the Stuarts had, until his time, been guilty."[13] Furthermore, we have Locke's own word that "their [the legislative's] power in the utmost bounds of it is limited to the public good of the society. It is a power that hath no other end but preservation, and therefore can never have a right to destroy, enslave, or designedly to impoverish the subjects."[14] Now *one* clear meaning of these passages is that Locke intended the government *of the day* in his political society to be a government of limited power, thus of limited sovereignty, thus non-sovereign; and if this were all that Professors Lamprecht and Laski intended to say, the statements we have quoted from them above would be quite unexceptionable from the point of view of the present study. The relation between the government of the day in Locke's system and the society from which it derives its powers is, quite simply, assimilable to that between principal and agent in Anglo-American law; and for the government to claim *vis-à-vis* the society for which it acts powers which the society has not entrusted to it *would,* on Locke's showing, be as preposterous as for an agent to claim, *vis-à-vis* his principal, a freedom to do in the latter's name things which the latter does not wish done.[15]

Locke might, to be sure, have spoken more clearly about the precise character of the limits upon the power of the

legislative (= the government)[16] and of the act by which it becomes the society's agent. There are passages from which, for example, we might get the impression that the legislative possesses a general power to take whatever action is necessary for the public good—a power similar to that which has, on occasion, been claimed for the government of the United States under the preamble and the general welfare clause of the constitution. The legislative may, he holds in such passages, "direct how the force of the commonwealth shall be employed for preserving the community and the members of it"[17]—a grant of power with which the most ambitious legislature might well be satisfied, and one which recalls the notion of "universal" agency in Anglo-American law. There are other passages which convey the impression (especially to an American reader, trained to think in such terms) that the legislative receives certain specific powers which—while it may not exceed them—it may subsequently exercise as a matter of right until it can be shown to have betrayed its trust. There are, again, passages in which critics have been able to see elements of a second, "governmental" *contract,* by which the society is itself bound not to disturb the legislature so long as it respects (the letter of? the spirit of?) the instrument of delegation.[18] "This legislative," he writes, "is not only the supreme power of the commonwealth, but sacred and unalterable in the hands where the com-

---

12 Harold J. Laski, *The Rise of Liberalism* (New York: Harper & Brothers, 1936), p. 127.

13 *Ibid.*   14 xi. 135.

15 Cf. Aaron, *John Locke,* p. 273.

16 Cf. xiii. 149: "In a constituted commonwealth...acting for the preservation of the community, there can be but one supreme power, which is the legislative, to which all the rest are and must be subordinate."

17 xii, 143.

18 But cf. Gierke, *Natural Law,* pp. 104–5: "The doctrine of the social contract developed in England, especially in the sense of popular sovereignty. The English theory gave the contract of rulership only secondary importance *if it did not drop it altogether*" (italics mine).

munity have once placed it."[19] And, again, the "legislative or supreme authority...is *bound* to dispense justice and decide the rights of the subject by promulgated standing laws, and known authorised judges."[20] We return below to both these questions, but we may anticipate by saying that the notion of a right in the legislative to continue to govern so long as it can point to the language of such a contract as justification for its actions will hardly survive a careful reading of the *Second Treatise*,[21] and that Blackstone was undoubtedly correct (however misguided from the democratic point of view) when he denounced Locke for not having given to his government adequate protection against popular whims.[22]

It seems highly probable, however, that in these quotations Lamprecht and Laski meant to do more than deny the sovereignty of the government of the day in Locke's system, and that their intention was to identify Locke with that tendency in political theory which —carried out to its logical implications —eventuates in a demand for institutional limitations upon *all* governments, even governments acting under express popular mandate. If so, it can easily be shown that they have misunderstood the bearing of what Locke said about these matters, and have mistaken Locke's wish to limit the power of the agent (in the relation he is discussing) to act against the will of the principal for a wish to limit the power of the principal to give instructions to his agent. *I.e.,* the interesting question (which Lamprecht and Laski have answered incorrectly if they meant to answer it at all) is not whether the government in Locke's system has the power to do to the society that which the latter *disapproves,* but whether the society can assign to it the power to do that which the society *approves*—however much it may conflict with previously received notions regarding the limits upon government. Had they asked themselves the second of these questions rather than the first, they would, as we shall show in (c) and (d) below, have used more cautious language in expounding Locke's ideas on sovereignty.[23]

(b) Nothing is easier, in writing about the *Second Treatise*,[24] than to forget that it is a book about politics and political institutions, and to proceed to treat it as if it were merely a book on ethics. All six of the aforementioned theses regarding the law of nature are, as we have shown, enunciated at some point in its argument; and none of

[19] xi. 134.

[20] xi. 136 (italics mine).

[21] Cf. D. L. Keir, *The Constitutional History of Modern Britain, 1485–1937* (New York: D. Van Nostrand Co., 1938), p. 271. But cf. Lamprecht, *op. cit.,* p. 145: "The people [in Locke's system] as much as the legislative are morally bound to abide by the contract, and cannot, with changing whims, annul one contract to make another."

[22] Sir William Blackstone, *Commentaries on the Laws of England* (Philadelphia: J. B. Lippincott & Co., 1859), i. 213: "The principles of Mr. Locke...would have reduced the society almost to a state of nature; would have levelled all distinctions of honour, rank, offices, and property; would have annihilated the sovereign power, and in consequence repealed all positive laws; and would have left the people at liberty to have erected a new system of state upon a new foundation of polity." This is strong evidence in favor of the interpretation of Locke urged in the present treatise.

[23] Cf. Carpenter, *The Development of American Political Thought*, p. 103: "In Locke's theory, sovereignty can exist nowhere except in the community as a whole. This is the original and supreme will which organizes the government and defines its just powers." Cf. John Neville Figgs, *The Divine Right of Kings* (Cambridge: University Press, 1914), p. 242.

[24] Kendall, *op. cit.,* Chap. IV.

them seems easy to square, at the limit, with the doctrine of unlimited sovereignty. We must, however, guard equally against the mistake of taking *one* of them as the doctrine of the "real" Locke and writing the others off as inconsistencies (for who can say which we should take?), and the mistake of confusing what we think he should (on his own ethical principles) have said about politics with what he in fact said. It is not improbable that behind the practical recommendations of every political theorist there lies a more or less articulate and more or less consistent thory as to what, in an ideal world, the limits upon governmental power ought to be. That governments should not violate the moral law, that they should not destroy or enslave or impoverish, that they should be stripped of authority when they begin to abuse it—these are propositions to which all (save only the perverse and sinful) who think about politics would unhesitatingly agree; and it is certain that Locke believed all of them. The differences between political theorists (in the light of which we distribute them into "schools") emerge when we consult them upon the *concrete institutional arrangements* which they are prepared to urge upon constitution-makers in a world in which the moral law must take its chances with the apparent necessity of placing the *legal* "right of making laws, with penalties of death and consequently all less penalties," in the hands of some person or group of persons—a world, furthermore, in which it is often difficult to decide whether or not a given law *is* one which destroys, enslaves, or impoverishes. Rules of morality and declarations of rights do get themselves written into constitutions, and perhaps, as Professor Laski maintains, it is well that they should.[25] But

American experience with (*e.g.*) the so-called "penal clause" of the Fourteenth Amendment suggests that they affect the course of subsequent events only where (a) persons yet living demand that they be respected, and (b) power to enforce them happens to be in the hands of those persons and not others.[26] And in that background, the way to discover how far a given political theorist is willing to go with the exponents of popular sovereignty is by fixing attention upon the facilities he would like to provide for the translation of popular will into governmental policy, and the facilities he would like to provide for preventing such translation when it might result in (*e.g.*) violation of the moral law, or action against the public good, *etc.* Locke never says, as Rousseau does,[27] that if a people wishes to do itself hurt no one has a right to prevent it from doing so, but his political system is that of a man who believes this; and as we shall see in (c) and (d) below, those seeking ammunition with which to defend America's peculiar institution will look in vain for it in the *Second Treatise*.[28]

(c) The drift of Locke's mind, where it concerns itself not with problems of

---

25 Laski, *Grammar of Politics*, p. 305.

26 Cf. *ibid.*, p. 103: "Rights are not merely, or even greatly, a matter of the written record. Musty parchments will doubtless give them greater sanctity; they will not ensure their realisation."

27 Rousseau, *op. cit.*, ii. 12.

28 Cf. Louis B. Boudin, *Government by Judiciary* (New York: William Godwin, Inc., 1932), I, p. 82: "Clearly, Locke's opinions were not favorable to the establishment of government by judiciary; and...the most influential of the Framers of the United States Constitution thought exactly as did Locke, both in the matter of the submission of the minority to the majority, as well as in the matter of there being 'no judge on earth' between the people and the Legislature, and the 'appeal to Heaven.' And, what is more to the point, they thought they had actually put Locke's doctrine into the Constitution."

pure right but those of right within the context of political organization, comes most clearly to light in those sections of the *Second Treatise* which deal with the right of revolution. It is in these sections that the significance of the limitations which he imposed upon his government may be seen in its most naked form. His doctrine is the simple one that "the community perpetually retains a supreme power of saving themselves from the attempts and designs of anybody, *even of their legislators,* wherever they shall be so foolish or so wicked as to lay and carry on designs against the liberties and properties of the subject";[29] that, in a word, "there remains . . . in the people a supreme power to remove or alter the legislative, *when they find* the legislative act contrary to the trust reposed in them."[30]

The problem posed by such passages is, as we have pointed out above, that of the meaning we should assign to the word "trust." Lord, for example, finds in Locke only a "modified" right of revolution,[31] and Sabine sees in him what Rousseau was (he thinks) entitled to regard as an "unwarranted limitation on the power of the people to govern itself as it saw fit"—on the grounds, apparently, that the people, in Locke's system, can resume its power only by dissolving the government![32] It cannot, however, be too strongly emphasized that Locke, though sufficiently familiar with the idea of contract to base upon it his entire account of political obligation, uses another vocabulary in describ-

ing the relation between people and legislative, and that *he makes no secret of the fact that such reciprocal obligations as may be conceived to have taken place between people and government are, at any given moment, merely what the people concede them to be.* In short, to think of the "trust" by which the government acts as a contract is to think of a contract whose terms are (by its own provision) to be interpreted unilaterally by one of the parties—*i.e.,* to deprive the term "contract" of all of its ordinary meaning; and the critics have, in point of fact, been overlooking the joker in Locke's description of the relation. To say that the people can remove the legislative when they are of the opinion (= "when they find")[33] that the legislative has acted against the public good (= action "contrary to the trust reposed in them") is merely to say that the character of that trust is defined from moment to moment by what *we* are accustomed to call public opinion. Locke even goes so far as to concede, at one point, that the solution which he is proposing for the problems of politics involves laying "the foundation of government in the . . . opinion and . . . humour of the people"![34]

Nor is this all that the critics have overlooked in Locke's account of this matter. One of the passages reproduced above continues as follows: "The trust must necessarily be forfeited, and the power devolve into the hands of those that gave it, *who may place it anew*

---

[29] xiii. 149 (italics mine).

[30] *Ibid.* (italics mine).

[31] A. R. Lord, *The Principles of Politics* (Oxford: The Clarendon Press, 1921), p. 59.

[32] Sabine, *A History of Political Theory,* p. 535. He sees in Locke the "persistence" of a tradition in which "a kind of indefeasibility in the right of the king and other governing organs" was regarded as compatible with "the right of a community to govern itself."

[33] Cf. xix. 240: "The people shall be judges." He is replying to his own question as to who shall determine when a violation of the trust has occurred.

[34] xix. 223: "To this, perhaps, it will be said that the people being ignorant and always discontented, to lay the foundation of government in the unsteady opinion and uncertain humour of the people, is to expose it to certain ruin. . . . I answer . . . [that] people are not so easily got out of their old forms as some are apt to suggest."

where they shall think best for their safety and security."[35] The right of revolution, that is to say, involves a right to put in the place of the legislative against which it is exercised one which *is* agreeable to the "opinion" and "humour" of the people—a right in the people to formulate their own notions as to what is "best for their safety and security" and, subsequently, to place power in the hands of men who will use it in accordance with those notions.[36]

It is a matter of some interest that Dunning, whose interpretation of Locke's theory coincides to a considerable extent with our own, finally falls back into the very error from which he appears to have written himself free. He says:

The society thus becomes, by the act of the individuals who form it, vested with the function of determining what are offences against the law of nature, and punishing violations of that law [wherefore anything is a violation of the law of nature which the society chooses to define as such?].[37]

And, again:

As that which underlies government and becomes active only when government is dissolved, the "community" [=the people?],... is held always to be the supreme power;. supremacy...belongs to that which is in the fullest sense the embodiment of [the public will of the society].[38]

So far in full agreement with our own interpretation; but not so in the sequel:

There is in this conception nothing of that absolute, unlimited, and uncontrollable sovereignty which was the soul of Hobbes' system.[39]

How are we to explain the fact that Dunning, having read Locke too carefully to attach to the limitations upon Locke's *government* the importance which they have assumed for other scholars, is yet unwilling to concede that what Locke ascribes to the society for which the government acts is *sovereignty?* Fortunately, Dunning has himself provided the answer to this question:

The natural rights of the individual limit the just power of the sovereign community precisely as they limited in the state of nature the just power of other individuals.[40]

In short, the explanation must be made in terms of the "persistence" of the notion (which we have already criticized in an earlier section) that Locke was, first, last, and always, the philosopher of inalienable individual rights. In the following section we shall examine the position of each of the individual members of Locke's political society *vis-à-vis* that society, attempting to show that the rights which he assigns to them are a function of, not a limitation on, the society's sovereignty.

(d) Before attempting to consider what Locke had to say about the obedience which the individual owes to the organized society of which he is a member, we must call attention to certain difficulties which the writer has deliberately ignored up to the present moment:

(1) We have, in the preceding section, taken no account of the possibility

---

35 xiii. 149 (italics mine).

36 Cf. xi. 141: "When the people have said, 'We will submit, and be governed by laws *made by such men* and in such forms,' nobody else can say other men shall make laws for them" (italics mine).

37 William Archibald Dunning, *A History of Political Theories from Luther to Montesquieu* (New York: The Macmillan Co., 1905), pp. 349–50.

38 *Ibid.*, p. 353.

39 *Ibid.*, pp. 349–350. Cf. *ibid.*, p. 353: *"So far as sovereignty is predicated by Locke in fact, if not in name, it is ascribed to the collective body which is created by the social pact"* (italics mine).

40 *Ibid.*, p. 350.

of differences of opinion between the members of a political society as to (*e.g.*) how it should employ its sovereignty, *i.e.*, its power of defining, and assessing penalties for, violations of the law of nature. We have, that is to say, simplified our discussion by equating the two questions: (a) what is the extent of the power which Locke claims for his political society? and (b) what is the extent of the power which Locke claims for the total membership of his political society—*i.e.*, for the people conceived in abstraction from the possibility of differences of opinion between them? Such a simplification has, be it noted, much to recommend it; since if we are to deal separately with the issues raised by the defenders of popular sovereignty (pure and simple) and those raised by the defenders of popular sovereignty plus majority-decisions regarding its exercise (= majority-sovereignty?) we must think, first of all, of a situation in which one might defend popular sovereignty without expressly committing oneself to majority-sovereignty; and the obvious example is a situation in which there *is* no dissident minority, thus unanimity. Or, to put the same thing in another way, we may tell ourselves that we have raised the question of the extent of the society's powers in its purest form when we state it with reference to a situation in which all methods of making decisions (except, possibly, decisions by lot)[41] about the use of those powers would come to the same thing. Purely aside, however, from the psychological improbability of unanimity, such a statement of the problem is unrealistic because all the interesting questions about the extent of a society's powers concern situations in which no problem would arise but

for the *existence* of differences of opinion among its members. These questions are always, that is to say, questions as to what should be done when one of the society's members, or a group of its members, steps forward to insist that what is about to be done in the society's name *should* not be done (because unjust, unwise, unnecessary, or unprecedented)—a statement which, be it noted, applies equally to decisions about internal and external policy, since a society whose members are unanimous in their support of a given external policy can evidently adopt no other. Historically, therefore, attacks upon the doctrine of sovereignty have come always from those who would like to make it possible for individuals and groups of individuals to prevent the action contemplated at such moments; and we are brought face to face with the curiosity that while we can (and must) distinguish between popular sovereignty and majority-sovereignty, by conceiving of the former in terms of unanimity, any particular exercise of popular sovereignty either ranges some of the society's members against others, thus (save in the improbable case of an unbreakable tie) a majority of those members against a minority, or poses no problem for theory to solve. Since, however, it is easy to conceive of arrangements whereby the power to make decisions regarding the exercise of the society's powers has been entrusted to a minority, the necessity of distinguishing between the sovereignty of the society and the sovereignty of the majority remains.

The simplification is further recommended by the fact that (along with the difficulty it involves) it is Locke's own—*i.e.*, he treats as a discrete question the claims of the majority of its members to exercise the power he attributes to the whole, and, in such a passage as that reproduced on page

---

41 "Possibly," because it appears improbable that a decision which nobody favors will be enforced.

210 above, he is clearly treating the society as (constructively) unanimous *although* the members of the legislative are evidently members of the society.[42]

(2) Locke was not especially concerned, in connection with his theory of popular sovereignty, with the problem for which (as we have just pointed out) modern liberalism has sought a solution, namely, that of the limits of the society's power over the individual member *as such* (rather than as an official of the society)—any more than, in his discussion of the majority's power over the minority, he was concerned with the question of possible abuse by a governing majority of its power over a governed minority. As Professor Lerner has lately reminded us, we live in a period in which things have happened to *governed* minorities and individuals which oblige us to give careful consideration to the problem of how they may be protected against "tyrannical" majorities.[43] Locke, in contrast, had clearly been seized of that which in his day was happening to governed majorities at the hands of minorities and individuals, and it was in this form that the problem involved most readily presented itself to his mind. Nevertheless, as we are about to show, he puts forward propositions which commit him on the issue as we discuss it today, and it is to these propositions that we direct the reader's attention in the following paragraphs:

Locke's teaching on this point is, quite simply, that which (erroneously, in the present writer's opinion) is usually attributed to Rousseau: The individual owes to the commonwealth of which he is a member a duty of obedience which is absolute and perpetual, and *must* be absolute and perpetual because the alternative is the anarchy of the state of nature:

The power that every individual gave the society when he entered into it can never revert to the individuals again, as long as the society lasts, but will always remain in the community; because without this there can be no community—no commonwealth.[44]

The power which the individual "gave up" includes *both* his power to "do whatever he thinks fit for the preservation of himself and others"[45] and his "power of punishing"[46]—and he gives them up, according to Locke, with the understanding that they are both to be exercised by the society,[47] which can subsequently call upon him to assist in the enforcement of its laws:

He has given up a right to the commonwealth to employ his force for the execution of the judgments of the commonwealth whenever he shall be called to it, *which,*

---

[42] Cf. Aaron, *op. cit.*, p. 276: "On... [Locke's] view the contract is between all the members of the society, as a consequence of which a trust is imposed upon one or more individuals. The ruler does not stand opposite to the people; he is one of them, but entrusted with exceptional duties."

[43] Although minorities have surely suffered least in the only country which has entrusted unlimited power to the numerical majority of its citizens. Cf. Lerner, *op. cit.*, p. 107: "What has happened to minorities in our day makes many of us fear majorities." Cf. Saripolos, *op. cit.*, p. 268: "Aujourd'hui, à la fin du XIXᵉ siècle, il s'agit en fin de fonder la vraie liberté et de protéger la minorité contre les *privilèges* de la majorité. La minorité demande aujourd'hui, comme la majorité avant la Révolution, à être quelque chose."

[44] xix. 243. Cf. Rousseau, *op. cit.*, i. 6, where we are told that the contract remains in force only "jusqu'à ce que, le pacte social étant violé, chacun rentre alors dans ses premiers droits, et reprenne sa liberté naturelle."

[45] Not, as Dunning incorrectly supposes, one power only. The misunderstanding is apparently due to Locke's unfamiliar use of the word "single" in the sentence (ix. 127): "It is this makes them so willingly give up every one his single [= private?] power of punishing, *etc.*" Cf. Dunning, *op. cit.*, p. 349.

[46] ix 128.   [47] ix. 130.

indeed, are his own judgments, they being made by himself or his representative.[48]

Furthermore,

...every man when he at first incorporates himself into any commonwealth, he, by his uniting himself thereunto, annexes also, and submits to the community *those possessions which he has, or shall acquire,* that do not already belong to any other government.... They become, both...person and possession, subject to the government and dominion of that commonwealth as long as it hath a being.[49]

Translated into the political vocabulary of our own day, these statements say as unambiguously as possible that (whatever may be the position of the individual *vis-à-vis* a *government* which he believes to have violated its trust and thus to have surrendered its title to act in the name of the commonwealth)[50] where the government's title to act in the name of the commonwealth is beyond dispute (or where the community itself acts as a legislature), the individual's rights (including his rights of property) are merely those vouchsafed to him by the positive law of his society. The individual may feel that a given law infringes upon his "natural" rights (*i.e.*, that it is morally outrageous), or that it is directed to some other end than "the peace, safety, and public good of the people";[51] but he cannot withhold his obedience, because membership in a commonwealth involves as a matter of course the surrender both of his private judgment and of his power to act upon his convictions. If, for example, he is a Quaker, and the law with which he is confronted is a declaration of war which provides for conscription, it becomes his duty not only to participate in the hostilities, but also, if called upon to do so, to assist in the coercion of conscientious objectors. Thus, while Carritt can find ample support in the *Second Treatise* for his statement to the effect that Locke "is one of those who think we ought to obey a government so long as it on the whole secures justice and happiness,"[52] he should not have gone on to say, on the strength of that statement, that "with all....[its] faults....his account of political obligation seems to me the best."[53] For in saying this he not only overlooks the major implications of Locke's real theory of *political* obligation (= that which describes the individual's obligation to the political unit of which he is a member), but also absolves Locke from responsibility for the introduction into modern political theory of the dangerous equivocation which was finally to develop into what Hobhouse has called the "metaphysical theory of the state."[54] For Locke (as we have seen) is saying, before Rousseau, two centuries before Bosanquet, that the commonwealth's judgments (= its laws = its will[55]) are the individual's own judgments (= his will), and is saying it in such fashion as to suggest that they are the individual's judgments *whether he agrees with them or not, i.e., they are the individual's judgments even when he consciously disagrees with them.* Nor can it be argued that this is to read into a single passage a meaning which is at variance

---

[48] vii. 88 (italics mine). Cf. vii. 89: "He authorises the society, or which is all one, the legislative thereof, to make laws for him as the public good of the society shall require, to the execution whereof his own assistance (as to his own decrees) is due." Cf. ix. 130.

[49] viii. 120 (italics mine).

[50] The reservation is necessary because Locke clearly intended that the commonwealth should regard itself as free to alter its government by revolution, and the revolution would of necessity be made by individuals.

[51] ix. 131.

[52] Carritt, *Morals and Politics,* p. 79.

[53] *Ibid.*

[54] L. T. Hobhouse, *The Metaphysical Theory of the State* (London: G. Allen & Unwin, 1918).

[55] xiii. 151.

with the remainder of Locke's argument, for he must be very deaf indeed to the nuances of political discourse who cannot detect in the following lines the elements of the distinction between the "actual" will of the individual and the "real" will which is his whether he thinks it is or not, as also of the insistence that freedom consists rather in the presence than the absence of constraint (*i.e.*, the insistence which Hobhouse treats as the essence of the "metaphysical" theory):

Law, in its true notion, is not so much the limitation as the direction of a free and intelligent agent to his proper interest [even when it directs him to that which he regards as against his interest?].... That ill deserves the name of confinement which hedges us in only from bogs and precipices. ...The end of law is not to abolish or restrain, but to preserve and enlarge freedom.[56]

Locke's use of the word "law" is, to be sure, ambiguous in the extreme, since it means now the positive law and now that which the positive law ought to be (= the law of nature); but since in the discussion cited he says "this holds in all the laws a man is under, whether natural or civil,"[57] we are entitled to suppose that it provides a reliable index to Locke's opinions regarding the individual's right to call into question the binding character of the law of his community.[58]

It is interesting to notice, in this background, that Locke, like more recent writers whose minds have run to an absolute obligation on the part of the individual to regard the will of his community as his own will, does not hesitate to press *à l'outrance* the analogy between the relation of the community to its members and the relation of the organism to its parts. "When," he writes, "any number of men have so consented to make one community or government, they are thereby presently incorporated, and make one body politic";[59] and political power is "that power...to make laws and annex such penalties to them as may tend to the preservation of the whole, by cutting off those parts, and those only, which are so corrupt that they threaten the sound and healthy, without which no severity is lawful."[60] Such a passage, furthermore, gives us the most concise answer we shall find to the question raised in the present chapter: Even the individual's right to life is valid only to the extent that it is compatible with the good (= preservation) of his community, and it is the people, not the individual, to whom Locke has clearly imputed the power to make the necessary judgments as to what is compatible with its preservation.[61] This, then, is our reply to Dunning: If that which Locke claims for his community is not

---

56 vi. 57.   57 vi. 59.

58 Cf. *ibid.*: "Is a man under the law of England? what made him free of that law— that is, to have the liberty to dispose of his actions and possessions, according to his own will, within the permission of that law? *a capacity of knowing that law*" (italics mine). Thus he can argue, a few lines later (vi. 60) that whilst he is incapable of "knowing the law, and so living within the rules of it," a man should be "continued under the tuition and government of others." This is, evidently, to say that the individual may take his choice between being treated like a child, on the one hand, and making his will conform to the law of the community, on the other hand.

59 viii. 95. Cf. Rousseau, *op. cit.*, iv. 1: "Tant que plusieurs hommes réunis se considèrent comme un seul corps, ils n'ont qu'une seule volonté." *I.e.*, so long as group of men have a single will they have a single will—a statement which is less startling than Locke's, but somewhat more convincing.

60 xv. 171. Cf. Rousseau, *De l'économie politique.* pp. 25–26, where he condemns this notion as "une des plus exécrables que jamais la tyrannie ait inventées."

61 Cf. Aaron, *op. cit.*, p. 287: "Locke is an individualist, and yet his individualism is left undefined; for no definite solution is to be found in his works of the vexed problem of the relations between the individual and the community."

unlimited sovereignty, where would one turn, in the literature of politics, to find a sovereignty which *is* unlimited?[62]

We now have before us the main elements of the individual promise which is presupposed by Locke's theory of popular sovereignty; and we may, without injustice to his argument, proceed at once to the line of criticism which we propose to direct against it. The individual has, it must be remembered, made the promise in order to escape the inconveniences which attach to existence outside an organized society: uncertainty as to the nature of his own rights and duties, and those of other men, inadequate guarantees of his own rights and duties, and those of other men, inadequate guarantees of impartial arbitration where differences of opinion arise between him and other men, insufficient machinery for the enforcement of his rights when the law is on his side. So long, therefore, as the individual is able to see that he has got a good bargain, that by keeping the promise he is in fact looking, in the best possible manner, to his own preservation and welfare, and insofar as Locke is prepared to overlook the second thesis above and stand by the first, the most that can be said about the promise he describes is that it is unnecessary—since under the first thesis he is apparently obligated to keep good bargains whether he has promised to or

not. But, as we have now seen at some length, the promise is to be kept even when the bargain turns out badly, and involves a previous commitment by the individual to accept the verdict of the remaining members of the society with regard to every difference of opinion between himself and them on matters of right; and (leaving to one side the first thesis and concentrating now on the fifth) he has made himself accountable for a demonstration that, in the presence of such a difference, the remaining members of the society will exercise their power *impartially*. That is, Locke must either show us that the remaining members of the society will, at such a moment, judge impartially, in which case the promise to obey was one which the individual could rightfully make and ought therefore to keep, or he must admit that his theory represents each individual as having subjected himself to the absolute, arbitrary will of the remaining members. In the latter case the promise would not (on Locke's showing) be a binding one.

What we cannot permit Locke to do, in all this, is to surround his doctrine regarding the society's sovereignty over the individual with the atmosphere of reasonableness and impersonality which attaches, superficially at least, to arrangements calling for decisions in accordance with the unanimity-principle—a principle to which Locke makes his appeal every time he says that a man can be bound only by his own consent. Or (what comes to the same thing) we must now demand of him that he pay the price for his attempt to have it more ways than one with his law of nature. According to the first thesis, the individual's obligation (thus also the society's sovereignty) would necessarily cease at that moment when further discharge of the obligation would clearly militate against preservation of his life, liberty, and estate. According to the

[62] Bearing in mind the fact that Lamprecht is one of the critics who have found in Locke no trace of the idea of sovereignty, the reader may profitably compare the account we have just given of the power of Locke's community over the individual with what, in another writer, Lamprecht regards as "absolutism" (*op. cit.*, p. 45): "While even Hobbes exempted men from obeying commands which ordered them to take their own lives or to give up their means of livelihood, Filmer refused to tolerate such slight exemptions. In Filmer the absolutism of the monarch reaches its most extreme statement."

sixth thesis, a man cannot give up his power to resist force when, in his own opinion, it is exerted upon him without right; and Locke clearly wants to reply that the question does not arise with regard to coercion by the community, because the right flows from the individual's own previous consent. When, however, we take him at his word about this, and proceed to examine what he has to say about consent, we discover (a) that the individual is represented as having consented only to the exercise of impartial authority, and thus, apparently, would not be bound to obey community authority when exercised in a partial manner, and (b) that the individual has, in Locke's belief, no right to consent to authority of any other kind. The obvious solution to the difficulty would evidently have been to propose a political system in which, as in his state of nature, laws would be made and governmental arrangements established only with unanimous approval, and subsequently changed only by unanimous approval—*i.e.*, approximately the kind of system which Burke defends. When, under such a system, the individual finds himself the victim of what be believes to be an unjust law, he can at least be reminded that he has himself, in a cool moment, set his seal to its reasonableness, and that, in any case, nothing can be changed in a sense unfavorable to himself except with his own approval. Locke was logically estopped from proposing such a system by the insight which we have presented as his fourth thesis—*i.e.*, by the knowledge that today's justice may be tomorrow's injustice because of a change of conditions; and, evidently with a view to preventing the indefinite perpetuation of ancient enactments which are no longer defensible, he proceeds to shift his ground from unanimity at some moment in the past as an ultimate criterion of right to virtual unanimity (either in the present or at some time in the past) as an ultimate criterion of right. The society can come into existence only by unanimous approval of its members; but subsequently, by making a revolution, the people (no longer represented as strictly unanimous) may change the society's character in any way they see fit, and require of the individual (*e.g.*, the individual member of the legislative they have turned out) the same duty of obedience which he owed before the revolution. The people have, in short, consented unanimously to something less than unanimity as an ultimate criterion of right; and Locke is evidently asserting that such consent is valid.[63]

The issue posed here may be stated very simply indeed, and since it is, in effect, the Great Divide which separates the defenders of popular sovereignty from their opponents (and, ultimately, the defenders of majority-rule from their opponents), we shall be well advised to grasp it as clearly as possible at this point. Here are a group of people united together in order to enjoy the benefits of just and reasonable government. A difference arises amongst them as to what is just and reasonable, and investigation reveals that the opposing factions consist of one individual, on the one side, and the remainder of the community, on the other side. Does either have a *right* to impose its view of what is just and reasonable upon the other? Can either judge impartially in what is, by definition, its own cause? Locke's theory of popular sovereignty obliges him to answer the second question in the affirmative, and the first

---

63 Here, again, Rousseau is much the more cautious of the two. Cf. Rousseau, *Contrat social,* i. 6: 'La loi de la pluralité des suffrages est...un établissement de convention, et suppose, *au moins* une fois, l'unamimité" (italics mine).

with the words, Yes, the rest of the community has such a right.[64] And, since the only difference between the two (the community minus one of its members, and the individual) which leaps to the eye is that the one is many individuals and the latter is only one, he is obliged to say that numbers guarantee impartiality.

An ocean separates those who, confronted with the above problem, are willing to make Lockes' answer, and those whose cast of mind makes it necessary for them to argue that no answer can be given on the facts stated —*i.e.*, that the community may be right, or the individual may be right, or they both may be wrong. (We repeat that Locke cannot seriously contend that the community is right because the individual has promised to regard it so, because unless there be reasons for regarding the community as right [= impartial] at such a moment, the promise is not a valid one.) We make no attempt to adjudicate the issue at stake, our purpose being merely to show what position Locke finally adopted with regard to it and what consequences the

___

[64] Cf. *ibid.,* ii. 4: "En effet, sitôt qu'il s'agit d'un fait ou d'un droit particulier sur un point qui n'a pas été réglé par une convention générale et antérieure, l'affaire devient contentieuse. C'est un procès où les particuliers intéressés sont une des parties, et le public l'autre, mais où *je ne vois ni la loi qu'il faut suivre, ni le juge qui doit prononcer"* (italics mine). It is interesting to notice that Professor Friedrich, who, as we have seen, regards Rousseau as in some sense responsible for the excesses of those who attach too much importance to "approximate majority support," is in this matter (as Rousseau clearly was not) a thorough-going majoritarian. Cf. Friedrich, *Constitutional Government and Politics,* p. 454: "The narrower the special interest is, the lower is the representative quality of those whose actions are directed towards its realization. And an interest is narrow or broad depending on the *number* of human beings whose interest is identified with it" (italics mine).

position involves for the consistency of his argument. And the charge we are bringing against him is that he has attempted to argue from unanimity as a criterion of right (a criterion which is, in some sense, consistent with the fifth thesis) to constructive, or virtual, unanimity (as revealed in his discussion of the right of revolution) as an equally acceptable criterion of right. If Locke had stayed with the unanimity-principle, we are saying, he would have made no distinction between a situation in which an individual wishes to alter existing arrangements, and one in which all individuals except one wish to alter them; for under the rule *pacta sunt servanda* the two situations are indistinguishable, the individual having the same right of revolution against the society as the society has against the individual, which is none at all. And we are insisting that Locke's right of revolution is, in effect, a right on the part of the bulk of the community to treat as non-members those who take exception to its opinions, a right which is wholly inconsistent with the fifth thesis.

There is much to be said against the unanimity-principle as a criterion of right in an organized society, but there is this to be said in its favor: that where action can be taken under it at all there is some sort of presumption that the action taken is the wisest and most reasonable of which the deliberators are, as a group, capable. Every disputant among them must have been heard and convinced before action becomes possible; every suggestion that the action about to be taken is unwise or unjust must have been refuted to the satisfaction of him who has put it forward. By providing a maximum of guarantees against new decisions of all kinds, it provides a maximum of guarantees against new decisions which are unwise or unjust. Thus, although unanimous decisions do become unanimous only by the accumulation of individual approvals, they do not owe their peculiar quality to the *number* of the approvals —or, at least, the further claim may be made for them that they are underwritten by the reasoning process itself insofar as the deliberators in question are capable of reasoning. The unanimity-principle, that is to say, forces the deliberators to observe the basic rules of the reasoning process: consideration of all evidence available, attribution of equal weight to all points of view, *etc.*; and of decisions made under it we may say not only that they have secured general approval, but also (with *some* confidence)[65] that they have been able to withstand all the criticisms urged against them by all the minds consulted with respect to them—which is apparently the most that can be said for any decision at any particular moment. This is important because those who take inadequate notice of this characteristic of unanimous decisions yield easily to the temptation of arguing that since unanimous decisions are best, almost unanimous decisions are next best, and thus the best possible where complete unanimity cannot be secured. The only theorist whom the writer has found ready to put this argument forward thus unambiguously is Starosolskyj;[66] but the ease with which Locke makes the transition from the one position to the other in his theory of sovereignty suggests that he had something of this kind in mind, and it cannot be too strongly emphasized that *there is no connection between the premise and the conclusion.* Where there is virtual unanimity only

there is opposition, *i.e.*, there are unsatisfied objectors, *i.e.*, minds which, by withholding approval, create a presumption against the decision—a presumption whose strength bears no demonstrable relation to the number of the unsatisfied objectors, and one which all of us have seen vindicated with disturbing frequency in situations in which the objectors have been few. The arguments in favor of the unanimity-principle cannot, therefore, be applied *a fortiori* to the defense of virtually unanimous decisions, because the distinctive quality of unanimous decisions is not a quality of which decisions may partake to a greater or lesser degree; either, that is to say, all the objections have been answered or they have not. This is not to say, of course, that the principle of unanimity is a better principle for political societies to adopt than a principle requiring only virtual unanimity, or that the right of nearly all the members of a commonwealth to revoke previous decisions is less susceptible of defense than that of all the members. What we can say is (a) that Locke could have claimed for decisions made under the *liberum veto* something of the impartiality and impersonality which would legitimate (under the fifth thesis) the promise which he demands of the members of his society, and (b) that the right of *nearly all* must be defended on different grounds than that of all. But Locke's attempts to find such grounds— as we shall encounter them in the next chapter—are remarkably unsuccessful, and as we present him here he is either not arguing at all (*i.e.*, merely asserting) or arguing (on what level of awareness we do not endeavor to say) from the proposition that all (thus also the few) are bound by that to which all *have* consented, to the proposition that the few are bound by that to which the rest *have consented* (as after a revolution), and thence to the proposition that

---

[65] With *some* confidence only, because of the possibility that objections have been withdrawn by objectors who, though by no means satisfied, have yet despaired of convincing others and are unwilling to stand in the way of action.

[66] Starosolskyj, *Das Majoritätprinzip*, p. 56.

the few are bound by that to which the rest *now consent*—wherefore he can insist, as he does, that the government which calls down on itself a revolution is itself rebellious, the "law" presumably having changed at the moment when the society (= the members minus the government and its supporters) recognized the necessity for making one.[67] Neither of these steps is legitimate.

Locke's failure to take account of the above difficulty is astonishing, but less astonishing, on the whole, than his failure to offer the sort of defense for the (virtually unanimous) community's right of revolution that we should expect from him in the light of his usual handling of the subject of rights and duties. As we have seen in an earlier chapter, Locke elsewhere reveals a profound insight into the problem of rights and duties, representing the former as, in a manner of speaking, merely another way of looking at the latter, and both as determined by a common or collective good. If, therefore, he proposes to speak in terms of a duty in the individual to obey the rest of his community and a right in the rest of the community to coerce the individual, he should tell us not only why the individual has (as compared to the rest of the community) that lesser duty to promote the public good which is the correlative of his lesser right to make laws and use the force of the community in its behalf, but also why the concession to the bulk of the community of a right to remove and install governments should result in the promotion of the public good. The latter problem would have led him into an analysis of that public opinion which he briefly mentions, and of the relation between the public good and widely-received opinion as to what is good. But neither problem appears to

have occurred to him, and we are obliged, therefore, to urge against the right he claims for the bulk of the community the objection that it will not bear examination in the light of his own theory of rights.

THE RIGHT OF THE MAJORITY

> When any number of men have... consented to make one community or government...the majority have a right to act and conclude the rest.[68]

This is Locke's clearest statement of his doctrine regarding what we have called in our Introduction the majority-principle, and it is, be it noted, so phrased as to fit very neatly into our interpretation of the compact. Wherever men live in community with one another, he is saying, the relations between them can be described in terms of an agreement which, in addition to assigning to the whole community that unlimited power which we have examined in the preceding section, assigns to its numerical majority a *right* to make decisions (regarding the use of that power) which are binding upon the minority. The majority-principle is, in a word, implicit in the logic of community life.

It is not only Locke's clearest commitment to the use of the majority-principle, but also the most concise statement of the faith of the majority-rule democrat that the present writer has been able to find in the course of his investigation; and we shall greatly clarify the problem of the present section if we face at once all that it implies. Assuming—as, in the context in which it is claimed, we must assume—that the right to which the statement refers is an ethical right, then it necessarily follows that decisions made by

---

[67] xix. 226.

[68] vii. 95.

the majority (= action taken by the majority) are in some definable sense ethically right decisions, since, in the absence of convicing proof to the contrary, it is necessary to suppose that there can be no such thing as an ethical right to make an ethically wrong decision. It follows, again, that any decision other than that of the majority is in some definable sense ethically wrong. It follows, yet again, that a decision comes to be right the moment it marshals majority support behind it, and ceases to be right the moment the "marginal" deliberator switches sides and reduces the erstwhile majority to a minority. And since these corollaries do clearly follow from it, it is to Locke, not to any recent writer, that Professor Friedrich should give credit for a "statement of the majoritarian position" which "avoids all subterfuges."[69]

We shall greatly clarify our problem, too, by facing at once the implications of Locke's proposition about the right of the majority with regard to the questions dealt with in the preceding sections. The individual has, as we have seen, an irrevocable obligation to obey the community of which he is a member; but the majority has a right to act for the community; and the individual's irrevocable duty of obedience thus turns out to be an irrevocable duty to obey the majority. The inalienable rights of the individual are, as we have seen, such rights as may be compatible with the public good of his society, and, as we have further seen, that public good is merely that which the "opinion" and "humour" of the

people designate as good; but since the majority of those people have a right to conclude the rest, the inalienable rights of the individual prove to be merely those which the majority of the people have not yet seen fit to withdraw.[70] The "proper interest" of each individual lies in obedience to a law decreed by a legislative which, as we have seen, is presumed to enjoy the confidence of the community; but since the majority can act for the community, and can thus exercise the community's right of revolution and its right to replace the old government with a new one to its liking, the proper interest of the individual becomes merely unquestioning obedience to the will of the majority. Here, in short, is the Rousseauism which is nowhere to be found in the *Contract social* and the *Gouvernement de Pologne*; and it is a matter of no little interest that Locke, apparently because the platitudes about morals which we have examined in the opening sections of this chapter cannot be squared with such a position, has got off with so little responsibility for the introduction of such notions into modern political theory.[71]

69 Friedrich, "One Majority Against Another," p. 43. Cf. Vaughan, *Studies in the History of Political Philosophy*, I, p. 166: "This [Locke's statement on the power of the majority] amounts to a blank cheque drawn in favour of 'the majority,' and eventually filled up either to tens or millions, as fortune may decide."

70 But cf. Wilson, *The Concept of Equality*, pp. 218–219: "Locke's *Two Treatises* put above the rough determination of majority vote the immutable natural rights of man."
71 Thus Vaughan, who in view of the comment reproduced in n. 69 above, can hardly be accused of having *overlooked* the majoritarian emphasis in Locke's theory, yet clings to the notion that that theory is "not merely anti-despotic, but also markedly individualist" (*op. cit.*, I, p. 134). "*The Essay of Civil Government*," he writes (*ibid.*), "is...an assault ...upon the very idea of sovereignty. Its shafts are aimed not merely against one particular form of sovereignty—doubtless the most oppressive and the least endurable—but against any form [thus against "blank cheques" to majorities?], even the mildest, that sovereignty can assume." Locke pleads for toleration for all save atheists and Catholics, and wins a reputation for having exercised "considerable" influence in "advancing

We now turn to consider the arguments by which Locke supports this proposition.[72]

First argument

The right to live under a government agreeable to the majority is a natural right of all men—or, in Locke's own language, men have a "native right... to have such a legislative over them as the majority should approve and freely acquiesce in."[73] This Locke does not seek to demonstrate; and we need only take notice of its presence in the *Second Treatise* and remind the reader of Ritchie's pleasantry[74] to the effect that the maxim, "No case; talk about the law of nature," plays in the profession of political theory a rôle analogous to that of the maxim, "No case; abuse

plaintiff's attorney," in the practice of law.[75]

Second argument

If the minority refused to be concluded by the majority, the society would speedily disintegrate; for, he insists, the only alternative is the unanimity-principle (= "nothing but the consent of every individual can make anything to be the act of the whole"[76]); and both because it is frequently impossible to consult everybody[77] and because "variety of opinions and contrariety of interests... unavoidably happen in all collections of men,"[78] such a principle would deprive the society of the strength it needs in order to fulfill the purposes for which it was created.[79] In short, "where the majority cannot conclude the rest, there they cannot act as one body, and consequently will be immediately dissolved again."[80]

This we may call the argument from *necessity and expediency*,[81] and the importance it has assumed in subsequent discussion of the case for majority-decisions is the most interesting indication we possess of the need for investigation of the problem by competent theorists. It is open to the following obvious objections:

---

the cause of toleration" (Lamprecht, *op. cit.*, p. 152); Rousseau pleads (*Contrat social*, iv. 8) for toleration for all save atheists and Catholics, and Vaughan (*The Political Writings of Rousseau* [Cambridge: University Press, 1915], I, p. 89) accuses him of advocating persecution. Rousseau writes (*op. cit.*, iv. 2) that provided "tous les caractères de la volonté générale sont encore dans la pluralité," I am more free when subjecting myself to the will of the majority than I would have been had I got my way—and wins recognition as a majoritarian! Locke, with no limiting conditions at all, equates the consent of the individual with that of the majority, and wins recognition as an individualist! Cf. Locke. xi. 140: "Governments cannot be supported without great charge, and it is fit everyone... should pay out of his estate his proportion for the maintenance of it. *But still it must be with his own consent, i.e., the consent of the majority*" (italics mine).

[72] It is instructive to notice than there is absolutely nothing in the *Contrat social* which can properly be called an argument for majority-right.

[73] xvi. 176. The writer has not attempted to list Locke's arguments in the order in which he introduces them.

[74] David G. Ritchie, *Natural Rights* (London: Swan Sonnenschein and Co., 1895), p. 31.

[75] Cf. Vaughan, *Studies,* I. pp. 140–141: "The answer of Locke is perfectly explicit: Those who make a social contract bind themselves to... regulate all their future proceedings by a bare majority: a provision imposed by that accommodating oracle, the law of nature, whose commands form the strangest assortment, ranging from *Thou shalt not kill* to *The odd man shall have the casting vote.*"

[76] viii. 98.

[77] Cf. *ibid.*: "Infirmities of health and avocations of business... will necessarily keep many away from the public assembly."

[78] *Ibid.*   [79] *Ibid.*   [80] *Ibid.*

[81] Cf. Wilson, *op. cit.*, p. 64: "Locke in his *Second Treatise* defends majority rule primarily on the ground of expediency, for without it civil society could not endure."

(a) It is simply not true that a commonwealth must choose between decisions by majority-vote and dissolution after a brief period of experiment with unanimous decisions, since, as Locke must have known very well, the power to make decisions binding upon all of its members may (and often does) become lodged in a minority of the society's members. That is, Locke's dilemma is, in the form in which he states it, a false dilemma.

(b) If it *were* true that the society must choose between dissolution and the lodgment of decision-making power in the majority, this would not constitute a valid argument in favor of the proposition that wherever men have "consented to make a community," the majority have a right to make that community's decisions. Even conceding the inarticulate premise that all commonwealths have a right to continue in existence and to thrive, the most that can be deduced from it is a decision-making right in that part of each commonwealth which is in fact most capable of assuring to it a healthy existence. It is possible to conceive of circumstances in which such a right might, on this showing, vest in the majority, but it is also possible to conceive of circumstances in which the majority-principle would conduce directly to the commonwealth's ruin. In such a case (leaving to one side the ever-present possibility of minority-rule) dissolution and majority-rule would appear to be equally undesirable.

For the rest, it seems improbable that the premise, according to which all commonwealths to which men happen at some time to have given their "consent," have a right to continue in existence and to thrive, can be successfully defended.

For all of its absurdity, in the form in which Locke states it, the argument contains the elements of a proposition which—although it still awaits its theorist—deserves (in the present writer's opinion) serious consideration as the point of departure for theoretically sound treatment of the majority-principle. For if, instead of saying that the society must either entrust decision-making power to the majority or face speedy dissolution, he had said that it must either entrust the decision-making power to the majority or cease to be *a society in which all can participate in the making of decisions,* he would not only have enunciated a proposition which cannot be so easily refuted as that which he does put forward, but also would have set his successors in the modern debate about majority-rule a problem worthy of their best speculative efforts.

Third argument

Denial of the right of the majority to conclude the minority would deprive the commonwealth of its title ' to govern.[82]

That which begins and actually constitutes any political society is nothing but the consent of any number of freemen capable of majority, to unite and incorporate into such a society [*i.e.,* one in which all necessary power has been given up to the majority] ... This is that, and that only,

---

[82] It is interesting to note the use which the members of a minority (in a society governed in accordance with Locke's ideas about majority-rule) might make of one of his pronouncements on absolute monarchy—*e.g.,* vii 90–91: "Absolute monarchy...is indeed inconsistent with civil society, and so can be no form of civil government at all...[The absolute prince] being supposed to have all... power in himself alone, there is no judge to be found, no appeal lies open to any one, who may fairly and indifferently, and with authority decide, and from whence relief and redress may be expected of any injury or inconveniency that may be suffered from him, or by his order."

which did or could give beginning to any lawful government in the world.[83]

Here, again, Locke is apparently very close to the idea which we have set forth at the end of our discussion of the second argument, and seems about to say that there are demonstrable differences between a society which does and one which does not make its decisions by majority-vote[84]—and differences which, from the ethical point of view, render the former distinctly preferable. But he does not say this; and since he adds that where the members have "expressly agreed in any number greater than the majority,"[85] that arrangement also is legitimate, it may well be that he does not intend even to imply it. (To stipulate in favor of decision-making by extraordinary majority is, obviously, to stipulate in favor of a *minority-right* to conclude the majority.) In short, the single clear implication of the statement, as it stands, is that any sort of government to which men have at some

time consented is lawful, and the safest conclusions seem to be (a) that the *Second Treatise* contains no unequivocal doctrine on this point, and (b) that the passage in question was intended merely as a reiteration of his general doctrine of consent as the basis of lawful government, its apparent emphasis upon majority-right being the result of careless wording.

Fourth argument

Political bodies, like all other bodies, must move in the direction in which they are impelled by the greater force, and in political bodies the greater force is the will of the majority.

This we may call the argument by analogy, and, like the argument from necessity, it has attracted many subsequent writers. What it amounts to is an insistence that majority-determination in political societies is natural, as it is natural for water to seek its level, for the heavier end of a seesaw to point downward, and (to follow the direction which Krabbe gives to the argument) for the human mind to make that decision to which it is drawn by the more weighty reasons. Its inarticulate major premise, when urged as an argument in favor of the right of the majority, is that the natural is not only natural but also right.

In Locke's hands the argument consists of the following steps: The motivating force of a community, in virtue of which alone it can act as a community, is the consent (past promise? present support?) of its individual members. Therefore the greater motivating force within it is the consent of the greater number of its individual members, and, at the limit, the consent of one half of those members plus one. If, then, we were to suppose it capable of responding to the force exerted by the smaller number of its individual members, we should have to suppose it

---

[83] viii. 99.

[84] It is on this level that Starosolskyj attacks the problem of majority-decisions. His book—the best we have on the subject—is an effort to demonstrate the theoretically necessary differences between what he calls the *Mehrheitsverband* and what he calls the *Herrschaftsverband* (*op. cit.*, pp. 22–34). Unfortunately, he defines the *Mehrheitsverband* in such fashion as to exclude any organization in which there exists a crystallized majority—*i.e.*, any organization in which the relations of subordination and superordination have ceased to be "indeterminate" (*ibid.*, p. 33). This means, of course, that the difference between the *Mehrheitsverband* and the *Herrschaftsverband* does not, at the limit, turn at all upon the fact that in the one decisions are made by the majority and in the other by an individual or a minority. Nevertheless, Starosolskyj has pointed the way to an adequate theoretical treatment of the problem, and if his theory could be restated in such fashion as to eliminate the confusion to which we have just directed attention, it might prove useful in the extreme.

[85] viii. 99.

different in this respect from all other bodies of which we possess knowledge.[86]

The argument is intensely interesting, if only as a reminder of the justice of Professor Catlin's acknowledgment of indebtedness to the contract theorists;[87] for here, in a paragraph, is the central conception of his admirable *Principles of Politics*. Those familiar with the refinement it has received in Professor Catlin's treatment will, therefore, see at once that it owes its plausibility (in Locke) to a carefully concealed *non sequitur*. The argument is unexceptionable insofar as it asserts that the motivating force of a community is consent—*if* we understand by consent present support rather than past commitment. It is unexceptionable, again, insofar as it asserts that the consent which motivates a community is a consent given (ultimately) by individuals. It is unexceptionable, finally, insofar as it asserts that more consent (for consent *is* additive) generates a greater motivating force than less consent. But it does not follow from these propositions that the consent which motivates a given society at any given moment is that of the greater number of its individual members, unless we are in a position to assume that the members are equally active in giving

and withholding their consent, and unless, further, we are in a position to assume that the consents given and withheld are of equal *intensity*.[88] No spectacle is more familiar in politics than that of a majority's abdication of responsibility for the making of decisions, unless it be that of the ease with which a smaller number of persons with intense convictions can make their consent count for more than that of a larger number of persons who, without joining the politically inactive majority, are yet not prepared, on the particular issue at stake, to offer resistance to the smaller number. The validity of Locke's conclusion rests, therefore, on two hidden premises (equal individual participation in the making of decisions, equal intensity of conviction on each issue to be decided) of whose necessity he reveals no sort of awareness; and we must conclude that that which he declares to be natural is natural only where certain indispensable conditions are satisfied.

If, *per impossibile*, we were to waive these objections, and grant for argument's sake that decisions by majority-vote are a natural phenomenon of community life, there would remain the difficulty that we cannot argue from the naturalness of the process by which the majority concludes the minority to a *majority-right* to conclude the minority—or, if the reader prefers, we cannot argue from the one to the other without first demonstrating our title to do so.

Fifth argument

Individual consents being, in any case, the only rightful title to the exercise of power, the right of the majority

---

86 viii. 96. The language in the text is a free but (the writer believes) faithful paraphrase.

87 Catlin, *Principles,* p. 169: "Men will become, not fugitive from society, but rebels against it, unless they are permitted to believe that they are acting freely in those things to which they attach most value. Restraint has no theoretical limit, but constraint can be imposed by no prudent statesman without a cautious calculation of his power to enforce it. *The theorists of the seventeenth and eighteenth centuries were, then, quite right in founding the contract upon the possibility of a rebellious attitude of will in every man.* It is not possible to quit society; but it is very possible to be anti-social, and, still more, anti-national, anti-group, impious, unconventional" (italics mine).

88 Cf. *ibid.,* p. 266: "If all men were equal, or if government were only possible if all men believed themselves to have an equal share, then only majority government (over-riding the 'equal shares' of the minority as a practical expedient) would be feasible."

flows as a matter of course from the fact that it can point to more consents than the minority.

This, in the opinion of the present writer, is what was really in Locke's mind as he wrote the paragraphs in which he attempts to defend the notion of majority-right, although, admittedly, some exegesis is needed in order to establish its presence in those paragraphs. A man, the argument runs, necessarily surrenders some of his liberty when he subscribes to the compact which makes him a member of a commonwealth.[89] The compact "would signify nothing, and be no compact if he be left free and under no other ties than he was in before in the state of Nature. . . . What new engagement [would there be] if he were no farther tied by any decrees of the society than *he himself thought* fit and did actually consent to?"[90] In consenting to be a member of a commonwealth, therefore, he consents beforehand to the acceptance of obligations which he does not himself approve, and it is right that he should do so because such an obligation is implicit in the nature of community life. And the character of the obligation, be it noted, is to be discovered in a situation in which the community, otherwise unanimous (as we are clearly asked to conceive it in the passage cited), is making a demand of the individual to which he is not prepared to give his consent. The compact would be all to the advantage of the individual, thus no compact, if it did not involve a duty on the part of the individual to fulfill the demand, thus also a right on the part of the community to make it, thus also a reciprocal obligation among all the individuals in the community to fulfill such a demand when it happens to be made of them. In other words, that community life to which all the individuals consent is

possible on no other basis; and therefore, Locke is saying, "every man, by consenting with others to make one body politic under one government, puts himself under an obligation to every one of that society to submit to the determination of the majority."[91]

Now the thing which Locke's critics have failed to perceive (thus overlooking the major emphasis of his defense of the majority-principle) is that, although he does not assist us with the deduction, the right of the majority to conclude the minority does follow as a matter of course from the right of the community to conclude the individual, *insofar as that right is defended in terms of the community's numerical superiority over the individual.* If one million persons have a right to conclude one because they are a million and he is only one, then there is no logical escape from the conclusion that five hundred thousand and one persons have a right to conclude five hundred thousand persons, and if one does not like the conclusion one must revise one's notions regarding the premise.

In a word, Locke had apprehended—on a half-conscious level—a tremendously important logical relation between the doctrine that the whole people have a right to have their way and the doctrine that the majority have a right to have their way. For either you mean, by the former doctrine, that the people must be really unanimous in order to exert their rightful authority, in which case there will be no one left upon whom it can be exerted, or you mean, as we have gone to some pains to show that Locke always did, that virtual unanimity is as good a title to authority as the people require, in which case you must be willing (as Locke was) to go ahead and defend—without any of those "subterfuges" to which Professor Friedrich refers—the majority-principle.

---

[89] viii. 97.   [90] *ibid.* (italics mine).   [91] *Ibid.*

We conclude: (a) that the first, second, third, and fourth of these arguments in favor of majority-right may properly be dismissed as unworthy of serious consideration; (b) that, insofar as he intended to show with his fourth argument that his theory of majority-right is logically implied in his theory of popular sovereignty, he was on safe ground; and (c) that our evaluation of his theory of majority-right must be dictated by our evaluation of his theory of popular sovereignty.

POLITICAL EQUALITY

The extent of Locke's verbal commitment to the position of the majority-rule democrats of our own day with respect to political equality may be inferred from the passages analyzed in the preceding chapter. As we have pointed out in our Introduction, to claim power for the majority of the individual members of a society is, *ceteris paribus,* to declare those individual members political equals, since it is to claim for each one the power to cast the deciding vote in virtue of which, at the limit, the majority *is* a majority—or since (to put the same thing in another way) it is to claim for each, before every decision, an equal capacity to affect the result of the ballot.[92] And, since Locke certainly makes the former claim, he may fairly be said to have committed himself (verbally) to the latter.[93] Broadly speaking, therefore, we may say of his theory of equality

that it is involved in his theory of the majority-principle, as, in the preceding chapter, we have shown his theory of the majority-principle to be involved in his theory of popular sovereignty; thus, also, that the three theories really constitute a *single* theory with three emphases which, for purposes of convenience, we have chosen to consider separately; thus, finally, that the three theories stand or fall together. This commentary upon Locke's theory of equality must, however, be read against the background of the following considerations:

(a) Because of the wide divergence between Locke's position and that of the majority-rule democrats of our own day with respect to the problem dealt with in the following chapter, his theory of equality admits of the possibility of vast political inequality over what (borrowing a phrase from the economists) we may call the "short period" (*i.e.,* the period between revolutions).

(b) It is a matter of some interest (in the light of what we have said in our Introduction regarding the advisability of keeping political problems separate in our minds from economic and social problems) that the equality Locke claims for the members of his society is *political* in the strictest sense of the word. Unlike many of the majority-rule democrats of our own day, and unlike Rousseau,[94] Locke was not prepared to dictate to the members of his commonwealth the principles of economic distribution which they must adopt, or to insist that men must be equal in all things in order to enjoy an equal voice in the making of laws. He explains at one point in the *Second Treatise:*

---

92 Cf. Aaron, *op. cit.,* p. 273: "For Locke ...a political community is an organization of equals...into which men enter voluntarily in order to achieve together what they cannot achieve apart."

93 Cf. Alfred Tuttle Williams, *The Concept of Equality in the Writings of Rousseau, Bentham and Kant* (New York: Teachers' College, Columbia University, 1907), p. 10: "The dictum that 'men are by nature free and equal,' which was accepted by the American Fathers as a self-evident proposition, may be traced immediately to Locke."

94 Cf. Rousseau, *op. cit.,* ii. 11, where he argues that without equality "la liberté ne peut subsister," and adds, "Quant à la richesse, que nul citoyen ne soit assez opulent pour en pouvoir acheter un autre, et nul assez pauvre pour être contraint de se vendre."

Though I have said above "That all men by nature are equal," I cannot be supposed to understand all sorts of "equality." Age or virtue may give men a just precedency. Excellency of parts and merit may place others above the common level. Birth may subject some, and alliance or benefits others, to pay an observance to those to whom Nature, gratitude, or other respects, may have made it due; and yet all this consists with...that equal right that every man hath to his natural freedom, without being subjected to the will or authority of any other man.[95]

(c) While lunatics, idiots, children, and (temporary) madmen are the only classes which he expressly excludes from the (equal) rights which attach to membership in his commonwealth,[96] it seems highly improbable that Locke was thinking in terms of extending those rights to women. Officially, his doctrine is that "we are born free [= equally free = equal] as we are born rational,"[97] a proposition of which much might be made in connection with a determined effort to enlist his support for the movement for woman suffrage; and the same

---

[95] vi. 54.

[96] vi. 60. Cf. Wilson, *op. cit.*, p. 120: "We must not forget...that neither Locke nor his follower Jefferson were democrats in the modern sense of the word, for neither believed in either universal or manhood suffrage." Cf. MacIver, *Leviathan,* p. 92: "The leaders of the [American] Revolution accepted the principle that the people were the locus of sovereignty, but the people were conceived in the *Lockian* sense. They were the substantial folk as distinguished from the rabble" (italics mine). Cf. Lamprecht, *op. cit.,* p. 140 n.: "To what extent Locke would wish to give political power to all classes of the population is uncertain. Even the Republicans like Milton and Harrington opposed universal suffrage, and would grant the ballot only to the competent or land-owing classes.... Whether Locke followed these predecessors...is difficult to determine. *His discussion of majority rule and the consent of the governed seems to point to a more broadly democratic point of view;* but if the general assumptions of his generation are considered, his failure to state explicitly that he favored universally shared political power can almost [!] be interpreted as satisfaction with the quite limited democracy of the English constitution in his day" (italics mine). Professor Lamprecht's admirable scholarly caution makes it difficult to say whether or not he would take issue with the point made in the text, where we are concerned less with what Locke thought in his heart of hearts (interesting as that would be to know) than with what Locke said in the *Second Treatise.* If Lamprecht had said that the discussion of majority-rule and the consent of the governed actually points to a more broadly democratic point of view (instead of only seeming to), or if he had said that we are entitled to attribute to Locke the general assumptions of his generation insofar as he does not expressly dissociate himself from them (instead of "almost"), we might safely observe that the latter point is doubtful and that, in any case, Locke *is* explicit about majority-rule and the consent of the governed (as Professor Lamprecht almost admits) and thus stands committed to that which (manhood suffrage) is implied in his treatment of them. Not, to be sure, manhood suffrage in elections held at regular intervals, but an equal right in every man to consent or refuse to form a part of a contemplated revolutionary majority. As for suffrage in parliamentary elections, where a majority of the society has decreed them, we have pointed out in the text that Locke's principles admit of political inequality in the short period. For the rest, men have been hanged for less explicit pronouncements upon the subject of political equality than the following words, hidden in Locke's account of the state of nature (ii. 4): "There...[is] nothing more evident than that creatures of the same species and rank, promiscuously born to all the same advantages of Nature, and the use of the same faculties, *should also be equal one amongst another, without subordination or subjection,* unless the lord and master of them all should, by any manifest declaration of his will, set one above another, and confer on him...an undoubted right to dominion and sovereignty" (italics mine). Note the final word of the quotation, and cf. Lamprecht's statement ("Hobbes and Hobbism," *loc. cit.*) that Locke could compose an entire treatise on government without mentioning it.

[97] vi. 61. Cf. vi. 59, where he directs attention to the "supposition" in English law that rationality begins at the age of twenty-one, and offers no objection.

thing may be said of his vigorous denunciation of Filmer for having overlooked the claims of mothers when he sought to rest the case for monarchy on the rights attaching to fatherhood.[98] But the following passage suggests that Locke's notions on the position of women were those of his age, thus that the "people" (thus also the majority) for whom he claimed power was a more restricted group than that which figures in the thinking of many more recent majority-rule democrats:

The husband and wife, though they have but one common concern, yet having different understandings, will unavoidably sometimes have different wills too. It therefore being necessary that the last determination (*i.e.*, the rule) should be placed somewhere, it naturally falls to the man's share as the abler and stronger.[99]

(d) Locke was apparently no more aware than the majority-rule democrats of our day of the considerations which make it necessary for *us* to write the reservation *ceteris paribus* into the proposition that the making of political decisions by majority-vote is compatible with (even formal) political equality. It is easy to see—once the problem has forced itself upon one's mind—that, in (*e.g.*) a group in which a "crystallized" majority (made up of persons who, whether out of conviction or out of self-interest or, what is perhaps more usual, a little of each, vote together on all issues) has arrogated to itself the function of making group decisions, a group in which the member of the minority knows, before deliberation takes place, that he is *not* in position to affect the result of the ballot, compliance with the majority-principle entails, for the minority, any degree of political subjection which the majority cares to impose upon them.[100] It is easy to see, again, that if with the passing of time the crystallized majority learns (as modern political parties have learned) to entrust to a majority of its own members the power to conclude the minority of its own members, fidelity to the majority-principle can come to involve political subjection for the *majority* of the members of the wider group.[101] It was this order of considerations which led Starosolskyj to limit his argument for the majority-principle to situations characterized by what he calls "indeterminacy of the relations of subordination and superordination,"[102] and which led Rousseau (to whom Starosolskyj does not express his indebtedness) to place so much emphasis upon (a) the prohibition of "partial" organizations within the political society,[103] and (b) the impossibility of eliciting a "general will" where many votes are cast by persons who place self-interest before the general interest.[104] Locke, we repeat, saw nothing of all this—a failure which is, in this writer's opinion, intimately related to the vagueness of his statements regarding the character of that "public good" to the promotion of which he represents his political society as dedicated. Here, as elsewhere, his central difficulty is the cavalier unconcern with which he (by implication) extends to existing commonwealths propositions which (as he should have seen) apply only to situations in which the phrase "the public good" can be filled up with meaning.

---

98 vi. 53.

99 vii. 82.

100 Cf. Jellinek, *Das Recht der Minoritäten,* p. 41.

101 Indeed, for all the members of the group except the two members who constitute a majority of the triad in which, if such a process were continued indefinitely, decision-making power would finally rest. The writer is indebted for this suggestion to Professor John A. Fairlie.

102 Cf. Starosolskyj, *op. cit.,* p. 65, p. 89.

103 Rousseau, *op. cit.,* ii. 3.   104 *Ibid.*

(e) While the existence of a public good which men are prepared to place above their selfish interests in a *necessary* condition for the compatibility of majority-decisions and political equality (*i.e.*, where no such good exists there seems to be no reason to expect for the minority any result other than political subjection), it must be noticed that, conceptually, the notion of a public good which is both public and *good* is not easy to reconcile with that of political equality. If, that is to say, we insist (with Locke at his best) that claims to rights must be granted or denied according as the rights claimed are or are not compatible with the public good, then we are logically committed either to the view that equal political rights are appropriate only to those situations in which men possess equal capacity and equal willingness to use their power (to affect decisions) in the general interest, or to the admission that Locke's political system presupposes not merely the existence of a public good, but the existence of a public good of a very special kind—*i.e.*, one which *by definition* ceases to be good unless achieved upon a cooperative and egalitarian basis. That it is such a good which the majority-rule democrats have in mind when they condemn as incompatible with the general interest any principle other than that of equality and decisions by majority-vote is a thing which becomes increasingly evident to the student of their thought, but one which none of them (except possibly Marx) has defined with any degree of precision.[105]

---

[105] It is interesting to note that this implication concerning the special nature of the public good in a democracy did not entirely escape notice in the ancient world. The Old Oligarch, in his ironic defence of the Athenian polity, argues that rule by the people must be considered as a good *per se,* for one is, he says, obliged to concede that the government best for the state would be a government administered by the most capable men and would thus necessarily deprive the many of participation in the making of decisions (Pseudo-Xenophon, *Constitution of Athens,* i. 8–9).

7

ROUSSEAU

Jean Jacques Rousseau (1712–1778) was the most important political thinker to emerge from the eighteenth-century circle of French *philosophes*. Before he turned to the writing, in the 1750's and 1760's, of political discourses, essays, and novels by which he is now remembered, he passed through a varied number of occupations. He was, in turn, an engraver, a domestic servant, a tax collector, a tutor, a diplomatic secretary, a musical performer, and a composer. He stood apart from his fellow *philosophes*, by inclination and by personality. More radical than they, he rejected the model of the enlightened despot in favor of a thoroughgoing democracy. While they applauded the technological advances of their enlightened age, he lamented the advances of culture and civilization; while they frequented the fashionable urban world and its salons, he, the country cousin, blasted the false world of Paris and its less than virtuous women.

Bertrand de Jouvenel, the distinguished French writer on politics, takes a fresh look at Rousseau's political writings in his article. Rousseau, he writes, was uniquely concerned not with prescription but with lamentation.

It is as a reactionary critic of social evolution that he must be read. Jouvenel suggests that, the Jacobin invocation of his ideas notwithstanding, Rousseau's ideas were far from revolutionary; indeed, he finds him nostalgically yearning for a lost past. George Kateb, a professor at Amherst College, is more concerned with working out a proper philosophical appreciation of Rousseau's ideas. In the course of this he deals with, and finds lacking, most of the current interpretations of Rousseau. He in turn uses contemporary philosophical approaches in an effort to better understand Rousseau's notions of justice and the general will.

BERTRAND DE JOUVENEL

Jean-Jacques Rousseau *

Rousseau had a profound impact upon the way of the late 18th century: thanks to him many parents became aware of and attentive to their children; he fostered enjoyment of natural beauties and contributed to a change in the style of gardening; he was instrumental in shifting the manner of personal relationships from polite restraint to excessive demonstrativeness; with a lag of a generation his political views fired Robespierre; with an even greater lag his Socinian religiosity was to pervade the 19th century. It would be hard to find another writer whose suggestions have proved effective so extensively.

Strangely enough, however, the very core of Rousseau's doctrine has been almost entirely disregarded. But is it so strange? In this respect, Rousseau was not only intellectually ahead of his day, but also he was affectively in direct opposition to the trend of his time, which has developed ever since. Rousseau is the first great exponent of social evolution. His was the first attempt to depict systematically the historical progress of human society: here he comes a full century before Engels and all the others who were to make the evolution

of human society a popular theme. His concern to mark out stages of social development and to bring out the factors which he deemed effective in the process, is impressive against the background of contemporary writings. Everybody was then talking about Progress but in a very loose manner, and Rousseau was the only one who thought of it as a process to be understood. Now the first author who offered an understanding of what everybody talked about should have been praised to the skies on that score. This, on the contrary, is what brought Rousseau the enmities which made the last part of his life a misery.

Rousseau attempting to place the manuscript of the *Dialogues* on the master-altar of Notre-Dame, because that then seemed to him the only chance of ensuring that his protest against his persecutors should reach posterity.... Rousseau balked in his attempt and wandering through the streets of Paris, clutching his justification, in despair because there is no one he can trust to procure its posthumous publication.... Rousseau standing at street-corners, distributing leaflets copied in his own hand, which are spurned by passers-by ...here are images which move us to pity, yet we feel that such conduct is pathological. Also when we read the

* Reprinted from *Encounter*, XIX (December, 1962), 35–42, by permission of the author.

Dialogues, we feel that Rousseau is mainly the victim of his disordered imagination. I said "mainly," not "solely." However much he exaggerated it, the evidence seems to me convincing that there was a continuing systematic attempt on the part of the *Philosophes* to discredit him. A war of derisive *bon mots* and ridiculous anecdotes was waged upon him which his own disposition made easy and which his sensitivity made effective. It will not do to plead that the *Philosophes* reacted without wilful malice to his being a "difficult" person: they treated him as a dangerous man, and took advantage of his being difficult, making him ever so more so by their expert teasing, finally driving him to desperate isolation.

But why did these lovers of Progress regard as dangerous the first systematic exponent of social evolution? For a solid and weighty reason: because Rousseau, while sketching evolution with a keen pencil, also painted it in dark colours. The *Philosophes* fought the Church, which they regarded as a restraining hand upon Progress, but an ever weakening hand. What if they now found standing in their path, coming from their own ranks, a new enemy, a voice warning against the dangers of Progress? To this challenger applied *a fortiori* the war-cry: *"Écrasons l'infâme!"* Rousseau points out that the *Philosophes,* having proved powerful enough to drive the Jesuits out of France,[1] found it child's play to get rid

of a single inconvenient individual.[2]

In a concise recapitulation of his doctrine, Rousseau provides the key to the enmity of the *Philosophes.* A speaker is supposed to sum up the lessons he has drawn from a second painstaking reading of all Rousseau's works: "I saw throughout the development of his great principle that nature has made man happy and good but that society corrupts him and causes his misery. Take the *Émile,* much read but much misunderstood; it is nothing other than a treatise on the spontaneous goodness of man, meant to show how vice and error, foreign to his constitution, invade it from outside and deteriorate it progressively. In his first writings, he is more concerned to destroy the delusive prestige which causes us to admire stupidly the very means of our misery, and he seeks to correct this false valuation which causes us to honour mischievous talents and to despise beneficial virtues. Everywhere he shows us

---

[1] Rousseau describes the conflict of the *Philosophes* with the Jesuits as "a duel of power like that of Rome with Carthage." He says: "These two bodies, equally domineering, equally intolerant, were therefore incompatible since each was committed to despotic rule; they could not reign together, they were mutually exclusive. The newcomer, following covertly the tactics of the older, managed to supersede it, by divesting it of its ancient allies, thanks to whose about-face the new destroyed the old. But already we see the new body repeating the behaviour of the old with the same boldness and greater success since the older had ever met with resistance while the new meets with none. Its intolerance is better hidden but no less cruel: its rigour is not so apparent because it has no rebels to contend with. But let there be some true defenders of theism, tolerance, and morality, we would not fail to see against them the rise of a philosophic inquisition." *Troisième Dialogue,* XXII, 175.

[2] Rousseau claims that this happened to him: "Since the philosophic sect has gathered itself into a body under leaders, these, thanks to the art of intrigue to which they have applied themselves, have become the rulers of public opinion, and thereby are masters of private reputations, indeed can determine the fate of private lives, and of the State itself. They tried their new-found power upon J.-J. and the extent of their success, which must have come as a surprise even to them, gave them the measure of their credit." p. 171.

mankind better, wiser, and happier in its primitive constitution; blind, miserable, and nasty as it moves away from it. His goal is to correct the error of our judgments in order to check the progress of our vices."

It is easy to understand how exasperating the *Philosophes* must have found so pessimistic a view of Progress. It is also easy to understand that, during two centuries of accelerating Progress, admirers of Rousseau were prone to cast Noah's mantle upon what they regarded as an absurdity of their hero. But whether absurd or not, a doctrine which a great author explicitly states to be the essence of his message can not be glossed over without a consequent misreading of his works. The respect due to the author requires that his books be read in the light of what he himself names as his central concept.

THE DETERIORATION OF DEMOCRACY

This dawned upon me many years ago, while studying the *Social Contract,* when I found it to be, not a hopeful prescription for a Republic to come, but a clinical analysis of political deterioration. It is hard to misconceive what Rousseau meant when he himself summarised it:

The principle which constitutes the various forms of Government is to be found in the number of members which compose it. The lesser this number the stronger this Government; the greater this number, the weaker the Government; and as sovereignty tends ever to loosen, the Government tends to reinforce itself. Thus the executive must in time overpower the legislative; and when Law is finally subjected to men, there remain only masters and slaves; the State is destroyed.

Before such destruction, the Government must, by its natural progress, change its form, and pass by degrees from the greater number to the lesser.[3]

This summary turns our attention to Book III, chap. I of the *Contract,* where Rousseau offers what would now be called "a dynamic model of political transformation." While men should be active partners in the formulation of the public interest and voluntary agents thereof in private capacity, Rousseau asserts that such active partnership declines as the number of citizens increases, that individual conducts are increasingly inspired by divergent particular interests, that the role and pressure of Government must therefore develop; that, as the governmental apparatus grows, authority therein must be more concentrated; that, in sum the more numerous the people, the smaller the number of rulers. These rulers exert a heavier control over subjects, while they are ever less answerable to the citizenry:

A (governing) body which acts all the time can not render account of each action; it renders account only of the more important, and soon it may render account of none. The more active the acting Power, the less important the Power that wills.[4] ...Thus perish in the end all Democratic States.[5]

In the *Social Contract,* Rousseau offered no recipe for turning the government of a large and complex society into a democracy: on the contrary, he offered a demonstration that on the one hand great numbers, on the other the requirement of great activity in Government inevitably led to the centralisation of political authority in a few hands, which he regarded as the opposite of

---

[3] *Lettres Écrites de la Montagne,* Sixth Letter, XII, 176.

[4] The Power that wills: in Rousseau's scheme the People itself.

[5] *Montagne,* Seventh Letter, XII, 186.

Democracy. Quite early, Rousseau had expressed alarm about plans for the radical reconstruction of the French political system,[6] and in the *Dialogues* designed for posthumous publication he complained bitterly:

His object could not be to bring back large population and big States to the initial simplicity but only to arrest, if possible, the progress of those small and isolated enough for their preservation from the perfection of Society and the deterioration of the species.... But the bad faith of men of letters and that silly vanity which forever persuades everyone that he is being thought of, caused great nations to apply to themselves what was meant for small Republics; and, perversely, one wished to see a promoter of subversion and troubles in the man who is most prone to respect national laws and constitutions, and who has the strongest aversion for revolution, and for *ligueurs* of all kind, who return the compliment.[7]

URBANISATION

It is perhaps characteristic that the instance which immediately comes to our minds when we think of the purest democracy, Athens, found no favour in the eyes of Rousseau. Not only does he disparage it by comparison with Sparta in the *Discours sur les Sciences et les Arts,* but speaking of a political incident in Geneva, he exclaims in a private letter: "Here are these misguided people making great strides in imitation of the Athenians, and thus racing towards the same fate, which they shall encounter soon enough without running to it."[8] Why this low valuation of Athens? "With all this, never was Greece, excepting Sparta alone, given as an example of good mores."[9] Since Athens was lacking in mores and not a good example of democracy, the two things are linked in Rousseau's mind, and linked to the urban character of Athens. Note that when he pictures his assembly of the people, he mentions peasants: "When in the happiest people, we see peasants gathered under an oak to transact public business and acquitting themselves always wisely, can we fail to despise the refinements of other nations which achieve their fame and misery with so much art?"[10]

Democracy sits well with a sturdy peasantry and perishes through the riff-raff of the big town (*Contract*, Bk. IV, chap. IV). "Men were not designed to live in ant-heaps.... The closer you pack them the more they spoil.... Towns are the sink of the human species."[11] "The happiest of all condi-

---

6 See *Jugement sur la Polysynodie de l'Abbé de Saint-Pierre* (1756, published posthumously 1782) in Vaughan I, 415–16: "The mere introduction of suffrage was bound to cause a fearsome upheaval and to foster continual and convulsive agitation of social fractions rather than infuse new vigour into the whole. Picture the danger of setting into motion the enormous masses which make up the kingdom of France. Who shall control the consequent agitation or foresee all the effects of which it is capable? Even if the advantages of the new plan were clear, would any sensible man undertake to abolish the old customs, to discard the old maxims and to give another form to the State than that to which it has come by degrees over thirteen centuries?"

7 *Troisième Dialogue,* XXI, 129–130. The word *ligueurs* refers of course to the Ligue under Henri III and to the violent agitation caused by the faction which then brought disorder to France. See also the *Dédicace* of *Inegalité*: "When the people have once been accustomed to masters, they cannot henceforth do without them. If they try to shake the yoke, they move further from liberty as they mistake for it a frenzy of licence which stands in direct opposition to it: thus their revolutions almost always deliver them into the hands of seducers who but add to their chains."

8 Letter to Moultou, April 6, 1770.

9 *Lettre à D'Alembert sur les Spectacles,* XI, 222.

10 *Social Contract,* Book IV, chap. I.

11 *Émile,* Book I, VII, 45–6.

tions," states Rousseau, "is that of a villager in a free State."[12] Now we have moved on from Rousseau's political views to his social views, quite naturally since they are closely connected.

Of course, in our day the most "advanced" countries are characterised in terms of occupational statistics by having a quite small proportion of their man-power in agriculture. The proportion is very large on the contrary in the "under-developed" countries, and, quite currently, the rate at which the land cedes manpower to the town is taken as a rough measure of the rate of progress. Here then we have a stark contrast between Rousseau's view of human welfare and that which is current among us.

For Rousseau, "the condition natural to man is to till the soil and live from the fruits thereof...this occupation is the only necessary one and the most useful: it is an unhappy estate only when others tyrannise it by their violence or seduce it by the example of their vices."[13] The "agriculture" which Rousseau has in mind is of course not "the food factory" producing essentially for the market, but it is the "subsistence farm" whereby the farming family is self-sufficient and then produces some surplus to support a small minority of non-farmers. Those who tyrannise the peasant, interfering with the natural happiness of his condition, are of course the "privileged classes" which levy too heavy a tribute upon him: and presumably Rousseau would have seen also as tyrannical the levy on peasants for the sake of "socialist industrialisation." But the happiness of the peasant is not jeopardised only by levies, but also by the temptation of the town: "Both the more substantial and the poorer peasants have the mania of sending their children into the towns, the former to make them students on their way to becoming gentlemen, the others to make them wage-earners...." It comes as something of a shock to the reader of 1962 that Madame de Wolmar's great maxim should be to do all that is possible towards the happiness of peasants, but to lend no hand towards individual promotion out of that condition. It is indeed stressed that the distribution of talents among men is independent of the class into which they are born: why then should the talents from the peasant class not be helped to positions consonant with their gifts? Because mores and happiness are the major considerations. Rousseau does not deny that promoting a man to a position wherein he can make full employment of his talent is to the advantage of Society but, he stresses, men should not be considered as "instruments," and therefore one should not so distribute employments as to put the best man in the place where he can be most efficient, but so as to put men in positions where they can be as good and happy as possible: "it is never permissible to deteriorate a human soul for the benefit of others."

Nothing perhaps is so foreign to the attitude of 1962 as Rousseau's view of the peasantry. A hasty reader must regard it as fantastically conservative: it is conservative from the angle of economics, since he advocates the preservation of a form of production, subsistence farming, which is inimical to economic development; moreover it is socially conservative since he does not want to afford the gifted individuals opportunities for promotion out of this condition! But Rousseau never pretended to be interested in economic and social development. Repeatedly he stated that his purpose was to reverse

---

[12] *La Nouvelle Héloïse*, Part V, Letter II, V 200.

[13] *La Nouvelle Héloïse*, Part V, Letter II.

our valuations. Throughout history, peasants have been the despised basis upon which the social pyramid has been reared: there have been a few exceptions to this "rule of contempt," such as early Rome, the pioneer age of the U.S., the simpler Swiss *cantons*. These are the social systems of which Rousseau approves. If peasants are exploited and spurned, then of course they cannot be happy and contented, but a society made up of peasant families would be a virtuous and contented Society. This Arcadian dream already lies at the core of the *Discours des Sciences et des Arts*.

This does not imply that men should remain ignorant of skills other than those of agriculture. There is a picture in the *Lettre à D'Alembert sur Genève* of a happy society in the neighbourhood of Neufchâtel: here equally spaced farms display the equality of land possessions of the farmers, and afford the inhabitants the advantages of privacy together with the benefits of society. These happy peasants are all in favourable circumstances, free from any levies, dues or taxes, they each live from their own produce; however they have leisure to display their natural creative genius in many handiworks, especially in the winter, each family isolated by snow in the nice house built by its own hands practises many arts which are both pleasurable and useful. "No carpenter, locksmith [etc.] ever entered the country; they have no need of specialised craftsmen, each is his own craftsman.... Indeed they even make watches; and, incredible as it may seem, each united in his own person the various professions which watchmaking, and its very tooling, seem to require."

The last phrase irresistibly suggests the contrast of Adam Smith's opening remarks: a pin is a simple object, yet many men are assembled to make it, and its manufacture is subdivided into "about eighteen different operations."

Adam Smith eulogises this massing of hands and sub-division of tasks in the production of a simple object: this is the diametrically opposite position from that of Rousseau who rejoices that a complicated object is made by a simple man. Surely Rousseau would have conceded to Smith that division of labour was more efficient and led to higher production, but he would have argued that the Neufchâtel procedure made the worker a happier and a better man.

The contrast with Adam Smith gives us a key to Rousseau's thinking: he cared little for efficiency, which has been ever more highly valued in the course of the two centuries elapsed. It is in terms of efficiency that we can call ourselves greatly superior to the men of 1762; it is by means of efficiency that we enjoy many goods and possibilities they lacked. The great "success story" of the West is the Story of Efficiency, our élites are efficiency élites, our new wisdom consists in efficient processes and maxims of efficiency. It is in that form, and in that form only, that the "wisdom of the West" is eagerly accepted throughout the world. As we shall see, Rousseau's "advice to an under-developed nation" stands in sharp opposition to ours.

What is the mainspring of Rousseau's contempt for efficiency? He understands that increasing mastery over Nature implies increasing material interdependence of men: this he regards as corrupting. His great concern is to promote a condition of mutual friendship. He considers the thesis according to which a practical equivalent is obtained when each man is moved, for his own personal advantage to serve that of his fellows, and he forcibly rejects this equivalence.[14] Not only is the feeling for the neighbour utterly different in quality if he is regarded as a means

14 Cf. *Préface* of *Narcisse* (1752) XV.

to services, however mutual, but it is not true that on this personal advantage basis, harmony will be achieved. On the contrary there will be in each man a propensity to feel that he is not getting as good a bargain as he should. Man feels less at home in his work if its nature and discipline are imposed, directly or not, by his fellows, and more dissatisfied with its proceeds, if these seem determined at the discretion of his fellows. Thus Rousseau sees in the division of labour, not the proceeds thereof, but feelings arising therefrom: unfreedom, frustration, and resentment.

ADVICE TO AN UNDER-DEVELOPED NATION

Nowadays we quantify Progress. We evaluate in current prices the sum of goods and services produced in a nation in a given year, and then measure against this the flow in some succeeding year, making corrections for price changes: this calculation, put on a per year and per inhabitant basis, yields us the per capita rate of growth, which we commonly identify with rate of progress. Also we use the "flow of goods and services per year" concept to compare the National Product per head in various countries and then we can place these countries on a graduated scale with India at the bottom and the U.S. at the top. It is indeed in terms of position on this graduated scale that we define "under-developed countries": in the case of the latter we deem it mandatory that they should adopt the policies and structures apt to move them up the scale at the fastest feasible pace.

In Rousseau's day there was no pressure of population problem and therefore we cannot presume to say what his view would have been in the case of the countries so afflicted. But taking the case of, say, African countries, it

seems quite clear from his writings that he would not have advocated the imitation of the Western economy. He would have said that maximising the flow of goods and service was a purpose different in kind from fostering a virtuous and happy community, and that his own purpose was the latter. Nothing is more telling in this respect than his advice on the political and social reformation of Poland. In his day Poland was an "under-developed country," lacking the administration, industry, and trade of the western kingdoms, although it possessed a cultural élite (which is also the case of a good number of now "under-developed" nations).

If you only want to become noisome, brilliant, formidable, and to make your weight felt to the other peoples of Europe, then follow their example. Cultivate the sciences, the arts, trade, industry, have a regular army, fortresses, academies, above all a good financial system which stirs up the circulation of money; make money indispensable to everyone in order to increase social dependence and toward that end foster material and intellectual luxury....

But if perchance you should prefer to shape a free, peaceful, and wise nation, self-sufficient and happy, then you should take quite another path, maintain or re-establish at home simple mores, healthy tastes, a martial spirit devoid of ambition, form courageous and disinterested souls, apply your people to agriculture and to the arts basic to living, make money despicable....[15]

In those days the suggestions of the French way of life had perhaps an even stronger "demonstration effect" than in our day the American way of life. This is what Rousseau feels about social imitation:

A great nation which has never been too intimately mixed with its neighbours must have many [civil and domestic customs]

15 *Considérations sur le Gouvernement de Pologne*, p. xi.

which are its very own, but which are presumably being adulterated, due to the general bent throughout Europe towards the adoption of French tastes and mores. You should maintain or re-establish any ancient custom of yours, and indeed introduce some which shall be specific to yourselves. Even if such specific customs are in themselves of no value, even if they are somewhat bad, provided they are not essentially so, their very difference is of value as tying the Poles more closely together and giving them a natural reluctance to mix with foreigners. I regard it as a boon that they have a national style of clothing. Carefully maintain this advantage: do exactly the reverse of that much vaunted Czar [Peter the Great]. Let neither king nor senator nor any public man ever appear in any other raiment than the national, let no Pole dare to produce himself at court in clothing of French style.

Keen to foster patriotism, Rousseau conceives it as an attachment to and pride in what is specific to the nation. Obviously he would have applauded the resurrection of Gaelic in Eire and of Hebrew in Israel. In contradiction to Voltaire's hatred of the Jews, Rousseau expressed the utmost admiration for their conservation of the national character throughout their ordeals.

Out of these vagabonds Moses dared to make a political body, a free people; while this herd wandered in the desert he instituted it in a manner invulnerable to time, mishaps, and conquerors, which the passage of five thousand years has neither destroyed nor altered, and which subsists in its pristine vigour even while the nation has ceased to form a body politic.

To prevent his people from melting into others, he gave it mores and customs incompatible with those of other nations; he burdened it with specific rites and ceremonies, he introduced a thousand constraints to keep it on the alert and to make it forever a stranger to other peoples; and all the bonds of brotherhood which he created between its citizens were as many obstacles to its absorption in other peoples.

Rousseau goes on to glorify the Jewish nation which shall subsist as such to the end of the world, whatever the persecutions.

The mere quoting of Peter the Great as a model of what should not be done suffices to stress that Rousseau deliberately advanced the view opposed to that the *Philosophes*. They all thought highly of Peter's efforts to "westernise" the Russian people; indeed in his day they were enamoured of Catherine the Great, who was pursuing the same object, denounced by Rousseau. Jean-Jacques' position here is consistent with the more general and extreme statement he made twenty years earlier in the preface to *Narcisse*:

Everything which facilitates communication between the several nations carries to each not the virtues but the vices of another, and alters in all the mores suitable to its climate and constitution.

Again his attitude is opposed to that of the Philosophers, and to the modern attitude, in terms of administration. They were all in favour of centralisation: he stands against it. He would like to see Poland "a confederation of thirty-three small States." This fully accords with his desire to involve all citizens in public affairs,[16] and with his finding that the proportion of those so involved

---

16 All citizens does not mean all adult inhabitants. If we were here dealing with the politics of Rousseau, we would have to stress what he says in chaps. VI and XIII of *Pologne,* where he warns against a sweeping abolition of bondage, stresses that liberty is a heady wine for those unaccustomed to it, who are more apt to mutiny than fit for citizenship. He recommends a slow and progressive course of emancipation. Provincial committees would sit every two years to single out families deserving by their moral behaviour of access into the civic body. When a sufficient number of families came, after a number of sessions, to be in full enjoyment of citizenship rights, then villages where such families were numerous would be collectively enfranchised.

declines as membership of the body politic increases. It seems strange that Rousseau should have been invoked as patron by the centralising Jacobins.

Political confederation rather than unification, limited rather than universal suffrage, systematic cultivation of national traits rather than westernisation, self-sufficiency rather than foreign trade, rural life rather than urbanisation, taxes in kind rather than in money, subsistence agriculture associated with cottage crafts rather than farming for the market and establishment of industrial complexes—at every point Rousseau's advice to the Poles stands in contradiction to that which is now currently given to under-developed countries.

VIEWPOINT

Undergraduates find it easy to think that Rousseau's views were "advanced" in their day, and have become "reactionary" in our own, due to the march of Progress. This will not do. At every point at which it clashes with now prevalent views, Rousseau's doctrine conflicted in his own day with the views of the *Philosophes*. It is in conflict with developments which have occurred because it was conceived in opposition to developments due to occur.

An analogy immediately comes to mind: Plato pictured his small, closed, self-sufficient City while he was well aware that Greek cities were being swept into larger wholes. Rousseau's recommendations now seem Utopian, but he knew them for such at the time. He sensed the accelerating pace of social evolution, but chose to dwell on what was being lost rather than on what was being gained. No doubt we can read in his works the bitter condemnation of the society he lived in, but in the name of a better past, not of a better future.

His attitude is fundamentally pessimistic: the course of social history cannot be reversed or indeed stopped, except in isolated cases.[17]

This pessimism explains the contradiction which has so often been noted between the *Social Contract* and *Émile*. The man of the *Contract* is essentially a patriot, while *Émile* is educated for a life of privacy: the *Contract* is offered as the recipe which can preserve small rustic communities from deterioration, while also describing the process of their inevitable corruption; *Émile* is offered as advice to the inhabitant of a corrupted society, who should as far as feasible avoid involvement. The *Contract* is for Corsica, *Émile* for a Frenchman.

But why does Rousseau regard social evolution with such horror? His enemies were wont to say that, having gained fame through a clever paradox, he had lacked the wit to extricate himself from it, and that the joker's mask had helped to mould the philosopher's face; but this is the sort of stupidity of which clever men become capable when obfuscated by unkindness. Rousseau replies with dignity: "His system may be false, but in its development he has painted himself truly." Jean-Jacques has left us in no doubt about his main personal need: it is to feel at peace with himself and in trusting harmony with his fellows. It seemed to him that these basic needs of the human heart were

[17] "But human nature does not move backwards, and never can we return to times of innocence and equality once we have departed from them: this is one of the principles which he most stressed. Therefore his aim could not be to bring back large nations and big States to their pristine simplicity, but only to arrest if possible the progress of those whose smallness and seclusion had preserved them from marching rapidly towards the perfection of society and the deterioration of the species."
—*Troisième Dialogue*, XXII.

increasingly thwarted by social evolution.

A century earlier, Hobbes had written in *Leviathan*: "Felicity is a continual progress of the desire from one object to another, the attaining of the former being still but the way to the latter.... The *power* of a man, to take it universally, is his present means to obtain some future apparent good. And therefore, man's desire moving from one object to another...I put for a general inclination of all mankind a perpetual and restless desire of power after power, that ceaseth only in death.... Competition of riches, honour, command, or other power, inclineth to contention, enmity, and war...."

These simple quotations suffice to evoke a questing and contentious being. Rousseau in *Inégalité* adopts this picture without reservation: "Indeed men are nasty, a sad and ceaseless experience is enough proof." But he swings the Hobbesian model right around: according to Hobbes, and according to Bayle, man is naturally avid, and therefore violent when he is crossed, but education and society tame him. Rousseau wants it the other way around: but "Man is naturally good"; he asserts it, believes that he has proved it, he feels it within himself:[18] man therefore must have deteriorated. "What can have depraved him other than the changes intervening in his constitution, the progress he has made, the knowledge that he has acquired? Admire if you will human society, it is no less true that, of necessity, it leads men to hate each other proportionately to the criss-crossing of their interests."

The seventeenth century had seen in Society mainly the mutual guarantee; more realistically the eighteenth century takes social co-operation as the *fons et origo*. This practically beneficial co-operation is morally corrupting, says Rousseau, because it arouses our imagination. While *in conditione naturali*, man's desires are limited; in the state of society, having others at hand to help him, he can dream up ends achievable if others sufficiently connive at his purpose, and having enjoyed such achievement in imagination, he then feels unhappy and resentful if others in fact do not help him to it. Nor is this to be thought of mainly in material terms.[19] The individual good which social commerce endows with a very high value is "consideration"; the individual learns to see himself through others' eyes, and suffers if he is not looked up to as much as he wants, as much as another: and however efficient society may become in multiplying material goods, esteem, being assessed relatively, is by nature a scarce good, which all come to desire and but few can enjoy. The greater social co-operation is, the higher the prospects it offers to the individual who takes his Ego as the centre, and the more bitter his disappointment when the others fail to treat him as the centre.

Thus he finds himself shifting from the unexacting selfishness of the natural condition to the demanding selfishness of the social condition, the more demanding, the more extensive and intensive the social co-operation is. In a small rustic society it is possible to shift the individual's intense *Ego* concern to a *We* concern,[20] but it requires that the community be small and immutable. It cannot be done in a large,

---

[18] He regards himself as "the man of Nature" and goes to the embarrassing extreme of stating: "I who feel better and more just than any man known to me...." *Troisième Dialogue*, XXII.

[19] Therefore it is incapable of being remedied by a social policy of equal material shares.

[20] This is the "recipe" of the *Social Contract*, fully explained in psychological terms at the beginning of *Émile*.

progressive society, and it is mere fancy in the case of the *societas humani generis*.[21] Therefore, given the large progressive society, the best that can be done is to so educate the individual as to deflate foolish desires. Émile shall make no bid for a large share or a high place at the social banquet, but seek happiness within himself, in domestic life and the quiet enjoyment of Nature. While the ecstasy of the Lake of Bienne is perforce a rare event, life can be well spent in a pleasant retreat with charitable attention to a very narrow circle of neighbours.[22] There is probably great symbolic value in Wolmar's garden with

---

21 See the "suppressed" chapter of the *Social Contract*.

22 "A small number of mild and peaceful people united by mutual needs and a reciprocity of good-will concur by various occupations to a common end; each finding in his condition the means of his contentment, and without desire of rising from it, has no other ambition than to properly fulfil its duties." *Héloïse*, Part V, Letter II.

Compare at the beginning of *Émile*: "Distrust these cosmopolitans to seek afar in their books duties which they disdain to fulfil in their neighbourhood. See this philosopher who loves the Tartars dispense himself from loving his neighbours!"

its closed horizon and its moderate re-arrangement of Nature.[23] There is rather unexpected *rapprochement* here with the final sentence of *Candide*. However this calls for some curbing not only of lower appetites but also of finer feelings (witness Julie).

I did not propose here to discuss the ideas of Rousseau. What I wanted to do is to display their consistency, which appears as soon as one envisages them from the centre which Rousseau many times indicates as his own: the search for "a true system of the human heart." Whether Rousseau found the "true" system is not my concern. But it is surely a singular merit to have considered the affective needs of Man. While the adoption of Rousseau's practical recommendations would have stopped us from progressing as we have done in the satisfaction of human material wants, our very advance on the road he so bitterly spurned quickens our sensitivity to the problems he raised.

---

23 An important page (*Héloïse*, Part II, Letter XI). In general I feel that *Héloïse* has been inadequately exploited for the understanding of Rousseau as a social philosopher.

GEORGE KATEB

Aspects of Rousseau's
Political Thought[*][1]

In a review of Sir Isaiah Berlin's *Two Concepts of Liberty*, which appeared in *The Times* (London) *Literary Supplement*, the anonymous writer complained of the "slanders" that have been lavished on the political philosophy of Rousseau.[2] The slanders—and slanders they are—which the writer had in mind have come from those who claim to see in Rousseau's thought a powerful and also influential defense of totalitarianism. The fashion which makes of Rousseau a *totalitarian democrat* must, of course, be as modern as the word "totalitarian" itself; and it is J. L. Talmon who has been primarily respon-

sible for this kind of attribution to Rousseau.[3] But there are slanders against Rousseau that go back to an earlier time: the view of Rousseau as a friend of *despotism* begins with Constant.[4] Later in the century, Taine thought he saw in Rousseau's writings a repellent theory of collectivism.[5]

* Reprinted with permission from the *Political Science Quarterly*, December 1961, Vol. LXXVI, No. 4.

[1] The author is greatly indebted to John Rawls' paper, 'Justice as Fairness," *The Philosophical Reveiw, LXVII* (April 1958), pp. 164–194; and to Kurt Baier, *The Moral Point of View* (Ithaca, 1958), esp. chaps. 8 and 10, for aid in understanding some of the concepts which figure in this paper. Of all the writing on Rousseau consulted, I found Robert Derathé's *Jean-Jacques Rousseau et le science politique de son temps* (Paris, 1950) to be the most valuable. Derathé's book is a work of profound scholarship.

[2] Anon., "A Hundred Years After," *The Times Literary Supplement*, Feb. 20, 1959, pp. 89–90, at p. 90.

[3] See J. L. Talmon, *The Rise of Totalitarian Democracy* (Boston, 1952), pp. 38–49. The idea of "democratic despotism" is to be found in Alexis de Tocqueville, *Democracy in America*, trans. by Henry Reeve, rev. by Francis Bowen (2 vols., New York, 1945), vol. II, chaps. 6–7, and *The Old Regime and the French Revolution*, trans. by Stuart Gilbert (New York, 1955), pt. 3, chap. 3. In the latter work, Tocqueville associates specific thinkers with this idea, but Rousseau is not among them. For other accusations against Rousseau in the totalitarian vein, see John W. Chapman, *Rousseau—Totalitarian or Liberal?* (New York, 1956), p. 74.

[4] For a discussion of Constant's criticism, and of the way in which Constant qualified his criticism, see Alfred Cobban, *Rousseau and the Modern State* (London, 1934), pp. 36–37.

[5] See Peter Gay's Introduction to his translation of Ernst Cassirer, *The Question of Jean-Jacques Rousseau* (New York, 1954), pp. 7–8. The most careful and sustained exposition of the view that Rousseau is a collectivist is to be found in C. E. Vaughan's Introduction to his edition of *The Political Writings of Jean-Jacques Rousseau* (2 vols., Cambridge, 1915).

Against these charges, as we know, Rousseau has had his defenders, whose strategy has been to try to show that Rousseau is not a collectivist, at all, nor some kind of perverted democrat, but an individualist.[6] And it would seem hopeless to expect that the exchange of arguments for and against Rousseau could ever be resolved: truces resulting from fatigue would seem in fact to be the only resolution. However, if the issue could somehow be given a different complexion; if, somehow, it could be shown that both sides are wrong and their battle folly, then perhaps intolerable debate would be quieted, and Rousseau's thought be allowed a different perspective. Such an enterprise is itself pretentious, but the pretentiousness may be forgiven by the results. In this paper, I will try to show what this enterprise, in its outlines, would be.

1

There is common agreement that the central idea in Rousseau's political thought is the idea of the general will. And though every one acknowledges that he is somewhat confused by Rousseau's analysis of this idea, almost everyone feels that he understands it well enough to make it the primary reason for saying that Rousseau is either a collectivist or despot or totalitarian, or an individualist. I have no wish to deny that the idea of the general will *is* the central idea in Rousseau's political thought; nor that some of the blame for the confusion belongs to Rousseau. But I would also say that whatever the occasional obscurities of the idea, it is possible to come to an

understanding of it that is quite certain; and thereby come to an understanding of Rousseau's political thought.

The essential fact is that the aim of the general will is justice. Once this has been seen, the problems of interpreting Rousseau become much less fierce. Once it has been seen that justice is at the center of Rousseau's concerns, no warrant is left for thinking that Rousseau is a collectivist, totalitarian, despot, or individualist. The concept of justice simply displaces these categories.[7] Accompanying justice are two other concepts which figure in Rousseau's political thought, the concept of moral autonomy and the concept of fair play. When these three concepts are located and related, I would say that Rousseau's political thought has been seen in its proper light.

To begin with, we must understand that the idea of justice to be found in Rousseau's writings is the idea of distributive justice, the idea of justice as "giving every man his due."[8] The polit-

---

[6] For a historical discussion of the individualist interpretation of Rousseau's political thought, consult Peter Gay, *op. cit.* (See note 5). See also the temperate pages of John W. Chapman, *op. cit.*, especially chapters 7 and 9.

[7] Some attention is given to the concept of justice in Rousseau's thought by John W. Chapman, *op. cit.*, chapter 5.

[8] See Rousseau, *Contrat Social*, First Draft, bk. II, chap. IV in Vaughan, vol. I, pp. 493–495. Rousseau cites the axiom *cuique suum*, "to each his own." According to Rousseau this axiom "to each his own," and the related axiom, "to do to others what one wishes done to oneself"—which together are the true principles of justice—are applications of the overriding principle, to seek the greatest good of all. This latter principle is the first principle of civil society. The rule of distributive justice is thus an indispensable *means* to the attainment of the greatest good of all. In the early state of nature, the natural feeling of compassion is operative; but this feeling leads men not to try to do good to others, but to "do good to yourself with as little evil as possible to others." (*A Discourse on the Origin of Inequality* in *The Social Contract and Discourses,* trans. by G. D. H. Cole (New York, 1950), p. 227.) Only when civil society is established does it become possible actively to seek the good of others without jeopardizing oneself, to be benevolent without

ical application of justice (so understood) is a condition in which the rights
of every citizen are protected. That
society is just in which the life, liberty,
and property of every citizen are protected. Next, we must understand that
by "autonomy" is meant something
very much like what Kant said it
meant. Rousseau does not use the word,
but his meaning is clear: a man is autonomous when the laws by which he
lives are given by that man to himself.
Last, we must understand that by "fair
play" is meant the willingness of every
man to obey the laws of his society,
even when such obedience imposes on
him some sacrifice, and therefore seems
to take back from him what society, in
the first place, gave him. The connections between justice, autonomy, and
fair play are of the following sort. In
the good society, every man takes part
directly in the framing of laws; those
laws are to be framed which embody
(distributive) justice, or which (in extraordinary circumstances) call into
being the operation of fair play. The
good citizen (who is the good man)
will not absent himself from the deliberations which conclude in the framing of
laws; will always seek to have laws
framed which are just, or which accord
with fair play, as the case may be; and
will obey these laws willingly, conscious
both of their importance to him and his
society, and of their moral character.
Rousseau's primary intent is precisely

to see these concepts guide political
reality wherever possible.[9]

Thus, in a society which remains
faithful to the correct political principles (as embodied in the social contract), no man can preserve his life,
liberty, and property without fulfilling
his obligations; and merely by fulfilling
his obligations, each man will be able
to preserve his life, liberty, and property. There can be no benefits without
obligations, and there will be no obligations without benefits.

Lest our description be taken as an
impertinent simplification of Rousseau's
complex thought, it would be well to
examine some of the major points that
Rousseau makes in *The Social Contract*
and elsewhere. Such an examination
would establish, I think, the validity of
what I have so far said. In addition, we

---

ruin. And in civil society everything must be
done to cultivate the feeling of benevolence,
which manifests itself not only in voting
according to the rule of justice, but also in
one's general deportment. Though respect for
the idea of distributive justice is to the interest of each man, benevolence supplies another
motive for that respect. The good man will be
glad that the rule of distributive justice serves
others besides himself, he will be glad that his
own protection is indissolubly connected to
the protection of his fellows.

[9] In the state of nature, each is entitled to
do as he pleases: he is born free of chains; he
has no obligations. The consequence, however,
of each doing as he pleases is that each stands
the chance of losing his life, or becoming
enslaved, or losing his possessions. Men place
restrictions on their will, men impose obligations on themselves, men take upon themselves the burden of morality, in order to
preserve themselves from death, slavery, or
loss. Civil society is the only condition in
which morality is inextricably joined with the
enjoyment of life, liberty, and possessions. In
nature, the good man will surely lose his life
or liberty or possessions, and bad men will
constantly war with each other; but in civil
society, under normal conditions, only the immoral man will lose his life or liberty or possessions. A man cannot afford to be moral in
nature; a man cannot afford to be immoral in
civil society. Civil society makes moral behavior both possible and necessary. Rousseau's
fullest discussion of the state of nature, and
of the hypothetically historical changes in it,
is to be found in his *A Discourse on the
Origin of Inequality*. See the commentary of
Arthur O. Lovejoy in "The Supposed Primi-
tivism of Rousseau's Discourse on Inequality"
in *Essays in the History of Ideas* (New York,
1955), pp. 14–37.

shall see how it has come about that Rousseau has been accused of collectivism, despotism, and totalitarianism, and defended by the counterclaim that he was an individualist.

2

Distributive justice is at the center of Rousseau's concerns, and the purpose for which men agree to live with each other in a society—the purpose for which they enter with each other into the agreement known as the social contract—is to set up the rule of distributive justice. With the formation of a society, a system of rights is for the first time established. In a condition of nature, men do what they must to live, and that means that they take what they can, often from each other, and keep it as long as they can. Each man has a natural right to preserve himself as he sees fit, and without the onus of blame. In the civil condition, however, precarious tenure is replaced by legal ownership, and the entire force of the society is employed to protect that ownership. Natural liberty gives way to a system of civil rights. There is, in Rousseau's political theory, no other purpose for which the social contract is made.[10] Marvelous benefits of every kind do in fact follow on the making of the social contract; most importantly, benefits moral, intellectual, and spiritual. But we must not think that in the past men were driven to enter civil society for the sake of these benefits; we must not think that today we live in civil society for the sake of these benefits. These benefits come as they can. So that it could be said that *prudence* dictates

the departure of men from their natural condition; and before we can call a society a good society, we must make sure that it accommodates that prudence. Rousseau begins where Hobbes begins.

Another comment by Rousseau strengthens the view that the protection of property (and, of course, of life and liberty) is the foundation stone of Rousseau's political thought. In a note to the last sentence of the first chapter of *The Social Contract,* Rousseau says:

Under bad governments, this equality (of convention and legal right) is only apparent and illusory; it serves only to keep the pauper in his poverty and the rich man in the position he has usurped. In fact, laws are always of use to those who possess and harmful to those who have nothing: from which it follows that the social state is advantageous to men only when all have something and none too much.[11]

When applied to a man without property, the principle of distributive justice is a mockery. He has no stake in society; he has nothing to be protected; he can only contribute to the protection of the property of others. He makes sacrifices, but receives no benefits, apart from mere existence. There is, as the saying goes, "nothing in it for him." But for those with property, there can be no higher blessing than to live in a society in which there is distributive justice.

What or who, then, deliberately offends against the principle of distributive justice in society? In *The Social Contract,* Rousseau finds in particular interests the source of offense; and in

---

[10] Let us note that the first moral idea Rousseau teaches his pupil is respect for the property of others. See Rousseau, *Émile,* trans. by Barbara Foxley (London, 1911), pp. 62–63.

[11] Jean-Jacques Rousseau, *The Social Contract,* trans. by G. D. H. Cole (see note 8, above), bk. I, chap. IX, p. 22. *The Social Contract* in this edition is hereafter cited simply as "Rousseau." *Cf. A Discourse on the Origin of Inequality,* pp. 251–52.

A Discourse on Political Economy, he finds that government (the executive power) can also offend.[12] In a phrase, to take, or to try to take, what is not one's own, constitutes the basic violation against the requirements of distributive justice. (Obviously, that is a matter of definition.) In a state of nature, one takes what one can, knowing that it may be taken by someone else. In society, however, one is enabled to keep what one has. In return, one must not try to take what belongs to another. Abstention from aggrandizement answers to the protection afforded against the aggrandizement of others. How does a man aggrandize? Clearly, whenever he commits a crime against the life, liberty, or property of another; that is, when he breaks a (putatively just) law. But it is also possible to aggrandize in accordance with the law, when the law is itself unjust. Laws are unjust, by definition, when they legitimize encroachments by particular interests (or by the government) on the property of others. Rousseau's great fear of particular interests, acting in solidarity, comes from his belief in the natural propensity of groups to expand at the expense of others. He prefers a society without organized interest groups just because of this propensity, not because he wished a levelled society at the mercy of the political power, or an equalitarian society of identical men. Of course, Rousseau did not want the energies and loyalties of citizens monopolized by the groups to which

they belonged, to the exclusion of their civic love and duty. But a major part of the reason for this position is the "realist" view which Rousseau had of the tendencies of all groups. Furthermore, Rousseau did not think it likely that any society could remain free of solidified interests. In a manner similar to that of Madison in *The Federalist* No. 10, he looked to the struggle of interest groups to produce a stalemate, from which the principle of distributive justice emerges as it were behind the backs of the participants in the struggle.[13] Presumably, the existence of numerous diverse groups would seriously interfere with the formation of a homogeneous majority opinion which sought basic transgressive changes in the pattern of economic relations. Rousseau says, "...take away from these same (particular) wills the pluses and minuses that cancel one another, and the general will remains as the sum of the differences."[14] The meaning of the arithmetic metaphor is simply this: when some try to flourish at the expense of others, they go, by definition, beyond the claims of the principle of distributive justice; but when these excessive claims are eliminated from the deliberations that conclude in law, dis-

---

[12] Rousseau, *A Discourse on Political Economy* in *The Social Contract and Discourses* (see note 8 above), p. 297. This discourse is hereafter cited as "Political Economy." The abuses of government which Rousseau discusses in bk. III, chap. X of *The Social Contract* are violations of the principle of autonomy and illegal changes in the structure of government.

[13] *Cf.* the view of John W. Chapman that, "Expression of the general will cannot be a purely mechanical process in which conflicting personal goods offset and cancel each other. This they do, but only if each of the participants is motivated by desire for the general welfare and actively seeks to discover the course of action that promotes it." (*op. cit.,* p. 45.)

[14] Rousseau, bk. II, chap. III. p. 26. See also note 1, pp. 26–27. See the discussion of this sentence in *Montesquieu and Rousseau, Forerunners of Sociology,* by Émile Durkheim, trans. by Ralph Manheim (Ann Arbor, 1960), pp. 107–8. For further discussion of the inevitability of particular interests, see "Political Economy," pp. 290–91.

tributive justice is served.[15] If society could not be made up of men who placed themselves in a direct, unmediated relationship with each other and who in the privacy of their conscience came to their own conclusions as to what was just and hence fit to be made law, then the next best thing was to have a society made up of interest groups of equal strength, each able to defend itself, and each prevented by the others from seeking to aggrandize. The good society will cultivate the sentiment of benevolence in every man; at the same time, its economic and social structure will be such as to make up for the inevitable lapses of that sentiment. When each group can keep what belongs to it, and cannot take what does not belong to it, justice rules.

But whatever the differences of wealth in society, the principle of distributive justice places restraints on the strong, for it morally disbars them from using their strength to the limit. The very reciprocity of the social contract works to the equal benefit of all; and if one is to be faithful to the terms of the social contract, one must never, in one's strength, take from the weak: the rich must not take from the poor, nor the many from the few.[16] Hopefully,

advantage and justice will not be at odds. Society should be such as to make it implausible for groups to think that they can thrive at the expense of other groups. At the same time, unjust actions will have a tendency to upset the social order, and thus threaten the protection of the property of the unjust; and therefore ultimately be imprudent.[17] Again, it is equality—not, of course, "absolutely identical" degrees of powers and riches for everybody—which helps to keep injustice from being advantageous, or justice from tending to appear as a harsh circumscription of the pursuit of advantage.[18]

We must now fit the general will into these considerations. There are a few things to be remembered about this concept. The general will is expressed only in laws. And laws should embody the principle of distributive justice; laws should be just. Rousseau (speaking of political agencies) says, "...it is needful only to act justly, to be certain of following the general will."[19] This is, of course, a matter of definition. We must also remember that Rousseau speaks of the common good: the general will looks only to the common good: laws should look only to the common good. Just as the aim of an individual's will is the good of that individual, so the aim of the general will is the good of

---

15 The principle of distributive justice not only prohibits the selfish augmentation of one's own interest, but may also hurt us in our legitimate interest. For example, we will have to keep our promises, and honor our contracts, even though shifts in circumstance make it difficult for us to do so. See Rousseau, "Political Economy," p. 312.

16 Rousseau, bk. II, chap. XI, p. 50; and "Political Economy," p. 305. It is the very security afforded by civil society that gives an interest enough strength to allow it to feel capable of aggrandizement. To employ that strength in aggrandizement is to accept the sacrifices of others in order to deny them the benefits which justify their sacrifices. Looked at in this way, aggrandizement violates the demands of fair play.

17 Rousseau, bk. I, chap. VII, p. 18.

18 In a society in which there are great distinctions of wealth, the social contract becomes an absurdity: "The terms of the social compact between these two estates of men (rich and poor) may be summed up in a few words: 'You have need of me, because I am rich and you are poor. We will therefore come to an agreement. I will permit you to have the honour of serving me on condition that you bestow on me the little you have left, in return for the pains I shall take to command you.'" ("Political Economy," pp. 323–24). Rousseau goes on to advocate a system of progressive taxation.

19 Rousseau, "Political Economy," p. 297.

society as a whole, the common good.[20] But what is the common good? Is it something mystical, some good different from, and higher than, the good of each man in society? The answer is an unequivocal No. The common good is "...the common element in...different interests."[21] What do all interests have in common? In a word: preservation. Rousseau says, "...individual interest always tends to privileges, while the common interest always tends to equality."[22] By "equality," Rousseau does not ever mean equality of property, equal holdings. He rather means equal consideration, equal entitlement to protection, whatever the size of the holding. In addition, every man has an equal interest in remaining alive (life) and in remaining master of his own will (liberty). There is no other common good or common interest: there is no other reason for which the social contract was first made: there is no other reason for which society exists. Rousseau also says, "The undertakings which bind us to the social body are obligatory only because they are mutual; and their nature is such that in fulfilling them we cannot work for others without working for ourselves."[23] Rousseau is not Hegel. The general will wills justice; and if a citizen wishes to be in accord with the general will, he must always vote in law-making deliber-

ations in the way by which he feels justice—the common good or the common interest—will be served. He may, of course, be wrong: hopefully, but not necessarily, more citizens will be right than wrong. More important, it is to be hoped that most citizens will *want* to be right; that is, will want to be in accord with the general will. Naturally, there is a constant temptation to pursue one's interest (or the interest of one's group) at the expense of others. But in the good society—which is the just society —things will conspire to produce just laws. And by "things" must be meant the virtuous inclinations of the citizenry combined with a proper economic and social structure.

3

The two concepts present in association with distributive justice are autonomy and fair play. On the concept of autonomy in Rousseau's political thought, there is abundant good writing.[24] Rousseau says, "...obedience to a law which we prescribe to ourselves is liberty."[25] We prescribe to ourselves when we take part in the deliberations that conclude in law: law imposed on us, or emanating from a (morally) distant source, no matter how good the law, leaves us in a condition of dependence. We ourselves must see what law is called for, and then go on to make it with others. Autonomy thus contains the procedural requirement for calling a law good; and that requirement is defeated even by representative government. For even representative government takes out of our hands the deliberations that con-

---

[20] Rousseau, "Political Economy," pp. 289–90.

[21] Rousseau, bk. II, chap. I, p. 23. See Derathé, *Jean-Jacques Rousseau et le science politique de son temps,* pp. 237–41, 353–57.

[22] Rousseau, *Émile,* p. 426. Rousseau's words are: "...l'intérêt privé tend toujours aux préférences, et l'intérêt public à l'égalité." (*The Political Writings of Jean-Jacques Rousseau,* ed. by C. E. Vaughan, vol. II. p. 153.) *Cf.* Rousseau, bk. II, chap. I: "—la volonté particulière tend, par sa nature, aux préférences, et la volonté générale à l'égalité." (Vaughan, Vol. II, p. 40.) See also Rousseau, bk. II, chap. III, p. 26.

[23] Rousseau, bk. II, chap. IV, p. 29.

[24] See, for example, G. D. H. Cole's Introduction (see note 8 above) pp. xli–l; Ernest Cassirer, *The Question of Jean-Jacques Rousseau,* esp. pp. 57–70, 96–107.

[25] Or: obedience to a law we did not make, but could repeal.

clude in law: when we live under a representative government we, in effect, alienate our wills. We may recognize a law made for us by our representatives, or by other political agents, as satisfactory or utilitarian. But unless we help to make the law ourselves, we are placed in the position of being (at best) wards in the care of some superior agency. On the other hand, we do not have liberty when we prescribe to ourselves any law whatsoever. There is a substantival requirement which the law must meet, if we are to be free; and this is the same as the substantival requirement for calling a law just; the law must look to the common good, it must realize the general will, it must embody the principle of distributive justice. The concept of autonomy cannot be understood apart from the concept of distributive justice. Alluding perhaps to an old Roman legal adage, Rousseau says, "...it (the general will expressed in law) must both come from all and apply to all."[26] Laws are to be made by the citizens, and the laws are to be just. Only then are the procedural and the substantival requirements for proper law satisfied. And only then are we in a condition of moral liberty, a condition immensely better than the condition of natural liberty. Moral liberty thus combines distributive justice (the protection of one's life, liberty, and property) with autonomy.

4

We must now turn to our third concept, the concept of fair play, and thereby complete our sketch of the outlines of Rousseau's political philosophy. We must ask: What brings into being the operation of fair play? The answer is: the need for some sort of sacrifice on the part of the citizen. In *The Social Contract,* Rousseau speaks of the sacrifice involved in defending one's country in time of war; in *A Discourse on Political Economy,* he speaks of the sacrifice involved in the payment of taxes. Rousseau says, "He who wills the end wills the means also, and the means must involve some risks, and even some losses. He who wishes to preserve his life at others' expense should also, when it is necessary, be ready to give it up for their sake."[27] Every society necessitates restrictions and sacrifices; and Rousseau, with his matchless sense of the real, does not think that even the good society can be free of them. For him, one splendid thing about the good society is that it is alone among societies in exacting sacrifices according to the demands of fair play. For only in the good society will there be a strict correspondence between benefits and sacrifices. The supreme benefit of the good society is the establishment of distributive justice through the medium of autonomy; everyone shares in the making of the laws by which he lives, and those laws will be, ideally, protective of everyone's life, liberty, and property. When, therefore, the citizenry, in its sovereign capacity, makes laws requiring military service or imposing taxes, the individual citizen can feel, in obeying those laws, that he is merely sharing *equally* in those things which make the continued existence of his society possible, and therewith, the continued existence of his civil liberty possible. No one in the good society is exempt. Everyone's benefit is tied to everyone else's. Both the benefits and the obligations of the good society are reciprocal. One cannot help oneself except by helping others; one must inevitably help oneself by helping others. In the good society, in all cases where sacrifice is

---

26 Rousseau, bk. II, chap. IV, p. 29.

27 Rousseau, bk. II, chap. IV, p. 32.

required for preservation, sacrifice for others will be the necessary and sufficient condition for preserving oneself and/or one's liberty and/or one's interest. Fair play demands that he who benefits must pay the *necessary* price for those benefits. But suppose men lose their lives, their all, in defense of their society? Isn't that to make a cheat of the social contract? Rousseau replies, "Their very life, which they have devoted to the State, is by it constantly protected; and when they risk it in the State's defense, what more are they doing than giving back what they have received from it? What are they doing that they would not do more often and with greater danger in the state of nature, in which they would inevitably have to fight battles at the peril of their lives in defense of that which is the means of their preservation."[28] Rousseau's answer adds a strict utilitarian consideration to the appeal to fair play.[29] If one is blind to the demands of fair play, there is always the utilitarian calculation to fall back on. If a man is incapable of moral feelings toward his fellows; or if a man chooses to ignore the fact that as he defends others they defend him, he must at least come to realize that at its most demanding, his civil condition (in the good society) is no worse than the natural condition. But in any case, Rousseau's stress is on the concept of fair play.

It will be noticed that common to the concepts of distributive justice and fair play is the element of reciprocity. In each case, a man does to others as he would be done to by them. On the one hand, he agrees to respect the civil rights of others, who in turn are to respect his. That is to be just. On the other hand, he agrees to make sacrifices for others, who in turn are to make the same sacrifices for him. That is to be fair. In both cases, mutual benefits result; and in both cases, self-interest and love of one's fellows work together in the mind of each man.

5

Out of these concepts of distributive justice, autonomy, and fair play, how have commentators extracted a theory of collectivism or despotism or totalitarianism or of individualism? Rousseau's whole aim is to advocate a small community in which all citizens share the responsibility to use their autonomy to frame laws that answer to the demands of distributive justice and fair play. One would think that if the above description is correct, Rousseau's political philosophy could be called "rationalist," if it had to have a tag. I do not wish to deny that there are statements in Rousseau's writings that seem to beg for one or another of the foregoing interpretations. Still, I would say that, despite appearances, whenever we think we have a reason for calling Rousseau collectivist, despotic, totalitarian, or individualist, we are wrong; and wrong because we have failed to notice that the principles of distributive justice, autonomy, and fair play (which are neither collectivist nor despotic nor totalitarian nor individualist) are at issue, singly or jointly. Let us see how these things can be so.

6

We shall first examine the charge that Rousseau was a collectivist: the charge that Rousseau looked to the submergence of the individual in his society, and the sacrifice of the individual's interests and aspirations to those of

---

[28] Rousseau, bk. II, chap. IV.
[29] See Rousseau's coupling of "duty and interest," bk, I. chap. VII. p. 17.

society as a whole. Now it is true that Rousseau speaks of the making of the social contract as an act which "... creates a moral and collective body, composed of as many members as the assembly contains voters, and receiving from this act its unity, its common identity, its life, and its will."[30] But these words, whatever unpleasant connotations they may have for the modern liberal reader, do not constitute a defense of any kind of collectivism, even the best sort we could imagine. In *A Discourse on Political Economy*, Rousseau is eloquent in his rejection of the view that the sacrifice of one man for the benefit of the rest is morally permissible.[31] Unless all stand ready to share risks, the sacrifice of even one man, for any reason at all, is, to Rousseau, unforgivable. The principle of fair play must *always* be respected, even though a utilitarian consideration could possibly dictate isolated abandonments of that principle. Though Rousseau uses the organic metaphor to speak of society,[32] he does not use it with the generally conservative intentions accompanying that metaphor.

Another reason why some have inclined to calling Rousseau collectivist is his great love of ancient city-states, and his stress on individual involvement in public affairs. It is often recognized that the idea of community was important to Rousseau. Rousseau says, "The better the constitution of a State is, the more do public affairs encroach on private in the minds of the citizens."[33] This may indeed seem ugly to us; something like a fascist slogan. But

Rousseau's preference for a political community in the form of a city-state allows of a very simple explanation; and that explanation is intimately connected to all we have so far said. The explanation is that only in a city-state, if anywhere, could the principles of distributive justice, autonomy, and fair play be simultaneously realized. Larger political units could, in theory, realize distributive justice and fair play, but not realize them in conjunction with autonomy. That is to say, these units could, in theory, have civil liberty; but not moral liberty in all its fullness. Size alone would prevent them. Only when all citizens could gather together and make the laws which bind them would it be possible to speak of moral liberty. (Furthermore, the chances are greater in a small community that men will desire the reign of justice. For only a small community could be so organized, and contain such practices and institutions as to breed in men an understanding of, *and* a love for, the right political principles.)[34]

---

[30] Rousseau, bk. I, chap. VI, p. 15. See also "Political Economy," pp. 289–90.

[31] Rousseau, "Political Economy," pp. 303–4.

[32] Rousseau, "Political Economy," p. 289. He complains of the inaccuracy of the metaphor. See also Derathé, *op. cit.*, pp. 410–13.

[33] Rousseau, bk. III, chap. XV, p. 93.

[34] See Rousseau, "Political Economy," p. 301. For a careful and stimulating discussion of Rousseau's advocacy of the small community, see Bertrand de Jouvenel's Introduction to his edition of *Du Contrat Social* (Geneva, 1947). Jouvenel shows how Rousseau thought it possible for each man in a small, stable and homogeneous society to include his fellows within his *amour de soi*, and to have his *amour-propre* weakened. On p. 131, Jouvenel summarizes his views. We could say that Rousseau favored the existence of an agrarian city-state because it alone could be small, economically simple and economically static. We have already seen that smallness is a precondition of autonomy; smallness also makes it possible for a man to love his fellow-citizens, and feel himself to be involved with them in a coöperative enterprise, namely, a community. If a society is economically simple, conflicting interests tend to be avoided. If a society is economically static, selfishness, acquisitiveness, tends to be avoided. See also *A Discourse on the Origin of Inequality*, p. 177; and Rousseau, bk. II, chap. IX, and bk. IV, chap. I.

7

We turn now to the charge that Rousseau advocates totalitarian principles. The passage in his writings which seems most favorable to the totalitarian interpretation of Rousseau is the following:

These clauses (of the social contract), properly understood, may be reduced to one—the total alienation of each associate, together with all his right, to the whole community. . . .[35]

It would appear that by the terms of the social contract the individual is left in helpless bondage to capriciousness: he cannot count on a minimum area of rights which the sovereign majority is permanently forbidden to invade. But to see Rousseau as a ruthless majoritarian is to misunderstand him. The only limits that Rousseau is interested in placing on liberty are the limits dictated by the principles of distributive justice and fair play.[36] In justice, rights entail obligations. Without corresponding obligations, there would be no rights, only privileges, a species of injustice or unfairness.[37] What is allowed to one, must be allowed to all;

what is to be given up by one, must be given up by all. And only that is to be given up which is necessary for the preservation of the civil rights of all. The lesser is given up for the greater. As long as society remains good, the only sort of encroachment made on rights will be encroachment made on the rights of all, in equal measure; and the only reason for encroachments will be necessity.[38] Of course, unscrupulous men can always use the argument of necessity for encroachments that will serve particular interests. But Rousseau's theories are meant for good societies alone. A critic of Rousseau could ask, Why does Rousseau not allow for some agency of government which would have the last word on encroachments, and judge whether necessity required any given encroachment? In this way, individual rights would be given total protection. To this it could be answered that such an agency (like, say, the Supreme Court of the United States) would, in effect, share the sovereign power with the citizenry; and by doing so, would dilute the principle of moral autonomy and keep the conscience of the people. It would cheapen the office of citizenship. It would make it seem that the good society did not depend on the virtue of its members. In a good society, it would thus be useless and morally harmful. When improper encroachments are made, the society in

---

[35] Rousseau, bk. I, chap. VIII, p. 14. But see Rousseau, bk. II, chap. IV, p. 23; "Each man alienates, I admit, by the social compact, only such part of his powers, goods, and liberty as it is important for the community to control; but it must also be granted that the Sovereign is sole judge of what is important." And bk. IV, chap, VIII, p. 138. note 1: " 'In the republic,' says the Marquis d'Argenson, 'each man is perfectly free in what does not harm others.' This is the invariable limitation, which it is impossible to define more exactly."

[36] See Alfred Cobban, *Rousseau and the Modern State,* pp. 121–22; and Derathé, *op. cit.,* pp. 157–58, 170–71, 342–44. Derathé shows how Rousseau recognized natural law as a limitation on the Sovereign. See also G. D. H. Cole's defense of Rousseau in his Introduction to his edition of Rousseau's writing (see note 8 above), p. xliv.

[37] Rousseau, bk. I, chap. VII, pp. 17–18. See also bk. I, chap. VI, p. 14.

[38] In *Émile,* Rousseau says, "If the sovereign power rests upon the right of ownership, there is no right more worthy of respect; it is inviolable and sacred for the sovereign power, so long as it remains a private individual right; as soon as it is viewed as common to all the citizens, it is subject to the common will, and this will may destroy it. Thus the sovereign has no right to touch the property of one or many; but he may lawfully take possession of the property of all, as was done in Sparta in the time of Lycurgus; while the abolition of debts by Solon was an unlawful deed" (p. 425).

which they are made is irretrievably gone. Rousseau's principles then lose their applicability. On the assumption, however, that the people in their sovereign capacity are seeking to make laws that serve the common good (properly understood: see above), there can be no limits to their will. Rousseau says, "...as each gives himself absolutely (in the making of the social contract), the conditions are the same for all; and, this being so, no one has any interest in making them burdensome for others."[39]

8

There are also two phrases in Rousseau's writings that have made trouble for him, and lent plausibility to the view that his principles favored totalitarianism. These phrases are "forced to be free" and "the reign of virtue"; phrases which are glittering, or at least, striking, and seem eminently to lend themselves to the designs of political maniacs. It is, therefore, quite urgent to try to understand what Rousseau could have meant by them.

Referring to the phrase, "forced to be free," Rousseau says:

In order that the social compact may not be an empty formula, it tacitly includes the undertaking, which alone can give force to the rest, that whoever refuses to obey the general will shall be compelled to do so by the whole body. This means nothing less than that he will be forced to be free; for this is the condition which, by giving each citizen to his country, secures him against all personal dependence.[40]

It is clear that for "forced to be free" to make sense, three things must be understood: the identity of those to whom the phrase applies, the meaning of "free," and the connection between being free (having liberty) and the general will.

From the preceding quotation it would seem, though not with absolute certainty, that the words "forced to be free" apply not to those who break the law—that is, to criminals—but to those who are tempted to evade the requirements of the law because it goes against their interests, and who must be persuaded or induced to obey; to *potential* criminals. This reading of these words is reinforced by another comment that Rousseau makes. Rousseau says, "At Genoa, the word 'liberty' may be read over the front of the prisons and on the chains of the galley-slaves. This application of the device is good and just. It is indeed only malefactors of all estates who prevent the citizen from being free. In the country in which all such men were in the galleys, the most perfect liberty would be enjoyed."[41] Rousseau does not here say that the man in chains is free, and imply thereby that whenever one is prevented from continuing in a life of criminality, one is "really" or "truly" free. Rather, Rousseau says that all *law-abiding citizens* are free when protected from those who transgress, from those who substitute their own selfish wills for the general will, the will which aims at distributive justice.

In addition to those who must be

---

[39] Rousseau, bk. I, chap. VI, p. 14.

[40] Rousseau. bk. I, chap. VII, p. 18. See also bk. I. chap, VI, p. 14: "Finally, each man, in giving himself to all, gives himself to nobody; and as there is no associate over which he does not acquire the same right as he yields others over himself, he gains an equivalent for everything he loses, and an

increase of force for the preservation of what he has." Also, in the Characters of La Bruyère, the following sentence occurs: "Les hommes souvent veulent aimer, et ne sauroient y' réussir: ils cherchent leur défaite sans pouvoir la rencontrer, et si j'ose ainsi parler, ils sont contraints de demeurer libres" (*Du Coeur,* p. 16). Rousseau uses *forcer,* where La Bruyère uses *contraindre.*

[41] Rousseau, bk. II, chap. II, p. 106, note 2.

persuaded or induced to obey the law, there are others to whom the phrase "forced to be free" applies. Rousseau says, "When therefore the opinion that is contrary to my own prevails, this proves neither more nor less than that I was mistaken, and that what I thought to be the general will was not so. If my particular opinion carried the day I should have achieved the opposite of what was my will; and it is in that case that I should not have been free."[42] Thus, those who attempt to have an unjust law passed—a law that promotes the interests of one or some at the expense of others—are, in effect, forced to be free when they allow themselves to be concluded by the majority, whose will is putatively the general will. In sum, those who indicate a readiness to disobey a just law, and those who try to have an unjust law passed, come within the scope of the phrase, "forced to be free."

We now must see how Rousseau is using the word, "free." Rousseau distinguishes between natural liberty (or independence) and moral liberty.[43] Moral liberty has two components: civil liberty and autonomy. Civil liberty is a condition in which there are no restrictions on doing what one pleases except for those restrictions set up by law; that is, restrictions applicable equally

to oneself and to all other men in one's society, and framed only in accordance with the terms of the social contract. Autonomy is the ability to take part in the framing of the laws which set up the restrictions. To be forced to be free is to be forced to preserve one's civil liberty and to be autonomous; to be forced to be free is to be forced to be in a condition of moral liberty.

In a state of nature there is only natural liberty. The fact is that the consequence of everyone's having natural liberty is the possibility that everyone can lose his natural liberty and become a slave, at some time or other. Civil society contains laws, restrictions on the will of all, precisely in order to remove the possibility. But when a man acts in such a way as to indicate that he is ready to disobey the law, he is risking a return to the state of nature, with its possibility of slavery for himself. His threatened disobedience, if undeterred, may culminate in an act which oppresses a neighbor, and which therefore may cause the neighbor to defend himself with any means at hand. In this struggle, the oppressor endangers his civil liberty. Rousseau says, ". . . for no sooner does one man, setting aside the law, claim to subject another to his private will, than he departs from the state of civil society, and confronts him face to face in the pure state of nature in which obedience is prescribed solely by necessity."[44] Or, his threatened disobedience, if undeterred, may help to bring about the dissolution of the *whole* civil society, and with it, a return of *all* to the state of nature, including the man who is inclined to disobedience. Precedent for successful evasion of the requirements of the law is established; the law is brought into disrepect; the obligations which bind society together are weakened. Rousseau says, "The con-

---

[42] Rousseau, bk. II, chap. II, p. 106.

[43] The distinctions between natural, civil, and moral liberty occur in Rousseau, bk. I, chap. VIII, p. 19. The distinction between independence and liberty occurs in *Letters from the Mountain,* no. VIII, in *The Political Writings of Jean-Jacques Rousseau,* ed. by C. E. Vaughan, vol. II, pp. 234 235. For a discussion of this latter distinction see Alfred Cobban, *Rousseau and the Modern State,* pp. 116–117. In bk. II, chap. VII of *The Social Contract,* Rousseau also says that one of the tasks of the Legislator is that of ". . . substituting a partial and moral existence for the physical and independent existence nature has conferred on us all" (p. 38). And in bk. I, chap. VI, Rousseau contrasts natural liberty and conventional liberty (p. 14).

[44] "Political Economy," p. 294.

tinuance of such an injustice could not but prove the undoing of the body public."[45] When civil society is undone, the possibility of slavery—perhaps for those whose disobedience destroyed civil society—revives.

In the case of the man who out of selfishness or ignorance tries to have an unjust law passed, similar considerations hold. The civil society which is the subject of Rousseau's discussion is the good society; and in the good society, unjust laws must eventually lead to antagonism, and perhaps to dissolution and a return to the state of nature. To live by a law which derives from the general will, even when one thinks that that law inhibits the pursuit of one's advantage, is to live by that which preserves one's life, liberty, and property. In the good society, however, one's life, liberty, and property can be preserved only when one respects the lives liberty, and property of all others; that is, only when justice reigns, only when the general will is realized. One's fate is tied to that of one's fellow-citizens.

Thus, intimidated obedience to the law (when necessary) works together with majority rule to prevent the re-emergence of the natural condition, and hence the re-emergence of the possibility of slavery for *all* men.[46] The intimidated man and the outvoted man are forced not to risk becoming slaves; they are forced to abide by the terms of the social contract; they are forced to retain their civil liberty at the expense of doing whatever they please, when what they please to do is contrary to justice.

But, we may ask, though one can be intimidated or outvoted and still have *civil liberty,* can one be intimidated or

outvoted and still be *autonomous?* Rousseau is quite aware that there seems to be something paradoxical here, and attempts to remove the paradox by saying:

The constant will of all the members of the State is the general will; by virtue of it they are citizens and free. . . .[47]

The temptation, however, is to feel that Rousseau has removed the paradox by resorting to an Idealist trick. That is to say, we feel that Rousseau is distinguishing between two selves in each person, a lower self which is aggressive or impulsive; and a higher self which is rational, moral, or perhaps altruistic, and is the seat of our "constant will." The lower self may get the better of the higher self, or the higher self may never be fully developed. Each man must, therefore, be constrained to live according to his higher self, or to live as if he had a higher self. The constraint may even come from some external source which claims superior insight into the nature and demands of the higher self. And when we notice that Rousseau says that ". . . the mere impulse of appetite is slavery. . . ,"[48] we may consider our Idealist reading of Rousseau correct.

We must realize, however, that Rousseau means nothing very extraordinary by "constant will." His assumption is that no man who is minimally rational could ever want to be a slave, or to risk becoming one. Since this is so, it follows that no rational man could want to do anything that would jeopardize that which keeps him from slavery; namely, civil society. When, however, civil society is the good society, civil society can be preserved only if the general will prevails; that is, only if distributive justice prevails, only if every man is protected in his own. As

---

45 Rousseau, bk. I, chap. VII, p. 18.
46 Naturally, society relies, in the last instance, on the punishment of crimes actually committed, to preserve itself from the natural condition.

47 Rousseau, bk. IV, chap. II, p. 106.
48 Rousseau, bk. I, chap. VIII, p. 19.

we have seen, Rousseau's premise is that violations against the principle of distributive justice in the good society will lead to disorder and possible dissolution.[49] The obligation to be just is thus reinforced by a pragmatic consideration. Consequently, every rational man's constant will must be the general will. To follow one's constant will is to be autonomous, is to live by the law that one would give oneself if one were not temporarily led astray by impulse, or excessive appetite. And when we remember that the general will looks to the preservation of the life, liberty, and property of even the man who voted against the general will, we see that the protection of legitimate interest remains at the center of Rousseau's considerations. Obedience to law *tout court* is not equivalent to freedom; acting on desire or impulse *tout court* is not slavery. Rather, obedience to nothing except laws which embody the general will (one's constant will) is equivalent to moral freedom; while acting from desire or impulse is to sacrifice one's moral freedom to one's independence, and threatens to throw one back into the natural condition with its threat of slavery. When we are forced to be free, nothing supererogatory is being demanded of us; nor is conformity to anything mystical or supra-personal being demanded of us.

Finally, we must recall that Rousseau acknowledges that one who dissents from a law may do so in the name of justice, and be right in his claim: the majority may have made an unjust law. But in that case, the phrase "forced to be free" would no longer apply; that phrase is relevant only when the principle of distributive justice is respected,

only when the general will has actually been embodied in the given law. An unjust law is analogous to the will of a master: to be forced to obey an unjust law is to be forced to be something very much like a slave. Rousseau's argument "...presupposes, indeed, that all the qualities of the general will still reside in the majority; when they cease to do so, whatever side a man may take, liberty is no longer possible."[50]

Referring to the second phrase, "the reign of virtue," Rousseau says:

The second essential rule of political economy is no less important than the first. If you would have the general will accomplished, bring all the particular wills into conformity with it; in other words, as virtue is nothing more than this conformity of the particular wills with the general will, establish the reign of virtue.[51]

(Rousseau is addressing the Legislator: him who would found a society or is entrusted with the task of reforming an existing one.) The first thing to say about this phrase is that it is not meant to apply to a condition in which a government takes it upon itself to impose virtue (or what it considers to be virtue) by legal sanction on a recalcitrant population used to living in the old bad ways. The reign of virtue is not the rule of Robespierre, nor of Angelo in *Measure for Measure*. The reign of virtue, rather, is a condition in which people make and obey laws in conformity with the general will, and do so with their heart in it. To repeat Rousseau's words, "...virtue is nothing more than ...conformity of the particular wills with the general will." For the vast majority, the conformity will be free, uncoerced; and it must be kept in mind that the general will looks only to the common good, the good of every single man in civil society.

---

[49] Rousseau, bk. I, chap. VIII, p. 18: "The continuance of such an injustice could not but prove the undoing of the body public." Implicit is the view that injustice *should* lead to undoing.

[50] Rousseau, bk. IV, chap. II, p. 107.

[51] Rousseau, "Political Economy," p. 298.

But how is virtue to reign? That is, how can men become good citizens who make the laws by which they live (and those laws good laws)? "To form citizens is not the work of a day; and in order to have men it is necessary to educate them when they are children."[52] This is only possible in a society newly founded or plastic enough to be radically reformed, for the Legislator must introduce customs and practices which provide the proper medium for the cultivation of all those sentiments favorable to the common good, and thus reinforce the effects of education. And Rousseau never forgets the connection between "virtue" and the legitimate (that is, unavaricious) interest of each man in society:

Do we wish men to be virtuous? Then let us begin by making them love their country: but how can they love it, if their country be nothing more to them than to strangers, and afford them nothing but what it can refuse nobody? It would be still worse, if they did not enjoy even the privilege of social security, and if their lives, liberties, and property lay at the mercy of persons in power, without their being permitted, or its being possible for them, to get relief from the laws.[53]

In sum, education in the principles of distributive justice, autonomy, and fair play, combined with a suitable social structure will produce "the reign of virtue" in the good society. Rousseau intends nothing more complicated or pernicious than that.[54]

---

[52] Rousseau, "Political Economy," p. 307. See Rousseau's discussion of education of children in common, pp. 307–311. In his very interesting book, op. cit., John W. Chapman says, "The question is whether his methods for intensifying social sentiment are consistent with both his view of human dynamics and his moral ideals" (p. 55). Chapman concludes that "The totalitarian aspect of Rousseau's political theory lies in his proposals for intensifying social sentiment.... The difficulty is that the means by which he seeks to secure social unity and sentiment transfers the individual from the center to the circumference of value. Authoritarian means do not achieve liberal ends" (pp. 86–87). What makes Chapman's conclusion so worthy of attention is that he does not find in Rousseau's doctrine of the general will, nor in other key parts of Rousseau's theory, grounds for holding Rousseau to be a totalitarian. Nevertheless, I do not think it could be said that Chapman has proved his case. That is, he has not shown that Rousseau's prescriptions for education and social arrangement diminish human *rationality*. That they may inhibit the full development of human *individuality,* in the modern sense, is doubtless true. But the latter tendency in Rousseau's thought neither amounts to a totalitarian aspect, nor defeats the ends of political life which Rousseau wished to prevail.

[53] Rousseau, "Political Economy," pp. 302–303.
[54] There are two other reasons which have inclined commentators to think of Rousseau as totalitarian or despotic: the place of the Legislator in Rousseau's political theory, and Rousseau's notion of civil religion. Limitation of space prevents a detailed consideration of these two points. But we can say here that neither can be part of any legitimate attempt to fix the label of totalitarian or despot on Rousseau. On the Legislator, we must notice that the Legislator is not a permanent component of the good society; that he does his work at the inception of a society; that he does not make laws, but initiates institutions, habits and practices which promote the workings of the political order; that the people of a country must give their permission before he can begin his work, and then must pass on his proposals; and that there is no provision in Rousseau's thought for an act of usurpation on the part of a would-be Legislator. So far was Rousseau from being a revolutionary that he has his pupil Emile settle down in his (Émile's) native country out of piety, rather than seek out some better land (see *Émile,* pp. 437–438). On the notion of civil religion, we can say that, of course, Rousseau's restrictions on freedom of opinion are intolerable. But we must remember that Rousseau himself believed in its major doctrines, namely, a provident God and an after-life. Rousseau has no theory of the noble lie. He seems to have been sincere in his profession that certain beliefs useful to society were, at the same time, true.

9

We turn now to the charge that Rousseau advocated individualist principles. It is correct to say, I think, that in one sense of the term Rousseau was an individualist theorist; but not correct in another sense. At the center of Rousseau's political philosophy, as we have seen, are the principles of distributive justice, autonomy, and fair play. That is to say, Rousseau's thought is focused on the individual man as a moral agent and as a creature of rights and duties. Society exists to make it possible for individual men to preserve themselves and their own by means of law: it has no other reason for being, no higher purposes. And in so far as this line of argument makes of a writer an individulist theorist, Rousseau is an individualist theorist. (Then, too, the way in which Rousseau favorably contrasts the natural condition with the civilization he knew, makes us want to call him an individualist theorist.) He is an individualist where, say, Hegel, Treitschke, and Maurras are not. But for Rousseau, the insistence on civil liberty and on the political application of moral autonomy—though radical for its day—is not the consequence of an individualist bias in temperament. Rather, the principles of distributive justice, autonomy, and fair play are principles, the absence of which reduce men in society to the status of slavery. They are the principles which, taken together, constitute the necessary conditions for the creation of a society of *persons,* in the strictest meaning of that word. They are the principles indispensable to the existence of morality, pure and simple.[55]

On the other hand, Rousseau is not an individualist in the sense in which Schiller, Humboldt, and, best of all, J. S. Mill, are. He did not delight in a society in which all tastes and talents and eccentricities were permitted and even encouraged. He believed in community and citizenship too much to espouse any doctrine that tends to isolate men from each other and to urge men to pursue private satisfactions and to refine private talents, at the expense of their concern with, and involvement in, public affairs.[56] The most pressing matter of all for Rousseau was to make of civil society a morally acceptable sphere. The cost of such an enterprise would perforce be the advanced development of "individuality" (to use Mill's word). And though one may find such a cost ridiculously exorbitant, one cannot find Rousseau's position contemptible, or deserving of the abuse which has been given it by friends of "the open society."

CONCLUSION

We could find many things in Rousseau's political theory as presented in *The Social Contract* and *A Discourse on Political Economy,* which seem irrelevant to our reasoned thought today. Rousseau's ideals, as he knew, were inextricably tied to the city-state and to a simple and unexpanding economy.[57] Relevance aside, however, it would be desirable to come to see what Rousseau

---

[55] In the words of Leo Strauss: "Hence Rousseau's answer to the question of the good life takes on this form: the good life consists in the closest approximation to the state of nature which is possible on the level of humanity. On the political plane that closest

approximation is achieved by a society with the requirements of the social contract." (*Natural Right and History,* Chicago, 1953, p. 282.) *Cf.* Bertrand de Jouvenel, *op. cit.,* pp. 91–94.

[56] Especially instructive, in this regard, is Rousseau's discussion of the respective merits of Socrates and Cato in "Political Economy," p. 302.

[57] See Rousseau, "Political Economy," pp. 306, 311, 313, 316.

was trying to say. We may find that Rousseau is saying things in an artificial or confusing way, which Hobbes or Locke or Hume or Kant said better. But we cannot find that he was defending collectivism, despotism, totalitarianism, or individualism. Are we then not entitled to say to his defenders: Watch how you defend him; and to say to his critics: Please, no more slanders?

8

BURKE

For nearly thirty years Edmund Burke (1729–1797) sat in the English Parliament convinced, as we know from his famous letter to his constituents, that only reasonable men like himself were suited to pass judgment on political events and the national interest. Many such judgments were forthcoming. He pleaded the cause of the American colonies, while also demanding reform of crown patronage at home. He attacked imperial policy in India and demanded the amelioration of England's harsh prescriptions against Roman Catholics. Burke stood adamantly opposed to the radical demand heard in the 1780's for reform of the English Parliament and extension of the suffrage. But it is his attack on the French revolutionaries which has endured as his most lasting comment on political events. The sins of the French, he wrote, were many, not the least of which were their misconceptions of the nature of politics, of thought, and of change. Would that the errant French were more like his fellow countrymen! Concerning the English, Burke wrote: "We fear God; we look up with awe to kings, with affection to parliaments, with duty to magistrates, with reverence to priests and with respect to nobility."

In the selection below, Francis P. Canavan, a Jesuit scholar at Fordham University, first describes the style of Burke's political thinking, which he calls "practical reason"; it is characterized by the avoidance of argument from abstract concepts and by the search for practical implementation of desired objectives according to principles of prudence. Canavan also contends that Burke's writings contain an important and useful theory of natural law. In his article, Russell Kirk, one of America's leading conservative thinkers, outlines the fundamental components of Burke's conservatism: his reverence for custom, history, and tradition. Central to this creed, according to Kirk, are Burke's defense of ancient ideas—prejudice—and ancient institutions—prescription.

FRANCIS P. CANAVAN, S.J.

Edmund Burke's Conception of the Role of Reason in Politics*

British and American scholars have generally taken Edmund Burke for a utilitarian and an empiricist with a keen sense of historical development, qualified by certain religious prepossessions which inclined him to conservatism. In the nineteenth century, to mention but two examples, Leslie Stephen understood Burke as rejecting metaphysics in favor of utilitarian principles derived solely from experience,[1] and John Morley took it as obvious that Burke's norm of political morality was "the standard of convenience, of the interest of the greatest number, of utility and expediency."[2] In the present century the late Harold Laski described Burke as "a utilitarian who was convinced that what was old was valuable by the mere fact of its arrival at maturity." According to Laski, political philosophy for Burke "was nothing...but accurate generalization from experience....

Nothing was more alien from Burke's temper than deductive thinking in politics. The only safeguard he could find was in empiricism."[3]

Laski, like several other writers, traced Burke's empiricism to what he considered to be its roots in the critical theories of David Hume. "The metaphysics of Burke," he said, "so far as one may use a term he would himself have repudiated, are largely those of Hume."[4] An American, Victor Hamm, surmised that Burke, in revolt against the "decadent nominalism" which he had studied in Trinity College, Dublin, had turned, not to Hume, but to the similar epistemological theory of David Hartley.[5] More recently Morton Frisch has advanced the thesis that Burke agreed with Aristotle in regard to practice but parted company with him, by rejecting the supremacy of theory. Rather, he says, Burke adopted the position taken by Hume in his *Treatise of Human Nature* and maintained that

* Reprinted from *The Journal of Politics*, XXI, No. 1 (February, 1959), 60–79, by permission of the editors and the author.

1 *History of English Thought in the Eighteenth Century* (2 vols., London, 1881), II, 223–227.

2 *Edmund Burke: A Historical Study* (London, 1867), p. 151.

3 *Political Thought in England from Locke to Bentham* (New York, 1920), pp. 236–237.

4 *Ibid.*, p. 157.

5 "Burke and Metaphysics," *Essays in Modern Scholasticism*, ed. by A. C. Pegis (Westminster, Md., 1944), pp. 207–208.

the passions, and not reason, form the natural basis of our morals, our opinions, and our lives.[6] It would follow, of course, that Burke, in adopting Hume's epistemology, did not so much accept Hume's metaphysics as agree with him in rejecting metaphysics altogether.

But the rejection of a rational metaphysic entails the denial that there is a rationally apprehended natural law which is the foundation of morality. That Burke drew this inference is also asserted. Thus George Sabine says that "in a sense Burke accepted Hume's negations of reason and the law of nature."[7] Samuel Huntington speaks of "Burke's denial of natural law," and asserts that the theory of natural law is inherently opposed to conservative doctrines such as his.[8] Finally, Maurice Cranston said, in an essay read on the British Broadcasting Corporation's Third Programme two years ago, that Burke dismissed natural law and liberty, equality and the rights of man "on wholly positivistic grounds." As Mr. Cranston reads Burke, natural law "which was not written down and which no authority administered" was "a fiction, a myth, a metaphysical abstraction with no real content. . . ." And so once again Burke is seen as an empiricist for whom the function once performed by the doctrine of natural law was fulfilled by "a deep emotional faith in tradition."[9]

All of these students of Burke, it is evident, agree in situating him in the tradition of British empiricism. The present writer finds this interpretation not wholly false but seriously defective, and in some respects flatly contrary to Burke's expressed convictions. Burke's denunciations of "metaphysics" and "theory," and his exhortations to reliance on "experience" and "expediency" are too well known to need documentation. But certain questions must be asked: what did he mean by theory and metaphysics, what did he think was to be learned from experience, and what was the relation of expediency to the moral principles which he also undoubtedly held? The answer to these questions lies in Burke's conception of the role of reason in politics. The purpose of this paper therefore is to analyze what Burke himself said about the way in which human reason properly functions when dealing with political matters, and then to relate this conception of political reason to the moral theory that lay behind it.

POLITICAL REASON AND PRUDENCE

Burke did not often use the term "political reason." More often he spoke simply of "reason," or of political or civil wisdom, or of prudence. All of these terms, however, are broadly interchangeable in his writings and need not be carefully distinguished. Burke's preoccupations were pre-eminently practical, and so reason for him was usually practical political reason, by the exercise of which the statesman prudently directed public action to public ends. "It is the business of the speculative philosopher to mark the proper ends of government," he said. "It is the business of the politician, who is the philosopher in action, to find out proper means towards those ends, and to employ them with effect."[10] Burke

[6] "Burke on Theory," *Cambridge Journal,* VII (1954), 292–297.

[7] *History of Political Theory* (New York, 1950), p. 607.

[8] "Conservatism as an Ideology," *American Political Science Review,* LI (June 1957), 459, n. 6.

[9] "Burke and the French Revolution," *The Listener,* LVII (Jan. 1957).

[10] *Thoughts on the Cause of the Present Discontents* (1770), *The Works of the Right Honourable Edmund Burke* (16 vols., London, the Rivington edition, 1803–1827: cited

thought habitually as "the philosopher in action." For him political reason was concerned with the adaptation of means to ends, or in more modern terminology, with policy formation and decision making.

The object of political reason

An analysis of Burke's doctrine of political reason should begin with its object, namely the political good to be achieved. As has been said, political reason directs political action. But action, as distinguished from pure thought, aims at the good and not *at the true;* and, therefore, political reason is concerned with what is good rather than with what is true. The good of which we speak here is not necessarily the good in the moral sense. Men may do what they know to be morally bad, but they always act for the sake of what they consider to be in some sense good for themselves. In Burke's phrase, "Man acts from adequate motives relative to his interest."[11] We shall point out below, on the other hand, that genuinely prudent action, as Burke conceived it, always supposed a morally good end. The point to be made here, however, is that action, and therefore that function of reason which directs action, is concerned with attaining goals which men find good rather than with propositions which they find true.

"Political problems," to use Burke's own words, "do not primarily concern truth or falsehood. They relate to good or evil."[12] Another way of saying the same thing would be that political questions are questions of right or wrong. That is right which is properly directed to its end. One does not ask whether a decision is true (a meaningless ques-

tion), but whether it is well calculated to attain the desired goal. In short, one asks whether the decision is right. That is to ask whether it will realize the good in view.

The end or good to be achieved is thus the standard of action, and so of practical judgment. Burke once wrote, "Proper action is an action directed to an End—& is tried by that End."[13] Political action consequently will be "tried" by the specifically political end, "the good of the commonwealth."[14] But the good of the community, in any form in which it can actually exist, is a concrete, practicable, complex, and imperfect good. The nature and mode of operation of political reason are therefore determined by these characteristics of its object.

First, then, the political good is *concrete.* Political reason is not concerned with the good in its abstract perfection. The object of the statesman's thought and effort is the concrete and limited good of the particular community which he has to govern, and not the good of man in the abstract. As Burke said, "the general character and situation of a people must determine what sort of government is fitted for them."[15] But "the general character and situation of a people" is not merely an objective fact; it has its subjective and psychological side too. "People must be governed in a manner agreeable to their temper and disposition; and men of free character and spirit must be ruled

---

hereafter as *Works*), II, 335.

[11] *Speech on Conciliation with the Colonies,* 22 March 1775, *Works,* III, 113.

[12] *Appeal from the New to the Old Whigs* (1791), *Works,* VI, 210.

[13] Notes for a speech, undated, to be found among the Wentworth-Woodhouse Muniments in the Central City Library in Sheffield, Burke Papers, Bundle 8i. Acknowledgment is made to the Right Honourable the Earl Fitzwilliam and the trustees of the Wentworth-Woodhouse Muniments for permission to quote from these manuscripts.

[14] *Letter to Sir Hercules Langrishe,* 3 Jan. 1792, *Works,* VI, 318. *Cf. Works,* III. 182.

[15] *Speech on Conciliation with the Colonies* (1775), *Works,* III, 76. *Cf. Works,* V, 330–333; VI, 133, 288; IX, 437ff.

with, at least, some condescension to this spirit and this character."[16] To be more specific, the Americans, of whom Burke was speaking at this time, valued liberty. But liberty, as an abstraction, is practically meaningless. "Abstract liberty, like other mere abstractions, is not to be found. Liberty inheres in some sensible object; and every nation has formed itself some favourite point, which by way of eminence becomes the criterion of their happiness."[17] In England this was the right of the people to levy their own taxes through their representatives, and so too in America. If then the British government wished to reason rightly about governing the Americans, it would not ignore their conviction that self-taxation was of the essence of liberty, and liberty of the essence of the political good. To put the matter in general terms, political reason seeks to realize the good of a particular people and must take into account *their* notion of what that good is.

Closely related to the foregoing is the principle that the political good must be *practicable*. "The question," Burke once said, restating a favorite theme of his, "is not concerning *absolute* discontent or *perfect* satisfaction in government; neither of which can be pure and unmixed at any time, or upon any system. The controversy is about that degree of good-humour in the people, which may possibly be attained, and ought certainly to be looked for."[18] Now, "practicable" means capable of being realized in the situation in which the statesman has to act. The elements of the existing situation necessarily limit the possibilities of

action and therefore narrow the range of good attainable. As Burke put it, "No politician can make a situation. His skill consists in his well-playing the game dealt to him by fortune, and following the indications given by nature, times, and circumstances."[19] Among the limiting factors may be mentioned the men with whom the statesman has to act and the resources available to him. "We have not the making of men," Burke said, "but must take them as we find them."[20] So too with resources. "Wisdom cannot create materials; they are the gifts of nature or of chance; her pride is in the use."[21] What the statesman can do is limited by circumstances beyond his control; and, therefore, the object of political reason is not an abstract ideal but a concrete reality within the boundaries of practical possibility.

Thirdly, the political good is *complex*. "The nature of man," in Burke's words, "is intricate; the objects of society are of the greatest possible complexity. . . ."[22] The good of the commonwealth is not a single and definable object, but rather is a vast network of relationships among men and goods which, as Burke said of the elements of the national economy, "in a length of time, and by a variety of accidents, have coalesced into a sort of body."[23] A particular political act or policy may aim at a definite goal. But it cannot aim at that alone. For the goal is always a part of or a means to the welfare of the

[16] *Observations on the State of the Nation* (1769), *Works*, II, 166.

[17] *Speech on Conciliation with the Colonies* (1775), *Works*, III, 49–50.

[18] *Thoughts on the Cause of the Present Discontents* (1770), *Works*, II, 268.

[19] Burke to G. Elliot, 22 Sept. 1793, *The Correspondence of the Right Honourable Edmund Burke* (4 vols., London, 1844: cited hereafter as *Correspondence*), IV, 154.

[20] Burke to Rockingham, 25 Sept. 1774, *Correspondence*, I, 483. Cf. *Works*, VIII, 354.

[21] *Reflections on the Revolution in France* (1790: cited hereafter as *Reflections*), *Works*, V, 286.

[22] *Ibid.*, p. 125.

[23] *Observations on the State of the Nation* (1769), *Works*, II, 132.

whole community. The goal must therefore be attained in such a way as to contribute to the great general object, the common good of society. This again qualifies the object of political reason. The object must not only be practicable as considered in itself, but also as considered in its relations to all the other ends of political action. It is thus doubly limited; and although a particular political goal may be in itself simple and clear, when set in its full context it will be seen to be part of a vast, intricate, and therefore not fully comprehensible order.

Finally, the realizable good of men in society, according to Burke, is not only limited but *imperfect*. It is necessarily conjoined with disadvantages and defects. In a letter written in November, 1789, to the young Frenchman, DePont,[24] to whom he was later to address the *Reflections on the Revolution in France,* Burke explained that

There is, by the essential fundamental constitution of things, a radical infirmity in all human contrivances; and the weakness is often so attached to the very perfection of our political mechanism, that some defect in it,—something that stops short of its principle,—something that controls, that mitigates, that moderates it,—becomes a necessary corrective to the evils that the theoretic perfection would produce.[25]

Statesmen, therefore, ought not to aim at perfection because they cannot attain it.

Twenty years earlier Burke had expressed the same thought in somewhat cynical terms: "Indeed, all that wise

men even aim at is to keep things from coming to the worst. Those who expect perfect reformations, either deceive or are deceived miserably."[26] Burke was not always so pessimistic in his attitude toward reform,[27] but his conviction that unmixed political good was unattainable remained constant throughout his life.

Political reason will therefore be prepared to tolerate evils, not because it is indifferent to good and evil, but because a "public-spirited prudence" sometimes demands a "compliance with the impracticable nature of inveterate evils."[28] Burke gave a fuller explanation of this principle in stating his views on religious toleration. He said:

Toleration being a part of moral and political prudence, ought to be tender and large. A tolerant government ought not to be too scrupulous in its investigations; but may bear without blame, not only very ill-grounded doctrines, but even many things that are positively vices, where they are *adulta et praevalida*. The good of the commonwealth is the rule which rides over the rest; and to this every other must completely submit.[29]

But on the other hand, the necessary imperfection of all human good ought not to serve as a pretext for doing no good at all. "An imperfect good is still a good," as Burke wrote to DePont, and government ought to accomplish whatever good lay within its power.[30] As a general rule, perfection was not attainable. But the practicable political good, with all its limitations and imper-

24 For the reasons why the name and date as given here are correct, see H. V. F. Somerset, "A Burke Discovery," *English*, VIII (1950/51), 171–178.
25 *Correspondence*, III, 117. *Cf. The Speeches of the Right Honourable Edmund Burke in the House of Commons and in Westminster-Hall* (4 vols., London, 1816: cited hereafter as *Speeches*), II, 161.

26 Burke to Shackleton, 15 Aug. 1770, *Correspondence*, I, 231.
27 See Thomas Copeland, *Our Eminent Friend, Edmund Burke* (New Haven, 1949), p. 164.
28 "On the State of Ireland," (1792), *Correspondence*, IV, 71. *Cf. Works*, II, 391.
29 *Letter to Sir Hercules Langrishe* (1792), *Works*, VI, 318.
30 *Correspondence*, III, 118. *Cf. Speeches*, III, 439; *Works*, II, 434.

fections, was attainable. That was and must be the object of political reason.

The mode of operation of political reason

It follows from what has been said concerning the object of political reason that the judgments of the statesman differ from those of the engineer. An engineer, working with purely mechanical forces, can determine the effectiveness of each force in mathematical terms and so predict with a high degree of accuracy the product even of complicated processes. The statesman cannot always do this. His "forces" are not often amenable to exact measurement. What is more, his judgments involve not only predictions of what will happen, but the comparison of values, some of which must be sacrificed to others, and a decision about which values are to be preferred. The process of political judgment in consequence is not the same as that of the engineer or the scientist. "Political reason," Burke said, "is a computing principle; adding, subtracting, multiplying, and dividing, morally and not metaphysically or mathematically, true moral denominations."[31]

It was Burke's belief, therefore, that there is an "unavoidable uncertainty, as to the effect, which attends on every measure of human prudence."[32] The reason is that the end sought for does not yet exist, but is to be brought into existence through action in a situation in which one cannot be sure that every factor has been taken into account and evaluated correctly. "The *means* to any end being first in order, are *immediate* in their good or their evil;—they are always, in a manner, *certainties*. The *end* is doubly problematical; first,

whether it is to be attained; then, whether supposing it attained, we obtain the true object we sought for."[33] In this uncertainty, it is impossible to be sure that the means chosen will be successful. One can only estimate which means, given the circumstances, are most likely to be successful. The more complex the end to be attained, the more difficult this estimation will be.[34]

In view of this uncertainty, which affects all practical reasoning, political reason distrusts *a priori* conclusions. Instead, it utilizes experience. "The science of government," said Burke, "being therefore so practical in itself, and intended for such practical purposes, [is] a matter which requires experience, and even more experience than any person can gain in his whole life, however sagacious and observing he may be...."[35] But even the lessons of experience, though indispensable, are not conclusive and too heavy a reliance on the past as a guide to the future could lead to disaster. As Burke explained:

The world of contingency and political combination is much larger than we are apt to imagine. We never can say what may, or may not happen, without a view to all the actual circumstances. Experience upon other data than those, is of all things the most delusive. Prudence in new cases can do nothing on grounds of retrospect. A constant vigilance and attention to the train of things as they successively emerge, and to act on what they direct, are the only sure courses.[36]

31 *Reflections* (1790), *Works*, V, 126.
32 *Letter to a Member of the National Assembly* (1791), *Works*, VI, 6. *Cf. Works*, II, 338.

33 Burke to DePont, Nov., 1789, *Correspondence*, III, 118. *Cf. Correspondence*, I, 373.
34 *Works*, V, 124; VIII, 78–80.
35 *Reflections* (1790), *Works*, V, 124–125. *Cf. Speeches*, III, 46, 226; IV, 34, 49; *Works*, II, 431; III, 48, 196; V, 97, 119, 304–306; XIII, 39.
36 *Thoughts on French Affairs* (1791), *Works*, VII, 50. *Cf. Correspondence*, II, 276; III, 204; *Works*, II, 165–166; VI, 271–273; VII, 197.

The nature of political reasoning, furthermore, makes it difficult for one man alone to avoid mistakes. This is particularly true when what is to be decided upon is not a single act or limited policy but a comprehensive plan of action. "Political arrangement, as it is a work for social ends, is to be wrought by social means. There mind must conspire with mind."[37] The conspiracy of mind with mind in turn makes compromise necessary and legitimate. The necessity of compromise arises from the attachment of men to their own opinions and interests, to be sure, but has the desirable effect of "preventing the sore evil of harsh, crude, unqualified reformations; and rendering all the headlong exertions of arbitrary power, in the few or in the many, forever impracticable."[38]

But compromise is required not only by human selfishness and obstinacy, but also by the nature of political reason. "For you know," Burke said, "that the decisions of prudence (contrary to the system of the insane reasoners) differ from those of judicature; and that almost all the former are determined on the more or the less, the earlier or the later, and on a balance of advantage and inconvenience, of good and evil."[39] The striking of a balance connotes the partial sacrifice of each of the advantages which it is desired to secure. But this sacrifice is not merely the result of the selfishness of men whose interests are at stake. It would still be necessary were they all wholeheartedly devoted to the common good. Compromise, "the balance of advantage and inconvenience, of good and evil," is of the essence of political reason, because it follows from the nature of realizable political good.

The rules of prudence

Burke's analysis of the nature of political good and of the mode of reasoning demanded by it led him to certain conclusions about the practical rules of political conduct. There were indeed rules: "the rules of prudence, which are formed upon the known march of the ordinary providence of God."[40] Men are to regulate their actions in the light of what they know ordinarily happens. But this knowledge does not sully them with certain or inviolable norms of conduct. "The rules and definitions of prudence can rarely be exact; never universal."[41]

The rules of prudence, therefore, have a certain flexibility. But they are not for that reason valueless. As Burke said:

No lines can be laid down for civil or political wisdom. They are a matter incapable of exact definition. But, though no man can draw a stroke between the confines of day and night, yet light and darkness are upon the whole tolerably distinguishable. Nor will it be impossible for a prince to find out such a mode of government, and such persons to administer it, as will give a great degree of content to his people; without any curious and anxious research for that abstract, universal, perfect harmony, which while he is seeking, he abandons those means of ordinary tranquillity which are in his power without any research at all.[42]

The rules of prudence thus have a certain usefulness if it is remembered that they are practical rules intended for the guidance of action and adjustable to the demands of particular situations, and not premises from which conclusions applicable to all situations can be drawn with strict logic.

---

[37] *Reflections* (1790), *Works*, V, 305. *Cf. Speeches*, III, 226.

[38] *Reflections* (1790), *Works*, V, 82.

[39] *Letter to Sir Hercules Langrishe* (1792), *Works*, VI, 309. *Cf. Works*, III, 110–111.

[40] *Second Letter on a Regicide Peace* (1796), *Works*, VIII, 222.

[41] *First Letter on a Regicide Peace* (1796), *Works*, VIII, 87.

[42] *Thoughts on the Cause of the Present Discontents* (1770), *Works*, II, 269.

The essential difference between Burke's political thought and the type of thinking of which he accused his opponents, is that he thought in terms of practical reason, and they, as he saw it, did not. That is to say, Burke thought primarily of the end to be achieved and then of the ways of attaining it in the given circumstances. The questions to be answered were: what do we really want? how must we act in order to obtain it?[43] But Burke's parliamentary adversaries during the American crisis and, later on, the French revolutionaries, if he understood them correctly, despised such practical considerations. They started from a premise of right and drew the logical conclusions regardless of consequences. Parliament had the right to tax the colonies and therefore would exercise it, though it led to rebellion. The French had the imprescriptible rights of men and would claim them, though they led to the ruin of existing society. Burke thought, in short, that his opponents, and in particular the French, were doctrinaires.

J. L. Talmon has described the climate of opinion prevailing in the second half of the eighteenth century, when men "were gripped by the idea that conditions, a product of faith, time and custom, in which they and their forefathers had been living, were unnatural and had all to be replaced by deliberately planned uniform patterns, which would be natural and rational."[44] It was this "faith in a natural order and the immutable, universal principles deduced from it,"[45] which produced the revolutionary mentality of the 1790s and led Rabaud de St. Etienne, to take but one example quoted by Burke, to say in the National Assembly at Paris that "il faut...tout détruire; oui, tout détruire; puisque tout est à recréer."[46] This was the sort of thinking which infuriated Burke and which he had in mind when he denounced "theory" and "metaphysics." He had told a Parliament bent on asserting its right to tax the American colonies that he was resolved "to have nothing at all to do with the question of the right of taxation." "The question with me," he said, "is, not whether you have a right to render your people miserable, but whether it is not your interest to make them happy."[47] The same practical cast of mind caused Burke to tremble with alarm when he heard the assertion of universally valid rights, derived immediately from the natural order, against which "let no government look for security in the length of its continuance, or in the justice and lenity of its administration," and which when recklessly preached to whole populations would "break prison to burst like a *Levanter,* to sweep the earth with their hurricane, and to break up the fountains of the great deep to overwhelm us."[48]

Against such "metaphysical" thinking in politics, Burke offered his conception of political reason operating according to the rules of prudence. Its function was to estimate properly a social end to be achieved in its relationship to all the other ends which must be achieved or safeguarded, to evaluate the means for attaining the end and the situation in which those means must be used, to combine all the elements of the situation into a consistent course of action,

[43] This preoccupation with ends and means appears with particular clarity in "Notes for Speeches—American War," undated, *Correspondence,* IV, 478.

[44] *The Origins of Totalitarian Democracy* (London, 1952), p. 3. *Cf.* Talmon's sketch of "The Doctrinaire Mentality," *ibid.,* pp. 135–138.

[45] *Ibid.,* p. 25.

[46] *Reflections* (1790), *Works,* V, 120. *Cf. ibid.,* 394ff.

[47] *Speech on Conciliation with the Colonies* (1775), *Works,* III, 74–75. *Cf. Works,* II, 131, 432–433.

[48] *Reflections* (1790), *Works,* V, 303, note.

and finally to make those decisions which would translate its purposes into reality. Political reason connoted a mind which was never doctrinaire yet respected consistency, which consulted history and experience but was not bound by them, and which had a clear eye both for desirable goals and for the actual world in which they were to be realized. All this was implied in Burke's notion of political reason and the virtue of prudence.

MORAL THEORY

Yet Burke's theory of prudence did not deny the existence of a natural moral order. Above the level of the rules of prudence were the principles of moral law. Burke devoted much thought to relating these two levels to each other but did not carry his analysis all the way through to a systematic study of moral principles at their highest and most general level. As we shall presently show, in contradiction to the authorities quoted at the beginning of this paper, Burke clearly took the postulates of his moral theory from a natural-law doctrine. But he always approached the doctrine from below, so to speak, from the discussion of a concrete political or legal question. He was therefore content to assume the principles of natural law and was little concerned with analyzing and elaborating the theory of natural law as such. That function, in his opinion, belonged to the schools, and there he was glad to leave it.

It would serve greatly to clarify Burke's thought, for example, if it could be shown that he distinguished, in the manner of the medieval schoolmen, between primary and immutable moral principles, and derived principles which are conditioned by circumstances and admit of exceptions in their application. Such a distinction would help to reconcile Burke's talk of "the eternal and immutable rules of morality,"[49] with his apparently contradictory statement, "Nothing universal can rationally be affirmed on any moral, or any political subject."[50] But although there are strong reasons for believing that Burke had studied Thomistic theory of natural law,[51] and while the distinction between conditioned and unconditioned moral principles seems to be implicit in his writings,[52] it is nowhere explicitly stated.

Nonetheless Burke did hold a natural-law doctrine. It is true that the sensistic epistemology which he espoused in his essay on *The Sublime and Beautiful* (1756) is quite inconsistent with such a doctrine, and this is one reason why some critics have assumed that he must have agreed with Hume's reduction of morality to passion, imagination, and custom. Yet even in *The Sublime and Beautiful* Burke protested against the application of his rather crudely materialistic aesthetic theory to the principles of morality. "This loose and inaccurate manner of speaking," he said, "has therefore misled us both in the theory of taste and of morals; and induced us to remove the science of our

---

49 Hastings Trial, 7 May 1789, *Works,* XIV, 221.

50 *Appeal from the New to the Old Whigs* (1791), *Works,* VI, 97.

51 Sanderson's *De obligatione conscientiae praelectiones decem* (London, 1670) contains a treatise on natural law recognizably derived from Aquinas, and Eustachius's *Ethica, sive summa moralis disciplinae* (Cambridge, 1655) is a handbook of Thomistic moral philosophy. Both books were studied in the regular course at Trinity College, Dublin, in 1736, and it is a safe assumption that they were still studied there when Burke was a student a decade later. For an account of these books see the present writer's "Edmund Burke's College Study of Philosophy," *Notes and Queries,* N.S. IV (1957), 538–543.

52 As when he speaks of "the dreadful exigence in which morality submits to the suspension of its own rules in favour of its own principles...." *Reflections* (1790), *Works,* V, 248. *Cf. ibid.,* 185.

duties from their proper basis (our reason, our relations, and our necessities) to rest it upon foundations altogether visionary and unsubstantial."[53] However incongruous with his epistemology it may have been, even in this early work Burke's moral theory was based upon "our reason, our relations, and our necessities," that is, upon an ontological and rationally cognizable foundation. In his properly political writings, which we shall now consider, it will be seen that he stated and used a full-blown theory of natural law, of whose metaphysical implications he was by no means unaware.

Universal order and natural law

The central idea in Burke's thought was that of order. As a statesman he was of course primarily concerned with the social and political order. But behind his conception of the order of society lay always the grand idea of the order of the universe. Sir Ernest Barker says of him, "The idea of the divine concordance of the Universe, which includes the State in its scheme, haunted the mind of Burke."[54] This feature of Burke's political thought is both undeniable and of primary importance. Despite his constant denunciations of "metaphysics," his thought had unmistakable metaphysical foundations and his understanding of the structure of the state and society was based on certain definite assumptions about the nature of the universe. "I love order so far as I am able to understand it," he once wrote, "for the universe is order."[55]

To this notion of a universal order we must therefore turn our attention, because it is the supposition without which Burke's theory of political reason cannot be understood.

Burke's fundamental premises may be summarized in two propositions. First, the moral law is the foundation and the framework of politics: "The principles of true politics are those of morality enlarged."[56] But secondly, the moral law itself requires the existence of an intelligible world order. Burke's views on this point appear plainly in a passage which he directed against sceptics, and in which, incidentally, he declared how thoroughly he disagreed with Hume when the latter said, "Objects have no discoverable connexion together; nor is it from any other principle but custom operating upon the imagination, that we can draw any inference from the appearance of one to the existence of another."[57] Burke wrote:

Not contented with shewing, what is but too evident, the narrowness and imbecillity of the human understanding, they [the sceptics] have denied that it is at all calculated for the discovery and comprehension of truth; or, what amounts to the same, that no fixed order existed in the world, so correspondent to our ideas, as to afford the least ground for certainty in any thing.... It is evident that, if such an opinion should prevail, the pursuit of knowledge, both in the design and the end, must be the greatest folly, instead of being an indication of some wisdom in the attempt, and in the progress a means of acquiring the highest. It is evident too, that morality must share the fate of knowledge, and every duty of life become pre-

53 *Works*, I, 234–235.
54 "Burke on the French Revolution," *Essays on Government* (Oxford, 2nd ed., 1951), p. 218, n. 1.
55 Burke to the Archbishop of Nisibi, 14 Dec. 1791, in H. V. F. Somerset, "Edmund Burke, England, and the Papacy," *Dublin Review*, CCII (Jan.–Jun. 1938), 140. *Cf. Works*, VIII, 30.

56 Burke to an unnamed correspondent, probably Bishop Markham of Chester, *Correspondence*, I, 332. *Cf. Works*, VI, 252; VIII, 189–191; XIII, 170; XV, 95.
57 *A Treatise of Human Nature* (ed. L. A. Selby-Bigge, Oxford, 1888, reprinted 1951), p. 103.

carious, if it be impossible for us to know that we are bound to any duties, or that the relations which gave rise to them have any real existence.[58]

In this passage Burke characteristically expresses his keen awareness of "the narrowness and imbecillity of the human understanding." But he also insists that there is a world order; that it can be known with certainty by man, despite the weakness of the human mind; and that our knowledge of the relations which form part of that order is the source of our moral obligations.

It is, however, in his statements concerning the natural moral law that Burke's conception of the relationship between the universal divine order and the rules of human conduct appears most plainly. There is not to be found in Burke's writings a formal treatise on the natural law; nor is this surprising in view of the practical and *ad hoc* nature of his work. But the doctrine is alluded to throughout his works and furnishes the premises of his most profound arguments. This is especially true of his early writings on Ireland, his criticism of British rule in India, and his attack on the revolutionary theory of the natural and imprescriptible rights of man. Perhaps the most explicit statement of Burke's natural law doctrine occurs in his speech opening the trial

of Warren Hastings, in which he said:

We are all born in subjection, all born equally, high and low, governors and governed, in subjection to one great immutable, preexistent law, prior to all our devices, and prior to all our contrivances, paramount to all our ideas, and all our sensations, antecedent to our very existence, by which we are knit and connected in the eternal frame of the Universe, out of which we cannot stir. This great law does not arise from our conventions or compacts; on the contrary, it gives to our conventions and compacts all the force and sanction they can have;—it does not arise from our vain institutions. . . . If then all dominion of man over man is the effect of the divine disposition, it is bound by the eternal laws of Him, that gave it, with which no human authority can dispense. . . .[59]

Burke's description of the natural law in this passage is strongly reminiscent of Cicero's, but differs significantly from the Roman orator's in that Burke assumes the Christian doctrine of divine creation as the source of moral order. "I allow," he said in another place, "that if no supreme ruler exists, wise to form, and potent to enforce, the moral law, there is no sanction to any contract, virtual or even actual, against the will of prevalent power."[60] The moral law therefore finds its archetype in God, for it is derived from "that eternal, immutable law, in which will

---

[58] Review of Beattie's *Essays on Truth* in *The Annual Register,* XIV (1771) 252. The book reviews in *The Annual Register* are unsigned, but the writer has felt safe in citing the above because it is one of those which Professor Thomas Copeland considers with almost complete certainty to have been written by Burke. See his article, "Edmund Burke and the Book Reviews in Dodsley's *Annual Register,*" *Publications of the Modern Language Association,* LVII (1942), 446–468. For a later statement by Burke of the relation of morality to a universal order, see the well-known passage in the *Reflections* (1790), which begins, "Society is indeed a contract. . . ." *Works,* V, 184. *Cf. Works,* IV, 84.

[59] 16 Feb. 1788, *Works,* XIII, 166. *Cf. Works,* III, 236, 422–423; V, 180; VI, 321; VIII, 185; IX; 349–351, 354–355, 368; *Correspondence,* I, 332; III, 145; IV, 463; *Speeches,* I, 75, 151; III, 414, for statements of or allusions to the natural law. For the argument from natural-law premises against the revolutionary rights of man, see *Works,* V, 184; VI, 200–207. For the reasons why Burke recurred directly to the natural law in speaking of India, but usually not when speaking of European affairs, see Peter J. Stanlis, *Edmund Burke and the Natural Law* (Ann Arbor, 1958), pp. 88–89.

[60] *Appeal from the New to the Old Whigs* (1791), *Works,* VI, 205.

and reason are the same."[61] But the moral law is not simply imposed on man from without: it is "the will of Him, who gave us our nature, and in giving impressed an invariable Law upon it."[62] The moral law therefore is not exclusively transcendent, but is also immanent to man; it springs from his nature, but from his nature as created and formed by God. In acting in accordance with the natural law, man obeys God, but is at the same time most true to himself.

"The laws of morality," therefore, "are the same everywhere."[63] They apply in India as well as in England, for the Indians and the English are "cemented" to one another by the "law of a common nature."[64] Laws made by men are subordinated to the moral law and, indeed, are derived from it. "All human Laws," Burke said, "are, properly speaking, only declaratory; they may alter the mode and application, but have no power over the substance of original justice."[65] "Justice," therefore, "is itself the great standing policy of civil society,"[66] and constitutes an obligation superior to the will of any government, superior even to "the demands of the people; whose desires, when they do not militate with the stable and eternal

rules of justice and reason (rules which are above us, and above them) ought to be as a law to a house of commons."[67]

The supremacy of the natural law of justice and reason were the ultimate explanation of Burke's statement that "government and legislation are matters of reason and judgment, and not of inclination,"[68] and lent him an air of sincerity when he said shortly before his death, "I have ever abhorred, since the first dawn of my understanding to this its obscure twilight, all the operations of opinion, fancy, inclination, and will, in the affairs of government, where only a sovereign reason, paramount to all forms of legislation and administration, should dictate."[69] There is a sense, then, in which Burke can be called a political rationalist. Basically it is this, that he believed in an intelligible universal order, the product of the divine intelligence and the ruling norm for the operation of human reason in politics. All his political thought moved within the framework of a rational and moral universe. That framework constituted what we have called the metaphysical foundation of his theory of the state and society.

Yet Burke did not understand the natural moral law as a rigidly deductive system. Rather, he had a subtle and empirical conception of it, which allowed him to say, "There are some fundamental points in which nature never changes—but they are few and obvious, and belong rather to morals than to politicks. But so far as regards

---

61 *Reflections* (1790), *Works*, V, 180.
62 *Tracts on the Popery Laws* (1761), *Works*, IX, 349–350.
63 Hastings Trial, 16 Feb. 1789, *Works*, XIII, 155–156.
64 Hastings Trial, 15 Feb. 1788, *Works*, XIII, 21. Cf. *Works*, IX, 351.
65 *Tracts on the Popery Laws* (1761), *Works*, IX, 351. Thirty years later Burke said much the same: "There is but one law for all, namely, that law which governs all law, of our Creator, the law of Humanity, Justice, Equity:—the law of Nature and of Nations. So far as any laws fortify this primeval law, and give it more precision, more energy, more effect by their declarations, such laws enter into the Sanctuary, and participate in the sacredness of its character." Hastings Trial, 28 May 1794, *Works*, XV, 90. *Cf. Works*, III, 418–419; VIII, 185.

66 *Reflections* (1790), *Works*, V, 283.
67 *Speech on Economical Reform*, 11 Feb. 1780, *Works*, III, 236. *Cf. Report on the Lords' Journals*, 30 April 1794, *Works*, XIV, 355, 385 for the subordination of the courts of law to "the immutable principles of substantial justice."
68 *Speech at Bristol*, 3 Nov. 1774, *Works*, III, 19. Cf. *Works*, XIII, 169; *Correspondence*, III, 107.
69 *Letter to a Noble Lord* (1796), *Works*, VIII, 23.

political matter, the human mind and human affairs are susceptible of infinite modifications, and of combinations wholly new and unlooked for."[70] If Burke has a reputation as an empiricist and an apostle of expediency, it is because of his insistence on the necessity of taking concrete actuality in all its variety and flux into consideration in the making of political judgments. He was aware not only of the element of moral necessity in such judgments, but also of the vast area of contingency and mutability in them. "Circumstances perpetually variable," he said, "directing a moral prudence and discretion, the *general* principles of which never vary, must alone prescribe a conduct fitting on such occasions."[71] The realm of prudence is situated by this passage: it lies between invariable general principles and constantly varying circumstances. The function of prudence is to synthesize the two in a single moral-political judgment. Prudence, therefore, in Burke's mind did not deny but complemented moral principle.

Prudence and principle

Since prudence is a virtue, it assumes a moral end and applies itself to determining the means of attaining it. "God forbid," Burke said, "that prudence, the first of all the virtues, as well as the supreme director of them all, should ever be employed in the service of any of the vices."[72] Nor does prudence have an unlimited scope in its choice of means. Burke held that "there are ways and means, by which a good man would not even save the commonwealth,"[73] and once wrote that all politics "are rotten and hollow at bottom...that are

founded upon any, however minute a degree of positive injustice."[74] It is safe to say that, in principle and in general intention, Burke's doctrine of prudence is compatible with and indeed supposes his theory of the moral order and the natural law.

But while Burke believed that "without the guide and light of sound well-understood principles, all reasoning in politics, as in everything else, would be only a confused jumble of particular facts and details, without the means of drawing out any sort of theoretical or practical conclusion,"[75] he did not stop there. He also believed that "no moral questions are ever abstract questions," and that before judgment could be passed upon "any abstract proposition," it "must be embodied in circumstances." For, he said, "things are right or wrong, morally speaking, only by their relation and connexion with other things."[76] "A statesman," therefore, "never losing sight of principles, is to be guided by circumstances; and judging contrary to the exigencies of the moment he may ruin his country for ever."[77]

The relationship between principles and prudence may be summarized in the phrase that principles are necessary but insufficient.[78] They are necessary because without them consistent, intelligent, and moral action is impossible. But principles are not enough because one cannot often argue from them alone

---

70 *Remarks on the Policy of the Allies* (1793), *Works*, VII, 197–198.

71 *Ibid.,* p. 155.

72 Hastings Trial, 17 Feb. 1788, *Works*, XIII, 275.

73 Notes for a speech in the Commons, 11 May 1792, *Speeches*, IV, 58 and *Works*, X, 45.

74 *Tracts on the Popery Laws* (1761), *Works*, IX, 368. *Cf. Works,* VII, 166; and *cf. Correspondence*, III, 115 for an instance in which Burke went about as far as he ever went in justifying the subordination of morality to expediency.

75 Notes for a speech in the Commons, 11 May 1792, *Speeches*, IV, 55 and Works, X, 41.

76 *Ibid.,* pp. 66 and 58. *Cf. Speeches,* III, 475–476; Works, V, 35–36.

77 *Ibid.,* pp. 55 and 42.

78 The writer is here indebted to Leo Strauss, *Natural Right and History* (Chicago, 1953), pp. 303–306.

to what ought to be done here and now. As Burke himself put it, "The lines of morality are not like the ideal lines of mathematicks. They are broad and deep as well as long. They admit of exceptions; they demand modifications. These exceptions and modifications are not made by the process of logick, but by the rules of prudence."[79] It is the function of prudence, therefore, to supply the deficiencies of principle in meeting the demands of practice.

It is significant that Burke's denunciations were reserved for those who argued with logical but impractical rigor from premises of right—the rights of the sovereign in the American crisis, the rights of man in the French revolutionary crisis. He seldom if ever denounces an argument from premises of duty, and he certainly would not admit, in general terms at least, the supremacy of expediency over duty. His attitude on this point is well expressed in his phrase, "as we never ought to go to war for a profitable wrong, so we ought never to go to war for an unprofitable right."[80]

Yet even the fulfillment of duties is often subject to the judgments of prudence. If a distinction may be made which Burke does not explicitly make (though it is implied in the phrase just quoted above), a positive duty must be performed, but not under all circumstances; and it is only a negative duty (i.e., the duty to refrain from an evil action) which binds everywhere and always. In regard to all positive duties as in regard to the exercise of all rights, knowledge of the principle alone is not sufficient. It is not enough for a man to know that he has a duty or a right. There must also be a judgment on the circumstances which demand performance of the duty or justify the exercise of the right. That will be a prudential judgment of practical reason by which the principle is applied to the actual situation.[81]

Burke's doctrine of political reason and prudence thus made it possible for him to advocate what may be called a principled pragmatism. In contrast to pure pragmatism—if there is such a thing—Burke's pragmatism was not without "absolutes" and fixed stars on which to set a political course. These unchanging points of reference were provided by the natural moral law, which in essence stated an order of ends, derived from human nature, which must ultimately be attained. The basic principles of moral law imposed the realization of these ends and forbade actions contrary to them. But within these limits, the realm of means and intermediate ends was the domain of prudence. In this area the mode of thought proper to the statesman was that of political reason, which was concerned with adapting means to ends in ever-changing circumstances, according to the norms of an intelligent and enlightened expediency.

Burke's theory of practical reason in politics furnishes a key to much of his thought. His conception of the proper structure of society, his doctrine of prescription, his theory of conservation and reform—these and other aspects of his thought cannot be understood if Burke is taken as merely an empiricist in the British philosophical tradition. It is well known that he distrusted abstract reason and objected to the introduction into political questions of arguments from original natural rights.

---

[79] *Appeal from the New to the Old Whigs* (1791), *Works*, VI, 97.

[80] In the Commons, 6 May 1790, *Speeches*, III, 492.

[81] See the preamble to the *Sketch of the Negro Code* which Burke submitted to the Home Secretary in 1792 for an example of his manner of reconciling moral principle with expediency through the exercise of prudence. *Works*, IX, 283.

His reliance on tradition and experience, his predilection for "prejudice" and custom, his insistence on the conventional and evolving character of human society are also well known. But to understand his thought as a whole, it is necessary to perceive that he did not oppose nature and convention, prejudice and reason, or tradition and reform. In his mind all these fell together into a vast and coherent pattern in which the designs of the Creator, the demands of nature, and the artificial social arrangements produced by the mind and will of man made one great and continuous whole. The central idea in Burke's thought, as we have said, was that of order. But this order, as he understood it, was neither wholly natural nor wholly conventional. It was a joint product of God and man, in which the order of society, derived from and reflecting the divinely-ordained order of the universe, was produced, maintained and improved by the constant exercise of man's political reason.

RUSSELL KIRK

Burke and the Philosophy of Prescription*

Conservatism, as a critically held system of ideas, is younger than equalitarianism and rationalism. For philosophical conservatism begins with Edmund Burke, who erected prescription and "prejudice"—by which he meant the supra-rational wisdom of the species—into a conscious and imaginative defense of the traditional ways of society.

When the age of Miracles lay faded into the distance as an incredible tradition, and

* Reprinted from the *Journal of the History of Ideas*, XIV (1953), 365–80, by permission of the editors and the author.

even the age of Conventionalities was now old; and Man's Existence had for long generations rested on mere formulas which were grown hollow by course of time; and it seemed as if no Reality any longer existed, but only Phantasms of realities, and God's Universe were the work of the Tailor and the Upholsterer mainly, and men were buckram masks that went about becking and grimacing there,—on a sudden, the Earth yawns asunder, and amid Tartarean smoke, and glare of fierce brightness, rises Sansculottism, many-headed, fire-breathing, and asks: What think ye of *me?* Well may the buckram masks start together, terror-struck; "into expressive well-concerted groups!"

Thus Carlyle on the events of 1789; his *French Revolution,* said Lord Acton, "delivered the English mind from the thraldom of Burke." Acton, by the way, would have hanged Robespierre and Burke on the same gallows, a judgment in this matter as philosophically representative of Liberal sentiment during the past century as its execution would have been abhorrent to Liberal practice. From Carlyle onward, a great part of the reflecting public maintained that the truth about the Revolution must lie somewhere between Burke and—why, Condorcet, if one must choose a name.

Throughout its century of ascendancy, indeed, Liberalism believed that Burke had erred woefully concerning the significance of the Deluge; Buckle went so far as to explain, in mournful pages, that Burke had gone mad in 1790.[1] But for all that, the intellectual defenses of the Revolution never recovered from the buffet Burke dealt them; Carlyle could not find it possible to share the ecstatic vision of Paine. Burke's *Reflections* had captured the imagination of a powerful section of the rising generation. His style "forked and playful as the lightning, crested like the serpent" (Hazlitt's description) had outshone the flame of Rousseau in the eyes of many a young man of mind and spirit; his great work had not only survived Paine's assault, but had eclipsed it. He had set the course for British conservatism, he had become a pattern for Continental theorists, and he had insinuated himself even into the rebellious soul of America. Buckram masks could not survive the Deluge which Burke himself proclaimed the revolution "most astonishing that has hitherto happened in the world." But Burke was other than buckram; nor did he belong to the age of Conventional-

ities. He believed in the age of Miracles —the old age of Miracles, not the new. He lit a fire to stifle a fire.

For Burke provided the principles to refute the abstractions of the equalitarians. The task was not congenial to his nature. Even when he set himself doggedly to it, as in the *Reflections* and the *Appeal from the New Whigs,* he could hold himself to the abstract expression of general principles only for a few consecutive paragraphs. This present essay, intended to systematize Burke's opinions, might itself be anathema to him, since generalities separated from contingenices were in his eyes almost impious. Yet he perceived the necessity of opposing ideas with ideas, and by 1793 his tremendous countermine had effectually thwarted the sappers from the equalitarian school. "Nothing can be conceived more hard than the heart of a thoroughbred metaphysician," he had written. "It comes nearer to the cold malignity of a wicked spirit than to the frailty and passion of a man. It is like that of the principle of evil himself, incorporeal, pure, unmixed, dephlegmated, defecated evil."[2] In 1798, nevertheless, admiring Hazlitt was telling Southey that "Burke was a metaphysician, Mackintosh a mere logician."[3] By the clutch of circumstance, Burke had been compelled to enter the realm of the abstract, but he never went one foot further into that windy domain than exigency demanded: "I must see the things; I must see the men." Never was statesman more reluctant to turn political philosopher, but never, perhaps, was the metamorphosis more happy.

Edmund Burke was impelled to undertake the delineation of a system

[1] Buckle, *History of Civilization in England,* I, 424–425.

[2] *Letter to a Noble Lord, Works* (Bohn edition), V, 141.

[3] P. P. Howe, *The Life of William Hazlitt,* 60.

of general principles by his alarm at the rapidly swelling influence of three separate schools of thought: that of Rousseau, that of the *philosophes,* and that of the heritors of Locke. The hostility between Rousseau's romanticism and the rationalism of, say, Voltaire has been remarked often, and Burke was not unaware of it; he assaulted both camps, though generally sighting his heavy guns upon Rousseau. As for Locke and his successors, the great Whig orator could not well disavow the defender of the settlement of 1688; yet his fealty to Locke's politics is only nominal,[4] and he wholly disclaims or ignores Locke's psychology and metaphysics. That Burke represented the actual *sentiments* of the Whigs throughout their supremacy, the perspective of history certainly discloses; but the *theories* of the Whigs, so far as they are embodied in the works of Locke, passed to such diverse legatees as Rousseau in Geneva, Price in the Old Jewry, Fox in St. Stephen's, Jefferson at Monticello.

Numerous differences of opinion divided these several camps, of course; but the later followers of Locke were agreed that change they must have, and that *change* for them was very nearly a synonym for *reform.* One may go further, fixing upon a half-dozen points of doctrine concerning which they reached consensus—these:

That God is a Being of a sort quite unlike Jehovah—at once incorporated in us, this God of the deists and of Rousseau, and yet infinitely distant.

That abstract reason or imagination may be utilized not only to study, but to direct, the course of society.

That man is naturally benevolent, generous, healthy-souled, but is corrupted by institutions.

That mankind is struggling upward toward Elysium, is capable of infinite improvement, and should fix its gaze upon the future.

That the aim of the reformer, intellectual and political, is emancipation—liberation from old creeds, old oaths, old establishments; that the man of the future is to rejoice in complete liberty, self-governing, self-satisfying.

To this catalogue of progressive philosophy, the Utilitarians and the Collectivists later submitted amendments; but it will serve for our present definition of that radical mind which Burke endeavored to discredit. Burke conceded his enemies not one premise. He began and ended his campaign upon the grand design of morality; for Burke, the whole of earthly reality was an expression of moral principle. This it is which lifts him so far above "political science" that many scholars have been unable to understand him; yet Burke remains, notwithstanding, so devoted to practicality that he leaves metaphysicians at a loss. It is wise to commence our view of Burke's reluctantly-produced system with an eye to his concept of the force which governs the universe. For him, the formulas upon which man's existence rested never had grown hollow.

"The Tory has always insisted that, if men would cultivate the individual virtues, social problems would take care of themselves." So Granville Hicks once wrote of Stevenson.[5] Extend the epithet "Tory" to "conservative," and the observation is sound enough. This is not the whole of Burke's opinion upon the ills of society, since no one knew better the power for good or evil that lies in establishments; but it is true that Burke saw politics as an exercise in morals and

---

[4] See Alfred Cobban's chapter "Burke and the Heritage of Locke" in his *Edmund Burke and the Revolt against the Eighteenth Century.*

[5] Hicks, *Figures of Transition,* 271–272.

that a great part of conservative doctrine on this point comes out of Burke's dicta. To know the state, we must first know the ethical man—so Burke tells us.

"Rousseau is a moralist, or he is nothing." After delivering this judgment, Burke rises to an assault upon the Genevese so merciless that one is tempted to add the obvious quip. But Burke was in earnest. A false morality, Rousseau's, but a pretentious, in the view of the old Whig statesman: against it must be set a nobler. A new-forged morality was a monstrous imposture, and so Burke turned, as he always did, to prescription and precedent, to old materials ready to the true reformer's hand, in order to produce this opposing morality. The praise of humility was often on Burke's lips, and in his construction of a system of thought he showed himself a humble man. Disdaining a vain show of creation, he turned to Aristotle and Cicero, to the fathers of the Church, to Hooker and Milton, and put new warmth into their phrases, made their ideas flame above the revolutionary torches. And he poured in a catalyst of his own that transformed blind tradition into deliberate adherence to ancient values. Rejecting the concept of a world subject to impulse and appetite, he revealed a world always governed by strong and subtle purpose.

There is a God; and He is wise; and this world is His design; and man and the state are God's creations. Such is Burke's philosophical fundamental. These were ideas accepted without question in most ages, but obscured by the vanity of the eighteenth century. How is God's purpose revealed? Through the unrolling of history. And how do we know God's mind and will? Through the prejudices and traditions which milleniums of human experience with divine judgments have implanted in the mind of the race. What is our purpose in this world? Not to indulge our impulse, but to render our obedience to divine intent.

Now this view of the cosmos may be true, or it may be delusory; but it is not obscure, let alone incomprehensible. The enduring influence of latter-day rationalism and utilitarianism, nevertheless, has prevented a number of writers in our day, scholars in philosophy and politics, from understanding how a great statesman and man of letters could hold such a view. We have stated Burke's position in the simplest terms: he makes his own case in language at once more lucid and more lofty. For many hundreds of years, all thinking men held this position to be supported by truths undeniable. Yet even by friendly critics, the dread word "obscurantism" is applied to Burke's affection for a moral tradition that was venerable when Socrates undertook its defense. R. M. MacIver remarks with a species of indignation, "It was no service to our understanding when Burke enveloped once more in mystic obscurity the office of government and in the sphere of politics appealed once more against reason to tradition and religion."[6]

But is not this begging the question? The Age of Reason, Burke protested with all his Irish fervor, was in reality an Age of Ignorance. If the basis of existence is genuinely divine will, limiting politics and ethics to a puny "reason" is an act of folly; it is this blindness to the effulgence of the burning bush, this deafness to the thunder above Sinai, this shrugging at *mene, mene, tekel, upharsin,* which Burke proclaimed a principal infatuation of the French "Enlightenment." Even Rousseau cried out against such overweening confidence in a reason which, though assertedly independent of providential guidance, proclaims its own infallibility. Here we

---

6 MacIver, *The Modern State,* 148.

are concerned with first principles, and Burke himself doubtless would have agreed that if the teleological arguments of Aristotle, Seneca, and the Schoolmen are rejected, there remains no means of converting the skeptic but revelation. To dismiss such postulates summarily, however, and resign man to an abstract "reason" (by which is generally meant analytic empiricism) was to Burke an act of intellectual impudence. For Burke's forceful imagination, there could be no suspension of judgment: either there was design, or there was chaos. If chaos is demonstrated, the fragile equalitarian doctrines and emancipating intentions of the revolutionaries had no significance; for in a world of chaos, only force and appetite are valid.

I allow, that if no supreme ruler exists, wise to form, and potent to enforce, the moral law, there is no sanction to any contract, virtual or even actual, against the will of prevalent power. On that hypothesis, let any set of men be strong enough to set their duties at defiance, and they cease to be duties any longer. We have but one appeal against irresistible power—

> Si genus humanum et mortalia
> temnitis arma,
> At sperate Deos memores fandi
> atque nefandi.

Taking it for granted that I do not write to the disciples of the Parisian philosophy, I may assume, that the awful Author of our Being is the Author of our place in the order of existence; and that having disposed and marshalled us by a divine tactic, not according to our will, but according to His, He has, in and by that disposition, virtually subjected us to act the part which belongs to the part assigned us. We have obligations to mankind at large, which are not in consequence of any special voluntary pact. They arise from the relation of man to man, and the relation of man to God, which relations are not a matter of choice. ...When we marry, the choice is voluntary, but the duties are not matter of choice. ... The instincts which give rise to this mysterious process of nature are not of our making. But out of physical causes, unknown to us, perhaps unknowable, arise moral duties, which, as we are able perfectly to comprehend, we are bound indispensably to perform.[7]

Was this aspect of the argument for Providence ever better expressed? If the sanction for human conduct be divine, the way of wisdom is comprehension of, and submission to, the divine injunction; if there be no such sanction, "reason," "enlightenment," "equality," and "natural justice" are so many figments of dreams, for men require neither knowledge nor charity in a world without purpose. MacCunn observes concerning Burke, "It seemed to him the sheet anchor of a true political faith that the whole great drama of national life should be reverently recognized as ordered by a Power to which past, present, and future are organically knit stages in one Divine plan."[8]

Polybius' contention that the ancients invented the myths of religion in order to shelter morality and property was repugnant to Burke. The arguments Burke advances to prove that society cannot subsist without divine sanction are so convincing that a skeptic might concede, "If there were no God, it would be necessary to invent one"; but this is inverting Burke's own conviction. His piety was fervent, and its source was innate conviction. A world away from that other great Whig, Locke, Burke frequently expounds the doctrine of innate ideas. For the rest, the great arguments of the Platonic tradition in behalf of a universe of purpose and order are implicit in his speeches and writings: the instinct toward perpetuation of the species; the conviction of

---

7 *Appeal from the New to the Old Whigs, Works,* III, 79.

8 John MacCunn, *The Political Philosophy of Burke,* 127.

conscience; the intimations of immortality; the awareness of immaterial soul. New proofs he does not attempt to introduce; a man always desperately busy, he leaves theology to the schools. We detect in him much of Doctor Johnson's exasperated, "Why, Sir, we *know* the will is free, and there's an end of it!" Christianity he believes established on foundations no one but the restless, the shallow, and the self-intoxicated would venture to assail; and the spectacle of Burke's great intellect thus convinced, his erudition supporting the common voice of centuries, his prudent, practical, reforming spirit submitting to the discipline of the Christian tradition, is as good a proof as any from the books of the Scholastics, perhaps, to attest the truth of Christianity. It is a Christian faith, Burke's, and also a Greek faith. Observe the Hellenic ring in this pronouncement:

He who gave our nature to be perfected by our virtue, willed also the necessary means of its perfection. He willed therefore the state. He willed its connexion with the source and original archtype of all perfection. They who are convinced of this His will, which is the law of laws, and the sovereign of sovereigns, cannot think it reprehensible that this our recognition of a signiory paramount, I had almost said this oblation of the state itself, as a worthy offering on the high altar of universal praise, should be performed as all public, solemn acts are performed, in buildings, in music, in decoration, in speech, in the dignity of persons, according to the customs of mankind taught by their nature; this is, with modest splendor and unassuming state, with mild majesty and sober pomp.[9]

Transcendent even of Christianity, Burke's piety; for he viewed with a corresponding reverence the rites of the Hindus and the Mohammedans: his fiercest indignation against Hastings was from the Governor-General's heavy-handed contempt for native religious ceremony.

Conceivably Burke's conservatism might stand of itself even though shorn of its religious buttresses. The doctrine of expediency in politics might suffice as an apology for a conservative order —and, indeed, seemed quite enough to such pupils of Burke as Sir James Fitzjames Stephen. But Burke himself found it impossible to envisage a social order worthy of respect from which the spirit of piety was absent. The state is a creation religiously consecrated, he tells us:

This consecration is made, that all who administer in the government of men, in which they stand in the person of God himself, should have high and worthy notions of their function and destination; that their hope should be full of immortality; that they should not look to the paltry pelf of the moment, nor to the temporary and transient praise of the vulgar, but to a solid, permanent existence, in the permanent part of their nature, and to a permanent fame and glory, in the example they leave as a rich inheritance to the world.[10]

Such consecration is necessary in a monarchy or an aristocracy—but even more necessary in a popular government:

The consecration of the state, by a state religious establishment, is necessary also to operate with a wholesome awe upon free citizens; because, in order to secure their freedom, they must enjoy some determinate portion of power.... All persons possessing any portion of power ought to be strongly and awfully impressed with an idea that they act in trust; and that they are to account for their conduct in that trust to the one great Master, Author, and Founder of society.[11]

---

9 *Reflections on the Revolution in France, Works*, II, 370.

10 *Ibid.*, 363–364.
11 *Ibid.*, 365.

To call such a faith "obscurantism" and "mysticism" illustrates the lexicographical Dark Age into which our time has been slipping. A lofty faith, Burke's, but also a practical man's, linked to public honor and responsibility. The rationalist may believe such a man wrong, but the rationalist is confused if he calls him a "mystic." And Burke proceeds, by reference and aside throughout his political career and his writings, to make his creed still more a part of private and public life. If the state of the world is the consequence of God's design, we need to be cautious about our reformations; for though it may be God's will to use us as His instruments of alteration, yet we should first satisfy our consciences and our intellects on that point. Again, Burke tells us there is indeed a universal equality; but it is the equality of Christianity, moral equality, equality in the judgment of God; equality of any other sort we may be foolish, possibly impious, to seek. That shrewdest of Socialists, Sir Leonard Woolf, remarks this bond between Christianity and social conservatism:

As soon as people began to believe that happiness was politically of supreme importance, that everyone had an equal right to happiness, or that government should aim at the greatest happiness of the greatest number, the conflict between political psychology and religious psychology began in their minds. Christianity envisages a framework for human society in which earthly miseries have a recognized, permanent, and honourable place. They are trials sent by Heaven to test and train us; as such, it is impious to repine against them.[12]

Burke would have taken up this gauntlet. Poverty, brutality, misfortune he did indeed view as portions of the eternal order of things; sin was a real and demonstrable fact; religion was the

consolation for these ills, not the product of them. Religious faith made existence tolerable; vain ambition without pious restraint would fail of accomplishment and destroy the beauty of reverence.

Burke was well aware of the powerful conservative effect upon society of the church, and recommended to parliament a decent concern for the well-being of the Roman clergy in Ireland, that their influence might be for the preservation of order, not its subversion. In the years that followed the restoration, de Maistre and de Bonald were to adapt the concepts of Burke to French clerical conservatism and ultramontane theories.

True religion is not only identical with national spirit, in Burke's view; it rises superior to law, and is, indeed, the origin of all law. With Philo and Cicero, both of whom he quotes, Burke proclaims the doctrine of the *jus naturale,* the creation of the divine mind, of which the laws of man are but a manifestation. "All human laws are, properly speaking, only declaratory; they may alter the mode and application, but have no power over the substance of original justice."[13] "Religion, to have any force on man's understandings, indeed to exist at all, must be supposed paramount to laws, and independent for its substance on any human institution. Else it would be the absurdest thing in the world; an acknowledged cheat."[14] The majority of the people "have no right to make a law prejudicial to the whole community, even though the delinquents in making such an act should be themselves the chief sufferers by it; because it would be made against the principle of a superior law, which it is not in the

---

12 Woolf, *After the Deluge,* 177.

13 *Tracts on the Popery Laws, Works,* VI, 22.

14 *Ibid.,* 32–33.

power of any community, or the whole race of man, to alter.—I mean the will of Him who gave us our nature, and in giving impressed an invariable law upon it. It would be hard to point out any error more truly subversive of all the order and beauty, of all the peace and happiness, of human society, than the position that any body of men have a right to make what laws they please; or that laws can derive any authority from their institution merely and independent of the quality of the subject-matter."[15]

By no means new, these concepts of the law; but powerfully presented, and that at a time when the world was infatuated with constitution-making, when Abbe Sièyes was drawing up organic documents wholesale. And these concepts are promulgated, too, by the spokesman of the Whigs, nominally the heritor of Locke the constitution-designer. America had just got fourteen new constitutions and was thinking of more. A man of strong conviction and original mind was required to find the basis of law in a transcendent plan, rather than in a neat parliamentary construction; and that man, paradoxically, was also the advocate of enlarged expediency as the guide to the conduct of affairs. But expediency, said Burke, always must yield to the dictates of right—the right which God teaches to man through the experience of the race.

Ours is a moral order, then, and our laws are representative of grander moral laws; the higher contentment is moral happiness, says Burke, and the cause of suffering is moral evil. Pride, ambition, avarice, revenge, lust, sedition, hypocrisy, ungoverned zeal, disorderly appetites—these vices are the true causes of the storms that trouble life. "Religion, morals, laws, prerogatives,

privileges, liberties, rights of men, are the *pretexts*. The pretexts are always found in some specious appearance of a real good. You would not secure men from tyranny and sedition, by rooting out from the mind the principles to which these fraudulent principles apply? If you did, you would root out everything that is valuable in the human breast. . . . You would not cure the evil by resolving, that there should be no more monarchs, nor ministers of state, nor of the gospel; no interpreters of law; no general officers; no public councils. . . . Wise men will apply their remedies to vices, not to names."[16]

Nor can this moral order be altered by counting noses. "When we know, that the opinions of even the greatest multitudes are the standard of rectitude, I shall think myself obliged to make those opinions the masters of my conscience. But if it may be doubted whether Omnipotence itself is competent to alter the essential constitution of right and wrong, sure am I, that such *things,* as they and I, are possessed of no such power."[17]

This doctrine of the moral order, the realm of divine injunction, may appear to march with the bog of metaphysical abstraction so loathed by Burke himself. But the Whig orator would have thundered his retort upon the doubter. Surely as indulgence brings disgust, surely as violence is repaid in kind, just so certain is the operation of other causes and effects in the moral world; they are matters of observation, not of conjecture, Burke would have rejoined. The illustration of the principle he left to the preachers and essayists of the age. How is the nature of the moral world to be comprehended? How are we to guide ourselves within its bounds?

15 *Ibid.,* 21–22.

16 *Reflections, Works,* II, 412–413.
17 *Speech previous to the Election at Bristol, Works,* II, 167.

By observance of tradition and prescription, says Burke.

"The reason first why we do admire those things which are greatest, and second those things which are ancientest, is because the one are the least distant from the infinite substance, the other from the infinite continuance, of God."[18] This was only a passing remark of Burke's, in a general conversation; but it holds the kernel of his philosophy of prescription.

What is the basis of authority in ethics, politics, public economy, law? Burke found it necessary to re-state for the eighteenth century the position of those who have faith in a permanent order of things. His answer, succinctly, was "Tradition tempered by expediency." The custom of mankind determines principles; expedience, its application. The contemner of abstraction was far from rejecting general principles and maxims; and his doctrine of divine purpose puts a gulf between his "expedience" and the expediency of the Machiavellians, just as it separates him from the geographical and historical determinism of his teacher Montesquieu and his pupil Taine.

Willfully or not, it was for a long time the fashion among the liberal admirers of Burke to look upon him as a sort of Benthamite, lauding his determination to deal with circumstances, not concepts; Buckle is as enthusiastic about this side of Burke as he is indignant concerning the *Reflections:*

We had, no doubt, other statesmen before him who denied the validity of general principles in politics; but their denial was only the happy guess of ignorance, and they rejected theories which they had never taken the pains to study. Burke

rejected them because he knew them. It was his rare merit that, notwithstanding every inducement to rely upon his own generalizations, he resisted the temptation; that, though rich in all the varieties of political knowledge, he made his opinions subservient to the march of events; that he recognized as the object of government, not the preservation of particular institutions, nor the propagation of particular tenets, but the happiness of the people at large. . . . Burke was never weary of attacking the common argument that, because a country has long flourished under some particular custom, therefore the custom must be good.[19]

Curiously perverse here, Buckle, translating Burke's exceptions into Burke's rules. Above all else, Burke's philosophy has principle and prescription written upon the face of it; not these, but *abstraction* and *abuse,* does Burke attack. "I do not put abstract ideas wholly out of any question, because I well know that under that name I should dismiss principles; and that without the guide and light of sound, well-understood principles, all reasoning in politics, as in everything else, would be only a confused jumble of particular facts and details, without the means of drawing out any sort of theoretical or practical conclusion."[20]

Abstraction, no; principle, yes. To the first, the guide was knowledge of nature and history, the expressions of divine purpose; to the second, that prudence Burke extols as "the director, the regulator, the standard" of all the virtues. Expedience serves principle, never supplants it. For principle is our cognizance of the divine intent.

History, for Burke, was the gradual revelation of a Supreme design—often shadowy and subtle to our eyes, but

---

[18] Burke was quoting from Hooker's *Ecclesiastical Polity,* Book V, chapter 69.

[19] Buckle, *The History of Civilization in England,* I, 424–425.
[20] *Speech on the Petition of the Unitarians, Works,* VI, 112–113.

quite resistless, wholly just. Burke stops far short of Hegel's mystical determinism, for his adherence to the doctrine of free will tells him that it is not arbitrary, unreasoning will, not material force or racial destiny, which make history, but rather human character and conduct. God makes history through the medium of human souls. It may become impious to resist the grand design, when once its character is irrefutably manifested; but a full comprehension of God's ends we are rarely vouchsafed. The statesman and the thinker must know more than history: they must know nature. Burke's "nature" is human nature, the revelation of universal and permanent principles through the study of mind and soul—not the Romantics' half-pantheistic nature. The phrase "state of nature" was often irritating to Burke's accurate mind; "natural rights," as demanded by Rousseau and other equalitarians, he denied; but the usage of "nature" which was Cicero's is Burke's also. Know history and nature, and you may presume to guess at God's intent.

How has the human species collected and condensed the wisdom of its experience, the written part of which we call history? Chiefly through tradition, "prejudice," prescription—generally surer guides to conscience and conduct than books or speculation. Habit and custom may be the wisdom of unlettered men, but they come from the sound old heart of humanity.

We are afraid to put men to live and trade each on his own private stock of reason; because we suspect that this stock in each man is small, and that the individuals would do better to avail themselves of the general bank and capital of nations and ages. Many of our men of speculation, instead of exploding general prejudices, employ their sagacity to discover the latent wisdom which prevails in them. If they find what they seek, and they seldom fail,

they think it more wise to continue the prejudice, with the reason involved, than to cast away the coat of prejudice, and to leave nothing but the naked reason; because prejudice, with its reason, has a motive to give action to that reason, and an affection which will give it permanence.[21]

Without reverence, man will not serve God, and so will destroy himself; prejudice, prescription, and custom bring reverence.

They bring reverence, but they are not modes of action, of course. When society needs to act, it should resort to an expedience which is founded upon these traditions and habits of thought. "Expedience is that which is good for the community, and good for every individual in it."[22] These words of Burke's are not very different from the definitions of Hume or of Bentham; for that matter, one notes the similarity of this sentence to Rousseau's identification of individual happiness with the gratification of the General Will. But Burke meant something very unlike the several concepts of Hume and Bentham and Rousseau. His qualifying phrase really is his premise. The good of the individual, for Burke, is the *test* of expediency—not its consequence. When Burke thought of the "good of the community" he had in mind a spiritual good, an enduring good without the alloy of incidental and private deprivation. He was unyieldingly hostile to a vision of society composed of a satisfied majority and a submitting minority. The statesman who properly understands the functions of expedience, or prudence, will have for his model a society in which every man has his prerogatives, his accepted station, and his correspondent duties; tradition and prescription will have taught every man

---

[21] *Reflections, Works,* II, 359.
[22] *Speech on the Reform of Representation, Works,* VI, 149.

to recognize the justice of this order, and he will not merely acquiesce in the stability of social institutions, but will support them out of a sound prejudice. An intelligent exercise of expedience will save man from the anarchy of "natural right" and the presumption of "reason." Prescription as a guide for the great mass of mankind, tradition illuminated by expedience as a guide for the philosopher and the statesman who are shepherds of the mass of men: this combination is Burke's recipe for a society at once pious and vigorous.

Burke's praises of custom and traditional wisdom, ancient usage that is surer guarantee than statute, knowledge of the species that is beyond our own little intellects, are repeated in all his principal works. Of the persecution of Catholics, "You punish them for acting upon a principle which of all others is perhaps most necessary for preserving society, an implicit admiration and adherence to the establishments of their forefathers."[23] Again, "If prescription be once shaken, no species of property is secure, when it once becomes an object large enough to tempt the cupidity of indigent power."[24] The British Constitution itself is his best example of right established by custom:

Our constitution is a prescriptive constitution; it is a constitution whose sole authority is that it has existed time out of mind. . . . Your king, your lords, your judges, your juries, grand and little, all are prescriptive; and what proves it is the dispute not yet concluded, and never near becoming so, when any of them first originated. Prescription is the most solid of all titles, not only to property, but, which is to secure that property, to government. They harmonize with each other, and give mutual aid to one another. It is accompanied with another ground of authority in the constitution of the human mind—presumption. It is a presumption in favour of any settled scheme of government against any untried project, that a nation has long existed and flourished under it. It is a far better presumption even of the *choice* of a nation, far better than any sudden and temporary arrangement by actual election.[25]

"Prejudice"—the half-intuitive knowledge that enables man to meet the problems of life without logic-chopping; "prescription"—the customary right which grows out of the implied conventions and compacts of many successive generations: employing these instruments, mankind manages to live together in some degree of amicability and freedom. They direct the individual conscience and the conscript fathers. Without them, society can be kept from destruction only by force and a master. "Somewhere there must be a control upon will and appetite; and the less of it there is within, the more of it there must be without." For if prejudice and prescription be eradicated, only one peaceful instrument remains for preventing man from relapsing into that primitive natural state from which he has so painfully crept up through milleniums, and which existence Burke (in most matters at war with Hobbes) also knew to be "poor, nasty, brutish, and short." That surviving instrument is reasons. And Reason, the darling of the *philosophes,* seemed to Burke a poor, weak servant. The mass of mankind, Burke implies, reason hardly at all; deprived of folk-wisdom and folk-law, which are a part of prescription and prejudice, they can only troop after the demagogue, the charlatan, and the despot. The mass of mankind are not ignorant, but their knowledge is a kind of collective possession, the sum of the

---

23 *Tracts on the Popery Laws, Works,* VI, 32.
24 *Reflections, Works,* II, 422.

25 *Speech on the Reform of Representation, Works,* VI, 146.

slow accretions of generations. This abandoned, they are thrown back upon their "own private stock of reason"; and that stock is very small, hopelessly inferior to the "general bank and capital of nations and of ages." Even the wisest and shrewdest of men are ridiculously conceited if they presume to set the products of their reason against the judgment of the centuries. It is possible, Burke concedes, that they may be right, and past humanity wrong; but the ordinary presumption is the other way; and in any case, it may be wiser to continue an old practice, even if it be the child of error, than to break radically with custom and run the risk of disturbing the body social merely to satisfy a doctrinaire affection for scientific precision. "You see, Sir, that in this enlightened age I am bold enough to confess, that we are generally men of untaught feelings; that instead of casting away all our old prejudices, we cherish them to a very considerable degree, and, to take more shame to ourselves, we cherish them because they are prejudices; and the longer they have lasted, and the more generally they have prevailed, the more we cherish them."[26]

Burke was not the first English philosopher to respect prejudice and prescription. Hume, for all his boldness, was aware of their social utility; and a writer whose ideas Burke generally disliked as much as Hume's, Chesterfield, praises prejudice nearly as eloquently as does Burke himself. In *The World*, Chesterfield has observed:

A prejudice is by no means (though generally thought so) an error; on the contrary, it may be a most unquestioned truth, though it be still a prejudice in those who, without any examination, take it upon trust and entertain it by habit. There are even some prejudices, founded upon error, which ought to be connived it, or perhaps encouraged; their effects being more beneficial to society than their detection can possibly be.... The bulk of mankind have neither leisure nor knowledge sufficient to reason right; why should they be taught to reason at all? Will not honest instinct prompt, and wholesome prejudices guide them, much better than half reasoning?[27]

Yet Burke's onslaught upon newfangled Reason clashed with the great fashionable intellectual current of his time, with the whole principle of the Encyclopedia. Courage was required for such declarations in support of prejudice; in a lesser man, this stand would have been dismissed with scorn by the literate public. Burke, however, they could not scorn. It is some indication of the strength of Burke's belief in Christian humility that he, with his acute and far-ranging mind, could be the partisan of the instincts of the race against the assumptions of the man of genius.

Men are by appetite voracious and sanguinary, Burke thinks; they are held in check by this collective and immemorial wisdom we call morality, prejudice; reason alone never can bind them to their duties. Whenever the veneer of prejudice and prescription is cracked at any point, we are menaced by the danger that the crack may widen and lengthen, even to the annihilation of civilization. If men are discharged from reverence for custom and usage, they will treat this frail world as if it were their personal property, to be consumed for their immediate gratification; and thus they will destroy in their lust for enjoyment the property of future generations, of their own contemporaries, and indeed their very own capital:

One of the first and most leading principles on which the commonwealth and the laws are consecrated, is lest the temporary pos-

---

26 *Reflections, Works*, II, 359.

27 *The World*, No. 112.

sessors and life-renters in it, unmindful of what they have received from their ancestors, or of what is due to their posterity, should act as if they were the entire masters; that they should not think it among their rights to cut off the entail, or commit waste on the inheritance, by destroying at their pleasure the whole original fabric of their society; hazarding to leave to those who come after them a ruin instead of a habitation—and teaching these successors as little to respect their contrivances, as they had themselves respected the institutions of their forefathers. By this unprincipled facility of changing the state as often, and as much, and in as many ways, as there are floating fancies or fashions, the whole chain and continuity of the commonwealth would be broken. No one generation could link with another. Men would become little better than the flies of a summer.[28]

Prejudice and prescription, despite their great age—or perhaps because of it—are delicate growths, slow to rise, easy to injure, hardly possible to revive. The abstract metaphysician and fanatic reformer, intending to cleanse, may find he has scrubbed society clean away:

An ignorant man, who is not fool enough to meddle with his clock, is however sufficiently confident to think he can safely take to pieces, and put together at his pleasure, a moral machine of another guise, importance, and complexity, composed of far other wheels, and springs, and balances, and counteracting and co-operating powers. Men think little how immorally they act in rashly meddling with what they do not understand. Their delusive good intention is no sort of excuse for their presumption. They who truly mean well must be fearful of acting ill.[29]

Then is alteration of any sort undesirable? Do prejudice and prescription compel mankind to tread perpetually behind their ancestors? No, says

Burke; change is inevitable; but let it come as the consequence of a need generally felt, not out of fine-spun abstractions. Both prejudice and prescription are altered by the newer experiences of humanity. This process should not be stifled, since it is a natural and providential means of prolonging life, quite like the physical renewal of the human body. But change should be considered as the manifestation of divine purpose, not simply as a mechanism for men to tinker with. The course of change is not truly a *conscious* process; some might call it a blind process. Our part is to patch and polish the old order of things, clothing ancient form with new substance, fitting recent experience and need into the pattern of the wisdom of our ancestors. We must try to distinguish between a profound, slow, natural alteration and some infatuation of the hour. Here again the instrument of expedience is required for the wise reconciliation of prescription with necessary alteration.

We must all obey the great law of change. It is the most powerful law of nature, and the means perhaps of its conservation. All we can do, and that human wisdom can do, is to provide that the change shall proceed by insensible degrees. This has all the benefits which may be in change, without any of the inconveniences of mutation. Everything is provided for as it arrives. This mode will, on the one hand, prevent the unfixing old interests at once: a thing which is apt to breed a black and sullen discontent in those who are at once dispossessed of all their influence and consideration. This gradual course, on the other side, will prevent men, long under depression, from being intoxicated with a large draught of new power, which they always abuse with a licentious insolence.[30]

Prescription and prejudice are themselves subject to change, and the man

28 *Reflections, Works,* II, 366–367.
29 *Appeal from the New Whigs to the Old, Works,* III, 111–112.

30 *Letter to Sir Hercules Langrische on the Catholics* (1792), *Works,* III, 340.

who obstinately rejects even such innovations as are manifestly the improvements of Providence is as rash as the devotee of Reason.

Prescription and venerable precept never have received a more consistent and courageous defense than Burke's championship of the wisdom of our ancestors. Yet Burke has very little to say concerning the greatest social quandary of our time: once prescription and prejudice *are* violated, once the mass of mankind have been cast adrift, with only miscellaneous scraps of custom and tradition left to mingle with their private stock of reason, how is society to be kept from disintegration? "Burke was sincerely convinced that men's power of political reasoning was so utterly inadequate to their task," comments Graham Wallas, "that all his life long he urged the English nation to follow prescription, to obey, that is to say, on principle their habitual political impulses. But the deliberate following of prescription which Burke advocated was something different, because it was the result of choice, from the uncalculated

loyalty of the past. Those who have eaten of the tree of knowledge cannot forget."[31]

"Prejudice renders a man's virtue his habit; and not a series of unconnected acts. Through just prejudice, his duty becomes a part of his nature"—thus Burke.[32] Can prejudice and prescription, once shattered, be restored? Wallas thinks not; and probably Burke would agree with him. Yet Wallas and other recent writers have come to agree with Burke that a private stock of reason is wholly inadequate to guide man and society. Perhaps Burke's confidence in the purposeful design of Providence would have prompted him to answer that out of the confusion of our century will be resolved a fresh set of prescriptions and prejudices remarkably like those his age knew; for prescription, he declared, has its true origin in the nature which God bestowed upon man.

---

[31] Wallas, *Human Nature in Politics* (4th ed., 1948), 182–183.
[32] *Reflections, Works,* II, 359.

9

HEGEL

Throughout most of his adult life, G.W.F. Hegel (1770–1831) taught in universities in Switzerland and Germany. From 1818 until his death he held the prestigious chair of philosophy at the University of Berlin. In these formative years of German nationalism he acquired a reputation as the philosopher of the Prussian regime since his writings offered some measure of metaphysical justification for the growing power of the Prussian state. Hegel's reputation has since suffered the fate of being measured mainly in terms of his later influence on Marx and subsequently on twentieth-century fascist thought. His ideas on historical inevitability and the course of the dialectic are cited with respect to Marx, and his contention that freedom is found only within the state is cited for the influence on fascism. Much less attention has been paid to Hegel's ideas on their own terms.

The two selections offered here, however, investigate Hegel's political thought for its own sake, while remaining aware of its seminal quality. Herbert Marcuse, in the selection from his great work on Hegel, investigates Hegel's interesting notion of civil society and then critically looks at his theory of the state. The selection ends with Marcuse's discussion of the *Philosophy of History* in which, he suggests, one can find Hegel's final teachings on the relationship of the state and society as originally outlined in the *Philosophy of Right*. George Sabine, the late professor of philosophy at Cornell University and distinguished historian of political thought, offers in his article a broad overview of Hegel's political thought in the perspective of both his general philosophical opinions and the proper historical context. Sabine's particular concern is with Hegel's theory of the dialectic, his distinction between the state and civil society, and finally with his theory of freedom, which Sabine contends should be read primarily as a reaction to the doctrinaire individualism fashionable in Hegel's time.

HERBERT MARCUSE

Reason and Revolution *

THE POLITICAL PHILOSOPHY

The state is essentially separate and distinct from society. The decisive feature of civil society is 'the security and protection of property and personal freedom,' 'the interest of the individual' its ultimate purpose. The state has a totally different function, and is related to the individual in another way. 'Union as such is itself the true content and end' for the state. The integrating factor is the universal, not the particular. The individual may 'pass a universal life' in the state; his particular satisfactions, activities, and ways of life are here regulated by the common interest. The state is a subject in the strict sense of the word, namely, the actual carrier and end of all individual actions that now stand under 'universal laws and principles.'

The laws and principles of the state guide the activities of free-thinking subjects, so that their element is not nature, but mind, the rational knowledge and will of associated individuals. This is the meaning of Hegel's terming the state 'Objective Mind.' The state creates an order that does not depend, as civil society did, on the blind interrelation of particular needs and performances for its own perpetuation. The 'system of wants' becomes a conscious scheme of life controlled by man's autonomous decisions in the common interest. The state therefore can be denoted as the 'realization of freedom.'

We have mentioned that for Hegel the state's fundamental task is to make the specific and the general interest coincide, so as to preserve the individual's right and freedom. Yet such a demand presupposes the identification of state and society, not their separation. For, the wants and interests of the individual exist in society and, no matter how they may be modified by the demands of the common welfare, they arise in and remain bound up with the social processes governing individual life. The demand that freedom and happiness be fulfilled thus eventually falls back upon society, and not upon the state. According to Hegel, the state has no aim other than 'association as such.' In other words, it has no aim at all if the social and economic order constitutes a 'true association.' The process of bringing the individual into harmony with the universal would

* Reprinted from Herbert Marcuse, *Reason and Revolution* (New York: Humanities Press Inc., 1954), pp. 213–37, by permission of the publisher. The footnotes found in the original have been omitted here.

295

engender the 'withering away' of the state, rather than the opposite.

Hegel, however, separated the rational order of the state from the contingent interrelations of the society because he looked upon society as civil society, which is not a 'true association.' The critical character of his dialectic forced him to see society as he did. Dialectical method understands the existent in terms of the negativity it contains and views realities in the light of their change. Change is a historical category. The objective mind, with which the *Philosophy of Right* deals, unfolds itself in time, and the dialectical analysis of its content has to be guided by the forms that this content has taken in history. The truth thus appears as a historical achievement, so that the stage man has reached with civil society fulfills all preceding historical efforts. Some other form of association may come in the future, but philosophy, as the science of the actual, does not enter into speculations over it. The social reality, with its general competition, selfishness, and exploitation, with its excessive wealth and excessive poverty, is the foundation on which reason must build. Philosophy cannot jump ahead of history, for it is a son of its time, 'its time apprehended in thought.'

The times are those of a civil society wherein has been prepared the material basis for realizing reason and freedom, but a reason distorted by the blind necessity of the economic process and a freedom perverted through competition of conflicting private interests. Yet this selfsame society has much that makes for a truly free and rational association: it upholds the inalienable right of the individual, increases human wants and the means for their satisfaction, organizes the division of labor, and advances the rule of law. These elements must be freed from private interests and submitted to a power that stands above the competitive system of civil society, in a specially exalted position. This power is the state. Hegel sees the state as 'an independent and autonomous power' in which 'the individuals are mere moments,' as 'the march of God in the world.' He thought this to be the very essence of the state, but, in reality, he was only describing the historical type of state that corresponded to civil society.

We reach this interpretation of Hegel's state by placing his concept in the socio-historical setting that he himself implied in his description of civil society. Hegel's idea of the state stems from a philosophy in which the liberalistic conception of state and society has all but collapsed. We have seen that Hegel's analysis led to his denying any 'natural' harmony between the particular and the general interest, between civil society and the state. The liberalist idea of the state was thus demolished. In order that the framework of the given social order may not be broken, the common interest has to be vested in an autonomous agency, and the authority of the state set above the battleground of competing social groups. Hegel's 'deified' state, however, by no means parallels the Fascist one. The latter represents the very level of social development that Hegel's state is supposed to avoid, namely, the direct totalitarian rule of special interests over the whole. Civil society under Fascism rules the state; Hegel's state rules civil society. And in whose name does it rule? According to Hegel, in the name of the free individual and in his true interest. 'The essence of the modern state is the union of the universal with the full freedom of the particular, and with the welfare of individuals.' The prime difference between the ancient and the modern world rests on the fact that in the latter the great questions of human life are to be decided not by some superior authority, but by the free 'I will' of man. 'This I will... must have its peculiar niche in the great building of State.' The basic principle of this state is the full development of the individual. Its constitution and all its political institutions are to express 'the knowledge and the will of its individuals.'

At this point, however, the historical contradition inherent in Hegel's political philosophy determines its fate. The individual who knows and wishes his true interest in the common interest— this individual simply doesn't exist. Individuals exist only as private owners, subjects of the fierce processes of civil society, cut off from the common interest by selfishness and all it entails. As far as civil society reaches, none is free of its toils.

Outside of society, however, lies nature. If there could be found someone who possesses his individuality by virtue of his *natural* and not his social existence, and who is what he is simply by nature and not by the social mechanisms, he might be the stable point from which the state could be ruled. Hegel finds such a man in the monarch, a man chosen to his position 'by natural birth.' Ultimate freedom can rest with him, for he is outside a world of false and negative freedom and is 'exacted above all that is particular and conditional.' The ego of everyone else is corrupted by the social order that molds all; the monarch alone is not so influenced and is hence able to originate and decide all his acts by reference to his pure ego. He can cancel all particularity in the 'simple certainty of his self.'

We know what the 'self-certainty of the pure ego' means to Hegel's system: it is the essential property of the 'sub-stance as subject,' and thus characterizes the true being. The use of this principle historically to yield the monarch's natural person again points up the frustration of idealism. Freedom becomes identical with the inexorable necessity of nature, and reason terminates in an accident of birth. The philosophy of freedom again turns into a philosophy of necessity.

Classical political economy described modern society as a 'natural system' whose laws appeared to have the necessity of physical laws. This point of view soon lost its magic. Marx showed how the anarchic forces of capitalism assume the quality of natural forces as long as they are not made subject to human reason, that the natural element in society is not a positive but a negative one. Hegel seems to have had some inkling of this. He sometimes seems to be smiling at his own idealization of the monarch, declaring that the decisions of the monarch are only formalities. He is 'a man who says yes and so puts the dot upon the i.' He notes that monarchs are not remarkable for intellectual or physical strength and that, despite this, millions permit themselves to be ruled by them. Nevertheless, the intellectual weakness of the monarch is preferable to the wisdom of civil society, Hegel feels.

The fault with Hegel lies much deeper than in his glorification of the Prussian monarchy. He is guilty not so much of being servile as of betraying his highest philosophical ideas. His political doctrine surrenders society to nature, freedom to necessity, reason to caprice. And in so doing, it mirrors the destiny of the social order that falls, while in pursuit of its freedom, into a state of nature far below reason. The dialectical analysis of civil society had concluded that society was not capable of establishing reason and freedom of its own accord. Hegel therefore put forward a strong state to achieve this end and tried to reconcile that state with the idea of freedom by giving a strong constitutional flavoring to monarchy.

The state exists only through the medium of law. 'Laws express the content of objective freedom...They are an absolute final end and a universal work.' Hence the state is bound by laws that are the opposite of authoritarian decrees. The body of laws is 'a universal work' that incorporates the reason and the will of associated men. The constitution expresses the interests of all (now, of course, their true, 'purified' interests), and the executive, legislative and judiciary powers are but the organs of constitutional law. Hegel repudiates the traditional division of these powers, as detrimental to the state's unity; the three functions of government are to work in permanent actual collaboration. The emphasis on the state's unity is so strong that it occasionally leads Hegel to formulations that come close to the organicist theory of the state. He declares, for instance, that the constitution, though 'begotten in time, should not be contemplated as made' by man, but rather as 'divine and perpetual.' Such utterances spring from the same motives that impelled the most far-seeing philosophers to set the state above any danger of criticism. They recognized that the tie that most effectively binds the conflicting groups of the ruling class is the fear of any subversion of the existing order.

We shall not spend time upon Hegel's outline of the constitution, since it hardly adds essentially to his earlier writings on the same subject, although some important features of his system are worthy of brief notice. The traditional trinity of political powers is altered to consist of the monarchic, the administrative, and the legislative power. These overlap so that the executive power belongs to the first two and includes the judicial, while the legislative power is exercised by the government together with the estates. The entire political system again converges towards the idea of sovereignty, which, though now rooted in the 'natural' person of the monarch, still pervades the whole structure. Alongside the state's sovereignty over the antagonisms of civil society, Hegel now stresses its sovereignty over the people (*Volk*). The people 'is that part of the State which does not know what it wants,' and whose 'movement and action would be elemental, void of reason, violent, and terrible' if not regulated. Here again, Hegel may have been thinking of the *Volksbewegung* of his time; the Prussian monarchy may well have seemed a paragon of reason compared to that Teutonic movement from 'below.' Yet, Hegel's advocacy of a strong hand over the masses is part of a more general trend, which threatens the whole constitutional structure of his state.

The state provides a unity for the particular and the general interest. Hegel's view of this unity differs from the liberalistic, inasmuch as his state is imposed upon the social and economic mechanisms of civil society and is vested in independent political powers and institutions. 'The objective will is in itself rational in its very conception, whether or not it be known by the individuals or willed as an object of their caprice.'

Hegel's exaltation of the state's political power has, however, some clearly critical traits. Discussing the relation between religion and the state, he points out that 'religion is principally commended and resorted to in times of public distress, disturbance, and oppression; it is taught to furnish consolation against wrong and the hope of compensation in the case of loss.' He notes the dangerous function of religion in its tendency to divert man from his search for actual freedom and to pay him fictitious damages for real wrongs. 'It would surely be regarded as a bitter jest if those who were oppressed by any despotism were referred to the consolations of religion; nor is it to be forgotten that religion may assume the form of a galling superstition, involving the most abject servitude, and the degradation of man below the level of the brute.' Some force has to interfere to rescue the individual from religion in such a case. The state comes to champion 'the rights of reason and self-consciousness.' 'It is not strength, but weakness which has in our times made religion a polemical kind of piety'; the struggle for man's historical fulfillment is not a religious but a social and political struggle, and its transplantation to an inner sanctum of the soul, of belief and morality, means regression to a stage long since past.

Nevertheless, these critical qualities are dwarfed by the oppressive trends inherent in all authoritarianism, which manifest their full force in Hegel's doctrine of external sovereignty. We have already shown how Hegel elevated the national interests of the particular state to the place of highest and most indubitable authority in international relations. The state puts forward and asserts the interests of its members by welding them into a community, in this way fulfilling their freedom and their rights and transforming the destructive force of competition into a unified whole. Undisputed *internal* authority of the state is a prerequisite for successful competition, and the latter necessarily terminates in *external* sovereignty. The life and death struggle of individuals in civil society for mutual recognition has its counterpart among sovereign states in the form of war. War is the inevitable issue of any test

of sovereignty. It is neither an absolute evil nor an accident, but an 'ethical element,' for war achieves that integration of interests that civil society cannot establish by itself. 'Successful wars have prevented civil broils and strengthened the internal power of the State.'

Hegel was thus as cynical as Hobbes on the subject of the bourgeios state, ending in a complete rejection of International Law. The state, the final subject that perpetuates competitive society, cannot be bound by a higher law, for such a law would amount to an external restriction of sovereignty and destroy the life-element of civil society. No contract is valid among states. Sovereignty cannot be circumscribed by treaties that imply in their very nature a mutual dependence of the parties involved. Sovereign states stand outside the world of civil interdependence; they exist in a 'state of nature.'

We note again that blind nature enters and elbows aside the self-conscious rationality of objective mind:

States find themselves in a natural more than a legal relation to each other. There is hence a continuous struggle between them. They conclude treaties and therewith establish a legal relation between themselves. On the other hand, however, they are autonomous and independent. Right, therefore, cannot be real as between them. They may break treaties arbitrarily, and they must constantly find themselves distrusting one another. Since they are in a state of nature, they act according to violence. They maintain and procure their rights through their own power and must as a matter of necessity plunge into war.

Hegel's idealism comes to the same conclusion as did Hobbes's materialism. The rights of sovereign states 'have reality not in a general will which is constituted as a superior power, but in their particular wills.' Accordingly, disputes among them can be settled only by war. International relations are an arena for 'the wild play of particular passions, interests, aims, talents, virtues, force, wrong, vice, and external contingency'—the moral end itself, 'the State's autonomy, is exposed to chance.'

But is this drama of chance and violence really final? Does reason terminate in the state and in that play of reckless natural forces in which the state must perforce engage? Hegel has repudiated such conclusions throughout the *Philosophy of Right*. The state right, though not bound by international law, is still not the final right, but must answer to 'the right of the World Mind which is the unconditional absolute.' The state has its real content in universal history (*Weltgeschichte*), the realm of the world mind, which holds 'the supreme absolute truth.' Furthermore, Hegel emphasizes that any relation between autonomous states 'must be external. A third must therefore stand above and unite them.' 'This third is the Mind which materializes itself in world history, and constitutes itself absolute judge over States.' The state, even laws and duties, are merely 'a determinate reality'; they pass up into and rest upon a higher sphere.

What, then, is this final sphere of state and society? How are state and society related to the world mind? These questions can only be answered if we turn to an interpretation of Hegel's *Philosophy of History*.

THE PHILOSOPHY OF HISTORY

Being, for dialectical logic, is a process through contradictions that determine the content and development of all reality. The *Logic* had elaborated the timeless structure of this process, but the intrinsic connection, between the *Logic* and the other parts of the system, and, above all, the implications of the dialectical method destroy the very idea of timelessness. The *Logic* had shown that the true being is the idea, but the idea unfolds itself 'in space' (as nature) and 'in time' (as mind). Mind is of its very essence affected by time, for it exists only in the temporal process of history. The forms of the mind manifest themselves in time, and the history of the world is an exposition of mind in time. The dialectic thus gets to view reality temporally, and the 'negativity' that, in the *Logic,* determined the process of thought appears in the *Philosophy of History* as the destructive power of time.

The *Logic* had demonstrated the structure of reason; the *Philosophy of History* expounds the historical content of reason. Or, we may say, the content of reason here is the same as the content of history, although by content we refer not to the miscellany of historical facts, but to what makes history a rational whole, the laws and tendencies to which the facts point and from which they receive their meaning.

'Reason is the sovereign of the world,' —this, according to Hegel, is a hypothesis, and the only hypothesis in the philosophy of history. This hypothesis, which distinguishes the philosophic method of treating history from any other method, does not imply that history has a definite end. The teleological character of history (if indeed history has such) can only be a conclusion from an empirical study of history and cannot be assumed *a priori*. Hegel states emphatically that 'in history, thought must be subordinate to what is given, to the realities of fact; this is its basis and guide.' Consequently, 'we have to take history as it is. We must proceed historically—empirically,' an odd approach for an idealistic philosophy of history.

The laws of history have to be demonstrated in and from the facts— thus far, Hegel's is the empirical method. But these laws cannot be known unless the investigation first has the guidance of proper theory. Facts of themselves disclose nothing; they only answer adequate theoretical questions. True scientific objectivity requires the application of sound categories that organize data in their actual significance, and not a passive reception of given facts. 'Even the ordinary, the "impartial" historiographer, who believes and professes that he maintains a simply receptive attitude, surrendering himself only to the data supplied him—is by no means passive as regards the exercise of his thinking powers. He brings his categories with him, and sees the phenomena...exclusively through these media.'

But how does one recognize the sound categories and the proper theory? Philosophy decides. It elaborates those general categories that direct investigation in all special fields. Their validity in these fields, however, must be verified by the facts, and the verification is had when the given facts are comprehended by the theory in such a way that they appear under definite laws and as moments of definite tendencies, which explain their sequence and interdependence.

The dictum that philosophy should provide the general categories for understanding history is not arbitrary, nor did it originate with Hegel. The great theories of the eighteenth century all took the philosophic view that history was progress. This concept of progress, soon to degenerate into a shallow complacency, originally pointed sharp condemnatory criticism on an obsolete social order. The rising middle class used the concept of progress as a means to interpret the past history of mankind as the prehistory of its own reign, a reign that was destined to bring the world to maturity. When, they said, the new middle class would get to shape the world in accordance with its interests, an unheard-of spurt in material and intellectual forces would make man master of nature and would intiate the true history of humanity. As long as all this had not yet materialized, history was still in a state of struggle for truth. The idea of progress, an integral element in the philosophy of the French Enlightenment, interpreted historical facts as signposts marking man's path to reason. The truth still lay outside the realm of fact—in a state to come. Progress implied that the given state of affairs would be negated and not continued.

This pattern still prevails in Hegel's *Philosophy of History*. Philosophy is the material as well as the logical *a priori* of history, so long as history has not yet won the level adequate to human potentialities. We know, however, that Hegel thought history had reached its goal and that idea and reality had found common ground. Hegel's work thus marks the apogee and end of the critical philosophic historiography. He still looks to freedom's interest in his dealing with historical facts, and still views the struggle for freedom as the only content of history. But this interest has lost its vigor and the struggle has come to an end.

The concept of freedom, as the *Philosophy of Right* has shown, follows the pattern of free ownership. As a result, the history of the world that Hegel looks out upon exalts and enshrines the history of the middle class, which based itself on this pattern. There is a stark truth in Hegel's strangely certain announcement that history has reached its end. But it announces the funeral of a class, not of history. At the close of the book, Hegel writes, after a description of the Restoration, 'This is the point which consciousness has attained.' This hardly sounds like an end. Consciousness is historical consciousness, and when we read in the *Philosophy of Right* that 'one form of life has grown old,' it is one form, not all forms of life. The consciousness and the aims of his class were open to Hegel. He saw they contained no new principle to rejuvenate the world. If this consciousness was to be mind's final form, then history had entered a realm beyond which there was no progress.

Philosophy gives historiography its general categories, and these are identical with the basic concepts of the dialectic. Hegel has summarized them in his introductory lectures. We shall get to them later. First, we must discuss the concepts he calls specific historical categories.

The hypothesis on which the *Philosophy of History* rests has already been verified by Hegel's *Logic:* the true being is reason, manifest in nature and come to realization in man. The realization takes place in history, and since reason realized in history is mind, Hegel's thesis implies that the actual subject or driving force of history is mind.

Of course, man is also part of nature and his natural drives and impulses play a material role in history. Hegel's *Philosophy of History* does more justice to this role than do many empirical historiographies. Nature, in the form of the sum-total of natural conditions for human life, remains the primary basis of history throughout Hegel's book.

As a natural being, man is confined to particular conditions—he is born in this or that place or time, a member of this or that nation, bound to share the fate of the particular whole to which he belongs. Yet, despite all this, man is essentially a thinking subject, and thought, we know, constitutes universality. Thought (1) lifts men beyond their particular determinations and (2)

also makes the multitude of external things the medium for the subject's development.

This double universality, subjective and objective, characterizes the historical world wherein man unfolds his life. History, as the history of the thinking subject, is of necessity universal history (*Weltgeschichte*) just because 'it belongs to the realm of Mind.' We apprehend the content of history through general concepts, such as nation, state; agrarian, feudal, civil society; despotism, democracy, monarchy; proletariat, middle class, nobility, and so on. Caesar, Cromwell, Napoleon are for us Roman, English, French citizens; we understand them as members of their nation, responding to the society and the state of their time. The universal asserts itself in them. Our general concepts grasp this universal to be the actual subject of history, so that, for example, the history of mankind is not the life and battles of Alexander the Great, Caesar, the German emperors, the French kings, the Cromwells and Napoleons, but the life and battles of that universal which unfolds itself in different guises through the various cultural wholes.

The essence of this universal is mind, and 'the essence of Mind is freedom... Philosophy teaches that all the qualities of Mind exist only through freedom; that all are but means for attaining freedom; that all seek and produce this and this alone.' We have discussed these qualities, and we have seen that freedom terminates in the self-assurance of complete appropriation; that the mind is free if it possesses and knows the world as its property. It is therefore quite understandable that the *Philosophy of History* should end with the consolidation of middle-class society and that the periods of history should appear as necessary stages in the realization of its form of freedom.

The true subject of history is the universal, not the individual; the true content is the realization of the self-consciousness of freedom, not the interests, needs, and actions of the individual. 'The history of the world is none other than the progress of the consciousness of freedom.' Yet, 'the first glance at history convinces us that the actions of men proceed from their needs, their passions, their characters and talents; and impresses us with the belief that such needs, passions and interests are the sole springs of action—the efficient agents in this scene of activity.' To explain history thus means 'to depict the passions of mankind, its genius, its active powers.' How does Hegel resolve the apparent contradiction? There can be no question that the needs and interests of individuals are the levers of all historical action, and that in history it is the individual's fulfillment that should come to pass. Something else asserts itself, however —historical reason. As they follow out their own interests, individuals promote the progress of mind, that is, perform a universal task that advances freedom. Hegel cites the example of Caesar's struggle for power. In his overthrow of the traditional form of Roman state, Caesar was certainly driven by ambition; but, in satisfying his personal drives he fulfilled 'a necessary destiny in the history of Rome and of the world'; through his actions, he achieved a higher, more rational form of political organization.

A universal principle is thus latent in the particular aims of individuals— universal because 'a necessary phase in the development of truth.' It is as if mind uses individuals for its unwitting tool. Let us take an example from Marxian theory that may elucidate the connection between Hegel's *Philosophy of History* and the subsequent evolution of the dialectic. Marx held that during a developed industrial capitalism individual capitalists are compelled to adapt their enterprises to the rapid progress of technology in order to assure their profits and outdo their competitors. They thereby reduce the amount of labor-power they employ and thus, since their surplus value is produced only by labor-power, reduce the rate of profit at the disposal of their class. In this way they accelerate the disintegrating tendencies of the social system they want to maintain.

The process of reason working itself out through individuals, however, does not occur with natural necessity, nor does it have a continuous and unilinear course. 'There are many considerable periods in history in which this development seems to have been intermitted; in which, we might rather say, the whole enormous gain of previous culture appears to have been entirely lost; after which, unhappily, a new commencement has been necessary.' There are periods of 'retrocession' alternating with periods of steady advance. Regress, when it occurs, is not an 'external contingency' but, as we shall see, is part of the dialectic of historical change; an advance to a higher plane of history first requires that the negative forces inherent in all reality get the upper hand. The higher phase, however, is finally to be reached; every obstacle on the road to freedom is surmountable, given the efforts of a self-conscious mankind.

This is the universal principle of history. It is not a 'law,' in the scientific sense of the term, such, for example, as governs matter. Matter in its structure and motion has unchangeable laws that carry on and maintain it, but matter is nowhere the subject of its processes, nor has it any power over them. A being, on the other hand, that is the active and conscious subject of its existence stands under quite different laws. Self-conscious practice becomes part of the very content of the laws, so that the latter operate as laws only in so far as they are taken into the subject's will and influence his acts. The universal law of history is, in Hegel's formulation, not simply progress to freedom, but progress 'in the self-consciousness of freedom.' A set of historical tendencies becomes a law only if man comprehends and acts on them. Historical laws, in other words, originate and are actual only in man's conscious practice, so that if, for instance, there is a law of progress to ever higher forms of freedom, it ceases to operate if man fails to recognize and execute it. Hegel's philosophy of history might amount to a deterministic theory, but the determining factor is at least freedom. Progress depends on man's ability to grasp the universal interest of reason and on his will and vigor in making it a reality.

But if the *particular* wants and interests of men are the sole springs of their action, how can self-consciousness of freedom ever motivate human practice? To answer this question we must again ask, Who is the actual subject of history? Whose practice is historical practice? Individuals, it would seem, are merely agents of history. Their consciousness is conditioned by their personal interest; they make business, not history. There are some individuals, however, who rise above this level; their actions do not repeat old patterns but create new forms of life. Such men are men of history *kat'exochen, welthistorische Individuen,* like Alexander, Caesar, Napoleon. Their acts, too, spring from personal interests, but in their case these become identical with the universal interest and the latter far transcends the interest of any particular group: they forge and administer the progress of history. Their interest must necessarily clash with the particular

interest of the prevailing system of life. Historical individuals are men of a time when 'momentous collisions' arise 'between existing, acknowledged duties, laws, and rights, and those potentialities which are adverse to this fixed system; which assail and even destroy its foundations and existence.' These potentialities appear to the historical individual as choices for his specific power, but they involve a 'universal principle' in so far as they are the choice of a higher form of life that has ripened within the existing system. Historical individuals thus anticipated 'the necessary... sequent step in progress which their world was to take.' What they desired and struggled for was 'the very truth for their age, for their world.' Conscious of 'the requirements of the the time' and of 'what was ripe for development,' they acted.

Even these men of history, however, are not yet the actual subjects of history. They are the executors of its will, the 'agents of the World Mind,' no more. They are victims of a higher necessity, which acts itself out in their lives; they are still mere instruments for historical progress.

The final subject of history Hegel calls the world mind (*Weltgeist*). Its reality lies in those actions, tendencies, efforts, and institutions that embody the interest of freedom and reason. It does not exist separate from these realities, and acts through these agents and agencies. The law of history, which the world mind represents, thus operates behind the backs and over the heads of individuals, in the form of an irresistible anonymous power. The transition from Oriental culture to that of the Greek world, the rise of feudalism, the establishment of bourgeois society —all these changes were not man's free work, but the necessary results of objective historical forces. Hegel's conception of the world mind emphasizes that in these previous periods of recorded history man was not the self-conscious master of his existence. The divine power of the world mind appeared then an objective force that rules over the actions of men.

The sovereignty of the world mind, as Hegel portrays it, exhibits the dark traits of a world that is controlled by the forces of history instead of controlling them. While these forces are as yet unknown in their true essence, they bring misery and destruction in their wake. History then appears as 'the slaughter-bench at which the happiness of peoples, the wisdom of States, and the virtue of individuals have been victimized.' Hegel at the same time extols the sacrifice of individual and general happiness that results. He calls it 'the *cunning of reason.*' Individuals lead unhappy lives, they toil and perish, but though they actually never win their goal, their distress and defeat are the very means by which truth and freedom proceed. A man never reaps the fruits of his labor; they always fall to future generations. His passions and interests, however, do not succumb; they are devices that keep him working in the service of a superior power and a superior interest. 'This may be called the *cunning of reason*— that it sets the passions to work for itself, while that which develops its existence through such impulsion pays the penalty, and suffers loss.' Individuals fail and pass away; the idea triumphs and is eternal.

The idea triumphs precisely because individuals perish in defeat. It is not the 'Idea that is implicated in opposition and combat, and that is exposed to danger. It remains in the background, untouched and uninjured' while 'individuals are sacrificed and abandoned. The Idea pays the penalty of existence and of transitoriness not from itself,

but from the passions of individuals.' But can this idea still be regarded as the incarnation of truth and freedom? Kant had emphatically insisted that it would contradict man's nature to use him as a mere means. Only a few decades later Hegel declares himself in favor of 'the idea that individuals, their desires and the gratification of them, are...sacrificed, and their happiness given up to the empire of chance, to which it belongs; and that as a general rule, individuals come under the category of means.' He confesses that where man is simply an object of superior historical processes he can be an end in himself only in the domain of morality and religion.

The world mind is the hypostatic subject of history; it is a metaphysical substitute for the real subject, the unfathomable God of a frustrated humanity, hidden and awful, like the God of the Calvinists; the mover of a world in which all that occurs does so despite the conscious actions of man and at the expense of his happiness. 'History...is not the theater of happiness. Periods of happiness are blank pages in it.'

This metaphysical subject, however, assumes concrete form as soon as Hegel raises the question of how the world mind materializes itself. 'In what material is the idea of Reason wrought out?' The world mind strives to realize freedom and can materialize itself only in the real realm of freedom, that is, in the *state.* Here, the world mind is, as it were, institutionalized; here it finds the self-consciousness through which the law of history operates.

The *Philosophy of History* does not discuss (as did the *Philosophy of Right*) the *idea* of the state; it discusses its various concrete historical forms. Hegel's well-known schema distinguishes three main historical stages in the development of freedom: the Oriental, the Greco-Roman, and the German-Christian.

The Orientals have not attained the knowledge that Mind—man *as such*—is free; and because they do not know this, they are not free. They only know that *one is free*. But on this very account, the freedom of that one is only caprice. . . . That *one* is therefore only a Despot, not free man. The consciousness of freedom first arose among the Greeks, and therefore they were free; but they, and the Romans likewise, knew only that *some* are free—not man as such. . . . The Greeks, therefore, had slaves; and their whole life and the maintenance of their splendid liberty, was implicated with the institution of slavery. . . . The German nations, under the influence of Christianity, were the first to attain the consciousness, that man, as man, is free: that it is the *freedom* of Mind which constitutes its essence.

Hegel distinguishes three typical state forms to correspond to the three main phases in the development of freedom: 'The East knew and to the present day knows only that One is free; the Greek and Roman world, that some are free; the German world knows that all are free. The first political form, therefore, which we observe in history, is despotism, the second democracy and aristocracy, the third monarchy.' At first, this is no more than the Aristotelian typology applied to universal history. The monarchic holds first rank as the perfectly free state form, by virtue of its rule of right and law under constitutional guarantees. 'In monarchy, . . . there is one lord and no serf, for servitude is abrogated by it; and in it Right and Law are recognized; it is the source of real freedom. Thus in monarchy, the caprice of individuals is kept under, and a common gubernatorial interest established.' Hegel's judgment here is based on the fact that he regards the modern absolutist state to be an advance over the feudal system.

He has reference to the strongly centralized bourgeois state that overcame the revolutionary terror of 1793. Freedom, he has shown, begins with property, unfolds itself in the universal rule of law that acknowledges and secures the equal right to property, and terminates in the state, which is able to cope with the antagonisms that attend freedom of property. Consequently, the history of freedom comes to an end with the advent of modern monarchy, which, in Hegel's time, achieved this goal.

The *Philosophy of Right* had concluded with the statement that the right of the state is subordinate to the right of the world mind and to the judgment of universal history. Hegel now develops this point. He gives the various state forms their place in the course of history, first coordinating each with its representative historical period. Hegel does not mean to say that the Oriental world knew only despotism, the Greco-Roman only democracy, and the German only monarchy. His scheme rather implies that despotism is the political form most adequate to the material and intellectual culture of the Orient, and the other political forms respectively to the other historical periods. He then proceeds to assert that the unity of the state is conditioned by the prevailing national culture; that is, the state depends on such factors as the geographical location and the natural, racial, and social qualities of the nation. This is the purport of his concept of national mind (*Volksgeist*). The latter is the manifestation of the world mind at a given stage of historical development; it is the subject of national history in the same sense as the world mind is the subject of universal history. National history must be understood in terms of universal history. 'Each particular National genius is to be treated as only one individual in the process of Universal History.' The history of a nation has to be judged according to its contribution to the progress of all mankind towards the self-consciousness of freedom. The various nations do not contribute equally; some are active promoters of this progress. These are the world-historical nations (*welthisto-rische Volksgeister*). The decisive jumps to new and higher forms of life occur in their history, while other nations play more minor roles.

The question as to the relation of a particular state to the world mind may now be answered. Every form of state must be evaluated according to whether it is adequate to the stage of historical consciousness that mankind has reached. Freedom does not and cannot mean the same thing in the different periods of history, for in each period one type of freedom is the true one. The state must be built on the acknowledgment of this freedom. The German world, through the Reformation, produced in its course that kind of freedom which recognized the essential equality of men. Constitutional monarchy expresses and integrates this form of society. It is for Hegel the consummation of the realization of freedom.

GEORGE H. SABINE

Hegel's Political Philosophy[*]

In his brilliant essays on the long un-published works of Hegel's youth, Wilhelm Dilthey proved that Hegel's philosophy was at bottom a philosophy of civilization, that it arose in an effort to grasp the meaning of certain critical phases in the evolution of European culture, and that it was only later brought to that abstract, dialectical and metaphysical mode of statement which became its best known characteristic. More recent analysis of Hegel's early writings has amply verified Dilthey's position. In short, Hegel's philosophy originated in an effort to deal scientifically or philosophically with quite concrete, often practical, problems presented by the state of religious, social, and political thought in his day, and only partly in the technical problems of Kant's and Fichte's metaphysics and epistemology. If Hegel's philosophy be approached as a system to be proved or disproved, the validity of his dialectic as a logical instrument is of major importance, but the end of merely understanding his thought, as a human creation and as a product of German

* Reprinted from *The Philosophical Review,* No. 41 (1932), 261–82, by permission of the editors. The footnotes found in the original have been omitted here.

and of European intelligence, is better served by trying to show the concrete difficulties from which it arose. It is the purpose of the present paper to investigate this question, so far as Hegel's philosophy of society and the state is concerned. The most distinctive characteristics of his philosophy are quite intelligible when they are placed side by side with the problems, as Hegel conceived them, which in that day confronted Germany.

Hegel's point of departure was the socialized history of the Enlightenment, history as it had been written most typically by Voltaire and Montesquieu, and the most original result of his early studies was an advance toward a truer and more adequate historicity. History as it was written by the great writers of the Enlightenment had been in spirit practical, utilitarian, directed toward a statesmanlike control of the political and social condiditions which it described. It had dealt typically with the causes of the rise, the greatness, and the decline of nations, with national character and its physical and economic conditions, with the adjustment of laws and institutions to national character and the exigencies of social existence. It set up reason, or what it took to be reason, as the standard of what is and what ought to be, and it looked with impatience upon custom, creed, speculation, metaphysics and upon all that it regarded as superstition and illusion. In the same breath, it glorified the rationality of human nature and condemned as folly the most of what human nature in its history had produced.

But Hegel, in common with the ablest of his German contemporaries, had been deeply stirred by a far-reaching renaissance of Greek studies. For him the two great historical forces in western civilization were Greece, with its free intelligence and its creative imagination,

and Christianity, with what he conceived to be its deeper religious and ethical insight. From Kant, Hegel had learned, what indeed was implicit in all the later forms of religious Platonism, that no formulation of religious or moral truth, in conceptual or sensuous terms, could be adequate to the inner truth toward which the spirit groped. Great Germans before Hegel had had the same thought, and had added its corollary, that if every formulation is inadequate, all perhaps contain some adumbration of the truth. This thought, in Herder and Lessing, had given the Enlightenment in Germany a tone significantly different from that which it possessed in France and England.

Thus Hegel's problem was set for him: Why should a purely spiritual religion, such as he conceived Christianity to be, have been forced to create for itself a framework of creeds and dogmas necessarily illusory from the standpoint of pure intelligence? Why must it transform its historic founder into a myth? Why must it express itself in the sensuous symbols of observance and build for itself an ecclesiastical organization in which too soon the free religious spirit of the early Christian community was lost? And having thus embodied its soul, wherein did it surpass and why did it supersede its predecessors and contemporaries, the religions of Greece, of Rome, and of the Jews? Profoundly as these historical questions touched Hegel, his interest in them was at no time antiquarian. Indeed, he started with the strictly practical purpose of revivifying popular religion, of finding for it something less doctrinaire than the religion of reason and something less benighted than ecclesiasticism. In such a religion even myth must find its not wholly irrational place. At no time is this practical purpose engulfed by theoretical or dialectical problems. In his mode of approaching Christianity there is an important clue for understanding his way of approaching any social problem: he characteristically seeks to criticize and evaluate an institution as one element of a larger social and cultural whole, partly indeed in the light of the past and of the surrounding circumstances, but also with an eye upon its probable development. The investigation is meant to promote understanding of the present and the future, and in this broad sense it may be called practical, but the sense is quite different from the planning and contriving and manipulating which the Enlightenment associated with the rational study of history. For Hegel it is the total cultural life of a people, the *Volksgeist,* which runs its appointed course and provides the arena in which the national hero meets his spiritual fate.

Out of Hegel's study of the formative period of Christianity there emerged what are obviously the germs of some of his most characteristic ideas. He came to see that a certain course of development was imposed upon Christianity merely by the growing size of the Christian community. He recognized that fundamental characteristics of Judaism were a natural consequence of the history and national experience of the Jews. He pictured to himself the myth of Jesus as the spontaneous expression of Christian ideals through the medium of religious imagination. He reached the conclusion that Christianity would in fact never have been able to conquer the ancient world, had that world not already lost its old free spirit, and thus he arrived at the broad generalization that important features in the spiritual life of the Hellenistic age—its mysticism, pessimism, and world-weariness—are correlated with the loss of civic freedom in the city-state. This social phenomenon he interpreted as a turning-back of the spirit upon itself,

a consequence of losing its natural and happy mode of self-expression and the condition both of other-worldliness and of a deeper consciousness of self. Thus there occurs that withdrawal of the spirit which is at once an alienation and the ground for its return to itself upon a higher level. In a word, Hegel arrived at the conception of religion as an integrated whole, including its myths and creeds and formularies, and as an outgrowth of the whole social consciousness of a people and an age, arising as a necessary response of the spirit to its ideals and the circumstances under which those ideals must be realized.

It is certainly true that, in this early period of his life, the absorbing social interest which guided Hegel's thought was religion. And yet, when we turn to his early writings on politics, we find a similarity both of purpose and conception. There is the same rather unusual combination of practical interest with historical study, the same conception of institutions as the expression of a national spirit and the organs of a national life, and the same sense of inward determination by an expanding social spirit. The frustration of spirit which Hegel regards as the key to the rise of Christianity he conceives to be also, *mutatis mutandis,* the mark of his own age and the key to vast social and spiritual changes which he hopes, or perhaps foresees, for Germany. Between the spirit of Germany and the actual state of German politics he finds a complete discrepancy which portends a new day, for the spirit will be served. Writing in 1789, doubtless still under the drive of a youthful enthusiasm kindled by the French Revolution, he says: "The silent acquiescence in things as they are, the hopelessness, the patient endurance of a vast, overmastering fate, has turned to hope, to expectation, to the will for something different. The vision of a better and a juster time has entered alive into the souls of men, and a desire, a longing, for a purer, freer condition has moved every heart and has alienated it from the existing state of affairs. . . . Call this, if you like, a fever-paroxism, but it will end either in death or in eliminating the cause of the disease." Had he been writing a few years later, Hegel would certainly have looked with less complacency upon the risks of disorder inherent in a fever-paroxism, yet it remained true always that he looked forward to a new philosophy and a new social life. At no time was he a revolutionist—he believed too fervently in the essential rightness of the institutions in which the national life had embodied itself—and yet his political writing was at once a prophecy and an appeal, but it was an appeal rather to the communal will of the nation than to the self-help of its individual members. For the spirit cannot remain forever alienated from its expression: "How blind are they who can imagine that institutions, constitutions, and laws can persist after they have ceased to be in accord with the morals, the needs, and the purposes of mankind, and after the meaning has gone out of them; that forms in which understanding and feeling are no longer involved can retain the power to bind a nation!" Such institutions must change or give place to new embodiments of national aspiration.

This thought is expanded and particularized, with special reference to the existing condition of Germany, in the essay which Hegel wrote in 1802 on the *Constitution of Germany*. The work begins with the striking assertion, "Germany is no longer a state". Hegel proceeds to make this good with an exceedingly able analysis of the decline of the Empire from the time of the Peace of Westphalia. Germany, he argues, has become merely an anarch-

ical collection of virtually independent states. It is a name which has the connotations of past greatness, but as an institution it is wholly out of accord with the existing realities of European politics. In particular, it is to be contrasted with the unified national governments which modern monarchy brought into being in France, England, and Spain, and which have failed to develop in Italy and Germany. Able as Hegel's historical analysis is, however, it is obviously a means and not an end. His purpose in examining the process of national unification elsewhere is to raise the question, How may Germany become a real state?

In common with many of his contemporaries, Hegel finds the cause of the Empire's weakness in the particularism and individualism and love of independence which he takes to be a national characteristic of the German people. Culturally the Germans are a nation, but they have never learned the subordination of parts to the whole which is essential both for a national government and for real political freedom. The love of freedom, by refusing to submit to the conditions which alone make national liberty possible, has proved self-defeating. The Empire has no power except what the parts give it, and the existing constitution has in fact no purpose except to keep the state weak. The free cities, the independent princes, the estates, the guilds, and the religious sects go their own way, absorbing the rights of the state and paralysing its action—and all with a good show of legal right in the antiquated feudal law that governs the Empire. The motto of Germany, as Hegel says with bitter irony, is, "Fiat justitia, pereat Germania". The fundaental weakness, as Hegel states it, is a thoroughgoing confusion of private and constitutional law, which is, of course, only another name for feudalism. There is in Germany no constitutional law according to principles. Legislative, judicial, ecclesiastical, and military privileges are combined and separated, bought and sold, like so many pieces of private property. This criticism of the existing situation in Germany must be kept in mind when we come to consider the distinction of the state and civil society, with its attendant separation of public and private law, which is one of the characteristic features of Hegel's finished political theory.

This diagnosis of Germany's ills leads Hegel to a definition of the state. A state is a group which collectively protects its property. The only powers which are necessary to it are a civil and a military administration adequate to this end. In other words, a state is *de facto* power; an expression, to be sure, of a unity of national will or a national aspiration to self-government, but fundamentally the power to make this will effective by civil government at home and by military defense abroad. A state exists wherever such a power is actually found. Accordingly, the existence of a state is quite consistent with any lack of uniformity which does not prevent effective defense. The form of government, equality of civil rights, uniformity of law throughout the national domain, the existence of privileged classes, even differences of customs, culture, language, and religion, are all indifferent in themselves. One is reminded strikingly of a sixteenth-century writer like Jean Bodin, not because Hegel copied Bodin but because the problem of national government in Germany when Hegel wrote really is in broad outline like that in France when Bodin wrote. One is reminded also of the tenderness of the historical school for differences of local custom. In the same spirit Hegel criticizes drastically the "pedantic" sort of centralized government which tries to do everything. Here he is evidently thinking of republican France and of Prussia. The upshot of the argument is that Germany may become a state despite its internal diversity.

As for the means by which this end may be brought about, Hegel looks to the rise of a great military leader or conqueror who will nonetheless consent to rule as a constitutional monarch. That strong and well unified national government must depend upon strengthening the monarch he takes to be proved by the experience of France, Spain, and England, in all of which local and feudal differences similar to those existing in Germany had been repressed and the national state amalgamated by the growing power of the sovereign. "From the period when these countries grew to be states dates their power, their wealth, and the free condition of their citizens under the law." For Hegel, obviously, freedom has almost the same meaning as for King James, when he spoke of the "True Law of Free Monarchy", though for Hegel more than for James the typical modern government is a constitutional rather than an absolute monarchy. Emphatically he does not believe that Germany will ever be unified by general consent, by mere national sentiment, or by any peaceful method. His bitterness sometimes suggests the terrible blast against Fries in the Preface of the *Philosophie des Rechts*, as when he remarks, with characteristic irony, that "Gangrene is not cured with lavender-water". It is war rather than peace that shows the health of a state. The two heroic figures of modern politics are, for Hegel, Machiavelli and Richelieu. The *Prince* he calls "the great and true conception of a real political genius with the highest and noblest intention". For the rules of private morality do not hold between states; a state has no higher duty than to preserve and strengthen itself. Richelieu's enemies—the French nobility and the Huguenots—went down not before Richelieu but before the principle of French national unity which he represented, and Hegel adds the characteristic remark, "Political genius consists in identifying yourself with a principle". The modernizing of Germany calls for an era of blood and iron—an estimate which the facts confirmed, though in 1802 Hegel expected more from Austria than from Prussia.

In conclusion it should be pointed out that Hegel, when he wrote this rather extraordinary essay on the *Constitution of Germany,* already had a pretty definite idea of the method which he was following. His purpose, as he explains, is to promote understanding of things as they are, to exhibit political history not as arbitrary but as necessary. For unhappiness results from the discrepancy between what is and what men are fain to believe ought to be. And they are prone to imagine that events are mere unrelated details and not "a system ruled by a spirit". Only when they realize that what is must be will they perceive that it also ought to be. But no one who reads the essay can imagine for a moment that Hegel's purpose is to instill political quietism. He is using the device of many strong spirits who prefer to show that the ends they seek are inevitable, rather than to commend them as desirable. What is necessary for Hegel is not the *status quo* but the modernizing and nationalizing of Germany.

We have now seen something of the sort of political problems which concerned Hegel in his early manhood and also the point of view from which he approached them. As yet he writes as a publicist rather than as a philosopher; indeed one wonders, as one reads his glowing tribute to Machiavelli, whether there may not have glittered before Hegel's eyes an ambition to be the Machiavelli of Germany. The astonishing array of dialectical abstractions which often makes the *Philosophie des Rechts* so hard to follow is very little in evidence. On the other hand, there is a firm grasp of historical actualities, indeed a kind of hard political realism, which appears in the later work only by flashes, though often it can be read between the lines. Let us turn now to Hegel's political philosophy in its final form to see how far we can trace a relation between the concrete difficulties that confronted Germany in the opening years of the nineteenth century, at least as Hegel understood those difficulties, and the theories at which he finally arrived. We cannot here undertake a lengthy exposition of Hegel's philosophy of the state, but must confine ourselves to a few chosen aspects which present its typical features. For this purpose we may take, first, the dialectical method as a device for interpreting social phenomena; second, the distinction which Hegel draws between the state and civil society; and third, his theory of freedom. In all three cases, it can easily be shown that his theories, whatever validity they may have, were at least not produced merely by manipulating concepts but had social actualities in view, especially those which bulked large in the experience of Germany.

I. Possibly it may be open to doubt whether the dialectical method ought to be counted as belonging typically to Hegel's social and political philosophy. Certainly it belongs also to his logic and metaphysics, and the problems which it involves in those connections are much too difficult to be discussed as mere incidents of one side of his system; of these problems nothing need be said here. Nevertheless, it is clear that the principles of the dialectic were deeply involved in his whole conception of social philosophy. We have already seen that, even when he wrote the essay on the *Constitution of Germany,* his intention was to show that what is is necessary, and that his purpose in so doing was to produce that reconciliation of the individual with reality which he regarded as necessary for effective action. Manifestly it is the same principle which appears later as the postulate that the real is rational. The further principle, that will is "thought translating itself into being or the impulse of thought to give itself existence", is evidently intended to provide the groundwork for the logical necessity of the historical process. At the same time, it is obvious that the necessity which Hegel attributed to history was really a moral necessity, the rational self-development of the Absolute. Necessity he always regarded as consistent with "transient existence (*Dasein*), external contingency, opinion, unessential appearance, untruth, illusion, etc." Underlying this he presumes a connected tendency or trend (*Begriff* or *Wirklichkeit*) which gives meaning and value. It is this union of logical necessity and historical or ethical significance in the dialectic which calls for a new logic, not of the understanding but of reason.

We have already seen that, very early in Hegel's career, he felt the need of a new instrument for understanding and evaluating culture, especially the rise of Christianity and its significance in European civilization. Thus he early formed the conception of religion, and indeed of morals, politics, and art, as expressions of a national spirit, working out its destiny in the historic situation peculiar to it and making its proper contribution to world-history. The free and harmonious expression of a nation's personality is at first instinctive and but half conscious. The breaking-up of this happy mode of life produces painful self-consciousness, alienation from the world as it is, and a sense of frustration, but this very disharmony is the means to a new harmony upon a higher level of spiritual self-expression. It was thus that Hegel conceived the other-worldliness of the Christian-Hellenistic period, supervening upon the natural grace and beauty of classical Greece. It was in some such terms also that he conceived the unhappiness of his own age. The disunion and feebleness of Germany are not marks of decay but rather the travail of the German spirit about to give birth to a new philosophy and a new social and political order. The only cure for the intolerable sense of futility and self-alienation lies in perceiving the necessity of what is, not, be it noted, in its literal factual existence, but as the transition to a higher realization of the human spirit.

As a working method, the dialectic apparently took form in Hegel's mind by a series of negations. That is to say, it followed a middle course between several extremes which he desired to avoid. Thus there is an unquestionable affinity between the dialectic and the historical study of philosophy, religion, law, and other products of civilization. This Hegel acknowledged, and it must be admitted that his own historical insight was often astonishingly keen. It was equally true, however, that the dialectic often falsified history, and certainly nothing was further from Hegel's intention than the writing of historical narrative. The dialectic is supposed to place facts, even down to the smallest details, in their proper philosophical perspective, but the facts by themselves cannot be made to display what he calls "the necessity of the concept". Accordingly, Hegel regards historical positivism as quite unphilosophical, and indeed as quite impractical. Thus he separates himself sharply from historical jurists in his preference for statutory and codified law over customary law. It is true that laws and constitutions grow rather than are made, but they do not grow without an effort toward intellectual organization. The dialectic makes room for history and uses it, but it is never merely history. It is intended always to serve as a measure of significance and hence it always stands, so to speak, between past and future time. It is not, in the usual sense of the word, practical, but it is designed to produce a certain sort of moral attitude—that of acquiescence and coöperation.

But Hegel has his own peculiar mode of moral exhortation. In nothing is he so unmeasured as in his condemnation of sentiment and mere good feeling, whether of a social or moral kind. Feeling belongs peculiarly to the sphere of what Hegel calls bitingly "the hypocrisy of good intentions", and as such it is either weak or fanatical, and in both cases futile. Unquestionably, Hegel carries this contempt of subjective attitudes to an unjustifiable extreme, but it is one of his most characteristic notes. It reflects his utter disbelief in the efficacy of unorganized emotion to accomplish anything in a world where effectiveness is the ultimate criterion of right. Had he not before his eyes the spectacle of German impotence, despite a very real sentiment of nationality? Hegel's heroes are not men of feeling but men of action, even men of brute strength, and his state is an embodiment of power. This conclusion represents both his reading of history and his expectation for Germany. But force for him is not mere strength; it is rather the outward and visible symbol of ethical right, which for Hegel is the same as logical necessity. Might is right for right makes might, and right prevails not because men like it but because of the inherent logic of history.

The spirit of a nation is not merely national sentiment. It is the national will to power, already embodied in moral and legal institutions, and this will is thought translating itself into being. The great man is the man who can tell the time what it wills. From this point of view, therefore, the dialectic connotes avoidance of mere aspiration. It is aspiration which sustains itself by belief in its inevitable success.

It is this same sense of the inevitable in social progress which leads Hegel to deny to philosophy the power to direct or control social change. "Minerva's owl begins its flight only in the gathering dusk." Philosophy brings reconciliation with reality, not the power to command its course. Hegel's whole conception of history is filled with a sense of the irony of life. Men build better and worse than they know; almost never does the accomplishment precisely equal the expectation. Hence from Hegel's point of view utilitarianism is always a superficial kind of philosophy. At the same time, it would be a total misreading of Hegel to suppose that the necessity of history connotes quietism or passive acquiescence. What it connotes is rather an active coöperation. Hegel's point of view is that which has often, perhaps usually, been taken by the reformer imbued with religious zeal, the position that made Luther and Calvin passionate enemies of the doctrine of free will, as it was taught by the intelligent but somewhat skeptical Erasmus. Nothing strengthens the sinews like believing that one stands at Armageddon and battles for the Lord, not because the issue is in doubt, but because one is ranged on the side of eternal right.

As a way of looking at social phenomena, therefore, the dialectic represents a point upon which Hegel's thought converged as it was thrown back from several alternative positions which he felt constrained to reject. It was designed to be not utilitarian and at the same time not quietist. It was meant to have at once the force of sentiment and the rigor of logic, to produce that acquiescence in the force and validity of the social system which will free all the individual's creative efforts to coöperate in the realization of social purposes. It is designed to provide an intelligible framework for a more accurate historicity without losing itself in the minutiae of historical positivism. This strange interweaving of motives is sufficient to account for the difficulty, if not the impossibility, of turning the dialectic into a clear-cut method. In particular, Hegel's effort to give it the status of rigid logic reacts in the most unfortunate way upon his social philosophy. Nothing is ever put forward on the simple ground that it is psychologically or historically sound. Abstract individualism, for example, is treated as a theory which is unexceptionable so long as we look at the social system from the point of view of the understanding and which therefore requires a new logic of reason to controvert it. The old position is left standing to be "mediated" later in the new. This works havoc with the organization of the *Philosophie des Rechts*. It leads to the anomaly that the sphere of abstract right is placed apparently outside the social system, with all the numerous artificialities in the arrangement of subject-matter which follows. The dialectic as actually applied goes far to conceal one of Hegel's most fruitful ideas, *viz.*, that economic, political, legal, and ethical institutions are all mutually interdependent.

II. The second main feature of Hegel's political theory which we shall examine is the broad distinction which he draws between the state and civil society. We have already seen how, in his essay on the *Constitution of Germany,* he stressed the confusion of public and private law as a major weakness of The Empire. For Hegel the state is no utilitarian institution, engaged in the commonplace business of providing public services, administering the law, performing police duties, and adjusting industrial and economic interests. All these functions belong to civil society. They must, of course, be adjusted to the needs of the state, which stand far above them in importance, and the state may regulate and supervise them as occasion requires, but the state does not itself perform them. The state is not the means but the end, the rational ideal in historical development, and the truly spiritual or intelligent element in civilization. Hence the romantic idealization so typical of Hegel's description of the state as the absolutely rational, the divinity which knows and wills itself, the eternal and necessary being of spirit, the march of God in the world, and much more to the same effect. Hence also the fact that for Hegel the essential nature of the state appears perhaps more clearly in war and in foreign relations than in the peace-time working of its internal constitution. In war the utilitarian nature of civil society is obviously subordinated, and in its relations with other states the supreme duty of the state to preserve itself, its superiority to treaties and any form of international organization, and its right to be judged only in the court of world-history, are manifest.

It should be noted, however, that Hegel's subordination of civil society to the state by no means implies contempt of the latter or an inclination to disregard the economic and administrative problems of society, but the contrary. The economic life of society and even the homely details of its administration are glorified as the humble but necessary agencies upon which the state, with its august mission, depends. Nothing is more characteristic of Hegel than his endless effort to trace a principle down to the smallest details. Among books upon political philosophy of its date, the *Philosophie des Rechts* is notable for the seriousness with which it treats trade and industry. Moreover, Hegel was undoubtedly charmed by the apparent paradox of civil society. It is founded, according to his view, explicitly upon individual self-seeking and yet it works out to a system of mutual coöperation. In this he sees, of course, the working of the universal upon the particulars, much as Adam Smith had seen in it the working of an "unseen hand". Out of a swarm of apparently accidental details and individual motives there arise necessary laws which govern the whole process, as gravitation governs the motions of the planets. The economic determination of history, which Karl Marx was later to erect upon the foundation of a modified Hegelianism, served a purpose quite different from those which Hegel had in view, and yet it was almost a legitimate deduction from Hegel's view of civil society, if once the orientation of civil society toward a national state be expunged from the theory.

Hegel's separation of the state from civil society is wholly out of accord with the English tradition in political philosophy, and to a large extent meaningless from the standpoint of English and French political experience. On the other hand, it corresponds quite accurately to the experience of Germany. Manifestly the problem of creating a central government in Germany, with its multitude of independent princes and free cities, was something quite different from the problem of existing national government in England and France. German national government was predetermined to be of the federal kind, arising by the association, but not

the amalgamation, of the existing local governments. Hegel himself was quite aware of the difference. We have seen that in his early work on the *Constitution of Germany* he had expressed a low opinion of French centralization; this he repeats in the *Philosophie des Rechts*. Highly centralized government such as the republican and Napoleonic eras had made effective in France he regards, with a good deal of justification, as merely the obverse of individualism; if the citizen is to figure only as an isolated person, the state will figure as the only form of corporate life. This Hegel held to be undesirable in itself and wholly impossible in Germany.

On the other hand, English parliamentarism appeared to Hegel to be merely a modified form of class-government by an aristocracy, a judgment not without justification at the time. A thoroughgoing dislike of government by an hereditary patrician oligarchy was one of Hegel's earliest political convictions, and that English government belongs essentially to this type was one of his maturest judgments; it lacks *der grosse Sinn von Fürsten*. His reading of modern history had convinced him that the monarchy had everywhere been the agency of national unification, and this led him to the conclusion that constitutional monarchy is the distinctively modern form of government, the form in which the spirit of nationality must realize itself. In the light of this conviction we can understand Hegel's mystical reverence for the monarch. In believing that national unity in Germany could be achieved only by attaching unique importance to the monarchy, Hegel was of course fully justified by the history of the nineteenth century.

From Hegel's point of view, therefore, the state is not composed primarily of its individual citizens. The organization of lesser communities and corporations is united in a political and social hierarchy of which the state is the apex. The people, considered as individuals, are merely a formless mass. Only as members of estates, of classes, of guilds and associations (*Genossenschaften*), and of local communities do they acquire moral dignity and the right to participate in the life of the state. The persistence of guild-organizations appeals to Hegel as a valuable feature of German economic life, and he comments upon their disappearance in England and France as accounting for distinctive aspects of English and French politics. For Hegel, therefore, the distinction of civil society from the state is essential. The individual is "mediated" by a series of communities from the family at the bottom, through the estates and the associations in the middle, to the state at the top. The state must be conceived by principles quite different from those which govern its subordinate members. Its strength lies precisely in this balance between the sovereign above and the subsidiary communities below. Hegel's conception of the state remained what it explicitly was in his early work on the *Constitution of Germany,* a statement of the conditions upon which it appeared to him possible that Germany might become a modernized state.

Much light is thrown upon this conception by Hegel's efforts to deal with the problem of political representation. For the reasons already stated the representation of individuals upon an arbitrary territorial basis appeared to Hegel to be almost meaningless. In a very early political work he already expresses his distrust of this device— supposed to be the very essence of responsible constitutional government— for a population mostly without political experience. In the *Philosophie des Rechts* the legislature is treated as the point at which the institutions of civil

society make contact with the state. What needs to be represented, therefore, is not the individual but the significant spheres (*Kreise*), or interests, or functional units, of civil society. In the essay on the English Reform Bill, written just before Hegel's death, the same principle is used in criticism of the projected popularization of the suffrage. Hegel speaks with approval of the conservative argument that the great interests of the nation ought to form the basis of representation. There was no doubt in Hegel's mind at any time that constitutional monarchy implied representation in some form, nor that representation by the estates was unsuitable to the existing state of society, but he felt only distrust for popular representation on the basis of numbers alone. His conception of the state was necessarily federal, but he envisaged federal government in a somewhat medieval form, not as a territorial but rather as a functional federalization. What he desired, and what for obvious reasons he was unable to formulate satisfactorily, was a revision of the estates to fit society as he found it. Undoubtedly, he failed to grasp the disintegrating force of modernized industry, and this is probably to be explained by the fact that these forces had not proceeded so far in Germany as in either France or England.

III. Hegel's theory of freedom, or of the relation between society and the individual, includes at once the most generally accepted and the most generally controverted part of his social philosophy. On the one hand, the theory brought into relief certain historical and psychological considerations which were, in general, obvious but which received no adequate consideration from the doctrinaire individualism of the revolutionary era. On the other hand, it drew certain deductions, or at least suggested them, which made the use of the word freedom seem a paradox. It will be best to consider these two phases of the theory of freedom separately.

In most general terms what Hegel undertook to do was to reunite the individual with the social system of which he is a member. He urges the obvious fact that civilization is, in general, not foreign to, or repressive of, individual self-expression; that social forces are a medium in which the individual always moves and from which he derives the elements even of his individuality; that to be a man at all requires participation in the life of some sort of communities; that education and culture are in general a means of liberation; and that there is little freedom in a vaunted state of nature, at least as savages experience it. Few parts of Hegel's work are more enlightening than his proof that economic wants are social, as distinguished from mere biological needs, that custom and law are at once distinctively human and distinctively social, and that rights and duties are correlative and fall within the legal system. Individual freedom is therefore itself a social phenomenon, produced in the moral development of a community and protected by legal and ethical institutions which the community alone can provide.

There can be no doubt that this is a valuable corrective to the theory of doctrinaire individualism, especially to the extravagant paradoxes of Rousseau's early essays. Hegel swung back in the direction of Greek political theory, toward the view that individual good implies the performance of a socially valuable task; the influence of Plato upon him is unmistakable. His theory was, moreover, part of a widespread reaction against the violence of the French Revolution, not unlike what we find in Edmund Burke. There was the best of reasons why the case against

the Revolution should first have been stated with philosophical clearness by a German philosopher. The theory of natural rights, while of course fully known to educated Germans, had never made itself at home in Germany. In England and France the seventeenth and eighteenth centuries had seen the theory transformed to a defense of revolution, and Germany was a country in which there was no revolution. Developed as an instrument in the hands of a religious minority to be used against a hostile centralized government, it was a theory which had few uses in the one country where differences of religion coincided in general with political boundaries. And after religious differences receded into the background of politics, and natural rights tended to be transformed into a doctrine of economic *laissez faire,* the relatively backward industrialization of Germany, as compared with England and France, again failed to furnish a soil in which the theory would naturally flourish. Hegel's conception of an organic society matures a tradition which had been present in German philosophy since the days of Leibniz, Herder, and Lessing.

But Hegel's theory of freedom was not designed merely to correct the speculative errors of the Revolution in France. We have seen that he very early came to regard extreme individualism as a fundamental defect of the German national character in its political dealings. The Germans desire to be free and to be a nation, but they have never learned the lesson that they must first create a state as the precondition of freedom. For modern men political freedom can exist only in a national state, and the national state, when combined with Protestant Christianity, is unique in producing the highest degree and kind of freedom. But the heaviest stress, under the circumstances, must fall upon the creation of the state. From this follow two of the most characteristic features of Hegel's political philosophy. First, it is continually implied that no genuine conflict of interest ever can arise between individuals and the society they belong to, and, second, the state is continually represented as standing for the highest possible ethical value. These two phases of Hegel's philosophy, though they are perfectly comprehensible when viewed in the light of the circumstances in which he wrote, are nevertheless the causes of very great confusion in his thought.

Starting from the position that individual good and right must always involve the finding of a significant social work with which private interests may be identified. Hegel is led at times to the conclusion that obligation is always clearly presented in existing social relationships. Quite characteristically he equates individual choice with mere caprice, sentimentality, and fanaticism. The belief that freedom involves the right to do as one pleases is a "superficial" view of the matter, and this adjective is Hegel's favorite term of condemnation. It is only the influence of caprice and self-will which prevents law from being identical with what is intrinsically right. In the ethical system all distinction of individual and social ends vanishes; only as a citizen in a good state does an individual attain true self-development. The implication appears to be that the primary moral obligation is simply obedience and conformity. The concessions which Hegel endeavors to make to the principle of subjective freedom are in fact little better than quibbles.

Nevertheless, Hegel certainly believed that, in some sense which he never made clear, the modern state succeeds better than the ancient in respecting the individual's independence and right of choice. A higher type of personal life he regarded as the unique contribution of Christianity to European civilization. Even on the political level he does himself less than justice when he implies that citizenship can be summed up in conformity; his heroes are one and all iconoclasts. To suppose that Hegel desired to perpetuate the political state of affairs in Germany as it was in his lifetime is manifestly false. Moreover, he is quite unable to show how the vast, impersonal modern state can serve as a centralizing principle for all of a modern man's interests, and therefore how citizenship can overlap and include all phases of personal morality. To identify private conscience with conformity or caprice is quite inconsistent with the value which Hegel placed upon Christianity.

The same sort of confusion is introduced into Hegel's whole system of social philosophy by his tendency to represent the state as embodying the highest ethical values. The place to be assigned to religion and art is highly ambiguous. These are frequently represented as if they were the creations of the national spirit, though it is quite clear that in general they are regarded as manifestations of something higher. As a consequence Hegel in his political philosophy never reached any clear theory of the relation between churches and the state. His hostile estimate of Roman Catholicism and of German pietism, and his quite uncritical admiration for Lutheran Protestantism, alike bear witness to the biasses which were inherent in the circumstances that provided the immediate occasion of his thought. Hegel's deification of the state is a reflection of the overmastering aspiration for German unity, for the state which he deifies is not Prussia or any other state that existed in 1817. If individual choice and conscience are overshadowed, this is exactly the fate which overtook German liberalism in '48. In Germany the dangers of particularism and provincialism quite eclipsed the dangers of political absolutism; the nation as a whole acquiesced in Hegel's assertion that the formation of a state is a condition precedent to freedom.

Hegel's political philosophy was an authentic expression of German experience and German aspiration in the dark days of Germany's bitter national humiliation. Over it broods a nation's effort to create a national government commensurate with its national culture and able to implement its national will to power. For an Englishman or a Frenchman of the same date such effort was the memory of an achievement long accomplished. For a German it was a subject of passionate aspiration, of bitter disappointment, and of almost religious hope. For him the national destiny was necessary, as is true so often with deeply felt ideals, precisely because the facts seem to belie it. For him the premonition of a new social order was cast not in the mold of a wider and surer area of personal choice, but in the mold of a national unity which should at once absorb and liberate the ambitions and the capacities of the individual. Like all absorbing ideals it could pervert as well as clarify; like all powerful passions it was potentially dangerous. Read as a human document in the light of the situation in which it was produced, Hegel's political philosophy, even in its confusions and exaggerations, is profoundly intelligible, even profoundly moving. The conceptual form in which Hegel chose to cast it, even its truth or falsity, does not cover its historic significance. For it belongs not only to science but to a phase of European political history. It is a phenomenon as significant in the creation of modern Germany as the careers of Stein and Hardenberg.

10

MARX

Karl Marx (1818–1883) was born in a small town in the German Rhineland. He studied first at the University of Bonn, and then at Berlin where he came under the influence of Hegelian thought. After obtaining his doctorate at the University of Jena in 1841, he began a career in radical journalism which was interrupted by the suppression of his newspaper in 1843. In Paris, where he had gone in exile, he met Friedrich Engels who became his lifelong collaborator. His radical journalism and political activity took him then to Brussels and finally to London where he settled down to research, writing, and the work of the Communist International. For a long while in London he was European correspondent for the then socialist *New York Tribune,* later to become the more respectable *Herald-Tribune.* No mean indication of Marx's great influence is the fact that his ideas have had a longer life than this paper for which he once wrote.

In the first of the two selections on Marx, Harold Laski, the late English socialist, gives a detailed exposition of Marxist ideas as found in a close reading of *The Communist Manifesto.* Laski discusses its biting attack on other socialists, its notion of class struggle, its theory of history, and the meaning of various key phrases like "the withering away of the state" and "the dictatorship of the proletariat." Laski's discussion represents the more traditional approach to Marx studies. The article by Karl Löwith, professor of philosophy at Heidelberg, is one of the earliest efforts at a new, and increasingly popular, interpretation of Marx. Löwith investigates the earlier writings of Marx which were more clearly under the influence of Hegel and which reflected a greater concern with philosophical and moral questions. Particularly concerned with Marx's notion of "alienation," Löwith lucidly demonstrates the relationship of the contemporary connotation to Marx's meaning of the concept.

HAROLD J. LASKI

The Communist Manifesto*

The actual construction of the *Communist Manifesto* is brilliantly simple. Affirming, with justice, the dread of communism felt by the governments of Europe, it goes on to insist that the struggle between classes is the central clue to historical change. But whereas in previous periods the structure of society is a "complicated arrangement," in the new "epoch of the bourgeoisie" society is being ever more "simplified" by being forced towards the dual division between bourgeoisie and proletariat. The *Manifesto* emphasises the revolutionary part the bourgeoisie has played in history, its relentless drive to make the "cash nexus" the only bond between men. It has dissolved innumerable other freedoms for the one freedom which gives it command of the world market—freedom of trade. It lives by exploitation, and its unresting search for markets means an unending and profound change in every aspect of life. It gives a "cosmopolitan character

to production and consumption in every country." It compels the breakdown of national isolation; as it builds an interdependent material universe, so it draws, as a common fund, upon science and learning from every nation. It means the centralisation of government, the supremacy of town over country, the dependence of backward peoples upon those with more advanced methods of production in their hands.

The *Manifesto* describes with savage eloquence how the development of bourgeois society makes the workman a wage-slave exploited by the capitalist. The latter spares neither age nor sex. He makes it increasingly impossible for the small producer to compete with him; on every side economic power is increasingly concentrated and the little man, in every category of industry and agriculture, is driven into the dependent condition of the working class. So ruthless is this exploitation that in sheer self-defence the workers are compelled to combine to fight their masters. They form unions, ever more wide, which come at last to fight together as a class and as a political party representative of that class. If the battle sways backwards and forwards, with gains here and losses there, the consolidation of the workers as a class hostile to their ex-

* Condensed from *Harold J. Laski on the Communist Manifesto*. © Copyright 1967 by Random House, Inc. Reprinted by permission of Pantheon Books, Inc., a Division of Random House, Inc., and by permission of George Allen and Unwin Ltd. (London). The footnotes found in the original have been omitted here.

ploiters has one special feature which distinguishes it from all previous struggles between rulers and ruled; the working class becomes increasingly the self-conscious, independent movement of the immense majority, in the interest of the immense majority. If at first it struggles within the framework of the national state, it soon becomes evident that this struggle is but one act in a vast international drama. A time comes in the history of capitalism when "its existence is no longer compatible with society." It cannot feed its slaves. It drives them to revolution in which a proletarian victory is inevitable.

The *Manifesto* then turns to the special functions of Communists in the working class movement. It insists that the Communists do not form "a separate party opposed to other working-class parties." They have no interest apart from the workers. More than this: "They do not set up any sectarian principles of their own," says the *Manifesto*, "by which to mould and shape the proletarian movement." Their task is to insist on the international solidarity of the working class, to stand in its vanguard in each country, to aid, by their deeper theoretical grasp of the movement of history, in the workers' drive to the conquest of power. They do not aim at the abolition of individual private property, but of that bourgeois form of the ownership of the instruments of production which deprives nine-tenths of society of the capacity to acquire individual property. Communists admit freely that they desire to abolish the bourgeois corruption of the family and to replace home education by social education. They do so because the bourgeois family is a means of exploiting the labour of women and children, and because bourgeois education means its subordination to the ends of the ruling class. If Communists are charged with seeking to abolish love of

country, the *Manifesto* answers that the workers can have no country until they are emancipated from bourgeois domination; with their acquisition of political power, the hostility between nations will disappear. So, also, it will change traditional ideas in religion and philosophy. Since it puts experience on a new basis, it will change the ideas which are their expression.

The *Manifesto* recognises that the emancipation of the workers will never come in exactly the same way in every country; differences in development make that inevitable. Yet it suggests a programme of measures, "generally applicable" in advanced countries, which will enable the workers to win the battle of democracy. When this victory has been won, under these conditions class distinctions will disappear and the state-power will wither away, since it is necessary only to preserve class-distinctions. In its place there will be a free association of citizens "in which the free development of each will be the condition of the free development of all."

Such a summary as this, of course, is bound to do injustice to the superb sweep of the *Manifesto* itself. But it is important to dwell upon it for the implications upon which it insists. First, perhaps a word is useful on the title of the document itself. It was to have been the "Catechism" by way of question and answer, from the Communist League; it became the *Communist Manifesto*. What is the reason for the change? Partly, no doubt, the decision of Marx and Engels to alter what would have been an essentially temporary domestic piece of propaganda into one that would have permanent historical value. It is hard not to believe that they called it a *Manifesto* in tribute to the memory of the Babouviste *Manifesto of the Equals*. They always recognised Babeuf as a real precursor, and do honour to him in their own work. The word *Com-*

munist, it may fairly be suggested, has a double implication. On the one hand, it emphasises the relation of their work to the Communist League, by which they were authorised to undertake it; on the other, it serves to mark their own sense of profound separation from the "true" socialists of Germany, and especially of Karl Grün, against whom their criticism was so violent in the *Manifesto* itself. They reproached "true" socialism with sentimentality, with pretentiousness, and with an abstract approach to concrete problems which deprived them of any sense of reality. One can already see the depth of their hostility to Grün in articles they had written against him in August and September, 1847. It would not be surprising that they should choose a title for their pronouncements which at once looked back to a great revolutionary predecessor, and avoided the danger of any confusion with a group whose "socialism" seemed to them no more than a vapid humanitarianism.

What lends support to this view is the emphatic declaration of Marx and Engels that the Communists do not form a separate party. On the contrary, they are ready to work with all working-class organisations genuinely dedicated to the socialist task; more, they repudiate any claim to "sectarian" doctrines of their own which might result in their separation from the rest of the working-class movement. It is vital to insist upon this emphasis. However critical Marx and Engels may be of other socialist principles than their own, their regard for unity among the working-class forces is paramount. That is shown by their careers from the very outset. Engels lent his support to Chartism even before the appearance of the *Manifesto;* yet there must have been few among its leaders who had any real insight into the doctrines of which he was the exponent. He and Marx were

often bitterly hostile to the German Social Democratic Movement; they attacked Lassalle, Liebknecht, Bebel, Kautsky. But they never sought to found a separate German Communist Party. The hostility of Marx to the dominant elements in French socialism is obvious from his attack on Proudhon as early as 1847; but though he and Engels always encouraged the "Marxist" elements in the French party, the *Civil War in France* (1871) of Marx himself shows their anxiety to assist it, even when they thought its policy mistaken. Indeed, Section IV of the *Manifesto* itself insists upon this view. The Communists support the Chartists in England and the Agrarian Reformers in America; they "ally themselves" with the Social Democratic Party in France; they support the radicals in Switzerland, "without forgetting that the party consists of contradictory elements"; in Poland they support "the party that has seen in an agrarian revolution the means to national freedom, that party which caused the insurrection of Cracow in 1846"; in Germany they fight with any bourgeois elements which see the need to "act in a revolutionary manner against the absolute monarchy, the feudal landlords, and the little middle class."

The *Manifesto,* without question, insists that the Communists enter into relations with other groups to give them direction, to spread their own revolutionary creed, to make the workers aware of the "hostile antagonism" between bourgeoisie and proletariat. They "openly declare that their ends can be attained only by the forcible overthrow of all existing social conditions." But this declaration follows upon the announcement of three purposes which must be kept closely in mind if it is to be fully understood. They support "every revolutionary movement against the existing social and political order of things." In every movement, moreover, whatever its stage of development, they put the question of property in the first place. "Equally," says the *Manifesto,* "they labour everywhere for the union and agreement of the democratic parties of all countries."

If all this is read in the context of Engels' famous introduction to Marx's *Class Struggles in France,* which he wrote in 1895, and of the joint *Address of the Central Council of the Communist League,* it is clear that the *Manifesto* is presenting a doctrine of permanent revolution. By that famous phrase they do not mean a continuous series of attempts to seize the state-power by the workers in the manner advocated by Blanqui. They had learned that revolution was an art, and that it needs certain special historical conditions if it is to be successful. They meant that when an alliance of the progressive forces in society overthrows the reactionary forces, the workers must not allow bourgeois democrats or social reformers to stop at the point where private ownership of the means of production remains unchallenged. They must always drive them on from this reformist outlook to the revolutionary stage where direct attack is made on private property. Even if the conditions do not permit of success, at least they will have done much to educate those workers who are not yet class-conscious into a realisation of their position. And, with the coming of universal suffrage, the revolutionary idea will, by force of historical circumstances, enable the Communists to "conquer the greater part of the middle section of society, petty bourgeois and small peasants, and grow into the decisive power in the land, before which all other powers will have to bow, whether they like it or not. To keep this growth going without interruption, until of itself it gets beyond the control of the ruling governmental sys-

tem, not to fritter away this daily increasing shock force in advance guard fighting, but to keep it intact until the day of the decision—that is our main task."

The continuation is not less significant. "The irony of world history," wrote Engels, "turns everything upside down. We, 'the revolutionaries,' the 'rebels,' we are thriving far better on legal methods than on illegal methods and revolt...The parties of order, as they call themselves, are perishing under the legal conditions created by themselves...and if we are not so crazy as to let ourselves be driven into street fighting in order to please them, then nothing else is finally left for them but themselves to break through this legality so fatal to them." Nothing here written by Engels means that he assumed the likelihood that the final transition from capitalism to socialism would be peaceful. On the contrary, it is quite evident that he expected the peaceful forces of socialism so to develop that their strength became a threat to the interests of property. That threat, he prophesied, would lead the interests of property themselves to break the Constitution. Where that occurred Social Democracy would then be free to act in its own defence. That, for him, is the moment when a revolutionary struggle would begin. He did not neglect the danger that progress towards socialism might be halted by war on a global scale. "No war is any longer possible for Prussia-Germany," he wrote,

except a world war, and a world war indeed of an extension and violence hitherto undreamed of. Eight to ten millions of soldiers will mutually massacre one another and, in doing so, devour the whole of Europe until they have stripped it barer than any swarm of locusts has ever done. The devastations of the Thirty Years' War compressed into three or four years: and spread over the whole Continent; famine, prestilence, general demoralisation both of the armies and of the mass of the people produced by acute distress; hopeless confusion of our artificial machinery in trade, industry and credit, ending in general bankruptcy; collapse of the old states and their traditional state-wisdom to such an extent that crowns will roll by dozens on the pavement, and there will be no one to pick them up; absolute impossibility of foreseeing how it will end, and who will come out of the struggle as victor; only one result is absolutely certain: general exhaustion, and the establishment of the conditions for the ultimate victory of the working class. This is the prospect when the system of mutual outbidding in armaments, driven to extremities, at last bears its inevitable fruits. This, my lords and gentlemen, is where, in your wisdom, you have brought old Europe. And when nothing more remains to you but to open the last great war dance—that will suit us all right. The war may perhaps push us temporarily into the background, may wrench from us many a position already conquered. But when you have unfettered forces which you will then no longer be able again to control, things may go as they will; at the end of the tragedy you will be ruined, and the victory of the proletariat will either be already achieved, or, at any rate, inevitable.

Nor does he fail to note, in a letter to Sorge, of January 7th, 1888, that "American industry would conquer all along the line, and push us up against the alternatives: either retrogression to production for home consumption...or —social transformation...but once the first shot is fired, control ceases, the horse can take the bit between his teeth."

To this should be added what Marx and Engels had to say in the edition, prepared by the latter, of Marx's famous address to the General Council of the First International on the Civil War in France which arose out of the defeat of Louis Napoleon in the Franco-Prussian War. "In reality," wrote Engels, in his preface of March 18th, 1871,

the state is nothing but a machine for the oppression of one class by another, and, indeed, in the democratic republic, no less than in the monarchy; and, at best, an evil inherited by the proletariat after its victorious struggle for class supremacy, whose worst sides, the proletariat, just like the Commune, cannot avoid leaving to lop off until such time, at the earliest possible moment, as a new generation, reared in new and free social conditions, will be able to throw the entire lumber of the state on the scrap-heap. Of late, the Social Democratic philistine has once more been filled with terror at the words: dictatorship of the proletariat. Well and good, gentlemen, do you want to know what this Dictatorship looks like? Look at the Paris Commune. That was the Dictatorship of the Proletariat!

No one can examine this section of the *Manifesto* honestly without coming to two conclusions, especially when it is set in the light of the subsequent comments upon its meaning by its own authors. They did not expect that capitalist society would be transformed into socialist society without violent revolution. They were insistent that the people who shared their views must never divide the organised working-class forces, that it was their duty to avoid sectarianism, and that they must not form a separate party. Their task was to be the vanguard of their party, to proclaim, indeed, their views, to do all in their power to get them accepted as the basis of action, but still to remain within the political ranks of the organised working class. More than this: in the last edition of the *Manifesto* edited by Engels, though he remained emphatic in his belief that violence would accompany the final disappearance of capitalism, was also emphatic that the workers would be foolish to rely upon the old methods of street-fighting at the barricades, because new methods and new weapons had altered the situation in favour of the armed forces and the police. Fighting might still be necessary, but it would be folly for the workers to abandon legal methods until a stage had been reached when the position they confronted compensated for the new strength a capitalist society possessed in the power at the disposal of the state authority.

Under what circumstances did the workers reach that position? The answer, surely, is given by the fact that Marx saw the dictatorship of the proletariat as the outcome of the Paris Commune when France was defeated by Prussia in the war of 1870. Engels saw it, as is evident from the preface of 1895 to the· *Manifesto,* and from his introduction to Borkheim's book, as the outcome of the catastrophic conditions produced by global war. It is of decisive importance to consider these views in the light of the interpretation that Lenin himself put upon them. He pointed out, with perfect fairness, the immense step taken by Marx between the publication of the *Manifesto* and the *Eighteenth Brumaire,* and between these pamphlets and both the *Letters to Kugelmann* and the *Civil War in France,* he draws attention, too, again quite fairly, to a similar change in the outlook of Engels between the production of the *Manifesto* and the careful analysis of the *Anti-Dühring,* but the vital outlook of Lenin is set out in his classic *State and Revolution* and the documents therewith connected. It is sufficient here to say that Lenin was here concerned to establish to the comrades in Leningrad the necessary conditions of successful revolution; for he, like Marx and Engels, was careful to distinguish his outlook from that of Blanqui. He thought it necessary, first, that the armed forces of the state-

power should be disloyal. He thought that the machinery of the state must be in ruins; there must be widespread revolutionary disturbance among the working class, as evidenced by strikes and demonstrations and there must be a solid and coherent working-class power able to lead the working class to the conquest of power. On these conditions, working-class victory was a possibility with a real prospect of success. Here, it will be noted that Lenin is considering a condition in which the overwhelming breakdown of the machinery of government opened the prospect of new orientations. The breakdown of ancient state-powers as the outcome of the war of 1939 had resulted in something akin to that which Lenin had foreseen. That was the result of defeat in war. The form of state has remained unaltered in the states which remained victorious in that struggle. Lenin was pretty clearly right in insisting that the "democratic republic," based on universal suffrage, was the last rampart of bourgeois socialism rather than the first of democratic socialism in the Marxian sense of that term; that can be seen from utterances like those of Macaulay and of Daniel Webster. But nothing in his discussion deals with the fundamental point of whether and why that extreme Left he represented was justified in dissenting from the continuous insistence of Marx and Engels that the working class opposed to the imposition of bourgeois capitalism should form a separate party from the old social democrats. In this regard, the famous split between Bolsheviks and Mensheviks, at the Congress in London in 1903, was an innovation unconsidered by his predecessors. Whether it was wise or unwise, together with all the immense consequences to which, since the foundation of the Third International in 1919, it has led, lies outside the scope of this introduction.

From this remarkable analysis, the *Manifesto* goes on, a little cursorily and haphazardly, to consider the literature of socialism which had appeared up to 1848. It condemns, first of all, what it calls "reactionary" socialism as a form of capitalism the roots of which lie deep in a feudal outlook. It seems probable that the author had in mind, without naming them, two groups of thinkers. On the one hand they were attacking the attempts of men like Herman Wagener and Bismarck who were seeking an alliance between the Prussian Crown and the proletariat, primarily at the expense, immediately, of the bourgeoisie, but ultimately, of the proletariat. These were seeking, in the old technique, how first to divide in order that their royal master might govern without question. They were in all probability attacking also the *soi-disant* socialism of Louis Rousseau and Villeneuve-Bargemont in France, who sought, by putting the French unemployed into agricultural colonies, to prevent them from strengthening the army of the proletariat by leaving the supporters of the "juste milieu" face to face with their bourgeoisie. Above all, they were dismissing that "Young England" group, of which Disraeli, as in *Sybil,* with some support from George Smythe and, at a remoter distance, Thomas Carlyle, supplied the ideas, and for which Lord John Manners provided, with occasional support from Lord Ashley (the later Earl of Shaftesbury), the political leadership. They, together with the Christian Socialists, of whom F. D. Maurice and Charles Kingsley were the outstanding figures, were groups of which Engels, with his accustomed prescience, had already seen the danger in his *Condition of the Working Class in England* in 1844.

Engels, at least, had not failed to understand the importance of Carlyle's *Chartism* (1840) and of his *Past and Present* (1843); he had already written about them in the *Deutsch Französische Jahrbücher*. He had fully understood the reality of their horror of the new factory system, the new poor law, the invasion of happy lives by the new and grim industrialism. But the *Manifesto* regarded this type of socialism as no more than feudalism, however much its plea might be garbed in eloquence. Marx saw that they loathed the effects of industrialism; but he realised that they wanted to go backwards to a paternalistic feudalism, not forward to a democratic socialism. They were afraid of a rebellion from the oppressed, and they hoped to buy it off by paternal concessions which would still leave Tory Democracy in power. Since this was in its essence aristocratic and would, as in the Ten Hours Bill, improve factory conditions without removing the indignity of an unemancipated class, the *Manifesto* rejects this attempt to return to "Merrie England" as an effort without serious meaning for socialists who had really grasped the problem before the proletariat.

They then turned to the analysis of petty-bourgeois socialism. The *Manifesto* admits freely the achievements of this school of doctrine, at the head of which, both for France and England, it places the distinguished name of Sismondi. But it argues that, apart from its important criticism of modern production, the petty-bourgeois school has no positive aim but to restore "the old property relations, and the old society." It is therefore dismissed as both "reactionary and utopian"; "this form of socialism," says the *Manifesto,* "ended in a miserable fit of the blues."

. . .

It may be that the abrupt brevity with which the "petty bourgeois school" is dismissed is partly due to their failure to depict the revolution, the coming of which is, of course, the main prophecy of the *Manifesto*; this leads naturally into the bitter attack that is made, in the next section, on "true" or German socialism.

This attack may be regarded as the final breach of Marx and Engels with that Hegelian Left to which both of them had once belonged. It is the demonstration not only that its leaders were living by concepts and not by things, but also that the result of their effort was merely to serve the ends of German reaction. It is here that Marx and Engels break with their own past. They have done with Ruge and Moses Hess, with Karl Grün and Hermann Kriege. The stride beyond Hegel which Feuerbach had taken, which was in large part the basis of "true" socialism, now is declared not only inadequate but also deceptive. The votaries of "true" socialism are using the great principles of revolutionary experience and thought in France to elucidate a situation to which they are inapplicable. They fail to see that French socialism is an attack upon a bourgeoisie already in power. In Germany this is not the case. There the bourgeoisie has only begun to fight against the feudal aristocracy. To fight for socialism under these conditions is to delay the success of the bourgeois revolution by frightening it with the threat of a proletarian attack for which the conditions are completely unripe. "True" socialism, the *Manifesto* argues, thus "served the governments (of Germany) as a weapon for fighting the German bourgeoisie." It thus delays the march of the necessary historical development by serving up as "eternal truths" concepts the value of which depends wholly upon their relevance to the concrete situation. The "true" socialists are thus guilty of an abstract philosophy which appears like a call to arms; but it is a call which can have

no other result than to aid the victory of feudal reaction by seeking a revolutionary temper in a class which has not yet decisively appeared upon the historic stage.

. . .

The section on literature continues with a discussion of "conservative or bourgeois" socialism. "The socialistic bourgeois," says the *Manifesto,* "want all the advantages of modern social conditions without the struggles and dangers necessarily resulting from them. They desire the present state of society without its revolutionary and disintegrating elements. They wish for a bourgeoisie without a proletariat." The "conservative" socialist may be an economist or a humanitarian; he is found among "hole and corner reformers of every kind." If he systematises his doctrine, he emerges with a body of ideas like those expounded by Proudhon in his *Philosophie de la Misère.* Or he may refrain from system-making, and devote his attention to attacks on revolutionary movements intended to persuade the workers of their folly. Political reform will not do. Nor is anything gained by abolishing the bourgeois relations of production. In the eyes of the "conservative" socialist the supreme need is a change in "the material conditions of existence." When we analyse what he means by this change, we find that it is no more than "administrative reforms" which, though they simplify the work and diminish the cost of government, leave the relations between capital and labour unchanged. He is in favour of free trade, or protective duties, or prison reform, for the benefit of the working class. What, nevertheless, is vital to his outlook is that the proletariat should cease to hate the bourgeoisie, and accept the capitalist system as final. By that means the "social New Jerusalem" can be built without the haunting fear that revolution is necessary to its establishment.

It is obvious enough that this attack is directed against the men whose palliatives Marx agreed with Proudhon in dismissing with contempt in his *Poverty of Philosophy*—Proudhon himself, be it noted, being added by Marx to the list of those to be so dismissed. Michel Chevalier, Adolphe Blanqui and Leon Faucher in France, with their remedies of technical education, profit-sharing and state-compensation for workers displaced by the development of machine-technology, are typical examples of this kind; they have, as the *Manifesto* says, to mitigate the harsher consequences of capitalism without interfering with the relations of production upon which it is based. The reference to free trade is, I think, pretty obviously an arrow launched against Cobden and Bright and their supporters in the Anti-Corn Law League who believed that the social problem would be solved by the adoption of universal free trade; and this view is the more likely since both Marx and Engels, and especially Engels, had seen at first hand how the propaganda of the League had done much to break the hold of the Chartist Movement upon the workers It is reasonable to suppose that the reference to tariffs is primarily a thrust at Friedrich List —who had died only the year before— and his system of German national economy based upon a closed customs union as the unit of prosperity. If this is so, it links the *Manifesto* to the growing economic literature from America, the famous *Report on Manufacture* (1791) of Alexander Hamilton, for example, and the works of Henry C. Carey, to which we know Marx and Engels gave careful attention, though without being convinced that the protectionists had found an answer to the central issue of productive relations.

What they were rejecting was the notorious doctrine of the "harmony of interest" between capital and labour, which, though Adam Smith at the rise and John Stuart Mill at the end of the first half-century of classical political economy had already seen it to be fallacious, was still the main ground upon which the growth of trade unions was discouraged and repressed. Men of good will, the *Manifesto* says in effect, can never build a society capable of justice by philanthropy of palliatives. It is nothing less than the whole system of productive relations that must be changed.

In a sense, the final section on previous socialist literature, which deals with what the *Manifesto* calls "critico-Utopian" writers, is a little disappointing. It quite properly emphasises the fact that the literature of the first proletarian strivings produces "fantastic pictures" of future society, that it thinks of the workers as a suffering rather than a revolutionary class, that it appeals, for the most part, to ethical principles beyond and above class-antagonism, that it seeks to change society "by peaceful means" and "by small experiments." It agrees that Babeuf, Owen, Cabet and Fourier attack the existing foundation of their civilisation at its roots, that they are "full of the most valuable materials for the enlightenment of the working class." But their proposals are dismissed as "purely Utopian," and though it is admitted that they were themselves "in many respects revolutionary," it is insisted that their followers have always "formed merely reactionary sects." "They therefore endeavour," wrote Marx and Engels, "and that consistently, to deaden the class struggle, and to reconcile the class-antagonisms. . . . They sink into the category of the reactionary conservative socialists, differing from them only by more systematic pedantry." They became, we are told, the violent opponents of working-class political action. Like the followers of Owen who oppose the Chartists, and the followers of Fourier who oppose the *Reformistes,* they have a "fanatical and superstitious belief in the miraculous effects of their social science."

. . .

The final section of the *Manifesto* is essentially an outline of the correct Communist strategy in view of the coming struggle. The Communists, it affirms, will fight for the immediate interests of the workers, without losing sight of the need to assist the emergence of the future in their aid to the present. Thus, if in France they support the social democrats—the party led by Ledru-Rollin—that will not prevent them from seeking to correct the tendencies in that party which are no more than an empty tradition handed down from the Revolution; if in Germany they support the bourgeoisie in its revolutionary struggle against absolute monarchy, the feudalism of the landlords and the reactionary outlook of the petty-bourgeois elements, that will not prevent them from awakening the workers to the realisation that, once the bourgeois revolution has been accomplished, the proletarian revolution must begin.

The Communists concentrate their effort on Germany, Marx and Engels say, because a successful bourgeois revolution there, in the conditions of the nineteenth century, where the proletariat is so much more advanced than it could have been either at the time of the English or of the French Revolutions, is bound to be the prelude to an "immediate and subsequent" proletarian revolution. Their general position assumes three clear principles. They must support every revolutionary movement

against the conditions of the time. They must make the question of property—that is, the ownership of the means of production—the central issue in every movement in which they participate. They must, finally, "labour everywhere for the union and agreement of the democratic parties of all countries." Their position is thus unmistakable. They will always support working-class parties, even when these are not communist, without forming a separate party of their own; even though such a party may have an inadequate programme, its proletarian character makes it the appropriate instrument through which to exercise communist influence. Where the party they support, like that of Ledru-Rollin, is not proletarian, they support it because it offers the workers the chance first of a greater rôle in politics, and second of great social reforms.

. . .

Time has added to the lustre of the *Communist Manifesto;* and it has achieved the remarkable status not only of being a classic, but a classic also which is directly relevant to the controversies which rage a century after it was written. Inevitably, therefore, it has become the subject of rival interpretations; and it is not seldom read as though its eminent authors were still fighting for one or another of the different schools of contemporary socialist thought.

. . .

No phrase has been subject to so much misinterpretation as the "dictatorship of the proletariat." Let us be clear at once that neither for Marx nor for Engels was it the antithesis of democracy; for them, its antithesis was the "dictatorship of the bourgeoisie" which, as they believed, obtained in every country, even when concealed by formally democratic political institutions, so long as the ownership of the means of production remained in middle-class hands. Marx and Engels meant by the "dictatorship of the proletariat" an organisation of society in which the state-power was in the hands of the working class, and used with all the force necessary to prevent it being seized from them by the class which formerly exercised its authority. They assume that the representatives of the working class will use the state-power to change the relations of production and to repress any attempt to interfere with this change. But it is obvious from Engels' indentification of the Paris Commune with proletarian dictatorship that he regards it as based on the support of the majority, that it employs the technique of universal suffrage, and that its acceptance of the people's right to frequent elections, and to the recall of their representatives implies full popular participation in the working of the dictatorship. It is obvious, further, from Marx's account of the Commune as a legislature and executive in one, that it denies the validity of the separation of powers, and assumes that the dictatorship is exercised through the elected body based upon popular choice and subject to public opinion through the right of each constituency to recall any representative it may have chosen; that, surely, was what Marx meant when he wrote that "nothing could be more foreign to the spirit of the Commune than to supersede universal suffrage by hierarchic investiture," Marx even points out that the "great bulk of the Paris middle class. . . .the wealthy capitalist alone excepted" admitted that "this was the first revolution in which the working class was openly acknowledged as the only class capable of social initiative"; he noted that it supplied the republic with the basis of really democratic institutions; and he com-

pares the peace and order it secured within Paris, with the fanatically repressive atmosphere of Versailles under the domination of Thiers.

From this angle, it seems to me inescapable that Marx and Engels did not conceive the dictatorship of the proletariat to mean the dictatorship of the Communist Party over the rest of the community, that is, the centralisation of the state-power in the hands of a single party, which imposes its will by force on all citizens outside its ranks. It is conceivable that the struggle for the state-power may be so intense that the government has no alternative but to proclaim a state of siege until it has consolidated its authority. It is undeniable, also, that a workers' government in possession of the state-power may find it necessary to penalise persons or parties who threaten its safety, in the same way as the British Government found it necessary to assume drastic powers when it was threatened by invasion after Dunkirk in 1940. It was, I think, this second situation that Marx and Engels had in view. They assumed that the use of the state-power by and for the workers would mean an expansion, and not a contraction, of democratic forces; it would permit, that is, vastly greater numbers to participate in social life effectively than is possible when democratic institutions operate only within the framework of capitalist production. They could not, therefore, have envisaged the Communist Party acting as a dictatorship over the working class and excluding all other parties from the right to share in, and influence over, the exercise of power.

I think this view is borne out by other evidence. The *Manifesto* itself declares quite explicitly that Communists are the vanguard of the working class. They are not its masters; they are in the forefront of the co-operative effort to abolish capitalist society. Still more important, the Communists do not form a separate party of their own. They ally themselves with other organisations, especially of the working class, which aim at the same end as themselves, or may objectively be regarded as assisting that end even though unconsciously. That was why, for example, the Communist League supported Ledru-Rollin in 1845, even though he hated Communism. That was why, also, they persuaded the First International to support the Paris Commune, and why those of its members, who were also members of the International, co-operated in its heroic struggle with others who did not belong to it. Unless, indeed, Marx and Engels had taken this view, they would have been arguing that the dictatorship of the proletariat means the rule of that party leadership to the guidance of which any political organisation of large size must give heavy responsibilities. They never argued for this outlook. On the contrary, their deepest concern was to make the state-power, when it passed into the workers' hands, not only the organ through which the capitalist relations of production were transformed into socialist relations of production, but the organ also through which the unreal democracy of capitalist society became the real democracy of socialist society. Repression in all its forms was for them a transitory necessity. That was why they could argue that, with the establishment of socialism, the state would "wither away."

The "withering away" of the state is another famous phrase that has been much discussed and much misunderstood. In one sense it is a purely logical inference from the definition of the *Manifesto*. The state is there defined as the "executive committee of the bourgeoisie." Obviously, therefore, as the power to govern is taken out of the hands of the bourgeoisie by the workers, the state as a bourgeois institution ceases to exist because being in the workers' hands it becomes transformed into a proletarian institution. Marx and Engels then argued that its coercive authority, the army, for example, the police, and the civil service, would have so to be adapted as to be capable of use by the workers for socialist purposes, as they had been adapted by the bourgeoisie to be used for capitalist purposes. They thought in 1872, as Marx had suggested 20 years before, that a socialist society would have to "break" the political machinery of the régime it took over in order to make the adaptation successful. What did they mean by "breaking" the machinery of the capitalist state? The answer is, I think, that it was to be deprived of that character of an "hierarchical investiture" which, as Marx had written in *Civil War in France*, prevented the defective power of numbers from being authoritative. The organs of government were to be genuinely democratised. They were to be in and of the new proletarian society, not, as in capitalist society, over and above the workers, separated from them by caste-like walls, so that they could impose upon the workers the discipline necessary to maintain in its fullness the capitalist mode of production. The defence forces, the police and the civil service were to have no special privileges, and no special place in the new régime. Their members were to be looked upon as workers performing a necessary social function in the same way as any other groups of workers. They were to be deprived of their "hierarchical" attributes.

It should be added that when Marx and Engels spoke of the "withering away of the state" there is no reason to suppose they believed that in a socialist country the hopes of the philosophical anarchists would be fulfilled and that all authority would be the outcome of express assent to its orders. No doubt both of them strongly believed that as the private ownership of the means of production passed away there would be far less need for a coercive apparatus in society. That was a natural view for them to take since they held that it was the private ownership of those means which was responsible for most of what was evil in the social process. Their insistence that the state-power was essentially used to protect that private ownership from attack was, of course, held with great emphasis by Adam Smith himself. "It is only under the shelter of the civil magistrates," Adam Smith wrote, "that the owner of that valuable property, acquired by the labour of many years, or perhaps many successive generations, can sleep a single night in security." Marx and Engels agreed with the implications in Adam Smith's statement, though the inference they would have drawn was different. But there is nothing to suggest in all they wrote that with the establishment of a socialist society government itself becomes unnecessary. They rarely spoke of what a socialist society would be like; and the few references they did make to its character only justfy us in saying that they looked to a fuller and freer expression of individuality when the capitalists' fetters upon the forces of production had been finally removed.

Some discussion is desirable of the materialist conception of history which is the vital thread upon which the whole of the *Communist Manifesto* hangs; the more so because it continues to be strangely misrepresented by historians and social philosophers. It is not a claim that all actions are the result of economic motives. It does not insist either that all change is economically caused. It does not mean that the ideas and behaviour of men are fatalistically pre-determined and that, whether he will or no, the emergence of a socialist society is inevitable. It is the argument that, as Engels puts it, "production and, with production, the exchange of its products, is the basis of every social order; that in every society which has appeared in history, the distribution of the products, and, with it, the division of society into classes or estates, is determined by what is produced, and how it is produced, and how the product is exchanged." This is the basis from which Marx and Engels were led to that philosophy of history which led them to part company with their former allies, the Left Hegelians, whose conceptions are attacked in the *Manifesto*. For it led them to see that the way in which the total social production is divided in a community is not the outcome of the purposes, either good or bad, of the members of the community, but of the legal relations which arise out of given modes of production, and that these legal relations are independent of the wills of those engaged in production. Since changes in the modes of production and exchange are ceaselessly taking place, legal relations which were, at one time, adapted to the conditions of that time, cease to be adapted to them. It is in this disproportion between legal relations in the community and the forces of production in it that the changes in men's ideas of good and bad, justice and injustice, are to be found. That class in a community which legally owns the means of production uses the state-power to sanction that division of the product of which it approves. It therefore seeks through the coercive authority at the disposal of the state-power, to compel the general acceptance of its approved division; and systems of values, political, ethical, religious, philosophical, are ways in which, directly or indirectly, men express their agreement or disagreement with the nature of the division which the owners of the instruments of production endeavour to impose.

This does not mean that changes may be regarded as irrelevant to the ideas of men; but it does mean that men's ideas are continually evolving as their minds come to realise that changes in the methods of production and exchange render some ideas obsolete and require new ideas. As feudalism became transformed into capitalism, the legal relations it implied hindered the full use of the forces of production. The values the feudal system had been able to maintain before the advent of the capitalist method of production emerged became no longer acceptable. Then, as Engels wrote, "the bourgeoisie shattered the feudal system, and, on its ruins established the bourgeois social order, the realm of free competition, freedom of movement, equal rights for commodity owners and all the other bourgeois glories." Now, the *Manifesto* argues, changes in the forces of production have rendered the legal relations of capitalism obsolete in their turn; and socialism emerges as the claim to new relations, and, therefore, to new values which the workers, as the class which suffers most from this obsolescence, seek to put in its place.

No serious observer supposes that the materialist conception of history is free from difficulties, or that it solves all the problems involved in historical interpretation. But no serious observer either can doubt that it has done more in the last hundred years to provide a major clue to the causes of social change than any other hypothesis that has been put forward. There can really be no valid reason to deny that, over the whole space of recorded history, class struggle has been a central principle of its development. Nor can it be denied that class-struggle is intimately bound up with the relations of production in some

given society and the ability to develop the full possibilities of the forces of production at any given time. It is equally clear, on any close analysis, that the class which owns the instruments of production uses the state-power to safeguard that ownership, and seeks to repress the emergence of ideas and values which call that ownership into question. Anyone, moreover, who examines objectively any period in which the mode of production is rapidly changing, the age of the Reformation, for example, or the period between the two world wars, cannot fail to note that they are also periods marked by the grave instability of traditional values and of traditional institutions. There is nothing in the theory of the *Manifesto* which argues more than that the occurrence of such a period means that, if the traditional values and institutions continue to function in the new economic setting, they will deprive large numbers of their means of living, and that they will, therefore, seek to emancipate themselves from a position of which they are the victims. To do so, as Marx and Engels point out, they must possess themselves of the state-power that they may adapt the relations of production to the implications of the new order. And, on the argument of the *Manifesto*, since the passage from capitalist to social ownership marks the end of a history in which the instruments of production have been predominantly the possession of one class, the transition to public ownership means, when it is successfully effected, the emergence of the classless society.

It is this doctrine which the *Manifesto* is concerned to get accepted by socialists as against the other doctrines with which it was competing. It was not enough, Marx and Engels were saying in effect, for some men or group of men to proclaim a new principle as true and hope by the force merely of rational argument to persuade others to see also that it is true. What makes the new principle acceptable is the fact that changes in the mode of production have produced the material environment which makes it seem the natural expression of what people want. The duty to be tolerant is rarely likely to receive wide acceptance when it is advanced as an abstract metaphysical obligation. But when intolerance hinders the attainment by society of a full command over its material resources, men begin to see a validity in arguments advanced on its behalf, some religious, some ethical, some political, some economic, the strength of which had not previously been apparent to them. All the world applauded Robert Owen so long as he made the operation of that "revolution" in the mind and practice of the "human race" a philanthropic experiment confined to his own factories in New Lanark. But when he argued that his principles were so obviously rational that all social organisation should be adapted to their application, the world turned angrily upon him and showed him that, in the absence of the necessary material conditions, a principle which has justice and truth and reason on its side will still be unable to conquer the world by the inherent force of its own virtue. It is not until men see that the "anarchy of social production" caused by capitalism in decay can be replaced "by a socially planned regulation of production in accordance with the needs both of society as a whole, and of each individual," that they are prepared to get rid of capitalism.

"The forces operating in society," wrote Engels, "work exactly like the forces operating in nature: blindly, violently, destructively, so long as we do not understand them and fail to take them into account. But when we once have recognised them, and understood how they work, their direction and their efforts, the gradual subjection of them to our will, and the use of them for the attainment of our aims, depends entirely upon ourselves. And this is quite especially true of the mighty, productive forces of the present day." That is, I think, the central principle which underlies the whole of the *Communist Manifesto;* it is the social application of Bacon's great aphorism that "nature, to be commanded, must be obeyed." It is our attempt to show that every pattern of social institutions presupposes a stage in the development of productive forces, and that those who seek for the achievement of the pattern in which they believe will succeed only if their aim is justified by the character of those productive forces at the time when they make their effort. That was why, though Carlyle and Ruskin saw the evils of their own day, their remedy was an anachronism when they preached it; they preached a sermon to men who, as it were, had already left their church. That was why, to take a contemporary instance, the New Deal of President Roosevelt was able only to assuage temporarily the wounds he sought to heal; for those wounds were not some temporary infliction, but the symptoms of a disease far more deep and deadly than he was prepared to recognise.

KARL LÖWITH

Man's Self-Alienation in the Early Writings of Marx [*]

I

The specific concept that Marx uses in his analysis of the bourgeois-capitalist world is that of "human self-alienation," which expresses itself in the political economy as the "anatomy" of the bourgeoisie. "Political economy" includes, for Marx, man's economic existence as well as his human consciousness of it. Marx considers the material conditions of production to be the "skeleton" of society, and thus he transfers the emphasis from Hegel's "bourgeois society" to the "system of needs" as such. At the same time Marx's idea implies the specifically "materialist" thesis that the material conditions of life are of fundamental significance for all other conditions. This led eventually to the vulgar Marxist thesis: that the so-called material "basis" is the foundation on which, as on an independent stratum, the superstructure is to rise; this superstructure must therefore be interpreted ideologically as derived from the

"foundation." It was chiefly in this vulgarized form that Marxist doctrine became subject to criticism. However strongly Marx himself supported this interpretation—and Engels even more strongly—the fact remains that Marx had come to terms with philosophy before his criticism of political economy began to dominate in his thinking.

In this respect Marx's development can be summed up as follows: at first he criticized religion philosophically, then he criticized religion and philosophy politically, and at last he criticized religion, philosophy, politics, and all other ideologies economically. According to Marx's own words, however, the economic interpretation of all manifestations of human life was but the "last result" into which his critical revision of Hegel's metaphysical and political philosophy developed—in Hegel's words, "a corpse which has left behind its living impulse." To rediscover this living impulse contained in Marx's analysis of man's self-alienation, we must turn from *Capital* to Marx's early philosophical writings; we can find, for example, the "living impulse" from which the first chapter of *Capital* resulted, in 1867,

* Reprinted from *Social Research,* No. 21 (1954), 204–30, by permission of the editors. The footnotes found in the original have been omitted here.

expressed as early as 1842 in a discussion of a theft of lumber, published in the *Rheinische Zeitung*.

The original form of Marx's critical analysis of the capitalist process of production is his analysis of the bourgeois world, which is characterized by the alienation of man from himself. To Marx, as an Hegelian, the bourgeois-capitalist world represents a specifically "irrational" reality, and a world that for rational man is inhuman, perverted, de-humanized. In the preface to his doctoral thesis and in a letter to Ruge in 1843, Marx called himself an "idealist" who had the "impertinence" to try "to make man a human being." Therefore we have first to show that man as such was Marx's primary concern, and that this remained true even after his discovery of the "new" man in the proletarian. For what Marx ultimately aimed at was a "human" emancipation of man, not merely a legal one—that is, at "real humanism."

Among the German philosophers who were Marx's contemporaries, the tendency to consider man as such was basic with Feuerbach, in the latter's attempt to transform philosophy as metaphysics into philosophy as anthropology. To Feuerbach, Hegel's philosophy of the absolute spirit was the last realization of pure philosophy; and in opposition to Hegel's view, Feuerbach, like Marx, developed a critical study of man as man. Man as such does not play a principal role in Hegel's philosophy of the absolute, objective, and subjective spirit; he defines man's universal "essence" as "spirit" and as "self-consciousness" (*Encyclopedia of the Philosophical Sciences*, §377). In Hegel's social and political philosophy man appears as "man" only under the title of a "subject of material needs," the "system" of which Hegel comprehends as bourgeois society. Therefore when Hegel speaks of "man," he has in mind exclusively the "bourgeois" as the subject of material, economic needs.

Neither Hegel nor Marx hold that in this determination man embodies his universal essence. He is a mere particularity—for Hegel, in relation to the universality of the ethical state; for Marx, in relation to the universality of a classless society. In his *Philosophy of Right* (§190) Hegel makes the following distinction: "In abstract right, what we had before us was the person; in the sphere of morality, the subject; in civil society as a whole, the burgher or bourgeois. Here on the level of needs what we have before us is the concrete idea which we call man. Thus, this is the first time, and indeed properly the only time, to speak of man in this sense."

It is true that Hegel did not completely dismiss the universal concept of man; but he acknowledged it only with regard to man as the subject of "civil rights and economy." This shows clearly Hegel's outstanding realism with regard to man's contemporary reality. He says that every man is first of all "man as such," regardless of his race, nationality, creed, social status, or profession (§209 and note to §270). He counts as man "by virtue of his manhood alone," and this—to be human—is by no means "a mere superficial abstract quality." Nevertheless, according to Hegel, the pith of this universal quality is the fact that only the recognition of civil rights creates self-respect in individuals who feel that they belong to bourgeois society and possess legal rights in it as persons. This specific kind of civic humanity, Hegel says, is "the root from which the desired equalization in the ways of thinking and disposition comes into being." He guards himself explicitly against absolutizing this determination of man as man. It is true that every man, in so far as he is valued as man at all (and not simply as an Italian or a German, a Catholic or a Protestant) is equal to every other man. But his self-consciousness—that is, his consciousness of being nothing but man—would become defective if it were crystallized in this way (as cosmopolitanism, for example), and thus were opposed to public life in one state as if it were something independent and fundamental, with a meaning of its own. Man's universal essence is not determined by his being "man" in any sense whatever, but by his being essentially "spirit."

When Hegel talks of self-alienation, therefore, he means something fundamentally different from what Feuerbach and Marx mean, although the formal structure of the idea is the same. The fact that being "man" means being a subject of material needs and civic rights is subordinated by Hegel to the ontological determination of man as *logos* or spirit. And only to man as the subject of rights and needs (of whom we can form only a "notion" but no proper philosophical "concept") does Hegel grant the name of "man." Obviously, he believed more in man's ontological essence, in his spirituality, than in his humanity.

It was Feuerbach's main endeavor to transform this philosophy of spirit into a human philosophy of man, and he characterized the task of his "new philosophy of the future" in this way: what is important at present [1843] is not to describe man but to pull him first out of the "idealistic mire" in which he is sunk; "to derive the necessity of a philosophy of man [that is, anthropology] from the philosophy of the absolute [that is, philosophical theology]; and thus to lay the foundation of a human philosophy by criticizing the divine philosophy" (Preface to *Principles of a Philosophy of the Future*). The tendency to make man the subject of philosophy has its motive, says Feuerbach, in making philosophy the

cause of humanity. In accordance with his anthropological principle, Feuerbach attacks Hegel's particularized determination of man. Referring to Hegel's definition, quoted above, Feuerbach continues polemically. The fact that man can be discussed in so many different ways—as a legal "person," as a moral "subject," and so on—implies that the whole human being is referred to, although each time in a different sense. It belongs to the very character of man that he can be defined as this one and as that one, as a private person, as a public person, as a citizen by his social role and by his economic relations. Feuerbach thus guards himself against Hegel's idea of particularity, though he does not show us how to reintegrate the particularized humanity of the modern bourgeois into the whole humanity of man. This indeed could not be achieved by the humanitarian communism of Feuerbach, by the love of "I and thou," but only through social criticism of the division of labor in general and of its class-character in particular, as undertaken by Marx.

Marx also took Feuerbach's anthropological principle as his starting point for criticizing the man of bourgeois society and the whole modern world. In *The Holy Family* he still identifies himself with Feuerbach's "realistic humanism." The first sentence reads: "Real humanism has in Germany no more dangerous enemy than spiritualism or speculative idealism, which puts 'self-consciousness' or 'spirit' in the place of real, individual man and teaches, like the Gospel: 'It is the Spirit that giveth life.' " And at the beginning of the *Critique of Hegel's Philosophy of Right*, Marx states that Feuerbach's reduction of theology to anthropology is the prerequisite to any criticism of man's mundane situation. His incidental polemics against Hegel's definition of man as a particularity show the same tendency. Marx compares the man of bourgeois society with a commodity—a product of simple labor. Like labor, man has a questionable double character in economic terms: a "value-form" and a "natural-form." As a commodity—that is, as embodied labor—a thing is worth this or that much money, and its natural quality remains irrelevant in comparison to its value; things having the same natural properties may have quite different values as commodities.

The same is true of the man of the world of commodities. In his bourgeois value-form he may play an important role for others as well as for himself—as a general, as a banker, in short as a specialist of some kind, fixed and divided by his objectified activity. As a plain "man as such," however—in his natural-form, as it were—he plays a "rather shabby" role. Here Marx refers, without further comment, to §190 of Hegel's *Philosophy of Right*. This reference has to be interpreted in the following way. If Hegel characterizes man as such as the subject of material needs and the rights of a citizen (besides other similarly particular determinations), this reflects nothing less than the factual dividedness of man's consciousness, the "spiritlessness"—or rather, the inhumanity—in the existential situation of modern humanity. To such a theoretical isolation, division, and fixation of man's existence corresponds the actually existing isolation, division, and fixation of particular modifications of human nature in abstract forms of existence. These do not concern man as such and as a whole, but as a specialist, objectified through his specific work and function. Examples of such living abstractions of human nature are the bourgeois and the proletarian classman, the man who performs mental or bodily labor, and so on.

Most important, however, is the way in which the man of bourgeois society is divided into two contradictory modes of existence: that of the private man with his private morality and property, and that of the citizen with his public morality and dignity. It is true that in all of these partial expressions of human nature man as a whole is co-present, but only in a self-contradictory way. Being essentially determined by this or that particularly, he is this particularity only with regard to some other particularity: he is a professional man over against an amateur or over against himself as a family man; he is a private person as distinct from himself in his public function. In all these particular and objectified expressions of human nature he is man only in a restricted and conditioned way. At most and at best he is man as private man—namely, within bourgeois society, which is a society of "isolated private individuals." Man as such does not play a fundamental role in our specialized, divided, and alienated society; what maters in this bourgeois society is not man as such but particularized man. Furthermore, a man's economic existence and material needs depend on his special skills and accomplishments; "life" means "to make a living." Consequently, Marx says, Hegel's definition of man as a particularity determined by economic needs is not at all a contrived construction, but is the adequate theoretical expression of the actual inhumanity in the social situation of modern man. Hegel's distinctions indicate that in bourgeois society man as man is indeed alienated from himself.

To sum up the concept of man's self-alienation, as it developed from Hegel via Feuerbach to Marx: both Feuerbach and Marx emphasize that Hegel's philosophy of spirit reflects man only in a particular function and not as a complete human being, not as that which ought to be fundamental in any philosophical concept of man. In his analysis of bourgeois society, Hegel discovers the total and intrinsic particularity of modern man, but at the same time he conceals it by the illusory assumption that any partial alienation can be taken back into the whole existence of man, who in essence is spirit. Since Marx, however, is interested first of all in man as such and as a whole, his concern is to lay bare that particularity in its total consequences. He wants to show the shaky foundation of modern existence, which pretends to be human while it is only bourgeois. He is not satisfied with pointing out a single particularity, but shows the total particularity and consequently the alienation which man necessarily represents in such a society.

To free man from his total particularity, and to abolish his self-alienation to a variety of specialized functions, the political and economic emancipation of man is not sufficient. Accordingly, Marx demands a "human" emancipation of man. By this term he does not refer, as Feuerbach does, to man as "ego and alter ego" or as "I and thou," but to the world of man; for man *is* his social world, since he is essentially a *zöon politikon*, a "common essence" (*Gattungswesen*). For this reason Marx's criticism develops as a criticism of modern society and economy—without losing, however, its basic anthropological, and thus its philosophical, meaning. "If man is social by nature, he develops his true nature only within society, and the power of his nature cannot be measured by the power of the single individual but only by the standard of society." Marx pursues the basic and universal alienation of man in all realms of reality, in its economic, political, and immediately social forms. The economic expression of this problem is the world of "commodities," its political expression is the contradiction between "state" and "society," and its immediate social expression is the existence of the "proletariat."

II

The economic expression of man's self-alienation is the commodity. As Marx employs the term, "commodity" does not mean one special kind of object contrasted with other kinds, but the "commodity-form," a fundamental ontological character which, in the modern world, all kinds of objects have in common. It is the commodity-form or commodity-structure which characterizes the alienation or estrangement of man from himself as well as from things. Consequently, *Capital* begins with an analysis of the commodity. The fundamental meaning of this analysis lies in its criticism of a bourgeois society and bourgeois man. In *Capital* this criticism finds direct expression only in casual notes and marginal remarks; it is, however, one main theme in an early debate concerning the law about the theft of lumber (*Holzdiebstahlgesetz*) of 1842. Here Marx undertakes his first brilliant unmasking of the perversion of "means" and "ends," of "thing" and "man"— the perversion that implies the self-estrangement of man, his externalization, his transformation from himself into a *thing*—lumber. This highest degree of externalization, to behave toward oneself in terms of something different and alien, is labeled by Marx, in his doctoral thesis, "materialism" or "positivism," and he calls himself, as one who aims to abolish this estrangement, an "idealist." The externalization of man into an object is alienation from himself because, in their proper sense, things are what they are for man, while man is man for himself.

What Marx wanted to make clear in this debate can be summed up as follows. Lumber, which belongs to a private owner (that is, to a capitalist), and which can therefore be stolen by a man who does not own it privately, is not mere lumber, but something of economic and social relevance and human significance, even though its significance is concealed in the lumber itself. Endowed with this human-social quality, lumber is not the same for its owner as it is for the man who owns nothing and steals the lumber. As long as one man is aware of himself solely or primarily as the owner of lumber, having only this narrow-minded, partial consciousness of himself, while the other man is accordingly regarded merely as a lumber-thief, but not as a human being—as long as these unphilosophical ideas prevail, no equitable punishment (equitable from a human viewpoint, that is—not merely "correct" from the legal viewpoint) can be imposed. Both humanly and legally a dead thing, an "objective power," something non-human, mere wood, determines man and "subsumes" him, unless he is capable of directing and controlling his material and objective relationships in a human-social way. The determination of man through mere lumber is possible, however, because lumber, like any other commodity, is itself an objectified expression of socio-political relationships. Like any other commodity, it has the character of a fetish. For this reason "wooden idols rise while human sacrifices fall." In the words of Marx's concluding passage: "If, therefore, lumber and owners of lumber as such make laws, these laws will differ in nothing but the place where they are made and the language in which they are written. This depraved materialism, this mortal sin against the Holy Spirit of peoples and of mankind, is a direct consequence of the doctrine that the Preussische Staatszeitung preaches to the lawgivers: that when making a law about lumber, they are to think of nothing but wood and lumber, and are not to try to solve each material problem in a political way —that is, in connection with undivided civic reasoning and civic morality."

When something like lumber, this seeming "thing in itself," becomes the standard for the being and behavior of man, man will necessarily be reified and alienated from himself. Interhuman relations also become reified, or materialized, inasmuch as the material relations of things become humanized to quasi-personal powers of man. This perversion is a "depraved materialism." Thus Marx insists on the fundamentally human character of his economic analysis. In *The Holy Family* he emphasizes, in opposition to the views expressed by Proudhon, that a merely economic interpretation of such facts—as expressed in claims for equality of property or wages —is still an "estranged form" of the universal self-alienation of man. Elsewhere Marx says:

The fact that Proudhon wishes to abolish not-owning [*Nichthaben*], as well as the traditional way of owning, is identical with his desire to abolish the actually alienated relationship between man and his own human essence; that is, he wants to abolish the economic expression of man's self-alienation. But since his criticism of social economy is still trapped in the presuppositions of social economy, his concept of the reappropriation of the world of objects is still seen under the economic form of property. Proudhon contrasts...the old way of owning—that is, private property— with "possession." Possession, he declares, is a "socal function." The significant point about a function, however, is not that it "excludes" another person but that it actualizes and realizes a man's own essential powers.... Proudhon has not succeeded in giving this thought adequate elaboration. His notion of "equal property" is the economic one—that is, the still alienated expression of the fact that the object, which exists for man, which is his objectified being, is at the same time his existence in relation to other men, the social behavior of man toward man.

Proudhon abolishes economic alienation within economic alienation [*Proudhon hebt die nationalökonomische Entfremdung innerhalb der nationalökonomische Entfremdung auf*]. This means, Marx contends, that Proudhon does not really abolish economic alienation in any radical sense.

In *German Ideology* Marx raises the same question as in the debate on lumber, though he no longer treats it in the same way. He asks again: Whence comes the strangeness with which men behave toward the products of their own labor, so that they no longer have power and control over their reciprocal relationships? Why, instead, do these products become independent forces, so that "the power of their lives overpowers their own makers"? How does it happen that the personal behavior of the individual has to reify itself and thereby estrange itself, while it exists at the same time as an independent power outside the individual?

Marx replies that this perversion is caused by the division of labor. Accordingly, the way in which men have worked up to the present time must be abandoned; it must be transformed into "total self-activity." This transformation will include not only abolition of the division of labor but also abolition of the separation between city and country—which is "the most striking expression of the subsumption of the individual under the division of labor." Abolition of the division of labor can be accomplished only on the basis of a universal communist order of society, which will not only make all property common property but will also make man's very being, in all of its self-expressions, a common—that is, a communist—matter. Wherever there is division of labor, the slavery of the social structure to objectified relations between things is inevitable, just as the division of any individual's life is inevitable because it is in part a personal life and in part subsumed under some branch of labor with its special conditions.

In 1856, ten years after *German Ideology* was written, Marx looked back at the so-called "revolution" of 1848 and summed up his view of the perverted world as follows:

There is one great fact characterizing the nineteenth century which cannot be denied by any party: on the one side, industrial and scientific powers have developed which no former period of history could have fancied; on the other side, there are symptoms of disintegration surpassing even the well-known terrors of the late Roman Empire. In our time everything seems to be pregnant with its contrast. The machine is endowed with the marvelous power to shorten labor and to make it more profitable; and yet we see how it produces hunger and overwork. The newly emancipated powers of wealth become, through a strange play of destiny, sources of privation. ... Mankind becomes master of nature, but man the slave of man or of his own baseness. The result of all our inventions and progress seems to be that material powers become invested with spiritual life, while human life deteriorates into a material force. This antagonism between modern industry and science, on the one side, modern misery and corruption, on the other side, this antagonism between the forces of production and the social conditions of our epoch, is a tangible, overwhelming and undeniable fact. Some parties may complain about it, others may wish to get rid of the modern capacities in order to get rid also of the modern conflicts. Or they may fancy that such evident progress in the realm of production cannot be achieved but by a corresponding regress in the social political life. But as for us, we recognize in this antagonism the clever spirit [Hegel's "cunning of reason"] which keenly proceeds in working out all these contradictions. We know that the new form of social production, to achieve the good life, needs only new men.

As shown by the introduction to the *Critique of Hegel's Philosophy of Right,*

Marx had already decided who those new men were who were qualified to abolish the universal self-alienation. "They are the workers." Thus Feuerbach's philosophy of "real humanism" found in Marx's "scientific socialism" its adequate "social praxis," the possibility of realization. In *German Ideology* Marx rejected Feuerbach's "real humanism," however, on the ground that it was a mere sentimental community of individual love.

Capital, too, is not simply a critique of political economy but a critique of the man of bourgeois society in terms of that society's economy. The "economic cell" of this economy is the commodity-form of the labor products; and the commodity, like the lumber in the lumber-theft debate, is an economic expression of self-alienation. Self-alienation consists of this: that a thing whose original purpose is to be useful is not manufactured and exchanged for anyone's actual needs, but appears on the commodity market as an object with an autonomous commodity value, independent of its utility. This is true whether economic or intellectual products are traded, whether the commodities are cattle or books. Only through the salesman, for whom the commodity has merely exchange value, can the commodity reach its consumer, the buyer. The fact that an object intended for use becomes autonomous as a commodity offers another illustration of the general situation in modern bourgeois society, namely, that products govern men, and not vice versa.

To uncover this hidden perversion, Marx analyzes the "object-like appearance" (the German word *Schein* means both "appearance" and "disguise") of modern conditions of labor as expressed in the "fetish-character" of the commodity. As a commodity, a table or a chair is a "sensuous-supersensuous" thing—that is, an object whose qualities are at the same time perceptible and imperceptible to the senses. We perceive without difficulty exactly what a table means as an object for use; but what it means as a commodity—as an object that costs money because of the invested labor (that is, the invested working time) that it represents—is at first a hidden social phenomenon. As Marx expresses it in *Capital* (vol. 1, book 1, chap. I, 4), "The table no longer stands with its feet firmly on the ground, but stands on its head in front of all the other commodities, spinning whims from its wooden skull, far more wonderful than if it were to begin dancing of its own free will."

The commodity-form is mysterious because in it the social character of man's labor appears disguised as an objective character stamped upon the product of that labor; therefore the relation of the producers to the sum total of their own labor is presented to them as a social relation which exists not among themselves but among the products of their labor. Later in the same passage of *Capital* Marx continues:

By means of this quid pro quo the products of labor become commodities, sensuous-supersensuous or social things.... It is exactly that definite social relation between men that assumes, in their eyes, the fantastic form of a relation between things. In order to find an analogy, we must have recourse to the misty regions of the religious world. Here the productions of the human brain appear as independent beings endowed with life and entering into relations both with one another and with the human race. So it is, in the world of commodities, with the products of men's hands. This I call the festishism which attaches itself to the products of labor as soon as they are produced as commodities, and which is therefore inseparable from the production of commodities.

At first the producers of commodities —that is, of any kind of objects in the ontological form of commodity—make their social contacts only by exchanging their products. As these contacts take place only through things, the social conditions that underlie the commodities do not appear to the producers as labor-conditions of men. On the one side, these social conditions appear as purely objective and material relations among the various producers of commodities. On the other side, because of the objective character of modern commodities, these social conditions acquire a quasi-personal character on the modern commodity market, which follows its own economic laws. At first, men are not aware of this perversion, their self-consciousness being reified at the same rate. Marx says that although this perversion had to come about, he does not consider it irrevocable. Like other social structures, it can be transformed through revolutionary action and theoretical criticism. At first this revolutionary possibility is hidden behind the fixed and ready-made value-form of the commodity, which is money.

Thus it seems that only the price of a commodity can be changed, not its form as such. If we compare the economic order of our society with other social and economic epochs in history, however, we see at once the historical character of the present perversion of the economic order, by which the products of labor as commodities have acquired authority over their producers. Whatever else we may think about the so-called Dark Ages and Middle Ages, with their conditions of personal dependence, at least the social conditions of labor appear in these centuries as the personal conditions of the people, and not disguised as the social conditions of things. For the very reason that personal relations of dependence constituted the social foundations of society, there was no necessity for labor and its products to assume a fantastic form,

different from their reality. . . . In those days the particular and natural form of labor, and not its general, abstract form —as is the case in a society based on capitalist production of commodities— was the immediate form of labor.

In the light of this historical perspective Marx develops the possibility of a future communist order of society, in order to contrast the "opaque" perversion of the modern world of commodities, its inhumanity, with the "transparency" in a communist society of men's social relations to the products of their own labor. The world of commodities cannot be abolished except through a fundamental revolution in all the concrete conditions under which men now live. Not only "de-capitalization" is needed to change the commodity-form to the utility-form; it will also be necessary to reintegrate the particularity of a reified man into "natural man," whose human nature is, according to Marx, fundamentally social. Man is a *zöon politikon*, though not in an ancient Aristotelian *polis* but in a modern industrial *cosmopolis*.

It is characteristic of the nineteenth century that Hegel could still justify as a productive externalization what Marx rejected as self-alienation or estrangement. In his *Philosophy of Right* (§67) Hegel explains that man, in view of his particular bodily and mental faculties and activities, may very well externalize single products and their use for a limited time, because if they are thus limited they have but an "external" relation to human "totality" and "universality." Hegel explicitly likens this personal externalization to man's relation to the object. Concerning this relationship he argues (§61) that an object reaches its proper determination through the use which man makes of it and for which it is intended by its nature. Only the full use of the object— which appears at first as "external" with regard to the object "itself" or per se—allows it to gain validity in the whole range of what it is. Thus the substance of the thing *is* its "externality," which man appropriates, through use, to himself. In using a thing one makes it one's own, one appropriates it properly; this is the original meaning of "property," and property is therefore constitutive for man. In the same way, the totality of human life and the total use of human powers are identical with the whole of substantial life itself. On the basis of this identity of the substance of personal life with the totality of its activities, or externalization, Hegel argues that a special, single activity, directed toward a single product for a limited time—in other words, a "limited" external relationship of man toward himself—cannot swallow up the totality of man, or determine man in the whole as a particularity, or alienate him from himself.

Hegel's philosophy, which holds that the "spirit," and therefore freedom to abstract and appropriate, is the "universal" character of man, was not greatly concerned about such particular externalization. This accounts for the following addition to the ideas previously expressed: "The distinction here explained is that between a slave and a modern domestic servant or day laborer. The Athenian slave perhaps had an easier occupation and more leisurely work than is usually the case with our servants, but he was still a slave, because he had alienated to his master the whole range of his activity" (§67). Marx concludes precisely the contrary from this. To him the modern wage-earner is less free than the ancient slave. Though he is legally the free owner of his working power and legally equal to the owner of the means of production, and though he does not sell himself in totality but "only" his working power for a limited time, he is nevertheless completely a "commodity" on the modern labor market because his working power is his only true property, which he is forced to alienate in order to live by it. To Marx the "free" slave-laborer incorporates the whole problem of modern society; the Greek slave, by contrast, stood outside the society of his free fellowmen, and his personal fate had no bearing on it.

III

In considering man's political self-alienation in terms of bourgeois society, Marx says (pp. 437, 495): "The abstraction of the state as such belongs to modern times only, because the abstraction of private life belongs to modern times. . . . The *true* man [of modern times] is the private man of the present political constitution."

The political expression of man's self-alienation is found in the inner contradiction between the modern state and bourgeois society; in the contradiction, that is, that exists in a man of the bourgeois state and society because he is partly a private person and partly a public citizen but in no way a whole man—what Marx would call "a man without contradictions." Indirectly, Marx's critique of the principle of economy as "political" economy criticizes at the same time the social and political conditions of this particular society with its particular kind of economy. While his criticism of the commodity as the essential character, the ontological structure, of all our objects, is directed against the perversion of man into a thing, he now directs his criticism of the bourgeois state and society against the bourgeois way of life—its bourgeois humanity, which is essentially "privacy," a privation. This criticism is a main topic in his *Critique of Hegel's Philosophy of Right* and also in his discussion of Bauer's essay on the Jewish problem. Both of these works give a systematic presentation of Marx's views about man's self-alienation in its social and political forms; his remarks on the same subject in *The Holy Family* are more or less incidental and can be omitted from consideration here.

In his critique of Hegel, Marx does not attack man as the owner of money and producer of commodities, but modern man's particularity as such, distinguished from his public life and opposed to it. The particularity of the bourgeois, the thing that distinguishes him and isolates him from the universality of public life—that is, political life—is that he is first of all a private person: he is "bourgeois" in this particular sense. Referring to Hegel's implicit criticism of bourgeois society—which Hegel had defined as a society of isolated, "atomized individuals," Marx says, "Hegel should not be blamed for depicting the modern state as it is, but for presenting it as the *essential* structure of the state" (p. 476). Marx holds that Hegel beclouds the empirical world of the nineteenth century in such a way that his arguments are "crass materialism" (p. 526). Hegel is a materialist in so far as he acknowledges what happens to exist as if it existed by reason of some essential necessity, and thus posits it philosophically. But according to Marx's interpretation, what Hegel really depicts is nothing else but the conflict between bourgeois society and the state. "Hegel is profound in this: that he perceives the separation of the bourgeois and political society as a contradiction. But he is wrong in this: that he is satisfied with the appearance of his dialectical solution" (p. 492). What Hegel had recognized as creating the "extremes" of bourgeois society Marx placed at the center of his analysis: the fundamentally private character of the man of bourgeois society. His social status is "private"—he is deprived of

his political status. Marx develops this idea further in the following passage (p. 494):

As a real bourgeois he finds himself in a twofold organization: in the bureaucratic one, which is an external, formal feature of the political organization which does not touch him and his autonomous reality; and in the social organization, which is bourgeois society. In the latter, however, he stands as a private man outside the state; the social organization does not touch the political state.... Therefore, in order to become a *real* citizen, in order to acquire political importance and effectiveness, he has to step out of his bourgeois reality, to abstract from it, to withdraw from the whole organization into his individuality. For the only existence that he finds for his citizenship is his empty individuality; the state as government is complete without him, and his existence within the bourgeois society is complete without the state. He can be a citizen only as an individual—only in contradiction to these communities, which are the only ones that exist. His existence as a citizen is an existence which lies outside a common essence and is therefore purely individual.

The division between particular and universal interests, which also divides man, living within them, into a person having a private existence and an inferior public existence, is conceived by Marx as a self-alienation of man. For the bourgeois—who is a private man in relation to himself—feels that his real self is as different, external, foreign to himself as a citizen as his private life is foreign to the state. His state is an "abstracting" one, because it is merely administrative and thus abstracts or separates itself from the real or private lives of its citizens, just as individuals, in turn, abstract or separate themselves from the state. Therefore bourgeois society as a whole represents the full application of the principle of individualism or egotism. Its ultimate purpose is the existence of the individual, and everything else is but a means to this end. Man's condition as a member of the state, to live in it as his own, remains necessarily an "abstract" determination as long as modern life presupposes such a great separation of real life from life in the community of the state. As a private person, separated from the public life of the state, modern man represents only a privation of man. In a communist commonwealth the contrary is true: every individual is supposed to take part in the *respublica* individually and in a most personal way.

Marx's purpose was to build a new world through theoretical criticism and practical destruction of the one that had grown old. Out of existing reality, with its specific forms of society and state (a state that is basically unpolitical because it is political in an abstract way), he wanted to develop the "true reality" in which essence and existence, or reason and reality, are one and the same. In 1852, ten years after he wrote *The Holy Family*, Marx gave an historical account of this world grown old in *The Eighteenth Brumaire* of Louis Bonaparte. He described that era of the bourgeois revolution as a caricature of the greater revolution of 1789. He contended that the passions of the later period were without truth, for its truth had no passion; that its reality was completely watered down and living on loans; that its development was merely a constant repetition of the same tensions and relaxations; that its conflicts inflamed each other only to end in dullness and collapse. Its history was a history without events, its heroes performed no heroic deeds, its supreme law was irresolution. His criticism may be compared with the contemporary analysis by Kierkegaard, *The Present Age;* both men turned against Hegel's philosophy of reconciliation, though in opposite directions.

According to Marx, the contradiction between private and public life must be resolved. The deficient private humanity of the man of bourgeois society is to be sublated in a commonwealth which embraces the whole existence of man— including his "theoretical" existence— shaping him from head to foot into a communistic, universally human being. Marx therefore explicitly distinguishes his philosophical communism from the "real" communism of Cabet, Weitling, and others, which he calls a "particular and dogmatic abstraction" because it is a "phenomenon of the old humanistic principle, infected by its opposite, privacy" (p. 573). The whole socialistic principle, if taken as a single phenomenon, is but one side of the full reality of the true human essence.

To this radical destruction of all the isolated modes of existence that have become independent corresponds the change of all particularities into man as such and as a whole. The real basis of any positive reform must be the recognition that human existence is now limited to private man, a limitation unknown to antiquity or to the Middle Ages. The private man of antiquity was the slave, for he had no part in the *respublica* and therefore was not "man" in the full sense of the word. Likewise, in the Middle Ages there corresponded to each private sphere of life a public sphere "In the Middle Ages the life of the people and that of the state were identical. The real principle of the state was man, but man *enslaved*" (p. 437). Only the French Revolution emancipated man politically as the bourgeois, thus changing man's private status to a specific status, notwithstanding the fact that it was the French Revolution that wanted to make every man a *citoyen*.

The destruction of the religious particularity of man is considered by Marx with reference to Bauer's essay on the Jewish problem. The concrete question of how to accomplish the political emancipation of the Jews in Germany is bypassed by Marx in his first sentence. He says that a political emancipation cannot mean anything unless the Jews are emancipated "as men." But in this sense they are no more emancipated than the Germans who are to free them. "Why do the Jews complain about their special yoke while they accept the general one?" As long as the state is Christian and the Jew Jewish, the first is as unfit to grant emancipation as the second is to receive it.

Thus far Marx agrees with Bauer; both consider that a change to purely "human" conditions is the only "critical" and "scientific" solution. But Marx blames Bauer for ending his criticism at the point where the problem ceases to be theological and begins to become real. What must be investigated is the relationship between political and human emancipation. The limitations of a merely political emancipation are found in the fact that "the state can be free even though man in it is not free." In order truly to emancipate the Jew as well as the Christian, freedom from all religion is needed, not merely a state that grants religious freedom. The problem is a universal and basic one, since it concerns emancipation from every particularity in the way of being man, including religious man as well as private man and modern professional man, in their respective abstractions from the universal interests of human society. Marx goes on to say (p. 585): "The difference between the religious man and the citizen is the difference between merchant and citizen, between wage-earner and citizen, between landowner and citizen, between the living individual and the citizen. The contradiction in which religious man finds himself in relation to political man is the same one in which the bourgeois finds himself in relation to the *citoyen;* the same in which the member of bourgeois society, with his political lion's skin, finds himself."

Bauer, says Marx, passes over the cleavage between the political state and bourgeois society, directing his polemics only against the religious aspect of these types of social organization. The disintegration of man into Jew and citizen, or into Protestant and citizen, is not really a contradiction of citizenship but a defective political way of emancipating oneself from religion. The particularity of religion is merely another expression of the thorough disintegration of modern man in bourgeois society; it is one more example of the universal "estrangement of man from man," of man's alienation from himself, of the inner-human diremption between his individual life and his group life. Consequently, according to Marx (p. 591):

We do not say to the Jews as Bauer does, it is not possible for you to become politically emancipated unless you emancipate yourselves radically from Judaism. We tell them, because your political emancipation is possible without your complete renunciation of Judaism, therefore political emancipation is not yet identical with human emancipation. If you Jews want to be emancipated politically without being emancipated humanly at the same time, the contradiction lies not in you but in the nature of a merely political emancipation. If your thinking is trapped in this concept, you partake of a general prejudice. Just as the state acts as an evangelist when it behaves, though it is a state, in a Christian manner toward the Jews, in the same way the Jew acts as a politician when he asks for the rights of a citizen though he is a Jew.

In Marx's view the same defective approach to emancipation characterizes the French and the American "Rights of Man." It is clear to him that the "Droits de l'Homme" were not rights of man at all, but bourgeois privileges, because that historical *homme* was, as a *citoyen,* divided from himself as a bourgeois. The Declaration of the Rights of Man presupposed that *de facto* the bourgeois man was the actual, true, and essential man. This assumption Marx contests as follows (p. 595): "None of the so-called Rights of Man eliminates man the egoist, man as a member of bourgeois society—that is, an individual withdrawn into his private interests and arbitrariness, separated from the community. Far from comprehending man as an essentially common existence [*Gattungswesen*], the common life, society itself, appears in these Rights as an external frame for individuals, as a limitation of their original independence. The only ties by which individuals are held together are natural necessity, material needs, private interests, and the conservation of their property and their egoistic persons. . . ."

Thus a declaration of the rights of man is insufficient: the truly human emancipation is still to be achieved. Marx describes it in these words (p. 599): "Political emancipation is the reduction of man to a member of bourgeois society, to an egoistic, independent individual on the one hand, and to a citizen on the other hand. . . . Only when the real, individual man reintegrates into himself the abstract citizen and becomes, as individual man—in his empirical everyday life, in his individual work, in his individual relations—a common existence; only when man has acknowledged and organized his *forces propres* as social forces, and therefore no longer separates these social forces from himself in the disguise of political forces—only then is his *human* emancipation accomplished."

The freedom to which man is to be emancipated is thus, in its formal structure, freedom as understood by Hegel: a "freedom of supreme community"

(*Freiheit der höchsten Gemeinschaft*), contrasted with the negative freedom of the isolated individual, which is only a freedom from external coercion. In this respect the man of the Greek *polis* was freer than the man of bourgeois society, and even the Christian idea of freedom is more democratic because it respects each individual as equally sovereign in his relationship with God. Thus Marx can say (p. 561): "Self-reliance [*Selbstgefühl*] of man, his freedom, has still to be reawakened in the hearts of modern men. Only this feeling, which disappeared from this world with the Greeks, and into the blue haze of the skies with the Christians, can once more create from society a community of men dedicated to their highest aims, a democratic state."

True personal freedom becomes possible only in a community that is related to man as such. It comes about through a social change in the way of being man but it cannot be achieved either by an internal or an external approach exclusively. The freedom of private man in bourgeois society exists only in his own imagination. It is dependent and subsumed under the "objective power of things."

IV

In discussing the social expression of man's self-alienation in terms of the proletariat, Marx says: "If socialist writers attribute a world-historic role to the proletariat, their reason for doing so is not . . . that they consider the proletarians gods—but rather the opposite." And in the introduction to the *Critique of Hegel's Philosophy of Right* we find the following statement: "The dissolution of the whole of modern society is represented in the particular class of the proletariat." In this group lies the positive possibility of a human emancipation, not because it is a class within bourgeois society but because it is itself a society outside of the established one. It is a society "which can no longer lay claim to any historical title but only to the human title, which does not stand in one-sided opposition to the actions of the German state but in absolute opposition to its fundamental principles. Finally, the proletariat is a sphere which cannot become emancipated without emancipating itself from all the remaining spheres of society, thereby in turn emancipating them; it is, in a word, the complete loss of man and therefore can regain itself only by completely regaining man" (pp. 619–20).

Marx's philosophy, in which man is a "common essence," has found its weapon in the proletariat, just as the proletariat found its weapon in his philosophy. "The head of this emancipation is philosophy, its heart is the proletariat." The possessing class and the proletariat represent, fundamentally, the same kind of estrangement of man from himself; the difference is that one class feels itself healthy and fixed in this state of alienation—though without any critical consciousness of it—while the other class is a dehumanization that is conscious of being dehumanized and therefore strives to overcome it. The proletariat is, so to speak, the self-consciousness of the commodity. It is forced to alienate itself, to externalize itself like a commodity; but for this very reason it develops a critical and revolutionary consciousness, a class-consciousness. In one way, however, the proletarian is less dehumanized than the bourgeois, since his dehumanization is a manifest one, not the unconscious, hidden, and spiritualized dehumanization of the bourgeois. Because the proletariat embraces in its own conditions of life the conditions of all contemporary society in "its inhuman extreme," it

cannot liberate itself without emancipating all of society as well. This universal function of the proletariat is elucidated as follows by Marx, in connection with the universality of the modern international world economy, in *German Ideology* (Moscow ed., p. 296):

Only the proletarians of our time who are completely excluded from any self-activity are in a position to enforce their complete and no longer limited self-activity, which consists in appropriating the totality of productive powers together with the corresponding development of a totality of faculties. All seizures and appropriations by former revolutionary movements were limited ones. Individuals whose self-activity was limited through the limitation of the instruments of production and traffic took hold of these limited instruments of production, producing thereby just another limitation. Their production instruments became their property, but they remained subsumed under the division of labor and under their own productional instrument. In all such appropriations a mass of individuals remained subsumed under one single instrument of production; in the proletarian appropriation a mass of productional instruments must be subsumed under each single individual, and property under all. There is no way of subsuming the modern global economy under individuals except by subsuming it under all.

Thus we find that Marx does not attribute fundamental and universal importance to the proletariat because he considers that its members are "gods," but because to him the proletariat embodies potentially universal humanity—man's common existence though he is now in the extremity of self-alienation. The fundamental importance of the proletariat corresponds exactly to the commodity-form of modern objects. The class of the wage-earner has a universal function because the wage-earner is completely externalized through "the earthly question in life size"; because he is merely a salesman of his own labor, a personified commodity and not a human being. In him the economic phase of life shows itself most clearly as human destiny and thus, with the proletariat as the nucleus of all social problems, the economy necessarily becomes the "anatomy" of bourgeois society—as was pointed out at the beginning of this paper. With the self-liberation of the proletariat as the universal class with no particular interests, private humanity—together with private property and the private capitalist economy, the foundation of bourgeois privacy—dissolves. Private humanity is sublated in universal humanity, based on a commonwealth which is indeed common to all, with common property and a common economy. The negative in-dependence of the bourgeois individual is replaced by the positive freedom of a supreme community, which is a community of public life and of direct mutual relationships among all single individuals.

Marx's investigations, unlike those of empirical sociology, are not concerned with mutual relations between single empirical fields, or with "factors" which are considered to be of equal significance and to represent, when added up, the whole of reality. He was no abstract empiricist, just as he was no abstract philosophical "materialist" who would deduce his theory from economic principles. Marx analyzes our entire self-contradictory human world in terms of man's self-alienation, of which the existence of the proletariat is the climax and the key to the whole. This self-alienation is investigated in terms of its possible abolition, and not—as in Hegel's work—in terms of its dialectical sublation. Marx intends no more and no less than the abolition of the contradiction of particularity and universality, of privacy and public life. This contradiction, which had been previously formulated by Hegel, must disappear in a classless society, because such a society rests on the universal essence of man as a social creature.

It is true that man's self-alienation is conditioned by the type and degree of development of the material conditions of production, by the division of labor, and by the sum of the concrete conditions of his life. But these conditions are structurally united in the social nature of man, who is his own world and whose self-consciousness is a world-consciousness. The sum of conditions cannot be derived from abstract economic factors; the latter must be integrated into the concrete system of historic human conditions. "Real" man is not man "in the irrationality of his existence...as he walks and stands... as he is externalized...through the whole organization of our society," a semblance of himself (p. 590). In his true reality man is an essence which has to be brought into existence through action. Marx was convinced that the reality that accounts for the problematic condition of our society drives with historic necessity toward the fulfillment of his views, just as his philosophy moves toward its historic realization.

In *German Ideology* Marx had "settled his accounts" with his former "philosophical conscience." Nevertheless he still—in contrast to the scientism of so many Marxists—possessed a philosophical conscience, derived from his study of Hegel. His endeavor was to realize Hegel's principle of the dialectical identity of reason and reality, or of essence and existence, thus transforming Hegel's philosophy to Marxism. A full discussion of Marx's analysis of self-alienation would have to take into account his philosophy of history, which underlies not only Hegelianism and Marxism but all post-Hegelian modern historical thinking.

11

MILL

An appreciation of the personal continuity of English philosophical life is gained by recalling that John Stuart Mill (1806–1873) was the godfather of Bertrand Russell. The more widely known feature of Mill's life, however, is probably the stern intellectual upbringing of his infancy, in which his father, the philosopher James Mill, insisted that John study Greek at the age of three. He eventually outgrew the influence of his father and his father's friend Jeremy Bentham and became, in his own right, the leading Victorian writer on politics and economics. He sat in the House of Commons for three years near the end of his life championing the cause of liberal and democratic reform. His most important contribution, however, was his short essay *On Liberty* (1859), which is, to this day, the liberal manifesto. Nowhere has the sacredness of the individual been more eloquently defended.

In his article, J. C. Rees, a contemporary English scholar, addresses himself to the criticism most often leveled at the argument in *On Liberty*: that Mill failed to realize that all human acts have consequences for others. Rees holds that this criticism rests on a misreading of *On Liberty*. Mill, he writes, did not mean acts which had no effect simply on other persons but acts which had no effect, more specifically, on other people's interests. Having made this clear, Rees then proceeds to a critical evaluation of Mill as reread. H. J. McCloskey, the Australian philosopher, turns in his article to a broader investigation of Mill as the alleged theorist of the limited liberal state. McCloskey contends that a close reading of Mill's political and economic works reveals that he envisioned a much more active, intervening, and purposive state.

J. C. REES

A Re-Reading of Mill on Liberty

I

My aim in this article is to discuss what Mill was trying to do in his essay *On Liberty*. Or, to put it more precisely, to consider whether the commonly accepted version of 'the very simple principle' asserted in the essay is a fair account of Mill's intentions. Before setting out what I take to be the traditional version and giving my reasons for questioning it, we ought to remind ourselves of the general purpose Mill had in publishing his work.

In his *Autobiography* Mill describes the essay as 'a philosophic text-book of a single truth...the importance, to man and society, of a large variety in types of character, and of giving full freedom to human nature to expand itself in innumerable and conflicting directions'.[1] The book deals with one of the recurring questions of politics but was written in circumstances which gave that question a new significance. For behind Mill's question—'What is the nature and extent of the power which society ought to exercise over the individual?'

—was his anxiety lest the tendencies which he claimed to see at work in the civilized world would eventually extinguish spontaneity in all the important branches of human conduct. 'Society has now [the manuscript was completed in 1857] fairly got the better of individuality...in our times, from the highest class of society down to the lowest, every one lives as under the eye of a hostile and dreaded censorship.'[2] The essay had, therefore, the practical aim of helping to ward off the dangers which the trends of the age seemed to carry with them and, in particular, to counter 'the general tendency of things throughout the world to render mediocrity the ascendant power among mankind'.[3] The work, Mill tells us, was conceived and written as a short essay in 1854.[4] In a letter to Harriet from Rome in January 1855 he wrote: 'On my way here cogitating thereon I came back to an idea we have talked about, and thought that the best thing to write and publish at present would be a volume on Liberty. So many things might be brought into it and nothing seems more to be needed—it is

* Reprinted from *Political Studies*, VIII (1960), 113–29, by permission of the Clarendon Press, Oxford.

1 *Autobiography* (World's Classics edition), p. 215.

2 *On Liberty* (Everyman edition), p. 119. Quotations are from this edition throughout.

3 Op. cit., p. 123.

4 *Autobiography*, p. 212.

a growing need too, for opinion tends to encroach more and more on liberty, and almost all the projects of social reformers of these days are really liberticide—Comte's particularly so'.[5] But Mill's fears and anxieties go back long before this period. They were clearly expressed in an essay on 'Civilization' published in 1836 and there are definite signs that they were taking root in even earlier years.[6]

One of the tasks Mill set himself in *On Liberty* was to fix a limit 'to the legitimate interference of collective opinion with individual independence'.[7] This seemed to him to be at least as important as 'protection against political despotism', for the 'yoke of opinion in England is perhaps heavier, that of the law is lighter, than in most other countries of Europe'.[8] The preservation of individuality and variety of character was possible, he believed, if a principle were observed whereby every person was accorded an area of liberty in thought and action. His father and Bentham had argued the case for representative government, but its practical consequences, whether in the United States as revealed by de Tocqueville or experienced in England since the Reform Act, were in his view by no means wholly favourable to liberty.[9] And even more menacing than the now apparent

weaknesses of a system of government whose establishment was the great aim of the orthodox Utilitarians were the informal pressures of society that the coming of democracy tended to strengthen and make still more relentless. Progress and the attainment of the truth were, as Mill saw it, the work of a select few; and to promote and safeguard the conditions for the distinctive activity of this *élite* in face of the growing power of the mediocre mass was a result he hoped his essay would help to achieve. Yet to a number who have shared his aspirations the specific principle he offered has always seeemed defective. Mill's attachment to liberty has been admired on all sides and the

---

[5] F. A. Hayek, *John Stuart Mill and Harriet Taylor* (1951), p. 216.

[6] The essay on 'Civilization' is reprinted in *Dissertations and Discussions,* vol. i. See also Mill's article on 'Genius' (1832), reprinted in Ruth Borchardt's edition of *Four Dialogues of Plato* (1946) ; and my article in this journal, 'A Phase in the Development of Mill's Ideas on Liberty' (vol. vi, pp. 33–44).

[7] Op. cit., p. 68.   [8] Op. cit., pp. 71–72.

[9] Before the publication of the first part of Tocqueville's work in 1835 the American Unitarian preacher and writer, William Ellery Channing, had uttered warnings similar to Tocqueville's at a number of points. Channing's writings were known in England and there were reviews of some of them in the *Edinburgh Review* and the *Westminster*

Review in 1829 and 1830. I argued in a previous article in this journal (Feb. 1958) that Mill was influenced by Channing's views. Apart from the 'Remarks on the Formation of Associations', which Mill certainly knew, there is the election sermon of 1830. The latter was reprinted in a two-volume edition of Channing's works published in Britain in 1835 (see vol. ii, pp. 255ff.). One or two passage are worth quoting. 'The advantages of civilisation have their peril. In such a state of society, opinion and law impose salutary restraint, and produce general order and security. But the power of opinion grows into a despotism, which, more than all things, represses original and free thought, subverts individuality of character, reduces the community to a spiritless monotony, and chills the love of perfection' (p. 268). 'An espionage of bigotry may as effectually close our lips and chill our hearts, as an armed and hundred-eyed police' (p. 271). 'Our great error as a people, is, that we put an idolatrous trust in free institutions; as if these, by some magic power, must secure our rights, however we enslave ourselves to evil passions. We need to learn that forms of liberty are not its essence; that whilst the letter of a free constitution is preserved, its spirit may be lost; that even its wisest provisions and most guarded powers may be made weapons of tyranny. In a country called free, a majority may become a faction, and a proscribed minority may be insulted, robbed, and oppressed. Under elective governments, a dominant party may become as truly a usurper, and as treasonably conspire against the state, as an individual who forces his way by arms to the throne' (p. 278).

many eloquent and moving passages he dedicates to its virtues have been widely acclaimed as classic utterances on behalf of one of the most cherished of western ideals, but, it has been generally said, the principle he advances for its protection cannot do what is expected of it. My purpose here is to look again at that principle and to discuss whether it has been properly understood by its critics.

II

'The object of this Essay', says Mill, 'is to assert one very simple principle ...that the sole end for which mankind are warranted, individually or collectively, in interfering with the liberty of action of any of their number is self-protection...to prevent harm to others. ...His own good, either physical or moral, is not a sufficient warrant.... The only part of the conduct of any one, for which he is amenable to society, is that which concerns others. In the part which merely concerns himself, his independence is, of right, absolute.'[10] This passage appears in the first chapter of the essay. In the last chapter, where Mill offers some examples of how his principle might be applied in practical cases, he restates 'the two maxims which together form the entire doctrine of this Essay...first, that the individual is not accountable to society for his actions, in so far as these concern the interests of no person but himself.... Secondly, that for such actions as are prejudicial to the interests of others, the individual is accountable, and may be subjected either to social or to legal punishment, if society is of opinion that the one or the other is requisite for its protection.'[11]

A study of the comments on Mill's essay during the century since its publi-

cation shows that the principle just stated has been widely criticized because it appears to rest on the possibility of classifying human actions into two categories—actions which concern only the agent and actions that concern others besides the agent. The distinction between these two categories, it has been repeatedly argued, is impossible to sustain. As one of the critics has put it: 'The greater part of English history since his day has been a practical commentary on the fallacy of this distinction. No action, however intimate, is free from social consequences. No human being can say that what he is, still less what he does, affects no one but himself.'[12] The crucial point in this criticism is clearly the supposition that Mill's principle depends for its validity on there being some actions, including some important ones, which are free from social consequences, i.e. that they affect no one but the agent himself.[13] I shall argue that this assumption on the part of the critics is false and that it derives from a failure to observe the form of words which Mill often employs in the text and to take at its full value Mill's firm asser-

---

[10] Op. cit., pp. 72–73.
[11] Op. cit., pp. 149–50.

[12] Leading article in *The Times Literary Supplement,* 10 July 1948. Reprinted as part of a pamphlet, *Western Values,* published by *The Times.*

[13] Including some important ones is necessary here in order to prevent the issue from being trivialized. When Mill's critics say that no action is free from social consequences they must be assumed to be ignoring many petty acts which are obviously free from social effects, or else they are mistaken in refusing to admit their existence. For example, if I shave in a well-lit room before a mirror that reflects the face with uniform clarity and I can, in these conditions, shave equally well no matter which side I begin to shave, then starting with the left or the right side is a matter which cannot be considered to have any effects on other persons. Hence it is of no concern to society how I, or anyone else, begins to shave each morning. The debate between Mill and his critics clearly does not hinge on trivial acts of this kind.

tion that actions of the so-called 'self-regarding' variety may frequently affect, even harmfully, persons other than the agent. Before elaborating this claim I want to pass briefly in review the evidence for my contention that the traditional account of Mill's principle makes just this assumption about his classification of human actions.

I begin with a commonly made criticism, drawn from among the first reviews of *On Liberty*. There is no conduct whose impact is confined to the agent, said the *London Review* in 1859, because 'no moral quality is limited in its action to the sphere of its possessor's own history and doings...society has an interest, over and above that of mere self-defence, in the conduct of everyone of its members'.[14] Fourteen years later, Fitzjames Stephen, whose *Liberty, Equality, Fraternity* has set the pattern for much of the criticism directed against Mill up to the present time, asserted with characteristic vigour that 'the attempt to distinguish between self-regarding acts and acts which regard others, is like an attempt to distinguish between acts which happen in time and acts which happen in space. Every act happens at some time and in some place, and in like manner every act that we do either does or may affect both ourselves and others...the distinction is altogether fallacious and unfounded.'[15] Further, in defence of the attitude of a temperance reformer whom Mill had attacked in the *Liberty*, Stephen remarks: 'It is surely a simple matter of fact that every human creature is deeply interested not only in the conduct, but in the thoughts, feelings, and opinions of millions of persons who stand in no other assignable relation to him than that of being his fellow-creatures.... A man would no more be a man if he was alone in the world than a hand

would be a hand without the rest of the body.'[16] The view of human relations expressed in this last passage was, of course, shared by the Oxford Idealists and we should expect from them too a decided lack of sympathy with Mill's principle. Thus Ritchie considers the conception of the individual implied in Mill's doctrine to be abstract and negative, for the individual finds his true self 'not in distinction and separation from others, but in community with them'. 'We may very well doubt', he continues, 'whether any acts, nay, even thoughts, of the individual can, in the strictest sense, be merely self-regarding, and so matter of indifference to other individuals.... The more we learn of human society, the more we discover that there are no absolute divisions, but that every atom influences and is influenced by every other. It may be very inexpedient to meddle with particular acts, or it may be practically impossible to do so; but we can lay down no hard and fast line, separating self-regarding acts from acts which affect others.'[17] And Bosanquet: '... every act of mine affects both myself and others.... It may safely be said that no demarcation between self-regarding and other-regarding action can possibly hold good.'[18]

[14] Vol. xiii, p. 274.
[15] p. x, preface to the 2nd edition, 1874.
[16] p. 128 (1st edition, 1873). Mill's remarks appear on pp. 145–46 of *On Liberty*.
[17] D. G. Ritchie, *The Principles of State Interference* (1891), pp. 96–98.
[18] *Philosophical Theory of the State*, p. 60. Writing about the same time Frederic Harrison (*Tennyson, Ruskin, Mill*: 1899) states: 'The attempt to distinguish between conduct which concerns oneself, and conduct that may remotely concern others, is quite fallacious. No distinction can be drawn, for human acts are organically inseparable' (p. 300). See also F. C. Montague's *The Limits of Individual Liberty* (1885), pp. 185–8: Mill's distinction, says Montague, is an offshoot of the doctrine of the social contract and 'is impossible to those who look upon man as receiving from society his whole character and his whole endowment, and as reacting upon society at every moment of his life'.

Closer to our own day, MacIver in his *Modern State* remarks of Mill's principle: 'This statement has a form which suggests that the full significance of the interdependence of social beings is hardly realized by Mill...he thinks of man as in certain categories social, but in others wholly "individual". But if we realize that the nature of man is a unity, that in every *aspect* he is a social being at the same time that he is also autonomous and self-legislating, so that his sociality and his individuality cannot belong to two different spheres...we can no longer be content with an abstract doctrine of liberty.'[19] In similar vein Sir Ernest Barker says that Mill's assumption of the existence of two different spheres of conduct is open to the criticism that Mill separates the inseparable. 'The conduct of any man', maintains Sir Ernest, 'is a single whole: there can be nothing in it that concerns himself only, and does not concern other men: whatever he is, and whatever he does, affects others and therefore concerns them.'[20] Finally, to conclude with a quotation from one of the best studies of Mill's philosophy that has appeared in recent decades, here is the view of Professor R. P. Anschutz. He is commenting on Mill's principle of self-protection ('the argument for insulation' as Anschutz calls it) and says: 'It is a completely untenable as well as a completely impracticable doctrine. It is quite impossible to distinguish between that part of a person's behaviour which affects himself and that part which also affects others: and there is nothing to be gained by attempting to make the distinction.'[21]

This, then, is the case which has been built up against Mill over the last hundred years. The essential point in the criticism is, as I have said, that Mill wrongly assumes some human actions to be free of social consequences. But if we look carefully at the two passages quoted above (p. 115) where Mill is explicitly stating his principle, it will be noticed that, although in the first case he writes of conduct which 'merely concerns' the agent and of conduct which 'concerns others', he introduces the word 'interests' in the second passage. He says that the individual is to be held accountable only for those actions which 'are prejudicial to the *interests* of others'.[22] Elsewhere in the essay both types of phrase appear, with a number of variations within each type. Thus we find on the one hand: 'what only regards himself', 'conduct which affects only himself', 'which concerns only himself', 'things wherein the individual alone is concerned'; and on the other: 'concern the interests of others', 'affects the interests of no one but himself', 'affect the interests of others', 'damage to the interests of others'. Traditional commentary has assumed that all these expressions were intended to convey the same meaning and that Mill's distinction was simply between actions which affect no one but the agent and actions which affect others. My case in this article is that we ought not to gloss over these different modes of expression, that there is an important difference between just 'affecting others' and 'affecting the interests of others', and that there are passages in the essay which lend support to the view that Mill was thinking of 'interests' and not merely 'effects'. As a first step I wish to support my claim that there is a significant difference between saying, on the one hand, that an action affects another person and, on the other, that it affects his interests.

---

19 pp. 457 and 459.
20 *Principles of Social and Political Theory* (1951), p. 217.
21 *The Philosophy of J. S. Mill* (1953), p. 48.

---

22 My italics.

It seems to me quite clear that a person may be affected by another's behaviour without his interests being affected. For example, when we speak of a man's equilibrium not being affected in trying circumstances we are not thinking of his interests. Indeed a man's interests may well be seriously injured without his equilibrium being affected to any marked degree. And even if it were, there would be two things affected, not one. Similarly, if we heard of someone's outlook on life being fundamentally affected by an event such as a religious experience we should not have to conclude that his interests had likewise been affected. True, a religious convert has an interest in religion that he did not have before, but we are not speaking of interests in that sense. My interests in literature can undergo a radical change without anything like business, professional, or property interests being affected to the slightest extent. To bring out the distinction I am trying to make between interests and effects, but with no pretence at offering a definitive account of the nature of interests, one might say that interests—and I do not wish to imply that they are necessarily legal—depend for their existence on social recognition and are closely connected with prevailing standards about the sort of behaviour a man can legitimately expect from others. A claim that something should be recognized as an interest is one we should require to be supported by reasons and one capable of being made the subject of discussion. On the other hand I could be very seriously affected by the action of another person merely because I had an extraordinarily sensitive nature and no claim to have others respect these tender spots would be recognized as amounting to an interest. How one is affected by a theatrical performance depends partly on one's tastes, but the interests of a businessman would be affected by a tax on business property no matter what his tastes or susceptibilities; just as the interests of a university are affected by a scheme to establish a research institute in the same area (in a common subject of course) whether the university authorities welcome the idea or not. Moreover, 'effects' is a concept applicable to plants and animals as well as human beings, but no one talks about the interests of plants. Crops are affected by fertilizers or drought in much the same way as a certain drug would have an effect on, say, chronic lassitude. And dogs are affected by thunder in the kind of way that I might be affected by the news that my favourite football team had been beaten in the cup-final. There are no interests necessarily at stake here, though drought could affect my interests as well as the crops, and gamblers stand to win or lose by a result that could also leave them dismayed. Apart from really trival actions—which we can ignore in this context—it is probably true that what I do or am like affects other people.[23] Any principle which rested on the assumption that other people are not (or may not be) affected would be open to precisely the objections brought against Mill. But deciding whether interests are affected is another matter and a principle that seeks to limit social interference to cases where interests are involved cannot be attacked because it fails to recognize the truth that 'every atom influences and is influenced by every other' or to realize that 'the nature of man is a unity'.

It might be objected at this stage that Mill does not consistently adhere to the term 'interests' and that one is entitled to assume from its appearance in some passages, coupled with the

_____

23 See note 13, above.

employment of such phrases as 'conduct which concerns only himself', that there is one unambiguous doctrine running through the entire essay. Our objector might well concede the distinction between a principle based on interests and one based on mere effects, but he feels we are not justified in attempting to produce a coherent theory when, from the variety of the terms used in the relevant passages, there is clearly not one there to extract. My answer to this objection, for the moment at least (whether one can find a single consistent principle running through the whole work I discuss below) is that if Mill is really trying to maintain two (possibly more) principles, and moves from one to the other at different points of the essay without really knowing what he is doing and hence with no warning to his readers of what he is about, then to recognize this fact is at least to notice something which commentators on Mill have, so far as I know, failed to discern in the past. But it need not necessarily follow that because Mill uses phrases like 'conduct which concerns only himself' along with 'conduct which affects the interests of no persons besides himself' this must be regarded as conclusive evidence of an unwitting affirmation of two distinct and potentially incompatible principles. For though the word 'concerns' has sometimes no more force than 'has reference to' or 'affects', with no implication that interests are being referred to or affected, it can also mean 'is of importance to' and could in some contexts carry with it the suggestion that interests are involved. Thus when Mill says that social control is permissible only in cases when one's conduct 'concerns others' we are not compelled to assume that he means actions which just have 'effects' on others. Hence it may well be that the ambiguity of the word 'concerns' is responsible for con-

cealing a coherent theory based on 'interests' rather than 'effects' and that we can so interpret the passages where the term 'interests' is not specifically used as to yield a single consistent principle.

However that may be, it should be observed that there are statements in the essay suggesting that Mill was quite aware of the manner in which individuals are constantly affecting one another. And so forthright are they that one wonders how it ever came to be thought of Mill that he wished to declare a whole area of human behaviour 'self-regarding' because the actions so named had no 'effects' on others (as opposed to 'affecting their interests'). Thus in the fourth chapter of the essay Mill discusses a possible objection to his principle in these terms: 'How (it may be asked) can any part of the conduct of a member of society be a matter of indifference to the other members? No person is an entirely isolated being; it is impossible for a person to do anything seriously or permanently hurtful to himself, without mischief reaching at least to his near connections, and often far beyond them. . . .'[24] And Mill concedes to this objection 'that the mischief which a person does to himself may *seriously affect,* both through their sympathies and their interests, those nearly connected with him and, in a minor degree, society at large'.[25] But he goes on to insist that only when conduct of this sort (i.e. conduct affecting others) violates 'a distinct and assignable obligation to any other person or persons' is 'the case taken out of the self-regarding class, and becomes amenable to moral disapprobation'.[26] A little farther on in the same chapter Mill speaks of a person

---

24 Op. cit., p. 136.
25 Op. cit., p. 137. My italics.
26 Op. cit., pp. 137–38.

preventing himself 'by conduct purely self-regarding, from the performance of some definite duty incumbent on him to the public' and thus being guilty of a social offence, but where the conduct 'neither violates any specific duty to the public, nor occasions perceptible hurt to any assignable individual except himself; the inconvenience is one which society can afford to bear, for the sake of the greater good of human freedom'.[27] It is surely obvious that Mill would be contradicting himself here in the most flagrant manner if we were to interpret 'purely self-regarding' to mean those actions which have no impact (i.e. no 'effects') on other members of society. And the case against this interpretation becomes even more conclusive if we consider Mill's remarks in the opening chapter where he is elaborating the central principle of the essay. He writes: '...there is a sphere of action in which society, as distinguished from the individual, has if any, only an indirect interest; comprehending all that portion of a person's life and conduct which affects only himself ...when I say only himself, I mean directly, and in the first instance; for whatever affects himself, may affect others through himself...'.[28] Further, in the fourth chapter, Mill talks of the 'self-regarding deficiencies' which a person may manifest and which 'render him necessarily and properly a subject of distaste, or, in extreme cases, even of contempt'. For vices of this kind, he says, a man may 'suffer very severe penalties at the hands of others for faults which directly concern only himself'.[29] Here, then, is a clear affirmation that what he calls, perhaps misleadingly, 'self-regarding conduct' can have effects on others. Even to the extent that those affected can retaliate with 'very severe penalties'!

Mill's critics, Fitzjames Stephen among them, have wondered how the division of human conduct into two spheres could be sustained if self-regarding actions might suffer severe penalties at the hands of others. Mill attempted to maintain the distinction, which is, of course, crucial for the viability of his principle, in these words: '...the inconveniences which are strictly inseparable from the unfavorable judgment of others, are the only ones to which a person should ever be subjected for that portion of his conduct and character which concerns his own good, but which does not affect the interests of others in their relations with him. Acts injurious to others require a totally different treatment... these are fit objects of moral reprobation, and, in grave cases, of moral retribution and punishment.'[30] And as if to meet the objections of the sceptical Stephen, who could not see how 'inconveniences strictly inseparable from the unfavourable judgment of others' could be differentiated from the 'moral retribution' to be visited when other people's interests were harmed, Mill went on to show why this distinction was not merely nominal, in his eyes at least. In the former case the offender incurs a loss of consideration by reason of his imprudence or lack of dignity, whereas in the latter reprobation is due to him 'for an offence against the rights of others'.[31] And, claims Mill, people will react differently if the conduct of which they disapprove is such that they think that they have a right to control the agent. Whether Mill makes his point or not I do not wish to discuss further, but the words 'for an offence against the *rights* of others' raise a very important question and seem to introduce a new element into the principle. Nor

---

[27] Op. cit., p. 138.   [28] Op. cit., p. 75.

[29] Op. cit., p. 134.   [30] Op. cit., p. 135
[31] Op. cit., p. 136.

is this the sole occasion when 'rights' are mentioned.[32] In the same chapter from which I have just been quoting, specifically devoted to discussing 'the limits to the authority of society over the individual', and therefore concerned to elaborate and give more detailed consideration to the principle mentioned and briefly treated in the opening chapter—it is in this fourth chapter that we should, I think, look for pointers to Mill's intentions—Mill attempts to demarcate the area of conduct for which we are to be made responsible to society. 'This conduct', he says, 'consists in not injuring the interests of one another; or rather certain interests which, either by express legal provision or by tacit understanding, ought to be considered as *rights*.'[33] Nor is this the complete extent of social control, for conduct may harm others 'without going to the length of violating any of their *constituted rights*'. In those cases punishment is inflicted by opinion rather than the law. Then, to sum up, Mill adds: 'As soon as any part of a person's conduct affects prejudicially the interests of others, society has jurisdiction over it', but no such question can arise 'when a person's conduct affects the interests of no persons besides himself. . .'.[34]

The paragraph from which these extracts have been taken, coming as it does at a crucial stage in Mill's argument, is of some significance for the interpretation of his leading principle. It serves, incidentally, as further proof of my claim that it is 'interests' rather than 'effects' with which Mill is concerned. But its main significance for us at this stage is the appearance in it of the term 'rights' and the relationship

Mill seems to suppose that term to have to the idea of 'interests'. From Mill's wording it is certain that the rights he has in mind are legal rights ('constituted rights'), for he envisages the law, rather than opinion, protecting some interests and these interests are then to be considered as rights. Other interests will not receive legal protection, though Mill does not exclude the possibility that these might be regarded as rights, though not legal ('constituted') rights. Certainly Mill is not saying that rights and interests are the same things, synonymous terms (and of course they are not), but he does seem to imply that they are very closely related to each other. It would be consistent with what he says here to suppose that when a person can be thought to have interests he is thereby possessed of a right, though not necessarily a right to the unqualified protection of his interests; perhaps only a right to have his interests taken into account. Moreover, by linking interests to rights in this way Mill leaves us with no excuse for confusing the notions of 'interests' and 'effects', which must now be seen as belonging to quite different categories. It may be true that because of the element of vagueness attaching to rights and interests (i.e. as to what a man may legitimately, I do not mean *legally*, account his rights or interests) the concepts would be much more difficult to operate as part of a principle of liberty than the relatively simple notion of effects, but that ought not to blind us to the difference it makes to a principle to have the one rather than the other type of concept as a component.

III

The case I have been trying to make out is that Mill's principle of self-protection rests on a division of conduct

32 See also op. cit., pp. 120 and 135. (My italics, J. C. R.)

33 Op. cit., p. 132. (My italics.)

34 Op. cit., p. 132. (My italics.)

into actions which either do or do not affect the interests of other persons rather than on what has generally been supposed to have been the division, namely, into conduct having or not having effects on others. This interpretation does not rely on the evidence of only one or two isolated passages where the word 'interests' appears. In fact the word appears at least fifteen times in the course of the essay and some of the passages where it is used are of the greatest importance in assessing Mill's intentions.[35] Furthermore, there is also the evidence I have already cited which shows how freely Mill admitted that what have commonly been thought of as literally self-regarding actions did have their effects on other persons. But having said that, I would be seriously misleading the reader if I failed to mention a number of difficulties which stand in the way of this interpretation or at least suggest that Mill was not always clear in his own mind as to what he wanted to say. The first difficulty arises out of a passage previously quoted in another context: '...there is a sphere of action in which society, as distinguished from the individual, has, if any, only an indirect interest; comprehending all that portion of a person's life and conduct which affects only himself.... When I say only himself, I mean *directly, and in the first instance*; for whatever affects himself, may affect others through himself....'[36] And we find phrases similar to the one italicized here in other parts of the essay; for example, 'things which do not *primarily* concern others' and 'the part of life in which it is *chiefly* the individual that is interested...[as opposed to] the part which *chiefly*

interests society'.[37] This seems to me a difficulty because if we are to take this passage seriously (and the repetition of like phrases elsewhere suggests it is not merely a case of careless writing) we should, on the account I have been giving, have to say that when Mill writes here of 'conduct which affects only himself' he means to say 'conduct which affects only his own interests'.[38] Further, since what affects my interests may also affect the interests of others, we should have to allow that 'self-regarding' conduct could affect the interests of others, though not 'directly' or 'primarily'. Hence the distinction Mill was attempting to make in his use of the self-regarding and other-regarding categories would seem to resolve itself into a division between (i) actions which primarily affect the interests of the agent but may affect the interests of others too, and (ii) actions which primarily affect the interests of others, though the agent's own interests may also be involved. It requires little imagination to foresee the immense complications that would be bound to arise in the application of such a formula. Nothing could be less appropriately described as a 'very simple principle'—Mill's own characterization in his opening chapter. Yet we should have to interpret these passages in some such manner or else admit, which is quite possible, that Mill falls occa-

[35] I have found the word on the following pages: 74 (twice), 75, 120, 132 (four times), 135, 138, 142, 149 (twice), and 150 (twice).

[36] Op. cit., p. 75. My italics.

[37] Op. cit., pp. 115 and 132. It should be noted, however, that 'primarily' and 'chiefly' are the equivalent to 'directly' or 'in the first instance'.

[38] In the first draft of this article the words 'to say' did not appear. I have inserted them in response to a remark made by Mr. J. M. Brown in some very valuable comments he kindly sent me on the draft. Mr. Brown pointed out that to allow 'conduct which affects only himself' to mean 'conduct which affects only his own interests' would undermine the distinction I have sought to make between these two types of statement.

sionally into the language of 'effects', without realizing that he thereby allows a second principle to peep through from time to time while adhering mainly to a doctrine based on 'interests'.

IV

Assuming, then, that Mill's doctrine involves the idea of 'interests' rather than 'effects', is it, interpreted thus, a useful working principle of liberty in the way that the traditional version is patently not? The revised version would read something like this: 'Social control of individual actions ought to be exercised only in cases where the interests of others are either threatened or actually affected.'[39] But how to decide when interests are affected? What are interests? Is there any commonly accepted criterion, or set of criteria, of an interest? Mill's principle, as reformulated, must inevitably provoke questions like these and its value will obviously depend on the answers to be given to them. They cannot be fully treated here and all I shall attempt are some preliminary and tentative remarks.

As it is commonly used, the concept of 'interests' is an elusive one. There is no precise and generally acceptable definition. As Mr. Plamenatz observed in this journal, the idea of 'interest', compared with notions like 'right' or 'duty', is extremely vague.[40] But there are many important concepts in our language which evade exact description and they remain none the less indispensable. Failure to bring the notion within the confines of a neat definition ought not to be a sufficient reason for rejecting out of hand a theory to which the concept is central. Moreover there are sociologists and jurists for whom

the term occupies an important place in their theories. MacIver, for example, conceives human activity through the two concepts 'interest' and 'will'. There is, he says, 'no will without an interest and no interest apart from a will'. And by an interest he means 'some object which determines activity', though it is more than mere desire; it has 'a certain permanence and stability'.[41] Another definition of interest he offers is, 'the object of consciousness...anything, material or immaterial, factual or conceptual, to which we devote our attention'.[42] Roscoe Pound, too, employs the word with the same kind of wide meaning. For him an interest is a *de facto* claim and he draws up a comprehensive classification of interests which covers a vast field, ranging from individual claims to privacy to the social interest in free science and cultural progress. Among other writers the term is confined to certain kinds of consciousness or a particular class of attitudes such as, for example, those based on needs; and an appropriate list is provided of the bodily and spiritual needs which are to count for this purpose.[43] How are these uses of the word related to the normal sense of the term? Indeed, is it possible to identify an 'ordinary' use of the word? There would seem to be some grounds for saying that in a normal context an interest should not be construed as just a claim, far less any sort of claim. Rather it seems to be the condition in which a person's claim to, or title to, or share in something is recognized as valid by others, or at least is regarded as worthy of consideration. That is to say, there is an objective element about it which precludes any fanciful demand from

---

39 I am leaving out the complications connected with 'primarily', 'chiefly', and 'directly.'

40 Vol. II, no. 1 (Feb. 1954), p. 3.

41 *Community* (3rd edition), pp. 98–101.

42 *Society* (1937), pp. 20–21.

43 See Alf Ross, *On Law and Justice* (1958), pp. 358–59.

being an interest. For interests are things we would generally look upon as deserving protection, to be prejudicially affected only by advantages likely to accrue in another direction. Certainly we feel that they ought not to be ignored even if there are compelling reasons for subordinating them to what we think are more important considerations. Interests, then, are not just arbitrary wishes, fleeting fancies, or capricious demands, though some of them may well have developed from forms to which these terms might have been particularly apposite at the time.

Mill does not say much to indicate how he understood the notion of interest, but there is nothing in the essay to suggest that he uses the term in any exceptional manner. There is a passage, however, which points to some of the problems inseparably connected with the idea of interests. The secretary of an association formed to secure prohibition had claimed a right to be protected from the consequences of the liquor trade which, he argued, 'destroys my primary right of security, by constantly creating and stimulating social disorder. ...It impedes my right to free moral and intellectual development, by surrounding my path with dangers, and by weakening and demoralising society, from which I have a right to claim mutual aid and intercourse.' Mill repudiates with indignation such a sweeping claim, amounting, as he saw it, to 'the absolute social right of every individual, that every other individual shall act in every respect exactly as he ought' and conferring on everyone 'a vested interest in each other's moral, intellectual, and even physical perfection'.[44] Mill and the prohibitionist are disputing what may legitimately be claimed as rights and what is to count as an injury to a person's interests.

According to the standards prevailing in Mill's day, and certainly by those current in our own time, the secretary's claims appear ludicrously excessive and there would be no point in taking his case seriously. But what is of importance is the very fact of disagreement as to what a man may hold to be his interests. The prohibitionist could have submitted the relatively modest claim that a man's interests are prejudicially affected by the noisy behaviour of groups of people gathering outside a public house adjoining, or close to, his home. If the noise became such a nuisance as to lower the value of the property it could not be denied that interests had been affected. But apart from depreciation of value, has a man's interest been adversely affected by the mere fact of disturbance of his privacy? He could be the tenant of the house and suffer no personal pecuniary loss, yet he might find the behaviour of the publican's clients extremely annoying and might set a high monetary value on its cessation. Is it part of a man's interests to be free from interference of this sort? From the noise of the radio in his neighbour's flat or from the machines on the airfield near his house? If we are going to say 'no' to the claim that interests are affected by interference such as noise, as opposed to monetary loss caused by noise, then this would seem to prevent Mill's principle from operating in spheres in which he clearly wanted it to work. But it is obvious that people can differ about what are to be regarded as interests, since standards and values enter into what will be recognized as interests (or what will *not* be recognized) at any given time in a way that they do not in the case of 'effects'.[45] Consequently,

_____
44 Op. cit., pp. 145–6.

45 And even if it came to be accepted that a man's interests were affected by the noisy interruption of his privacy there is still the

whether one takes a wide or narrow view of interests, the principle of self-protection must necessarily harbour value-ingredients which will inevitably render its use a controversial operation. That a drug affects a certain disease is a strictly empirical matter. There are objective procedures for tracing its 'effects'. It is true that there are also cases when it would be a relatively simple matter to decide if my interests have been affected: legal interests, for example. But there are also occasions when, because standards differ, people will disagree about what their interests are. And this is likely to make a principle based on 'interests' rather than 'effects' difficult to apply in many situations. For not only is the concept 'interest' in itself vague: what are to count as interests, even supposing there were a commonly accepted definition, would be an open question in an indeterminate number of cases. Had Mill formulated his principle in terms of rights rather than interests he would have met the same difficulty precisely because what a man's rights are is a question which can be reasonably answered in more than one way.

Mill's principle raises yet another problem. Social interference, he says, is justifiable only when the interests of others are affected but, he adds, 'it must by no means be supposed, because damage, or probability of damage, to the interests of others, can alone justify the interference of society, that therefore it always does justify such interference'.[46] Evidently the principle is not intended to absolve us from deciding cases on their merits even when interests have actually been affected. We should

have to weigh up the advantages and disadvantages of social interference on each occasion. As Mill puts it: '...the question whether the general welfare will or will not be promoted by interfering with [another person's conduct], becomes open to discussion'.[47] One of the examples he gives is the unsuccessful candidate in a competitive examination.[48] Others have gained at his expense, but no one would have it otherwise. A recent example would be the publicity given to statements warning of the harmful effects of heavy smoking. No one would wish to suppress information about the relation between smoking and lung cancer merely because it affected the interests of the tobacco firms. However, says Mill, in the case of conduct which affects no person's interests but one's own there can be no question of permitting social control and restraint: 'in all such cases, there should be perfect freedom, legal and social, to do the action and stand the consequences'.[49] So the principle provides us with a clear directive only when we can be sure that other people's interests are *not* involved; where interests *are* affected we are left with a margin of discretion and are advised to consider whether the general welfare is or is not likely to be promoted by interference in each particular instance. Hence the range of matters covered by the 'automatic' application of the rule is limited to those occasions on which it can be said that no one's interests have been injured. And it seems to be assumed that the question of interests being injured or not is one that can be readily determined.

It would be uncharitable to reject Mill's principle out of hand merely because it fails to provide an automatic and definite solution in an extensive

---

question of whether these interests should be protected against other claims, such as, for example, freedom to converse outside public houses, the demand for air travel, or the desire to listen to music.

[46] Op. cit., p. 150.

[47] Op. cit., p. 132.   [48] Op. cit., p. 150.

[49] Op. cit., p. 132.

range of cases (i.e. actions which *do* affect the interests of others). For how many of the principles we constantly wield in everyday life supply us with quick and certain answers? From Mill's point of view the important thing was to check the growing tendency to interfere in cases where intervention should be totally banned and for this purpose what had to be done was to demarcate the area of non-intervention from that in which a prima facie right to control could only be overridden by an appeal to the 'general welfare'. We have seen that with all its indefiniteness Mill's principle is emphatic on one point, namely, that when the interests of others have *not* been affected society should not intervene. But even here a serious doubt emerges. Are there not some actions we should want to control or prohibit which do not seem to injure the interests of others? Take the case of obscenity. It may be that some acts and some kinds of publications which the present law in the United Kingdom prohibits would be permitted in a more enlightened society, but there are certainly many which are, and ought to continue to be, prevented. Mill, too, seems to take this view. He refers to 'offences against decency', acts which, when done publicly, violate good manners, and places them 'within the category of offences against others' and therefore to be prohibited. But he remarks that offences of this nature 'are only connected indirectly with our subject'.[50] Why this should be so he does not explain and it is difficult to see what reasons he could have for saying it. Perhaps he realized that to prohibit offences against decency on the ground that they caused harm to other people's interests would involve a dangerous extension of the conception of 'interests'. For whose interests are threatened

or injured by the appearance of obscene publications (or the sale of opium, to take an example from a related field)? The interests of those who concern themselves with public morality? Or the social interest in maintaining standards of public decency? But if we are allowed to bring in considerations of this sort, how could Mill have maintained his opposition to a prohibition on the eating of pork in a predominantly Muslim country?[51] Measures against the dropping of litter or the emission of black smoke from chimneys in specified areas are taken in order to protect the *public interest,* not because they affect the interests of particular persons. That Mill recognized the claims of the general interest is clear enough from his discussion of the case of the person who instigates or counsels others to do acts which if done of one's own free and unaided will would be 'blameable' but not subject to social penalties because 'the evil directly resulting falls wholly on the agent'.[52] On the one hand, argues Mill, people must be allowed 'to consult with one another... to exchange opinions, and give and receive suggestions', but the question becomes 'doubtful only when the instigator derives a personal benefit from his advice' and is gainfully occupied in promoting 'what society and the State consider to be an evil'; for we would then be faced with a class of persons having an interest 'opposed to what is

---

50 Op. cit., p. 153.

51 This is one of Mill's examples (pp. 141–42). 'There are few acts which Christians and Europeans regard with more unaffected disgust than Mussulmans regard this particular mode of satisfying hunger', says Mill. He goes on to argue that the only good reason for condemning an attempt to ban the eating of pork in a country where the Mussulmans were a majority would be 'that with the personal tastes and self-regarding concerns of individuals the public has no business to interfere'.

52 Op. cit., pp. 153–55.

considered as the public weal'. Mill has in mind such people as the pimp and the keeper of a gambling house. He fails to come to a definite conclusion about the justifiability of prohibiting these activities, remarking that 'there are arguments on both sides'. What is interesting in Mill's discussion here is —apart from the confirmation that his principle can yield no clear directive in questions of this kind—his appeal to 'the public weal' as a factor we have to take into account before deciding on the legitimacy of social control. Does he intend that we should classify actions as being harmful to the interests of others if it could be shown that they are contrary to 'the public weal'? We are thus led back to the problem of how widely (or narrowly) we are to construe the notion of interests. Are we to interpret interests so narrowly as to exclude the public interest or so widely as to involve consideration of the general interest and social morality? On the former interpretation we should find ourselves unable to prohibit activity we should want to prohibit; on the latter we should be able to prohibit actions that Mill would certainly wish to be left unrestrained. And if standards and values enter into what we conceive to be a man's interests even in a restricted sense of the term, *a fortiori* they will shape what we take the public interest to require.

H. J. McCLOSKEY

Mill's Liberalism[*]

In his reply to Devlin's *The Enforcement of Morals*[1] H. L. Hart explains "the liberal point of view" as follows:—

One of the Committee's (the Wolfenden Committee on Homosexual Offences and Prostitution) principal grounds for this rec-

* Reprinted from *The Philosophical Quarterly*, XIII (1963), 143–56, by permission of the editor and the author.
1 Maccabaean Lecture in Jurisprudence of the British Academy, 1959, Oxford University Press, London.

ommendation was expressed in its report in this way: 'There must remain a realm of private morality and immorality which in brief and crude terms is not the law's business'. I shall call this the liberal point of view: for it is a special application of those wider principles of liberal thought which John Stuart Mill formulated in his essay on *Liberty*. Mill's most famous words, less cautious perhaps than the Wolfenden Committee's, were:

'The only purpose for which power can be rightfully exercised over any member of a civilized community against his will is to prevent harm to others'. . . .[2]

Because he is aware that if this is really the liberal view, it too is exposed to difficulties, Hart qualifies it thus:—

Mill's formulation of the liberal point of view may well be too simple. The grounds for interfering with human liberty are more various than the single criterion of 'harm to others' suggests: cruelty to animals or organized prostitution for gain do not, as Mill himself saw, fall easily under the description of harm to others. Conversely even where there is harm to others in the most literal sense; there may well be other principles limiting the extent to which harmful activities should be repressed by the law. So there are multiple criteria, not a single criterion, determining when human liberty may be restricted.

In so alluding to Mill's writings as landmarks in the development of liberalism and even as reasonably adequate expressions of liberal thought, Hart is typical of contemporary British liberal thinkers. It is important, therefore, to examine Mill's writings to determine what precisely is the nature of Mill's liberal political philosophy and, in particular, his answer to the question, What is the function of the State? I shall argue that even a superficial reading of Mill's writings reveals that it is a myth that Mill has stated a coherent, defensible, liberal view of the state. It is true, as Hart suggests, that Mill stressed the importance of liberty, and that he gave intelligent, thoughtful answers to specific problems such as the rights to freedom from interference of pimps, brothel keepers, gaming-house owners, and those cruel

to animals. But we cannot uncritically accept Mill's high praise of liberty without examining its grounds, as they may qualify the praise, both in general and in particular contexts. Again, because Mill made intelligent comments on awkward social issues it cannot be assumed that he has shown that liberalism can deal with such issues—for Mill's thoughtful answers may involve a departure from the liberal view. A consistent coherent liberal political philosophy must be set out in terms of general principles about liberty and the rôle of the state; and not simply as a collection of conclusions of limited generality and scope, accepted on all sorts of grounds and subject to various conditions and qualifications which spring from an unclear acceptance of other basic principles which may collide head-on with the principle they are said to qualify.

Some liberals have suggested that the question, What is the function of the state? misses the point of liberalism, being concerned with the different problem, of liberty in the state; i.e., the liberal is one who is concerned to insist on the maximum liberty possible and who enquires how it may best and most fully be realized. But unless the demand for liberty is qualified by reference to the proper function of government, it would imply anarchism; or it would become the view that it is the function of government to maximise liberty. Liberals often suggest the latter to be the true liberal view, but once it is explicitly stated and developed it would be seen to involve disregard of considerations of justice, happiness, well-being, except where concern for liberty coincided with them. Further, no notable liberal has explained liberalism in this way. All have noted the relevance of demands of justice, even where they conflict with consideration of liberty; and they have admitted some coercion to reduce suffering or to promote happiness even when such interferences are not with harmful, other-regarding actions. Liberalism, therefore, can be neither a simple view about the place of liberty in the state, nor the view that the function of the state consists solely in the promoting of liberty; instead, it must be a view which explains the place of liberty in the context of a general view of the proper function or functions of the state. Mill's writings have the merit those of so many liberals lack, of showing some awareness of this.

In his most celebrated and most quoted contribution to political philosophy, the essay *Liberty* (1859), Mill is concerned primarily to argue that liberty is essential if a state composed of civilized people is to be legitimate. He explains:—

The object of this Essay is to assert one very simple principle as entitled to govern absolutely the dealings of society with the individual in the way of compulsion and control, whether the means used be physical force in the form of legal penalties, or the moral coercion of public opinion. That principle is, that the sole end for which mankind are warranted, individually or collectively, in interfering with the liberty of action of any of their number, is self-protection. That the only purpose for which power can be rightfully exercised over any member of a civilized community, against his will, is to prevent harm to others. His own good, either physical or moral, is not a sufficient warrant. . . . The only part of the conduct of any one, for which he is amenable to society, is that which concerns others.[3]

In defending and circumscribing the right to liberty, Mill implicitly develops

3 *Liberty* (Everyman, J. M. Dent & Sons, London, 1910), pp. 72–73. All subsequent references to *Liberty* are to this edition.

a view of the function of the state; in brief, that the end of the state is to maximise the goods of true knowledge, rational belief, self-direction, self-perfection, moral character and responsibility, happiness and progress. Mill develops this theory further in his discussion of its applications, suggesting that it is part of the function of the well-run state to restrain people from thoughtless errors in the major decisions of their lives, and, more important, to make moral judgments and to aid morality and to impede immorality, indirectly by non-coercive methods such as education, and directly, by using force to ensure the fulfilling of "assignable duties" and to prevent people profiting from the immorality of others, although on this latter point Mill expresses uncertainty. Thus, whilst the precise view of the function of the state that Mill assumes or develops in *Liberty* is not always clear, it is obvious that he does not regard liberty as the sole or main end of the state, nor even as always a necessary condition of its legitimacy. The same general view is expressed in *Representative Government* (1861) and *Principles of Political Economy* (1848, People's Edition, 1866), it being most clearly, fully and explicitly developed in the latter work.

In *Liberty* Mill claims that he will justify liberty in terms of its utility (74); but the term 'utility' is misleading and obscures from Mill the character of his own arguments. He does try to defend liberty in terms of its utility, but not in the sense suggested by his utilitarianism, for most of his arguments are directed at showing the utility of liberty as a means to knowledge, truth, rationality, rational belief, progress, moral responsibility, and self-perfection. He also notes some considerations which relate to liberty as an aid to happiness, but more usually the arguments linking liberty and happiness relate to happiness expanded to include liberty as part of rather than as a means to the end.

Mill's best known arguments about liberty relate to freedom of speech; but he nowhere explains exactly what he is defending, as all his definitions relate to freedom of action. He seems to hold that there should be complete freedom of speech provided that its exercise does not incite others to immediate harmful riotous behaviour, this qualification being added almost as an after-thought (114). Mill's four arguments are: (i) The view being suppressed may be true. A claim to infallibility which cannot be sustained is involved in intolerance. (ii) The view being suppressed may be false, but suppressing it will cause the true view to be held in the manner of a prejudice, with little understanding and appreciation of its grounds. (iii) The view being suppressed may be false, but suppressing it will cause the prevailing favoured view to become enfeebled, lost and deprived of its vital effect on character and conduct. (iv) The view being suppressed may be only partly false, and the prevailing view only partly true, hence complete knowledge of the truth will entail tolerance of both. This is a special application of the first argument and need not concern us further.

(i) The first argument supports liberty (and the state's safeguarding it) on the basis of an evaluation of truth and knowledge—an evaluation which, if Mill's argument is sound, rests on an illegitimate claim by the state of infallible knowledge. As Joad observed, this evaluation of true (and of rational) belief of the masses has been disputed, e.g., by Nazis, Marxists, and others.[4] Besides being self-refuting, this argument implies that all restrictions on

freedom of speech, including censorship in war, are illegitimate, as they presuppose indefensible claims to infallible knowledge. But we shall not be concerned here with the soundness or otherwise of Mill's arguments but solely with the view of the state and of liberty that follow from them. This argument suggests the view of the state as a 'good-producer' which produces the good of true knowledge by promoting liberty of speech as the means to this good; and it implies that if true knowledge were better promoted by intolerance, intolerance would be as desirable as Mill thought tolerance to be.

(ii) The second argument also defends liberty as a means of promoting some other good, rational, understanding belief; and it presupposes the view that it is the function of the state so to act as to ensure maximum rational belief; and it implies that if it were discovered that freedom of speech impedes the realization of this good, the state should then suppress freedom of speech.

(iii) The third argument entails that the state should interfere to ensure that falsehood have a voice if it has no actual exponents. And it, too, is an argument about the value of knowledge and rational belief, with the further good mentioned, the good of moral improvement, liberty of speech being defended as a means of promoting these goods. And it presupposes the view that the state should concern itself not simply with promoting the goods of knowledge and rational belief, but with right behaviour as well. Hence, if intolerance were shown to produce lively, vital beliefs, which effectively influenced our moral conduct, the argument would imply that the state should suppress freedom of speech. Behind these arguments is the suggestion that the enjoyment of these goods is part of happiness

---

[4] C. E. M. Joad: *Liberty Today* (Watts & Co., London, 1934), Ch. 4.

and a means to happiness and that the state's business consists in promoting goods.

Slight and inadequate though it is, the qualification that freedom of speech is permissible only if its exercise does not incite others to riotous behaviour, is nonetheless significant. The arguments about freedom of speech justify it as a means to other goods which the state should promote or safeguard. By contrast, this qualification invokes a principle over-riding liberty and involves an admission that the state cannot always treat adult civilized people as responsible, rational beings, as some forms of public speech will cause them to act irrationally, irresponsibly, violently. It is difficult to determine what the additional principle is that this qualification involves. It is not that of limiting liberty for the sake of liberty, as it is directed at protecting the property or person of another; nor is it that of limiting freedom of speech whenever such freedom results in harm to another's person or property; for Mill wishes to allow freedom of speech which results in harm to people's persons and property, e.g., by a persuasive communist, provided the harm is not due to immediate violence directly consequent on the speaker's oratory. To become a defensible qualification it must be enlarged and restated in terms of "speech which causes determinate harm"; and it then becomes a substantial qualification of freedom of speech.

The qualification in terms of harm to others is made explicit in Mill's account of freedom of action as follows:—

The only freedom which deserves the name, is that of pursuing our own good in our own way, so long as we do not attempt to deprive others of theirs or impede their efforts to obtain it (75).

Acts, of whatever kind, which, without justifiable cause, do harm to others, may be, and in the more important cases absolutely require to be, controlled by the unfavourable sentiments, and, when needful, by the active interference of mankind: The liberty of the individual must be thus far limited; he must not make himself a nuisance to other people (114).
Each will receive its proper share, if each has that which more particularly concerns it. To individuality should belong the part of life in which it is chiefly the individual that is interested; to socety, the part which chiefly interests society (132).

Mill urges the limiting of liberty of action for the sake of preventing harm or injury, these being construed very narrowly to mean physical harm or harm in respect to one's property or happiness, not harm in respect to knowledge, moral integrity or virtue. Mill thereby implicitly admits that liberty is a lesser good, and a lesser good than a good commonly regarded as itself a lesser good than other goods. Mill sometimes writes as if he is suggesting that the limitations to freedom of action should be confined to actions which interfere with other people's freedom; but he does not consistently hold such a view as he contends that causing harm constitutes a ground for restricting liberty, even when the harm is not itself a restriction on liberty. (Not all harm is an impediment to another's freedom.) This suggests that the formula 'coercion to prevent coercion' used by some liberals is distinct from Mill's 'coercion to prevent harm'. And both are distinct from Mill's other formula in terms of self and other-regarding actions. An action may be other-regarding, not productive of harm, and yet be a proper object of state interference, as Mill acknowledges in his discussion of applications of his theory; and, as Mill also notes, our actions may harm others, but be such that the state should not interfere with them—e.g., in competitive situations (150). Yet Mill's definition of freedom is intended to indicate at least when the state is not entitled to act, i.e., necessary but not sufficient conditions for state interference.

The qualification of freedom of action in terms of harm to others is substantial, for it may exclude many of the more interesting experiments of living, since most of them often involve harm to others—e.g., asceticism, devotion to art, science or learning to the exclusion of other obligations; life in accord with most moral theories, e.g., Kantianism, pacificism, or even vegetarianism; social experiments such as prohibition and legalized betting shops; *laissez-faire* capitalism, socialism, Nazism, etc.

Mill suggests that the arguments for freedom of speech also hold for freedom of action. Thus, here too, he uses arguments which imply that it is the business of the state to promote goods, in particular, the goods of true belief, self-improvement, rationality and rational belief. Mill argues:—

That mankind are not infallible; that their truths, for the most part, are only half-truths; that unity of opinion, unless resulting from the fullest and freest comparison of opposite opinions, is not desirable, and diversity not an evil, but a good, until mankind are much more capable than at present of recognizing all sides of the truth, are principles applicable to men's modes of action, not less than to their opinions. As it is useful that while mankind are imperfect there should be different opinions, so it is that there should be different experiments of living; that free scope should be given to varieties of character, short of injury to others; and that the worth of different modes of life should be proved practically, when any one thinks fit to try them (114–5).

Thus the arguments imply, as when stated for freedom of speech, that if truth, rational belief and self-perfection

can be achieved with greater success through intolerance and coercion, then freedom of action will lose its justification. To show further that freedom of action does achieve these goods, in particular the good of self-perfection, Mill invokes other considerations, including the argument "each is the best judge and guardian of his own interests". But in *Liberty* it is simply one of a number of supporting considerations. Mill argues that our personal peculiarities constitute a ground for freedom of action, in that individual perfection entails the development of these personal traits, and we should have a better knowledge and a keener interest in our self-perfection, and that, in seeking it freely we should develop and improve further our mental and moral powers:—

It is not by wearing down into uniformity all that is individual in themselves, but by cultivating it, and calling it forth, within the limits imposed by the rights and interests of others, that human beings become a noble and beautiful object of contemplation (120).

The interference of society to overrule his judgment and purposes in what only regards himself must be grounded on general presumptions; which may be altogether wrong, and even if right, are as likely as not to be misapplied to individual cases, by persons no better acquainted with the circumstances of such cases than those are who look at them merely from without. In this department, therefore, of human affairs, individuality has its proper field of action (133).

Although it is used as a subsidiary argument in *Liberty,* the argument "each is the best judge" is one of which Mill, in company with other liberals, makes extensive use elsewhere. It receives its clearest statement in *Representative Government.*[5] Interpreted lit-

5 *Representative Government* (Everyman), pp. 208–10.

erally, it is an argument for anarchism. It implies even a condemnation of legislation preventing "force and fraud" as Mill noted in *Principles of Political Economy*. It must, therefore, as Mill notes in the latter work, be qualified in various ways, e.g. to allow interference to prevent harm, to promote goods. Again, whether interpreted as claiming that we may secure most effectively our happiness, self-perfection, or simply our selfish interests, the argument defends liberty as a means to other goods, and, in some versions of the argument, also as part of the end. Thus if it could be shown that each was not the best judge, or though the best judge each was not the best guardian of his own interests, the principle of the argument would suggest that liberty be restricted and reliance placed on those who were the best judges or guardians of our interests. Mill himself accepts this implication within a limited area in *Principles of Political Economy*. But before these qualifications be considered, I wish to complete our examination of the view of the function of the state suggested or stated in *Liberty*.

What new principle, if any, is introduced by the qualification that the state may never interfere with self-regarding, and only sometimes with other-regarding actions? Mill's critics have suggested that this formula virtually destroys his theory, since few if any actions are self-regarding. Mill noted this objection:—

The distinction here pointed out between the part of a person's life which concerns only himself, and that which concerns others, many persons will refuse to admit. How (it may be asked) can any part of the conduct of a member of society be a matter of indifference to the other members? No person is an entirely isolated being; it is impossible for a person to do anything seriously or permanently hurtful to himself, without mischief reaching at least to his near connections, and often far beyond them (136).

Every act has social repercussions which may be beneficial or harmful to others. Does Mill's qualification then allow liberty to be restricted *whenever* the general good requires it? Mill's reply is unconvincing but important:—

I fully admit that the mischief which a person does to himself may seriously affect, both through their sympathies and their interests, those nearly connected with him, and in a minor degree, society at large. When, by conduct of this sort, a person is led to violate a distinct and assignable obligation to any other person or persons, the case is taken out of the self-regarding class, and becomes amenable to moral disapprobation in the proper sense of the term.... But with regard to the merely contingent, or, as it may be called, constructive injury which a person causes to society, by conduct which neither violates any specific duty to the public nor occasions perceptible hurt to any assignable individual except himself; the inconvenience is one which society can afford to bear, for the sake of the greater good of human freedom (137–8).

Mill then suggests that society can help the individual by non-coercive means, e.g., by education, implying thereby the right of the state to promote these goods provided it does not use direct coercion. Thus Mill meets the difficulty that few if any acts are purely self-regarding by conceding the state's right to make moral judgments, and to enforce "assignable duties" (which his discussion there, and of the application of his theory, suggests to be anything the state regards as a fairly determinate inter-personal duty), and to promote self-regarding moral behaviour (presumably also judged to be so by the state) by non-coercive means. And his ground here for limiting coercion in respect of private morality is the one rarely invoked by him, namely that he sees freedom as a distinct good, which outweighs the good of that private morality which is to be achieved only through state coercion.

Mill's discussion of the *applications* of his theory introduces new qualifications and reaffirms those already noted. The discussion of marriage and the family brings out the importance of the qualification that the state may enforce morality where it takes the form of "assignable duties". Mill argues that the state may properly enforce the duties of parents in respect to their children. Since adultery and neglect of needy, invalid parents or spouses are as much "assignable duties" as those of parents to young children, the state may on Mill's qualified self-regarding, other-regarding principle interfere with a large area of conduct on moral grounds and repress much immorality. After all, are not lies, cheating, promise-breakings, etc., breaches of assignable duties? Thus Mill's liberal theory allows the enforcement of a very considerable amount of morality, when it is expedient so to enforce it; and equally important, his admission of the right of the state to enforce, and hence to judge our assignable duties, involves a very substantial qualification of his infallibility argument.

In his discussion of gambling and prostitution for gain, Mill virtually qualifies his infallibility argument out of existence, for he suggests that it *may* be right to restrict the liberty of those who make a livelihood out of the immorality of others. He observes:—

If people must be allowed, in whatever concerns only themselves, to act as seems best to themselves, at their own peril, they must equally be free to consult with one another about what is fit to be so done; to exchange opinions, and give and receive suggestions. Whatever it is permitted to do, it must be permitted to advise to do. The question is doubtful only when the instigator derives a personal benefit from his advice; when he makes it his occupation, for subsistence or pecuniary gain, to promote *what society and the State consider to be an evil* (154; my italics).

The fornicator and gambler must be tolerated, but Mill has grave doubts about the pimp, the prostitute and the gaming-house keeper. He notes the arguments for interference, but states:—

There is considerable force in these arguments. I will not venture to decide whether they are sufficient to justify the moral anomaly of punishing the accessary, when the principal is (and must be) allowed to go free (155).

The fact that Mill so sympathetically considers the possibility of such laws suggests that he was vaguely aware that such state interference may be essential in a well-ordered state. If Mill decides in favour of intolerance here, much possibly harmless immorality would be legally banned. Mill suggests that the gambler could still gamble privately, and presumably that the fornicator could fornicate with amateurs. But obviously, such restrictive legislation would make many immoral activities impossible or less accessible. Artificial methods of birth-control were, until this century, almost universally judged to be immoral; and they are still widely judged to be so. On Mill's principle, the state might be justified in preventing the manufacture and sale of instruments of birth-control; and this would be to prevent a very important form of private "immorality". Thus this suggested solution to the problem of prostitution for gain, etc., would drastically qualify Mill's liberal theory. It confers on the state the right to make moral judgments—and to enforce them up to a point—on every important moral issue. Thus if any religious or moral view—atheism, pacifism, euthanasia, family planning, etc., is judged evil, the state can make illegal the having of paid advocates of the view—e.g., clergy; and it can ban all gainful manufacture upon which the practice of these immoral views is dependent. That this is not a stupid lapse on Mill's part, but a qualification suggested by the needs of his theory is evident from the fact that much the same principle underlies his discussion of the state's right to tax "stimulants" heavily to gain necessary revenue.

Mill's discussion of the state's right to take steps to prevent crimes and accidents—e.g., by insisting on the signing of a poison register and on warning labels on poisons—is significant only as showing an awareness that the individual may not always be the best judge or guardian of his own interests.

The suggested means test for marriage and Mill's discussion of offences against decency throw light on his qualification of liberty in terms of harm to others. The former brings out the extensive restrictions of liberty "harm to others" might justify, whilst the latter extends the concept of harm, from injury to person, happiness or property, to offences against manners. They are included in the class of acts "—which, if done publicly, are a violation of good manners, and coming thus within the category of offences against others, may rightly be prohibited" (153). Such an extension is needed if Mill is to justify restrictive laws about clothing, from "the liberal point of view".

Even with all these qualifications, explanations and additions, Mill nowhere in Liberty indicates the justification of intolerance of those cruel to animals. However, even without any further additional qualifications to explain this very proper restriction on liberty, it is clear that the liberal point of view expressed in Liberty is a very complicated one, and one which allows a great deal of activity by the state towards promoting goods, and in restricting and preventing immoralities.

The essay Representative Government touches more directly on the problem of the function of the state. Mill rejects the two prevailing views, in terms of Order and Progress, as inadequate, and suggests that the end of the state is the promotion of the well-being of its members:—

We have now, therefore, obtained a foundation for a twofold division of the merit which any set of political institutions can possess. It consists partly of the degree in which they promote the general mental advancement of the community, including under that phrase advancement in intellect, in virtue, and in practical activity and efficiency; and partly of the degree of perfection with which they organise the moral, intellectual, and active worth already existing, so as to operate with the greatest effect on public affairs.[6]

That Mill regards the state as very properly concerned with the moral and intellectual well-being of its citizens is further apparent from the many references he makes in Representative Government to the danger from bad government to these goods, and from the fact that he so often argues that certain kinds of measures are good or bad by reference to well-being so conceived.

In spite of the celebrity of Liberty and Representative Government, it is Principles of Political Economy that contains Mill's most thoughtful treatment of the problem. In Bk. V, ch. 1, Mill explicitly considers the problem of the proper sphere of activity of the state and of state interference, and rejects many formulae relating to it, including various of those used by himself in his later writings. He drastically qualifies the formula 'each is the best judge and guardian of his own interests', and rejects the "force and fraud" formula

6 Representative Government, p. 195.

popular with earlier liberals, and he seriously qualifies the self-regarding, other-regarding formula he himself so often uses. His discussion of "the province of government" throws light on the movement of his thought, and his lack of clarity and certainty in his other writings. Mill observes:—

But enough has been said to show that the admitted functions of government embrace a much wider field than can easily be included within the ring or fence of any restrictive definition, and that it is hardly possible to find any ground of justification common to them all, except the comprehensive one of general expediency; nor to limit the interference of government by any universal rule, save the simple and vague one that it should never be admitted but when the case of expediency is strong.[7]

Mill states this after noting the following varied, legitimate (necessary and optional) activities of government, involving as they do authoritative and non-authoritative interference: preservation of peace and order; laying down laws of inheritance; definitions of property; laws about contracts—defining them and how to set them out and determining which are fit to be enforced, and enforcing them; setting up civil tribunals to settle disputes, e.g., with laws about wills and forms of wills; registry of births, marriages, deaths and general statistical data; monopoly of money; prescribing standards of weights and measures; paving, lighting, and cleaning streets; making and improving harbours, lighthouses, surveys, maps, etc.; fostering exploration, colonization, culture, research and universities. Mill later suggests that many of these activities can be explained in terms of these formulae ("each is best judge",

"force and fraud", "self-regarding and other-regarding", authoritative and non-authoritative interference, necessary and optional state activities); but his well-considered view is that expressed above, that the function of the state consists in the promotion of happiness and that concern for liberty and non-interference has its justification as a dictate of expediency (which for Mill is the imposing of a moral point of view). However, he writes:—

The supporters of interference have been content with asserting a general right and duty on the part of government to intervene, wherever its intervention would be useful: and when those who have been called the *laisser-faire* school have attempted any definite limitation of the province of government, they have usually restricted it to the protection of person and property against force and fraud; a definition to which neither they nor anyone else can deliberately adhere, since it excludes, as has been shown in a preceding chapter, some of the most indispensable, and unanimously recognized, of the duties of government.

Without professing entirely to supply this deficiency of a general theory, on a question which does not, as I conceive, admit of any universal solution, I shall attempt to afford some little aid towards the resolution of this class of questions as they arise, by examining, in the most general point of view in which the subject can be considered, what are the advantages, and what the evils or inconveniences, of government interference (Bk. v, ch. 11, sec. 1, p. 568).

This Mill does by reference to particular issues, but his "solutions" are often in terms of non-liberal or illiberal principles; yet such principles emerge from thoughtful attempts to explain the state's rights and duties.

After discussing the province of government early in the last chapter of *Principles of Political Economy*, Mill states:—

We have observed that, as a general rule,

---

[7] *Principles of Political Economy* (Longmans, Green, London: People's Edition, 1866), Bk. v, ch. 1, sec. 2, p. 482. All subsequent references in my article are to this work.

the business of life is better performed when those who have an immediate interest in it are left to take their own course, uncontrolled either by the mandate of the law or by the meddling of any public functionary (*Ib.*, sec. 7, p. 575).

But he then goes on to qualify this conclusion, stating: "The proposition that the consumer is a competent judge of the commodity, can be admitted only with numerous abatements and exceptions" (*Ib.*, sec. 8, p. 575). Mill intends his qualifications to justify state compulsion in respect of education; state protection of children, lunatics, and animals; state interference with joint stock companies; compulsion in the sphere of labour and industry; state charity; state supervision and control of colonization; state promotion of goods such as culture, science, research, etc. The drastic nature of some of these qualifications reveals that Mill invokes principles of a radically different kind from those usually associated with liberalism.

To look at Mill's discussion of these exceptions. First, he allows that the ordinary citizen may not be a competent judge of his own interest in certain areas, e.g. education. He argues:—

The uncultivated cannot be competent judges of cultivation. Those who most need to be made wiser and better, usually desire it least, and if they desired it, would be incapable of finding the way to it by their own lights (*Ib.*, sec. 8, p. 575).

In the matter of education, the intervention is justifiable, because the case is not one in which the interest and judgment of the consumer are a sufficient security for the goodness of the commodity (*Ib.*, sec. 9, p. 577).

Since this argument admits of indefinite extension if the empirical facts warrant, it may be significant that Mill uses it rather than that stated elsewhere in terms of the state's right to enforce assignable duties, or that which liberals

more generally use, in terms of the rights of the child. That mature adults are not always the best judges of their own interests is also suggested in Mill's discussion of state interference where irrevocable contracts are, or may be, involved:—

A second exception...is when an individual attempts to decide irrevocably now, what will be best for his interest at some future and distant time. The presumption in favour of individual judgment is only legitimate, where the judgment is grounded on actual, and especially on present, personal experience; not where it is formed antecedently to experience, and not suffered to be reversed even after experience has condemned it (*Ib.*, sec. 10, p. 579).

Mill here has in mind slave and marriage contracts, but his comment suggests that the individual is the best judge of his own interest only when his judgment is grounded on personal experience. If taken seriously, this entails the illiberal conclusions that the state must insist on trial marriages, even where the parties are opposed, or alternatively, forbid the legal enactment of life-long marriage contracts, even where the parties wish to enter into unbreakable contracts. In either event, the thought behind his position represents a considerable qualification which admits of wide application.

Some of Mill's comments suggest that he invokes the same argument to justify state interference to protect children, lunatics, and animals; but Mill also suggests the alternative account that children, lunatics, and animals are weaker parties in a "contractual" situation, in need of state protection. In either case, the argument involves the remarkable suggestion that animals have a status comparable with that of lunatics. Possibly because he is uneasy about this suggestion, Mill offers the third account:—

It is by the grossest misunderstanding of

the principles of liberty, that the infliction of exemplary punishment on ruffianism practised towards these defenceless creatures, has been treated as a meddling by government with things beyond its province; an interference with domestic life. . . . What it would be the duty of a human being, possessed of the requisite physical strength, to prevent by force if attempted in his presence, it cannot be less incumbent on society generally to repress (*Ib.*, sec. 9. p. 578).

This illiberal suggestion is Mill's most convincing account of the state's right to punish cruelty to animals.

A further qualifiction condones state compulsion to ensure uniformity of action where the individual on his own cannot achieve what he judges to be his own interest. Mill sees in this a justification of labour and factory legislation—workers see their interest to lie in shorter hours under better conditions for higher wages, but only compulsory uniformity will allow them to realize their good. The argument assumes that the state has the right and competence to make this value judgment; and in effect it is claimed to justify coercion of others against what they judge to be their own interests. Again, the judgment may apparently involve uniformity to achieve moral ends that can be achieved only by compulsory uniformity of action. Hobhouse saw in this argument a justification for restraining individuals so as to permit unpopular religious processions, whilst Joad saw it as justifying the compulsory wearing of clothing in our society, and compulsory nudism among primitives.

Mill concedes the right of the state to provide help for the needy, provided various conditions, which amount to such aid being beneficial in its total effects, are fulfilled. He argues:—

The argument against government interference grounded on the maxim that indi-

viduals are the best judges of their own interest, cannot apply to the very large class of cases, in which those acts of individuals with which the government claims to interfere, are not done by those individuals for their own interest, but for the interest of other people. This includes, among other things, the important and much agitated subject of public charity (*Ib.*, sec. 13, p. 583).

Mill argues that the state is entitled to interfere with colonization engaged in by individuals judging rightly concerning their own interest, for the good of later generations, and that the same principle holds here as with state charity. He observes:—

If it is desirable, as no one will deny it to be, that the planting of colonies should be conducted, not with an exclusive view to the private interests of the first founders, but with a deliberate regard to the permanent welfare of the nations afterwards to arise from these small beginnings; such regard can only be secured by placing the enterprise, from its commencement, under regulations constructed with the foresight and enlarged views of philosophical legislators; and the government alone has power either to frame such regulations, or to enforce their observance (*Ib.*, sec. 14, p. 585).

The principle involved here is the fundamentally distinct one of interference for the good of future generations; and it is really an extension of the qualification about harming others, but one which amounts to a new principle, involving as it does, reference to the well-being of unborn generations. Such an extension of the principle would qualify liberty in all its contexts, and opens the way for wholesale intervention of the Russian and Chinese kinds; yet Mill is forced to admit this principle to explain and justify what is undoubtedly a necessary and proper activity of government.

Mill further noted that there are goods which are not any one person's goods, which ought to be promoted by the state; and he accordingly notes the desirability of state interference in the form of taxation and state subsidy to promote goods such as science, culture, research and exploration.

In brief, then, the argument "each is the best judge" holds only for rational beings; and then only where it holds, i.e., where the goods are goods of particular individuals, and where the individual is in fact the best judge or guardian of his own interest. He is not the best *judge* of certain commodities, and where irrevocable decisions are involved, his judgment is suspect. Hence the state may properly interfere in such matters. Mill gives no clear generally applicable principle by which to judge when the individual is the best judge of his own interest, and neglects to consider here the very relevant, important areas of morality and religion. The "individual" may also not be the best *guardian* of his own interest, e.g., if he is a child, a lunatic, or an animal, or if compulsory joint action is essential for him and others to realize their interests; and here, too, state interference is allowed. This means that much moral behaviour may properly be enforced, if it is expedient to enforce it, for compulsory observance of duties such as truth-telling, promise-keeping, marital fidelity, etc., is essential if most are to realize effectively their individual interests. Further, even where the individual is the best judge and guardian of his own interest, the state may interfere for the good of future generations, or to promote those goods which are not any one individual's goods. These essential qualifications represent a very substantial modification of the non-interference thesis. In the light of Mill's discussions here and elsewhere in *Principles of Political Economy, Liberty,* and *Representative Government,* the view of the function and proper activi-

ties of the state which results from Mill facing the concrete problems of political life is seen to be a very different theory to the non-interference theory commonly ascribed to him and which, no doubt, he sometimes believed himself to be advancing.

Mill's view is that it is the business of the state to secure and promote goods such as happiness, truth, rational belief, self-perfection, self-direction, moral character, and culture; and that it may interfere with liberty in special cases to promote these goods, even when the behaviour of those interfered with is not harmful to others. Mill does not regard it as part of the function of the state to promote moral conduct for its own sake; but he does argue that the state may legitimately take steps which in effect make much private immorality impossible. He suggests that it may possibly be legitimate to suppress, indirectly, those private immoralities which can usually or only be practised if organized in some way by others for their own gain. And this would make impossible or less easy to engage in, such immoralities as gambling, the private enjoyment of pornography, the practice of birth-control, and fornication. Again, all immorality which results in harm to others (where harm is construed in a very elastic way, sometimes narrowly, sometimes widely to cover offences against good manners, and harm to unborn generations) may be punished—if this results in less harm occurring. Again, any immoralities which involve failure to fulfil "assignable duties" may be suppressed; and the state (or society) is to be judge both of what is an assignable duty, and of what is an evil practice from which gainful employment may not lawfully be made.

There are still very significant differences between Mill's view and those of the Thomists and of Devlin; but Mill's liberal theory is not the simple theory Hart suggests that it is, nor is it the simple multiple criteria theory he suggests that it could readily be modified into becoming. It is a very complex theory and such that if it were consulted today, it would probably result in substantially more moral legislation than prevails in Great Britain and vastly more than most liberals would regard as permissible or desirable.